THE SYNTAX OF ARGUMENT STRUCTURE

Each verb in natural language is associated with a set of arguments, which are not systematically predictable from the verb's meaning and are realized syntactically as the projected sentence's subject, direct object, etc. Babby puts forward the theory that this set of arguments (the verb's "argument structure") has a universal hierarchical composition which directly determines the sentence's case and grammatical relations. The structure is uniform across language families and types, and this theory is supported by the fact that the core grammatical relations within simple sentences of all human languages are essentially identical. Babby determines and empirically justifies the rigid hierarchical organization of argument structure on which this theory rests. The book uses examples taken primarily from Russian, a language whose complex inflectional system, free word order, and lack of obligatory determiners make it the typological polar opposite of English.

LEONARD H. BABBY is Professor of Slavic Languages and Linguistics in the Slavic Department at Princeton University.

CAMBRIDGE STUDIES IN LINGUISTICS

General Editors: P. AUSTIN, J. BRESNAN, B. COMRIE, S. CRAIN,
W. DRESSLER, C.J. EWEN, R. LASS, D. LIGHTFOOT, K. RICE,
I. ROBERTS, S. ROMAINE, N.V. SMITH

The Syntax of Argument Structure

In this series

74 ALICE C. HARRIS and LYLE CAMPBELL: *Historical syntax in cross-linguistic perspective*
75 LILIANE HAEGEMAN: *The syntax of negation*
76 PAUL GORREL: *Syntax and parsing*
77 GUGLIELMO CINQUE: *Italian syntax and universal grammar*
78 HENRY SMITH: *Restrictiveness in case theory*
79 D. ROBERT LADD: *Intonational phonology*
80 ANDREA MORO: *The raising of predicates: predicative noun phrases and the theory of clause structure*
81 ROGER LASS: *Historical linguistics and language change*
82 JOHN M. ANDERSON: *A notional theory of syntactic categories*
83 BERND HEINE: *Possession: cognitive sources, forces and grammaticalization*
84 NOMT ERTESCHIK-SHIR: *The dynamics of focus structure*
85 JOHN COLEMAN: *Phonological representations: their names, forms and powers*
86 CHRISTINA Y. BETHIN: *Slavic prosody: language change and phonological theory*
87 BARBARA DANCYGIER: *Conditionals and prediction*
88 CLAIRE LEFEBVRE: *Creole genesis and the acquisition of grammar: the case of Haitian creole*
89 HEINZ GIEGERICH: *Lexical strata in English*
90 KEREN RICE: *Morpheme order and semantic scope*
91 APRIL McMAHON: *Lexical phonology and the history of English*
92 MATTHEW Y. CHEN: *Tone Sandhi: patterns across Chinese dialects*
93 GREGORY T. STUMP: *Inflectional morphology: a theory of paradigm structure*
94 JOAN BYBEE: *Phonology and language use*
95 LAURIE BAUER: *Morphological productivity*
96 THOMAS ERNST: *The syntax of adjuncts*
97 ELIZABETH CLOSS TRAUGOTT and RICHARD B. DASHER: *Regularity in semantic change*
98 MAYA HICKMANN: *Children's discourse: person, space and time across languages*
99 DIANE BLAKEMORE: *Relevance and linguistic meaning: the semantics and pragmatics of discourse markers*
100 IAN ROBERTS and ANNA ROUSSOU: *Syntactic change: a minimalist approach to grammaticalization*
101 DONKA MINKOVA: *Alliteration and sound change in early English*
102 MARK C. BAKER: *Lexical categories: verbs, nouns and adjectives*
103 CARLOTA S. SMITH: *Modes of discourse: the local structure of texts*
104 ROCHELLE LIEBER: *Morphology and lexical semantics*
105 HOLGER DIESSEL: *The acquisition of complex sentences*
106 SHARON INKELAS and CHERYL ZOLL: *Reduplication: doubling in morphology*
107 SUSAN EDWARDS: *Fluent aphasia*
108 BARBARA DANCYGIER and EVE SWEETSER: *Mental spaces in grammar: conditional constructions*
109 HEW BAERMAN, DUNSTAN BROWN and GREVILLE G. CORBETT: *The syntax–morphology interface: a study of syncretism*
110 MARCUS TOMALIN: *Linguistics and the formal sciences: the origins of generative grammar*
111 SAMUEL D. EPSTEIN and T. DANIEL SEELY: *Derivations in minimalism*
112 PAUL DE LACY: *Markedness: reduction and preservation in phonology*

113 YEHUDA N. FALK: *Subjects and their properties*
114 P. H. MATTHEWS: *Syntactic relations: a critical survey*
115 MARK C. BAKER: *The syntax of agreement and concord*
116 GILLIAN CATRIONA RAMCHAND: *Verb meaning and the lexicon: a first-phase syntax*
117 PIETER MUYSKEN: *Functional categories*
118 JUAN URIAGEREKA: *Syntactic anchors: on semantic structuring*
119 D. ROBERT LADD: *Intonational phonology, second edition*
120 LEONARD H. BABBY: *The syntax of argument structure*

Earlier issues not listed are also available

THE SYNTAX OF
ARGUMENT STRUCTURE

LEONARD H. BABBY
Princeton University, New Jersey

CAMBRIDGE UNIVERSITY PRESS
Cambridge, New York, Melbourne, Madrid, Cape Town, Singapore, São Paulo, Delhi

Cambridge University Press
The Edinburgh Building, Cambridge CB2 8RU, UK

Published in the United States of America by Cambridge University Press, New York

www.cambridge.org
Information on this title: www.cambridge.org/9780521417976

© Cambridge University Press 2009

This publication is in copyright. Subject to statutory exception
and to the provisions of relevant collective licensing agreements,
no reproduction of any part may take place without
the written permission of Cambridge University Press.

First published 2009

Printed in the United Kingdom at the University Press, Cambridge

A catalogue record for this publication is available from the British Library

Library of Congress Cataloging-in-Publication Data
Babby, Leonard Harvey.
The syntax of argument structure / Leonard H. Babby.
   p. cm. – (Cambridge studies in linguistics; 120)
ISBN 978-0-521-41797-6
1. Grammar, Comparative and general – Syntax.   2. Grammar, Comparative
and general – Verb phrase.   I. Title.   II. Series.
P291.B25   2009
415–dc22
                                                                      2008053260

ISBN 978-0-521-41797-6 hardback

Cambridge University Press has no responsibility for
the persistence or accuracy of URLs for external or
third-party internet websites referred to in this book,
and does not guarantee that any content on such
websites is, or will remain, accurate or appropriate.

To my wife, Kathleen Parthé, who helped me get through the rough spots and enjoy the smooth ones.

"The more outré and grotesque an incident is the more carefully it deserves to be examined, and the very point which appears to complicate a case is, when duly considered and scientifically handled, the one which is most likely to elucidate it."

Sherlock Holmes

Contents

	List of abbreviations	*page* xv
	Introduction	1
1	**The structure of argument structure**	**11**
1.0	Introduction	11
1.1	The internal structure of the diathesis	13
1.2	The hierarchical organization of argument structure	18
1.3	The autonomy of the theta and categorial tiers	19
1.4	External subcategorization	23
	1.4.1 The typology of external arguments	24
1.5	The final form of the diathesis	26
	1.5.1 The theta tier's fourth position	27
	1.5.2 Causativization in Turkish	28
	1.5.3 Passivization in Russian	28
1.6	Projecting phrase structure from argument structure	32
	1.6.1 The universal law of diathesis conservation	32
	1.6.2 The mapping between argument structure and syntactic structure	33
1.7	Projected syntactic asymmetries	36
1.8	Monadic verbs	37
	1.8.1 The impersonal ~ derived unaccusative alternation	40
1.9	Causativization and the universal architecture of the diathesis	45
	1.9.1 Language-specific diversity	50
1.10	Romance causativization	52
1.11	Nominalization and causativization	54
	1.11.1 The properties of Russian derived nominals	56
	1.11.2 The *by*-phrase in derived nominal phrases	57
	1.11.3 The *by*-phrase in causative sentences and derived nominal phrases	58
	1.11.4 The nominalization of monotransitive verbs	62
	1.11.5 The possessive genitive in derived nominals	66

xii   *Contents*

1.12	Constraints on alternations	67
1.13	Arguments, adjuncts, and complex predicates	69
1.14	Theta-role conversion	71
1.15	Concluding remarks	72

2	**The argument structure of adjectives**	**74**
2.0	Introduction	74
2.1	Russian adjectives	75
2.2	The predicate LF paradox	78
2.3	Dedicated and understood subjects	80
2.4	The syntactic properties of the LF and SF	82
2.5	The structure of SF small clauses	83
2.6	The control of depictive adjectives	84
	2.6.1 Object-controlled aP_i	87
	2.6.2 Russian noun phrases	88
2.7	The predicate LF	89
2.8	Head suppression	93
2.9	nP diagnostic I: agreement with *vy* 'you (polite)'	95
2.10	nP diagnostic II: third person personal pronouns	96
	2.10.1 *tak* + SF and *takoj* + LF	97
2.11	nP diagnostic III: the predicate genitive	98
2.12	nP diagnostic IV: *kak* + $nP_{<i>}$	100
2.13	Predicate nominals with unsuppressed heads	103
2.14	$aP_{<i>}$ adjoined to nP	107
2.15	The derivation of **-en-** participles	110
	2.15.1 Departicipial **-enn-** adjectives	114
2.16	The copula: syntactic merger or diathetic composition	115
	2.16.1 *buduči* + SF	115
2.17	Summary	122

3	**Hybrid verbal adjuncts**	**123**
3.0	Introduction	123
3.1	The syntactic representation of hybrid categories	124
3.2	Participles in Russian	127
	3.2.1 **-šč-**participles and **-en-**participles	131
	3.2.2 The interaction of external-argument altering suffixes	134
	3.2.3 Accusative case assignment	137
	3.2.4 Reflexive binding in participle phrases	141
	3.2.5 **-em-**participles	143

3.3	Hybrid adverbials in Russian	148
	3.3.1 Earlier analyses of gP_i	151
	3.3.2 The s-predicate analysis of hybrid adverbials	152
3.4	The syntactic distribution of gP_i	156
	3.4.1 gP_i in participle phrases	156
	3.4.2 gP_i in gP_i	159
3.5	gP_i in infinitive projections	159
	3.5.1 SAM$_i$ in infinitival complements	162
	3.5.2 Agreement of SAM$_i$ adjoined to gP_i	165
3.6	Hybrid adverbials in derived nominals	168
3.7	Hybrid adverbials in passive sentences	169

4 The derivation and control of infinitives — 172

4.0	Introduction	172
4.1	Independent infinitive clauses	176
4.2	Control	177
4.3	Nonfinite verbal categories	179
4.4	Subject control and infinitive s-predicates	181
	4.4.1 Subject-controlled infinitive clauses	183
4.5	Object control	186
	4.5.1 Infinitive clauses with overt dative subjects	188
4.6	The case agreement and binding of kP_i	190
	4.6.1 The default nominative	194
4.7	Diachronic change in progress: object-controlled infinitive s-predicates	195
	4.7.1 Depictive adjectives in infinitive complements	196
4.8	Locality restrictions on vertical binding	199
	4.8.1 Infinitive complements of nouns	199
	4.8.2 Infinitives with complementizers	201
	4.8.3 Infinitive clauses as subjects	202
	4.8.4 Conjoined subject-controlled infinitive complements	203
4.9	Hybrid adverbials in infinitive complements	205
4.10	Nominative direct objects in Old Russian infinitive clauses	208
4.11	*obeščat'* 'to promise'	213
4.12	The bare infinitive complement of auxiliary verbs	220
	4.12.1 Infinitive complements of impersonal verbs	224

5 Deriving the predicate instrumental — 228

5.0	Introduction	228
5.1	The distribution of the PI, LF, and SF	228
5.2	The Bailyn–Bowers hypothesis	231

5.3	The PI in the light of the LF and SF	232
5.4	Evidence that PIs head bare adjective phrases: argument I	234
	5.4.1 The case of predicate adjectives in infinitive clauses	236
	5.4.2 The case of depictive adjectives in infinitive clauses	237
5.5	*Buduči* + PI predicate adjectives: argument II	237
	5.5.1 Diathetic composition vs. syntactic merger	239
5.6	Evidence that PIs head s-predicates: argument I	243
5.7	*Byt'* + PI: argument II	245
	5.7.1 An anomalous agreement pattern?	248
5.8	Assigning the PI	249
5.9	Licensing the PI	251
5.10	Depictive adjectives in infinitive clauses	253
	Notes	260
	Bibliography	291
	Index	302

Abbreviations

A	adjective stem
A	adjective (head of syntactic AP)
-a	adjectival suffix; head of aP
ABL	ablative case
ACC	accusative case
ADV	adverb, adverbial
-af-	any affix
-af$_c$-	causative suffix
-af$_n$	final affix in a derivation
afP$_i$	affixal phrase with unbound unlinked external theta role
afP$_{<i>}$	affixal phrase with vertically bound unlinked external theta role
AP	adjective phrase
aP	phrasal projection of adjectival suffix: [$_{aP}$ [$_{a'}$ [A-a] AP]]
aux	auxiliary
C	complementizer
caus	causative
cop	copula
CP	complementizer phrase
c-selection	categorial selection (subcategorization)
D	determiner
DAT	dative case
DN	derived nominal
DP	determiner phrase: [$_{DP}$ [$_{D'}$ D nP]]
EPP	extended projection principle
FEM	feminine
GEN	genitive case
g^P	verbal adverb phrase
i	external argument theta role of lexical heads
i$_c$	external agentive theta role of causative suffix
IMPERF	imperfective aspect

XV

inf	infinitive (head of infP)
-inf	infinitive suffix
infP	infinitive phrase
INST	instrumental case
j	internal argument theta role (merges in spec-VP)
k	internal argument theta role (sister to V)
kP	*kak* 'as' phrase
LF	long form of adjectives and participles
lit.	word-for-word translation
M	masculine
MDP	minimal-distance principle
mod	modal
mP	modal phrase
N	noun stem
N	noun (syntactic head of NP)
N	neuter
n	small n (syntactic head of nP)
n-	small n (affixal head of nP)
NOM	nominative case
NP	noun phrase
nP	small nP ([$_{nP}$ [$_{n'}$ [N-n] NP])
obliq	oblique morphological case
P	preposition or postposition
PASS	passive
PERF	perfective aspect
PI	predicate instrumental case of adjectives
PL	plural
PP	prepositional or postpositional phrase
PRO	null subject of an infinitive clause ('big PRO')
pro	null form of an overt pronoun ('small pro')
prt	particle
s-selection	theta role selection (s here = s[emantic])
s-clause	small clause
SF	short form of adjectives and participles
SG	singular
SOV	subject-object-verb word order
spec	specifier

s-predicate	small / secondary predicate, i.e. a phrasal projection with an unlinked external theta role: $\{i\text{^-}\}_1$
SVO	subject-verb-object word order
T	head of tense phrase TP
t	trace/copy
TBC	theta binding chain
TP	tense phrase
UTAH	the Uniformity of Theta (role) Assignment Hypothesis
V	verb stem
V	verb (syntactic head of VP)
v	small v (syntactic head of vP)
-v	finite affix
V_{aux}	auxiliary verb
V-bound	vertically bound (an unlinked external theta role bound by a higher **i** or **j** theta role
V_{cop}	copula verb
VP	verb phrase
vP	small vP ($[_{vP}\,[_{v'}\,[\text{V-v}]\,\text{VP}]$)
w	internal portion of a diathesis (positions 2 to 4)
w	word
~	alternates with
<=>	a reversible (biunique) relation
^	is linked to (linear diathesis notation)
|	is linked to (box diathesis notation)
+	composes with (a diathesis-level operation)
=>	projection of a verb's final diathesis to syntax
>	argument-structure level operation
>>	automatic/obligatory argument-structure level operation
–>	syntactic-structure level operation
{x^y}	bipartite argument with a theta role (x) linked to a categorial head (y)
[…]	a constituent at any level of representation
#	intonation contour (prosodic gap) at major constituent boundary
*	ungrammatical
!	archaic but grammatical
*!	archaic and ungrammatical
**	morphologically and syntactically ill-formed

*?	ungrammatical for many but not all speakers
∠	grammatical but degraded (infelicitous)
α	variable case feature
θ	any theta role
<θ>	vertically bound theta role
Q	gloss for enclitic interrogative *li* 'whether' in Russian
-	absence of theta role or categorial head in diathesis (see s-predicate)
X'	denotes intermediate phrasal projection in syntax ([$_{XP}$ nP [$_{X'}$ X nP]]) and palatalization in Russian words (e.g. *brat'* 'to-take' vs. *brat* 'brother').
...	denotes irrelevant material in diathesis
(...)	parentheses denote optionality
‖	division of sentence into topic and comment
≈	link in a theta binding chain

Introduction

While current generative theory acknowledges the importance of argument structure and productive morphological processes, it nevertheless continues to be essentially syntactocentric and has therefore failed to produce a fully integrated, balanced theory of the relation between argument structure, the productive affix-driven operations that alter it, and the syntactic structures it projects. In *The Syntax of Argument Structure* I propose an explicit, unified theory of the mapping between a verb's argument structure representation and the core syntactic structure of the sentence it heads.[1] This theory's primary hypothesis is that *a sentence's core syntactic representation is the direct projection of the main verb's final argument-structure representation*, which entails that there is an isomorphic mapping relation between the positions in argument-structure representation and the corresponding positions in its syntactic projection, and that *the former determine the latter*. In slightly different terms, the premise on which this theory is based is that a sentence's core *grammatical (syntactic) relations are the direct projection of the internal relations of the main verb's final (derived) argument structure*. It follows that determining and substantiating the internal architecture of argument-structure representation, to which chapter 1 is devoted, is an indispensable precondition for the theory of the relation between argument structure and morphosyntactic structure presented in *The Syntax of Argument Structure*.

Extensive empirical evidence will be presented demonstrating that argument-structure based morphosyntactic theory is better able than the more familiar syntax-based theories to explain the universal relations between argument structure, the operations (canonically affix-driven) that alter the verb's *initial* (basic) argument structure, and syntactic structure. It will be demonstrated that many of the syntactic structures whose derivations have been assumed in the generative literature to be primarily syntactic are in fact the syntactic projection of affix-driven operations on the main verb's argument structure. In other words, the main computational action often occurs in argument structure rather than in syntactic structure. The crucial assumption here is that *function words and productive affixes have their own argument structures*, which interact with the lexical verb's argument structure, producing a single derived composite argument structure. For example, the active ~ passive alternation results from different affix-driven argument-structure level operations on the same verb stem's initial argument structure; active sentences are thus not transformed into passive ones by syntactic operations. More specifically, the verb stem's initial (underived 'active') argument structure is made passive by an affix-driven argument-structure level rule and the passivized verb's *final* derived *passive argument structure* projects to syntax as a passive sentence (see Jaeggli 1986, Roberts 1987; see below for details).[2] In more general terms, argument-structure level rules or operations canonically involve the *composition* or, more accurately, the *amalgamation* of a lexical verb stem's argument structure with a productive affix's argument structure; the projection-to-syntax of the resulting composite argument structure is perceived as having systematic *syntactic effects*, many of which have been misinterpreted as primary syntactic rules or operations.[3]

It will be argued that the internal organization of a verb stem's argument structure (**V**'s diathesis) and the type of operations that alter it are linguistic universals. Many of the systematic language-specific differences we observe among the world's languages are encoded in the diatheses of the overt and null affixes (**-af**) that drive argument-structure level derivations. This is why the theory presented in *The Syntax of Argument Structure* is characterized as *morphosyntactic* (rather than *syntactic* with a subsidiary morphological component): the *final* argument-structure representation (diathesis), which projects as the sentence's core syntactic structure, is canonically derived by the affixation of one or more of a relatively small set of productive, argument-structure-bearing, language-specific affixes.[4]

In order to help readers to better orient themselves, I present the following outline of the theory's terminology, notation, and criterial properties, all of which will be discussed in greater detail in the chapters to follow.

- All verbs are represented in the mental lexicon as *stems*, which have an *initial* argument structure.[5]
- The lexicon of each language has a distinct set of productive *paradigmatic affixes*, which have their own argument structures; they include what are traditionally classified as both *inflectional* and *productive derivational* affixes.
- Argument-structure level operations involve the *composition* of a verb stem (**V**) and its argument structure (diathesis) with one or

more paradigmatic affixes and their diatheses. Each paradigmatic affix composes with an initial stem **V** or a derived stem **[V...af-]**, inducing a specific change in the argument structure of the initial or derived stem it composes with.

- It is essential to bear in mind in what follows that all diatheses have the same internal skeletal structure (i.e., the same number (x) of positions or places, some or all of which may be unfilled) and that when two diatheses, each with x places, *compose*, they *amalgamate*, the result being a *derived diathesis* with precisely x places (not 2 x places). A corollary of this conception of diathesis composition is that no matter how many lexical and affixal diatheses compose in a given derivation, the result is a final diathesis with x places – it is the 'contents' of these positions that change; we see below that in natural language x = 4. Given that a **V**'s diathesis may have unfilled positions, another corollary of diathesis theory is that, whereas the number of positions in a **V**'s diathesis is immutable (x = 4), its *valence* (the number of *arguments* it selects to fill these positions) can range between zero and three; the fourth position is occupied by **V** itself (see (1); the reason for this will be explained in chapter 1).

- The argument structures of stems and paradigmatic affixes have the same universal hierarchical internal organization, which, I argue, is responsible for the universal aspects of syntactic structure.

- **V**'s *initial* diathesis is altered in highly restricted ways by the diathesis of the first paradigmatic affix it composes with; **[V-af-]**'s derived diathesis is further altered by the diathesis of the next paradigmatic affix, and so on. The derived argument structure of **[[[V-af] -af] ... -af$_n$]** is the derivation's *final diathesis* (argument structure representation), which projects to syntax. **[[[V-af] -af] ... -af$_n$]** is a well-formed *word*, whose internal structure cannot be accessed by the syntactic rules that operate on its syntactic projection (see Di Sciullo and Williams 1987).[6]

- The theory proposed in *The Syntax of Argument Structure* is a successive, 'in-line' morphosyntactic derivational theory: first, **V**'s initial diathesis composes with the diatheses of a subset of the language's paradigmatic affixes, producing **[[V-af]...-af$_n$]** (a *word*, which is a barrier to subsequent diathetic operations) and **V**'s *final* diathesis, which projects to syntax as the initial syntactic structure from which the sentence's final syntactic structure is derived by successive *syntax-level operations* (e.g. the merging of the higher functional projections,

- *wh*-movement, topicalization, raising to A'-positions, expletive merger, etc.).[7]
- Our most important assumption, which is implicit in other theories (see below), is that **V** cannot have more than three syntactic arguments; what appear to be 'fourth arguments' turn out to be *adjuncts*.[8]
- Much of *The Syntax of Argument Structure* is devoted to presenting empirical evidence that argument structure has the 2×4 bipartite organization represented by the *diathesis* in (1), according to which **V**'s argument structure consists of two related *tiers*, a *theta-role-selection tier* (theta-selection, s-selection, theta-grid) and a corresponding *linked categorial tier* (subcategorization frame, c-selection). Since each argument's categorial head is *linked* to a corresponding theta role *in argument structure*, an argument is bipartite.[9] Since the maximal number of arguments **V** can have is three, argument structure has the four positions represented in (1): **i, j**, and **k** are theta roles, **N** is a categorial noun head, and **V** is a lexical verb-stem head.[10] A theta role may be linked to **V** in *derived* diatheses only (e.g., see the *by*-phrase in passive derivations and the causative derivation of Turkish *ditransitive* (three-argument) verbs in §1.9).

(1)   The diathesis of a ditransitive verb:

i	j	k	-
N	N	N	V
1	2	3	4

The following is an alternative, linear representation of the two-tiered box structure in (1) (read " ^ " as "is linked to"; the curly brackets represent the bipartite arguments; the outer curly brackets demarcate **V**'s diathesis):

(2)   {{i^N}$_1$ {j^N}$_2$ {k^N}$_3$ {- ^V}$_4$}

- The argument structure representation in (1)/(2) is universal: *all* predicators and productive affixes have this skeletal 2×4, eight-slotted structure, regardless of their initial *valence* (which ranges from zero to three).[11] The reason for this is that initially unfilled slots like the theta-slot in {- ^V}$_4$ in (1)/(2) will be shown to play an active role in many argument-structure level operations. Unfilled argument positions (e.g., {-^-}$_3$ in the diathesis of monotransitive verbs) that are not affected by diathetic operations do not project to syntax.

- Given the bipartite structure of arguments, argument-structure rules, unlike syntactic rules, can operate on a theta role without affecting the **N** it is linked to (e.g., $\{i\wedge N\}_1 > \{-\wedge N\}_1$ *dethematization* in passive derivations) or can delete **N** without affecting **i** (e.g., $\{i\wedge N\}_1 > \{i\wedge -\}_1$ in the derivation of *s(mall)-predicates* (see below). Syntactic rules as presently conceived cannot delete an NP (DP) but not its theta role, or delete a theta role, stranding its NP.
- The two-tiered, four-positioned diathesis in (1)/(2) does not involve *redundancy* (see Lasnik and Uriagereka 2005: 3–7): (i) Since the unfilled positions in impersonal (zero valence), unergative, unaccusative, monotransitive, and ditransitive diatheses play a crucial role in constraining diathesis-level operations involving the *rightward displacement* of initial arguments, they must be explicitly represented in each verb's diathesis (see §1.9). (ii) Conclusive evidence will be presented that the two tiers in diathesis representation are *autonomous*, i.e., **V**'s c-selection (subcategorization tier) *cannot* be predicted from its theta-selection tier, as has been claimed (see Pesetsky 1982, Bošković 1997, and others).[12] (iii) Empirical evidence will also be presented for the existence of *external subcategorization* in Russian and other languages, which entails that Chomsky's Extended Projection Principle is not an absolute universal: not all *verbs* have external arguments and, accordingly, not all *sentences* have subjects (e.g., the external argument of an impersonal verb is $\{-\wedge-\}_1$, which does not project to syntax).[13] It appears that subject-optionality is a special case of a more general parameterizable universal, which I tentatively call the Spec-Parameter: the fact that the spec-position in Russian noun phrases and the subject position in Russian clauses (spec-vP) may be unfilled is an instantiation of the same parameter setting.
- The representation of argument structure by the diathesis in (1) is *hierarchical* in the sense that **[V-af$_n$]** in the final diathesis *merges* with **[V-af]**'s arguments *one at a time, from right-to-left*, projecting the sentence's core syntactic structure, which is the input (initial syntactic structure) to the syntactic phase of a sentence's derivation. Note that the bottom-to-top direction of syntactic projection and the binary branching of syntactic representation assumed in *The Syntax of Argument Structure* and in other theories are a consequence of the right-to-left merger of **V** and its arguments, which is determined by the diathesis's internal organization in (1)/(2).
- (1)/(2) projects the sentence's core syntactic structure (Extended Lexical Projection) in (3); 'small v' is the *finite affixal head* of vP:

6   *Introduction*

(3)   {{i^N}$_1$ {j^N}$_2$ {k^N}$_3$ {- ^V-}$_4$} => [$_{vP}$ NP$_i$ [$_{v'}$ [V-v] [$_{VP}$ NP$_j$ [$_{v'}$ t$_V$ NP$_k$]]]]

Since {i^N}$_1$ is the left-most argument in **V**'s diathesis, it is the last to merge syntactically and, given that VP has only two argument positions (spec-VP and sister-to-V), {i^N}$_1$'s syntactic projection is *VP-external*: it projects to spec-vP as the sentence's subject.[14] The vP s (mall)-clause in (3) canonically *merges* with higher functional heads and the subject NP$_i$ canonically moves to the spec-position of a higher functional phrase (not shown in (3)). Once vP is projected to syntax from **V**'s final diathesis, all subsequent operations are syntactic.

- The theory outlined above has the following corollaries: (i) *The 2×4 hierarchical structure of the final diathesis exhaustively determines the projected sentence's core grammatical (syntactic) relations.* (ii) Syntactic rules do not change a sentence's basic grammatical relations or the cases that express them, i.e., there are no syntactic movement rules that induce abstract or morphological case-change. All operations that alter **V**'s initial diathesis and, therefore, its projected syntactic relations, are diathesis-based and are canonically the result of the composition of **V**'s 2×4 initial diathesis with the 2×4 diatheses of its affixes or functional verbs (e.g., auxiliary verbs). Thus *alternations*, including voice alternations, are alternative realizations of a given **V**'s initial diathesis; the complete set of a given **V**'s alternations is its *morphosyntactic paradigm*. For example, the movement of direct object to subject position (with accompanying change of accusative to nominative case) in middle, passive, and unaccusative derivations does not by hypothesis involve syntactic movement. (iii) There are no rules of any kind at any level that change the value of a theta role. For example, when a Turkish unergative **V**'s initial external agent theta role is right-displaced by the causative suffix's diathesis and realized as **[V-af$_{CAUS}$]**'s direct object, it is an agentive accusative direct object: the agent role is not nor can it be converted to patient role (see §1.9).

- The initial and final diatheses of verbs and paradigmatic affixes always have 2×4 structure, which entails the following universal: there are no operations of any kind at any level that can alter the basic 2×4, eight-slotted *skeletal structure* of the diathesis; all argument-structure level operations begin and end with the diathesis's eight slots intact; rules may of course act upon the contents of the slots, adding, displacing, deleting, and delinking arguments. This is the foundation of the theory proposed in *The Syntax of Argument Structure*. We shall see below that diathesis-level operations may: (i) delink a theta role and its categorial head (e.g., *dethematization* and right-displacement of external **i** in passive derivations, which may be schematically represented as: $\{\{i^\wedge N\}_1...\{-^\wedge V\}_4\} > \{\{-^\wedge N\}_1...\{i^\wedge[V\text{-}af_{pass}]\}_4\})$; (ii) create *s-predicates* by deleting V's external N, i.e.: $\{\{i^\wedge N\}_1...\{-^\wedge V\}_4\} > \{\{i^\wedge\text{-}\}_1...\{-^\wedge [V\text{-}af]\}_4\}$;[15] (iii) add new arguments to V's initial diathesis in productive applicative and causative derivations *provided that appropriate positions are available*.[16] Given that a sentence's core syntax is determined by V's final diathesis, the immutability of the diathesis's 2×4 structure predicts that the core syntax of clauses should be cross-linguistically *uniform* (allowing for variation due to the parameterization of universal principles like the headedness parameter); it also predicts the absence of *construction-specific grammatical relations* (see below).

- *s-predicates*, which are derived diatheses with unlinked external theta roles, i.e., $\{i^\wedge\text{-}\}_1$, will be shown to play a central role in the building of morphosyntactic structures. For example, the following are s-predicates: attributive (but not predicate) forms of the adjective (chapter 2), hybrid verbal adjuncts (chapter 3), and subject-controlled infinitive complements (chapter 4). Now, if there are productive operations in natural language that dissociate (delink) theta roles and their categorial heads (e.g., $\{i^\wedge N\}_1 > \{i^\wedge\text{-}\}_1$ [s-predicate] or $\{i^\wedge N\}_1 > \{-^\wedge N\}_1$ [dethematized verb]), there must be a computational level of representation at which such operations are possible. Whereas syntactic rules are not able to dissociate an NP and its theta role (e.g., delete or move an NP, stranding its theta role), the 2×4 structure of the diathesis, in which *arguments are bipartite* (i.e., their theta roles and categorial heads are distributed over two autonomous tiers), predicts the existence of precisely this kind of delinking operation in argument-structure level derivations.

The theory outlined above is characterized as an integrated *morphosyntactic* theory because diathesis-level operations, which are canonically *affix-driven*, derive final diatheses, which *project core morphosyntactic structure*. In other words, if verbs are represented in the lexicon as stems, their derivations necessarily involve the composition of the stem's diathesis with the diathesis of at least one affix to create a *word*, which is the 'atom' of the syntactic phase of the derivation (see Di Sciullo and Williams 1987). If this theory is correct, a sentence's universal Extended Lexical Projection is a morphosyntactic structure (see vP in (3), where the head v is the finite verbal affix).

Explicit theories have a way of taking on a life of their own, making falsifiable predictions and suggesting solutions to problems that were not initially envisaged. This phenomenon is responsible for my decision to expand my original circumscribed goal of exploring the mapping between argument structure and syntax into a comprehensive theory of morphosyntax in which argument structure is promoted from its accessory status in Government and Binding theory and the Minimalist Program to a far more central role. For example, since, as we shall see below, s-predicates turn out to play a fundamental role in syntactic structure building and, since the unbound projection of $\{i^\wedge\text{-}\}_1$ is syntactically ill-formed, diathesis-based theory requires an explicit theory of *control*, which will be demonstrated to derive entirely from Binding theory and which is far broader than infinitive control (see chapters 2–5). Furthermore, theta binding chains (TBC), in which s-predicates are *vertically bound* (Williams 1994), turn out to also account for case, number, and gender *agreement*: the vertically bound tail of a TBC agrees with the TBC's head. Thus an explicit theory applied systematically to the full range of data both provides new solutions to old problems (e.g. the use of noun phrases as both arguments and predicates) and, equally important, identifies new problems based on old data that were erroneously thought to be well understood (e.g., see the similarities and differences between copula and auxiliary verbs in chapters 2, 3, and 4).

While data in *The Syntax of Argument Structure* comes from English, Turkish, Icelandic, French, and other languages, the star of the show is Russian.[17] The reason for this is the same as the reason I have been working on Russian morphosyntax since 1965: Russian, with its rich inflectional system and concomitant free word order, is essentially the typological polar opposite of English and perforce plays an important role in getting beyond English-specific phenomena in our search for morphosyntactic universals. For example, Russian's elaborate system of impersonal sentences provides robust empirical evidence against the English-biased claim that all sentences in all languages have a null or overt subject (see the Extended Projection Principle) and against Burzio's Generalization (see §1.8). Russian's rich case and agreement morphology provides precisely the kinds of data and problems that a coherent morphosyntactic theory must be able to account for (see Franks 1995, Lavine 2000). Note too that, as we shall see in chapter 1, it is overt case morphology in tandem with argument structure that licenses 'scrambling' (see Bailyn 1995a, 1995b, 2006, Junghanns and Zubatow 1997, Slioussar 2005). Russian's systematic gender, number, and case agreement serves a critical diagnostic function, enabling us to pinpoint the presence and absence of null categories; e.g., see chapter 4 where the case agreement of the adjunct s-predicate pronominal adjectives *sam* '(by) himself', *odin* 'alone', and *ves'* 'all' provides incontrovertible empirical evidence that infinitive complements come in three sizes: *infinitive s(mall) clauses*, which have *null* dative subjects when controlled: [$_{infP}$ PRO$_{i,DAT}$ inf'$_{<i>}$]; *infinitive s(econdary) predicates*, which, like all anaphors, must be bound: [$_{infP<i>}$ inf'$_{<i>}$]; and *bare infinitive phrases*: [$_{infP}$ inf'], which obligatorily cooccur with auxiliary verbs (see §4.12). I assume that many of the categories, distinctions, relations, operations, and constructions analyzed in the following chapters, which are overtly realized in Russian, are morphosyntactic universals which happen not to have formal realizations in English and many other languages.

The theoretical scaffolding of *The Syntax of Argument Structure* is Government and Binding theory and the Minimalist Program enriched by the insights of Williams' *Thematic Structure in Syntax* (1994). Williams' influence has been profound (e.g., the crucial notions of *vertical binding* and *external argument* are his). The influence of what I will call the Russian School has also been substantial: I first encountered the two-tiered diathesis and its use as the basis for a typology of alternations in Mel'čuk and Xolodovič 1970 and Xolodovič 1974.[18] Relational Grammar has also exerted an influence, but more as a theory of argument structure than syntax (see Channon 1979, Perlmutter 1983, Perlmutter and Rosen 1984, Blake 1990, Farrell 2005: ch. 6). The following publications influenced my conception of argument structure in this book's early stages: Fillmore 1968 (see Cook 1989), all references to Bowers, Marantz 1984, Pinker 1984: ch. 8, Zubizarreta 1987, Baker 1988b, Grimshaw 1990, Speas 1990, Wechsler 1995, Alsina 1996, Epstein *et al.* 1998, and all the references to Levin and Rappaport Hovav.

Since *The Syntax of Argument Structure*, which presents what I take to be a new theory of the mapping between argument structure and morphosyntactic structure, has unfamiliar terminology and notation, and is based primarily on Russian, which I do not assume my readers know, the book's readability has been a constant concern. To this end I have in most cases avoided protracted polemical discussions, preferring instead to devote the limited space at my disposal to working out the details implicit in diathesis theory.[19] My assumption is that the best way to introduce a new theory is to demonstrate its explanatory power on the basis of a broad range of data rather than dwell on the perceived weaknesses of its competitors. My argumentation is accordingly data based (empirical) rather than theory internal.

I would like to thank my past and present colleagues and graduate students at Cornell and Princeton who have either read and commented on early drafts of *The Syntax of Argument Structure* or participated in seminars based on its contents: Cori Anderson, John Bailyn, John Bowers, Vrinda Chidambaram, Bob Freidin, Steve Franks, Stephanie Harves, Anton Koychev, Jim Lavine, Anna Maslennikova and the Sankt-Peterburg Linguistics Society, Lucie Medova, Tarald Taraldsen, and Edwin Williams. I would also like to thank my colleagues at the following conferences for their papers and their comments on my presentations: The Argument Structure Workshop (University of Tromsoe, Norway, November 4–6, 2004) and The Workshop on Argument Structure and Syntactic Relations (University of the Basque Country, Vitoria-Gasteiz, Spain, May 23–25, 2007). Special thanks go to Vrinda Chidambaram, who proofread the manuscript, and to Ken Safir, who suggested the title.

1 *The structure of argument structure*

1.0 Introduction

One of recent generative theory's leading ideas is that *syntax is a projection of the lexicon*.[1] The primary goal of this book is to explore this hypothesis and to propose an explicit theory of the mapping between the lexicon and morphosyntactic structure. I will argue that this hypothesis is correct if by 'lexicon' we understand *predicate argument structure*, which is an integral part of the lexical entry of every verb and, more generally, of every *predicator* in the mental lexicon.[2]

My main hypothesis is that a sentence's *core syntactic structure* (vP) is the direct projection of **V**'s argument structure.[3] More specifically, argument structure has its own syntax, i.e., it has hierarchical internal structure which is operated on by argument-structure specific rules. This entails that vP is fully determined by the homologous structure of the head verb's *final derived argument structure*.[4] In other words, in the argument-structure based theory of morphosyntax presented in this book, the grammatical (syntactic) relations of a sentence's arguments are fully determined by the internal organization of **V**'s diathesis. It is in this sense that **V** *heads* its clause.

This theory requires that we pay careful attention to whether the rules responsible for a sentence's derivation operate on argument structure (**V**'s diathesis) or on the syntactic structure it projects: many operations that were thought to be syntactic will be shown to be diathetic. For example, *wh*-movement, which does not involve a change of grammatical relations or case, is patently a syntactic rule. But rules involving NP-movement, which involve a change of grammatical relations and case, will be shown to be operations on argument-structure representation that have predictable syntactic effects. A corollary of this theory is that *syntactic rules do not alter a sentence's basic (core) grammatical relations and the cases that lexicalize them*. In other words, operations that alter core grammatical relations must by hypothesis be diathesis-level operations.

My approach to *argument realization* is different from theories like that of Levin and Rappaport Hovav (2005), who posit a direct relation between a verb's lexical semantics and the syntactic realization of its arguments. The chapters of this book can be read as a protracted argument against the hypothesis that a verb's lexical semantics systematically determines the syntactic structure of the sentence it projects. We shall see that verbs with the same lexical semantics and even the same ordered set of theta roles routinely have different argument realizations, i.e., project different syntactic structures in the same language and cross-linguistically.[5]

An explicit theory of the mapping between argument structure and morphosyntactic structure must be able to encode the *arbitrary, semantically unmotivated aspects of argument realization* as well as its systematic aspects. My position is that if the relation between syntactic form and verbal meaning were direct and systematic, **V**'s projected syntax would always be predictable and there would be no need for argument structure as an autonomous level of representation (see Alsina 1996, Stowell 1992: 14, Sadler and Spencer 2001: 218, Zubizarreta 1987).

In the theory I am proposing, lexical semantic representation maps onto **V**'s diathesis, which, in turn, maps onto syntactic representation. Our focus will be the mapping between **V**'s diathesis and the core syntactic structure it projects. Since the diathesis mediates between lexical semantic and syntactic representations, it can be thought of as a *rectifier* that aligns the information in semantic representation, presenting it in a form facilitating the *direct projection of* **V**'s *arguments to syntactic structure.*[6]

Lexical semantic representation ideally involves the universal aspects of **V**'s event/participant meaning, whereas certain aspects of argument structure are, by hypothesis, necessarily language-specific, verb-specific, and *arbitrary*; e.g., it is in **V**'s diathesis that the unpredictable argument-realizations of *jealous* and its Russian counterpart *revnovat'* are encoded (see note 5). But the hierarchical organization of diathesis representation (see below), the kind of rules that operate on it (which are canonically driven by diathesis-bearing affixes), and the final diathesis's isomorphic relation to core syntactic structure are, I argue, formal universals. This book will thus be primarily concerned with the universal hierarchical structure of the diathesis, the constraints on the affix-driven operations that alter it (e.g., causativization, passivization, nominalization, infinitive-formation, etc.), and the projection of **V**'s final derived diathesis to vP, its Extended Lexical Projection, which can be represented as [VP nP$_{i.NOM}$ [$_{v'}$ [**V-v**] VP]] (**i** is **V**'s external theta role, nP$_i$ is its subject, v is the productive finite verbal *suffix*, [**V-v**] is a word [verb]). Thus the diathesis simultaneously encodes argument structure's immutable universal formal properties and the unpredictable, arbitrary properties of individual verbs in particular languages (see §1.8.1).

Languages typically have a closed class of productive, diathesis-altering, paradigm-creating affixes (**-af**), which have their own diatheses.[7] Since these affixes both alter **V**'s initial diathesis and head their own projections in the syntax (afP), diathesis theory provides a natural setting in which an important lexicalist dictum can be formalized: in addition to parameter-setting, the morphosyntactic differences we observe among languages can in large part be attributed to the language-specific properties of their diathesis-bearing *affixes*. A diathesis-level rule is thus the *composition* of **V**'s initial diathesis with the diathesis of a paradigmatic affix, which projects as [$_{afP}$ nP$_{i.\alpha}$ [$_{af'}$ [**V-af**] VP]] (α = case).

Summary: A sentence's Extended Lexical Projection is the syntactic projection of **V**'s final diathesis (i.e. **V**'s initial diathesis in composition with the diathesis of at least one affix), which encodes [**V-af**]'s syntactically relevant information in a form that maps directly and isomorphically onto binary-branching phrase-structure representation. The information encoded in **V**'s final diathesis includes: its syntactic category (syntactic features), its *valence* (the number, type, and obligatoriness of its arguments), the binary-branching and grammatical relations of the sentence it projects, the lexical (quirky) cases and prepositions it selects, and other unpredictable properties. However, far from simply being a repository of unsystematic, unpredictable properties, diathetic representation is in fact the seat of syntactic structure in the sense that its internal organization determines the projected sentence's syntactic organization. This conception of argument structure entails that **V**'s diathesis and the diathesis-bearing affixes it composes with play a far greater role in determining syntactic structure than allowed for in syntax-centered theories. In the next section we look more closely at the hypothesis that **V**'s final diathesis encodes the grammatical (syntactic) relations of the sentence it projects.

1.1 The internal structure of the diathesis

Russian provides a great deal of evidence that **V**'s diathesis must explicitly represent its theta-role selection and its category selection (c-selection or subcategorization) as *autonomous* but related *tiers* since it is easily demonstrated that neither can be systematically predicted from the other.[8] I shall argue below that: (i) **V**'s theta-selection and c-selection cannot be systematically predicted from its lexical meaning. (ii) c-selection is not predictable from theta-selection (see the notion of Canonical Structural Realization in Chomsky 1986; Levin and Rappaport Hovav 2005: 8): it is quite common in Russian for **V**s with identical ordered sets of theta roles to have different c-selections and, therefore, different morphosyntactic projections (see §1.8.1). (iii) There is overwhelming empirical evidence that the diathesis of Russian verbs must contain *external subcategorization* since it is not predictable whether a **V** that does not select an external theta role **i** projects a subject nP: (see the comparison of impersonal verbs, which are *subjectless* in Russian, and unaccusative verbs below).[9] (iv) It is also not predictable whether the direct object of a **V** that does not select an external theta role will *externalize* in **V**'s diathesis, projecting to syntax as the nominative subject (e.g. unaccusative **V**s), or remain in situ, projecting to syntax as the accusative direct object of an impersonal (subjectless) sentence (see *Menja$_{ACC}$ tošnilo$_N$* '(lit.) Me nauseated'):[10] whether or not an internal argument of a **V** that does not assign an external theta role can externalize in these derivations depends directly on whether or not **V** selects an unlinked external **N**, which is the diathesis-level analogue of a landing site in syntax (see {-^-}$_1$ vs. {-^N}$_1$ below). Since c-selection, especially *external c-selection*, is unpredictable in terms of **V**'s lexical semantics and theta-role selection, and plays a crucial role in the derivation of Russian morphosyntactic structure (see chapters 2–5), it must be explicitly represented as an autonomous c-selection tier in the diatheses of all predicators (see Grimshaw 1990: 70).[11]

The internal organization of the diathesis is based on the *linking* of the positions in **V**'s theta-selection tier to the corresponding positions in its autonomous categorial (subcategorization) tier. An *argument* is thus bipartite: it is a theta role *linked* to a categorial head in **V**'s diathesis. Arguments are arranged in strict linear order, which is determined in large part by the UTAH (see Baker 1997). An argument is thus represented as: {θ^X}$_n$, where "^" is to be read "is linked to," **X** is a categorial head in **V**'s lower tier (canonically a noun **N**), θ is a theta role in **V**'s upper tier (see Jaeggli 1986: 588, Zubizaretta 1985), and **n** indicates the relative position of the argument in **V**'s diathesis (see below). We can define argument structure as the *ordered set* of **V**'s {θ^X}$_n$ arguments, which maps onto homologous positions in **V**'s hierarchical syntactic projection vP (Extended Lexical Projection). This definition will be fine tuned as we proceed through this chapter. A verb can have no arguments or as many as three (see below).

The external argument of a transitive or unergative verb is represented as {i^N}$_1$, i.e., an external theta role **i**, which is canonically an agent, linked to a noun head **N**. {i^N}$_1$, the left-most argument in **V**'s diathesis and thus the last to merge in syntax, projects to spec-vP as **V**'s *dedicated subject* nP$_i$ (vP is the

1.1 The internal structure of the diathesis

syntactic projection of **-v-**, which is a finite verbal suffix whose complement is VP).[12] Thus: $\{i^\wedge N\}_1$ => $[_{vP}\ nP_{i.NOM}\ v']$.[13] The external argument of an impersonal (subjectless) **V** is $\{-^\wedge-\}_1$, where "- " denotes absence of a theta role or categorical head: $\{-^\wedge-\}_1$ => $[_{vP}\ v']$ (see §1.4.1 for a complete typology of external arguments).

Diathetic representation determines the core hierarchical syntactic structure of the sentence it projects in the following way: **V**'s diathesis encodes the *order in which its arguments merge*, one-by-one, from right-to-left, to form progressively larger syntactic constituents.[14] I am thus equating *merge* (in syntax) and *project* (from **V**'s diathesis). Note that a diathesis does not project to syntax all at once: the diathesis encodes the information that **V** merges first with the right-most argument in its diathesis, then this expression merges with the next argument in **V**'s diathesis, etc.[15] It is in this sense that syntax is a projection of the lexicon; more accurately, a sentence's binary-branching, hierarchical syntactic structure is directly encoded in **V**'s diathesis as the right-to-left ordering of the bipartite arguments it selects; the first argument that **V** merges with projects to syntax as the sentence's most deeply embedded argument ($\{k^\wedge N\}_3$) and the last argument merged is **V**'s *external argument*, which is the sentence's subject. Since $\{i^\wedge N\}_1$ is merged in spec-vP, it is *external* in the sense that it is the only one of **V**'s arguments to merge VP externally: $\{\{i^\wedge N\}_1\ \{j^\wedge N\}_2\ \{k^\wedge N\}_3\}$ => $[_{vP}\ nP_{i.NOM}\ [_{v'}\ [V-v]\ [_{VP}\ nP_{j.ACC}\ [_{v'}\ t_v\ nP_{k.oblique}]]]]$ (**i**, **j**, and **k** represent **V**'s theta roles; nP_k is the sister of **[V-v]** and nP_j merges in spec-VP).

Assuming that verbs cannot have more than three arguments, argument structure can be represented by the diathesis in (1), which has the following internal organization: (i) It has two horizontal tiers: the upper tier encodes theta selection, whose *order* is determined by the UTAH, and the lower category selection tier. (ii) **i**, **j**, and **k** in the upper tier are variables representing theta roles: the *external* theta role **i** is typically the *agent* if **V** selects one, **j** is the theta role of the direct object (typically theme), and **k** is the theta role of the indirect or oblique object, which is realized morphosyntactically as an oblique case or a preposition, depending on **k**'s value (see *theta case* in Babby 1994a). (iii) Each diathesis thus has four bipartite positions: three argument positions and **V**'s right-most position. (iv) There are thus eight *slots* or *cells* in every diathesis, not all of which are filled. (v) While the contents of the eight slots can be operated on and altered by diathesis-based operations, there are no operations that can alter the diathesis's basic 2×4 skeletal frame. (vi) All **V**'s and paradigmatic affixes have a 2×4 diathesis no matter what their valence is since there are diathesis-level operations that make use of unoccupied slots (e.g., see causativization and nominalization in §1.11). (vii) Empty diathesis positions, i.e., $\{-^\wedge-\}$,

16 *The structure of argument structure*

are not projected to syntax. ("|" in (1) represents the *linking* between theta roles in the upper tier and corresponding categorial heads in the lower tier.)

(1)   Diathesis of **V** with three arguments (ditransitive verb):

```
i   j   k   -
|   |   |   |
N   N   N   V
1   2   3   4
```

(2a) is the diathesis of the verb *revnovat'* 'to-be-jealous' discussed above in note 5: *k* 'to' in the lower tier is a preposition, which assigns quirky dative case to its complement (don't confuse the theta role **k** and the preposition *k* 'to' in (2a)); (2b) is the diathesis of the transitive impersonal verb *tošnit'*.

(2a)   Diathesis of *revnovat'* 'to-be-jealous':

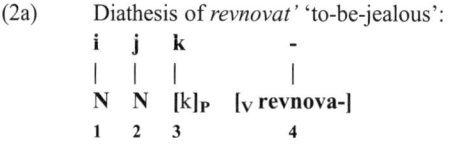

(2b)   Diathesis of impersonal transitive *tošnit'* 'to experience nausea':

```
-   j   -      -
|   |   |      |
-   N   -    [v tošni-]
1   2   3      4
```

The diatheses in (1) and (2) can be represented by the alternative linear notation in (3), which is convenient when referring to individual arguments and when representing diathesis-based derivations, which often involve the composition of **V**'s diathesis with several affixal diatheses.[16]

(3)   a. $\{\{i{\wedge}N\}_1\ \{j{\wedge}N\}_2\ \{k{\wedge}N\}_3\ \ \{\text{-}\wedge V\}_4\}$ (= (1))
       b. $\{\{i{\wedge}N\}_1\ \{j{\wedge}N\}_2\ \{k{\wedge}\ [k]_P\}_3\ \{\text{-}\wedge V\}_4\}$ (= (2a))
       c. $\{\{\text{-}{\wedge}\text{-}\}_1\ \{j{\wedge}N\}_2\ \{\text{-}{\wedge}\text{-}\}_3\ \ \{\text{-}\wedge V\}_4\}$ (= (2b))

Summary: The 2×4 representation of **V**'s diathesis encodes the systematic mapping between the diathesis's four ordered positions and the homologous positions in its morphosyntactic projection. For example, the diathesis of a ditransitive verb in (4a) encodes the right-to-left order in which **V** merges syntactically with its three arguments, which is made explicit by the diathesis-to-syntax projection 'rules' in (4b). (4c) is the core syntactic structure projected from the diathesis in (4a) via (4b): first (b.i) applies, then (b.ii), finally, (b.iii)), which results in the *bottom-to-top* building up of the hierarchically structured, binary-branching syntactic representation in (4c) ("⇒" denotes projection from positions in the diathesis to corresponding positions in syntactic structure). Since the phrase structure in (4c) is entirely encoded in the diathetic representation in (4a), the 'rules' in (4b) are redundant: they play an expository role here, making the merge/project operations encoded in (4a) explicit, and will play no role in what follows.

(4)   a. Representation of a ditransitive verb's diathesis:

b. Projection of positions in **V**'s diathesis to homologous positions in its syntactic structure: merger:
  i. $\{k \wedge N\}_3 + V \Rightarrow [_{V'} \; V \; nP_{k.oblique}]$
  ii. $\{j \wedge N\}_2 + V' \Rightarrow [_{VP} \; nP_{j.ACC} \; V']$
  iii. $\{i \wedge N\}_1 + VP \Rightarrow [_{vP} \; nP_{i.NOM} \; [_{v'} \; v \; VP]]$

c.

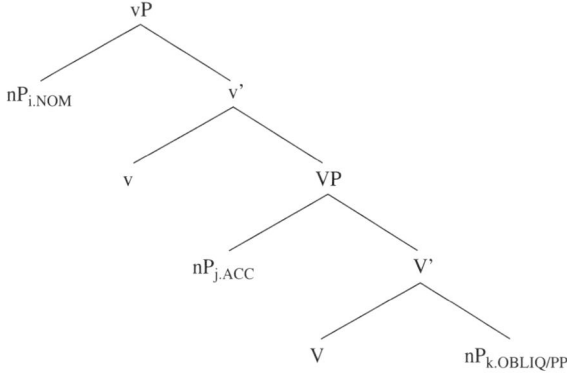

Speaking metaphorically, the 2×4 frame of the diathesis in (4a) is the substructure of syntactic form and the binary-branching, hierarchical structure in (4c) is its superstructure.

Diathetic theory correctly predicts the absence of *construction specific syntax*: operations on **V**'s initial diathesis may reorder arguments, delink theta roles from the categorial head they are linked to in the initial diathesis, delete arguments or parts of arguments, or add new arguments,[17] but they cannot alter the basic 2×4 architecture of diathetic representation. In other words, slots in argument-structure representation cannot be created or destroyed. The theory correctly predicts that the eight slots in **V**'s final (derived) diathesis always projects the same basic syntactic structures no matter what the slots' contents are, which explains both the absence of construction-specific syntax and the cross-linguistic uniformity of core syntactic structure and of grammatical relations (see below for details). (4) makes it clear why the ordering of the diathesis's three arguments vis-à-vis **V** in diathetic representation is the cornerstone of syntactic structure.

1.2 The hierarchical organization of argument structure

In this section we look more closely at the hypothesis that argument structure has the internal structure of the diathesis in (4a). Let us begin by considering two earlier proposals that argument structure has hierarchical organization. Williams (1981) had hierarchical structure in mind when he posited the existence of the *external argument* as a component of a verb's argument-structure representation. His underlining notation ($\underline{i}$ = external argument) encodes *partial* hierarchical structure, i.e., the external argument vs. the internal arguments; the former maps onto subject, which is *VP-external* (see (4c)), the latter map onto **V**'s objects, which are *VP-internal*. We can represent Williams' notation in (5), where $\underline{i}$, **j**, and **k** represent the external, direct internal, and indirect (oblique) internal arguments (theta roles) respectively. Williams assumes that arguments in argument-structure representation are theta roles and that a given **V** can have no more than three arguments:

(5)   Williams 1981: **V ($\underline{i}$ (j, k))**

Williams was on the right track, but he did not go far enough. The evidence from Russian, Turkish, and French presented below demonstrates that there must be additional hierarchical structure imposed on **V**'s two internal agruments. This is implicit in Bowers' 1993 notation, which can be represented in our terms in (6); Bowers too assumes that argument structure is represented solely in terms of theta roles and that **V** can have up to three theta-arguments (see Moro 2008: 18).

(6)   Bowers 1993: **V (((i) j) k)**

According to the embedded-parenthesis notation in (6), **k** is the first argument to merge with **V** and is therefore the most deeply embedded argument in syntactic structure (see (4c)). **j** is next, merging with **[V+k]** and projecting to spec-VP; **i** merges last and is external, i.e, projects to spec-vP, which is VP-external (see (4c)). According to (6), the argument structure of a ditransitive verb consists of three hierarchically ordered arguments, which project *three hierarchically distinct argument positions in syntactic structure* (see Bailyn 1995b: 13): [$_{vP}$ nP$_{i.NOM}$ [$_{v'}$ [V-v] [$_{VP}$ nP$_{j.ACC}$ [$_{v'}$ t$_V$ nP$_k$]]]].[18]

I argue below that single-tiered representations of argument structure like (5) and (6) do not encode enough information to account for **V**'s projected syntactic structure. For example, we shall see in §1.8.1 that although the Russian verbs *tošnit'* and *korčit'* have the same theta tiers (identical hierarchically ordered sets of theta roles), they nevertheless project sentences with entirely different morphosyntactic structures. Thus (6) is the correct representation of **V**'s theta tier, but it is only half the story: a second, c-selection tier is needed.

We shall be concerned primarily with the mapping between **V**'s final derived diathesis and its Extended Lexical Projection; see (4c), where small v, the head of vP, is the finite affixal head, which does not itself assign theta roles.[19] While our attention will be focused on the vP domain as the direct projection of **V**'s diathesis, we cannot account for a sentence's *word order* in a 'free' word-order language like Russian without reference to higher functional heads like T (tense) and C (complementizer). For example, although Russian is a SVO language, consider the neutral OV order in transitive impersonal sentences like (7), where the accusative direct object pronoun *menja* 'me' moves from spec-VP to spec-TP in the absence of a nominative subject to satisfy T's EPP property (see Lavine and Freidin 2002); (8) is a schematic representation of (7)'s syntactic structure.[20] This type of movement is *syntactic* since the sentence's projected case and grammatical relations are unaffected by it: *menja* in (7) is still the direct object despite its displacement from spec-VP.

(7) Menja   tošnilo   ot   zapaxa   krepkogo   tabaka
     me:ACC   nauseated:N.SG   from   smell:GEN   strong   tobacco:GEN.
     'The smell of the strong tobacco nauseated me.'

(8) a. [$_{TP}$ menja [$_{T'}$ T [$_{VP}$ [$_v$ tošnilo] [$_{v'}$ ...]]]]   or
     b. [$_{TP}$ menja [$_{T'}$ [$_T$ tošnilo] [$_{VP}$ t$_V$ [$_{v'}$ ...]]]]

1.3 The autonomy of the theta and categorial tiers

We saw above that argument structure encodes **V**'s theta selection, which is represented as a hierarchically ordered set of the theta roles.[21] The nesting representation in (6) encodes the information that the merger of **V** and its arguments procedes from right to left, from the most deeply embedded **k** argument to the external **i** argument. The argument structures of the most common verb types are represented in Bowers' notation in (9); (9a–e) are found in both English and Russian; (9f), which is not found in English and was not taken into consideration by Bowers, is illustrated above in (7)/(8).[22]

(9) a. Ditransitive: (((i) j) k) V
     b. Monotransitive: (((i) j) -) V

c. Unergative: $(((i)-)-)V$
d. No arguments: $(((-)-)-)V$
e. Unaccusative: $(((-)j)-)V$
f. Transitive-impersonal: $(((-)j)-)V$

Notice however that the single-tier, theta-role-only representations of unaccusative and transitive-impersonal verbs in (9e) and (9f) are *identical*: both have a single internal **j**-argument in second position, which is correct as far as it goes. But this is a serious problem for argument structure representation, whose function is to encode all **V**'s syntactically relevant information: the single-tier argument structures in (9e) and (9f) predict that unaccusative and transitive-impersonal verbs should have *identical* morphosyntactic structures, whereas they in fact have *entirely different morphosyntactic realizations*. The **j**-argument of unaccusative verbs obligatorily *externalizes* and is realized syntactically as the sentence's nominative subject; but the **j**-argument of transitive-impersonal verbs cannot *externalize* and is accordingly realized as the accusative direct object of an impersonal (subjectless) sentence, as in (7).[23]

(9e–f) and the sentences they project demonstrate that ordered theta-selection representations of argument structure cannot predict **V**'s c-selection (see Stowell 1992: 11, Bošković 1997), and thus cannot predict the morphosyntactic realization of **V**'s arguments. Our next step will be to enrich single-tiered representations like (9) so that they are able to encode unpredictable morphosyntactic differences in the argument structure of verbs with *identical theta-selection*. As we saw above, my proposal is that argument structure representation must consist of **V**'s hierarchically ordered set of theta roles, as in (6) and (9), and its c-selection (subcategorization), arranged in a *two-tiered structure* in which the corresponding theta and categorial heads are *linked*, forming bipartite arguments: $\{i^{\wedge}N\}_1$ $\{j^{\wedge}N\}_2$ $\{k^{\wedge}N\}_3$, as in (3a)/(4a). Since c-selection is not predictable from **V**'s theta-selection or lexical semantics, these two tiers are *autonomous*: see (10) for the two-tiered diathesis of a ditransitive verb (to be revised below); (11) is its Extended Lexical Projection. The *binary-branching* and *grammatical relations* in (11) are fully encoded in the diathesis's two-tiered hierarchical structure (see Stowell 1992: 13) and projected directly to syntactic structure as consecutive right-to-left mergers of **V** and its arguments.[24] We see in (12) and (13) that it is the lower, c-selection tier that encodes the morphosyntactic differences between the unaccusative and transitive-impersonal verbs discussed above (the vertical lines represent the linking between theta roles and their categorial heads). This entails that theta roles are not assigned to nPs (DPs) in syntax.

1.3 Autonomy of theta and categorial tiers   21

(10)   (((i) j) k)
          | | |
         (((N) N) N)
           1   2   3

(11) $[_{vP} nP_i [_{v'} [V\text{-}v] [_{VP} nP_j [_{V'} t_v nP_k]]]]^{25}$

(12)   Unaccusative argument structure:
         (((-) j) -)
          | | |
         (((N) -) -)
           1   2   3

(13)   Transitive-impersonal argument structure:
         (((-) j) -)
          | | |
         (((-) N) -)
           1   2   3

Since the upper, theta-selection tiers of (12) and (13) are identical, it is the lower, c-selection tiers that must encode the verbs' unpredictable morphosyntactic differences. The c-selection tier in (13) captures the fact that $\{j{\wedge}N\}_2$ of transitive impersonal verbs like *tošnit'* cannot *externalize*: there is no external N_1 for **j** to relink to. Thus $\{j{\wedge}N\}_2$ in (13) must remain in situ in the second position of **V**'s diathesis, which projects to spec-VP as the accusative direct object, just as in (10) => (11); see (14a–c). The morphosyntactic differences between unaccusative and transitive-impersonal verbs are thus encoded as follows: the initial unaccusative diathesis in (12) has an unlinked external N_1 for unlinked **j** to relink to: $\{\{\text{-}{\wedge}N\}_1 \{j{\wedge}\text{-}\}_2...\} >> \{\{j{\wedge}N\}_1 \{\text{-}{\wedge}\text{-}\}_2...\}$, whereas the impersonal diathesis in (13) has no external N_1; everything else in their derivations follows from this distinction.[26] Note that the explanation of the differences between unaccusative and transitive impersonal syntax proposed here depends crucially on the verbs' *external subcategorization*: $\{\text{-}{\wedge}N\}_1$ vs. $\{\text{-}{\wedge}\text{-}\}_1$.

(14) a. Menja   tošnilo   ot   zapaxa   krepkogo tabaka.[27]
         me:ACC nauseated:N.SG from smell:GEN strong   tobacco:GEN
         'The smell of the strong tobacco nauseated me.'
      b. *Zapax   krepkogo   tabaka   menja   tošnil.
         smell.NOM.M strong   tobacco.GEN   me.ACC   nauseated.M
         'The smell of the strong tobacco nauseated me.'
      c. *Ja   tošnilsja   ot   zapaxa   krepkogo tabaka.[28]
         I.NOM   nauseated+sja   from   smell   strong   tobacco
         'I was nauseated from the smell of strong tobacco.'

22 The structure of argument structure

Let us look more closely at the analysis of unaccusative verbs in (12). Unlinked **j** obligatorily externalizes, i.e., links to N_1, giving $\{j^\wedge N\}_1$, which projects to spec-vP as a nominative subject, just as initial external $\{i^\wedge N\}_1$ does in transitive and unergative derivations.[29] This captures the fact that unaccusative verbs have thematic subjects (**j** = theme). We can represent the derivation of unaccusative sentences in (15), according to which it is the absence of both the external theta role **i** and the internal categorial head N_2 that makes the externalization (advancement) of **j** to $\{-^\wedge N\}_1$ obligatory. Given unaccusative V's initial diathesis in (12), no unaccusative-forming affix is needed and there is no specialized unaccusative syntax. There is also no need to posit accusative case absorption or any other such mechanism to explain why unaccusative verbs do not have accusative direct objects: according to (12), there is no N_2 in V's initial diathesis to assign accusative case to (see Chomsky 1981, Haegeman 1995). Given (12), **j** obligatorily externalizes since $\{-^\wedge N\}_1$ and $\{j^\wedge-\}_2$ do not project well-formed arguments in syntax.[30]

(15) Derivation of Unaccusative Sentences:
   a. $\{\{-\wedge N\}_1\ \{j\ \wedge\ -\}_2\ \{-\ \wedge\ -\}_3\ ...\} >>$
   b. $\{\{j\ \wedge\ N\}_1\ \{-\ \wedge\ -\}_2\ \{-\ \wedge\ -\}_3\ ...\} =>$
   c. $[_{vP}\ nP_{j.NOM}\ v']$

The criterial property of unaccusativity is the $\{\{-^\wedge N\}_1\ \{j^\wedge-\}_2...\}$ configuration in V's diathesis, which may be *initial*, as in (12)/(15), or *derived*: e.g., see the unaccusativizing function of the **-sja** suffix in the derivation of passive verbs from initial transitive Vs in (27)/(28), which can be represented schematically as: $\{\{i^\wedge N\}_1\ \{j^\wedge N\}_2...V\} > \{\{-^\wedge N\}_1\ \{j^\wedge-\}_2...V\text{-sja}\} >> \{\{j^\wedge N\}_1\ \{-^\wedge-\}_2...V\text{-sja}\}$. If the diathesis of basic (underived) unaccusative Vs were $\{\{-^\wedge N\}_1\ \{j^\wedge N\}_2... V\}$, **-sja** would be needed to delete N_2, thereby freeing **j** to relink to $\{-^\wedge N\}_1$.[31] But this makes the incorrect prediction that *all* unaccusative verbs, initial as well as derived, should be affixed with **-sja** when in fact only *derived unaccusatives* involve affixation of **-sja** and the composition of its diathesis with V's (see (27)/(28)).

Given the diathesis in (13), the derivation of transitive impersonal verbs like *tošnit'* in (14) is entirely straightforward: since *tošnit'* has neither an external theta role nor an external **N** in its initial diathesis (i.e. $\{-^\wedge-\}_1$), **j** in $\{j^\wedge N\}_2$ cannot externalize as it does in (15) because there is no external **N** for it to relink to; it thus remains in situ in $\{j^\wedge N\}_2$ and projects to the syntax as the accusative direct object, as in (14a).[32] The projection of transitive impersonal verbs is schematically represented in (16); affixation of the past-tense suffix *-l-* and the non-agreement suffix *-o* are not shown here (see below).

(16) a. {{- ^ -}$_1$ {j ^ N}$_2$ {- ^ -}$_3$ V} =>
  b. [$_{vP}$ [$_{v'}$ [V-v]$_v$ [$_{vP}$ nP$_{j.ACC}$ V']]]

Summary: The diatheses of unaccusative and transitive impersonal Vs in (12) and (13) both have a **j** theta role and an **N** categorial head; since **j** is in the same position in both diatheses ({- j$_2$ - -}), it follows that the syntactic properties that differentiate unaccusative and transitive impersonal sentences are encoded by the position of **N** in the verbs' c-selection tiers: {N$_1$ - - -} in unaccusative diatheses vs. {- N$_2$ - - } in transitive impersonal diatheses.

The hierarchical ordering of **V**'s arguments in its diathesis determines the projected sentence's basic syntactic relations because it encodes the right-to-left binary merging of **V** and its arguments (see the projection of (4a) to (4c)). This entails that: (i) **V**'s 'diathetic relations' (the hierarchical organization of its arguments) are primary and the grammatical relations of the sentence it projects are *derived* from them and thus epiphenomenal; (ii) changes of grammatical relations and the cases/PPs that instantiate them are due to diathesis-driven operations: there is no evidence in Russian that *syntactic* rules can alter grammatical relations; (iii) there is no *construction-specific syntax* because argument-structure level operations cannot alter the diathesis's skeletal 2×4 structure and, therefore, diathesis-to-syntax projection is not sensitive to what is *initial* and what is *derived* in **V**'s final diathesis: all derivations begin and end with the diathesis's 2×4 structure in (4a), each of whose positions projects to isomorphic positions in the sentence's syntactic representation: (see (4a–c)).[33] If argument structure consisted solely of theta structure, as in (6) and (9), verbs with identical theta selection would be predicted to project sentences with identical syntax. But we have seen above and will see again below that this prediction is patently false. **V**'s c-selection cannot be predicted from its theta-selection and it plays a crucial role in **V**'s morphosyntactic realization.

1.4 External subcategorization

The internal organization of the diathesis in (1)/(3a) requires that each **V** have an external categorial slot in its lower c-selection tier (cf. (12) and (13)). Thus the initial diatheses of transitive, unaccusative, and transitive-impersonal verbs contain an external categorial slot, which is not obligatorily filled: compare {i^N}$_1$ in (10) and {-^N}$_1$ in (12) with {-^-}$_1$ in (13). In other words, the two-tiered diathetic representation of argument structure necessarily includes *external subcategorization*, which means that **V**'s external argument, which projects as subject, as well as its internal arguments, which project as objects, involve autonomous c-selection. This means that there are sentences in Russian and other languages that do not have subjects and that subject ~ subjectlessness is a selectional property of the main **V** (cf. (15a) and (16a)). A fundamental parametric difference between English and Russian is that, in the former, subject is a structural property of the sentence (expletives are not projected from **V**'s diathesis), whereas in the latter, subject is a selectional property of the main verb. This correlates with the presence of expletives (syntactic placeholders) in English and their absence in Russian.[34]

We shall see in the following chapters that: (i) *external subcategorization* in Russian is highly explanatory; (ii) subjectlessness (i.e. {-^-}$_1$) is *not* predicable from **V**'s lexical semantics; (iii) all the systematic morphosyntactic properties of impersonal verbs can be shown to follow from the fact that their external argument is {-^-}$_1$ (see their highly defective syntactic paradigm in chapters 3 and 4).

If subject is an obligatory position in English sentences, it follows that the expletive *it* is necessary in impersonal sentences and sentences with extraposed subjects to lexicalize this obligatory position: *It does not make sense [for him to study music]* ~ *[For him to study music] does not make sense*. But if subject in Russian is c-selected by individual verbs, the absence of expletive subjects in Russian impersonal and extraposed sentences is what we expect (*Emu*$_{DAT}$ *ne imeet smyla*$_{GEN}$ [t$_N$ *zanimat'sja muzykoj*$_{INST}$] '(lit.) for-him does-not make sense [to study music]').[35] Positing null expletives in Russian impersonal sentences obscures an important typological difference between Russian and English rather than explaining it: the positing of null expletives has the effect of making Russian and English seem to be underlyingly identical (null vs. overt expletive is a superficial phonological difference) at just the point where we should be attempting to capture a primary parametric difference between them (see Perlmutter and Moore 2002).

1.4.1 The typology of external arguments

The bipartite definition of argument and the two-tiered architecture of the diathesis that it entails predicts the existence of the four types of external argument in (17). The fact that these are precisely the four external arguments found in Russian is a striking piece of independent evidence supporting the diathetic representation of argument structure being proposed (parenthesis notion denoting optionality predicts the existence of subtypes, all of which are attested).

(17) The four types of external argument:
   a. {i ^ N }$_1$
   b. {- ^ - }$_1$

c. {- ^ N }₁
d. {i ^ - }₁

We have already encountered the first three types: (17a) is found in the diatheses of unergative and transitive verbs. All impersonal verbs have the external diathesis in (17b). In addition to verbs like *tošnit'*, many but not all meteorological verbs are impersonal in Russian: e.g.: *Stemnelo.* 'It-got-dark,' (*S utra*) *morosit.* 'It-has-been-drizzling (since morning)' (see Birjulin 1994, Ruwet 1991).[36] As we saw above, unaccusative verbs have the external argument in (17c).

(17d) is the external argument of a *secondary-predicate* (s-predicate), which is an afP$_i$, i.e., [$_{afPi}$ [$_{af'<i>}$ [$_{af}$ V-af] VP$_{<i>}$]], where af = affix). Since the external **i** theta role is not linked to an external **N** in [V-af]'s final diathesis, it must be satisfied *syntactically* by vertical binding (Williams 1994), i.e., **i** of afP$_i$ must be bound by the **i** or **j** theta role of the matrix **V**, forming *a theta binding chain* (TBC); the matrix **k** theta role is too low in VP to be a vertical binder. S-predicates thus behave like verbal anaphors: an afP$_i$ that is not vertically bound by the closest theta role in its clausal domain is syntactically ill formed.

There are no **V**s with (17d) as their initial external argument: {i^-}₁ is always *derived* by an affix-driven operation on **V**'s diathesis that deletes its external **N**, leaving external **i** unlinked; {i^-}₁ projects-to-syntactic as an s-predicate. This affix-driven {i^N}₁ > {i^-}₁ operation is responsible for the derivation of *hybrid deverbal adjuncts* (see chapter 3), long-form adjectives and participles (chapter 2), and subject-controlled infinitive complements (chapter 4). Finite verbs are predictably never s-predicates: there is no higher clausemate to vertically bind them, which is analogous to the absence of the nominative case of reflexive pronouns.[37]

For example, let us briefly consider the derivation of the uninflected deverbal hybrid adverbial *vernu-vši-s'* '(when you) return' (*vernu-t'-sja* 'to-return [intransitive]') in (18), which is an adjunct s-predicate whose *understood subject* (i.e., its unlinked external theta role **i**) is obligatorily construed as coreferential with the matrix **V**'s subject *ty*$_i$ 'you'; the diathesis of the hybrid-adverbial forming suffix -v(ši)- composes with **V**'s initial diathesis and is responsible for deleting **V**'s external **N**. In (19), -**af**- = -*vši*, and the s-predicate phrase [$_{afP<i>}$ *vernuvšis' domoj tak pozdno*] is vertically bound by the subject [$_{nPi}$ *ty*], which is the head of its TBC (angle brackets "<i>" denote a V(ertically) bound external theta role) (see chapter 3 for details). (20) is the derivation of *vernuvšis'*. The blank slots in the affix's diathesis are *unspecified*, and are 'filled in' (valued) by the corresponding slots in the diathesis of the **V** it composes with; this type of composition will be referred to as *inheritance*, which is common in derivations involving paradigmatic affixes and auxiliary verbs.

(18) Čto ty skažeš' žene, vernuvšis' domoj tak pozdno.
what.ACC you.NOM say wife.DAT having-returned home so late
'What do you say to your wife when you return (*she returns) home so late?'

(19) [$_{CP}$ Čto$_j$ [$_{TP}$ ty$_i$ skažeš' t$_j$ žene$_k$, [$_{afP<i>}$vernuvšis' domoj tak pozdno]]].

(20) The derivation of *vernu-vši-s*':[38]
(a) {{i ^ N}$_1$ ... {- ^ **vernu-sja**}$_4$} + (composes with)
(b) {{ ^ -}$_1$ ... { ^ -vši-}$_4$} > (yields)
(c) {{ i ^ -}$_1$ ... {- ^ vernuvšis'}$_4$} => (projects-to-syntax)

Impersonal verbs like *tošnit'*, whose initial external argument is {-^-}$_1$, predictably do not form hybrid adverbials, which must be *controlled* in syntax, i.e., have an unlinked external theta role {i^-}$_1$ that can be V-bound (vertically bound).

1.5 The final form of the diathesis

Since the set of alternations projected from **V**'s diathesis is canonically determined by the language's set of diathesis-bearing paradigmatic affixes, what I have been referring to as diathesis-level rules or operations are simply the *composition* of the affix's diathesis with **V**'s diathesis when **-af** is affixed to the verb stem **V**. This means that the affix and **V** must be represented as the fourth position in their respective diatheses.[39] The diathesis of a ditransitive verb is therefore represented in (21), where **V** occupies the fourth slot in the lower tier.

(21) ((((i) j) k) -)
       | | | |
      ((((N) N) N) V)
         1   2   3   4

We will employ the version of (21) in (22), which is unencumbered by nested parentheses and linking lines; the crucial hierarchical arrangement of **V**'s arguments that is explicit in (21) manifests itself in (22) as the implicit right-to-left order of merger of **V** and its arguments (see (4)). The diathesis of the hybrid adverbial suffix **-vši** is represented in (23). (24) represents the composition of (22) and (23) (cf. (20)). I follow Williams 1994 in assuming that an affix is the *head of the word* it derives and its properties thus take precedence over those of **V** when they 'compete' for a position or slot: the { ^-}$_1$ external argument of *-vši* thus takes precedence over **V**'s external {i^N}$_1$ argument, deriving the {i^-}$_1$ external argument that characterizes s-predicates (afP$_i$) in (24). ("+" = composes with.)

1.5 The final form of the diathesis 27

(22)

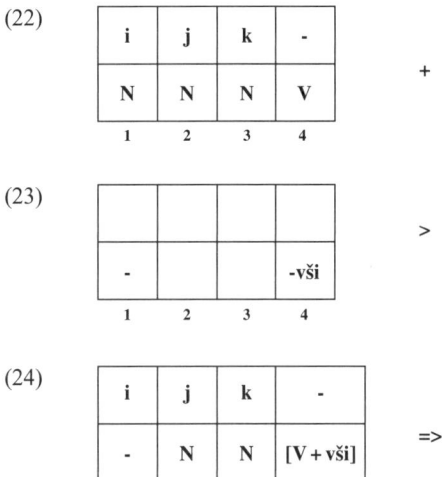

(23)

(24)

This derivation can be represented in linear notation in (25):

(25)   a. {{i ^ N}₁ {j ^ N}₂ {k ^ N}₃ {- ^ V}₄ }   +
       b. {{ ^ - }₁ { ^ }₂   { ^ }₃   { ^ -af}₄ }   >
       c. {{i ^ -}₁ {j ^ N}₂ {k ^ N}₃ {- ^ [V-af] }₄} =>
       d. [afPi [af' [V-af] VP]]

1.5.1 The theta tier's fourth position

The addition of **V** to the lower tier in (22) as the diathesis's fourth position has the effect of creating a corresponding fourth theta slot in the upper tier, i.e., {-^V}₄. Since there is no evidence for the existence of **V**s with more than three theta roles or with one of their theta roles *initially* linked to **V**, we must enquire whether this eighth slot ("-" in {-^V}₄) is a *spandrel*, the functionless residue of diathesis's 2×4 architecture, or whether it has a demonstrable function. If the potential theta-slot in {-^V}₄ turned out not to have a function, the hypothesis that each position in the diathesis maps onto an isomorphic position in syntactic structure would be weakened. However, if it can be demonstrated that this fourth theta slot is necessary (explanatory), it would be a stunning confirmation of the diathesis's proposed 2×4 structure since it is predicted to exist by the diathesis's bipartite organization (cf. the four types of external argument predicted to exist by the diathesis's 2×4 structure in (17)). The best way to motivate {-^V}₄ is to present empirical evidence that there is a derivation in which one of the theta roles in **V**'s initial diathesis relinks to the free theta slot in {-^ [V-af]}₄. We shall see evidence below in §§ 1.5.2 and 1.5.3 that {-^V}₄ is in fact highly explanatory in Russian and other languages.

1.5.2 Causativization in Turkish

The affix-driven derivation of Turkish causative sentences demonstrates conclusively that the initially unused theta slot in $\{\text{-}^\wedge V\}_4$ plays an explanatory role: the syntactic realization of **V**'s initial external argument $\{i^\wedge N\}_1$ as a *tarafindan*-phrase (*by*-phrase) occurs in causative sentences *when a ditransitive verb is causativized*. More specifically, the causative suffix **-af**$_c$ (**-dir-**) has its own external argument $\{i_c{}^\wedge N\}_1$ (see (26b)), which becomes the composite [**V-dir-**] stem's external argument when the diatheses of **-af**$_c$ and **V** compose (i_c is the causative suffix's external (agent) theta role). Their composition necessitates the *internalization* or right-displacement of **V**'s initial external argument $\{i^\wedge N\}_1$ to the first available (left-most) position in the composite diathesis, which must be the fourth position when **V** is ditransitive since all the other positions are occupied and double-occupancy is ill-formed. The resulting $\{i^\wedge[\text{V-af}]\}_4$ licenses the *by*-phrase in causative as well as in derived-nominal and passive derivations (see Babby 1997a–b). Thus the theta slot in $\{\text{-}^\wedge[\text{V-af}]\}_4$ enables us to capture the generalization that the *by*-phrase is not a construction-specific realization of dethematized **i** in passive derivations; it is associated with **i** in the $\{i^\wedge[\text{V-af}]\}_4$ diathetic configuration no matter how it gets there.

(26)   The causative derivation of a ditransitive Turkish verb.
    a. **V**: $\{i\,^\wedge N\}_1$ $\{j\,^\wedge N\}_2$ $\{k\,^\wedge N\}_3$ $\{\text{-}\,^\wedge V\}_4$ +
    b. **-af**$_c$-: $\{i_c\,^\wedge N\}_1$ $\{\,^\wedge\,\}_2$ $\{\,^\wedge\,\}_3$ $\{\,^\wedge\text{af}_c\}_4$ >
    c. a+b: $\{i_c\,^\wedge N\}_1$ $\{j\,^\wedge N\}_2$ $\{k\,^\wedge N\}_3$ $\{i\,^\wedge[\text{V-af}_c]\}_4$ =>

The 2×4 architecture of the diathesis in (26a)/(22) correctly predicts that if a derived diathesis has four theta roles, as in (26c), one of them must have relinked to $\{\text{-}^\wedge[\text{V-af}]\}_4$.[40] The 2×4 structure also correctly predicts that when an unergative **V** is causativized, $\{i^\wedge N\}_1 > \{i^\wedge N\}_2$ and projects to syntax as an agentive direct object, since $\{\text{-}^\wedge\text{-}\}_2$ is the left-most vacant position in an unergative verb's diathesis which displaced $\{i^\wedge N\}_1$ can occupy (see §1.9 for Turkish examples).[41]

1.5.3 Passivization in Russian

Let us now look at the evidence for *implicit i* (i.e. **i** in $\{i^\wedge[\text{V-af}]\}_4$) provided by passivization in Russian which, like causativization in Turkish, is an affix-driven operation on **V**'s initial diathesis that has systematic morphosyntactic effects. Passivization's universal invariant is *dethematization* of **V**'s initial external theta role, i.e., **i** is delinked from its initial external position and relinked to $\{\text{-}^\wedge V\}_4$: $\{\{i^\wedge N\}_1 \ldots \{\text{-}^\wedge V\}_4\} > \{\{\text{-}^\wedge N\}_1 \ldots \{i^\wedge[\text{V-af}_{\text{PASS}}]\}_4\}$.[42] Since **i** in passive derivations is right-displaced, not deleted, as it is in other derivations

1.5 The final form of the diathesis

(e.g. *Dver'$_j$ otkrylas'* [**Annoj$_i$*] 'The-door opened [*by-Anna]'), and cannot be linked to either of passivized **V**'s internal argument positions because they are occupied by **V**'s two initial internal arguments when **V** is ditransitive, it must link to [**V-af**$_{PASS}$] in the fourth theta tier postion. Thus the diathesis's 2×4 structure correctly predicts that dethematized **i** in passive derivations relinks to {-^[**V-af**$_{PASS}$]}$_4$ and, as we saw in the causative derivation, implicit **i** in {**i**^[**V-af**]}$_4$ licenses the *by*-phrase.[43]

Implicit in this analysis of passivization is the assumption that *externalization* of **V**'s direct internal argument {**j**^**N**}$_2$ is epiphenomenal: (i) Unergative verbs, which have no internal arguments, can passivize in many languages, where they project to syntax as *impersonal passives* (see Babby 2008).[44] (ii) The {**j**^**N**}$_2$ argument of passivized transitive verbs can remain *in situ* in the passive diathesis and project as the accusative direct object of a *transitive impersonal passive* (e.g., see Lavine 2000 for the analysis of transitive impersonal passives in Ukrainian and Polish).

Passivization of an imperfective ditransitive verb in Russian, which is driven by the *derived-unaccusative* suffix **-sja**, is represented in (27) and (28).[45]

(27)   Diathetic representation of ditransitive passivization:

a.

i	j	k	-
N	N	N	V
1	2	3	4

+

b.

-			
	-		-sja
1	2	3	4

>

c.

-	j	k	i
N	-	N	V-sja
1	2	3	4

>>

d.

j	-	k	i
N	-	N	V-sja
1	2	3	4

30 *The structure of argument structure*

(28) Diathetic represention of ditransitive passivization, linear notation:[46]
    a. V's diathesis: $\{\{i \wedge N\}_1 \; \{j \wedge N\}_2 \; \{k \wedge N\}_3 \; \{\text{-} \wedge V\}_4\}$ +
    b. -sja's diathesis: $\{\{\text{-} \wedge\}_1 \;\; \{\wedge\text{-}\}_2 \;\; \{\wedge\}_3 \;\; \{\wedge\text{-sja}\}_4\}$ >
    c. a + b: $\{\{\text{-} \wedge N\}_1 \; \{j \wedge \text{-}\}_2 \; \{k \wedge N\}_3 \; \{i \wedge \text{[V-sja]}\}_4\}$ >>
    d. final diathesis: $\{\{j \wedge N\}_1 \; \{\text{-} \wedge \text{-}\}_2 \; \{k \wedge N\}_3 \; \{i \wedge \text{[V-sja]}\}_4\}$

V's initial diathesis (28a) composes (+) with the diathesis of the derived-unaccusativizing suffix -**sja** (28b) to produce (>) the derived (composite) unaccusative diathesis in (28c). -**sja**'s external argument $\{\text{-}\wedge\;\}_1$ in (28c) is responsible for the dethematization of V's initial external **i** theta role: (28a) + (28b) > (28c), which cannot project a well-formed syntactic structure and **j** in $\{j\wedge\text{-}\}_2$ obligatorily (>>) externalizes (relinks to unlinked N_1). This yields **[V-sja]**'s final diathesis in (28d), which projects to syntactic structure (=>). Dethematized **i** in (28) cannot relink to the 2-position because it is occupied by **j** when dethematization applies, and it cannot link to the 3-position, which is also occupied. Thus the rightmost available theta-slot for it is $\{\text{-}\wedge\text{[V-sja]}\}_4$. (29) is a concrete example of the imperfective passive in Russian.[47]

(29)   a. Xozjain$_{\text{i.NOM}}$ otkryvaet dver'$_{\text{j.ACC}}$ (ključom$_{\text{INST}}$) ~
           'The-owner opens   the-door (with-a-key).'
     b. Dver'$_{\text{j.NOM}}$ otkryvaetsja xozjainom$_{\text{INST}}$ (ključom$_{\text{INST}}$)
           'The-door is-opened   by-the-owner (with-a-key).'

(30) is an example of perfective passivization, where the **-en-** participle plus copula is used. Unlike the **-en** suffix, which carries adjectival features, -**sja** does not have its own categorial features and thus does not affect V's category (see chapter 3 for details).

(30)   a. Oni$_{\text{i.NOM}}$ privezli s soboj$_{\text{INST}}$ vse oborudovanie$_{\text{j.ACC}}$.
           they   brought with self   all equipment
           'They brought all the-equipment with-them(selves).'
     b. Vse oborudovanie$_{\text{j.NOM}}$ bylo privezeno imi$_{\text{INST}}$.
           'All the-equipment   was brought   by-them.'
     c. Vse oborudovanie$_{\text{j.NOM}}$ bylo privezeno s soboj$_{\text{INST}}$.
           'All the-equipment   was brought   with them(selves).'

We know that implicit **i** in $\{i\wedge\text{[V-sja]}\}_4$ projects to syntax in passive derivations because, in addition to the semantic contribution it makes to the sentence (enabling us to explicitly represent the difference between passive and non-passive derived unaccusative sentences[48]), it is *syntactically active* since it can bind reflexive *adjuncts* (e.g. *s soboj* 'with themselves' in (30c) and (31)). Assuming that reflexive pronouns must be bound in their binding domain, which is the clause in Russian, the reflexive pronoun *s soboj* 'with self' in

1.5 The final form of the diathesis

(31) too must be bound, but the inanimate subject *vse oborudovanie* 'all the equipment' cannot be construed as the reflexive's antecedent (binder):[49]

(31)   (Oni snjali nebol'šoj domik.) [Vse oborudovanie, privezennoe s **soboj**]
(They rented a-small house.) all equipment$_{NOM}$ brought$_{LF.NOM}$ with self$_{INST}$
bylo rassovano po škafam.
was crammed into shelves
'(They rented a small cottage.) [All the-equipment brought with them (lit. 'with themselves')] was crammed into shelves.'

(32)   K čaju byla podana [vodka, privezennaja s **soboj** v kačestve obmennoj valjuty].
'[The-vodka, which-was-brought with us (lit. ourselves) as a medium of exchange], was served at tea.'

Reflexive [$_{PP}$ *s soboj*] in (31) is construed as coreferential with the subject *oni* 'they' of the preceding sentence, but *oni* cannot bind *s soboj* because they are not in the same binding domain. This means that it must be the implict **i** theta role that binds reflexive *s soboj*.[50] (32) is another example of the same phenomenon; here there is no clause-external potential binder; the implicit **i** linked to the matrix passive participle *podana* 'served' is not coreferential with the implicit **i** associated with *privezennaja* 'brought,' which modifies the subject *vodka*.[51]

The 2×4 structure of the diathesis also *explains* why dethematized **i** always relinks to $\{-\wedge[\text{V-sja}/\text{-en-}]\}_4$ in passive derivations, which is an important piece of corroborating evidence. While there is no other option in the case of ditransitive diatheses, what happens to displaced **i** in the passive derivation of monotransitive **V**s, i.e., why doesn't **i** occupy the available $\{-\wedge-\}_3$ position, which is what happens in the causativization of French and Turkish monotransitive **V**s (see §1.9)? The answer to this question, which was posed by Richard Larson (personal communication), falls out naturally from the architecture of the diathesis. To see why this is so, let us run through the passive derivation of the monotransitive **V** represented in (33) (see *otkryvat'* 'to-open' in (29)).

(33a)   Well-formed passive derivation of a monotransitive **V**:
    i. $\{\{i \wedge N\}_1 \{j \wedge N\}_2 \{-\wedge-\}_3 \{-\wedge V\}_4\}$ +
    ii. $\{\{-\wedge\}_1 \quad \{\wedge-\}_2 \quad \{\wedge\}_3 \quad \{\wedge\text{-sja}\}_4\}$ >
    iii. $\{\{-\wedge N\}_1 \{j \wedge -\}_2 \{-\wedge-\}_3 \{i \wedge [\text{V-sja}]\}_4\}$ >>
    iv. $\{\{j \wedge N\}_1 \{-\wedge-\}_2 \{-\wedge-\}_3 \{i \wedge [\text{V-sja}]\}_4\}$

(33b)   Ill-formed passive derivation of a monotransitive **V**:
    i. $\{\{i \wedge N\}_1 \{j \wedge N\}_2 \{-\wedge-\}_3 \{-\wedge V\}_4\}$ +
    ii. $\{\{-\wedge\}_1 \quad \{\wedge-\}_2 \quad \{\wedge\}_3 \quad \{\wedge\text{-sja}\}_4\}$ >
    iii. *$\{\{-\wedge N\}_1 \{j \wedge -\}_2 \{i \wedge -\}_3 \{-\wedge [\text{V-sja}]\}_4\}$ >>
    iv. *$\{\{j \wedge N\}_1 \{-\wedge-\}_2 \{i \wedge -\}_3 \{-\wedge [\text{V-sja}]\}_4\}$

32 *The structure of argument structure*

Dethematized **i** in (33) cannot relink to {-^-}₃ because it *has no categorial head for i to link to* (cf. the ill-formed structure in (33b.iii)); but the fourth position is always available because there is always a **[V-af]**₄ in the lower tier for delinked **i** to relink to.[52]

We now have an entirely natural explanation in terms of the diathesis's 2×4 skeletal structure for why internalization works differently in causativization and passivization: the difference is a function of the causative and passive suffixes' individual properties. We saw above in (26) that **V**'s entire {i^N}₁ external argument is internalized when the causative suffix introduces its own external argument {i_c^N}₁, which means that displaced {i^N}₁ is able to occupy the available {-^-}₃ position (and project to syntax as a dative agentive nP) when **V** is monotransitive (see (75) and (76) for Turkish examples): the causative suffix does not involve dethematization, i.e., **V**'s initial external {i^N}₁ is not delinked in causative derivations and thus occupies the left-most {-^-} in the composite causative diathesis. But in passive derivations, which create derived unaccusative diatheses, **i** is dethematized (delinked from **N**₁) and thus only unlinked **i** (not the entire bipartite external argument {i^N}₁)) is internalized (right-displaced), which entails that the {-^-}₃ position is not available for it to relink to because it does not contain an unlinked categorial head **N** in its lower tier; only {-^[V-af]}₄ can provide an unlinked categorial head for dethematized **i** to link to in passive derivations.

1.6 Projecting phrase structure from argument structure

Now that we have seen some of the argumentation that the diathesis's 2×4 architecture has explanatory power, we will look more closely at the constraints it imposes on diathetic operations and at the mapping between **V**'s final diathesis and the projected sentence's Extended Lexical Projection.

1.6.1 The universal law of diathesis conservation

Productive diathesis-level operations like passivization, causativization, and nominalization, which are canonically affix-driven (see Bobaljik 2001, Marantz 1984), apply to **V**'s initial diathesis, altering it in *highly restricted ways* (see Stowell 1992: 2). The most consequential restriction is this: the diatheses of all predicators – whether they have zero, one, two, or three arguments – and of all paradigmatic affixes are represented by a 2×4 diathesis whose eight-slotted skeletal structure (frame) *remains invariant under all operations*: while arguments may be added, deleted, relocated, or delinked, these operations cannot alter the diathesis's 2×4 frame in any way. Since a derivation's final derived diathesis determines the right-to-left syntactic *merger* of **V** and its arguments, the law of diathesis conservation ensures that there will be no difference in the 2×4 skeletal structure of initial and final diatheses and, therefore, that the mapping between argument structure and syntactic structure is not sensitive to the results of diathetic operations. This explains why languages do not have *construction-specific syntax*: specific constructions do not have specialized syntactic relations; e.g., there are no specialized passive or causative syntactic structures or case marking because all these syntactic 'constructions' are projected from 2×4 final diatheses. Thus an *alternation* is simply the syntactic projection of two final diatheses derived from the same **V**'s initial diathesis (e.g. active ~ passive sentences). The set of a given verb stem's alternations is its *diathetic paradigm*; cross-linguistic differences in the makeup of diathetic paradigms are due to the language-specific properties of the 2×4 affixal diatheses that drive the derivations.

1.6.2 The mapping between argument structure and syntactic structure
The most common diatheses are summarized below:[53]

(34)   Ditransitive diathesis.
        $\{\{i \wedge N\}_1 \{j \wedge N\}_2 \{k \wedge N\}_3 \{- \wedge V\}_4\}$

(35)   Monotransitive diathesis:
        $\{\{i \wedge N\}_1 \{j \wedge N\}_2 \{- \wedge -\}_3 \{- \wedge V\}_4\}$

(36)   Unergative diathesis:
        $\{\{i \wedge N\}_1 \{- \wedge -\}_2 \{- \wedge -\}_3 \{- \wedge V\}_4\}$

(37)   Transitive impersonal diathesis:
        $\{\{- \wedge -\}_1 \{j \wedge N\}_2 \ldots \{- \wedge V\}_4\}$

(38)   Unaccusative diathesis:
        a. basic: $\{\{- \wedge N\}_1 \{j \wedge -\}_2 \ldots \{- \wedge V\}_4\}$
        b. derived: $\{\{- \wedge N\}_1 \{j \wedge -\}_2 \ldots \{- \wedge [\text{V-af}]\}_4\}$

(39)   Impersonal diathesis:
        $\{\{- \wedge -\}_1 \{- \wedge -\}_2 \{- \wedge -\}_3 \{- \wedge V\}_4\}$

(40)   s-predicate diathesis (derived only):
        $\{\{i \wedge -\}_1 \ldots \{- \wedge [\text{V-af}]\}_4\}$

The purpose of this section is to make explicit precisely what it means to claim that a sentence's basic grammatical (syntactic) relations are encoded in **V**'s diathesis. The ditransitive diathesis in (34) encodes the right-to-left order of the syntactic merger of **V** and its arguments, i.e., it governs the diathesis-to-syntax projection of the Extended Lexical Projection in (41) (= (4c)), which is the basic 'molecule' of syntactic structure. However, according to representations like (41), the merger of **V** and **v** is syntactic,[54] which is problematic if **V** is a verb *stem* and **v** is the finite verbal *affix*, as I am claiming. My assumption is that the smallest expression that syntactic rules can operate on is the fully formed *word*, not stems and the affixes. We saw above that [V-v] is formed when the diatheses of **v** and **V** *compose*, not when V raises to v by syntactic head movement; see (44), which is the correct form of (41).

(41)

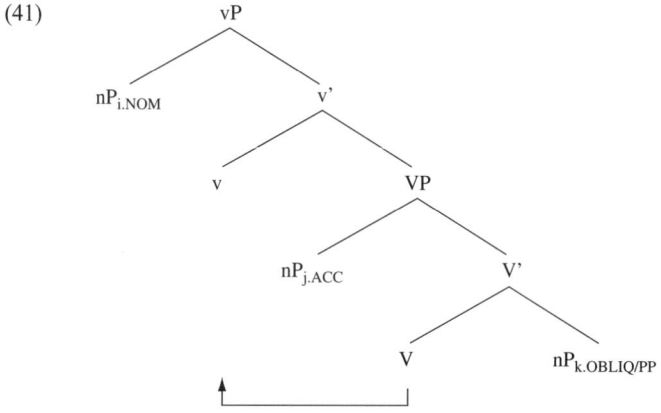

First the composite **[V-v]** head merges with **{k^N}$_3$** (the right-most argument in the diathesis and therefore the most deeply embedded argument in its syntactic projection), projecting the binary-branching structure in (42). nP$_k$, which is headed by **N$_3$**, is realized as an oblique-case nP or [$_{PP}$ P nP], which is determined by the specific value of **k** in a given **V**'s diathesis (see Babby 1994a–b for details of *theta determined case*). In contrast, the 'structural' cases assigned to nPs in vP and VP spec-positions in nominative-accusative languages are not determined by their theta roles.

(42)

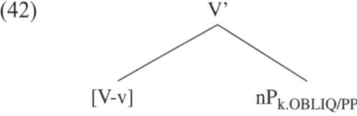

{j^N}$_2$ is next in line to merge: nP$_j$ forms the VP constituent with V', which was formed by the preceding merger: nP$_j$ is the sister of V' in the spec-VP position, where it is assigned/checks structural accusative case (see §3.2.3 for details of case assignment to nP in spec-position):

1.6 Projecting phrase structure 35

(43)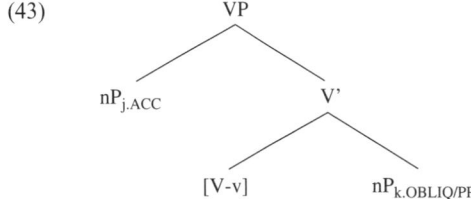

VP in (43) has only two syntactic argument positions. But, according to the diathesis in (34), the ditransitive **V** has one more argument to merge, its VP-external argument: [V-v] thus 'raises' and merges with VP, forming v'; and **V**'s external argument nP$_i$ (the projection of $\{i^{\wedge}N\}_1$) merges with v', creating (44), which is the sentence's neutral SVO word order (see Speas 1990: 17). Thus, rather than the stem V raising to the suffix v, [V-v] projects to syntax as VP's head and then raises to head vP.

(44)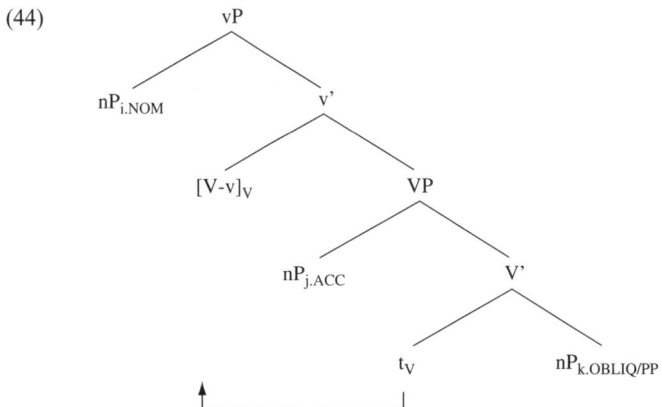

$\{-^{\wedge}-\}_3$, the third position in the monotransitive diathesis in (35) and, in general, all initially unfilled $\{-^{\wedge}-\}$ positions in **V**'s initial diathesis, must be indicated since, as we saw above, they play a crucial role in many affix-driven operations (e.g., all the 'unused' positions in **V**'s diathesis come into play in the case of Turkish and French causativization). Thus, in what follows, the diathesis of all verbs will be specified for the four positions we see in (34) to (40). If $\{-^{\wedge}-\}$ in **V**'s initial diathesis is not used to accomodate a new or displaced argument in the course of the sentence's diathesis-level derivation, it is passed over and not projected to syntactic structure. Thus the monotransitive diathesis in (35), repeated here as (45), projects the syntactic structure in (46).

36 *The structure of argument structure*

(45) Monotransitive diathesis:
  {{i ^ N}₁ {j ^ N}₂ {- ^ -}₃ {- ^ V}₄ }

(46)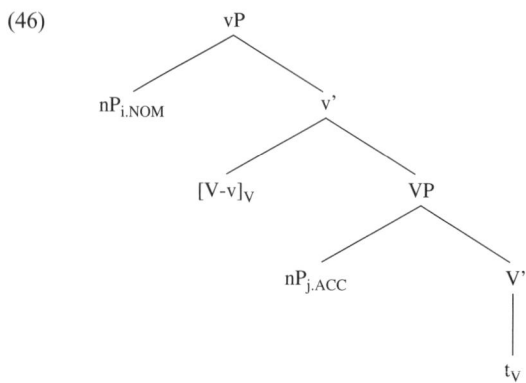

The projection of the positions (arguments) in **V**'s diathesis to isomorphic positions in phrase-structure representation is absolute, not relative (cf. Baker 1997: 120), i.e., each argument position in **V**'s diathesis projects to a specific position in phrase structure without regard to the projection or non-projection of other arguments.[55] For example, we saw in the case of transitive impersonal verbs like *tošnit'* in (37) that the internal {j^N}₂ argument does not automatically advance and become external (subject) in the absence of an external argument (cf. Speas 1990: 104; Grimshaw 1990). While the accusative direct object *menja* 'me' in (47) moves to spec-TP in the absence of a nominative subject, it nevertheless remains the accusative direct object, and the projected sentence's core grammatical relations and case remain unchanged.[56]

(47) Menja   tošnilo   ot   zapaxa krepkogo tabaka
      me:ACC   nauseated:N.SG from smell   strong   tobacco:GEN.
      'The smell of the strong tobacco nauseated me.'

1.7 Projected syntactic asymmetries

The right-to-left projection of the arguments in **V**'s diathesis determines that only nP$_k$ is the sister (complement) of [V-v] (see (44)). nP$_i$ and nP$_j$ form a natural class and are opposed to oblique nP$_k$ since both merge in spec-positions where they are assigned structural case: [$_{VP}$ nP$_{j.ACC}$ V'] and [$_{vP}$ nP$_{i.NOM}$ v']. We shall see below that this complement vs. spec asymmetry has a number of important morphosyntactic consequences. A **N$_k$** that *advances* to the 1-position or 2-position as the result of a diathetic operation projects to the isomorphic spec-position in syntactic structure and is assigned structural case; nP$_k$ which projects to the sister-of-V complement position is realized as either an oblique case or PP, depending on the theta-value of **k**.[57] In contrast to 'theta-case', structural and quirky case tell us nothing about the theta role of the nP they are assigned to.

The subject nP$_i$ in (44) asymmetrically c-commands nP$_j$ and nP$_k$ and thus can antecedent-bind reflexive direct and oblique objects. The direct object nP$_j$ c-commands nP$_k$, which predicts that accusative direct objects can bind reflexive oblique objects, as in (48). nP$_k$ does not c-command any of **V**'s arguments, which correctly predicts that it does not normally bind any of its clausemates. The reflexive pronoun [$_{PP}$ *iz sebja*$_k$] 'from self' in (48a) is bound by the direct object *menja*$_j$.

(48) a. Inogda   [ego tupost'$_{i.NOM}$] vyvodit   [$_{VP}$ **menja**$_{j.ACC}$
         sometimes his obtuseness   drives   me
         [$_{V'}$ t$_V$ [$_{PP}$ iz   **sebja**$_{k.GEN}$]]].
                          from (my)self
         'Sometimes his obtuseness drives me crazy.'
     b. Interesno   sravnivat'   **ix**$_{ACC}$ meždu **soboj**$_{INST}$.
         '(It is) interesting to-compare **them** among **themselves**.'

The descriptive generalization based on sentences like (48) is: Reflexive pronouns are *spec-oriented* since only nPs in spec-position are high enough in phrase structure to asymmetrically c-command other nPs and thus bind them.[58] This generalization correctly predicts the possibility of the binding relation illustrated in nonstandard but grammatical sentences like (49)/(50), where the accusative direct object *ee* 'her' has moved to spec-TP where it asymmetrically c-commands the lower bracketed *nominative subject nP* and binds the reflexive possessive adjective *svoej* contained in it.

(49) **Ee**   ne   trogajut   [$_{nPi}$ stradanija   **svoej**   podrugi].
      her:ACC   neg   touch.PL   sufferings:NOM.PL   her.GEN   girlfriend.GEN
      '[The-suffering [of her girlfriend]] does-not touch (move) her.'

(50) [$_{TP}$ ee [$_{T'}$ ne trogajut [$_{vP}$ [$_{nP.NOM}$ stradanija [$_{nP.GEN}$ svoej podrugi]] v']]]

1.8   Monadic verbs

This section is devoted to the comparison of the argument structures and derivations of the following types of Russian monadic verbs, none of which have an external theta role: impersonal-transitives like *tošnit'* (see (47) and (51)), basic and derived unaccusatives, *korčit'* 'writhe' type verbs, which are important because they combine the properties of impersonal and derived unaccusative verbs, and *atrofirovat' sja* 'atrophy' type verbs, which are basic transitive verbs that always cooccur with the **-sja** suffix in morphosyntactic structure and whose existence is predicted by diathetic representation. The purpose of this section is to demonstrate that the 2×4 architecture of the diathesis predicts precisely this monadic typology, which serves as additional evidence that it is explanatory.

The comparison of *tošnit'* and *korčit'* type verbs is especially important since it demonstrates the crucial role played by external c-selection in languages in which subject is a selectional property of **V**: *tošnit'* and *korčit'* have identical theta-selection ({- **j** - -}), which means that the differences in the morphosyntactic structures they project are due to the differences encoded in their external subcategorization (c-selection), which are arbitrary, i.e., patently not predicted by their lexical semantics (they both denote physical symptoms of illness); cf. the impersonal verbs in (51).

(51) a. Menja$_{ACC}$ mutit / vorotit ot   zapaxa$_{GEN}$ tabaka$_{GEN}$.
         me   sickens   from smell   of-tobacco
         'The-smell of-tobacco makes me feel sick.'
      b. Menja$_{ACC}$ znobilo.
         me   made-feel-feverish
         'I was feeling feverish.'
      c. Ego$_{ACC}$ rvet.
         'He is-vomiting.'

Before comparing *tošnit' (*sja)*, *korčit'(sja)*, and *atrofirovat'*(sja)*, we need to look more closely at the **-sja** suffix. While the **j** externalizes (relinks to {-^N}$_1$) in the derivation of both basic and derived unaccusatives, it is only in the latter that **-sja** is required. This was explained above as follows: the diathesis of basic unaccusative **V**s is represented in (52):

(52)   Initial (underived) unaccusative diathesis:
        {{- ^ N}$_1$ {j ^ -}$_2$ {- ^ -}$_3$ {- ^ V}$_4$ }

j obligatorily links to {-^N}$_1$, giving {j^N}$_1$, which projects to the spec-vP position and is realized as the sentence's nominative nP$_j$ subject. Since externalization of **j** is determined by initial {{-^N}$_1$ {j^-}$_2$ ...}, **-sja** is not needed. But in passive and agentless derived unaccusative (middle) derivations (e.g. *Jama*$_{j.NOM}$ *napolnilas' vodoj*$_{k.INST}$ 'The-pit filled with-water'), the unaccusative configuration in (53c) is derived from **V**'s initial diathesis in (53a) by composition of **-sja** and its diathesis in (53b) to (53a). The fate of **V**'s external **i** when **V** and **-sja** compose depends on the derivation: it is relinked to {-^ [V-sja]}₄ in passive derivations and is *deleted* in middle derivations: see *Frukty bystro portjatsja kogda žarko* 'Fruit quickly spoils when (it is) hot' (an agentive/passive reading here is excluded on semantic grounds).

(53) Derived unaccusative diathesis.
    a. {{i ^ N}₁ {j ^ N}₂ ... {- ^ V}₄ }   +
    b. {{- ^ }₁ { ^ - }₂ ... {- ^ -sja}₄ }   >
    c. {{- ^ N}₁ {j ^ - }₂ ... {- ^ [V-sja]}₄ }   >>
    d. {{j ^ N}₁ {- ^ - }₂ ... {- ^ [V-sja]}₄ }[59]

The diathesis of transitive impersonal Vs in (37) is repeated here as (54); their basic external argument {-^-}₁ predicts that: (i) like basic unaccusatives, they cannot passivize since there is no external **i** to dethematize; (ii) unlike unaccusatives, **j** cannot externalize in (54) because there is no external {-^N}₁ receptor for it to relink to.

(54) Transitive-impersonal diathesis
    {{- ^ -}₁ {j ^ N}₂ {- ^ -}₃ {- ^ V}₄ }

My first argument for the autonomy of categorial-selection and theta-selection was based on the fact that the upper theta tiers of unaccusative and transitive-impersonal Vs are identical (see (9e) and (9f)): their radically different morphosyntactic projections are therefore encoded in terms of differences in their c-selection, which constitutes direct evidence that a **V**'s c-selection cannot be predicted from its theta-selection and that c-selection is thus an autonomous tier in diathesis representation. A comparison of the diatheses in (52) and (54) captures the fact that it is the *absence* of an unlinked external **N** that blocks **j**'s externalization in the case of impersonal transitive Vs and that it is the *presence* of an unlinked external **N** in the case of unaccusative Vs that makes **j**'s externalization obligatory. Thus (52) and (54) provide evidence for *external c-selection* as well as for the autonomy of c-selection; additional evidence for the centrality of external c-selection is presented below in the discussion of *korčit'* and *atrofirovat'sja*.

The existence of *tošnit'* type Vs (see (51)) also provides empirical evidence against: (i) Burzio's generalization, which claims that Vs with accusative direct objects must also assign an external theta role; (ii) early versions of the Extended Projection Principle, which stipulate that every clause must have a syntactic subject; (iii) the claim that if there is no external argument, the most prominent argument in **V**'s argument structure automatically becomes the subject (see Grimshaw 1990, Stowell 1992: 12, Sadler and Spencer 2001: 211); (iv) the hypothesis in Kratzer 1996 that subject is not an argument of

V: if subject in Russian is c-selected by **V**, it must be **V**'s subject, i.e., it must be an argument of **V**, not **v**.

1.8.1   The impersonal ~ derived unaccusative alternation
Verbs like *korčit'* 'to writhe' and *korobit'* 'to warp' belong to another distinct class of Russian monadic verbs that has no counterpart in English: on the one hand, *korčit'* can be realized syntactically as an impersonal transitive verb whose theta-selection and morphosyntax are identical to that of *tošnit'*, as in (55a). But, unlike *tošnit'*, **j** can *optionally* externalize and be realized syntactically as the nominative subject of *korčit'*: just as it is in the case of derived unaccusatives (see (53)), **-sja** obligatorily affixes to *korčit'* in the derivation of (55b), deleting N_2, which delinks **j**, enabling it to externalize. (56) and (57) are additional examples. The b-sentences in (55) to (57) cannot be passive.

(55)   a. Ego$_j$ korčilo   ot   boli.
          him.ACC.M   writhed.N   from   pain.GEN
          'He was writhing in pain.'
       b. On$_j$ korčilsja   ot   boli.
          he.NOM.M   writhed.M.-sja   from pain
          'He was wrIthing in pain.'
       c. *Ego$_{ACC}$ korčilos'$_N$ ot boli.^{60}
       d. *On$_{NOM.M}$ korčil$_M$ ot boli.
       e. *Ego$_{ACC}$ korčila$_F$ bol'$_{NOM.F}$.

(56)   a. Faneru$_j$ korobit   ot   syrosti.
          plywood:ACC.F   warps   from   dampness:GEN
       b. Fanera$_j$ korobitsja   ot   syrosti.
          plywood:NOM.F   warps:-sja from   dampness

(57)   a. Ego$_j$ korežilo   ot   boli.
          him:ACC.M   writhed:N   from   pain:GEN
       b. On   korežilsja   ot   boli.
          he:NOM.M   writhed:M-sja in   pain:GEN

Since the morphosyntactic differences between *tošnit'* and *korčit'* cannot be predicted from their lexical semantics or from their theta-selection tiers, which are *identical*, they must be encoded in their c-selection tiers. We therefore need to answer the following questions: (i) How can we represent in **V**'s c-selection tier that *korčit'* heads either a personal or impersonal sentence and that **-sja** occurs only when *korčit'* has a subject, whereas *tošnit'* does not compose with **-sja** and is always impersonal? (ii) Is there a class of transitive monadic **V**s that *obligatorily* composes with **-sja**, which is a possibility predicted to exist by diathetic representation?

1.8 *Monadic verbs* 41

Speaking in strictly descriptive terms, a transitive **V** composes with **-sja** when its internal **j**-argument is realized as the projected sentence's nominative subject. Since **-sja** is most frequently used in passive and middle derivations, it is routinely assumed that its primary function is dethematization of **i**. But this hypothesis cannot be correct because (55a–b) is not an active ~ passive alternation: *korčit'* has no external **i** theta role in its initial diathesis, so it cannot passivize. The behavior of *korčit'* demonstrates that the common denominator in all derivations involving the affixation of **-sja** to transitive **V** is deletion of N_2 in **V**'s c-selection tier, i.e.: {... {j^N}$_2$ ... {-^V}$_4$} > {... {j^-}$_2$ ... {-^[V-sja]}$_4$}. The resulting unlinked **j** then obligatorily links to unlinked external N_1, just as in the case of basic unaccusatives (see (53)). If N_1 is not available for relinking with **j**, the resulting *{{i^N}$_1$ {-^j}$_2$...{-^[V-sja]}$_4$} or *{{-^-}$_1$ {-^j}$_2$...{-^[V-sja]}$_4$} diathesis cannot project a well-formed morphosyntactic structure and the derivation crashes.

Unlinked external N_1 (i.e., {-^N}$_1$) has three sources: (i) external **i** can be *dethematized* (relinked to {-^V}$_4$} in passive derivations); (ii) external **i** can be *deleted*, as in nonpassive derived unaccusative (middle) derivations (e.g., *Jama$_j$ napolnilas' vodoj$_k$ (*rabočimi)* 'The-pit filled with-water [*by-the-workers]'); (iii) **V**'s initial diathesis can have no external **i** to begin with, as in the case of *korčit'*. Thus **-sja** is first and foremost a *detransitivizer*, reducing the number of **V**'s categorial heads in its c-selection tier by one (N_2 is deleted), without directly affecting its theta-selection. *Korčilsja* (55b) is therefore a special type of *derived unaccusative*: its initial diathesis in (58a), like initial unaccusative diatheses, has no external theta role, but, unlike initial unaccusatives, it has a linked {j^N}$_2$ argument and **-sja** is required to delete N_2. (58) represents the derivation of (55b) (recall that {-^-} does not project to syntax).[61] (The dotted line is used to indicate separate phases in a diathesis-level derivation; its function is strictly expository. -l- in (58e) is the past-tense suffix).

(58)   The derivation of (55b):
a. {{- ^ N}$_1$ {j ^ N }$_2$ ... {- ^ korči-}$_4$}   +
b. {{- ^ }$_1$ { ^ - }$_2$ ... { ^ -sja}$_4$}   >
c. {{- ^ N }$_1$ { j ^ - }$_2$ ... { - ^ korči-sja}$_4$}   >>
d. {{j ^ N }$_1$ { - ^ - }$_2$ ... { - ^ korči-sja}$_4$}   +
....
e. {{ ^ }$_1$ { ^ }$_2$ ... { ^ -l-}$_4$}   >
f. {{j ^ N }$_1$ { - ^ - }$_2$ ... { - ^ korčilsja}$_4$}   =>

Our next step is to account for the personal ~ impersonal alternation that we observe in the case of *korčit'* in (55a–b) but not in the case of *tošnit'* in (59).

(59) a. Menja tošnilo ot zapaxa krepkogo tabaka.
me:ACC nauseated:N.SG from smell strong tobacco:GEN.
'The smell of the strong tobacco nauseated me.'
b. *Ja$_{NOM.M}$ tošnilsja$_M$ ot zapaxa krepkogo tabaka.
'The smell of the strong tobacco nauseated me.'

If the diatheses of **-sja** and *tošnit'* were to compose, the latter's internal N_2 would delete, but, since there is no external N_1 here for **j** to relink to, $\{j^\wedge\text{-}\}_2$ would project to syntax as an unlinked internal theta role, which is syntactically ill-formed: recall that unlinked *internal* theta roles cannot be V-bound. Thus the initial diatheses of *tošnit'* in (60b) and **-sja** in (60c) correctly predict that **tošnit'sja* is ill-formed. These facts suggest that the correct diathesis of *korčit'*, which, as noted above, combines the properties of transitive-impersonal and derived-unaccusative verbs, is (60a): the parenthesis indicates the *optionality* of external N_1 (cf. the specified absence of N_1 in (60b)).[62] Notice that it is the *external c-selected argument* that encodes the morphosyntactic differences between these two closely related verb types.

(60) a. **korči-**: $\{\{\text{-}^\wedge (N)\}_1 \{j^\wedge N\}_2 \{\text{-}^\wedge\text{-}\}_3 \{\text{-}^\wedge \text{korči-}\}_4\}$
b. **tošni-**: $\{\{\text{-}^\wedge\text{-}\}_1 \{j^\wedge N\}_2 \{\text{-}^\wedge\text{-}\}_3 \{\text{-}^\wedge \text{tošni-}\}_4\}$
c. **-sja**: $\{\{\text{-}^\wedge\ \}_1 \{^\wedge\text{-}\}_2 \{\text{-}^\wedge\text{-}\}_3 \{^\wedge \text{-sja}\}_4\}$

If the optional external **N** in (60a) is not selected, its external argument is $\{\text{-}^\wedge\text{-}\}_1$ and it thus has the same morphosyntactic projection as *tošnit'*: a subjectless sentence with an accusative direct object, as in (55a). But if the optional external **N** in (60a) is selected, giving $\{\text{-}^\wedge N\}_1$, which cannot project to syntax, **-sja** must be added to the derivation as a 'last resort,' creating the unaccusative configuration by deleting N_2, which frees $\{j^\wedge\text{-}\}_2$ to relink to $\{\text{-}^\wedge N\}_1$; $\{j^\wedge N\}_1$ projects as the nominative nP$_j$ subject.

This comparison of *korčit'* and *tošnit'* provides particularly robust evidence for: (i) the autonomy of c-selection and theta-selection and, therefore, the need to represent them as autonomous tiers in argument-structure representation; (ii) the crucial role played by *external c-selection* in Russian syntax: the fact that *korčit'* can select an external N_1 and *tošnit'* cannot, which is an entirely arbitrary fact, accounts for all their morphosyntactic differences. For example, encoded in $\{\text{-}^\wedge(N)\}_1$ is the information that *korčit'* can compose with **-sja** (when N_1 is selected), giving $\{j^\wedge N\}_1$, which enables *korčitsja* to form a hybrid adverbial *korč-a-s'*, as in (61); *korč-a is ill-formed because it has no external theta role and thus cannot be controlled (V-bound) (see chapter 3 for details).

(61) On$_i$ otskočil ot nee, korč-a-s'$_{<j>}$ (*korč-a) ot boli.
he jumped-away from it, writhing from pain
'He jumped away from it, writhing in pain.'

Summary: The theta-selection tiers of basic-unaccusative *tošnit'*, and *korčit'* type verbs are identical: {- j - -}. If syntactic structure could be predicted from V's hierarchically ordered set of theta roles alone (see (5) and (6)), we would expect the syntactic projections of all three to be identical. But we saw above that all three verb types are morphosyntactically different and that the differences are fully encoded in the verbs' c-selection tiers, with *external c-selection* playing the dominant role; the unergative diathesis in (62d) is included for comparison:

(62) Monadic verbs in Russian:
    a. unaccusative: {{- ^ N }$_1$ {j ^ -}$_2$ ... {- ^ V(-sja)}$_4$
    b. tošnit': {{- ^ - }$_1$ {j ^ N}$_2$ ... {- ^ V}$_4$
    c. korčit' {{- ^ (N)}$_1$ {j ^ N}$_2$ ... {- ^ V}$_4$
    d. unergative: {{i ^ N }$_1$ {- ^ -}$_2$ ... {- ^ V}$_4$

The 2×4 structure of diathesis representation predicts the potential existence of another type of {- j - -} monadic verb; whereas its diathesis in (63) has the same theta-selection as (62a–c), its c-selection makes it distinct: unlike the unaccusative diathesis in (62a), it has an N_2 linked to **j**; unlike *korčit'*, its external N_1 is *obligatory*:

(63)   {{- ^ N}$_1$ {j ^ N}$_2$ ... {- ^ V}$_4$}

The diathesis in (63) *predicts* that, if this type of **V** exists in Russian, it will have the following distinctive set of morphosyntactic properties:

(i) It cannot passivize because it has no initial external theta role.
(ii) Since external N_1 is obligatory and unlinked, **j** must, like the **j** of basic unaccusatives, obligatorily externalize (link to N_1) since {-^N}$_1$ does not project a well-formed sentence.
(iii) But (ii) entails that **V**s with the hypothetical diathesis in (63) must be affixed with **-sja** (or **-en-**), which deletes N_2, thereby enabling **j** to relink to {-^N}$_1$; {j^N}$_1$ projects as the sentence's nominative subject.[63] Thus the diathesis in (63) encodes the information that the verb in the sentence it projects will *always* be affixed with **-sja** or **-en-** but will never be passive.
(iv) Since unlinked N_1 is not optional, this type of **V** should not be able to project an impersonal sentence; cf. *tošnit'*, whose external argument is {-^-}$_1$ and whose morphosyntactic projection is thus *always* impersonal (subjectless), and *korčit'*, whose projection is *optionally* impersonal because its external argument is {- ^ (N)}$_1$.

44 *The structure of argument structure*

The sentences in (64) demonstrate that there does exist a class of Russian monadic Vs with the set of morphosyntactic properties predicted in (i)–(iv) on the basis of the diathesis posited in (63). See *atrofirovat' sja* (**atrofirovat'*) 'to atrophy' and *zasnežit' sja* 'to get covered with snow'.

(64) a. Ruka   u   nego   atrofirova-l-a-s' (*atrofirovala).
         arm:NOM.F at   him:GEN   atrophy-PAST-F-SJA
         'His arm atrophied.'
      b. Ruka   u   nego   atrofirova-n-a.
         arm:NOM.F at   him:GEN   atrophy:-(E)N-SF.NOM.F
         'His arm has atrophied.'
      c. *Ruku$_{ACC}$ u nego   atrofirova-l-o$_N$.

We see in (64) that *atrofirovat'sja*: (i) must be affixed with **-sja** or **-en-**; (ii) unlike *korčit'* and *tošnit'* but like basic unaccusatives, it has no impersonal counterpart (cf. (64c)). We know that *atrofirovat' sja* is a verb with *a basic transitive stem* (**atrofirova-**) rather than a verb like *bojat' sja* (**bojat'*) 'to fear', where *-sja* has become part of its stem, because its paradigm includes the **-en-** participle in (64b), which is formed only from *transitive V*s in standard Russian. (64b) is stative not passive (see Babby 1993a). The derivation of *atrofirovalas'* in (64a) is represented in (65) (**-l-a-** is the past feminine singular suffix).

(65) a. {{- ^ N}$_1$ {j ^ N}$_2$ {- ^ -}$_3$ {- ^ **atrofirova-**}$_4$}   +
      b. {{- ^ }$_1$ { ^ - }$_2$ { ^ }$_3$ { ^ **-sja**}$_4$}   >
      c. {{- ^ N}$_1$ {j ^ -}$_2$ {- ^ -}$_3$ {- ^ **[atrofirova-sja]**}$_4$} >>
      d. {{j ^ N}$_1$ {- ^ -}$_2$ {- ^ -}$_3$ {- ^ **atrofirova-sja**}$_4$}   +
      ....
      e. {{ ^ }$_1$ { ^ }$_2$ { ^ }$_3$ { ^ **l-a**}$_4$}   >
      f. {{j ^ N}$_1$ {- ^ -}$_2$ {- ^ -}$_3$ {- ^ **atrofirovalas'**}$_4$}   =>

Although the theta-selection tiers in (62a), (62b), (62c) and (65a) are identical, the morphosyntactic realization of all four monadic verb-types is different. I have shown above that the differences in each case project from systematic differences encoded in the verbs' c-selection tier. This analysis of the properties of monadic verbs constitutes crucial empirical evidence for the correctness of the bipartite representation of arguments in argument structure, the autonomy of the c-selection and, in particular, for *external c-selection*.

In the next section we shall see empirical evidence from other languages that the diathesis's 2×4 structure has extraordinary explanatory (predictive) power and, therefore, that it is in all probability a formal linguistic universal.

1.9 Causativization and the universal architecture of the diathesis

We shall see in the following sections that the diathesis's 2×4, eight-slotted internal organization *predicts* the morphosyntactic realization of **V**'s initial external argument when its diathesis composes with the diathesis of a causative suffix, as in Turkish and Japanese, or with the diathesis of a causative auxiliary verb, as in French and Italian (§1.10).[64] §1.11 demonstrates that diathesis representation enables us to account for the observation that the morphosyntacic realization of **V**'s arguments in derived nominal noun phrases is virtually identical to their realization in causative sentences.

The diathesis of the causative suffix $\mathbf{af_c}$ in (66) has its own external argument $\{i_c{}^\wedge N\}_1$, where i_c is an agent that is *construed* as the causative agent when **V**'s external theta role **i** is itself an agent (the *direct agent* or *causee*).[65] All the other positions in $\mathbf{af_c}$'s diathesis are *unspecified* and are therefore determined by the corresponding positions in the lexical **V**'s diathesis. For example, the composition of (66) and (67) derives the causative diathesis in (68), where **V**'s external argument $\{i{}^\wedge N\}_1$ is displaced by $\{i_c{}^\wedge N\}_1$ and occupies the available $\{-{}^\wedge-\}_2$ position; $\{i{}^\wedge N\}_2$ projects to syntax as [**V-af_c**]'s agentive accusative direct object (see (71)–(72)).

(66)   Diathesis of the causative suffix $\mathbf{af_c}$:
       $\{\{ i_c {}^\wedge N\}_1 \ \{{}^\wedge\}_2 \ \ \{{}^\wedge\}_3 \ \ \{{}^\wedge \mathbf{af_c}\}_4\}$ +

(67)   Diathesis of the unergative verb stem:
       $\{\{ i {}^\wedge N\}_1 \ \{-{}^\wedge-\}_2 \ \{-{}^\wedge-\}_3 \ \{-{}^\wedge V\}_4\}$ >

(68)   Composition of (66) and (67): the 'derived transitive' causative diathesis:
       $\{\{ i_c {}^\wedge N\}_1 \ \{i {}^\wedge N\}_2 \ \{-{}^\wedge-\}_3 \ \{-{}^\wedge \mathbf{[V\text{-}af_c]}\}_4\}$ =>
       $[_{vP}\ nP_{ic.NOM}\ [v'\ [V\text{-}af_c]\ [_{VP}\ nP_{i.ACC}\ V']]]$

$\mathbf{af_c}$ is the head of **[V-af_c]** and, therefore, its initial external argument $\{i_c{}^\wedge N\}_1$ becomes the external argument of the causativized **V**'s diathesis in (68) and projects to syntax as the causative sentence's nominative subject. This entails that **V**'s initial $\{i{}^\wedge N\}_1$ argument in (67) must *internalize*, i.e., it is right-displaced to position 2, 3, or 4, since two arguments cannot occupy the same diathetic position, which would entail their projection to the same position in the syntax, a violation of the Theta Criterion. It is thus this restriction on diathetic well-formedness that explains why a clause cannot have two subjects.

This much is unproblematic and may appear at first glance to be a restatement in diathetic terms of the analysis of the Japanese morphological causative proposed by DiSciullo and Williams (1987: 92) in (69): *-sase* is the causative suffix; A stands for **V**'s external argument (agent) and for -*sase*'s external argument (agent); Th is **V**'s internal (thematic) argument. When the argument structures of the verb *yomi* (A , Th) 'read' and the suffix -*sase* (A) compose in (69), the external argument A of -*sase* becomes the external argument of [*yomi-sase*] and the initial external argument of *yomi* is internalized, which is represented by the removal of A's underlining. Note that no bracketed internal structure is designated for [*yomi-sase*]'s internal argument structure in (69c).

(69)   a. V (A, Th) +
        b. -sase (A) =
        c. V+sase (A (A , Th))

(70)   Tanaka-ga John-ni hon-o yomi-sase masu.
        T:-NOM   J:-DAT   book-ACC   read-af$_{caus}$ tense/aspect
        'Tanaka made John read the book.'

There are three closely related problems with the representation of causativization in (69): (i) argument structure is represented solely in terms of theta roles, which was demonstrated above to be insufficient; (ii) the hierarchical relation between internalized A (dative *John-ni*) and Th (accusative *hon-o*) in (69c) is not indicated (cf. the discussion of (5) and (6) in §1.2); (iii) there is no indication of which principle or principles determine how the lexical verb's internalized external argument A is realized morphosyntactically (e.g., how *John*, the external argument of *yomi*, is realized as dative *John ni* in (70)).

The diathesis-based analysis, which eliminates these problems, is based on the following observation: unlike passive derivations, **V**'s external **i** in causative derivations is *not* delinked from **N$_1$** (*dethematized*) and relinked to $\{- \wedge \text{[V-af]}\}_4$, giving $\{i \wedge \text{[V-af]}\}_4$. Rather, **V**'s intact bipartite external argument $\{i \wedge N\}_1$ is internalized (*right-displaced*) by the causative affix's external argument $\{i_c \wedge N\}_1$ and realized morphosyntactically *in several different ways*. Most important, $\{i \wedge N\}_1$'s morphosyntactic realization is entirely predictable: it depends directly on whether **V** is intransitive, monotransitive or ditransitive. My hypothesis is that this crucial empirical fact follows directly and automatically from the diathesis's 2×4 structure.

Argument structure representations like (69) do have not sufficient internal structure to predict the position occupied by the internalized agent A and, therefore, its position and case in the causative sentence's projected syntactic structure. In the diathetic representation I am proposing, the derived position of displaced $\{i \wedge N\}_1$ and, therefore, its morphosyntactic realization, is exhaustively determined by the left-most *unoccupied* (i.e., $\{-\wedge-\}$) position in **[V-af$_c$]**'s composite diathesis; (e.g., see $\{i \wedge N\}_1 > \{i \wedge N\}_2 \Rightarrow [_{VP} nP_{i.ACC}V']$ in (66) to (68)).

1.9 Causativization   47

To see how this works in vivo, let us begin with the causativization of unergative Vs in Turkish. As we saw above in (66) to (68), when the unergative diathesis in (66) composes with the causative suffix af_c's (-*dir-/-t-*) diathesis in (67), the result is the derived causative diathesis in (68): $\{i_c\wedge N\}_1$ becomes the external argument of [V-af_c] and V's initial $\{i\wedge N\}_1$ is right-displaced to $\{-\wedge-\}_2$, which is the left-most unoccupied position in V's initial diathesis, i.e., $\{i\wedge N\}_1 > \{i\wedge N\}_2$, which projects to the spec-VP position in syntax, just as the initial $\{j\wedge N\}_2$ argument of basic transitive Vs does, and it is realized syntactically as the accusative direct object. Thus causativization of an unergative V produces a *derived monotransitive* diathesis whose projected subject and direct object are both linked to agent theta roles, which is the theta-configuration responsible for the sentence's causative interpretation.[66]

This derivation also accounts for the following corollary of diathesis-based theory: there is no causative-specific syntax: the unergative V's derived causative diathesis in (68) ($\{\{i_c\wedge N\}_1 \{i\wedge N\}_2 \{-\wedge-\}_3 \{-\wedge[V-af_c]\}_4\}$ => [$_{VP}$ nP$_{i.c.NOM}$ [v' [V-af_c] [$_{VP}$ nP$_{i.ACC}$ V']]]) has the same final diathetic structure as a *basic monotransitive* V, and they thus both project the same morphosyntactic structures. However, while there is no causative-specific syntax, there are causative-specific affixes, which alter V's initial diathesis without altering its skeletal 2×4 structure. (71) is the causative derivation of the Turkish unergative V in (72b).

(71)   Causativization of unergative verbs (*gez-mek* 'to take a walk')
       a. initial diathesis: $\{\{$ i $\wedge$ N$\}_1$ $\{-$ $\wedge$ $-\}_2$ $\{-$ $\wedge$ $-\}_3$ $\{-$ $\wedge$ gez-$\}_4\}$ +
       b. affix diathesis: $\{\{$ i$_c$ $\wedge$ N$\}_1$ $\{$ $\wedge$ $\}_2$ $\{$ $\wedge$ $\}_3$ $\{$ $\wedge$ -dir-$\}_4\}$ >
       c. a+b: $\{\{$ i$_c$ $\wedge$ N$\}_1$ $\{$i $\wedge$ N$\}_2$ $\{-$ $\wedge$ $-\}_3$ $\{-$ $\wedge$ [gez-dir-]$\}_4\}$ +
       d. -d-im: $\{\{$ $\wedge$ $\}_1$ $\{$ $\wedge$ $\}_2$ $\{$ $\wedge$ $\}_3$ $\{$ $\wedge$ -d-im$\}_4\}$ >
       e. c+d: $\{\{$ i$_c$ $\wedge$ N$\}_1$ $\{$i $\wedge$ N$\}_2$ $\{-$ $\wedge$ $-\}_3$ $\{-$ $\wedge$ [gezdirdim]$\}_4\}$ =>

(72)   a. Çocuk   bahçe-de   **gez-di.** (unergative)
           child.NOM   garden.LOC   walk.PAST
           'The-child walked in-the-garden.'
       b. (Ben)   çocuğ-u   bahçe-de   **gez-dir-d-im.** (causative)
           I:NOM.i$_c$ child:ACC.i   garden:LOC   walk-CAUS-PAST-FIRST-PERSON SG
           '(lit.) I walked-the-child (= took the child for a walk) in-the-garden.'

When the causative affix's diathesis composes with the diathesis of an *unaccusative* verb, $\{i_c\wedge N\}_1$ again becomes the external argument of [V-af_c] and V's external argument $\{-\wedge N\}_1$ internalizes, linking to $\{j\wedge-\}_2$, giving $\{j\wedge N\}_2$, which projects as [V-af_c]'s *accusative* direct object, as in (73i): cf. internalized $\{-\wedge N\}_1$ + internal $\{j\wedge-\}_2$ > internal $\{j\wedge N\}_2$ in causative derivations vs. external $\{-\wedge N\}_1$ + externalized $\{j\wedge-\}_2$ > external $\{j\wedge N\}_1$ unaccusative derivations. Thus

af$_c$ converts an unaccusative **V**'s initial diathesis into a two-place, monotransitive diathesis, just as in the causativization of unergative **V**s. The final derived diatheses of causativized unergative and unaccusative diatheses are identical except for the theta role linked to **N$_2$**, which is an agent **i** in the former case and the initial theme **j** in the latter; cf. {j^N}$_2$ in (73i) and {i^N}$_2$ in (73ii).

(73)   i. Causativization of unaccusative verb:
   a. initial diathesis: {{ - ^ N}$_1$ {j ^ -}$_2$ {- ^ -}$_3$ {- ^ V}$_4$} +
   b. affix diathesis: {{ i$_c$ ^ N}$_1$ { ^ }$_2$ { ^ }$_3$ { ^ af$_c$}$_4$} >
   c. a + b: {{ i$_c$ ^ N}$_1$ {j ^ N}$_2$ {- ^ -}$_3$ { - ^ [V-af$_c$]}$_4$}
  ii. Causativization of unergative verb:
   a. initial diathesis: {{ i ^ N}$_1$ {- ^ -}$_2$ {- ^ -}$_3$ {- ^ V}$_4$} +
   b. affix diathesis: {{ i$_c$ ^ N}$_1$ { ^ }$_2$ { ^ }$_3$ { ^ af$_c$}$_4$} >
   c. a + b: {{ i$_c$ ^ N}$_1$ {i ^ N}$_2$ {- ^ -}$_3$ { - ^ [V-af$_c$]}$_4$}

Our two-agent-construal analysis of causative meaning correctly predicts that, since causativized unaccusative verbs have only one agent (**j** is a theme), they should not have causative meaning: the external agent of causativized unaccusative verbs is construed as the direct agent, just as it is in initial monotransitive sentences. See (74): when unaccusative *öl-mek* 'to-die' is causativized, *öl-dür-mek* means 'to kill,' which is semantically not a causative verb because the **i$_c$** agent here is construed as the direct agent in the absence of an internal **i** agent.[67] It is only the double-causative *öl-dür$_{caus}$-t$_{caus}$-mek* 'to have someone kill someone' that has causative semantics, since here there are two agents, a causative agent (the instigator) and a direct agent (the killer): there are two cauasative suffixes and the diathesis of each introduces one external agent argument to the initial unaccusative **V**, whose initial diathesis has no agents.

(74) a. Hasan$_j$ öl-dü.
    Hasan:NOM died:PAST
   b. Orhan$_{ic}$ Hasan$_j$ öl-dür-dü.
    Orhan:NOM Hasan-ACC die:af$_c$-PAST
    'Orhan killed Hasan.'
   c. Hasan$_j$ Orhan tarafından öl-dür-ül-dü
    Hasan:NOM Orhan by   die-af$_c$-af$_{PASS}$-af$_{PAST}$
    'Hasan was-killed by Ali.'
   d. Attila$_{ic}$ Orhan-1$_j$ Hasan-a$_{ic}$ öl-dür-t-tü.
    A.NOM O.ACC H.DAT die-af$_c$-af$_c$-PAST
    'Attila had Hasan kill Orhan.'

Note that passivized causatives like (74c) demonstrate that causativization must be an argument-structure level operation (diathesis composition), not a syntactic rule (clause union). Since, as we saw in §1.5.3, passivization is patently a diathetic operation and causativization *precedes* passivization

1.9 Causativization   49

(cf. *öl-dür*$_{caus}$-*ül*$_{pass}$-*dü* vs.*öl-ül$_{pass}$-*dür*$_{caus}$-*dü* in (74c); see Baker 1985), causativization too must be a diathetic operation: the output of a syntactic operation cannot feed a diathetic operation (double causatives also passivize: *öl-dür-t-ül-mek*).

Now let us see what happens when we causativize a monotransitive diathesis, whose first two positions are occupied; see (75) and (76). Monotransitive **V**'s initial diathesis predicts that its external argument should be realized morphosyntactically as a *dative agentive* object under causativization. More specifically, monotransitive **V**'s initial diathesis in (75a) predicts that its internalized $\{i^\wedge N\}_1$ should occupy the available 'third position', i.e., $\{i^\wedge N\}_1 > \{i^\wedge N\}_3$ when $\{i_c^\wedge N\}_1$ becomes the external argument of **[V-af$_c$]**; see (75c) and (76). $\{i^\wedge N\}_3$ is assigned structural dative case in Turkish (cf. the dative projection of $\{i^\wedge N\}_3$ in Japanese in (70) and French in (81a)). (76b) has a causative reading because it contains two agents; cf. (74d).

(75) Causativization of monotransitive verbs.
    a. initial diathesis: $\{\{\,i\,\wedge\,N\}_1\;\{j\,\wedge\,N\}_2\;\{-\,\wedge\,-\}_3\;\{-\,\wedge\,V\}_4\}$ +
    b. affix diathesis: $\{\{\,i_c\,\wedge\,N\}_1\;\{\,\wedge\,\}_2\;\;\;\;\{\,\wedge\,\}_3\;\;\{\,\wedge\,af_c\}_4\}$ >
    c. a + b: $\{\{\,i_c\,\wedge\,N\}_1\;\{j\,\wedge\,N\}_2\;\{i\,\wedge\,N\}_3\;\{\,V\,\wedge\,af_c\}_4\}$

(76) a. Hasan$_i$ bütün paket-ler-in-i$_j$ aç-tı.
       Hasan-NOM all   package-PL-POSS-ACC open-PAST
       'Hasan opened all his packages.'
    b. Polis$_{ic}$ Hasan$_i$-a   bütün paket-ler-in-i$_j$ aç-tır-dı.
       police-NOM Hasan-DAT all package-PL-POSS-ACC open-CAUS-PAST
       'The police made Hasan open all his packages.'

We come now to the crucial case of the ditransitive diathesis. Since, as we see in (77a), all three of its argument positions are occupied, the diathesis's 2×4 structure predicts that: (i) the only position available to accomodate **V**'s displaced external argument is the unlinked 4-position; (ii) implicit i (i.e., $\{i^\wedge[V\text{-}af_c]\}_4$) licenses a *tarafından by*-phrase. This is precisely what we see in (78).[68]

(77) Causativization of ditransitive verbs.
    a. initial diathesis: $\{\{\,i\,\wedge\,N\}_1\;\{j\,\wedge\,N\}_2\;\{k\,\wedge\,N\}_3\;\{-\,\wedge\,V\}_4\}$ +
    b. affix diathesis: $\{\{\,i_c\,\wedge\,N\}_1\{\,\wedge\,\}_2\;\;\;\{\,\wedge\,\}_3\;\;\{\,\wedge\,af_c\}_4\}$ >
    c. a + b: $\{\{\,i_c\,\wedge\,N\}_1\;\{j\,\wedge\,N\}_2\;\{k\,\wedge\,N\}_3\;\{i\,\wedge\,[V\text{-}af_c]\}_4\}$

(78) a. Müdür   Hasan-a mektub-u göster-di.
       director-NOM H.-DAT letter-ACC show-PAST
       'The director showed the letter to Hasan.'
    b. Baba-m   Hasan-a mektub-u [$_{PP}$ müdür tarafından] göster-t-ti.
       father-POSS-NOM H-DAT letter-ACC [director by]   show-CAUS-PAST
       'My father made the director show the letter to Hasan.'

50 *The structure of argument structure*

Given the derivations of passive sentences in (27)/(28) and the causative sentences above, I conclude that *by*-phrases are licensed by an implicit **i**, i.e., $\{i^\wedge[\text{V-af}]\}_4$. Since the *by*-phrase is not the unique property of passives, there is no need to posit an 'intermediate passive rule' in the derivation of ditransitive causatives in order to account for the presence of the *by*-phrase (see Comrie 1989). My analysis predicts that any diathetic derivation in which **i** is linked to $\{-\wedge[\text{V-af}]\}_4$ licenses a *by*-phrase. The occurrence of *by*-phrases in *derived nominals* confirms this analysis; see §1.11 below; Babby 1997a–b.

We see in (79a) that *başlamak* 'to begin' in Turkish assigns quirky dative case to its internal object *okul-a* 'school'. (79b), the causative of (79a), demonstrates that the initial diathesis of *başlamak* in (80a) encodes the information that the left-most free position for $\{i^\wedge N\}_1$ to occupy is $\{-\wedge-\}_2$.[69] $\{i^\wedge N\}_2$ is realized morphosyntactically as the agentive accusative direct object in spec-VP. Thus the realization of *çocuk* as the nominative subject in (79a) and as the agentive accusative direct object in (79b) is entirely encoded in (80a) and (80b).

(79)   a. Çocuk   okul-a   başla-dı.
            boy:NOM   school:DAT   begin:PAST
            'The boy began school.'
       b. Baba-m   çocuğ-u   okul-a   başla-t-tı.[70]
            father-POSS-NOM   boy-ACC   school-DAT   begin-CAUS-PAST
            'My father made the boy begin school.'

(80)   Causativization of lexical-case assigning monotransitive verbs.
          a. initial diathesis: $\{\{i \wedge N\}_1 \ \{-\wedge-\}_2 \ \{k \wedge N_{\text{DAT}}\}_3 \ \{-\wedge V\}_4\}$ +
          b. affix diathesis: $\{\{i_c \wedge N\}_1 \ \{\wedge\}_2 \ \{\wedge\}_3 \ \{\wedge \text{af}_c\}_4\}$ >
          c. a + b: $\{\{i_c \wedge N\}_1 \ \{i \wedge N\}_2 \ \{k \wedge N_{\text{DAT}}\}_3 \ \{-\wedge [\text{V-af}_c]\}_4\}$ =>
          d. projection of c: $[_{\text{VP}} nP_{\text{ic.NOM}} \ [_{v'} \ [_{\text{VP}} nP_{\text{i.ACC}} \ nP_{\text{k.DAT}}] \ [\text{V-af}_c]]]$

We have seen above that while there are causative-specific affixal diatheses, there are no causative-specific syntactic relations or cases. The *by*-phrase is not passive-, causative-, or derived-nominal-specific: it is $\{i^\wedge[\text{V-af}]\}_4$-specific. This follows from the fact that the diathesis-encoded projection rules do not distinguish between basic and derived diatheses: both have the same 2×4 diathesis, which projects the same core Extended Lexical Projection. This means that the absence of construction-specific syntactic structure and case is epiphenomenal, an automatic consequence of the diathesis's immutable 2×4 structure.

1.9.1 Language-specific diversity

There are essentially two sources of language-specific diversity in causative sentences, and both are constrained by the diathesis's 2×4 architecture. The first involves the morphosyntactic realization of {i^[V-af_c]}_4. Since implicit **i** licenses an *argument-adjunct* (see Grimshaw 1990), various language-specific adjunct realization strategies are possible in addition to the canonical *by*-phrase. For example, displaced {i^N}_1 can be realized in Turkish ditransitive causative derivations by *case doubling*, i.e., by *adjoining* displaced {i^N}_1's nP_i projection to the initial dative indirect object, in which case the sentence has two datives, one **V**'s initial dative argument, the other an adjunct agreeing with it in case (see Comrie 1989: 178 for details). This strategy is relatively uncommon because most languages have a *blocking mechanism* that filters out two nPs with the same morphological case in the same clause (see Guasti 1997: 149). Manner adverbs have a limited use in place of *by*-phrases: e.g., see Turkish *ben-ce* (lit. 'I-ly') for *ben-im*_GEN *taraf-ım*_POSS*-dan*_ABL 'by me (lit. side-my-from [i.e., from-my-side]).'[71]

The second type of diversity is *position-skipping*, which is important because it demonstrates another way in which the syntactic realization of internalized {i^N}_1 is constrained by the diathesis's 2×4 structure. Position-skipping is common in Romance causativization: when {i^N}_1 is internalized, it may skip over the nearest available {-^-} position in the derived causative diathesis and occupy a more distant available position (but it cannot skip out of the diathesis). In practice, position-skipping is restricted to the causativization of initial monotransitive verbs: instead of occupying {-^-}_3 (and being projected to syntax as a dative nP_i or PP), displaced {i^N}_1 skips over it to {-^[V-af_c]}_4 and the resulting implicit {i^[V-af_c]}_4 licenses the *by*-phrase, which is the *par*-phrase in French.[72] For example, consider the causativization of monotransitive **V**s in French: we see in (81a) that {i^N}_1 can occupy {-^-}_3 (the left-most available position) and be realized as the dative (*à* 'to'), just as in Turkish; but *par* 'by' may be used instead, which means that the nearest available 3-position has been skipped and the available 4-position used instead, as in (81b).[73]

(81)   a. Hasan a   fait   manger les pommes   à Ali.
           H.NOM has made to-eat   the apples.ACC to Ali.
           'Hasan made Ali eat the apples.'
        b. Hasan a   fait   manger les pommes   par Ali.
           H.NOM has made to-eat   the-apples.ACC by Ali
           'Hasan made Ali eat the apples.'

What is significant about the 'alternation' in (81a–b) is that even a peripheral, language-specific phenomenon like position-skipping is constrained by the diathesis's 2×4 skeletal frame. Note too that while position-skipping is not a legitimate syntactic operation, its existence, rightward direction, and final position are predicted by the diathesis's 2×4 structure.

1.10 Romance causativization

The explanatory power of the diathesis's 2×4 internal organization receives stunning confirmation from the Romance type of causativization, which looks superficially like the bi-clausal, object-control causative sentences in Russian and English, but will be shown below to be virtually identical to the monoclausal affix-driven Turkish morphological causative. Most important: (i) in French and Italian, **V**'s initial external argument {i^N}$_1$ is *displaced* (*internalized*), which happens in Turkish causative derivations, but not in English and Russian; (ii) the morphosyntactic realization of internalized {i^N}$_1$ in French and Italian is determined by **V**'s initial diathesis, just as it is in Turkish, and, I argue, for the same reason.

French causative sentences, like English, have a finite causative verb *faire* 'make' whose infinitive complement is headed by **V**. But there is a crucial difference in word order: the infinitive in French must follow immediately after the auxiliary *faire*; this order is not possible in the corresponding English causative sentences: see (82)–(84).[74]

(82) a. J'ai fait courir Paul.
    I-have made run:INFIN Paul:ACC
    'I made Paul run.' (cf. Turkish (71)–(73ii))
    b. *J'ai fait Paul courir.

(83) a. J'ai fait manger les pommes à Paul.
    I-have made eat:INFIN the apples:ACC to Paul
    'I made Paul eat the apples.' (cf. Turkish (75)–(76))
    b. *J'ai fait Paul manger les pommes.

(84) a. J'ai fait écrire une lettre au directeur par Paul.
    I-have made write:INFIN a letter:ACC to-the director by Paul
    'I made Paul write a letter to the director.' (cf. Turkish (77)–(78))
    b. *J'ai fait Paul écrire une lettre au directeur.

This seemingly superficial difference in word order actually reflects the radically different derivations and syntactic structures of causative sentences in French and English. More specifically, *faire* is a true *auxiliary* **V**, i.e., its diathesis has the same structure as the causative suffix in Turkish and it therefore *composes* with **V**'s diathesis in argument structure, not syntax (see §4.12). *Make* in English and *zastavit'* 'make' in Russian are not auxiliary verbs: they are ordinary *object-control verbs*, i.e., ditransitive verbs that select a direct object that antecedent binds the null (PRO) subject of the their infinitive-clause complement, as in (85) and (86) (infP denotes an infinitive clause; see chapter 4 for details).

(85) a. I$_i$ made Paul$_j$ [$_{infP}$ PRO$_i$ run]. (cf. (82)–(84))
 b. I$_i$ made Paul$_j$ [$_{infP}$ PRO$_i$ eat the apples$_j$].
 c. I$_i$ made Paul$_j$ [$_{infP}$ PRO$_i$ write a letter$_j$ to the director$_k$].

(86) a. Ja zastavil Paula$_{ACC}$ [$_{infP}$ PRO$_i$ begat'].
 c. Ja zastavil Paula$_{ACC}$ [$_{infP}$ PRO$_i$ s"est' jabloki$_{ACC}$].
 d. Ja zastavil Paula$_{ACC}$ [$_{infP}$ PRO$_i$ napisat' direktoru$_{DAT}$ pis'mo$_{ACC}$].

According to the analysis I am proposing, causative sentences in English and Russian are *bi-clausal*, whereas in French and Turkish they are the result of the diathesis-composition of **V** and the causative auxiliary or causative suffix and, therefore, their final diatheses project to syntax as *monoclausal* structures. In other words, English and Russian causative sentences involve *syntax-level clause union* (*merger*), whereas Turkish and French involve *argument-structure-level diathesis union* (composition).

What sets auxiliaries off as a separate verb class is that, like paradigmatic affixes, their diatheses contain *unspecified slots*, which must be filled in by the corresponding slots in **V**'s diathesis. This entails that the diatheses of the causative auxiliary *faire* and the lexical verb stem **V** *compose*, and that the 2×4 structure of their composite diathesis, which determines the position of **V**'s internalized {i^N}$_1$, projects to syntax as a single clause. This explains why the [auxiliary + infinitive] in French forms what is perceived to be a maximally tight 'syntactic bond': they form a composite lexical head [V$_{aux}$+V$_{lex}$], which accounts for the fact noted above that nothing can intervene between *faire* and its infinitive complement (see (82)–(84)).

Let us run through the derivation of the French causative sentences in (82) to (84), comparing them to the corresponding Turkish sentences. If **V** is unergative, displaced {i^N}$_1$ occupies the {-^-}$_2$ position in [*faire courir*]'s composite diathesis and is realized syntactically as the accusative direct object (cf. (71) and (82)). If **V** is monotransitive, its {j^N}$_2$ position is occupied and internalized {i^N}$_1$ thus occupies {-^-}$_3$, which projects to syntax as the dative oblique object (sister-to-V') (see dative *Hasan-a* in (75)/(76) and dative *à Paul* in (83)). If **V** is ditransitive, both its internal argument positions are occupied in its initial diathesis, and {i^N}$_1$ occupies the fourth position. This yields {i^[*faire écrire*]}$_4$ and implicit **i** licenses the adjunct *par by*-phrase, just as in Turkish (cf. the *tarafından* postpositional *by*-phrase in (78)/(79) and the *par* phrase in (84)).

I conclude on the basis of these facts that the diathesis of the causative auxiliary *faire*, like the Turkish causative suffix *-dir-*, has its own external {i$_c^N_1$ argument and composes with the diathesis of lexical **V** (see §4.2.2; Baker 1988a, Chomsky 1988: 56 ff., DiSciullo and Williams 1987, Comrie

1989, Guasti 1997). The syntactic structures of (82)–(84) are schematically represented as (87a–c). Guasti 1997 presents evidence from clitic placement and clitic climbing in Italian that [$_{Vaux}$V$_{aux}$V$_{inf}$] is the correct structure and that the causative auxiliary is the head. Compare (87i) to the English and Russian causative sentences in (87ii–iii) (= (85) and (86)).

(87) i: French causative sentences:
  a. J'ai [[fait] [$_{inf}$ courir]] [$_{VP}$ Paul$_i$ v'].
  b. J'ai [[fait] [$_{inf}$ manger]] [$_{VP}$ les pommes$_j$ [$_{v'}$ t à Paul$_i$]].
  c. J'ai [[fait] [$_{inf}$ ècrire]] [$_{VP}$ [$_{VP}$ une lettre$_j$ [$_{v'}$ t au directeur$_k$]]] par Paul].

(87) ii: English causative sentences:
  a. I$_i$ made Paul$_j$ [$_{infP}$ PRO$_i$ run].
  b. I$_i$ made Paul$_j$ [$_{infP}$ PRO$_i$ eat the apples$_j$].
  c. I$_i$ made Paul$_j$ [$_{infP}$ PRO$_i$ write a letter$_j$ to the director$_k$].

(87) iii: Russian causative sentences:
  a. Ja zastavil Paula$_{ACC}$ [$_{infP}$ PRO$_i$ begat'].
  b. Ja zastavil Paula$_{ACC}$ [$_{infP}$ PRO$_i$ s"est' jabloki$_{ACC}$].
  c. Ja zastavil Paula$_{ACC}$ [$_{infP}$ PRO$_i$ napisat' direktoru$_{DAT}$ pis'mo$_{ACC}$].

The structures in (87) explain why English and Russian ditransitive causative sentences never have a *by*-phrase: they are bi-clausal and thus never need one: the causative agent **i**$_c$ is the subject of the finite matrix clause and the direct agent **i** is the subject of the complement clause and thus not displaced: it is the object-controlled subject (PRO$_i$) of the infinitive clause complement. Thus neither the finite matrix clause nor the infinitive complement clause in the analytic causative construction has more than three arguments. The French causative sentence is monoclausal because its infinitive complement *is not a clause* and thus has no subject nP of its own. [*faire* + infinitive] has a single 2×4 diathesis, which predicts the use of the diathesis's fourth position to accomodate {i^N}$_1$ when a ditransitive verb is causativized; this is precisely what happens in Turkish (see chapter 4 for discussion of the *bare infinitive complements* of auxiliary verbs).

1.11 Nominalization and causativization

In this section we will compare the derivations of derived nominals (DN), passives, and causatives, the three constructions which cross-linguistically license *by*-phrases. It is based on the following empirical facts and assumptions: (i) Derived nominals have hybrid VP-in-nP structure, i.e., [$_{nP}$ [$_{n'}$ [$_n$ V-n] [$_{VP}$ nP$_j$ [$_{v'}$ t$_v$ nP$_k$]]]], where **n** is the DN-forming suffix;[75] (ii) the *by*-phrase is always

1.11 Nominalization and causativization 55

licensed by the derived $\{i\wedge[V\text{-}af]\}_4$ configuration ($\{i\wedge[V\text{-}n]_n\}_4$ in DNs); (iii) Russian nPs do not have an obligatory determiner-phrase shell and there is no equivalent of the English [$_{DP}$ nP's D'...] construction in Russian. (i) to (iii) raise the following question: what happens to **V**'s external $\{i\wedge N\}_1$ argument when the diatheses of **V** and the DN-forming suffix **n** compose? More specifically, how is the $\{i\wedge[V\text{-}n]_n]\}_4$ *by*-phrase licensing configuration derived in the case of derived nominals: unlike causative derivations involving initial ditransitive **V**s, **n**'s diathesis does not introduce a 'new' subject that is responsible for displacing **V**'s initial $\{i\wedge N\}_1$? Positing an intermediate passive phase in the derivation of DNs to account for the occurrence of the *by*-phrase is not explanatory since it makes several incorrect predictions.

I will argue that, despite superficial differences, the derivation of derived nominals is the nP-internal analogue of the affix/auxiliary-driven causative derivation we saw above: **V**'s external $\{i\wedge N\}_1$ argument is displaced and occupies the first $\{\text{-}\wedge\text{-}\}$ position in the composite 2×4 diathesis of **[V-n]$_n$**; what is crucial here is that **[V-n]$_n$** projects an nP rather than a vP (finite clause), as in causative derivations.[76] Although the suffixes used in the derivation of Russian DNs are not predictable from **V**, i.e, the stem-specific value of the **n** affix is not predictable in terms of the verb stem's form or meaning, the mapping between the positions in **V**'s diathesis and their nP-internal morphosyntactic realization in the DN's phrasal projection is entirely systematic and, I shall argue, makes an important contribution to the now substantial body of evidence that the diathesis's 2×4 structure is explanatory. I will demonstrate below that the relations between the argument positions in **V**'s initial diathesis and the positions of these arguments in syntactic structure are identical in the derivations of causative clauses and DN noun phrases.

It was assumed in early generative theory that nominalization is a *syntactic rule* that transforms sentences into noun phrases, preserving the former's grammatical relations. There is now general agreement that it is a *lexical rule* which combines a verb stem and a nominal affix to form the derived-nominal head of a noun phrase (cf. Chomsky 1970, Grimshaw 1990; see also Lees 1966, Giorgi and Longobardi 1991). An explicit account of nominalization as a lexical rule must be able to explain why sentences and their corresponding DNs appear to have the *same grammatical relations* (see the traditional notions like *genitivus subjectivus* and *genitivus objectivus*).[77] This is not a problem for diathesis theory, one of whose main hypotheses is that the argument positions in **V**'s diathesis encode the projected vP's – and nP's – grammatical relations.[78] We shall thus be interested below in how the positions in **V**'s diathesis map onto homologous positions in the derived nominal's nP projection. Since Russian DNs, unlike English DNs, do not have a prehead -'s genitive, we will focus on how {i^N}$_1$ is realized morphosyntactically when it is displaced in DN derivations. I begin my analysis with the following examples (note the word order in (88a–c)), but first I will outline the salient properties of Russian DNs.

(88)   a. Rabočie$_i$ napolnili jamu$_j$ vodoj$_k$.
              workers:NOM   filled:PL   pit:ACC   water:INST.
              'The-workers filled the-pit with-water.'
     b. napolnenie   jamy$_j$ vodoj$_k$ (rabočimi$_i$)
              DN:NOM   pit:GEN   water:INST   workers:INST
              'the-filling of-the-pit with-water (by-the-workers)'
     c. napolnenie (rabočimi) jamy vodoj.
     d. *napolnenie jamy (rabočimi) vodoj.
     e. *[$_{DP}$ rabočix$_{GEN}$ [$_{nP}$ napolnenie$_{NOM}$ jamy$_{GEN}$ vodoj$_{INST}$]
        'the-workers' filling the-pit with-water'

(89)   a. Sud$_i$ lišil   prestupnika$_j$ svobody$_k$.
              court:NOM   deprived   criminal:ACC   freedom:GEN
              'The-court deprived the-criminal of-(his)-freedom.'
     b. lišenie (sudom$_{INST}$) prestupnika$_{j·GEN}$ svobody$_{k·GEN}$ [79]
        '(lit.) the-deprivation of-the-criminal of-his-freedom (by the court)'
     c. lišenie prestupnika$_{j·GEN}$ svobody$_{k·GEN}$ (sudom$_{INST}$)

1.11.1   *The properties of Russian derived nominals*

- All **V**'s nP arguments *follow* the head, as in (88b).
- The Russian nP has two distinct genitive positions: adnominal genitive follows the head and precedes possessive genitive, e.g.: [$_{nP}$ *tablica élementov Mendeleeva*] 'Mendeleev's table of elements (lit. the-table of-elements of-Mendeleev)' (cf. *[$_{nP}$ *tablica Mendeleeva élementov*]). The left-most (adnominal) genitive nP in DNs is the direct projection of one of **V**'s *arguments* ({j^N}$_2$ in the case of transitive **V**s) while the possessive genitive has an *adjunct* function (see below).[80]
- Under neutral word order, the optional instrumental-case *by*-phrase in Russian ditransitive DN phrases occupies a position at either the right-periphery of the phrase or its left-periphery, the latter being the position immediately following the DN phrase's head (see (88b–c) and (89b–c)): e.g., [*obnaruženie det'mi$_{INST}$ trupa$_{GEN}$*] 'the-discovery by-the-children of-a-corpse' or [*obnaruženie trupa$_{GEN}$ det'mi$_{INST}$*] 'the-discovery of-a-corpse by-the-children' (cf. *Deti$_{i.NOM}$ obnaružili trup$_{j.ACC}$* 'The-children discovered a-corpse').

1.11 Nominalization and causativization

- V's {k^N}₃ argument is realized in DN phrases just as it is in the VP of finite clauses (see $vodoj_{INST}$ 'with-water' in (88a–b)) since its case is determined by its theta role when it remains in situ in VP (see Babby 1994a, Woolford 2006).
- If **V** selects a *quirky* case, which is specified in its initial diathesis as a c-selected case feature, it is 'inherited' by the DN, as in (89). Quirky case in Russian is canonically assigned to **V**'s {k^N}₃ position.[81]
- Both tiers of **V**'s diathesis play a role in determining the morphosyntactic realization of its arguments in DN phrases (see Rozwadowska 1988: 157 for a different hypothesis).

These facts suggest that (90) is the internal structure of the DN phrases in (88b–c) (cf. Moro 1997: 80): the adnominal genitive nP$_j$ (*jamy*) precedes the oblique **k**-argument (*vodoj*); the bare instrumental-case *by*-phrases (*rabočimi*) adjoins to VP, which accounts for the fact that it can occupy either of the two peripheral adjunct positions (which is denoted by the parentheses and dashed lines): [$_{VP}$ nP$_{INST}$ VP] or [$_{VP}$ VP nP$_{INST}$].[82] The representation in (90) expains why {i^N}₁ canonically maps onto a *by*-phrase in DN derivations when **V** is *ditransitive*, which is parallel to causative derivations.

(90) Internal structure of Russian derived nominals.

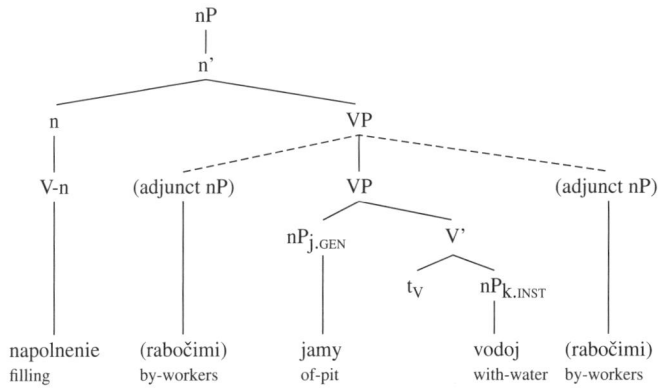

(91) a. [$_{nP}$ [$_{n'}$ [V-n]$_n$ [$_{vP}$ nP$_j$:GEN V']]]
      b. [$_{vP}$ [$_{v'}$ [V-v]$_v$ [$_{VP}$ nP$_j$:ACC V']]]

1.11.2 The by-*phrase in derived nominal phrases*

We will consider two proposals: (i) nominalization is the nP-internal analogue of passivization; (ii) nominalization is the nP-internal analogue of causativization.

It has been proposed that DNs like (88b c)/(90) have *by*-phrases because, like passives, they involve *dethematization* of V's external theta role, with the resulting *implicit* theta role licensing the *by*-phrase (e.g., see Cinque 1980, Comrie 1980: 217, Grimshaw 1990).[83] However, there are several problems with this analysis. First, explaining the occurrence of the *by*-phrase in DNs in terms of passivization fails to explain why *causatives* have *by*-phrases: we saw above that causativization does not involve dethematization or a "hidden intermediate passive rule." Second, the passive-analysis predicts that Vs that are unable to passivize should not nominalize, which is also patently incorrect: unaccusative verbs are incorrectly predicted not to nominalize because they have no external **i** to dethematize. Third, the passive/dethematization-analysis makes the patently incorrect prediction that V's external **i** should *always* be realized as a *by*-phrase in DNs. In Russian DNs, the argument of intransitive Vs is always realized as the adnominal genitive, as in (92)–(93); the PP in (94) is the projection of $\{k^{\wedge}[na]_P\}_3$. However, given the realization of V's arguments in causative sentences and derived-nominal phrases described above, it is immediately obvious that only the *displacement* analysis, i.e., the causative analogue, is explanatory.

(92) priezd Ivana (*Ivanom)
arrival:NOM Ivan:GEN(*INST)
'the arrival of (*by) Ivan'

(93) a. Vrag otstupil.
enemy:NOM.M retreated:M
'The-enemy retreated.'
b. otstuplenie vraga (*vragom)
retreat:NOM.N enemy:GEN.M (enemy:INST)
'the-retreat of (*by) the-enemy'

(94) a. naezd na nee [p'janogo voditelja] (*p'janym voditelem)
running:NOM over her:ACC drunk driver:GEN (*INST)
'(lit.) the-running over her [of a drunk driver]'
b. Na nee naexal [$_{nP}$ p'janyj voditel'].
over her:ACC ran:M drunk:NOM driver:NOM.
'A-drunk driver ran her over.'
c. **Ona$_{NOM}$ byla naexana na [pjanym voditelem$_{INST}$].
She was run over (by a) drunk driver.

1.11.3 *The* by-*phrase in causative sentences and derived nominal phrases*
We saw above that the fundamental difference between passivization and causativization is this: the primary function of passivization is to *dethematize*

1.11 Nominalization and causativization 59

(*delink*) **V**'s external theta role **i**, relinking it to {-^[**V-af**]}$_4$, which leaves {-^**N**}$_1$ available for **j** to relink to, i.e.: {{**i**^**N**}$_1$ {**j**^**N**}$_2$ ...{-^**V**}$_4$} > {{-^**N**}$_1$ {**j**^-}$_2$ ... {**i**^[**V-af**]}$_4$} >> {{**j**^**N**}$_1$ {-^-}$_2$ ...{**i**^[**V-af**]}$_4$}. In contrast, the primary function of causativization is to add a new external argument to **V**'s initial diathesis; the *internalization* of **V**'s {**i**^**N**}$_1$ argument is thus epiphenomenal, and internalized {**i**^**N**}$_1$ occupies the left-most free argument position {-^-} in **V**'s diathesis.[84]

According to the displacement analysis of DNs, the principle determining the morphosyntactic realization of **V**'s initial {**i**^**N**}$_1$ argument is the same in causative and DN derivations: it depends directly on whether **V**'s diathesis has an internal valence of one, two, or three arguments, which determines the location of [**V-af**]'s left-most available {-^-} position (**af** here is **af**$_C$ or **af**$_{DN}$); see Williams 1987: 173, Speas 1990: 105, Baker 1997: 98.

In causative derivations, it is **af**$_C$'s external {**i**$_C$^**N**}$_1$ argument that is responsible for the right-displacement of **V**'s external {**i**^**N**}$_1$ argument. The parallel displacement analysis of DNs entails that **af**$_{DN}$ too has its own external argument that induces the right-displacement of **V**'s {**i**^**N**}$_1$. But it is an empirical fact that nominalization does not add an additonal nP argument to **V**'s initial set of arguments. The problem is how to implement this scenario, i.e., what property of **af**$_{DN}$ (**n**) is responsible for internalizing {**i**^**N**}$_1$?

It has been proposed that nPs, unlike clauses, do not have dedicated subjects because their external argument is **R**, which accounts for nP's *reference* (see Grimshaw 1990, Zubizarreta 1987). Assuming that some version of this proposal is correct, when **V**'s diathesis composes with **af**$_{DN}$'s diathesis, **V**'s external {**i**^**N**}$_1$ argument is right-displaced by **af**$_{DN}$'s external {**R**^-}$_1$ argument (see Williams 1987: 367). It is here that the parallelism between nominalization and causativization becomes clear: in the diathesis-based derivation of both DNs and causatives, the external argument of both **af**$_{DN}$ and **af**$_C$ *displaces* **V**'s {**i**^**N**}$_1$ to [**V-af**]'s left-most available position. This parallelism is somewhat obscured by the fact that, in DN derivations, **V**'s final diathesis maps onto the internal structure of an nP whereas in the latter, **V**'s final diathesis maps onto the structure of a finite clause.

The grammatical relations in DN nPs and in causative vPs are perceived as being the same because both are projections of diathesis's 2×4 structure; the cases that realize the grammatical relations are necessarily different because the *structural* cases in nPs and vPs are different. In the ditransitive diathesis, where all the potential argument positions in the diathesis's 2×4 structure are occupied, **V**'s displaced external argument must link to {-^[**V-af**]}$_4$ and the consequent implict **i** licenses the *by*-phrase: cf. (95) and (96); (98) and (100) is an example of (95); (99) are additional examples.

60 *The structure of argument structure*

(95) Nominalization of ditransitive verbs in Russian ($af_{DN} = n$):
 a. V's diathesis: $\{\{ i \wedge N\}_1 \{j \wedge N\}_2 \{k \wedge N\}_3 \{- \wedge V\}_4\}$ +
 b. affix diathesis: $\{\{ R \wedge -\}_1 \{ \wedge \}_2 \quad \{ \wedge \}_3 \quad \{ \wedge n\}_4\}$ >
 c. a + b: $\{\{ R \wedge -\}_1 \{j \wedge N\}_2 \{k \wedge N\}_3 \{i \wedge [V\text{-}n]\}_4\}$

(96) Causativization of ditransitive verbs in Turkish (see (77)–(78)):
 a. V's diathesis: $\{\{ i \wedge N\}_1 \quad \{j \wedge N\}_2 \{k \wedge N\}_3 \{- \wedge V\}_4\}$ +
 b. affix diathesis: $\{\{ i_c \wedge N\}_1 \{ \wedge \}_2 \quad \{ \wedge \}_3 \quad \{ \wedge af_c\}_4\}$ >
 c. a + b: $\{\{ i_c \wedge N\}_1 \{j \wedge N\}_2 \{k \wedge N\}_3 \{i \wedge [V\text{-} af_c]\}_4\}$

(97) Passivization (position 2 and 3 are not relevant):
 a. V's diathesis: $\{\{ i \wedge N\}_1 \ldots \{- \wedge V\}_4\}$ +
 b. affix diathesis: $\{\{ - \wedge \}_1 \ldots \{ \wedge af_{PASS}\}_4\}$ >
 c. a + b: $\{\{- \wedge N\}_1 \ldots \{i \wedge [V\text{-} af_{PASS}]\}_4\}$

The $\{R^\wedge\text{-}\}_1$ analysis itself is not crucial. What is crucial is the claim that the derivation of DNs, like that of causatives, involves *right-displacement* of V's intact external $\{i^\wedge N\}_1$ argument to the first free position in $[V\text{-}af_{DN}]$'s diathesis, rather than *dethematization* of V's external theta role i and its obligatory relinking to $\{-^\wedge[V\text{-}af]\}_4$ in derived unaccusative (i.e., passive and middle) derivations (the quirky dative in (98) and (99) is selected by *ob"javit'* 'to-declare').

(98) a. Germanija$_i$ ob"javila vojnu$_j$ evropejskim deržavam$_k$.
  G:NOM declared war:ACC European powers:DAT (see 100c))
  'Germany declared war on the European powers.'
 b. ob"javlenie Germaniej vojny$_j$ evropejskim deržavam$_k$.
  declaration:NOM G:INST war:GEN European powers:DAT
  'the-declaration of-war by-Germany on-the-European powers'

(99) a. okazanie [finansovoj pomošči]$_j$ [bednym fermeram]$_k$ Kongressom
  'the-giving [$_{nP:GEN}$ of-financial aid] [$_{nP:DAT}$ to-poor farmers] by-Congress$_{INST}$'
 b. vyplata vami$_{INST}$ denegj.$_{GEN}$ [ee materi$_{k.DAT}$]
  'the-payment by-you of-money [(to) her mother]'

When the diatheses in (95a) and (95b) compose, $\{R^\wedge\text{-}\}_1$ becomes the external argument in (95c) and $\{i^\wedge N\}_1$ is right-dislocated. Since the 2 and 3 positions are occupied, $\{i^\wedge N\}_1$ has no alternative other than to link to $\{-^\wedge[V\text{-}af_n]\}_4$, giving $\{i^\wedge[V\text{-}af_n]\}_4$, which licenses the instrumental-case *by*-phrase *Germaniej* in (98b). The internal structure of the DN phrase in (90) correctly predicts that the instrumental *by*-phrase is canonically located either between the DN head and the adnominal genitive nP, or at the end of the DN phrase. The structure of (98b) is represented in (100a–b); (100c) is the finite clausal structure of (98a).

1.11 Nominalization and causativization 61

(100a)
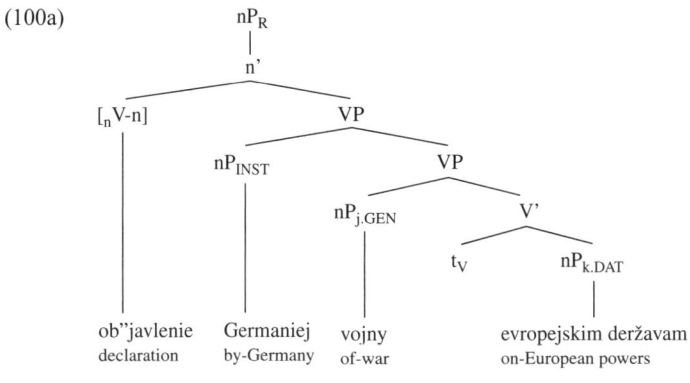

(100b)
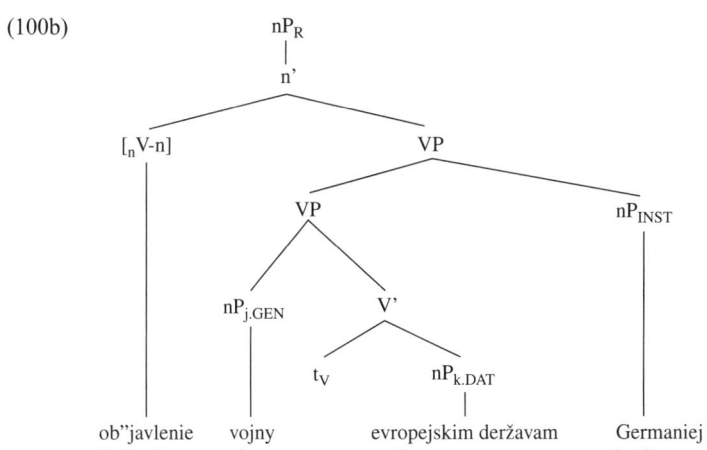

(100c)
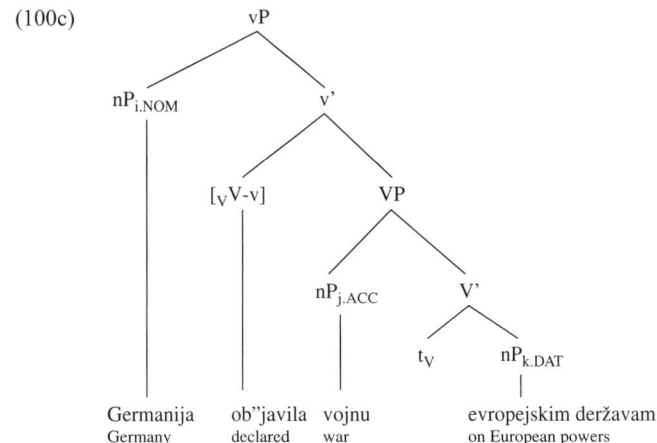

The common denominator of passivization and the causativization and nominalization of ditransitive verbs is $\{i\wedge[V\text{-}af]\}_4$, which is derived in two different ways: (i) **i** is *dethematized* in passive derivations and **V**'s internal positions are irrelevant. (ii) $\{i\wedge N\}_1$ is *internalized* and linked to $\{\text{-}\wedge [V\text{-}af]\}_4$ in causative and DN derivations involving a ditransitive **V**.

Let us run through the derivation of monadic, monotransitive, and ditransitive DNs, comparing them to the corresponding causative derivations. As we saw above, the causativization of unergative and unaccusative verbs gives the same morpho-syntactic results: **V**'s initial external argument is realized in spec-VP as the accusative direct object. The displacement analysis of DNs correctly predicts that the argument of a nominalized monadic verb should be realized in spec-VP as the adnominal genitive, as in (92) and (93). When (101a) and (101b) compose, the **n** affix's external argument $\{R\wedge\text{-}\}_1$ becomes the external argument of the DN diathesis in (101c): $\{i\wedge N\}_1$ is displaced and occupies the $\{\text{-}\wedge\text{-}\}_2$ position, which is **V**'s left-most free position; $\{i\wedge N\}_2$ projects to spec-VP, where it is assigned (checks) structural *adnominal genitive case* by $[V\text{-}n]_n$. The only difference in the derivation of *unaccusative* DNs is that N_2 and **j** link up (see (103)). Thus we have seen so far that the derivations of Russian DNs and Turkish causative sentences from monadic and ditransitive **V**'s are point-by-point identical, which is what our hypothesis predicts.

(101) Nominalization of unergative verbs:
    a. V's diathesis: $\{\{i \wedge N\}_1 \{\text{-}\wedge\text{-}\}_2 \{\text{-}\wedge\text{-}\}_3 \{\text{-}\wedge V\}_4\}$ +
    b. affix diathesis: $\{\{R\wedge\text{-}\}_1 \{\wedge\}_2 \{\wedge\}_3 \{\wedge\text{-}af_n\}_4\}$ >
    c. a + b: $\{\{R\wedge\text{-}\}_1 \{i \wedge N\}_2 \{\text{-}\wedge\text{-}\}_3 \{\text{-}\wedge [V\text{-}af_n]\}_4\}$

(102) Causativization of unergative verbs:
    a. V's diathesis: $\{\{i \wedge N\}_1 \{\text{-}\wedge\text{-}\}_2 \{\text{-}\wedge\text{-}\}_3 \{\text{-}\wedge V\}_4\}$ +
    b. affix diathesis: $\{\{i_c \wedge N\}_1 \{\wedge\}_2 \{\wedge\}_3 \{\wedge af_c\}_4\}$ >
    c. final diathesis: $\{\{i_c \wedge N\}_1 \{i \wedge N\}_2 \{\text{-}\wedge\text{-}\}_3 \{\text{-}\wedge [V\text{-}af_c]\}_4\}$

(103) Nominalization of unaccusative verbs:
    a. V's diathesis: $\{\{\text{-}\wedge N\}_1 \{j \wedge \text{-}\}_2 \{\text{-}\wedge\text{-}\}_3 \{\text{-}\wedge V\}_4\}$ +
    b. affix diathesis: $\{\{R\wedge\text{-}\}_1 \{\wedge\}_2 \{\wedge\}_3 \{\wedge\text{-}af_n\}_4\}$ >
    c. final diathesis: $\{\{R\wedge\text{-}\}_1 \{j \wedge N\}_2 \{\text{-}\wedge\text{-}\}_3 \{\text{-}\wedge [V\text{-}af_n]\}_4\}$

(104) Causativization of unaccusative verbs:
    a. V's diathesis: $\{\{\text{-}\wedge N\}_1 \{\text{-}\wedge j\}_2 \{\text{-}\wedge\text{-}\}_3 \{\text{-}\wedge V\}_4\}$ +
    b. affix diathesis: $\{\{i_c \wedge N\}_1 \{\wedge\}_2 \{\wedge\}_3 \{\wedge af_c\}_4\}$ >
    c. final diathesis: $\{\{i_c \wedge N\}_1 \{j \wedge N\}_2 \{\text{-}\wedge\text{-}\}_3 \{\text{-}\wedge [V\text{-}af_c]\}_4\}$

1.11.4 The nominalization of monotransitive verbs

Now let us consider the derivation of Russian DN phrases and Turkish causative sentences from the diathesis of *monotransitive* V; note that $\{i\wedge N\}_1 > \{i\wedge N\}_3$ in both.

1.11 *Nominalization and causativization* 63

(105) Nominalization of monotransitive verbs in Russian.
    a. V's diathesis: $\{\{\ i\ \wedge\ N\}_1\ \{j\ \wedge\ N\}_2\ \{-\ \wedge\ -\}_3\ \{-\ \wedge\ V\}_4\}$ +
    b. affix diathesis: $\{\{\ R\ \wedge\ -\}_1\ \{\ \wedge\ \}_2\ \ \ \{\ \wedge\ \}_3\ \ \ \{\ \wedge\ af_n\}_4\}$ >
    c. final diathesis: $\{\{\ R\ \wedge\ -\}_1\ \{j\ \wedge\ N\}_2\ \{i\ \wedge\ N\}_3\ \{\ -\ \wedge\ [V\text{-}af_n]\}_4\}$

(106) Causativization of monotransitive verbs in Turkish.
    a. V's diathesis: $\{\{\ i\ \wedge\ N\}_1\ \{j\ \wedge\ N\}_2\ \{-\ \wedge\ -\}_3\ \{-\ \wedge\ V\}_4\}$ +
    b. affix diathesis: $\{\{\ i_c\ \wedge\ N\}_1\ \{\ \wedge\ \}_2\ \ \ \{\ \wedge\ \}_3\ \ \ \{\ \wedge\ af_c\}_4\}$ >
    c. final diathesis: $\{\{\ i_c\ \wedge\ N\}_1\ \{j\ \wedge\ N\}_2\ \{i\ \wedge\ N\}_3\ \{\ -\ \wedge\ [V\text{-}af_c]\}_4\}$

However, we see in (107), which gives typical examples of Russian monotransitive DN phrases, that the syntactic realization of monotransitive DNs do *not* appear to be parallel to the causativization of monotransitive verbs in Turkish, where displaced $\{i\wedge N\}_1$ is realized, as expected, as the *dative* case; see in (76): $\{i\wedge N\}_1$ in (107) is canonically realized in Russian as the instrumental *by*-phrase rather than the expected dative case, which is an instance of *position-skipping* (cf. *position-skipping* in the French monotransitive causative sentences in (81)).[85]

(107) Realization of $\{i\wedge N\}_1$ as the *by*-phrase in monotransitive DNs.
    a. Mendeleev$_i$ otkryl   periodičeskij zakon$_j$.
       M:NOM   discovered   periodic law:ACC
       'Mendeleev discovered the periodic law.'
    b. [$_{nP}$ otkrytie   Mendeleevym   periodičeskogo   zakona$_j$]
       discovery:NOM   M:INST   periodic:GEN   law:GEN
       'the-discovery by-Mendeleev of-the-periodic law'
    c. *[$_{nP}$ otkrytie$_{NOM}$ periodičeskogo$_{GEN}$ zakona$_{j.GEN}$ Mendeleevu$_{i.DAT}$]
    d. ∠[$_{nP}$ otkrytie Mendeleeva$_{i.GEN}$ periodičeskogo$_{GEN}$ zakona$_{j.GEN}$]
    e. Èto ne dolžno prinimat'sja prisjažnymi$_{INST}$ vo vnimanie [$_{PP}$ pri
       [$_{nP}$ vynesenii$_{DN.LOC}$ imi$_{i.INST}$ verdikta$_{j.GEN}$]].
       'That should not be taken into consideration by the jurors during [the-rendering by-them of-a-verdict'.
    f. [$_{PP}$ posle [$_{nP}$ vzjatija$_{GEN}$ bol'ševikami$_{INST}$ vlasti$_{GEN}$]]
       'after the-seizure$_{GEN}$ of-power$_{GEN}$ by-the-bolsheviks$_{INST}$'
    g. ∠[$_{PP}$ posle [$_{nP}$ vzjatija$_{GEN}$ bol'ševikov$_{GEN}$ vlasti$_{GEN}$]]

It can, however, be demonstrated that the derivation of Russian monotransitive DNs in (105) is indeed parallel to the derivation of Turkish and French causative sentences from monotransitive Vs. All we need do is take into consideration two case-related phenomena, which have the effect of obscuring the parallelism between nominalization and causativization that comes through so clearly in the monadic and ditransitive derivations presented above.

The derivation in (105) correctly predicts that when a Russian monotransitive V is nominalized, its $\{i\wedge N\}_1$ is right-displaced to $\{-\wedge-\}_3$, which is the leftmost free position in its diathesis, giving $\{i\wedge N\}_3$ (cf. (105c) and (106c)). The perceived deviation between the causative and DN derivations starts here: in the Turkish causative derivation, $\{i\wedge N\}_3$ is realized morphosyntactically as a *dative* nP, which is a *structural* case in Turkish: only *initial* in situ $\{k\wedge N\}_3$ in Turkish and Russian is realized as theta-case. But dative in Russian is not a structural case in clauses or DPs. Since the only structural case in the domain of the Russian nP is the genitive, we therefore expect $\{i\wedge N\}_3$ in (105c) to be realized as the genitive case. We see in (108)–(109) that this prediction is correct: the nominalization of monotransitive Vs does result in the realization of displaced $\{i\wedge N\}_1$ as a genitive nP, which, however, derives DN phrases with *two structural-genitive nPs* (see Rozental' 1967: 344 for examples of double-genitive DNs).

(108) Double-genitive monotransitive DNs in Russian:
    a. ∠poiski$_{NOM}$ Čexova$_{i.GEN}$ [svoej tvorčeskoj manery$_j$]$_{nPGEN}$
    '(lit.) the-seeking of-Chekhov of-his creative style'
    b. poiski Čexovym$_{i.INST}$ [svoej tvorčeskoj manery$_j$]$_{nPGEN}$
    'the-seeking by-Chekhov of-his creative style'

(109) a. izloženie$_{NOM}$ učitelja$_{GEN}$ (učitelem$_{INST}$) [učebnogo materiala]$_{GEN}$.
    '(lit.) the-outlining of-the-teacher$_{i.GEN}$ (by-the-teacher) of-the-academic material$_{j.GEN}$'
    b. zaxvat angličan$_{i.GEN}$ Indii$_{j.GEN}$
    '(lit.) the-seizure of-the-English of-India = of-India by-the-English'

But *double-structural-genitive* DN phrases are considered to be *degraded* (grammatical but infelicitous) because they often result in mapping opacity and unacceptable ambiguity.[86] Given that the post-head word-order of nP and PP arguments in Russian DN phrases is 'free' (determined in part by discourse factors), the mapping between the arguments' case realization and their grammatical relations, the latter determined by their position in **[V-af]**'s diathesis, is obscured. For example, it is not clear without discourse context or real-world knowledge who denounced whom in:[87] *razoblačenie Xruščeva Stalina* '(lit.) the-denunciation of-Khrushchov of-Stalin.'

Thus *double-structural-genitive* DN phrases are systematically avoided in standard Russian, and what happens in these monotransitive Russian DN phrases is exactly what we saw above happens in monotransitive French causative sentences: V's displaced $\{i\wedge N\}_1$ *skips* the $\{-\wedge-\}_3$ position and links instead to $\{- \wedge $ **[V-af$_n$]**$\}_4$, which licenses the *by*-phrase (cf. (109) and (81a–b)), thereby restoring transparency to the mapping between grammatical relations, case, theta role, and syntactic position.

We conclude that the nominalization of monotransitive Vs, like those of monadic and ditransitive Vs, is parallel to the causativization of monotransitive

1.11 Nominalization and causativization   65

Vs (allowing for the language-specific case phenomena described above), right down to the 3-to-4 position-skipping phenomenon.

The derivation of DNs outlined above makes a number of additional correct predictions, which further support my analysis of DNs and, more generally, of the 2×4 diathetic representation of argument structure.

If a bivalent intransitive V's internal argument is an infinitive, a quirky-case nP, or a PP, as in (110a),[88] the 2×4 structure of the diathesis correctly predicts that the displaced $\{i^\wedge N\}_1$ is realized as the adnominal genitive rather than the instrumental case (*by*-phrase) because it occupies the available $\{-^\wedge-\}_2$ position, and $\{i^\wedge N\}_2$ projects to spec-VP, where it is assigned genitive case by $[V\text{-}n]_n$. $\{i^\wedge N\}_1$ does not skip to the 4-position because the syntactic projection of final diatheses like (110c) does not involve mapping opacity (cf. the causativization of Turkish *başlamak* 'to-begin' in (79)/(80)).

(110)   Nominalization of bivalent intransitive verbs in Russian.
    a. V's diathesis: $\{\{i \wedge N\}_1 \{-\wedge-\}_2 \{k \wedge X\}_3 \{-\wedge V\}_4\}$ +
    b. affix diathesis: $\{\{R \wedge -\}_1 \{\wedge\}_2 \quad \{\wedge\}_3 \quad \{\wedge af_n\}_4\}$ >
    c. a+b: $\qquad\qquad \{\{R \wedge -\}_1 \{i \wedge N\}_2 \{k \wedge X\}_3 \{-\wedge [V\text{-}af_n]\}_4\}$

(111)   a. Učenye$_{NOM}$ pytajutsja [$_{infP}$ usoveršenstvovat' sistemu$_{ACC}$].
        'Scientists are-trying to-perfect the-system.'
    b. popytka$_{NOM}$ učenyx$_{GEN}$ [$_{infP}$ usoveršenstvovat' sistemu$_{ACC}$]
        'the-attempt of-scientists to-perfect-the-system'

(112)   a. [$_{nPNOM}$ Glagoly, označajuščie zabotu] upravljajut [$_{nPINST}$ datel'nym padežom].
        '[Verbs denoting concern] govern [the dative case].'[89]
    b. upravlenie   [datel'nym padežom] [glagolov, označajuščix zabotu]
        government   [dative case]$_{nP.INST}$ [verbs denoting concern]$_{nP.GEN}$
        'government [of-the-dative-case] [by-verbs-denoting-concern]'

(113)   a. Deti$_{NOM}$ podražajut [$_{nP.DAT}$ rotditeljam].
        'Children imitate (their) parents.'
    b. podražanie detej   roditeljam
        imitation   children$_{GEN}$ parents$_{DAT}$
        'the-imitation by-children of-(their)-parents'

(114)   a. Odni$_{NOM}$ pol'zujutsja [podnevol'nym trudom$_{INST}$ drugix$_{GEN}$].
        some   use   forced   labor   of-others
        'Some people make-use-of the involuntary labor of-others.'
    b. Rabstvo est' [pol'zovanie odnix$_{i.GEN}$ [podnevol'nym trudom$_{INST}$ drugix$_{GEN}$]].
        'Slavery is [the-use [by-some (people)] [of-the-forced labor of-others]].'

Two genitive nPs are perfectly natural in standard Russian DN phrases provided that they are not both structural:[90] the first genitive *Anny*$_{j.GEN}$ in (115b) is structural and the second is quirky (which is clear in the corresponding finite clause in (115a)).[91] There is no mapping opacity here because the quirky genitive is specified in **V**'s diathesis as a case feature on N_3, which makes it possible to keep track of the nPs' grammatical relations (structural case is not specified in the diathesis); cf. (115b–c).

(115) a. Sud$_{i.NOM}$ lišil Annu$_{j.ACC}$ svobody$_{k.GEN}$.
court deprived Anna freedom
'The court deprived Anna of-her-freedom.'
b. lišenie (sudom$_{INST}$) Anny$_{j.GEN}$ svobody$_{k.GEN}$
'(lit.) the-deprivation of-Anna of-her-freedom (by the court)'
c. lišenie Anny$_{j.GEN}$ svobody$_{k.GEN}$ (sudom$_{INST}$)

By the same token, the cooccurrence of the two instrumental case nPs in bivalent DN phrases like (116) is well formed because one is an adjunct *by*-phrase and the other is a quirky-case marked argument (but double-instrumental DN phrases like (116) are nevertheless felt by many speakers to be degraded (see Livšic 1964: 130)).

(116) a. Tibetskie lamy pol'zujutsja telepatiej.
tibetan lamas:NOM use telepathy:INST
b. telepatija i [pol'zovanie$_{NOM}$ eju$_{INST}$ tibetskimi lamami$_{INST}$]
'telepathy and [the-use of-it by-Tibetan lamas]' (Kurennov)

1.11.5 The possessive genitive in derived nominals
We see in (117) that when a ditransitive verb like *priznat'sja* 'confess', neither of whose internal arguments is assigned structural case, is nominalized, the 2×4 structure of the diathesis predicts that, since there is no danger of mapping opacity here, $\{i^{\wedge}N\}_1$ can be realized as either a genitive nP or the bare instrumental *by*-phrase (see Zubizarreta 1987: 65). The preposition *v* 'in' and dative case in (117) are both c-selected by *priznat'sja*.

(117) a. Klient$_{i.NOM}$ priznalsja detektivu$_{j.DAT}$ [$_{PP}$ v prestuplenii$_{k.LOC}$].
client confessed to-detective in crime
'The-client confessed (his) crime to-the-detective.'
b. priznanie$_{NOM}$ klienta$_{GEN}$ detektivu$_{j.DAT}$ [$_{PP}$ v prestuplenii$_{k.LOC}$].
confession of-client to-detective [$_{PP}$ in crime]
'the-client's confession of-(his)-crime to-the-detective'
c. priznanie$_{NOM}$ klientom$_{INST}$ detektivu$_{j.DAT}$ [$_{PP}$ v prestuplenii$_{k.LOC}$].
'the-confession by-the-client to-the-detective [of-(his)-crime]$_{PP}$'

Our next step is to determine what kind of genitive *klienta* in (117b) is. Since all three argument positions in *priznat'sja/priznanie*'s initial diathesis are occupied, the diathesis's 2×4 structure determines that *klienta* must be an *argument adjunct* since there is no third internal argument position. More specifically, *klienta* is a 'possessive genitive' adjunct nP (cf. the English gloss in (117b)), which is in complementary distribution with the instrumental *by*-phrase in Russian DN phrases: both are *argument adjuncts* licensed by implicit **i** (i.e., {i^[V-af$_n$]}$_4$); they compete to occupy one of the two peripheral nP-adjunct positions (see (90) and (100)). This phenomenon is parallel to the syntactic realization of displaced {i^N}$_1$ as the structural dative instead of the *by*-phrase when a ditransitive Turkish **V** is causativized (see §1.9.1). (118) is the structure of (117b).

(118)

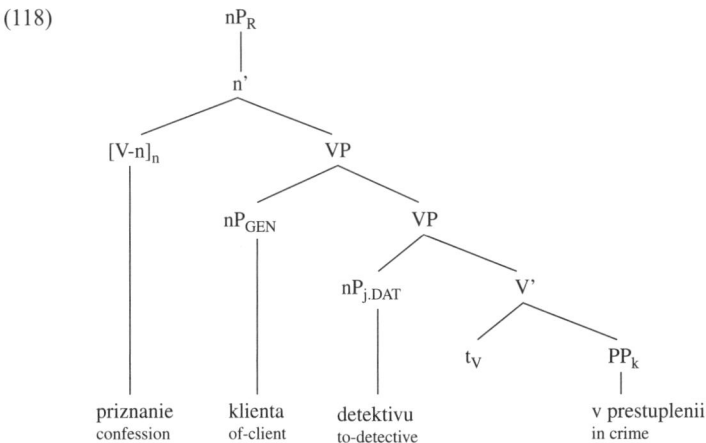

My analysis correctly predicts that the nominalization of ditransitive verbs can have both the *adnominal genitive* realization of {j^N}$_2$ and the *possessive genitive* realization of implicit {i^[V-n]$_n$}$_4$. The Double-Genitive Filter encountered in §1.11.4 above accounts for the fact that the *by*-phrase in (120) is felt to be more felicitous than the possessive genitive (119); (121) is an additional example:

(119) [$_{PP}$ nakanune [$_{nP}$ predstavlenija$_{GEN}$ Avstrii$_{GEN}$ ul'timatuma$_{j.GEN}$ Serbii$_{k.DAT}$]]
'just-before Austria's presentation of-an-ultimatum to-Serbia'

(120) [$_{PP}$ nakanune [$_{nP}$ predstavlenija$_{GEN}$ Avstriej$_{INST}$ ul'timatuma$_{j.GEN}$ Serbii$_{k.DAT}$]]
'just-before the-presentation by-Austria of-an-ultimatum to-Serbia'

(121) [$_{PP}$ nakanune [$_{nP}$ ob"javlenii$_{GEN}$ japoncev$_{GEN}$ ~ japoncami$_{INST}$ vojny$_{j.GEN}$ Rossii$_{k.DAT}$]]
'just-before the-declaration of-war on (lit. to) Russia by-the-Japanese'

1.12 Constraints on alternations

In this section we continue to explore the relation between the diathesis's 2×4 structure, the constraints it imposes on argument-structure level operations,

68 *The structure of argument structure*

and the types of alternations predicted by it to occur (or not occur) in human language.[92]

We saw above that diathetic structure predicts that if an affix's diathesis has an argument of its own, the final position of the corresponding argument in **V**'s initial diathesis is determined by the first available {-^-} position in the composite diathesis of **[V-af]**. This right-displacement phenomenon is neither construction-specific nor language-specific, and *it is not limited to external arguments*. For example, if an affix's diathesis has its own $\{j^\wedge N\}_2$ argument, the diathesis's 2×4 structure predicts that **V**'s own initial $\{j^\wedge N\}_2$ argument will be right-displaced to the first free position, which is {-^-}$_3$ when **V** is monotransitive:

(122) a. **V**: $\{\{i \wedge N\}_1 \ \{j \wedge N\}_2 \ \{-\wedge -\}_3 \ \{-\wedge V\}_4\}$ +
   b. -af: $\{\{\wedge\}_1 \ \{j \wedge N\}_{2.af} \ \{\wedge\}_3 \ \{\wedge \text{af-}\}_4\}$ >
   c. a + b: $\{\{i \wedge N\}_1 \ \{j \wedge N\}_{2.af} \ \{j \wedge N\}_3 \ \{-\wedge \text{[V-af]}\}_4\}$

While the hypothetical derivation in (122) is not as common as the causative derivation, where the affix has its own *external* argument, what is important for the typology of alternations is that this type of derivation is well attested. For example, the diathesis of a small class of *prefixes* in Russian (and German) have a $\{j^\wedge N\}_{2.af}$ argument and, in accordance with (122), **V**'s initial $\{j^\wedge N\}_2$ argument undergoes 2-to-3 diathesis displacement and is realized morphosyntactically as an oblique-case nP or PP, depending on the value of **j**:

(123) a. My$_i$ kopali   kanavy$_j$.
          we:NOM   were-digging   ditches:ACC
          'We were-digging ditches.'
   b. My$_i$ **o**-kopali   dom$_j$ kanavami$_j$ (*kanavy)
          we:NOM   prefix-dug   house:ACC   ditches:INST (*ACC)
          '(lit.) We around-dug the-house with-ditches' = 'We surrounded the house with ditches.'[93]

(124) a. Nikita$_i$ pil   pivo$_j$.
          N.:NOM   drank   beer:ACC
          'N. was-drinking beer.'
   b. Nikita$_i$ **za**-pil   piljulju$_j$ pivom$_j$.
          N.:NOM   za-drank   pill:ACC   beer:INST
          'N. washed-down the pill with-beer.'

(125) a. Nikita **za**-lil   rubašku   sousom. (*lit'sous*$_{ACC}$ 'pour sauce').
          N.   za-poured   shirt:ACC   sauce:INST
          'N. poured sauce on (his) shirt.'
   b. Grozilis'   **za**-kidat'   nas   arbuzami.   (*kidat'* 'throw')
          threatened   za-throw   us:ACC   water-melon:INST
          'They-threatened to-throw water-melons at us (all over us).'

c. Ee   zabrasyvali   gnilymi   fruktami.
   her:ACC za-threw   rotten   fruit:INST
   'Unspecified-agent(s) threw rotten fruit at her.'

The derivation of (124b) is represented in (126):

(126)   a. V: {{i ^ N}₁ {j ^ N}₂   {- ^ -}₃   {- ^ pil}₄ }   +
        b. af: {{ ^ }₁   {j ^ N}₂.af { ^ }₃   { ^ za-}₄ }   >
        c. a + b: {{i ^ N}₁ {j ^ N}₂.af {j ^ N}₃ {- ^ [zapil]}₄ }   => (124b)

If the -**af** were *productive* (paradigmatic), (126) would represent the derivation of a subtype of the *applicative* construction, which is common in the Bantu languages.[94]

If an affix is productive and its diathesis specifies that transitive **V**'s initial {j^N}₂ is right-displaced, the verbal paradigm of such a language has the *antipassive* construction: {j^N}₂ is displaced to { ^ }₃ where it is realized as the appropriate language-specific oblique case or PP (see Babby 1994a), e.g.:

(127)   Antipassive derivation:
        a. V: {{i ^ N}₁ {j ^ N}₂   {- ^ -}₃   {- ^ V}₄ }   +
        b. -af: {{ ^ }₁   {- ^ -}₂   { ^ }₃   { ^ af-}₄ }   >
        c. a + b: {{i ^ N}₁ {- ^ -}₂   {j ^ N}₃ {- ^ [V-af]}₄ }

The antipassive suffix in effect detransitivizes **V** by right-displacing {j^N}₂ without introducing an argument of its own; it should be called the antitransitive since **V**'s external argument is not dethematized or otherwise affected, and the derivation thus has nothing to do with passivization. Since the antipassive is typically productive in ergative~absolute languages (e.g., Dyirbal), we can assume that its function is to affect the subject's case: when the main verb is transitive, the subject is assigned ergative case, but subjects of intransitive and detransitivized verbs are assigned absolute case, which facilitates certain syntactic operations (e.g., conjunction). For examples and discussion, see Marantz 1984, Baker 1988b, Comrie 1989, Palmer 1994, Klaiman 2005, Payne 2006: 219–220.

This brief mention of constructions like the antipassive and applicative in addition to more familiar constructions like the causative, derived-unaccusative, and passive is intended to demonstrate that the diathetic theory of argument structure makes the following falsifiable prediction: all the systematic alternations attested in the world's languages should be constrained by the 2×4 structure of the diatheses of **V** and the affixes it composes with.[95]

1.13 Arguments, adjuncts, and complex predicates

Inherent in diathesis-based theory is a clear-cut distinction between *arguments* and *adjuncts*: an argument is specified in **V**'s diathesis; an adjunct is a phrasal projection whose head is not specified in **V**'s diathesis. We saw in §1.0 (note 5) that what is an argument in one language may be an adjunct in another, and that the choice is often arbitrary. The *by*-phrase in passives, causatives, and DNs, which has been referred to an as "argument-adjunct" (Grimshaw 1990) is an adjunct that is *licensed* by an *implict* theta role, i.e., {i^ [V-af]}$_4$.

In practice, however, it is often difficult to determine whether an nP or PP is an argument or an adjunct. For example, consider human dative nPs in sentences like the following; the construal of *emu* 'him' in (128a–b) as a possesive in English suggests that it is not an argument of **V**:

(128)   a. Ja   nastupila   **emu**   na nogu. (*na emu nogu)
            I.NOM   stepped   him.DAT   on foot
            '(lit.) I stepped him on the foot' = 'I stepped on his foot.'
        b. Ja   požal   **emu**   ruku.
            I.NOM   shook   him.DAT   hand.ACC
            'I shook his hand.'

Ditransitive sentences like the following provide additional evidence that these dative human nPs are adjuncts (assuming that there are no four-argument predicators in natural language): since *glaza* and *tabakom* are the internal arguments of *zaporošil* in (129) and the subject *on* is its external argument, the dative reflexive pronoun *sebe* must be an adjunct.

(129)   On dunul v portsigar i (on$_1$)   zaporošil sebe   tabakom$_3$ glaza$_2$.
                                    he:NOM powdered self:DAT tobacco:INST eyes:ACC
        'He blew into his cigarette case and (he) got tobacco in his eyes.'

Sentences like the following may seem at first to complicate the picture, but they in fact further demonstrate the diathesis's explanatory power. Transitive idiomatic verb + PP expressions like *sbit'* [$_{PP}$ *s tolku*] 'to confuse', *zadet'* [$_{PP}$ *za živoe*] 'to hurt someone's feelings', etc. appear to be ditransitive **V**s with a 'variable' subject and direct object:

(130)   Nikita$_i$ sbil   Annu$_j$ s   tolku.
        N.NOM   deflected   A.ACC   from sense:GEN
        'N. distracted A.'

(131)   {{i ^ N}$_1$ {j ^ N}$_2$ {? ^ [s tolku]}$_3$ {- ^ sbit'}$_4$ }

If **?** in (131) is **V**'s **k** theta role, then *s tolku* is a *specified argument*. But if *s tolku* has no theta role, i.e., {-^[s tolku]}$_3$, it is neither an argument nor an adjunct; rather *sbit's tolku* is a discontinuous complex predicate, which seems to be the correct analysis. The distinction between *specified argument* and *complex predicate* enables us to capture the intuiton that idiomatic expressions like *sbit's tolku* and specific direct objects in the case of verbs like *vysmorkat' nos* 'blow one's nose', which can only have *nos* 'nose' as its object, are fundamentally different. If this is correct, the initial diathesis of *sbit's tolku* is (132a), of *vysmorkat' nos* is (132b), and *sbit'* in its nonidiomatic use is (132c) (e.g. *Anna sbila jabloki s dereva* 'A. knocked/shook apples from the-tree'):

(132)   a. {{i ^ N}₁ {j ^ N}₂   {- ^ [s tolku}₃ {- ^ sbit'}₄ }
        b. {{i ^ N}₁ {j ^ nos}₂ {- ^ -}₃   {- ^ vysmorkat'}₄ }
        c. {{i ^ N}₁ {j ^ N}₂   {k ^ [ₚ s]}₃   {- ^ sbit'}₄ }

1.14 Theta-role conversion

We have seen above that the theta roles in **V**'s diathesis may be delinked and relinked, left-displaced (advanced) or right-displaced, deleted or added, but there are two a priori possible argument-structure level operations that appear not to be attested in natural language. We have already encountered the first: the 2×4, eight-slotted skeletal frame of the diathesis cannot be altered in any way; derivations begin and end with a 2×4 diathesis. In other words, diathetic positions cannot be created or eliminated, which accounts for the cross-linguistic uniformity of the core syntactic structures and grammatical relations found in all languages.

The second potentially possible but non-occurring diathetic operation is *theta-role conversion*: the specific *value* (agent, theme, goal, etc) of the theta roles in **V**'s initial diathesis cannot be *changed* by diathetic, syntactic, or any other type of operation. A corollary of this putative universal is that sentence pairs like (133a–b) are not *alternations* as defined above since they cannot be related in terms of an operation that changes the value of the adjective's theta role from nominative theme in (133a) to dative experiencer in (133b). This entails that there is a large, semantically distinct class of adjectives that can be impersonalized, i.e., the diathesis of the adjective stem (**A**) in (133a) composes with the diathesis of the non-agreement (impersonalizing) suffix -**o**, which deletes **A**'s external argument (e.g., *Tut*_ADV *krasiv-o* '[It is] pretty here', *Tam*_ADV *ne očen' čist-o* '[It is] not very clean there', *V èto utro bylo sux-o* '[It] was dry on that morning', *Doma*_ADV *poln-o kaminov*_GEN.PL '[lit.] At-home (is) full-of fireplaces = Our house is full of fireplaces'). The dative experiencer in (133b) is thus an adjunct, which is common in impersonal sentences that can be construed as affecting human beings (Babby 2008); see (134a–b); in (134c–d) the dative adjunct is in a sentence whose predicator is a verb (cf. (128)).

(133)   a. On   skučnyj (skučen).
            he.M.NOM   boring.M.LF(SF)
            'He is (a) boring (person) = others find him boring.'

b. Emu   skučno.
   him.M.DAT   boring.N.SG
   'He is bored = he is-experiencing boredom.'

(134) a. - Vam$_{DAT}$ ne$_{NEG}$ xolodn-o?
         to-you   not   cold
         'Are you cold / do you feel cold?'
         - Net. Mne$_{DAT}$ očen' daže normal'n-o.
         'No. (lit.) to-me (is) even very normal = I'm just fine.'
      b. Emu   stal-o   trevožn-o   ot   ètix   slov.
         him:DAT became   anxious   from these   words:GEN
         'These words made him feel anxious.'
      c. Vo vremja vzryva   emu   sil'no izuvečil-o nogu.
         during   blast:GEN him:DAT   badly   injured   leg:ACC
         'His leg was badly injured during the explosion.'
      d. Emu   otorval-o ruku$_j$ snarjadom$_k$.
         him:DAT tore-off arm:ACC   shell:INST
         'His arm got-torn-off by-a-shell.'

Bol'n- has different meanings in (135a–b), which is additional evidence that they do not constitute an alternation:

(135) a. Ona   bol'n-a.
         she:NOM.F sick:SF.F
         'She is sick.'
      b. Ej   bol'n-o.
         to-her:DAT.F painful
         'She is experiencing pain.'
      c. Mne   bol'n-o vzdoxnut'
         me:DAT painful to-breath
         'It hurts me to breathe.'
      d. *Ona bol'na vzdoxnut' (cf. (135a))

1.15 Concluding remarks

My primary hypothesis is that syntactic principles are, ideally, linguistic universals and that the morphosyntactic diversity we observe in individual languages is a reflex of both the parameterization of these principles and the unpredictable properties of a given language's lexical and affixal diatheses (see chapters 2 to 5). However, while a verb's *lexical entry* may specify all manner of syntactically relevant idiomatic, unpredictable information (e.g. (132)), this should not obscure the fact that the *form* of the diathesis itself is universal and that it has its own 'syntax', i.e., it has 2×4 internal hierarchical structure which is the locus of systematic operations (e.g. passivization,

1.15 Concluding remarks

causativization, and nominalization) that modify argument-structure representation in highly restricted ways, which is responsible for the *uniform grammatical relations* and the morphosyntactic alternations found in all human languages: languages that look different do not have different grammatical relations. Since most presyntactic (argument-structure level) operations are affix-driven and since the diathetic properties of syntactic-paradigm-building affixes with the same or similar functions may differ from language to language, I assume that a great deal of language-specific diversity can be traced to the argument structure of *paradigmatic affixes*. What sets these affixes off as a separate class is that they have their own diatheses.[96] 'Lexical rules' thus boil down to the composition of lexical stems and paradigmatic affixes accompanied by the amalgamation of their respective diatheses.[97] The following chapters are devoted to the composition of lexical and affixal diatheses, and to their morphosyntactic projections.

2 The argument structure of adjectives

2.0 Introduction

This chapter explores the composition of the diatheses of the adjective stem **A** with adjective suffixes (**-a**) and the morphosyntactic projection of **[A-a]**'s final diathesis (cf. **[V-v]** and **[N-n]** in chapter 1). My initial hypothesis is that **[A-a]** is canonically realized as the head of either the adjective *small clause* (s-clause or aP) in (1a), which has a dedicated subject nP_i (the projection of **A**'s external $\{i^\wedge N\}_1$ argument), or the adjective *secondary predicate* (s-predicate or aP_i) in (1b).[1]

(1) a. adjective s-clause: $[_{aP}\ nP_{i.NOM}\ [_{a'<i>}\ [A\text{-}a]\ [_{AP<i>}\ t_A\ ...]]]$
     b. adjective s-predicate: $[_{aPi}\ \ \ \ \ \ \ \ \ \ \ [_{a'<i>}\ [A\text{-}a]\ [_{AP<i>}\ t_A\ ...]]]$

We see in (1) that an adjective is a complex head **[A-a]** whose diathesis is the product of the composition of the diatheses of its stem **A** and suffix **-a**. The diatheses of the suffixes are responsible for the systematic changes in **A**'s initial diathesis that create the adjective's *morphosyntactic paradigm*. As in the case of verbs, the crucial changes of **A**'s initial diathesis involve its external $\{i^\wedge N\}_1$ argument.

Since the s-predicate aP_i in (1b) has an *unlinked* external theta role **i**, and since sentences containing unlinked theta roles are syntactically ill formed, aP_i's external **i** must be *vertically bound* in syntax. This entails that aP_i cannot merge *directly* with copula verbs (V_{cop}), which do not have their own theta roles and thus cannot V-bind aP_i. In contrast, adjective s-clauses obligatorily merge with V_{cop} (see (5)).[2]

These facts account for the syntactic complementary distribution of aP and aP_i: the unlinked external theta of aP_i must be vertically bound by a theta role of the *predicator* phrase it adjoins to, whereas the s-clause's dedicated subject nP_i (a projection of **A**'s initial $\{i^\wedge N\}_1$) must raise to the spec-position of the matrix copula projection. In other words, (1a) must merge with a *functor*, which does not assign theta roles, whereas the aP_i in (1b) must merge with a *predicator* (a theta-role assigner), one of whose theta roles vertically binds and thus *controls* it. We shall see below that the aP and aP$_i$ projections of **A** and the natural constraints on their licensing fully account for the syntactic distribution and function of Russian adjectives and participles (participles in Russian are verb-adjective hybrids with the inflectional morphology and syntactic distribution of adjectives; see chapter 3 for details).[3]

2.1 Russian adjectives

Russian plays an important role in the substantiation of the analysis in (1) because **A** in Russian canonically composes with two different sets of inflectional suffixes, the *long form* endings (LF) and *short form* endings (SF), which, I claim, morphologically mark whether **[A-a]** heads an aP$_i$ or aP. In other words, there is a biunique relation between the syntactic structure in (1a) and the SF suffix, and between (1b) and the LF suffix, as in (2).

(2) The morphosyntactic projections of the diatheses of the SF and LF:[4]
 a. SF s-clause: [$_{aP}$ nP$_{i.NOM}$ [$_{a'<i>}$ [A-a$_{SF}$] [$_{AP<i>}$ t$_A$ ...]]]
 b. LF s-predicate: [$_{aPi}$ [$_{a'<i>}$ [A-a$_{LF}$] [$_{AP<i>}$ t$_A$ ...]]]

Since the SF and LF suffixes and the lexical stem **A** they compose with each has its own diathesis, the derivation of the LF and SF is an *affix-driven*, diathesis-based operation: see (3) and (4). Note that the crucial syntactic difference between the SF and LF adjectives is encoded in the *external c-selection* slots of -a$_{SF}$ and -a$_{LF}$: { ^ }$_1$ in (3b) and { ^ -}$_1$ in (4b) (see §1.4).[5]

(3) Diathesis-based derivation of the SF:
 a. A-stem: {i ^ N}$_1$ ... {- ^ A}$_4$ +   (composes with)
 b. SF-affix: { ^ }$_1$ ... { ^ -a$_{SF.NOM}$}$_4$ >   (yields)
 c. SF: {i ^ N}$_1$ ... {- ^ [A-a$_{SF.NOM}$]}$_4$ => (projects to (2a))

(4) Diathesis-based derivation of the LF (α denotes a variable case feature):
 a. A-stem: {i ^ N}$_1$ ... {- ^ A}$_4$ +
 b. LF-affix: { ^ - }$_1$ ... { ^ -a$_{LFα}$ }$_4$ >
 c. LF: {i ^ - }$_1$ ... {- ^ [A-a$_{LF.α}$]}$_4$ => (2b)

(5) [SUBJECT+COPULA+SF-ADJECTIVE] sentences in Russian:
 Vino   bylo   vkusno.
 wine:NOM.N was:N   good:SF.NOM.N
 'The-wine was good.'

The LF suffix in (4) deletes **A**'s initial external **N₁** and the final diathesis in (4c) projects to syntax as (2b): $\{\{i\wedge\text{-}\}_1 \ldots \{\text{-} \wedge [\text{A-a}]_{\textbf{LF}}\}_4\} \Rightarrow [_{aP_i} [_{a'_{<i>}} [\text{A-a}]_{LF} \text{ AP}_{<i>}]]$.[6] In contrast, while the SF suffix in (3) leaves **A**'s external argument {i^N}₁ intact, it introduces an inherent nominative case feature, which captures the fact that the SF in modern Russian occurs only in the nominative case; LFs always *agree* in case with the head of the theta binding chain (TBC) in which they are V-bound and thus appear in all the cases that nouns do (see below).

Encoded in (4b) is the crucial fact that LFs (aP$_i$) *never* have dedicated subjects, and there are thus no LF clauses; aP$_i$ is always a *controlled adjunct*.[7] In contrast, the SF's aP projection always has a subject and is never an adjunct: its only function is to combine with the copula to form a sentence with a SF predicate adjective. The fact that LF and SF adjectives are in syntactic complementary distribution has the following corollaries: (i) they do not conjoin; (ii) when they occur in the same clause, they are in different syntactic configurations and, therefore, have different syntactic functions: e.g., in (6a), the SF *doroga* 'valuable' is the primary predicate and the LF *živaja* is a depictive adjunct controlled by the SF's subject *ryba*.[8]

(6) a. Ryba   tebe   doroga$_{SF}$ byla   živaja$_{LF}$ (*živa$_{SF}$).
       fish:NOM.F you:DAT   valuable:SF.NOM.F was:F   alive:LF.NOM.F
       'The-fish was valuable to-you (when it was) alive.'
    b. Segodnja ty   mne   nužen   trezvyj (*trezv$_{SF}$)
       today   you:NOM.M me:DAT   necessary:SF.M   sober:LF.NOM.M
       '(lit.) You are-necessary$_{SF}$ to-me today sober$_{LF}$.'
    c. Nikita byl spokoen$_{SF}$, uverennyj$_{LF}$ v tom, čto on skažet neobxodimoe.
       'Nikita was calm$_{SF}$, (since he was) sure$_{LF}$ that he would-say what-was-essential.'

We will be concerned primarily with the diathesis-to-syntax derivations of the phrasal projections headed by the LF and SF of adjectives and participles.[9] Since the SF always occurs in syntax with a form of the copula, [COPULA+SF] *must be accounted for in tandem*.

The minimal syntactic projections of the ditransitive SF and LF diatheses in (3c) and (4c) are represented in (7a) and (7b). If the trace t$_N$ is present in (7a), aP is a small clause whose subject nP$_i$ raises to spec-V$_{cop}$; if there is no t$_N$, aP is a *bare adjective phrase* with **A**'s external {i^N}₁ *inherited* by V$_{cop}$. In either case nP$_{i.NOM}$ in (7a) is **A**'s displaced initial external argument. The difference boils down to whether V$_{cop}$ *merges* with aP in syntax or *composes* with **A**'s diathesis in argument structure (see §2.16).

(7a)   SF syntactic projection:

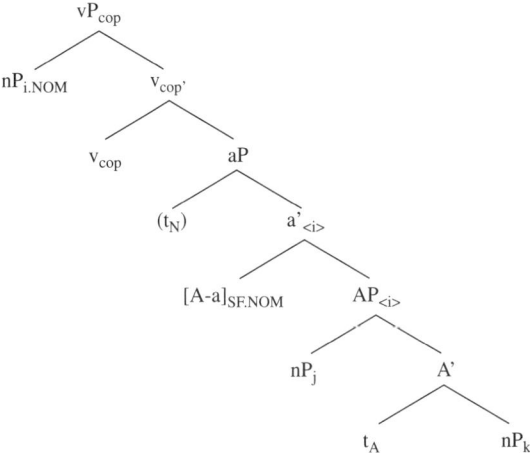

(7b)   LF s-predicate phrasal projection.

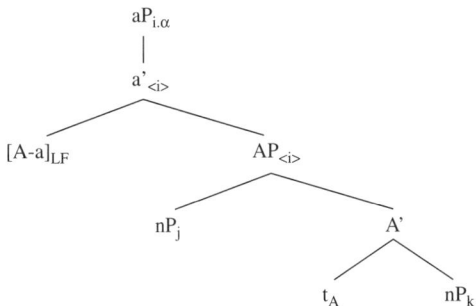

The derivations of the SF and LF in (3) and (4) provide additional evidence supporting one of chapter 1's central hypotheses, namely, that the diathesis of every predicator has a 2×4 structure and thus encodes *external subcategorization*. According to (3a) and (4a), the SF and LF have a common stem-diathesis and thus have the same ordered set of theta roles: the minimal distinctive difference between them is that the SF's *final*, pre-projection diathesis in (3c) inherits **A**'s intact *external* argument {i^N}$_1$, which projects as the sentence's dedicated nominative subject, whereas in the final diathesis of the LF in (4c), **A**'s external **N**$_1$ has been deleted; unlinked external {i^-}$_1$ is the signature of the s-predicate.[10] This is the core hypothesis being proposed in this chapter. Since the upper, theta tiers of the SF and LF diatheses are identical, it follows that their morphosyntactic differences are a function of the differences projected from their lower, c-selection tiers. More specifically, the different syntactic properties of SF and LF phrases derive from the differences encoded in their *suffixes' external c-selection*: see $\{i\wedge N\}_1$ vs. $\{i\wedge-\}_1$ in (3) and (4). If argument-structure representation were limited to A's theta roles only (see §1.3), LFs and SFs would have the same argument structure and their syntactic complementarity would not be accounted for.

2.2 The predicate LF paradox

Russian has the three kinds of [SUBJECT + COPULA + ADJECTIVE] sentence in (8):

(8)   [SUBJECT + COPULA + ADJECTIVE] sentences in Russian:
    a. SF: Vino   bylo   vkusn-o.
           wine:NOM.N   was:N   good:SF.NOM.N
           'The-wine was good.'
    b. LF: Vino   bylo   vkusn-oe.
           wine:NOM.N   was:N   good:LF.NOM.N
    c. PI: Vino   bylo   vkusn-ym.
           wine:NOM.N   was:N   good:PI.N

Sentences like (8b) are of particular interest because, given what was said above in §2.1, they appear to involve a paradox: if LFs are the morphological realization of the s-predicate structure in (7b) above, which is my main hypothesis, how can *vino* merge with the copula and be the subject of *vkusnoe*$_{LF}$ in (8b) if LFs, by hypothesis, are inherently aP$_i$ adjuncts and do not license a subject nP$_i$? In other words, if the diathesis of the LF in (4c) ($\{\{i\wedge-\}_1...\{-\wedge[A-a_{LF}]\}_4\}$) projects an external theta role but no external nP, as in (4)/(7b), (8b) should be ungrammatical. But (8b) is perfectly grammatical and entirely felicitous.

My solution to this problem may appear initially to replace one paradox with another: I will argue below that *vino* is indeed the subject in (8b), but it is not the subject of *vkusnoe*$_{LF}$, which is an adjunct in (8b), just as it is in all the other syntactic constructions in which it occurs. More specifically, my hypothesis is that *vino* is the subject of (8b) but *vkusnoe* is not the predicate, and, therefore, *vino* is not predicated of *vkusnoe*$_{LF}$.

This analysis entails that the [SUBJECT+COPULA+ADJECTIVE] sentence pattern in (8a) and (8b) is the morphosyntactic realization of two radically different diathesis-to-syntactic projections. I will present extensive empirical evidence that the correct syntactic structure of (8b) is represented in (9).

(9)
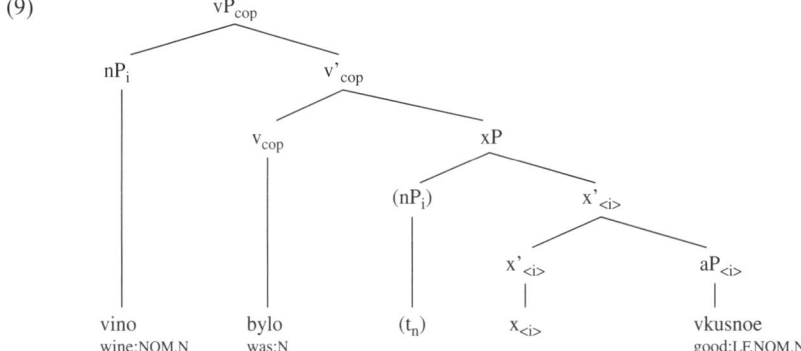

xP is a 'hidden' phrasal projection that comes between the copula *bylo* and *vkusnoe*$_{LF}$, which *adjoins* to x'$_i$ and is V-bound by it. The syntactic structure of (9) entails that:

(i) [*bylo* xP]$_{V'cop}$ is the main predicate in (8b), which means that *vino*$_i$ receives its external theta role from x, not [$_{aPi}$ *vkusnoe*$_{LF}$], which is an adjunct: [$_{x'<i>}$ x'$_{<i>}$ aP$_{<i>}$].

(ii) *Vino* is the subject of xP and raises to spec-vP$_{cop}$ (or is *inherited* by *bylo* in argument structure; cf. the parentheses in (9) and (7a)).

(iii) *Vkusnoe* is an xP internal adjunct that *modifies* the head of xP and is therefore V-bound inside xP by x's external theta role.

(iv) *Vkusnoe* in (8b) should appear to behave syntactically like an xP because it is its only overt constituent.

(v) xP is 'hidden' only in the sense that its head x is canonically null (but not obligatorily null, as we shall see in §2.13).

(vi) The difference in meaning attributed to *vkusno*$_{SF}$ and *vkusnoe*$_{LF}$ in (8a) and (8b) derives directly from their syntactic structures: (8a) has no xP between the copula and aP.[11]

(vii) LFs cannot merge directly with the copula and are therefore never predicate adjectives.[12]

(viii) The subject *vino* in (8b) is the raised/inherited subject of xP; *vkusnoe* agrees with x, not *vino*.

The structure of (8b) in (10) is ill-formed because it violates the Projection Principle: {i^-}$_1$, the external argument in [$_{aPi}$ *vkusnoe*]'s diathesis, cannot project a subject nP.

80 *The argument structure of adjectives*

(10)

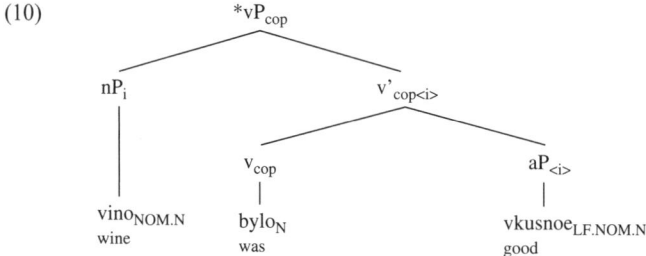

Note that a Projection Principle violation in diathesis theory is simply a mismapping or mismatch between a predicator's final derived diathesis and its syntactic projection; the mismatch here can be schematically represented as: *{{i^-}$_1$...} => [$_{vPcop}$ nP$_i$ v'$_{cop}$].

My next step is to present empirical evidence that there really is a null-headed xP in (8b)/(9) and to determine its lexical category. But it is necessary first to sharpen our definition of *subject*, and to provide a complete inventory of the constructions in which the LF occurs; the SF occurs only as the main predicate of copula sentences, as in (8a).

2.3   Dedicated and understood subjects

All Russian nP-subjects are *dedicated subjects*, i.e., the syntactic projection of a predicator's final linked external argument, e.g.: {{i^N}$_1$ ...} => [$_{vP}$ nP$_{i.NOM}$ v']; nP$_i$ canonically raises to spec-TP to check its nominative case feature and to satisfy T's EPP requirement (see McCloskey 1997). In the case of unaccusative verbs, externalized nP$_j$ projects as the sentence's dedicated subject: {{j^N}$_1$ ...} => [$_{vP}$ nP$_{j.NOM}$...]. *Vino* is accordingly the dedicated subject of *vkusno*$_{SF}$ in (7a)/(8a), but not of *vkusnoe*$_{LF}$ in (8b) /(9).[13]

Now let us consider sentences like (11a), which has a *subject-controlled* nominative LF depictive adjunct *golodnyj* 'hungry'; the PI *golodnym* is also possible, but not the SF *goloden*.

(11)   a. Nikita$_{i.NOM}$ vernulsja domoj [$_{aP<i>}$ golodnyj$_{LF.NOM}$] (*goloden$_{SF.NOM}$).
           Nikita   returned   home   hungry
           'Nikita came home hungry.'
       b. My$_{i.NOM.PL}$ uložili   Annu$_{j.ACC.F}$ v postel' [$_{aP<i>}$ odetuju$_{LF.ACC.F}$].
           'We   put   Anna   to bed   dressed.'

Nikita is simultaneously the dedicated subject of *vernulsja* and the 'understood' subject of [$_{aP<i>}$ *golodnyj*$_{LF}$], which is V-bound by [$_{v'i}$ *vernulsja domoj*]; the latter assigns its external i to the matrix subject *Nikita*, forming a TBC whose head is *Nikita* and whose tail is *golodnyj*. This TBC accounts for the nominative

2.3 Dedicated and understood subjects

case agreement between *Nikita* and *golodnyj*, and for the *subject control* of *golodnyj* by *Nikita* (cf. the object control and accusative case agreement in (11b), where $Annu_{j.ACC.F}$ is the head of the TBC in which the LF $odetuju_{<i>.ACC.F}$ is bound). It is in this sense that the head of a TBC is the tail's 'understood subject.'

AP is the maximal projection of the adjective **A** stem. Like **V**, **A** can have up to three arguments: two AP internal and one AP external. While **A**-diatheses normally have one internal argument in addition to its external argument, we see in (12) that two are possible, which is what is predicted by the diathesis's 2×4 structure (both internal arguments are assigned quirky case, which is specified in **A**'s initial diathesis); (14) is the AP projection headed by *objazana*. **A**'s external argument $\{i^\wedge N\}_1$ merges AP-externally in the spec-position of the immediately dominating aP projection headed by $\text{-}a_{SF}$. An aP with **A**'s dedicated subject in its spec-position is an *adjective s-clause*, as in (15). Each argument position in (13) maps onto an isomorphic position in the syntactic representation in (15).

(12) Ja$_{NOM}$ objazana$_{SF}$ emu$_{DAT}$ žizn'ju$_{INST}$.
      I   owe   him   life
      'I owe him my life.'

(13) $\{\{i \wedge N\}_1 \{j \wedge N_{DAT}\}_2 \{k \wedge N_{INST}\}_3 \{\text{-} \wedge [A\text{-}a_{SF}]\}_4\}$

(14)
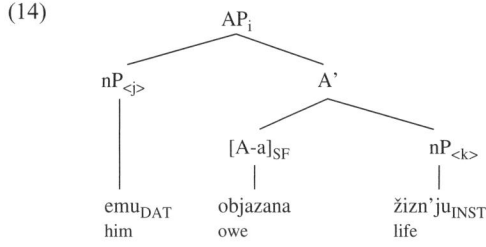

(15)
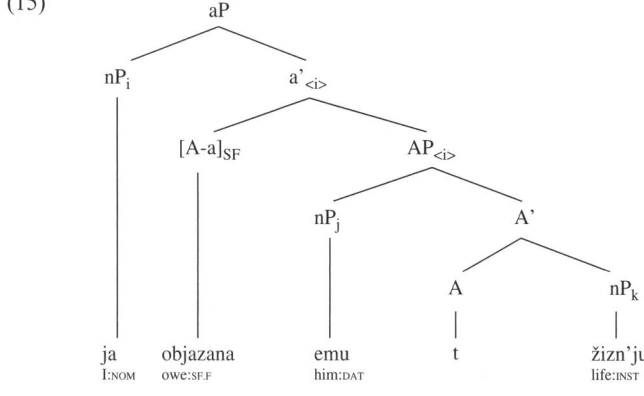

82 The argument structure of adjectives

When **A**'s diathesis composes with the diathesis of -a_{LF}, its external **N** is deleted, creating the s-predicate in (16), whose unlinked external theta role **i** (aP_i) must be V-bound in syntactic structure (see Moro 1997: 86, Rothstein 2001). The s-predicate *objazanaja*$_{LF}$ is represented in (17), where aP_i is adjoined to matrix n'$_i$, which V-binds aP_i's external **i**, making aP_i an nP-internal attributive s-predicate adjective phrase that modifies the head noun *devuška* 'girl': [$_{nPNOM}$ *devuška* [*objazannaja*$_{LF.}$ $_{NOM.F}$ *emu*$_{DAT}$ *žizn'ju*$_{INST}$]] 'the-girl (who) owes him (her) life.'

(16) {{i ^ -}$_1$ {j ^ N}$_2$ {k ^ N}$_3$ {- ^ [A-a]$_{LF}$}$_4$ }

(17)

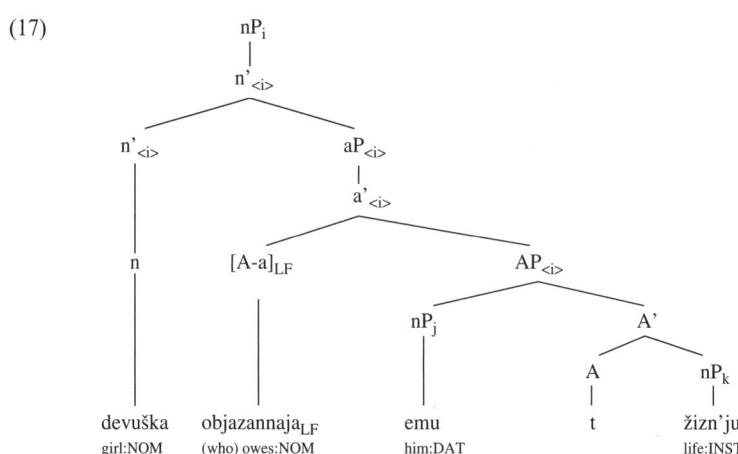

2.4 The syntactic properties of the LF and SF

The criterial properties of the LF and SF are summarized in (18) and (19).[14]

(18) The LF:
    (a) agrees in gender, number, and case with the head of the TBC in which it is vertically bound;
    (b) has an unlinked external theta role **i**, which is what makes it an s-predicate;
    (c) always functions as a controlled adjunct aP_i (including (8b)); see (11);[15]
    (d) always adjoins to a phrasal projection of a predicator one of whose theta roles V-binds it;
    (e) cannot merge directly with the copula, which is a functor and has no theta roles to bind aP_i (cf. (10)).

(19) The SF:
    (a) inflects for gender, number, and case, but, unlike the LF, it occurs in the nominative case only; its nominative case is inherent, i.e., specified in the lower tier of the SF suffix's diathesis;

(b) is always the head of an aP (never an aP$_i$);
(c) its {i^N}$_1$ is always realized as the copula's subject;
(d) always merges with a functor (copula), never with a predicator.

In addition to sentences like (8b), LF adjectives occur in the following constructions.

(20) The nP-internal, attributive realization of **A** (cf. (17)):
a. *SF: [$_{nP:NOM}$ vkusn-o vino]
b. LF: [$_{nP:NOM}$ vkusn-oe vino]
  'good wine'
c. *PI: [$_{nP:NOM}$ vkusn-ym vino]

(21) Subject-controlled depictive adjunct:
a. *SF: Anna ljubit tancevat' pered zerkalom gola$_{NOM.F}$.[16]
b. LF: Anna ljubit tancevat' pered zerkalom golaja$_{NOM.F}$.
c. PI: Anna ljubit tancevat' pered zerkalom goloj$_{PI.F}$.
  'Anna loves to-dance in-front-of the-mirror naked.'

(22) On pil i p'janyj$_{LF.NOM.M}$ (*p'jan$_{SF}$) izbival ženu$_{ACC}$.
    he drank and drunk   beat   wife
  'He drank and (when) drunk (he) beat (his) wife.'

(23) Object-controlled depictive adjuncts:
a. *SF: Ona obnaružila, čto ee$_{ACC.F}$ uložili$_{PL}$ v postel' odeta$_{SF.NOM.F}$.
b. LF: Ona obnaružila, čto ee$_{ACC.F}$ uložili$_{PL}$ v postel' odetuju$_{LF.ACC.F}$.
  'She discovered that (unknown person) put her to bed dressed.'
c. PI: Ona obnaružila, čto ee$_{ACC.F}$ uložili$_{PL}$ v postel' odetoj$_{PI.F}$.

(24) aP$_i$ adjoined to nP$_i$: [$_{nPi}$ aP$_{<i>}$ # nP$_{<i>}$] (# denotes a *prosodic gap*).
a. [$_{nPi}$ [$_{aP<i>}$ golodnye$_{NOM.LF}$] # [$_{nP<i>}$ tarakany$_{NOM}$]] snovali po stenam.
        hungry   roaches   scurried on walls
  'Cockroaches were-scurrying around the walls (because they were) hungry.'
b. [$_{nPi}$ [$_{n'<i>}$ [$_{aP<i>}$ golodnye$_{NOM}$] [$_{n'<i>}$ tarakany$_{NOM}$]]] snovali po stenam.
  'The cockroaches (who were) hungry were-scurrying around the walls.'
c. [*golodny$_{SF}$ / *golodnymi$_{PI}$ (#) tarakany] snovali po stenam.

2.5 The structure of SF small clauses

Given that the SF obligatorily cooccurs with a copula, I will initially assume the standard analysis that aP is the s-clause complement of V$_{cop}$ and that the SF's nominative subject *raises* from spec-aP to spec-vP$_{cop}$, which is a syntactic operation. (8a) can thus be represented as (25); empirically motivating the structure of predicate LF proposed in (9) is the goal of the rest of

84 *The argument structure of adjectives*

this chapter. The bottom-to-top *syntactic* derivation of (8a)/(25) proceeds as follows:

- AP is built up.
- A's (*vkusn-*) external argument {i^N}$_1$ projects from [A-a$_{SF}$]'s final diathesis to spec aP as the nominative subject *vino*.
- The [A-a$_{SF}$] head of AP, which was created by diathesis composition in (3), raises to the head of aP position by head movement (see Matushansky 2006).
- aP merges with the copula *bylo*, which heads vP$_{cop}$.
- *Vino* moves from spec-aP to spec-vP$_{cop}$.

(25) The syntactic structure of (8a):[17]

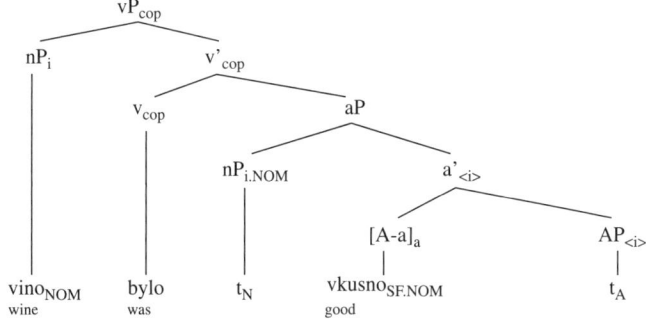

2.6 The control of depictive adjectives

Vzvolnovannyj$_{LF.M.SG}$ 'agitated' in (26b) is a nominative subject-controlled depictive LF adjective (see Bowers 2001: 326 ff.); (27) is the syntactic representation of (26b)'s finite vP (the depictive-control TBC is in boldface); (28) gives additional examples.

(26) Subject-controlled depictive s-predicates:
    a. *SF: On   vernulsja   domoj   vzvolnovan.
            he:NOM.M   returned   home$_{ADV}$ agitated:SF.NOM.M
    b. LF: On   vernulsja   domoj   vzvolnovannyj.
            he:NOM.M   returned:M   home   agitated:NOM.LF.M
    c. PI: On   vernulsja   domoj   vzvolnovannym.
            he:NOM.M   returned:M   home   agitated:PI.M

(27)

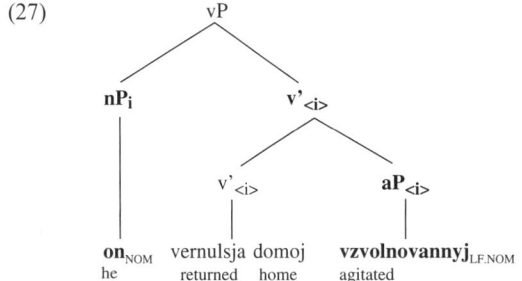

on_{NOM} vernulsja domoj vzvolnovannyj_{LF.NOM}
he returned home agitated

(28) a. **Anna**_{i.NOM} nužna_{SF.F} nam_{DAT} [_{aP<i>} **živaja**_{LF.NOM.F}].
Anna necessary to us alive
'Anna is necessary to us [alive].'
b. **Anna**_i stojala na pervoj stupen'ke, [_{aP<i>} **gotovaja**_{LF.NOM.F} prygnut' vniz].
'Anna stood on the-first step [ready to-jump down].'
c. Ja_{NOM.M} ložilsja_M spat' [_{aP<i>} **golodnyj**_{LF.NOM.M}].
'I went to bed hungry.'
d. Kstati, [_{aP<i>} **ryžen'kaja**_{LF.NOM.F}] **ty**_{NOM.F} mne_{DAT} nravilas'_F bol'še.
red you to-me liked more
'By-the-way, I liked you better [red] (= when your hair was red).'
e. Prosto **golaja**_{LF.NOM} **ja**_{NOM.F} raza v dva tolšče, čem **odetaja**_{LF.NOM.F}.
simply naked I twice fatter than dressed
'(It's) simply (that) I'm twice as fat naked than dressed.' (Truskinovskaja)

(27) demonstrates that, although LFs always have a case feature, they are not always nP-internal constituents, as in (17). *Vzvolnovannyj*_{LF.NOM.M} is V-bound by *on* (the nominative subject of the sentence and head of the boldface TBC) and thus *agrees* with it in case, number, and gender.

Next we compare the derivations of subject- and object-controlled depictive adjuncts, which demonstrate that classic GB contol theory, which reduces all instances of control to the antecedent-binding of a nonfinite clause's PRO-subject, makes the wrong predictions in the case of Russian depictives.

The depictive aP_i *vzvolnovannyj*_{LF.NOM} in (27) is V-bound by finite matrix v'_i, whose external **i** is assigned to the nominative matrix subject nP_i (*on*), creating the boldface TBC with *on* as the head and *vzvolnovannyj*_{LF} as the tail. This explains why *vzvolnovannyj* is nominative despite the fact that it is a constituent of v': s-predicates always agree in case with the head of the their TBC; their own immediate constituency is not relevant. The syntactic structure in (27) thus explains both the nominative case of *vzvolnovannyj* and its control relations, i.e., the fact that *on* is simultaneously the dedicated subject of *vernulsja* and the controller (understood subject) of *vzvolnovannyj* without having to claim that

86   *The argument structure of adjectives*

on is assigned two theta roles (see Hornstein 1999) or that LF depictives have PRO subjects. (29) cannot be the correct structure of (26b) because, as established above, s-predicates do not have a subject nP of any kind, including a null [nP PRO] subject (see the ill-formed structure in (10)).

(29)

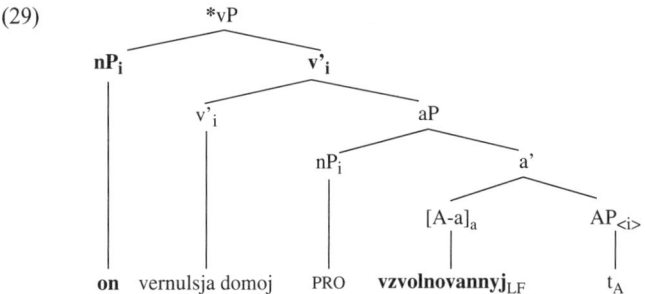

Note that (29) actually predicts that LF subject-controlled depictives like *vzvolnovannyj* in (26b) should be ill-formed, while SFs, which have subject nPs, should be well-formed subject-controlled depictives: the PRO subject of the SF s-clause would be antecedent-bound by the proximate nominative subject. But, as we see in (26), just the opposite is true: LFs are well-formed depictives and SFs are ill-formed: compare (29) with (30).

(30)

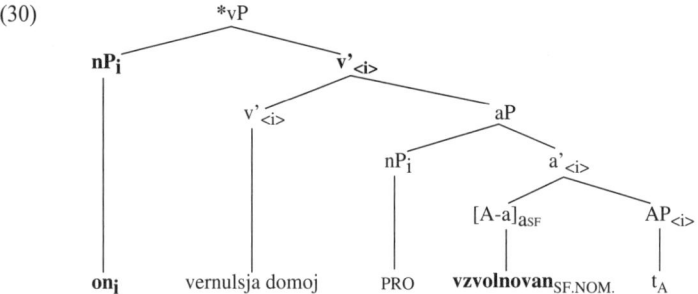

While it is clear from (29) why the well-formed LF's control cannot be captured in terms of an antecedent-bound PRO subject, it may not be immediately clear why SF s-clauses cannot have a depictive function in modern Russian, i.e., what precisely is it that makes (30) ungrammatical?[18] The ill-formedness of (30) (and (29) for that matter) emerges clearly from comparing the properties of LFs and SFs listed in (18) and (19): it is an empirical fact that SFs in well-formed sentences must cooccur with a form of the copula, which is not possible in structures like (30). We must wait for

2.6 The control of depictive adjectives 87

an explanation for why the SF must cooccur with the copula until §2.16.1, where the syntactic merger + raising analysis of the copula we are assuming is revised (see footnote 3).[19]

SFs cannot be object-controlled for the same reason they cannot be subject-controlled: a form of the copula is not possible here either; see (31a), where, *ee* and PRO are coreferential; the accusative direct object *ee* in (31b) is the head of the TBC in which accusative *odetuju*$_{\text{LF.F}}$ is V-bound.

(31) a. *My uložili ee$_{\text{ACC.F}}$ v postel' [PRO odeta$_{\text{SF.NOM.F}}$].
       we put her in bed dressed
   b. My uložili ee$_{\text{ACC.F}}$ v postel' **odetuju**$_{\text{LF.ACC.F}}$ (odetoj$_{\text{PL.F}}$).
      'We put her to bed dresed.'

The vertically bound s-predicate analysis of the LF unifies its nP-*external* agreement (see (27)) and nP-*internal* agreement ([$_{\text{nPi}}$ *vkusnoe*$_{\text{LF<i>}}$ (**vkusno*$_{\text{SF}}$) *vino*]) 'good wine,' both of which involve gender, number, and case agreement. The LF's unlinked external theta role **i** in (26b) and (31b) is satisfied nP-*externally* by V-binding: the head of the TBC in which it is bound determines its number, gender, and case agreement features. Since the LF is the only morphosyntactic realization of **A** that occurs nP-*internally* (see (20)), and since it canonically agrees in case, gender, and number with the nP's head, the simplest hypothesis is that the LF's agreement is determined nP-internally the same way it is nP-externally, namely, LF's unlinked external theta role is V-bound by the external theta role **i** of the nP containing it. In other words, n in (20a) is simultaneously the head of nP and the head of the TBC in which the attributive aP$_i$ is V-bound.[20] More generally: xP$_i$ agrees with and is controlled by the head of the TBC in which it is V-bound; a sentence in which xP$_i$ is not a link in a TBC is ill-formed.

2.6.1 Object-controlled aP$_i$

In this section we look more closely at the *syntactic* derivation of object-controlled aP$_i$ depictives. (33) is the structure of (32a); (34) gives additional examples.

(32) Object-controlled depictive adjectives:
   a. My$_i$ uložili ee$_j$ v postel' [$_{\text{aP<i>}}$ **odetuju**].
      we:NOM put her:ACC.F in bed dressed:LF.ACC.F
      'We put her to bed dressed.'
   b. My uložili ee v postel' odetoj (*odeta).
      we:NOM put her:ACC.F in bed dressed:PL.F (*SF)

88 The argument structure of adjectives

(33)

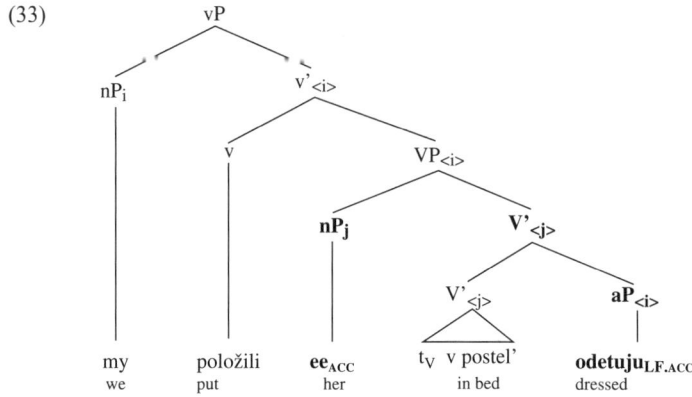

(34) a. General prikazal dostavit' **komandira** **živogo**.
    general ordered to-deliver commander:ACC.M alive:LF.ACC.M
    'The-general ordered (them) to-bring (him) **the-commander alive**.'
  b. Uvidev **ee goluju**, on oščutil želanie poznakomit'sja s nej.
    'Upon-seeing **her**$_{\text{ACC.F}}$ **naked**$_{\text{LF.ACC.F}}$, he felt the-desire to-meet her.'
  c. Oni podralis' iz-za bol'šoj morkovki, **kotoruju**$_{\text{ACC}}$ kto-to počti **celuju**$_{\text{LF.ACC}}$ brosil v otxody.
    'They fought over a big carrot, **which** someone threw in the-trash almost **whole**.'

The accusative LF [*odetuju*]$_{\text{aP<i>}}$ in (32a)/(33) is adjoined to the matrix V'$_j$ and is V-bound by **j**, giving [$_{\text{V'}_j}$ V'$_{<j>}$ [$_{\text{aP<i>}}$ *odetuju*]]. V'$_j$ then merges with the accusative direct object **ee**, creating an object-control TBC, which is parallel to the subject-control TBC in (27). Compare the boldface TBCs in (27) and (33): subject-control involves adjoining aP$_i$ to v'$_i$, where it is vertically bound by matrix external **i**; object-control involves adjoining aP$_i$ to V'$_j$, where it is vertically bound by **j**. In both cases, aP$_{<i>}$ agrees in case, gender, and number with the head of its TBC, which is the subject nP$_{i.\text{NOM}}$ in spec-vP in subject-control structures and the direct object nP$_{j.\text{ACC}}$ in spec-VP in object-control structures. These two derivations capture the close relation between binding, control, and case agreement in terms of the sentences' TBCs.

2.6.2 Russian noun phrases

I have been assuming that noun phrases in Russian have the following minimal phrase structure: [$_{\text{nP}}$ [$_{\text{n'}}$ [N-n] NP]], where N heads the lexical NP projection, n is the head of the affix projection nP, and the composite head [$_{\text{n}}$ N-n] is the product of diathesis-composition; cf. [A-a] in [$_{\text{aP}}$ [$_{\text{a'}}$ [A-a] AP]] (adjective phrase), [V-v] in [$_{\text{vP}}$ [$_{\text{v'}}$ [V-v] VP]] (finite vP phrase), [V-inf] in [$_{\text{infP}}$ [$_{\text{inf'}}$ [V-inf] VP]] (infinitive phrase), and [nP [n' [V-n] VP]] in hybrid derived nominal phrases (see (90) in chapter 1). Given that Russian nPs do not have articles, which are obligatory determiners, base-generated preposed genitives like -'s in English, obligatory possessives (*On podnjal ruku* 'He lifted (his) arm'), and that determiners are morphologically adjectives, I conclude that nPs in Russian are not obligatorily contained in a DP shell: [DP [D' D nP]].

The evidence we shall see below suggests that the noun phrase is realized as either nP or nP$_i$, parallel to aP and aP$_i$ in (1) and to infP (infinitive s-clause) and infP$_i$ (infinitive s-predicate) in chapter 4. [nP nP$_{i.NOM}$ [n'$_{<i>}$ [N-n] NP$_{<i>}$]] is the structure of *predicate nominals*, whose nP$_{i.NOM}$ subject raises to the spec-position of the copula it *obligatorily* merges with. The structure of *On byl učitel'* 'He was a-teacher' is accordingly represented as (35): *on* raises from spec-nP to spec-vP$_{cop}$. [nPi [n'$_{<i>}$ [N-n] NP$_{<i>}$]] is the structure of nP-*arguments*.[21] These facts suggest the following X-bar generalization: a lexical stem X has three potential morphosyntactic realizations, which depend on the affixal head's (x) diathesis: (i) the *s-clause* structure in [xP nP$_i$ [x'$_{<i>}$ [X-x] XP$_{<i>}$]]; (ii) the *s-predicate* structure in [xPi [x'$_{<i>}$ [X-x] XP$_{<i>}$]]; and (iii) the *bare-phrase* structure in [xP [x' [X-x] XP]].[22]

(35)

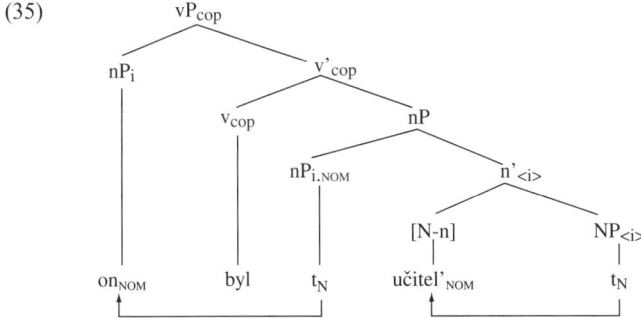

2.7 The predicate LF

We can now return to the predicate LF in sentences like (8b) (*Vino bylo vkusnoe* 'The-wine was good'), which has the structure in (36a) or (36b), depending on whether we treat copula introduction as merger + raising in syntax, as in (36a) (see (9)), or as composition + inheritance in argument structure, as in (36b), where there are no traces;[23] (37) to (39) are additional examples of the predicate LF. We consider only (36a) raising analysis until §2.16, where evidence is presented that the copula's diathesis *composes* with **A**'s diathesis and, therefore, that the copula *inherits* **A**'s external argument in argument structure.

(36a)
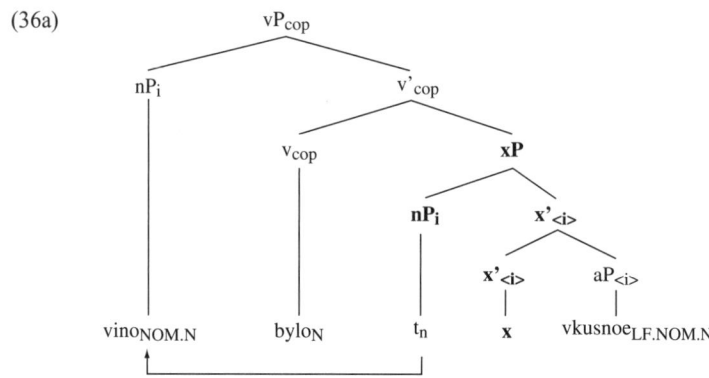

(36b)
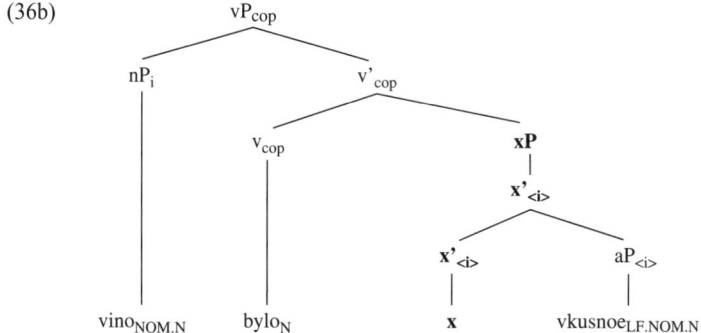

(37) a. Ona   edinstvennaja   zdorovaja.
       she:NOM.F   only:LF.NOM.F   healthy:LF.NOM.F
       'She is the only healthy (one/person/woman).'
    b. *Ona   edinstvenna   zdorova.
       she:NOM.F   only: SF.NOM.F healthy:SF.NOM.F

(38) a. Počemu ty takaja$_{LF.NOM.F}$ (*tak$_{ADV}$) umnaja$_{LF.NOM.F}$?
       'Why are you so smart?'
    b. Počemu ty tak$_{ADV}$ (*takaja$_{LF.NOM.F}$) umna$_{SF.NOM.F}$?
       'Why are you so smart?'

(39) a. Vy nenormal'nyj$_{LF.NOM.SG.M}$ (*nenormal'nye$_{LF.NOM.PL}$).
       'You're not (a) normal (person/man/one, etc.).'
    b. Vy nenorma'ny$_{SF.NOM.PL}$ (*nenormalen$_{SF.NOM.SG.M}$).
       'You're not normal.'
    c. Iz vsex brat'ev, on samyj$_{LF.NOM.SG.M}$ umnyj$_{LF.NOM.SG.M}$.
       'Of all the-brothers, he is the-smartest (one/brother).'
    d. *Iz vsex brat'ev, on samyj umen$_{SF.NOM.SG.M}$.

2.7 The predicate LF   91

LFs are s-predicates and therefore cannot combine *directly* with the copula *bylo*, which gets its external argument from the nP or aP it composes with: since the external argument of the LF is {i^-}$_1$, the direct merger/composition of the LF *vkusnoe* and the copula *bylo* would result in a *finite s-predicate* [$_{vPcop.i}$ *bylo vkusnoe*], which is ill-formed because there is no higher theta role in the sentence to vertically bind it.[24] If the LF cannot merge directly with the copula, there must be an intermediate xP in (8b)/(36), which licenses the subject nP *vino*$_i$ and whose head x the predicate LF modifies and agrees with.

The hidden xP in (36) is the sentence's main predicate and *vino* is its subject. The LF [$_{aPi}$ *vkusnoe*] in *Vino bylo vkusnoe*$_{LF}$ adjoins to x'$_i$ and thus modifies x, not *vino*. xP is hidden because its head x is canonically null. In the following sections I will present extensive empirical evidence that xP exists, intervenes between vP$_{cop}$ and aP$_i$ as in (8b)/(36), and that this xP is not present in (8a) (*Vino bylo vkusno*$_{SF}$). According to (36), xP has the following properties:

(40) a. In (36a), xP is an [$_{xP}$ [$_{nPi}$ *vino*] x'$_{<i>}$] s-clause and *vino* is its subject; in (36b), xP is a bare phrase whose external argument (*vino*) is inherited by the copula. In either case, xP must be the source of the sentence's subject (*vino*) because neither the s-predicate LF adjunct *vkusnoe* nor the functor *bylo* can be the source of the sentence's subject.
   b. [*vkusnoe*]$_{aPi}$ adjoins to x'$_i$ and is vertically bound by it: [$_{x'i}$ x'$_i$ aP$_{<i>}$].
   c. The structures in (36) correctly predict that the LF in copula + LF constructions like (38) and (39) should appear to have the syntactic distribution of an xP since the LF is canonically its only overt constituent.
   d. *Vkusnoe* agrees in case, number and gender with x, the head of xP, not with *vino*.

Since x in (36) has inherent case, number, and gender features for *vkusnoe* to agree with, it must be a noun and, therefore, predicate LFs are *nP-internal attributive adjectives*, as in (42)/(43) (cf. (36a)/b)) More specifically, xP in (36) is an nP, which means that in sentences like (8b), the LF is *modifying* the null head of a *predicate nominal nP* and, according to (40c), should itself appear to behave syntactically like a predicate nominal. In other words, *Vino bylo vkusnoe* 'The-wine was good' in (8b) should have the structure of the predicate nominal in (35) and the sentences in (41b–c); see (42)/(43) (boldface **n** abbreviates [$_n$ N-n] and denotes the null head of the predicate nominal phrase):

(41) a. Vino [$_{nP}$ [$_{aP<i>}$vkusnoe] **n**].
      'The-wine (is) good.'
   b. Vino [$_{nP}$ [$_{aP<i>}$vkusnoe$_{LF.NOM.N}$] pit'e$_{LF.NOM.N}$].
      'Wine (is a) good drink.'
   c. Vino [$_{nP}$ [$_{aP<i>}$vkusnyj$_{LF.NOM.M}$] napitok$_{LF.NOM.M}$].
      'Wine (is a) good drink.'

92 *The argument structure of adjectives*

(42)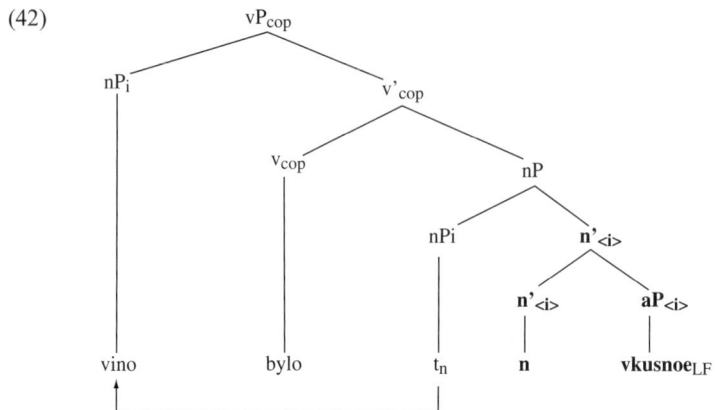

(43)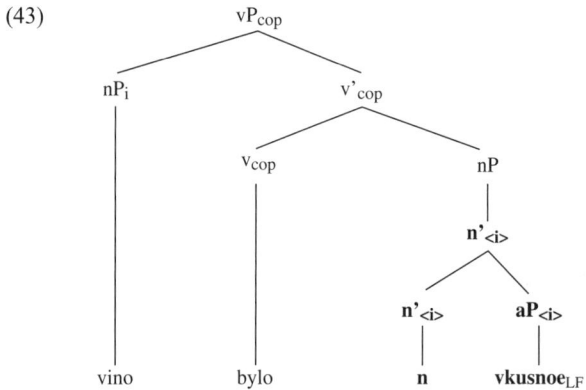

A *predicate nominal* phrase is schematically represented in (44a), which has the structure of an s-clause; an *argument nominal* phrase is an nP$_i$, i.e., a noun phrase that functions as an argument of a predicator, not as a predicator (see (44b)). Compare (44) and (45).

(44)   a. predicate nominal: [$_{nP}$ nP$_{i.NOM}$ [$_{n'}$ [N-n] NP]]
        b. argument nominal: [$_{nPi}$ [$_{n'}$[N-n]   NP]]

(45)   a. SF small clause: [$_{aP}$ nP$_{i.NOM}$ [$_{a'}$ [A-a]$_{SF}$ AP]]
        b. LF s-predicate: [$_{aPi}$ [$_{a'}$ [A-a]$_{LF}$ AP]]

(46)   The syntactic structures of (8a) and (8b):
        a. SF: [$_{vPcop}$ Vino$_i$ [$_{v'cop}$ bylo [$_{aP}$ (t$_n$)   [$_{a'<i>}$ vkusno]]]]
        b. SF: *[$_{vPcop}$ Vino$_i$ [$_{v'cop}$ bylo [$_{nP}$ (t$_n$) n [$_{aP<i>}$ vkusno]]]]

c. LF: [$_{vPcop}$ Vino$_i$ [$_{v'cop}$ bylo   [$_{nP}$ (t$_n$) **n**   [$_{aP<i>}$ vkusnoe]]]]
d. LF: *[$_{vPcop}$ Vino$_i$ [$_{v'cop}$ bylo   [$_{aP}$ (t$_n$)   [$_{a'<i>}$ vkusnoe]]]]

The aP$_{<i>}$-in-predicate-nP analysis of the predicate LF construction in (42)/(43) and (46c) appears to be correct because of the many correct, empirically verifiable predictions it makes.

2.8   Head suppression

I argue in this section that *suppression* of an nP's head, which is a vital component in the analysis of the predicate LF, is not construction specific, i.e., the null **n** posited above is not confined to the head of predicate nominal nPs like [*Vino$_i$ bylo* [$_{nP}$ **n** [$_{aP<i>}$ *vkusnoe*$_{LF}$]]]: see the null-headed nPs in (47) through (50).[25] The descriptive generalization unifying most instances of nP head-suppression in Russian is this: a head n modified nP-internally by a LF adjective or participle is phonetically unrealized (suppressed) if it can be easily recovered from the immediate discourse. Head suppression, which is virtually obligatory when identical head nouns are in close proximity, as in (47), is far more common in Russian than in English because the number, gender, and case agreement morphology of the LF attributive adjective makes it much easier to recover the missing noun. English uses the pronoun *one* in many but not all the contexts in which Russian suppresses the nP's head, in effect stranding the LF modifier as the only overt constituent of the nP.

(47)   a. Ee   xolodnye   kak   led   guby   vstretilis' s   ego   **pylajuščimi**.[26]
          her   cold   as   ice   lips   met   with   his   burning
          'Her lips (which were) cold as ice met with his **burning**$_{LF.INST.PL}$ (lips).'
       b. [$_{nP.NOM}$ ee xolodnye kak led guby] vstretilis' [$_{PP}$ s [$_{nP.INST}$ ego [$_{aP<i>}$ pylajuščimi$_{LF.INST.PL}$] **n**]].

(48)   a. Bol'šoj nož – edinstvennyj **režuščij** vo vsem dome.
          '(lit.) The big knife is the only **cutting** (one) in the whole house / … the only one that cuts…'
       b. [$_{nP.NOM}$ Bol'šoj nož] – [$_{nP.NOM}$ [$_{aP<i>}$ edinstvennyj$_{LF.NOM}$ režuščij$_{LF.NOM}$] **n**] vo vsem dome.

(49)   a. On brosil vzgljad na te neskol'ko stranic, kotorye predšestvovali [**vynutoj** im]$_{nP.DAT}$.
          'He glanced at those few pages which preceded [(the one) **removed** by-him].'
       b. …, kotorye predšestvovali [$_{nP.DAT}$ [$_{aP<i>}$ **vynutoj**$_{LF.DAT.F.SG}$ im$_{INST}$] **n**].[27]

(50)   a. Xvost poxož [$_{PP}$ na [$_{nP.ACC}$ [$_{aP<i>}$ oslinyj$_{LF.ACC.M.SG}$] **n**]].
          'The-tail looks like a donkey('s) (tail) / *a donkey one.'

b. On dokazal, čto [$_{PP}$ pomimo [$_{nP.GEN}$ **n** [$_{aP<i>}$ rabovladel'českoj$_{LF.GEN.F}$]]], est' Amerika$_{NOM.F.SG}$ borcov$_{GEN.PL}$ za svobodu.
'He (Lincoln) proved that besides [slave-holding$_{LF}$ (America/?one)], there existed an America of fighters for freedom.'
c. U Anny našlis' i drugie motivy, [$_{PP}$ pomimo [$_{nP}$ **n** ukazannyx vami]].
'Anna had other motives [besides (the ones) **pointed-out** by-you].'
d. On ženilsja na devuške, ne imevšej ni opyta aktrisy, [$_{nPGEN}$ ni **kakogo** by to ni bylo voobšče].
'He married a girl who had neither an actress's experience nor **any** (experience) at all.' (L. Ulickaja)
e. Botinki$_{ACC.PL}$ ‖ ja$_{NOM}$ nadel [$_{nP.ACC}$ [t]$_N$ [$_{afP<i>}$ grjaznye$_{LF.ACC.PL}$]].[28]
  shoes   I   put-on   dirty
'I put on dirty shoes (lit. Shoes ‖ I put on dirty [ones]).'

The preposition *pomimo* in (50c) assigns quirky genitive case to its complement. Since prepositions select nP complements, not adjective/participle ones, and since LFs always agree in case with the head of their TBC, the PP in (50c) must contain a null-headed ('hidden') nP between PP and aP$_i$: [$_{PP}$ *pomimo* [$_{nP}$ **n** *ukazannyx vami*]] 'besides (the-ones) indicated by-you'; see also (47), (50a–b), and (52). The possessive pronoun *ego* 'his' in (47a) modifies covert **n**, not overt [$_{aP<i>}$ *pylajuščimi*], which is another piece of evidence that the LF *pylajuščimi* 'burning' is an attributive participle in a null-headed nP.

In (51a) we see the suppression of a repeated noun in *parallel constructions*, where the suppressed nP-head is particularly easily to recover, despite the absence of an nP-internal LF (cf. the predicate genitive construction in §2.11 below). Thus (51a) and (51b) have the same syntactic structures, the only difference being that the repeated noun in the second conjunct is not suppressed in (51b).[29]

(51) a. Tak možet vesti sebja ili [p'janyj čelovek]$_{nP}$ ili [$_{nP}$**n** [$_{CP}$ [$_{PP}$u kogo] ne vse doma]].
'Only [a drunk person] or [(a person) at whom not everything (is) at-home (= is not all there)] can act that way.'
b. Tak možet vesti sebja ili p'janyj čelovek ili [$_{nP}$ **čelovek** [$_{CP}$ u kogo ne vse doma]].
'Only a drunk person or [a person who is not all there] can act this way.'
c. [$_{nP}$ ([$_n$ čelovek]) [$_{CP}$ [$_{PP}$ u kogo] [$_{TP}$ t$_P$ ne vse doma]]]

LFs modifying null head nouns are common in nPs referring to human beings; the suppressed head in the following examples is either generic (people in general) or refers to a specific person whose identity has been established in the immediately preceding discourse:

(52)   – Ona očen' **rasstroena**$_{\text{SF.NOM.F}}$.[30]
       'She is very upset.'
       – Ničego, my umeem razgovarivat' [$_{\text{PP}}$ s [$_{\text{nP}}$ [$_{\text{aP<i>}}$ **rasstroennymi**$_{\text{LF.INST.PL}}$] **n**]].
       'No problem, we know-how to-talk with [(people who are) **upset**].'

(53)   [$_{\text{nP.NOM}}$ [$_{\text{aP<i>}}$ **Pozvonivšij**$_{\text{LF.NOM.M}}$ **n**]] skazal, čto...
       '[(The person who) called] said that...'

(54)   [$_{\text{nP}}$ Nikogda i ni v čem ne **somnevajuščijsja**$_{\text{LF.NOM.M}}$ **n**] mertv$_{\text{SF.M}}$ dušoj.
       '[(One who) never has doubts about anything] is spiritually dead.'

(55)   **Sytyj**$_{\text{LF.NOM.M}}$ **golodnogo**$_{\text{LF.ACC.M}}$ ne pojmet.
       '(A person/one who is) full cannnot understand (a person/one who is) hungry.'

Summary: head suppression in the predicate LF ([$_{\text{nP}}$...**n** aP$_{<i>}$...]) is a special case of the nP head suppression phenomena illustrated in §2.8. The following sections present other types of empirical evidence that the predicate LF has the morphosyntactic structure of a null-headed predicate nominal nP.

2.9 nP diagnostic I: agreement with *vy* 'you (polite)'

The following evidence for the presence of the null-headed predicate nominal nP posited in (8b) ([$_{\text{vPcop}}$ *Vino*$_i$ [$_{\text{v'cop}}$ *bylo* [$_{\text{nP}}$ (t$_{\text{N}}$) **n** [$_{\text{aP<i>}}$ *vkusnoe*$_{\text{LF}}$]]]]) is based on the *number agreement* of SFs and LFs in SUBJECT+COPULA+ADJECTIVE constructions whose subject is *vy* 'you (pl.)' referring to *one* person in polite discourse (cf. *Sie* and *du* in German, *vous* and *tu* in French).[31] The aP$_i$-in-nP analysis of the predicate LF in (42)/(43) correctly predicts that the LF should pattern like the predicate nominal nP in (56), whose overt head *durak* is *singular* even though *vy* is formally plural: the head of a predicate nominal nP does not agree in number with the head of the subject nP (their features tend to *coincide*); cf. (56) and (57a). The copula *byli* in (56) is plural since it agrees directly with plural *vy*. The SF should, like the copula, be plural since it is the main predicator and agrees directly with *vy*. This is precisely the agreement pattern we find in (57): the SF in (57b) is *plural*, while the predicate LF in (57a) is *obligatorily singular* even though the copula is plural, just as in (56): the predicate LF agrees with the singular null head of the predicate nominal nP, not with the plural head *vy* of the sentence's subject nP.

(56)   Vy   (byli)   [$_{\text{nPNOM}}$ durak / *duraki].
       you:PL   (were:PL)   fool:SG (*PL)
       'You are (were) a fool.'

96 *The argument structure of adjectives*

(57) a. LF: Vy   (byli)   umnaja (*umnye).
          you:PL (were:PL) smart:LF.F.SG. (*PL)
          'You are (were) smart.'
     b. SF: Vy   (byli)   umny (*umna).
          you:PL (were:PL) smart:SF.PL.(*SG.F)
          'You are (were) smart.'
     c. PI: V oblasti nauki, esli (vy) budete$_{PL}$ priležnym$_{PI.SG}$, dob'etes'$_{PL}$ uspexa.
          'In the realm of science, if you are diligent, you will-achieve success.'

The two number-agreement patterns in (57a–b), i.e., [*vy* + V$_{cop.PL}$ + singular adjective] and [*vy* + V$_{cop.PL}$ + plural adjective], fall out automatically from my hypothesis, which is summarized in (58) and (59): the predicate LF in (57a) is *singular* because it agrees in number, case, and gender with the nominative singular head **n** of the predicate nominal nP containing it (see (58a–b)), not with the plural subject *vy*: the head of the predicate nominal nP is singular when polite *vy* is the subject. The SF in (57b) is plural because it is *not* contained in an nP and thus agrees *directly* with its plural subject *vy*, which is formally plural but semantically singular.

(58) a. Vy byli$_{PL}$ [$_{nP}$ [$_n$ durak$_{SG}$]].   (= (56))
        'You were a-fool.'
     b. Vy byli$_{PL}$ [$_{nP}$ **n** [$_{aP<i>}$umnaja$_{LF.SG}$]].   (= (57a))
        'You were smart.'
     c. Vy byli$_{PL}$ [$_{nP}$ ženščina$_{NOM.F.SG}$ [$_{aP<i>}$umnaja$_{LF.SG}$]].
        you were   woman   smart
        'You were a smart woman.'
     d. Vy byli$_{PL}$ [$_{aP}$ umny$_{SF.PL}$].   (= (57b))
        'You were smart.'

(59) a. SF: Vino$_i$ bylo   [$_{aP}$ (t$_N$) [$_{a'<i>}$ vkusno$_{SF}$]].^{32}
     b. LF: *Vino$_i$ bylo   [$_{aP<i>}$ vkusnoe$_{LF}$].
     c. LF Vino$_i$ bylo   [$_{nP}$ (t$_N$) [$_{n'<i>}$ **n** [$_{aP<i>}$ vkusnoe$_{LF}$]]].

Summary: Given my analysis of the SF and LF in (58) and (59), any subject-predicate agreement pattern other than the complex one we observe in (56) and (57) would be unexpected. The agreement pattern in (56) and (57) is entirely regular: anything that agrees *directly* with *vy* in number is plural (the copula and the SF); the predicate nominal nP is singular because it does not agree in number with *vy* and, therefore, given my analysis in (59c), neither should the predicate LF.

2.10 nP diagnostic II: third person personal pronouns

Sentences like (60a–b) provide another kind of evidence supporting the aP$_i$-in-nP analysis of the COPULA+LF construction. The third person personal pronoun has a use in Russian that it does not have in English: it can have the same function as the pronoun *one*. This can serve as an nP-diagnostic since the pronoun's antecedent must be an nP (see (61)). My aP$_i$-in-nP analysis of the predicate LF correctly predicts the well-formedness of (60a) and the unnaturalness of (60b): the SF *tak žestok* is not dominated by an nP and we thus do not expect it to antecede *im*$_{INST}$ ('it/him') in (60b): in (60a) it is the **n** head of [$_{nP}$ [$_{aP<i>}$ *takoj žestokij*] **n**] that antecedes *im*: we do not expect adjectives to antecede pronouns.

(60)   a. Ty vsegda byl [$_{nP}$ takoj žestokij$_{LF.NOM.M}$] ili stal **im**$_{INST.M}$ posle vojny?
you always was   such cruel   or became him after war
'Were you always [such a cruel person] or did you become one after the war?'
      b. ?* Ty vsegda byl [tak žestok$_{SF}$] ili stal **im** posle vojny?
'*Were you always so cruel or did you become one after the war.'

(61)   a. Ja   ne   trus   i   nikogda **im**   ne   byl.
I:NOM NEG coward:NOM and never   it:PI NEG was
'I am not a coward and never was one (lit. it/him$_{PI}$).'
      b. Ja ne krasavica$_{NOM.F}$ i nikogda ne smogu eju$_{PI.F}$ byt'. (A. Marinina)
'I (am) not a-beautiful-woman and I will never be able to be one (lit. her).'
      c. – Est' li u vas oružie$_{NOM.N}$? 'Do you have a weapon'?
– U menja est' ono$_{NOM.N}$. '(Yes) I have one (lit. it).' (Ju. Kopcov)
      d. Ètim kutilam ne podxodilo nazvanie *učenyx*, no oni$_{NOM.PL}$ byli *imi*$_{INST.PL}$.
'(lit.) These drunkards did not deserve the title of *scholars*, but they were them.' (A. Šaxnovič)

While there is complete agreement among Russian speakers that (60a) and (61) are natural and that (60b) is not, many speakers do not flatly reject (60b) as ungrammatical, as my hypothesis predicts they should. Since speaker judgments about (60b) are widely divergent, I will leave its status to future research. But what is crucial for us here is that the well-formedness and felicity of *takoj žestokij* in (60a) is predicted by its aP$_i$-in-nP predicate nominal structure.

2.10.1   tak + SF and takoj + LF
The distribution of *tak* and *takoj* in (60a–b) is itself an independent nP-diagnostic: *takoj* is formally an LF pronominal adjective that modifies nouns, *Nam*$_{DAT}$ *nužen*$_{SF.M}$ [$_{nP}$ *takoj*$_{NOM.M}$ (**takoj*) *rabotnik*$_{NOM.M}$] 'We need [such a-worker]', which means that *takoj* in (60a) is licensed by and agrees with the suppressed head **n** of the putative predicate nominal nP, not with the overt attributive LF *žestokij*.[33] *Tak* is an uninflected adverb and *tak* (**takoj*) *žestok*$_{SF}$ 'so cruel' in (60b) follows from the fact that SFs are the main predicates and are thus modified by adverbs, not adjectives. Thus SFs cannot be modified by *takoj*$_{LF}$ because they are not nP-internal (see (25)).

98   The argument structure of adjectives

(62)   On byl tak$_{ADV}$ (*takoj$_{LF}$) žestok$_{SF}$, čto ego$_{GEN}$ storonilis'$_{PL}$.
       'He was so cruel that (people) avoided him.'

2.11 nP diagnostic III: the predicate genitive

The V_{cop} + predicate-nominal nP analysis of the predicate LF is supported by the existence of the *predicate genitive* construction in sentences like (63a), whose properties can be accounted for in the same terms as the predicate LF, i.e., in terms of a predicate nominal nP whose suppressed head **n** is modifed by an adnominal genitive nP, as in (63b), rather than a LF adjective, as in (63d). Thus (63a) has the same syntactic structure as (63c), the only difference being that in (63c), the head of the predicate nominal nP is overt, i.e., SUBJECT + V_{cop} + [$_{nP}$ (t$_N$) **n** + MODIFIER], where the modifier is an agreeing LF adjective or a non-agreeing nP$_{GEN}$.

(63)   a. On$_{NOM}$ [$_{nPGEN}$ viskogo rosta].
          he (is) [of-tall   stature]
          'He is tall.'
       b. On (byl) [$_{nPNOM}$ (t$_N$) [$_{n'}$ [$_N$ **n**] [$_{nPGEN}$ vysokogo rosta]]].
       c. On (byl) [$_{nPNOM}$ (t$_N$) [$_{n'}$ [$_N$ čelovek] [$_{nPGEN}$ vysokogo rosta]]].
          'He is (a-person) of tall stature = He is a tall person.'
       d. Vino$_{NOM.N}$ (bylo) [$_{nPNOM}$ (t$_N$) [$_{n'}$ [$_N$ **n** / vino] [$_{aPi}$ vkusnoe$_{LF.NOM.N}$]]].
          '(The) wine is (was) (a) good (wine).'

(64c) is somewhat odd precisely because the repeated head of the predicate nominal has not been suppressed:

(64)   a. Odežda dlja putešestvija dolžna byt' [$_{nP}$ (t$_N$) **n** [$_{nP}$ sportivnogo pokroja]].
          'Clothing for travel   should be   of a-sporty cut.'
       b. [$_{nPNOM}$ odežda [$_{nPGEN}$ sportivnogo pokroja]]
          'clothing of a-sporty cut'
       c. ?Odežda dlja putešestvija dolžna byt' [$_{nP}$ odežda [$_{nP}$ sportivnogo pokroja]].
          'Clothing for travel should be clothing of a sporty cut.'
       d. Pokroj ee odeždy vsegda byl [$_{nP}$ **n** [$_{aP<i>}$ sportivnyj$_{LF}$]].
          'The-cut of her clothing was always sporty.'

Sentences like (65a) are crucial because [$_{nP}$ *bomba*$_{NOM}$ [$_{nPGEN}$ *zamedlennogo dejstvija*]] 'delayed action bomb (lit. bomb of slowed action)' is a fixed expression and **n** avoids the repetition of the easily recoverable second occurence of *bomba* (cf. (65c)); (66) is the syntactic structure of (65a). (67) to (69) are additional examples.

(65)   a. Bomba byla [$_{nP}$ **n** [$_{nPGEN}$ zamedlennogo dejstvija]].
          'The-bomb was (a) delayed-action (bomb).'

b. [nPNOM bomba [nPGEN zamedlennogo dejstvija]]
   'delayed-action bomb ([lit.] bomb of delayed action)'
c. ?Bomba byla [nP bomba [nPGEN zamedlennogo dejstvija]].
   'The-bomb was a delayed action bomb.'

(66)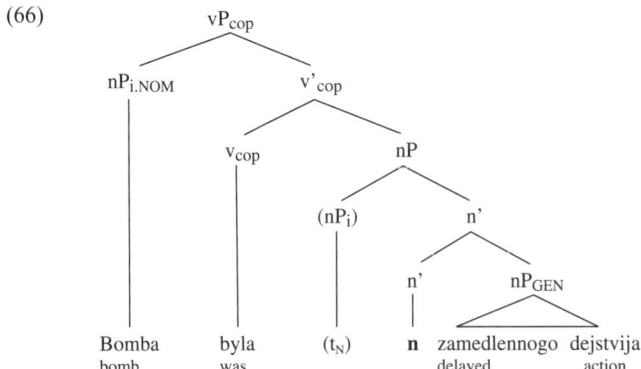

(67) a. Ženščina byla [nPGEN **n** dovol'no groznogo vida].
     '(lit.) (The) woman was [of quite scary appearance].'
   b. Dver' otkryla [nP ženščina dovol'no groznogo vida].
     '[A-woman [of quite scary appearance]] opened the-door.'
   c. ?Ženščina byla [nPNOM ženščina [nPGEN dovol'no_ADV groznogo vida]].

(68) a. Nikita – [nPNOM morjak [nPGEN staroj zakvaski]].
     'Nikita (is) (a) sailor [of the old school].'
   b. Èti morjaki – [nPNOM **n** [nPGEN staroj zakvaski]].
     'These sailors (are) [of the old school].'

(69) a. Sumka dolžna byt' [nPNOM **n** [nPGEN nebol'šogo razmera]].
     'The-bag should be [of small size].'
   b. Zamok byl [nPNOM **n** [nPGEN pružinnogo tipa]].
     'The-lock was [of (the) spring type].'
   c. Nikita [nPNOM **n** [nPGEN krupnogo telosloženija]].
     'Nikita (is) [(a man/person) of large build].'

The structures of the predicate genitive in (66) and the predicate LF in (42)/(43) suggest the following generalization: the nP$_i$ subject of copula-sentences is the initial external {i^N}$_1$ argument of the predicate phrase's head (see Moro 2000); cf. (68), (42)/(43), and the SF in (25).

In (70) and (71), the overt head of the accusative direct object nP has been extracted and preposed (topicalized), which is parallel to sentences like (50e): *Botinki*$_{ACC.PL}$ || *ja*$_{NOM}$ *nadel* [nPACC [t]$_N$ [afP<i> *grjaznye*$_{LF.ACC.PL}$]] 'Shoes I put on dirty' ("||" separates the *topic* from the *comment*).

(70) a. Material$_{ACC}$ || želatel'no vybrat' [$_{nPACC}$ t$_N$ [$_{nPGEN}$ skromnoj rascvetki]].
'(It is) desirable to-select [a material of modest color-scheme] ([lit.] Material ||
(it is) desirable to select [of modest color-scheme]).'
b. Želatel'no vybrat' [$_{nPACC}$ material [$_{nPGEN}$ skromnoj rascvetki]].

(71) a. Tufli$_{ACC}$ || ona$_{NOM}$ nosila [$_{nPacc}$ t$_N$ [$_{nPGEN}$ očen' malen'kogo razmera]].
'She wore [shoes [of a very small size]] ([lit.] Shoes || she wore of a very small size]).'
b. Ona nosila [$_{nPACC}$ tufli [$_{nPGEN}$ očen' malen'kogo razmera]].[34]

Summary: The structure of the predicate genitive in (66), which is virtually identical to (42)/(43), is independent evidence supporting the aP$_i$-in-nP structure of the predicate LF.

2.12 nP diagnostic IV: *kak* + nP$_{<i>}$

In this section we see another type of evidence that the predicate LF is adjoined to the projection of the **n** head of a predicate nominal nP. *Kak* 'as' in (72a) selects an nP complement: [$_{kP}$ [$_{k'}$ *kak* [$_{nP}$ *plenicu*]]] 'as a-prisoner' (kP = *kak*P phrase). The fact that *plenicu*$_{ACC}$ agrees in accusative case with its matrix-clause controller *ee*$_{ACC}$ tells us that *kak*'s phrasal projection must be an s-predicate kP$_i$, which is the vertically bound tail of the TBC headed by the accusative matrix direct object *ee*. Since *kak* is a functor and does not assign theta roles, kP$_i$ must inherit its unlinked external theta role **i** from its nP$_i$ complement. The fact that [$_{kPi}$ *kak* [$_{nP<i>}$ *plenicu*$_{ACC}$]] is a vertically bound s-predicate adjunct explains both the accusative case agreement of *plenicu* and kP$_i$'s *object control* by the direct object *ee*; cf. (72c), where kP$_i$ is *subject-controlled* and its nP$_i$ complement *sel'di* 'herring' is accordingly nominative.

(72) a. Nam   pridetsja vzjat'   **ee**$_j$ s   soboj
         us:DAT must   take   her:$_j$.ACC.F with   self:INST
         [$_{kP<i>}$ kak [$_{nP<i>}$ **plenicu**]].
                    as   hostage:ACC.F
         'We must take her$_{ACC}$ with us (lit. ourselves) [as a-hostage$_{ACC}$].'
      b. **Ego**   vstretili kak   **geroja**.
         him:ACC.M.SG met:PL   as   hero:ACC.M.SG
         '(Unspecified persons) greeted him [as a-hero].'
      c. **My**   tesnilis'   v vagone kak **sel'di**   v bočke.
         we:NOM   crowded   in car   like herrings:NOM in barrel
         'We$_{NOM}$ were-squeezed in the railway-car [like herrings$_{NOM}$ in a-barrel].'
      d. My   ne   možem prenebregat' **eju**   kak   **svidetelem**.[35]
         we:NOM NEG able to-disregard   her:INST as   witness:INST
         'We cannot disregard her as a witness.'

The analysis of kP$_i$ as a controlled s-predicate adjunct with an nP$_{<i>}$ complement (i.e. [$_{kPi}$ [$_{k'}$ *kak* nP$_{<i>}$]]) correctly predicts that LFs but not SFs can be the complement of *kak*: according to my analysis, only LFs can occur nP-internally, and the complement of kP$_i$ is an nP$_i$. Consider the following *kak* + LF sentences.

(73) Object-controlled kP$_i$:
 a. Storonilis' **menja** [$_{kP<i>}$ kak **zaražennogo**].
    avoided:PL me:GEN.M   like infected:LF.GEN.M
    '(People) avoided me like (one) infected (= like the plague).'
 b. On obnaružil neskol'ko otpečatkov, **kotorye**$_{j.ACC.PL}$ on opredelil t$_k$ [$_{kP<i>}$ [$_{k'}$ kak [$_{nP<i>ACC}$ **n** [$_{aP<i>}$ **prinadležaščie**$_{LF.ACC.PL}$ generalu$_{DAT}$]]]].[36]
    'He discovered several fingerprints, which$_{ACC}$ he identified [as belonging$_{ACC}$ to the general].'
 c. položenie, **kotoroe**$_{ACC.N}$ možno rassmatrivat' kak **komprometirujuščee**$_{LF.ACC.N}$.
    situation which   possible to-view   as compromising
    'a-situation which$_{ACC}$ (it is) possible to-view [as compromising$_{ACC}$]'

(74) Subject-controlled kP$_i$ (see (72c)):
 a. **Takaja gibel'**$_{NOM.F}$ ne možet rassmatrivat'sja [$_{kP<i>}$ kak [$_{nP<i>}$ **n**$_{NOM}$ [$_{aP<i>}$ slučajnaja$_{LF.NOM.F}$ (*slučajna$_{SF}$)]]].
    'Such destruction cannot be viewed [as accidental (destruction)].'[37]
 b. **Ona**$_{NOM.F}$ stojala$_F$ [kak gromom **poražennaja**$_{LF.NOM.F}$ (*poražena$_{SF}$)].
    'She stood [as-though struck by-lightning].'
 c. **Ona** xoxotala, kak **bezumnaja**$_{LF.NOM.F}$ (*bezumna$_{SF.NOM.F}$).
    '(lit.) She laughed like (a) crazy (person) (= as though she were crazy).'
 d. Naše **otdelenie**$_{NOM.N}$ sozdavalos' kak **èlitnoe**$_{LF.NOM.N}$. (A. Marinina)
    'Our department was-created as (an) elite (one/department).'

Since *kak* selects an nP, *kak* + LF has the following structure: [$_{kPi}$ kak [$_{nP<i>}$ **n** aP$_{<i>}$]], where kP$_i$'s unlinked external theta role i is inherited from nP$_i$, which V-binds aP$_i$. This supports my hypothesis that predicate LFs are V-bound in predicate nominal nPs with a suppressed head **n** (see (59c)).

However, we need to consider the possibility that the LF merges directly with *kak* and is therefore not contained in an nP, which is a priori possible because kP$_i$'s nP$_i$ or nP$_j$ antecedents are arguments of the matrix verb, i.e., [$_{vP}$...nP$_{i/j}$...[$_{kP<i>}$ [$_{k'<i>}$ kak aP$_{<i>}$]]]: nP$_{i/j}$ is the head of the TBC in which [*kak* aP$_i$] would be V-bound. But sentences like (75a), in which the *kak*-phrase functions not as an adjunct as above, but as the *main predicate of a copula sentence*, demonstrate that [$_{kP}$ kak [$_{nP}$ **n** aP$_{<i>}$]] is the correct structure, i.e., *kak* 'as, like' always selects an nP, which can be either an nP predicate nominal or an nP$_i$ s-predicate complement; in the former case, the obligatory copula's subject is inherited from the predicate nominal nP (see §2.6.2 and §2.11).

(75) a. Kniga   byla   [kak novaja$_{LF}$ (*nova$_{SF}$ / *novoj$_{PI}$)].
     book:NOM.F was:F like new:LF.NOM.F (*SF / *PI).
     'The-book was like new.'
  b. Ruka$_{NOM.F}$ byla$_F$ kak stekljannaja$_{LF.NOM.F}$ (tol'ko čto ne zvenela)].
     '(Her) hand was like glass (it all but rang).' (L. Ulickaja)
  c. A   sejčas ty kak v vodu opuščennaja.
     but   now   you like in water submerged:LF.NOM.F
     '(lit.) But now you are like (someone who has been) submerged in water.'

(75a) cannot have the structure in (76), where *novaja*$_{LF}$ and *kak* merge directly, for the same reason that, in the derivation of *Kniga byla novaja*$_{LF}$ 'The-book was new,' the LF *novaja* cannot merge directly with the copula *byla* and have the structure in (10) above: in both cases the LF, which is an s-predicate (aP$_i$), cannot license the subject nP (*kniga*). In other words, (76) is ill-formed because kP$_i$, which is an s-predicate, is functioning as the main predicate, which entails a Projection Principle violation. The correct structure of (75a) is thus (77).

(76)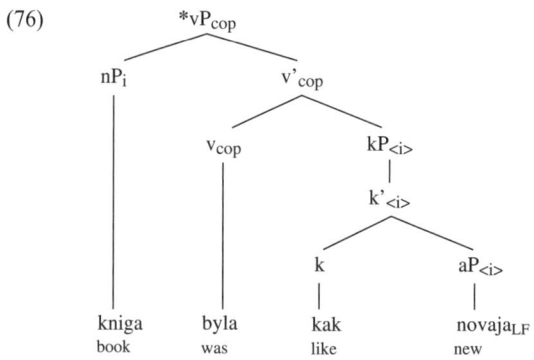

(77)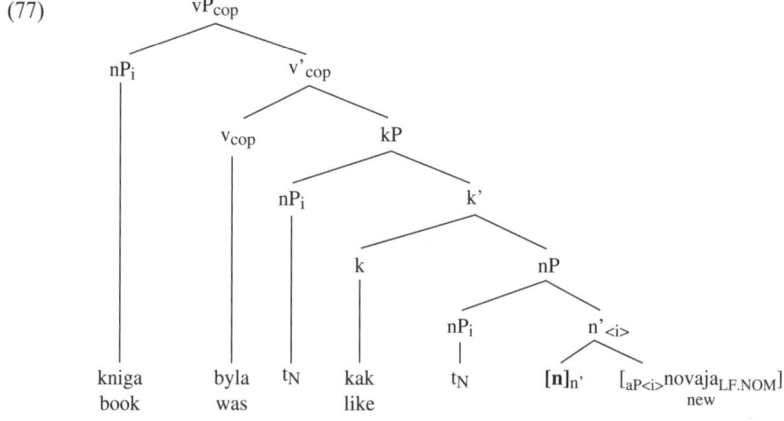

According to (77), the LF *novaja* is contained in a null-headed predicate nominal nP complement of *kak*, which licenses the nominative subject *kniga*, just as the predicate nominal nP licenses the nominative subject nP in (35) above: cf. [$_{vPcop}$ *On byl* [$_{nP}$ (t$_N$) [$_{n'}$ *učitel'*]]] 'He was a teacher.'

We conclude on the basis of this analysis that *kak* selects either an *nP$_i$ s-predicate* complement when it is an adjunct (as in (73) and (74)) or an *nP s-clause* complement (i.e., [$_{nP}$ nP$_{i.NOM}$ n'$_{<i>}$]) when it is the main predicate, in which case it must compose with the copula (see (75a)/(77)). More specifically, in the case of (75a)/(77), since *kak* does not assign theta roles, the subject of the sentence *kniga* merges first in spec-position of the nP predicate nominal and then raises to spec-vP$_{cop}$ via spec-kP (see (77)) (we return to the copula and the structure of (77) in §2.16).

This derivation also explains why [*kak* SF] is ill-formed (see (75a)): as demonstrated above, *kak* selects a noun phrase as its complement, and SFs are never nP-constituents. The ill-formedness of the PI (**Kniga$_{NOM.F}$ byla$_F$ kak novoj$_{PL.F}$*) in (75a) is treated in §5.9.

Summary:

(78)   a.   Kniga$_{NOM.F}$ byla$_F$ [$_{nP}$ (t$_N$) **n** [$_{aP<i>}$ novaja$_{NOM.LF.F}$]].
           'The-book was new.'
       b.   Kniga$_{NOM.F}$ byla$_F$ [$_{kP}$ (t$_N$) kak [$_{nP}$ (t$_N$) **n** [$_{aP<i>}$ novaja$_{NOM.LF.F}$]]].
           'The-book was like new.'
       c.   *Kniga byla [$_{kP}$ kak [$_{nP}$...nova$_{SF.NOM.SG}$...]].
       d.   *Kniga$_i$ byla [$_{aP<i>}$ novaja].
       e.   *Kniga$_i$ byla [$_{kP<I>}$ kak [$_{aP<i>}$ novaja]].

2.13   Predicate nominals with unsuppressed heads

The syntactic structures of SF and predicate LF sentences proposed above and summarized in (79) also account for the meaning that has been attributed to the LF and SF in sentence pairs like (80a–b).[38] For example, Isačenko's (1963: 75) understanding of the semantic difference between these constructions is best reflected in his paraphrase of (80a–b) in (81a–b); cf. also his German translation of (82a) in (82b).[39]

(79)   a.   SF: [$_{vPcop}$ Vino$_i$ [$_{v'cop}$ bylo [$_{aP}$ (t$_N$) [$_{a'<i>}$ vkusno$_{SF}$]]]]
       b.   SF: *[$_{vPcop}$ Vino$_i$ [$_{v'cop}$ bylo [$_{nP}$ **n** [$_{aP}$ [$_{a'<i>}$ vkusno$_{SF}$]]]]]
       c.   LF: [$_{vPcop}$ Vino$_i$ [$_{v'cop}$ bylo [$_{nP}$ (t$_N$) **n** [$_{aP<i>}$ vkusnoe$_{LF}$]]]]
       d.   LF: *[$_{vPcop}$ Vino$_i$ [$_{v'cop}$ bylo [$_{aP<i>}$ vkusnoe$_{LF}$]]]

(80)   a.   LF: Kitajskij   jazyk   očen'   trudnyj.
              Chinese   language:NOM.M   very   difficult:LF.NOM.M
              'The-Chinese language is a very difficult language.'

b. SF: Kitajskij jazyk očen' truden.
Chinese language very difficult:SF.NOM.M
'The-Chinese language is very difficult.'

(81) a. LF: Kitajskij jazyk otnositsja k klassu trudnyx jazykov. (= (80a))
'Chinese belongs to the class of difficult languages.'
b. SF: Trudnost' – svojstvo kitajskogo jazyka. (= (80b))
'Difficulty is a property of the Chinese language.'

(82) a. Ètot vopros političeskij.
this question:NOM.M political:LF.NOM.M
'This question is (a) political (one).'
b. Diese Frage ist eine politische.
'This question is a political (one).'

Since my hypothesis is that the predicate LF *vkusnoe* in (79c) and *trudnyj* in (80a) modify the null **n** head of a predicate nominal nP, their semantic interpretation is predictably akin to that of a *restrictive relative clause*, i.e., the property denoted by the predicate LF adjective is construed as being attributed to the subject of the sentence with respect to the class (set) of objects it belongs to (see Babby 1975 and 1998b, Stepanov 1981: 152, Isačenko 1963, Švedova 1952: 92). The meaning of (79c) is thus '*This/the wine is* [$_{nP}$ *a-good-wine/one*]', i.e., good with respect to other wines.[40] SFs, which are not contained in a predicate nominal nP, do not have this meaning: they are *unmarked* for class-membership (see (80b) = (81b)). In other words, the SF in (79a) conveys the same real-world information as the LF in (79c) without reference to the subject's class membership.[41] This analysis entails that the difference in meaning characterized in (80) and (81) above is not an inherent property of the LF and SF suffixes; it derives from the overall syntactic configurations which these suffixes lexicalize.

The structure-based meaning of the predicate LF proposed above makes a series of correct predictions. For example, nouns that have unique denotation, i.e., belong to a class of one, or denote actions/events, predictably cannot be the subject of a sentence with a predicate LF in standard Russian. For example, only the SF is natural in (83) because there is only one *outer-space*, i.e., in ordinary usage, there is no class of *outer-spaces* such that one can be singled out by the *restrictive* semantics associated with the predicate LF.[42]

(83) Prostranstvo beskonečno (*beskonečnoe).
space:NOM.N infinite:SF.NOM.N (*LF)
'Space is infinite (*Space is an infinite one).'

(84) Prestupnik ponjal, čto soprotivlenie bespolezno$_{SF}$ (*?bespoleznoe$_{LF}$).
'The-criminal understood that resistence was futile (*a futile one).'

The LF-in-nP structure of the predicate LF also predicts that pronouns like *èto* 'this', *vse* 'everything', and (*to*) *čto* '(the fact) that, what,' which cannot be modified by a relative clause, cannot be the subject of a predicate LF sentence (see Švedova 1952: 97).

(85) Èto bylo vozmožno$_{SF.N}$ (*vozmožnoe$_{LF.N}$).
    'This was possible.'

(86) Važno$_{SF.N}$ (*važnoe$_{LF.NOM.N}$) [$_{nP.NOM}$ to, [$_{CP}$ čto Nikita$_{NOM}$ ponjal Annu$_{ACC}$]].
    '[The-fact that Nikita understood Anna] is important$_{SF(*LF)}$.'

In sentences like (87), which have infinitive-clause subjects, the predicate LF is predictably excluded: *-o* of *neželatel'n-o* here is the nonagreeing (default) suffix, which is used when the subject has no inherent agreement features, as in the case of infinitive and CP subjects.

(87) [Perenosit' doklad na bolee pozdnij srok] bylo neželatel'n-o (*neželatel'noe$_{LF}$).
    [to-postpone the-report to a later date] was undesirable
    'It was undesirable [$_{infP}$ to-postpone the-report to a later date].'

(88) Teper' ponjatn-o (*ponjatn-oe$_{LF}$), [$_{CP}$ čto delat' dal'še].
    'Now (it is) clear (*a clear one) [what to-do next].'

The following piece of evidence supporting the LF-in-nP structure of the predicate LF is crucial: although the head **n** of the predicate nominal nP in (42)/(43) is canonically null, it can be made overt for stylistic reasons (cf. *This wine is really good ~ This wine is a really good wine (one)!*), provided that it is identical to the subject or is a nonreferential, semantically bleached classifier like *čelovek* 'person', *vešč'* 'thing', etc., which do not normally head predicate nominals unless they are modified by an adjective or nP$_{GEN}$ (see §2.11). Since the LF is the *focus* of these overtly headed predicate nominals, it is *postposed* (attributive adjectives normally precede the noun they modify in Russian) (see Kustova *et al.* 2005: 9). Siegel 1976 identifies the head of the nP in sentences like (79c) as a free variable ranging over common nouns. Compare the predicate LF in [*Anna* [$_{nP}$ (*ženščina*) *xitraja*$_{LF}$]] 'Anna is (a) clever (woman)' and the 'predicate genitive' in [*Anna* [$_{nP}$ (*ženščina*) [$_{nPGEN}$ *krepkogo zdorov'ja*]]] 'Anna is (a woman) of robust health.'

The overt head **n** of the COPULA + [$_{nP}$ **n**...LF$_{<i>}$] construction, in keeping with its reduced semantic role, is pronounced with accelerated tempo, reduced stress, and precedes the LF, which has the effect of defocusing the nP's head and shifting focus to its postposed LF modifier. Traditional grammars of Russian attempt to capture this relation by classifying the predicate nominal's overt head in sentences like (89) as a "copula word" whose function is to link the subject to the "predicate LF" (cf. Tolstoy 1966: 181); e.g., it is claimed that (89a) has the following structure: [*Ona*]~subject~ + [*ženščina*]~copula~ + [*umnaja*~LF~]~predicate adjective~.

(89)   a. Ona [~nP~ (ženščina)   umnaja~LF~].
              she   woman   smart
              'She is (a) smart (woman).'
       b. Teper'-to ja nejtralen~SF~ ... Povtorjaju, teper' ja [~nP~ čelovek nejtral'nyj~LF~].
           'Now I (am) neutral. I-repeat, now I (am) (a) neutral person.'
       c. Vy~PL~ (ženščina~F.SG~) krasivaja~LF.NOM.F.SG~, èlegantnaja~LF.NOM.F.SG~.
           'You are (a) beautiful, elegant (woman).' (see §2.9)
       d. Knigi – vešč' xorošaja.
           'Books (are a) good thing.'

The intuition that the defocused head of the predicate nominal in (89a) has a special semantically reduced copula function follows naturally from the fact that here it is the postposed LF *umnaja* 'smart' that carries the essential information.[43] However, as far as syntactic structure is concerned, the generic, semantically bleached head noun and its postposed modifier are constituents of the same predicate nominal nP, whose head noun is not a copula in any syntactic sense.

In (90) we see typical examples of the V_{cop} + [~nP~ **n** LF] construction where the reference of the suppressed head **n** is clear from the immediate context.

(90)   a. Mama priznavala, čto Maša~NOM~ [~PP~ iz dvux sester~GEN~] glavnaja~LF.NOM~.
           mama admitted   that Maša   from two sisters   main
           'Mama admitted that [of the two sisters] Masha (is) (the) main~LF~ (sister/one).'
       b. Bol'šoj nož – edinstvennyj~LF~ režuščij~LF~ vo vsem dome.
           big   knife   only   cutting   in entire houses
           'The-big knife is the only knife/one that cuts (lit. only cutting~LF~) in the whole house.'
       c. Prjamoj put' ne vsegda samyj vygodnyj~LF~.
           'The direct path is not always the most advantageous~LF~ (path/one).'
       d. Èto prokljatoe delo~NOM.N~ [takoe~LF.NOM.N~ (*tak~ADV~) zaputannoe~LF.NOM.N~].
           'This damned case is [such an intricate~LF~ (case/one)].' (see §2.10.1)
       e. Suščestvujut dve versii~GEN.F~ ètogo èpizoda, i mne plevat', [kakaja~LF.NOM.F~ iz nix pravil'naja~LF.NOM.F~].
           'There-exist two versions of-this episode, and I couldn't care less, [which of them (is) (the) correct~LF.NOM.F~ (version/one)].'
       f. On byl   samyj~LF~   sposobnyj~LF~.
           'He was (the) most   capable (one).'

Režuščij 'cutting' in (90b) is a *-šč*-participle, which is an inherent s-predicate and thus occurs in the LF only (see chapter 3). Since an LF cannot be a primary predicate, *režuščij* must be contained in a null-headed predicate nominal nP and its unlinked external theta role [*režuščij*]₍ₐP<ᵢ>₎ is therefore V-bound nP-internally by **n**. This is confirmed by the fact that the LF adjective *edinstvennyj* 'only' in (90b) must be modifying the [n' [aP<i> *režuščij*] **n**] consituent since LF adjectives do not directly modify other LF adjectives and participles; cf. (90f).

2.14   aP<i> adjoined to nP

We have seen aP$_i$ when it is adjoined nP-internally, as in (79c) and (20), and nP-externally, as in (21) and (23): *Ee*$_{ACC.F}$ *uložili*$_{PL}$ *v postel' odetuju*$_{LF.ACC.F}$ '(Someone) put her to bed dressed.' There is a third possibility, namely, aP$_i$ adjoined to nP$_i$: [$_{nPi}$ nP<i> aP<i>] and [$_{nPi}$ aP<i> nP<i>], as in: [$_{nPi}$ [aP<i> *Golodnye*$_{LF.NOM.PL}$] # [$_{nP<i>}$ *tarakany*$_{NOM.PL}$]] *snovali po stenam* '(Because they were) hungry, the-cockroaches were-scurrying around the- walls.' This construction provides additional empirical support for my analysis of the LF and SF (see (24)), which predicts the ill-formedness of SFs and the well-formedness of LFs in sentences like (91), (92), and (95) to (97).

We will look first at the LF adjective adjoined to the nP complement of a preposition: [$_{PP}$ [$_{P'}$ P [$_{nPi}$ nP<i> aP<i>]]]; both the SF and PI are ill-formed in this configuration. The preposition *na* 'at' in (91) assigns accusative case to its nP complement, which is headed by the reflexive pronoun *sebja*. The LF *goluju* agrees in case, gender, and number with *sebja*, which is the head of its TBC; the antecedent of *sebja* is the subject *ja*, which is thus construed as the understood subject (controller) of *goluju* (see §2.3); (92) contains additional examples.[44]

(91)   Ja ne ljublju smotret'   na **sebja**   **goluju** (*gola / *goloj)
       I NEG like to-look   at self:ACC.F naked:LF.ACC.F (*SF / *PI)
       'I don't like to look at myself (when I am) naked (in the mirror).'

(92)   a. Naručniki   snimut   s   **nego**   **mertvogo** (*mertvym).
          handcuffs:ACC remove:PL from him:GEN.M dead:LF.GEN.M (*PI)
          '(Unspecified agent) will remove the handcuffs from him (only when he is) dead.'
       b. Ty dolžen streljat' v **nego**$_{ACC}$ **pervogo**$_{LF.ACC}$ (*pervym$_{PI}$).
          'You must shoot at him first = he has to be the first one you shoot at.'
       c. Ty dolžen streljat' v **nego**$_{ACC}$ **pervyj**$_{NOM}$ / **pervym**$_{PI}$.
          'You must shoot at him first = you have to be the first one to shoot at him.'
          (*pervyj* 'first' here adjoins to v'$_i$ and the subject *ty* is the head of its TBC)
       d. Žesty xarakterny [$_{PP}$ dlja **nego rasserzennogo**].
          '(These) gestures (are) characteristic [for him$_{GEN}$ (when he is) angry$_{LF.GEN}$].'

108 *The argument structure of adjectives*

Given the obligatory case agreement between *sebja*$_{ACC.F}$ and *goluju*$_{LF.ACC.F}$ (91), the aP$_i$-to-nP$_i$ adjunction analysis in (93a) below is the only option: [$_{aP<i>}$ *goluju*] is V-bound by [$_{nPi}$ *sebja*] in [$_{nPi}$ [$_{nP<i>}$ *sebja*$_{ACC}$] [$_{aP<i>}$ *goluju*$_{ACC}$]] and thus agrees with it in case, gender, and number.[45] (93b) is not an option because LFs do not license subjects nPs of any kind and are never primary predicates.

(93) a. [$_{PP}$ na [$_{nPi}$ [$_{nPi}$ sebja$_{ACC}$] [$_{aP<i>}$ goluju$_{LF.ACC}$]]]
'at herself (when she is) naked'
b. *[$_{PP}$ na [$_{nPi}$ [$_{nPi}$ sebja] [$_{aP}$ PRO$_i$ [$_{a'<i>}$ goluju]]]]
c. *[$_{PP}$ na [$_{nPi}$ [$_{n'}$ [$_{n'}$ sebja] [$_{aP<i>}$ goluju]]]]

(93c), where *sebja* and [*goluju*]$_{aP<i>}$ are inside the *same* minimal nP, cannot be the correct structure of (91) because it gives the wrong meaning: when aP$_i$ (LF) is bound inside nP, it has an attributive, relative-clause-like reading. It is only when aP$_i$ adjoins to the root nP$_i$ node (maximal projection), as in (93a), that it is construed, depending on context, as a *when* or *because* clause, not a relative clause. Speaking in general terms, (94a) below represents modification (attribution) and (94b) represents *secondary predication*. Since both involve the vertical binding of aP$_i$, we must conclude that predication is a theta relation between maximal phrasal projections (see McCloskey 1997: 221).

(94) a. aP$_i$ in its *attributive* function: [$_{nP}$ [$_{n'}$ n'$_i$ aP$_{<i>}$]] or [$_{nP}$ [$_{n'}$ aP$_{<i>}$ n'$_i$]]
b. aP$_i$ in its *predicational* function: [$_{nPi}$ nP$_{<i>}$ aP$_{<i>}$] or [$_{nPi}$ aP$_{<i>}$ nP$_{<i>}$]

The efficacy of the complementary definitions of attribution and predication in (94) is nicely illustrated by the sentence pair in (95a–b), where the preposed LF *golodnyj* 'hungry' appears to be in the same linear position in both sentences. The only perceptible difference between them is the prosodic gap (#) in (95a) and its absence in (95b). This difference correlates with a clear-cut, systematic difference in meaning: *golodnyj* 'hungry' in (95b) is construed as having essentially the same restrictive meaning as a relative clause (cf. (96b)), while *golodnyj* in (95a) can be paraphrased by a *because*-clause.

(95) a. Golodnyj #   mal'čik   otpravilsja domoj.
         hungry:NOM.LF.M   boy:NOM.M   went   home.
         'The-boy went home because he was hungry.'
      b. Golodnyj   mal'čik   otpravilsja domoj.
         hungry:LF.NOM.M   boy:NOM.M   went   home
         'The hungry boy went home = the boy who was hungry…'
      c. *Goloden$_{SF}$ # mal'čik otpravilsja domoj.
      d. *Goloden$_{SF}$ mal'čik otpravilsja domoj.
      e. Ispugannyj$_{LF.NOM}$ # golodnyj$_{LF.NOM}$ mal'čik$_{NOM}$ otpravilsja domoj.
         frightened   hungry   boy   went   home
         '(Because he was) frightened the-boy (who was) hungry went home.'

(96)   a. Golodnyj # on otpravilsja domoj.
       'He went home (because he was) hungry.'
       b. *Golodnyj on otpravilsja domoj.
       *'Hungry he went home.'
       c. [$_{nP}$ **n** [$_{aP<i>}$ Golodnyj]] otpravilsja domoj.
       '[(The-person who was) hungry] went home.'

The semantic difference between sentences like (95a–b) can be accounted for directly in terms of the difference in their syntactic structures, which are schematically represented in (97) and (98) (see McCloskey 1997: 221).

(97)   [$_{nPi.NOM}$ [$_{aP<i>}$ golodnyj] # [$_{nP<i>}$ mal'čik / on]] otpravilsja domoj.
              hungry   boy / he   went   home
       '(Because/when he was) hungry, the-boy / he went home.'

(98)   [$_{nPi.NOM}$ [$_{n'<i>}$ [$_{aP<i>}$ Golodnyj] [$_{n'<i>}$ mal'čik / *on]]] otpravilsja domoj.
       'The hungry boy /*he went home.'

My analysis of the SF correctly predicts that an ill-formed sentence results if we replace the LF *golodnyj* with the SF *goloden*, as in (95c–d): SFs have an intact external {i^N}$_1$ argument, which, as we have seen above, must be realized syntactically as the subject of V$_{cop}$, which is impossible in (95c–d).

The [$_{nPi}$ aP$_{<i>}$ nP$_{<i>}$] adjunction configuration proposed above to account for the form and meaning of (97) makes another correct prediction: since the [$_{nPi}$ aP$_{<i>}$ nP$_{<i>}$] predicational relation is wholly contained inside nP, it should not be limited to the subject nP and, therefore, to the nominative case, which is precisely what we saw above in (91) and (92), where the case of [$_{nPi}$ nP$_{<i>}$ aP$_{<i>}$] is determined by the head of the PP containing it: *Ja ne ljublju smotret'* [$_{PP}$ *na* [$_{nPi·ACC}$ [*sebja*$_{nP<i>ACC}$] [$_{aP<i>}$ *goluju*$_{LF.ACC.F}$]]] 'I don't like to-look [at [myself (when I'm) naked]].' The specific prediction that my analysis makes is that [$_{nPi}$ aP$_{<i>}$ nP$_{<i>}$] should be able to occur in any nP position and, therefore, that the case of aP$_{<i>}$ should be determined by the case assigned to the dominating nP by virtue of its function in the sentence, i.e., [$_{nPi.α}$ aP$_{<i>α}$ nP$_{i.α}$] (α is a variable case feature). Sentences with preposed [$_{nPi.α}$ aP$_{<i>α}$ nP$_{i.α}$] are in fact very common: see (99) and (100). In (99a), [$_{nPACC}$ *Vkonec izmučennogo # ego*] is the preposed accusative direct object nP of the impersonal transitive verb *vybrosilo* (-*o* is the nonagreeing suffix); see Babby 1994c.

(99)   a. [$_{nPi}$ Vkonec   izmučennogo #   ego]   vybrosilo na bereg.
              completely exhausted:LF.ACC.M him:ACC.M threw   on shore
       'He was washed-up completely exhausted on the beach.'

110   *The argument structure of adjectives*

        b. [$_{nPi.ACC}$ [$_{aP<i>}$ Vkonec izmučennogo$_{ACC}$] # [$_{nP<i>}$ ego$_{ACC}$]] vybrosilo na bereg.
        c. *Vkonec izmučennyj$_{LF.NOM}$ # ego$_{ACC}$ vybrosilo na bereg.
        d. *Vkonec izmučennogo ego vybrosilo na bereg.

(100)   a. Imenno teper', bol'nomu$_{LF.DAT}$ # emu$_{DAT}$ ponadobilas' Liza$_{NOM}$. (I. Grekova)
        '(It was) precisely now, (since/when he was) sick, he needed Liza.'
        b. *Imenno teper', bol'noj$_{NOM}$ # emu$_{DAT}$ ponadobilas' Liza$_{NOM}$.

2.15   The derivation of -en- participles

The diathesis of the **-en-** participle suffix composes with the diathesis of perfective transitive **V**s to form stative participles, one of whose functions is expression of **V**'s passive voice, as in (101a).[46] **-en-** participles are of interest because, as we see in (101b) and (102), unlike lexical adjectives, they cannot be 'predicate LFs' despite the fact that, like lexical adjectives, they compose with LF and SF suffixes.

(101)   a. Prestupnik   byl   pojman   (Annoj).
          criminal:NOM.M   was:M   captured:SF:NOM.M   (Anna:INST)
          'The-criminal was captured (by Anna).'
        b. *Prestupnik byl pojmannyj:LF.NOM.M (*pojmannym:PI.M).
          'The criminal was captured.'
        c. [$_{nP}$ pojmannyj$_{LF}$ (*pojman$_{SF}$) prestupnik]
          'the captured criminal'

(102)   Kniga byla izdana$_{SF}$ (*izdannaja$_{LF}$ / *izdannoj$_{PI}$) v prošlom godu.
        'The-book was published last year.'

Since **-en-** carries adjectival categorial features, composes with adjectival inflectional endings, and is the head of derived **[V-en-]**, **-en**-participles are morphosyntactically adjectives with encapsulated verbal properties inherited from **V**'s diathesis (see chapter 3 for the derivation of *hybrid* categories). We see in (103) that **V**'s external theta role **i** is *dethematized* ({i^N}$_1$ > {-^N}$_1$), i.e., *right-displaced* in passive derivations or *deleted* in middle derivations (*Frukty*$_{j.NOM.PL}$ *isporč-en-y*$_{SF.PL}$ 'The-fruit (is/has) spoiled'). **V**'s internal **j** theta role *externalizes* when **i** is dethematized:

(103)   Derivation of the **-en**-participle stem:
        a. {{i ^ N}$_1$ {j ^ N}$_2$ {k ^ N}$_3$ {- ^ V-}$_4$}   +
        b. {{- ^ }$_1$ { ^ - }$_2$ { ^ }$_3$ { ^ -en- }$_4$}   >
        c. {{- ^ N}$_1$ { j ^ - }$_2$ { k ^ N}$_3$ {(i) ^ [V-en-] }$_4$}   >>
        d. {{j ^ N}$_1$ { - ^ - }$_2$ { k ^ N}$_3$ {(i) ^ [V-en-] }$_4$}

2.15 The derivation of -en- participles

V's diathesis in (103a) composes with **-en**-'s diathesis in (103b) to yield the derived unaccusative diathesis in (103c); **j** in {j^-}$_2$ obligatorily *externalizes*, i.e., relinks to {-^N}$_1$, yielding the **-en**-participle *stem* diathesis in (103d), which projects a well-formed morphosyntactic structure only after it composes with the diathesis of either the SF or LF suffix (see below), creating a *word*, the basic unit of the syntactic phase of the derivation. **-en**-participles are passive when dethematized **i** is made *implicit* (i.e., {-^[V-en-]}$_4$ > {i^[V-en-]}$_4$); they are realized as nonpassive stative/middle participles if **i** is deleted. Only implicit **i** licenses the *by*-phrase. The passive ~ stative distinction is encoded in (103) by the parenthesis notation **(i)**, which specifies the option of deleting dethematized **i** or making it implicit.

The last step in the derivation in (103) is composition of (103d) with the diathesis of either an SF or LF suffix. If the SF suffix is selected, **[V-en-]** > **[[V-en-]-a$_{SF}$]** and externalized {j^N}$_1$ projects to syntax as the sentence's nP$_j$ nominative subject (recall that **-a** is an adjective affix). Like the SF of lexical adjectives, SF **-en**-participles must combine with the copula. The syntactic structure of (101a) is (104) or (105), depending on whether we treat aP as an s-clause whose subject *raises* from spec-aP to spec-V$_{cop}$ in syntax, as in (104), or as a *bare* aP, which is formed when the diatheses of **[V-a]** and the copula *compose* and the copula inherits **[V-a]**'s external {i^N}$_1$ argument, as in (105). We shall see below and in chapter 5 that (105) is correct: there are no adjective, participle, or predicate nominal nP s-clauses in Russian syntax. Note that the difference between the syntactic vs. diathetic derivations of *byl pojman* 'was captured' in (101a) shows up in syntactic representation only as the presence vs. absence of a trace t$_N$ in (104) and (105): recall that diathetic operations do not leave traces.

(104)

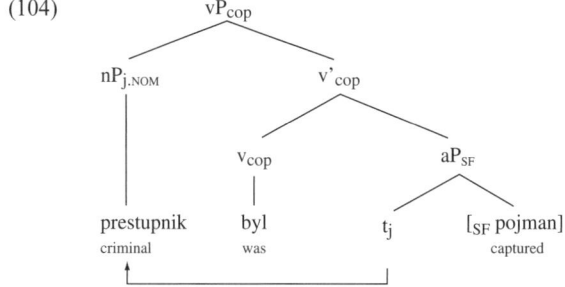

112   *The argument structure of adjectives*

(105)

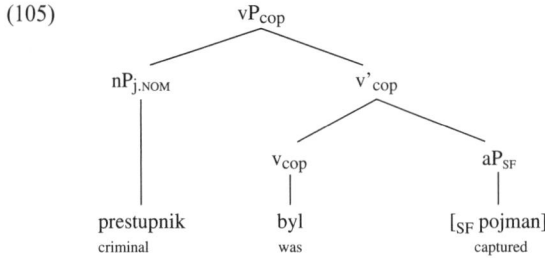

If the [**V-en**] stem in (103d) composes with the LF suffix, **V**'s initial external **N** is deleted, which means that externalized **j** is left unlinked, creating an **-en**-participle s-predicate aP$_j$, which cannot merge directly with the copula for the same reason that the LF of lexical adjectives cannot; see (106) and (107), both of which are ill-formed because they violate the Projection Principle: the subject nP cannot have been projected from the LF's final diathesis.

(106)

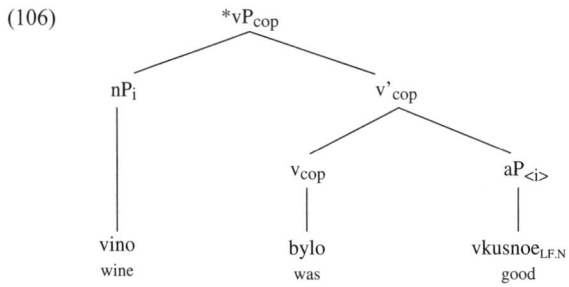

(107)

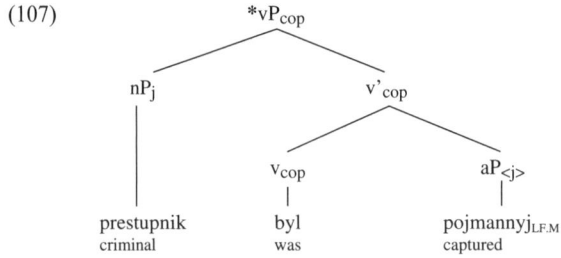

But there is still a loose end: why is the predicate LF of **-en**-participles ill-formed in passive sentences like (101b) (*Prestupnik byl *pojmannyj$_{LF}$ / pojman$_{SF}$* 'The-criminal was captured')? If predicate LFs have the structure in (46c) ([$_{vPcop}$ *Vino$_i$* [$_{v'cop}$ *bylo* [$_{nP}$ (t$_N$) **n** [$_{aP<i>}$ *vkusnoe*]]] 'The-wine was good', as I am claiming, (101b) has the structure in (108), which is morphosyntactically well-formed.

(108)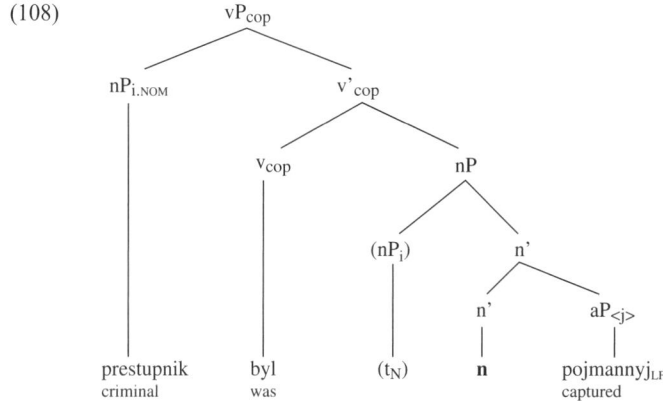

If (108) is well-formed (cf. the predicate LF of adjectives in (42)/(43)), the problem with (101b) (*Prestupnik byl pojmannyj$_{LF.NOM.M}$ 'The-criminal was captured') must be due to the meaning associated with an **-en-** participle in a structure like (108). More specifically, [pojmannyj]$_{aPj}$ is modifying the null head **n** of the predicate nominal, which, as we saw above, induces a relative-clause-like, class-membership reading (see §2.13): *The-criminal was the one who was captured*, which, although semantically well-formed, is nevertheless *not* the passive of active *Oni pojmali prestupnika*$_{j.ACC}$ 'They captured the-criminal.' My analysis of the SF and predicate LF thus correctly predicts that only the SF of **-en-** participles (*pojman*) can function as a simple passive predicate: *pojmannyj*$_{LF}$ in (108) obligatorily denotes a property of the subject *prestupnik* with respect to the discourse-specific class it belongs to, which is the reason it is infelicitous in isolation (cf. (80a–b)). ?*Prestupnik byl pojmannyj*$_{LF.NOM.M}$ 'The-criminal was (the one) caught' would be felicitous in a situation where a specific group (set) of criminals has been identified and we need to single out the one who had been recently (re)captured. The following is more felicitous since the discourse situation is clearer: *Oni edinstvennye*$_{LF.NOM.PL}$ *zainteresovannye*$_{LF.NOM.PL}$ *v tom, čtoby ego pojmali* 'They are (the) only (ones) interested in his being captured.'

Summary: the semantic oddness of (101b) is predicted by its morphosyntactic structure in (108), which lends further support to my aP$_i$-in-nP analysis of the predicate LF (see §2.13, where it is argued that the different meanings of the SF and predicate LF derive from their respective syntactic structures). (101b) is *ungrammatical* as the passive of active *(Oni) pojmali prestupnika* '(They) captured the-criminal' and *infelicitous* as the predicate LF equivalent of 'The-criminal was (the one who was) captured' (unless bolstered by the discourse situation).

114 *The argument structure of adjectives*

2.15.1 Departicipial *-enn-* adjectives

The sentences in (109) to (111) below are morphosyntactically and semantically well-formed because the predicate LFs are not LF **-en-** participles: they are LF departicipial **-enn-** *adjectives* (diachronically reanalyzed participles) which, as expected, behave like lexical adjectives (see Babby 1993a for details). The following morphosyntactic properties demonstrate that we are dealing with adjectives, not participles:

- **-enn-** adjectives cannot cooccur with the *by*-phrase because lexical adjectives never have an implicit **i** to license it.
- The meaning of **-enn-** adjectives may be radically different from the basic meaning of the corresponding **-en-** participle: e.g., the **-en-** participle of *rassejat'* 'to-scatter' is *rassejannyj*$_{LF}$ (*rassejana*$_{SF.F}$) 'scattered', whereas the corresponding **-enn-** adjective is *rassejannyj* (*rassejanna*$_{SF.F}$) 'absentminded, scatterbrained.' Note the **-nn-** in the SF of **-enn-** adjectives and the single **-n-** in the SF of participles (see (109b)).
- Like lexical adjectives and unlike **-en-** participles, **-enn-** adjectives can be felicitous predicate LFs: *Počemu èto ona takaja*$_{LF.F}$ *rassejannaja*$_{LF.F}$? 'Why is it that she is so scatterbrained (such a scatterbrained woman)?'; see Babby 1993a.[47]
- Unlike participles, they form the comparative (e.g., *Ona*$_{NOM}$ *rassejannee* (**rassejanee) sestry*$_{GEN}$ 'She (is) more-absentminded (than her) sister').
- Unlike participles, **-enn-** adjectives freely form **-o** manner adverbs (e.g., *rasssejanno* 'absentmindedly' and (114c)).

(109) a. Detskoe voobraženie takoe ograni**čenn**oe$_{LF}$ (*roditeljami).
   'A child's imagination is so limited (in comparison to adults').'
  b. Vozmožnosti nauki byli očen' ograni**čenn**y$_{SF}$ (*pravitel'stvom).
   '(lit.) The-possibilities of-science were very limited (*by the government) = there was very little science could do.'

(110) a. Bol'šinstvo voditelej disciplinirov**ann**y$_{SF}$.
   'The-majority of-drivers are disciplined (= trained, have self-control).'
  b. Bol'šinstvo voditelej disciplinirov**ann**y$_{SF}$ (miliciej).
   'The-majority of-drivers have been disciplined (= punished) (by the police).'
  c. Bol'šinstvo voditelej taksi disciplinirov**ann**ye$_{LF}$ (*miliciej).
   'The-majority of taxi drivers are well-trained (drivers) (*by the police).'

(111) a. Vopros očen' zaput**ann**yj$_{LF.NOM}$ (*dokladčikom).
   'The-question is (a) very intricate/involved (one) (*by-the-lecturer).'
  b. Ceny byli vpolne umer**enn**ye$_{LF}$. (cf. *umerit'* 'to-moderate')
   'The-prices were quite moderate (*moderated).'

(112) a. Ja ne spokojnyj$_{LF}$, a trenirovannyj$_{LF}$.
'I'm not (a) calm (person), but (a) well-trained (one).'
b. Vy sil'ny$_{SF.NOM.PL}$ i trenirovanny$_{SF.NOM.PL}$.
'You are strong and well-trained.'

(113) On ubedilsja, čto ego podozrenija obosnovanny$_{SF.PL}$.
'He was-convinced that his suspicions (were) well-founded.'

(114) a. Lico ego bylo serdito$_{SF.N}$ i nasupl-enn-o$_{SF.N}$. (cf. *nasupit'(sja)* 'scowl')
'(His) face was angry and sullen.'
b. Ty čego segodnja takaja nasuplennaja$_{LF.NOM.F}$?
'Why are you so sullen today?'
c. Odin put' garantirova-nn-o$_{ADV}$ prineset uspex.
'One path is guaranteed to bring success (lit. One path will guaranteedly bring success).'

2.16 The copula: syntactic merger or diathetic composition

This section is devoted to the hybrid adverbial *buduči* 'being' + SF/*LF construction, which is important for two reasons: First, it adds to the already considerable body of evidence supporting my aP ~ aP$_i$ analysis of the SF and LF. Second, and most important, it provides the decisive evidence alluded to above that the copula is introduced by a diathesis-level operation (*composition* of the SF's and copula's diatheses) rather than by a syntax-level operation (syntactic *merger* of copula with an aP$_{SF}$ s-clause followed by the raising of the clause's subject nP$_i$ to spec vP$_{cop}$).[48] The composition analysis entails that aP is a *bare adjective phrase* rather than an s-clause and, therefore, (43), not (42), is the correct structure of the predicate LF (*Vino bylo vkusnoe*$_{LF.NOM}$ 'The-wine was good'); cf. (108).

2.16.1 buduči + SF
(115) appears to be problematic for the [$_{aP}$ nP$_i$ a'$_{<i>}$] s-clause analysis of the SF: although the SF *golodna*$_{SF.F}$ in (115a) cooccurs with the copula, [*buduči golodna*$_{SF}$] does *not have a subject nP*: conclusive evidence is presented in chapter 3 that [*buduči golodna*$_{SF}$] does not have a null (PRO) subject nP (see §1.4.1) and is thus an s-predicate; I will argue below that *golodna* is a *bare aP phrase*, as in (116a).

(115) a. Buduči **golodna**, devuška otpravilas' domoj.
being hungry:SF.NOM.F girl:NOM.F went home
'The-girl went home because she was hungry.'
b. *Buduči **golodnaja**, devuška otpravilas' domoj.[49]
being hungry:LF.NOM.F girl went home

116 *The argument structure of adjectives*

We shall see below that, far from being problematic, (115a) is an instance of the coveted 'exception that proves the rule.' But first we need some descriptive background on which to base our argumentation. Russian hybrid [**V+af**$_{ADV}$] adverbials do not inflect for gender, number, or case, and do not have a subject nP, null or overt, because **V**'s initial external **N₁** is *deleted* as part of the diathesis-based derivation in which the diatheses of **V** and the adverbial suffix **-g** (**-af**$_{ADV}$) compose (see (117) below). The resulting unlinked external **i** in {**i^-**}₁ projects to syntax as a controlled adverbial gP$_i$ s-predicate (**-g**'s exponents are *-a* / *-v* / *-či* / *-všis'*). gP$_i$'s unlinked external **i** is V-bound by the matrix VP$_i$, to which it obligatorily adjoins. The resulting [$_{VP_i}$ VP$_{<i>}$ gP$_{<i>}$] configuration explains why gP$_i$ is always *subject controlled*: since gP$_i$ in (116b) is adjoined to and vertically bound by the matrix VP$_i$, the matrix clause's subject nP$_i$ is the head of the TBC in which gP$_i$ is V-bound and it thus gP$_i$'s understood subject or controller (see §2.3); the relevant TBC is in boldface and v is the finite verbal affix.

(116a)

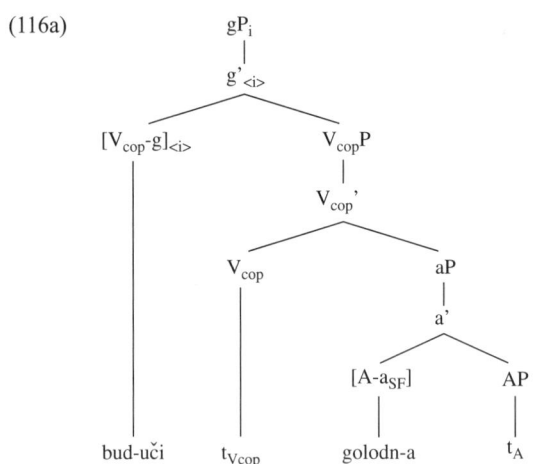

(116b)

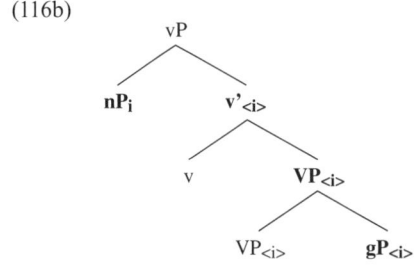

2.16 The copula   117

The putative problem is this: why is (115a), where the SF *golodna* has no subject nP, grammatical (SFs were defined above as having an intact $\{i\wedge N\}_1$ external argument), while in (115b), the LF s-predicate *golodnaja*, which has no subject nP, is ungrammatical? A priori, we expect just the opposite. It turns out upon closer inspection, however, that the well-formedness of (115a) and the ungrammaticality of (115b) are entirely regular and predictable. As a matter of fact, the well-formedness of (115a) and the ill-formedness of (115b) constitute dramatic evidence that my analysis of the SF and LF is essentially correct; it is the analysis of the copula that needs to be revised.

Since the derivation of *buduči golodna* is relatively complex, I will first present the entire derivation in (117), and then explain each step in greater detail (*golodn-* is the adjective lexical stem **A** ; "…" denotes **A**'s internal arguments [positions 2 and 3], which are irrelevant here). Note that copula-introduction in (117) is treated as diathesis-level composition, which is necessitated by the fact that the composition of the SF in (117c) and the copula must *precede* the composition of the adverbial-forming suffix **-g** (see (116a)).

(117)   Derivation of *buduči golodna* in (115a):
    a. $\{i \wedge N\}_1$ … $\{\text{-} \wedge \textbf{golodn-}\}_4$ + (**A**-'s initial diathesis)
    b. $\{\wedge\}_1$ … $\{\wedge \textbf{-a}_{\text{SF.NOM}}\}_4$ > (the suffix's diathesis)
    c. $\{i \wedge N\}_1$ … $\{\text{-} \wedge \textbf{golodna}_{\text{SF.NOM}}\}_4{}^{50}$ + (composition of (a) and (b))
    ....
    d. $\{\wedge\}_1$ … $\{\wedge \textbf{bud-}\}_4$ > (copula's diathesis)
    e. $\{i \wedge N\}_1$ … $\{\text{-} \wedge \textbf{bud-} [\text{golodna}]\}_4$ + (composition of (c) and (d))
    ....
    f. $\{\wedge \text{-}\}_1$ … $\{\wedge \textbf{-g}\}_4$ > (-g's diathesis)
    g. $\{i \wedge \text{-}\}_1$ … $\{\text{-} \wedge \text{buduči} [\text{golodna}]\}_4$ => (projection to (115a)/(116a))

The **A** stem's initial diathesis in (117a) composes with the SF suffix's diathesis in (117b), yielding the diathesis of the SF *golodna* in (117c); *golodna* is a complete *word* (the primitive unit of syntax) and thus henceforth diathetically inert and syntactically opaque. (117c) serves as input to the next phase of the derivation: it composes with the diathesis of the copula stem *bud-* and its diathesis in (117d) to yield the copularized SF in (117e). This step is critical: the copula's initial external argument in (117d) is $\{\wedge\}_1$ and it therefore *inherits* the SF's external $\{i\wedge N\}_1$ argument in (117e), making it its own external argument. *Inheritance* is the diathetic analogue of syntactic raising, but diathetic operations do not leave traces.[51] Since the copula *inherits* the SF's external $\{i\wedge N\}_1$ argument in argument structure, there is no point in the subsequent *syntactic* derivation where the SF heads an s-clause. The SF's syntactic aP projection is neither an s-predicate nor an s-clause: it is a third type of phrase, namely, a *bare phrase*, which has neither a dedicated subject nP_i nor an unlinked external **i**. Bare phrases occur only when a lexical diathesis composes with a copula or an auxiliary verb (see the [V_{aux} + *bare infinitive complement*] in chapter 4).[52]

(117e) now serves as the input into gP_i-formation, i.e., (117e) composes with (117f), the diathesis of the hybrid adverbial forming suffix **-g** (which is realized as *-či* with the *bud-* stem), yielding (117g), which is the derivation's *final diathesis*. We see in (117f–g) that the suffix **-g** deletes the copula stem's inherited external N_1, creating an adverbial s-predicate [$_{gP_i}$ *buduči golodna*] (**-g** has inherent adverb features, just as **-en-** has inherent adjective features). The diathesis in (117g) encodes the *merger conditions* for projecting the well-formed syntactic structure of (115a): given its unlinked external **i** and obligatory subject control, [$_{gP_i}$ *buduči golodna*] merges with matrix VP_i, which vertically binds its external theta role **i** thereby ensuring that the matrix subject nP_i in (116b) is the head of its TBC (see Babby and Franks 1998 for details).

To see why the diathesis-composition analysis in (117) is superior to the syntactic merger + subject-raising analysis of the copula assumed earlier in this chapter (cf. (42) vs. (43) and (104) vs. (105)), we need only look more closely at the last, decisive step in (117), which contains the crucial argument that the copula's introduction takes place in argument structure rather than in syntax. Recall that the **-g** (*-či*) suffix deletes the copula's inherited external N_1 (see { ^-}$_1$ in (117f)), creating the s-predicate gP_i. Now, since *buduči*, like all copula and auxiliary verbs, has an *unspecified* { ^ }$_1$ external argument in its diathesis, the external N_1 deleted in the formation of the *buduči* must have been inherited from the SF diathesis it composes with. In other words, the SF *golodna* must compose with **bud-** *before* **-g** since it is **bud-**'s *inherited* N_1 that **-g** deletes, i.e., the adjective that composes with **bud-** must be an SF since its diathesis (117c) provides the external {i^N}$_1$ that the **-g** suffix selects. My initial claim that the SF has an intact external {i^N}$_1$ argument is thus correct (see (117c)), whereas my initial claim that this {i^N}$_1$ projects to syntax as the subject nP_i of an SF-headed s-clause is not (see (117f–g) and the bare aP in (116a)).

Since gP_i-formation is patently an affix-driven diathetic operation, the derivation of *buduči golodna* requires that the union of the SF and the copula *must itself be a diathetic operation*. This is because [copula+SF], which inherits the SF's external {i^N}$_1$ argument, *is the input to gP_i formation*, which is a diathetic operation, not a syntactic one, and the output of syntactic operations cannot feed diathetic operations. Only the *final* diathesis projects to syntax, and subsequent syntactic operations do not have access to the diathetic derivation or representation (i.e., cannot add or delete affixes and cannot operate on the diathesis's individual slots). In other words, if the copula merged with aP as a syntactic operation, copula + aP could not then be the input to gP_i formation, which is an affix-driven diathetic operation. I thus conclude that the syntactic-merger analysis of copula union is descriptively inadequate: a *syntactic* rule cannot delete the copula's external nP leaving behind the theta role it is linked to; only diathetic operations can operate on the individual slots (cells) of arguments and thus *only a diathetic operation can create an s-predicate*. In other words, (118) is ill-formed because syntactic rules are not capable of deleting the raised nP_i subject of the SF s-clause but not the **i** theta role it is linked to.

(118)

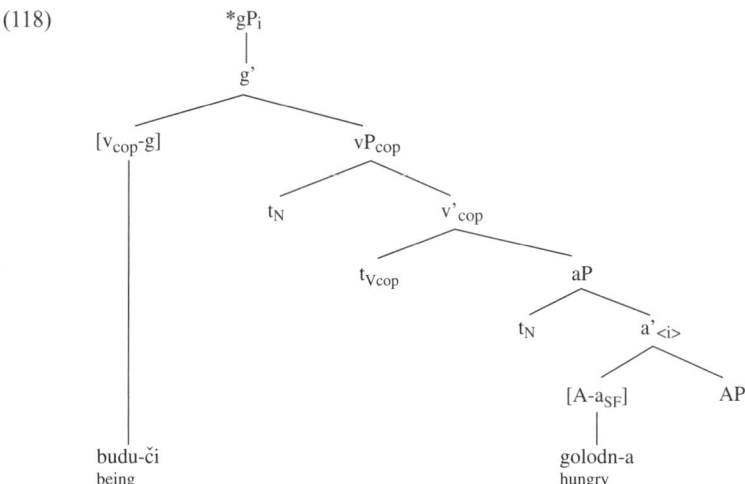

The derivation in (117) also provides an explanation for the ill-formedness of *buduči golodnaja$_{LF.NOM.F}$ in (115b). Since **A**'s c-selected external N_1 is deleted in the derivation of the LF itself, it is not available later in the derivation to be inherited by the copula and deleted by the adverbial forming suffix -**g**. Thus (115b) is ill-formed because its derivation involves a violation of -**g**'s selectional properties: the -**g** suffix selects Vs with $\{i\wedge N\}_1$, not $\{i\wedge-\}_1$. This is this same selectional restriction that accounts for the fact that impersonal verbs like *tošnit'*, which have $\{-\wedge-\}_1$ external arguments, cannot form gP_is. Note that *external c-selection* plays a crucial role here, which serves as additional evidence that the c-selection tier is autonomous and that external c-selection is not redundant (see chapter 1).

120   *The argument structure of adjectives*

My initial assumption that the SF's external {i^N}$_1$ projects to syntax as the dedicated subject of an aP *s-clause* and then raises to spec-vP$_{cop}$ as the sentence's subject has been demonstrated to be wrong. This is a welcome result since it follows from an earlier axiom of my theory that all grammatical-relation changing rules operate on argument-structure representation (the 2×4 diathesis). The derivation in (117) provides unambiguous evidence that the copula, like the auxiliary verb, *composes* with its lexical complement in argument structure (see §4.12 for the composition of V$_{aux}$ and bare infinitive phrases). This means that the derivation and syntactic projection of V$_{cop}$ + SF sentences must be as in (119)/(120) rather than (25). (117) also demonstrates that (105) not (104) must be correct, and that correct structure of the predicate LF is the bare nP (43) not the nP small clause + subject raising in (42). Thus the SF does project an aP, but it is a bare [$_{aP}$ a'] phrase, not an [$_{aP}$ nP$_i$ a'$_{<i>}$] s-clause.

(119)   Revised derivation of the SF (cf. (3)):
   a. A-stem: {i ^ N}$_1$ ...   {- ^ vkusn-}$_4$ +
   b. SF-affix: { ^ }$_1$ ...   { ^ -0$_{SF.NOM}$}$_4$ >
   c. SF: {i ^ N }$_1$ ... {- ^ [vkusno$_{SF.NOM}$]}$_4$ +
   ....
   d. copula: { ^ }$_1$ ...   { ^ by-}$_4$ >
   e. c + d: {i ^ N}$_1$ ...   { - ^ by-[vkusno$_{SF.NOM}$]}$_4$ +
   ....
   f. v-affix: { ^ }$_1$ ...   { ^ -lo}$_4$ >
   g. final: {i ^ N}$_1$ ...   { - ^ bylo [vkusno$_{SF.NOM}$]}$_4$ => (120)

(120)   The correct syntactic structure of (5a):

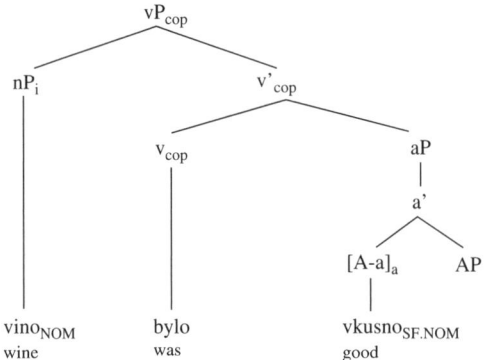

aP in (120) is a bare adjective phrase, not an adjective s-clause as in (25), repeated here as (121).

(121)
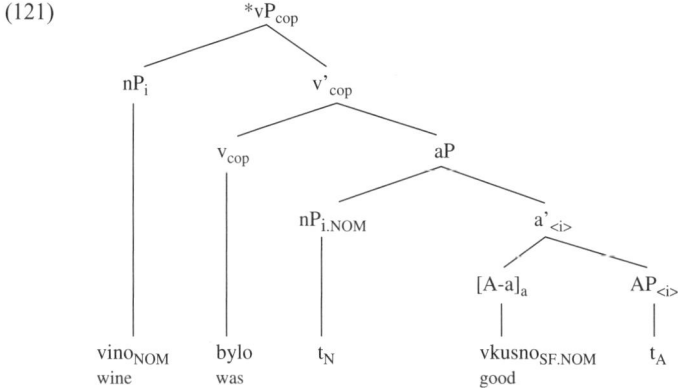

The problem with (121) is that it represents a diathesis-level operation as a syntactic operation.

The revised structure of (77), repeated as (122b), is (122a). First the diathesis of nP composes with the diathesis of *kak*, which inherits the nP's external argument (*kniga$_i$*); the copula *byla* is next to compose and it inherits *kniga*, which projects to syntax as the sentence's nominative subject. This entails that both nP and kP are bare phrases.

(122a)
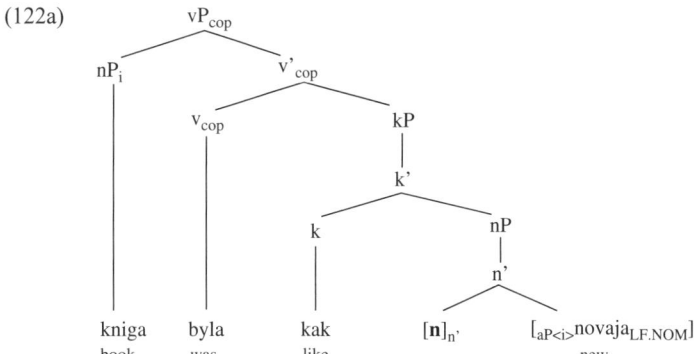

122   *The argument structure of adjectives*

(122b)

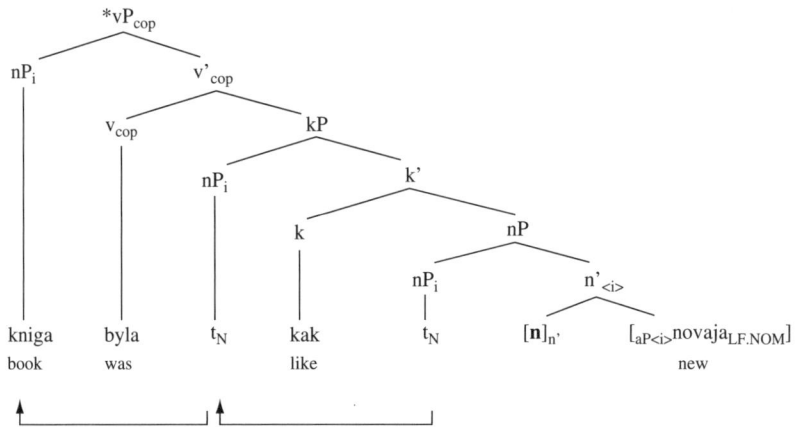

2.17   Summary

The derivations of LFs and SFs proposed above provide independent evidence for the claim made in chapter 1 that a Russian predicator's diathesis must specify whether or not is has a c-selected (subcategorized) external N_1. Since both LFs and SFs have case, number, and gender features, and identical theta tiers, the criterial difference between them is that the **A**-stem's external N_1 is deleted in the derivation of LFs (which creates an $\{i^\wedge\text{-}\}_1$ s-predicate) but not in the derivation of the SF, whose intact $\{i^\wedge N\}_1$ external argument is inherited by the V_{cop} that it obligatorily composes with. If the diathesis of adjective stems did not have an initial external N_1 specified in $\{i^\wedge N\}_1$ to begin with, this crucial difference could not be captured.

3 *Hybrid verbal adjuncts*

3.0 Introduction

The primary purpose of this chapter is to further illustrate the explanatory power of diathesis theory by applying it to the analysis of *hybrid verbal categories*, which I define as an **[X-x]ₓ**, which is a productively derived composite head, where **X** is a lexical stem and **-x** is an affixal head, and **X** and **-x** *belong to different categories*, i.e., have different sets of categorial features (cf. Grimshaw 2005: 2). **[X-x]ₓ** is created by the composition of the diatheses of **X** and **-x**. For example, English **[V-n]ₙ** *gerundive nominals* combine the properties of verbs and nouns.[1] In contrast, the LF and SF of the adjective are *homogeneous categories*: both the lexical stem **A** in **[A-a]ₐ** and the adjectival suffixes it composes with (**-aSF** or **-aLF**) have the same categorial features. It will be demonstrated below that the diathesis's 2×4 structure accounts for the unique set of morphosyntactic properties that characterize hybrid categories cross-linguistically.

Russian has two fully productive hybrid verbal categories, both of which are *adjunct s-predicates*:

(i) Deverbal *adverbials*: **[X-x]ₓ = [V-g]g** (see §2.16). The hybrid adverbial suffix **-g** has inherent adverbial features and it deletes **V**'s external **N₁**, creating an s-predicate hybrid category (see (8)/(9)).

(ii) Participles are deverbal *adjectives*, i.e., **[X-x]ₓ = [V-af]af**, where **-af-** is the participle-forming suffix, which has adjectival features. Russian has three types of participle, each of which has radically different morphosyntactic properties: **-en-** participles (see §2.15) and **-šč-** participles are treated below; **-em-** participles, which combine the essential properties of the other two, are treated in §3.2.5. Each suffix has several exponents.

The morphosyntactic properties of deverbal adjuncts differ from language to language. For example, unlike Russian hybrid adverbials, which are s-predicates, Lithuanian **-ant** hybrid adverbials project s-clauses with overt dative subjects: *Virve*~NOM~ *truko* [~advP~ *jiems*~DAT~ *lip-ant*] 'The-rope broke [(when) they~DAT~ (were)-climbing]' (see (3b)). My hypothesis is that hybrid verbal categories all have the same categorially heterogeneous VP-in-afP syntactic structure (-**af**- having nonverbal features); their morphosyntactic differences are encoded in the language-specific diatheses of the affixes that drive their derivations.

3.1 The syntactic representation of hybrid categories

The analysis of hybrid categories I am proposing is based on the following empirical observation: the verbal and nonverbal properties of hybrid categories are rigidly segregated. Russian hybrid verbal adjuncts clearly show that the verbal properties are internal (lower or embedded) while the nonverbal, affix-specific properties are external (higher) and therefore determine the syntactic category and distribution of the hybrid phrase as a whole. The English gerundive nominal has the syntactic distribution and function of an NP (DP), with its verbal properties encapsulated inside the VP complement of the NP's head.[2] This organization is reflected in the morphology of hybrid categories, with the verbal suffixes being closer to **V** than the non-verbal suffixes; see the *mirror principle* in Baker 1985.[3]

This bipartite, upstairs-downstairs structure of hybrid categories is nothing more than the bipartite Extended Lexical Projection, which results from the composition of the diatheses of **V** and the nonverbal affix it composes with (see §1.11). More specifically, all members of a **V**'s finite and nonfinite diathetic paradigm have the same afP basic *bipartite* morphosyntactic structure schematically represented in (1): a 'downstairs' lexical VP projection of **V** that is embedded as the complement of an 'upstairs' affixal head's projection, which can be realized as either an s-predicate, as in (1a), or an s-clause, as in (1b); (1a) and (1b) are both Extended Lexical Projections of **V**. (1a–b) are *hybrid* if **af**'s categorial features are not verbal and *homogeneous* if they are.

(1) a. [~afPi~   [~af'<i>~ [V-af]~af~ VP]]
      b. [~afP~ nP~i~ [~af'<i>~ [V-af]~af~ VP]]

Both Russian hybrid verbal adjuncts have the s-predicate structure in (1a). Lithuanian **-ant** hybrid adverbials have the s-clause structure in (1b), where **V**'s external theta role **i** is linked to the adverbial's overt dative subject (see (3b)). Turkish affix-headed adverbials have nominative subjects. The immutable 2×4 structure of the diathesis correctly predicts that there is no *hybrid-specific syntax*.

(2) Russian homogeneous infinitive s-predicate and s-clause (**-inf** is verbal):
 a. [$_{infP}$i [$_{inf'}$ [V-inf]$_{inf}$ VP]]
 b. [$_{infP}$ nP$_{i.DAT}$ [$_{inf'<i>}$ [V-inf]$_{inf}$ VP]]

(3) Hybrid s-clauses:
 a. English gerundive nominal: [$_{nP}$ nP$_i$'s [$_{n'<i>}$ [V-n]$_n$ VP]]
 b. Lithuanian adverbial clause: [$_{advP}$ nP$_{i.DAT}$ [$_{adv'<i>}$ [V-adv]$_{adv}$ VP]]
 c. Turkish adverbial clause: [$_{advP}$ nP$_{i.NOM}$ [$_{adv'<i>}$ VP [V-adv]$_{adv}$]]^4

The derivation of a hybrid verbal category and its syntactic projection are schematically represented in (4) and (5), which captures the crucial VP-inside ~ afP-outside structure of hybrid categories: (4a) is a ditransitive **V**'s initial diathesis, (4b) is the diathesis of a nonverbal affixal head **-af**.^{5}

(4) a V: {{i ^ N}$_1$ {j ^ N}$_2$ {k ^ N}$_3$ {- ^ V-}$_4$}   +
 b. affix: {{ ^ }1 { ^ }$_2$ { ^ }$_3$ { ^ **-af**}$_4$}   >
 c. a + b: {{i ^ N}$_1$ {j ^ N}$_2$ {k ^ N}$_3$ {- ^ [V-af]}$_4$}   => (5)

(5) Bipartite Extended Lexical Projection of **V**:

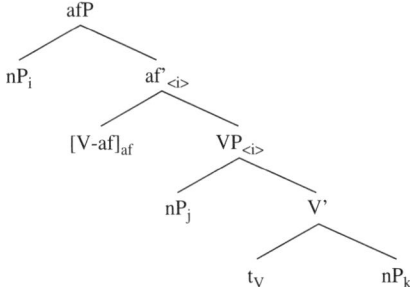

According to (4c) => (5), all that happens in this derivation is that **V** composes with **-af**, which introduces the hybrid's non-verbal categorial features (not shown). However, in practice, **-af**'s diathesis induces other changes in **V**'s initial diathesis. In the derivation of the Russian hybrid adjuncts, **-af** is also responsible for the deletion of **V**-'s external **N$_1$**, which delinks **i**, creating the s-predicate in (1a). The derivation of Russian hybrid verbal adjuncts is schematically represented in (6) => (7).

(6) a. {{i ^ N }$_1$ {j ^ N}$_2$ {k ^ N}$_3$ {- ^ V}$_4$}   +
 b. {{ ^ - }$_1$ { ^ }$_2$ { ^ }$_3$ { ^ **-af**}$_4$}   >
 c. {{i ^ - }$_1$ {j ^ N }$_2$ {k ^ N }$_3$ {- ^ [V-af]}$_4$}   => (7)

(7)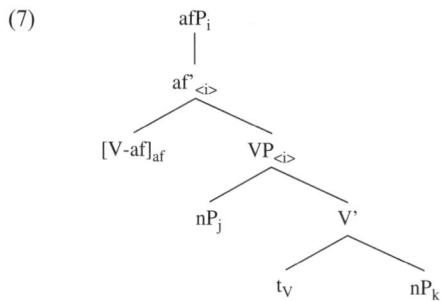

The projected syntactic structure in (7) explains why the verbal (**V**) and nonverbal (**-af**) properties of hybrid categories are *segregated*: there is an intact VP whose internal structure is identical to the VP in finite clauses. The verbal properties are perceived as internal because VP is encapsulated (embedded) as the complement of nonverbal **-af**, whose afP projection is thus external vis-à-vis VP. For example, Russian -šč-participles, which are adjective-verb hybrids, have the external syntactic distribution and inflectional morphology of adjectives but the internal structure of VP, e.g., a transitive -šč-participle's direct object is assigned structural accusative case, just as in finite VPs (see §3.2.3 below for structural case assignment).

All members of **V**'s *diathetic paradigm* (finite forms, infinitives, participles, hybrid adverbials, gerundive nominals, etc.) inherit **V**'s 2, 3, and 4 positions (its *internal diathesis*) intact, which projects to syntax as the encapsulated VP_i in (5) and (7); **[V-af]** verbal categories differ in terms of the categorial features introduced by their specific -**af** suffix and the effect -**af**'s external argument has on **V**'s initial external argument (e.g., deletion of N_1 in the case of Russian hybrid adjuncts).

There are no specialized hybrid-category specific syntactic rules or principles: **[V-af]**'s final diathesis always has 2×4 structure, which projects the Extended Lexical Projection in (5) and (7). Construction-specific and language-specific differences are due entirely to the properties of the affixes. For example, see (9), the syntactic structure of (8) (-**af** = -**g**, whose exponent is -*a*; see §3.3 for details): the s-predicate hybrid adverbial phrase gP_i is vertically bound by the upper finite VP_i, which assigns its external theta role **i** to the matrix subject *Nikita*, accounting for the *subject control* of [$_{gP<i>}$ *čitaja knigu*]. There is nothing gP_i-specific in the syntactic derivation or structure of (8); what is special about (8)/(9) is that the -**g** *suffix's diathesis* creates a *controlled uninflected hybrid adverbial phrase* (small v in (9) is the finite verbal suffix).

(8) Nikita$_i$ sidel v kresle [$_{gP<i>}$ čitaj-a knigu].
     N:NOM sat in easy-chair reading book:ACC
     'Nikita was-sitting in (his) easy-chair, reading a-book.'

(9)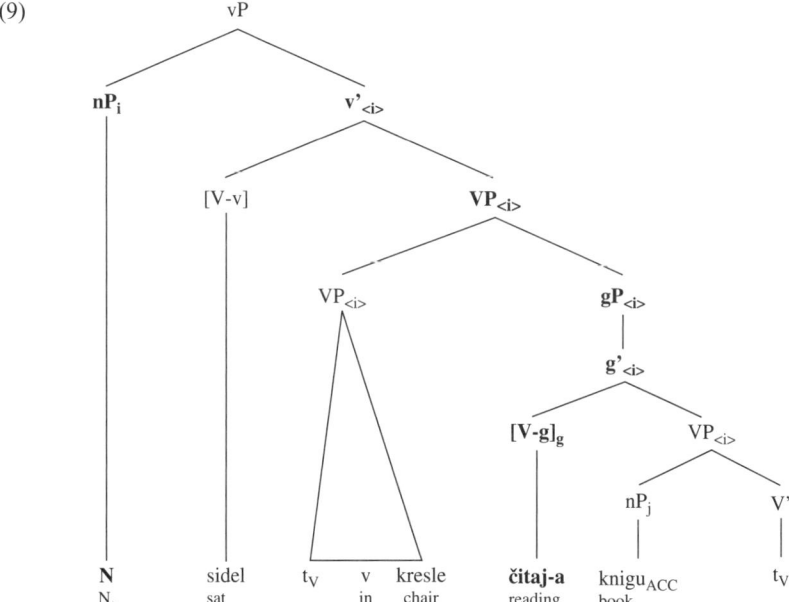

3.2 Participles in Russian

A *paradigmatic suffix* **-af** is a productive suffix that has its own diathesis and categorial features; it composes with **V** and its diathesis.[6] Since **-af** is the head of the derived word **[V-af-]**$_{af}$, its properties take precedence over competing properties in **V**'s diathesis (see causativization in §1.9).

This section is devoted to what are traditionally called 'active' (**-šč-**) and 'passive' (**-en-**) participles. However, since active participles are not always in the active voice (see (14)) and **-en-** participles are not always passive (see §2.15), I will refer to them simply as **-šč-** and **-en-** participles.[7]

The **[V-en-]** participle stem projects to syntax as either the LF or SF (see §2.15). The **-šč-**-participle is always an s-predicate (see (6)/(7)) and therefore obligatorily composes with LF suffixes and, like LF adjectives, has an exclusively adjunct function and cannot compose directly with the copula to form a **-šč-**-participle clause: **Nikita byl čitajuščij*$_{LF.NOM.M}$ *knigu*$_{ACC}$ 'Nikita was reading the-book.' For example, **zavjad-** 'wilt' in (10) is a perfective V, **-š-** is the participle-forming allomorph it selects, and **-ix** is the genitive plural LF inflectional suffix, which agrees with *rastenij*$_{GEN.PL}$, the head of its TBC; **zavjadaj(u)-** is the imperfective stem of the same verb.

(10) a. [$_{nP}$ Sotni$_{NOM.PL}$ različnyx rastenij$_{GEN}$, [$_{afP<i>}$ zavjad-š-ix$_{LF.GEN}$ i zavjadaju-šč-ix$_{LF.GEN}$]], stojali$_{PL}$ na polkax.
'[Hundreds of different plants, [wilted and wilting]], stood on shelves.'

b. (i) [**zavjad-**]$_{V\text{-stem}}$ +
   (ii) [**-š-**]$_{\text{-suffix}}$ >
   (iii) [**zavjad-š-**]$_{\text{participle stem}}$ +
   (iv) [**-ix-**]$_{LF.GEN \text{ suffix}}$ >
   (v) [zavjadšix]$_{\text{participle}}$ => zavjadšix in (10a)

We see in (11) that **-šč**-participles, like finite forms, infinitives, and hybrid adverbials, all of which have an encapsulated VP, can compose with the unaccusativizing suffix *-sja* (afP$_i$ in (10a) and elsewhere in this chapter denotes ščP$_i$).

(11) a. Kalitku$_{ACC.F}$ otkryvajut$_{3\text{-PL}}$.
'(unidentified person) is-opening the-gate.'
b. Kalitka$_{NOM.F}$ medlenno otkryvaetsja.
'The-gate is slowly opening / being-opened.'
c. [$_{nP}$ [$_{afP<i>}$ medlenno otkryvaju-šč-aja$_{LF.NOM.F}$-sja] kalitka$_{NOM.F}$]
        slowly   opening/being-opened   gate
'the gate which is slowly opening/being opened'

(12) to (15) demonstrate that: (i) the syntactic distribution of **-šč**-participles is determined by the need to V-bind their unlinked external theta role **i** and by **-šč-**'s adjectival categorial features; they have the same function and distribution as LF-adjectives; (ii) like finite clauses, their 'voice' can be active, middle (derived unaccusative), or passive.[8]

(12)   -šč-participles in the active voice:
a. [$_{nP}$ rabočie$_{NOM.PL}$ [$_{afP<i>}$ **napolni-vš-ie**$_{LF.NOM.PL}$ jamu$_{j.ACC}$ vodo$_{jk.INST}$]]
'the-workers [(who)-filled the-pit with-water]'
b. rabočie, kotorye$_{i.NOM.PL}$ napolnili$_{PL}$ jamu$_j$ vodo$_{jk}$
'the-workers, who filled the-pit with-water'

(13)   -šč-participles in the middle (derived unaccusative) voice :
a. [$_{nP}$ jama$_{j.NOM.F}$ [$_{afP<i>}$ **napolni-vš-aja**$_{LF.NOM.F}$**-sja** vodoj$_{INST}$ (*rabočimi)]].
'the-pit (which) filled with-water (*by-the-workers)'
b. [$_{nP}$ jama, kotoraja napolnilas' vodoj (*rabočimi)]
'the-pit which filled with-water'

(14)   -šč-participles in the passive voice:
a. Zapadnye deržavy soglasilis' na konferenciju s učastiem [$_{nP}$ Sovetskoj Rossii$_{GEN.F}$, [$_{afP<i>}$ [$_{ADV}$ do tex por] imi$_{INST}$ ne **priznava-vš-ej**$_{LF.GEN.F}$**-sja**]].

3.2 *Participles in Russian*   129

'The-western powers agreed to a-conference with the-participation of [Soviet Russia, [(which was) not recognized by-them [up to that time]]].'
b. Sovetskaja Rossija$_{j.NOM}$ do tex por imi$_{INST}$ ne priznava-l$_{PAST}$-a$_{F.SF}$-s'.
'Soviet Russian was not recognized by them until then.'

(15) Other uses of the **-šč-** participle parallel to the LF adjective:
a. Ja   zastal rabočix$_{ACC}$ [$_{afP<i>}$ napolnjaju-šč-imi$_{PI}$ jamu$_{ACC}$ vodoj$_{INST}$].
   I   found workers   filling   pit   with-water
   'I found (came-upon) the-workers [filling the-pit with-water].'
b. Poblednevšij$_{LF.NOM.M}$, on$_{NOM.M}$ vskočil s kresla.
   'Having-turned-pale, he jumped from the-chair.'

The derivation of *napolnivšie* in (12a) is represented in (16)/(17) (-**šč**- = -*vš*-). The derived head **[V-vš]** inherits **V**'s external **i** theta role and its entire *internal diathesis*; -*vš*'s diathesis in (16b) is responsible for the deletion of **V**'s external **N$_1$**, which leaves **i** unlinked; afP$_i$ in (17) is the **[V-vš]** composite hybrid head's maximal projection.

(16) The derivation of (12a):
a. {{i ^ N}$_1$ {j ^ N}$_2$ {k ^ N}$_3$ {- ^ **napolni-**}$_4$}   +
b. {{ ^ -}$_1$ { ^ }$_2$ { ^ }$_3$ { ^ -**vš**}$_4$}   >
c. {{i ^ -}$_1$ {j ^ N}$_2$ {k ^ N}$_3$ {- ^ **[napolni-vš-]**}$_4$}   +
....
d. {{ ^ -}$_1$ { ^ }$_2$ { ^ }$_3$ { ^ - **ie**$_{LF.NOM.PL}$}$_4$}   >
e. {{i ^ -}$_1$ {j ^ N}$_2$ {k ^ N}$_3$ {- ^ **[napolnivšie]**}$_4$}   =>

(17)

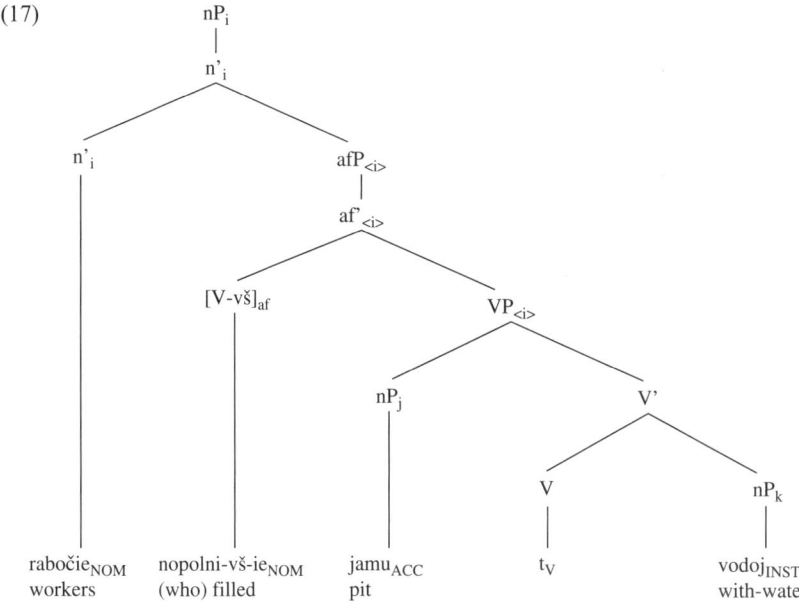

The s-predicate structure of afP$_i$ in (17) explains why -šč-participles cannot serve as primary predicators. *On byl napolnjajuščij$_{LF.NOM.M}$ (napolnjajuščim$_{PL.M}$) jamu vodoj 'He was filling the-pit with-water' is ill-formed for the following two reasons: (i) the subject nP on is unlicensed since it cannot have been projected from the final diathesis in (16e), which has no external **N**; (ii) LF s-predicates in Russian have an exclusively adjunct function.

(18) and (19) are not counterexamples: they are well-formed because -šč-participles, like -en-participles, are often reanalyzed as lexical adjectives (see §2.15.1), and can thus be used in the SF, as in (18a), or in the copula + [$_{nP}$ **n** aP$_{<i>}$] predicate LF construction, as in (18b) (cf. *potrjasat'* 'to-astound').

(18) a. Pričeska$_{NOM.F}$ byla$_F$ prosto potrjasaju-šč-a$_{SF.NOM.F}$.
    '(Her) hair-do was simply sensational (stunning).'
  b. Pričeska byla prosto potrjasaju-šč-aja$_{LF.NOM.F}$.

(19) a. Rasskazy$_{NOM.PL}$ zaxvatyvajušči$_{SF.NOM.PL}$.
    'The-stories (are) absorbing.' (cf. *zaxvatyvat'* 'to-grab; fascinate')
  b. Spisok$_{NOM.M.SG}$ nepravilnyx form$_{GEN}$ byl isčerpyvajušč$_{SF.NOM.M.SG}$.
    'The-list of irregular forms was exhaustive (*exhausting).'

This reanalysis correctly predicts the existence of -šč-manner adverbs (-šč- + -*o* > -šče): adjectives but not participles form manner adverbs by affixation of the nonagreeing -o suffix to their stem (cf. manner adverbs in -enn-o from departicipial -enn-adjectives in §2.15.1); see Babby 1986a.

(20) a. Pes   zavorčal   predosteregajušče.
    'The-dog   began-to-growl   threateningly.'
  b. Anna byla potrjasajušče otkrovenna$_{SF.NOM.F}$.
    'Anna was amazingly candid.'

My analysis correctly predicts that -šč-participles cannot be formed from impersonal verbs like *tošnit'*: since they do not have an external theta role in their initial diathesis (see (21a)), a -šč-participle (or hybrid adverbial) formed from them is not *syntactically* well-formed because it has no unlinked external **i** to V-bind and therefore *cannot be controlled*:

(21)   The derivation of -šč-participles from impersonal verbs:
  a. {{- ^ -}$_1$ {j ^ N}$_2$ {- ^ -}$_3$ {- ^ **tošni-**}$_4$}   +
  b. {{ ^ -}$_1$ { ^   }$_2$ { ^ }$_3$ { ^ **-šč-**}$_4$}   >
  c. {{- ^ -}$_1$ {j ^ N}$_2$ {- ^ -}$_3$ {- ^ **[tošnja-šč]-**}$_4$}   => *tošnjašč-

Summary: Given the derivation in (16) => (17), I conclude that participles are 'hybrid' because, in their Extended Lexical Projections, the downstairs head **V** and the upstairs adjective suffixal head -šč- have different categorial features.

(16)/(17) explain why the participle's verbal and adjectival properties are discrete and segregated, and why the suffix's adjectival properties are syntactically visible whereas the hybrid's verbal properties are *encapsulated* in VP, i.e., unable to interact with the syntax of the clause in which the afP$_i$ containing it is a constituent.

3.2.1 *-šč-particles and -en-participles*

Although both -šč- and -en-participles project the same bipartite, VP-in-afP syntactic structure (see (5) and (7)) and both participle-forming suffixes contribute the same adjective features to their hybrid **[V-af]** head, -**en**-participles are nevertheless felt to be somehow less verbal, more adjectival than -šč-participles. This intuition can be explained by simply comparing the two participles' derivations and their morphosyntactic properties:

(i) The -**šč**- suffix *obligatorily* deletes **V**'s external **N$_1$**, creating an s-predicate; the -**en**- suffix leaves **N$_1$** intact.

(ii) Since -šč-participles are inherently s-predicates, they compose with LF suffixes only (see chapter 2); -**en**-participle stems, like lexical adjectives, compose with both the SF and LF suffixes. Like basic adjectives, SF -**en**-participles compose with the copula and function as a sentence's primary predicate, e.g., [$_{nPj}$ *Gruppa*$_{NOM.M.SF}$ *škol'nikov*$_{GEN}$] *byla prived-en-a*$_{SF.NOM.F.SG}$ *v muzej* '[A-group of-schoolchildren] was taken to the-museum.' -šč-participles cannot compose directly with the copula.

(iii) -**en**- is a derived-unaccusative suffix and thus always *dethematizes* V's external theta role **i**, whereas affixation of the -**šč**-suffix *has no effect on V's theta roles*, i.e., the finite form of **V** and the corresponding -**šč**-participle *always have the identical ordered set of theta roles*, which is simply the inherited theta tier of **V**'s initial diathesis. In contrast, the finite form of **V** and its -**en**-participle *never* have the identical ordered set of theta roles. Thus the effects that the two participle-forming suffixes have on **V**'s initial external argument are diametrically opposed:

(22) a. {i ^ N}$_1$ + -šč- > {i ^ -}$_1$
      b. {i ^ N}$_1$ + -en- > {- ^ N}$_1$

{i^-}$_1$ projects to syntax as an s-predicate; {-^N}$_1$ cannot project to syntax.[9] It is a virtue of diathesis theory that it can capture this type of generalization.

(iv) Since -**en**- always dethematizes **V**'s external theta role **i**, and since {-^N}$_1$ does not project to syntax, **V**'s internal theta role **j** *externalizes* (i.e., links to {-^N}$_1$) and {j^N}$_1$ projects to syntax as the sentence's nominative subject.

(v) It follows from (iii) and (iv) that, like finite verbs, -šč-participles can have *agentive* external theta roles, while -**en**-participles, like primary (underived) adjectives, never have agentive external theta roles. In standard Russian, like primary adjectives, **-en**-participles do not have direct objects; but **-šč**-participles, like the corresponding finite transitive verb, have accusative direct objects (see §3.2.3).

(vi) **-šč**-participle stems can compose with the unaccusativizing **-sja** suffix to form passive and middle voice, as in (12) to (14) (e.g., *Oboi otryvajutsja* 'The-wallpaper is-pealing-off' ~ *otryvaju-šč-ie-sja oboi* 'the pealing-off wallpaper'); without **-sja** they are the participial counterpart of active voice, which is simply the projection to syntax of the intact theta tier of **V**'s initial diathesis. In contrast, **-en**-participles are never in the active voice since their initial **i** theta role is always dethematized: they are middle (stative) or passive, depending on whether dethematized **i** is deleted, as in middle derivations (*Ona*$_j$ *prostuž-en-a*$_{SF.NOM.F}$ 'She has-caught-cold'), or, as in passive derivations, relinked to [**V-en**], which licenses the *by*-phrase i.e., {i^[**V-en**]}$_4$ (*Takie že pis'ma byli poluč-en-y vsemi členami komiteta* 'Similar letters were received by all the-members of-the-committee'). **-en**-participles do not compose with **-sja** because they are already derived unaccusatives.

(vii) **-en-** canonically composes with perfective **V** stems, creating *stative* participles (see (vi)), while the **-šč**-suffix composes with imperfective as well as perfective **V**, creating participles that have the same aspectual meaning as the corresponding finite verb: *čitaju-šč-ij*$_{IMPERF}$~ *pro-čita-vš-ij*$_{PERF}$ 'reading.' Thus whereas **-šč**-participles retain the perfective ~ imperfective aspect opposition of finite verbs, **-en-**participles do not.

(viii) **-šč**-participles express (relative) tense morphologically (*čitajuščij* 'is-reading' ~ *čitavšij* 'was-reading'), while **-en**-participles, like adjectives, express tense analytically by means of the copula (see Timberlake 2004: §6.3.6).

We see in (i) through (viii) that **-šč**-participle phrases retain many more of **V**'s verbal properties, which explains why they are perceived as being closer to the structure of finite clauses than **-en**-participles, whose projections are closer to the structure of adjective phrases. Given that both types of participle are hybrid verbal categories with identical VP-in-afP structures, we may conclude that it is the properties of the **-šč-** and **-en**-suffixes that are responsible for the differences summarized in (i)–(viii).

(23) represents the core syntactic structure of a sentence whose predicate is [copula + SF *bare* adjective/**-en**-participle phrase]: its nP$_j$ subject is *inherited* from the **-en**-participle stem's derived external {j^N}$_1$ argument.[10] (24) is the structure of an LF **-en**-participle heading an *s-predicate*: its unlinked external theta role {j^-}$_1$ is V-bound by the head of its TBC, which is not shown here.[11] Compare the diathesis-based derivation of **-šč-** and **-en**-participle

stems in (25) and (26); see (17) for the syntactic structure of **-šč-**participle phrases.

(23)   Copula + SF **-en-**participle:[12]

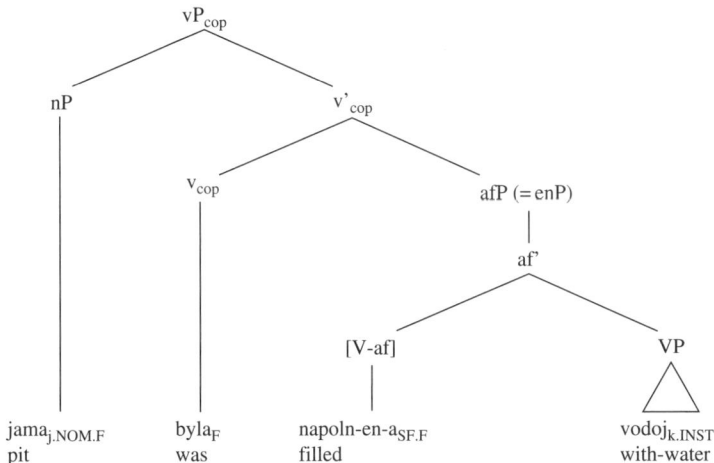

(24)   **-en-**participle s-predicate:

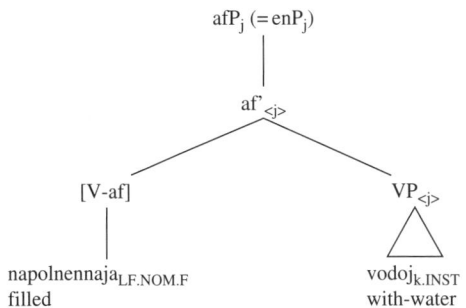

(25)   The derivation of **-šč-**participles:
a. {{i ^ N}$_1$ {j ^ N}$_2$ {k ^ N}$_3$ {- ^ **napolni-**}$_4$ +
b. {{ ^ -}$_1$ { ^ }$_2$ { ^ }$_3$ { ^ **-vš-**}$_4$ >
c. {{i ^ -}$_1$ {j ^ N}$_2$ {k ^ N}$_3$ {- ^ [**napolni-vš-**]}$_4$ +
....
d. {{ ^ -}$_1$ { ^ }$_2$ { ^ }$_3$ { ^ **-aja**$_{LF}$}$_4$ >
e. {{i ^ -}$_1$ {j ^ N}$_2$ {k ^ N}$_3$ {- ^ [**napolnivšaja**]}$_4$ =>

134 *Hybrid verbal adjuncts*

(26) The derivation of LF **-en**-participles:
  a. {{i ^ N}$_1$ {j ^ N}$_2$ {k ^ N}$_3$ {- ^ **napolni-**}$_4$} +
  b. {{- ^   }$_1$ { ^ - }$_2$ { ^   }$_3$ { ^ **-en-**}$_4$} >
  c. {{- ^ N}$_1$ {j ^ - }$_2$ {k ^ N}$_3$ {(i) ^ **napoln-en-**}$_4$} >>
  d. {{j ^ N}$_1$ {- ^ - }$_2$ {k ^ N}$_3$ {(i) ^ **napoln-en-**}$_4$} +
  ....
  e. {{   ^ - }$_1$ { ^   }$_2$ { ^   }$_3$ { ^ **-aja**$_{LF}$}$_4$} >
  f. {{j ^ - }$_1$ {- ^ - }$_2$ {k ^ N}$_3$ {(i) ^ **napolnennaja**}$_4$} =>

3.2.2 The interaction of external-argument altering suffixes

In this section we examine the interaction of the **-šč-**, **-af**$_{LF}$, and **-sja** suffixes: each has its own diathesis and each affects **V**'s external {i^N}$_1$ argument. We will naturally be interested in the *order* in which these suffixes and their diatheses compose in the same derivation. Our inquiry will be guided by the following question: Does the obligatory **V+šč+af**$_{LF}$**+sja** order of the stem **V** and its suffixes illustrated in (27) and (28) reflect the order in which their diatheses compose (see the Mirror Principle in Baker 1985)? I will argue that, although **-sja** is obligatorily *word-final*, it is nevertheless the first suffix to compose with **V** and that this order does *not* falsify the Mirror Principle. The [[V]-sja] stem then composes with the other suffixes, which determine [[V]-sja]-'s syntactic category. Finite verbs, infinitives, hybrid adverbials, and **-šč-**-participles (but not **-en**-participles) all compose with **-sja**.

The **-sja** suffix in modern Russian is a *word-level enclitic suffix*, i.e., [$_W$ W-**sja**], with two allomorphs: *-sja* and *-s'*; W denotes 'word,' which is simultaneously the lexical stem's maximal projection and the head of the syntactic phrase it projects. Since **-sja** is the only word-level enclitic in Russian, it obligatorily occurs at the right edge of the word no matter where in the diathetic derivation it is introduced.[13] Consider the participles in (27) and (28), each of which is composed of a **V** stem and the three suffixes under discussion.

(27) a. [$_{nP}$ [otkryvaju-šč-aja-sja] dver']
         opening   door
         'the door which is opening'
     b. [$_{nP}$ [afP$_{<j>}$ otkryvaju-**šc-aja**$_{LF.NOM-F-SG}$-**sja**] dver'$_{NOM-F-SG}$]
     c. [[[verb-stem+participle-forming suffix]+LF suffix]$_W$+sja]$_W$

(28) a. [$_{nP}$ [afP$_{<j>}$ plotno$_{ADV}$ zapiraju-šč-aja-sja$_{LF.NOM.F}$] dver'$_{NOM.F}$]
         '(the) [tightly locking] door'
     b. [$_{nP}$ [afP$_{<j>}$ vsju žizn'$_{ACC}$ tjanu-**vš-ij**$_{NOM}$-**sja** k obrazovaniju$_{DAT}$ čelovek$_{NOM}$]
         '[$_{nP}$(a) person [afP$_{<i>}$ (who) all (his) life has-been-drawn to education]]'

The left-to-right order of **V** and its suffixes can be easily explained if we bear in mind that:

3.2 *Participles in Russian* 135

(i) The unlinked external theta role of the participles in (27) and (28) is **V**'s *externalized* **j**, not its *initial* external **i**.

(ii) Affixation of **-sja** creates derived unaccusative **V**s and is thus responsible for the dethematization of **i** and the subsequent externalization of **j**.

(iii) The **-šč-** suffix deletes **V**'s external N_1, but does not affect its external or internal theta roles: the **-šč-**participle and its corresponding finite verb thus both have the same ordered set of theta roles, which is **V**'s inherited initial theta tier.

(iv) **-sja** has the same function in all Russian finite and nonfinite projections.

(v) **-sja**, unlike **-en-**, does not have its own categorial features and thus does not affect the category of **[[V]-sja]** (see the notion of *relativized head* in Williams 1994).

I will argue that the order of composition of **V** and its three suffixes is *intrinsic*, i.e., the properties of the suffixes themselves can be shown to determine their order of composition: any order other than the one in (29) results in an ill-formed structure (see (30)). **V** first composes with enclitic **-sja**, creating a derived unaccusative diathesis. **[[V]-sja]** then composes with **-šč-**, creating the participle stem **[[V-šč-]-sja]**, which then composes with the LF inflectional suffix, creating **[[V-šč-af$_{LF}$]-sja]**, the head of the participle phrase. To see how this works *in vivo*, let us work through the derivation of *otkryvaju-šč-aja-sja* 'opening' in (27).[14]

(29) The derivation of *otkryvaju-šč-aja-sja*:
  a. {{i ^ N}$_1$ {j ^ N}$_2$ {- ^ - }$_3$ {- ^ otkryvaju-}$_4$}   +
  b. {{- ^   }$_1$ { ^ - }$_2$ { ^   }$_3$ { ^ -sja-}$_4$}   >
  c. {{- ^ N}$_1$ {j ^ - }$_2$ {- ^ - }$_3$ {(i) ^ [[otkryvaju]-sja]}$_4$}   >>
  d. {{j ^ N}$_1$ {- ^ - }$_2$ {- ^ - }$_3$ {(i) ^ [[otkryvaju]-sja]}$_4$}   +
  ....
  e. {{ ^ -}$_1$ { ^ }$_2$ { ^   }$_3$ { ^ -šč-}$_4$}   >
  f. {{j ^ - }$_1$ {- ^ -}$_2$ {- ^ - }$_3$ {(i) ^ [[otkryvaju-šč]-sja] }$_4$}   +
  ....
  g. {{ ^ -}$_1$ { ^ }$_2$ { ^   }$_3$ { ^ -aja$_{LF}$}$_4$}   >
  h. {{j ^ - }$_1$ {- ^ -}$_2$ {- ^ - }$_3$ {(i) ^ [otkryvajuščajasja]}$_4$}   => (27)

(29a) is **V**'s initial diathesis, which composes with the diathesis of **-sja** in (29b), yielding the derived unaccusative diathesis in (29c).[15] Since, as we saw in chapter 1, {{-^N}$_1$ {j^-}$_2$ ...} in (29c) does not map onto a well-formed syntactic structure, **j** obligatorily relinks (*externalizes*) to delinked (dethematized) N_1, yielding (29d), ending the derivation's first phase.[16] The diathesis in (29d) is the common denominator underlying the derivation of finite verbs (*otkryvaetsja*), infinitives (*otkryvat'sja*), participles (*otkryvajuščajasja*), and hybrid adverbials (*otkryvajas'*). Next, -šč- and its diathesis in (29e) composes with (29d), producing the participial stem in (29f), which is an s-predicate; -šč- is responsible for the deletion of N_1 (see $\{j{\wedge}N\}_1 > \{j{\wedge}\text{-}\}_1$ in (29d) > (29f)). The final phase in this derivation is the introduction of the adjectival inflection suffix, which must be the LF since -šč-participles are inherent *s-predicates*.

It may at first seem plausible to claim that, given the s-predicate forming function of the LF suffix when affixed to *adjective* stems in chapter 2, the only contribution -šč- makes to the derivation is introduction of the adjectival categorial features that convert **V** into a hybrid participle stem. This entails that the LF suffix deletes **V**'s external N_1 in the derivation of both -šč-participles and LF primary adjectives, which seems to capture a generalization. The problem with this alternative is that it requires the stipulation that -šč-participle stems cannot compose with SF suffixes (*Ona_{NOM} byla čitaju-šč-a_{SF} knigu$_{ACC}$ 'She was reading the-book'); but this stipulation follows automatically in the derivation proposed in (29). The down-side of (29) is that, while the LF suffix is responsible for the deletion of N_1 in the derivation of LF adjectives, it is selected by $\{i{\wedge}\text{-}\}_1$ and $\{j{\wedge}\text{-}\}_1$ in the derivation of -šč-participles.

A natural question here is therefore: Does affixation of the LF suffix create s-predicates or do s-predicates select LF suffixes? This is the same kind of chicken-or-egg pseudo-problem we encounter in the derivation of impersonal sentences: does the 'nonagreement' **o**-suffix create subjectless diatheses (i.e., $\{i{\wedge}N\}_1 + $ -o $ > \{\text{-}{\wedge}\text{-}\}_1$) or is -o selected by the $\{\text{-}{\wedge}\text{-}\}_1$ external argument, as in the case of underived impersonal verbs like *tošnit'* (see *Menja*$_{ACC}$ *tošnilo* '(lit.) Me nauseated')? The solution I propose is this: when -o is affixed to a diathesis with a $\{i{\wedge}N\}_1$ external argument, it is responsible for its deletion, and this derived diathesis projects as an impersonal (subjectless) sentence, i.e., $\{i{\wedge}N\}_1 + $ -o $>$ $\{\text{-}{\wedge}\text{-}\}_1$ (see Babby 2008). In the case of an underived impersonal verb like *tošnit'*, -o must be affixed to it since its initial external argument is $\{\text{-}{\wedge}\text{-}\}_1$ to begin with and, therefore, no other suffix is possible. This type of biunique, reversible relation can be represented in the form of a bidirectional rule-schema: $\{\text{-}{\wedge}\text{-}\}_1 <=> $ -o. What is important here is the *relation* between argument structure and morphology, not the derivational history. The LF suffix works in essentially the same way: when its diathesis composes with a lexical-stem diathesis whose external argument is $\{i{\wedge}N\}_1$, -af_{LF} deletes N_1 (as in the case of primary adjective stems). In the case of the -šč-participle stem, which already has a delinked $\{i{\wedge}\text{-}\}_1$ external argument, -af_{LF} must be affixed to it. This relation too can be represented in templatic terms as $\{\theta{\wedge}\text{-}\}_1 <=> $ -af_{LF} (where $\theta = $ **i**, **j**, or **k**), which means in derivational terms that whichever member of the <=> equation is introduced first requires the introduction of the other. We will return to the affixation of -šč- and the LF below.

It is not necessary to stipulate that affixation of -sja must precede that of -šč- in (29): if the order is reversed, the final diathesis projects an ill-formed syntactic structure:

(30)   a. $\{\{i \wedge N\}_1 \{j \wedge N\}_2 \{- \wedge -\}_3 \{- \wedge \text{otkryvaju-}\}_4\}$ +
        b. $\{\{\wedge -\}_1 \{\wedge\}_2 \{\wedge\}_3 \{\wedge \text{-šč-}\}_4\}$ >
        c. $\{\{i \wedge -\}_1 \{j \wedge N\}_2 \{- \wedge -\}_3 \{- \wedge [\text{otkryvaju-šč}]-\}_4\}$ +

        d. $\{\{- \wedge\}_1 \{\wedge -\}_2 \{\wedge\}_3 \{\wedge \text{-sja-}\}_4\}$ >
        e. *$\{\{- \wedge -\}_1 \{j \wedge -\}_2 \{- \wedge -\}_3 \{(i) \wedge [\text{otkryvaju-šč-sja}]\}_4\}$

(30a) is **V**'s initial diathesis, which composes with the diathesis of -šč- in (30b), yielding (30c), which is an s-predicate participle stem. (30c) now composes with the diathesis of -sja in (30d): since the function of -sja is to create unaccusative diatheses from transitive diatheses, **V**'s external theta role **i** is dethematized. But this produces the *impersonal* $\{-\wedge-\}_1$ external argument in (30e), which is an ill-formed -šč-participle diathesis because it has no unlinked external theta role and its syntactic projection cannot be V-bound (controlled). Note too that $\{j\wedge-\}_2$ in (30e) cannot *externalize* because -šč- has already deleted **V**'s N_1 and there is therefore no external $\{-\wedge N\}_1$ linking site for **j** to relink to, and $\{j\wedge-\}_2$'s syntactic projection is thus ill-formed for the following reason: an unlinked *internal* theta role cannot be V-bound in syntactic structure and is ill-formed since it violates the diathesis theory version of the Theta Criterion: an unlinked and unbound theta role is syntactically ill-formed. Since composing **V** with -af$_{LF}$ first also derives a nonviable final diathesis, the [[V-šč-af$_{LF}$]-sja] word-internal order is the only possible one. Since this order follows naturally from the suffixes' diatheses, I conclude that the order of diathesis-composition in (29) is *intrinsic*.[17]

The reason that the word-level enclitic -sja suffix is not the *head of the word*, which is canonically the right-most suffix, is this: unlike -en-, -sja has *no inherent categorial features* and, therefore, cannot be the head, which is the source of the categorial features that project to the word's maximal node: the suffix immediately to the left of -sja is thus the categorial head of the word (see the notion of *relativized head* in Williams 1994).

3.2.3 Accusative case assignment

Russian sentences have two complementary structural cases: the nominative, whose domain is VP-external, and the accusative, whose domain is VP-internal. I will be concerned here with accounting for the accusative case only since

Russian nonfinite verbal categories do not have nominative subjects.[18] What needs to be explicitly accounted for is this: Why is the direct object (nP_j) of finite verbs, -šč-participles (which are syntactically LF *adjectives*), hybrid adverbials (gP_i), infinitives, and gerundive nominals (in English) assigned structural accusative case? I will argue below that, according to the analysis proposed above, this case distribution is due to the fact that all verbal categories have a syntactic common denominator, namely, VP-in-afP structure (see (5) and (7)), and the fact that structural accusative case is assigned to the nP in spec-VP. But there is a hitch: transitive derived nominals and **-en-** participles also have an encapsulated VP, but nevertheless do not have accusative direct objects, which means that, as we shall see below, accusative case assignment cannot be accounted for solely on the basis of an intact $[_{VP}\ nP_j\ V']$.

All verbal categories, hybrid and homogeneous, finite and nonfinite, s-predicate and s-clause, share an intact VP complement of an **-af**, i.e., $[_{af'}\ [V\text{-af}]_{af}\ VP]$, where **-af** is the affixal head of the afP or afP_i containing VP. The direct object nP is projected from **V**'s initial $\{j{\wedge}N\}_2$ position in the diathesis to the spec-VP position in syntax, i.e., $\{j{\wedge}N\}_2 \Rightarrow [_{VP}\ nP_{j.ACC}\ V']$; see (31):

(31) $[_{afP(i)}\ (nP_i)\ [_{af'}\ [_{af}V\text{-af}]\ [_{VP}\ nP_{J.ACC}\ V']]]$

Assuming that all transitive verbal categories have the structure in (31), the nP_j in spec-VP is the common denominator unifying the assignment of accusative case to direct objects. The obvious candidate for the accusative-case *probe* (assigner/checker) is the proximate affixal head $[V\text{-af}]_{af}$ in (31). This proposal correctly predicts that it is the $[_{af'}\ [V\text{-af}]_{af}\ [_{VP}\ nP_{j.ACC}\ V']]$ configuration that is relevant for accusative case assignment: it makes no difference whether $[_{afP}...af'...]$ is finite or nonfinite, an s-predicate or s-clause. Accusative is a *structural* case because it is not assigned by a specific lexical item or a *particular* suffix (quirky case) or a particular theta role (theta or semantic case): any *verbal* suffixal head **[V-af]** assigns accusative case to the nP in spec-VP, which explains why transitive -šč-participles, hybrid adverbials, infinitives, and finite verbs all have accusative direct objects: the **-af** in derived nominal phrases is nominal (i.e. [+N] [–V]), not verbal, and the structural case in nPs is genitive: $[_{n'}\ [V\text{-n}]_n\ [_{VP}\ nP_{j.GEN}\ V']]$ (n is the derived-nominal forming suffix and head of nP).[19]

Let us look at the concrete example in (32a), where the preposition *s* 'with' assigns quirky instrumental case. The case of *roli* 'roles,' the direct object of the transitive -šč-participle *otrepetirova-vš-imi*$_{INST.PL}$, is accusative, which tells us the following: (i) since the direct objects of participles and finite verbs are accusative, accusative case assignment has nothing to do with finiteness; (ii) the

3.2 Participles in Russian   139

case assigned to the participle itself does *not* in any way affect the accusative case of its direct object (see (32a–c)).[20]

(32)   a. [$_{PP}$ s [$_{nPINST}$ [$_{afP<i>}$ otrepetirovavšimi   **roli**]   akterami]]
          with   rehearsed:LF.INST.PL roles:**acc**.PL actors:INST.PL
          'with actors (who have) rehearsed (their) roles'
    b. k [$_{nPDAT}$ [otrepetirovavšim$_{DAT}$ **roli**$_{ACC}$] akteram$_{DAT}$]
        'to actors (who have) rehearsed (their) roles'
    c. [$_{nPNOM}$ [otrepetirovavšie$_{NOM}$ **roli**$_{ACC}$] aktery$_{NOM}$]

(33)   a. Ja izbegal devuški, čitajuščej   **knigu** / *knigi.
         'I avoided the-girl$_{GEN.F}$, reading$_{LF.GEN.F}$ the-book$_{ACC/*GEN}$.'
    b. Ja   podražal devuške, čitajuščej   **knigu**/*knige.
         'I$_{NOM.M}$ imitated$_M$ the-girl$_{DAT.F}$, reading$_{DAT.F}$ the-book$_{ACC/*DAT}$.'
    c. Ja sklonilsja k [[uže zanjavšemu$_{DAT}$ **svoe mesto**$_{ACC}$] ministru$_{DAT}$].
         'I leaned-over to the minister$_{DAT}$ [(who had) already occupied$_{DAT}$ his seat$_{ACC}$].'

The participle phrases in (32) and (33) are nP-internal attributive modifiers, which agree in case, number, and gender with the head noun: the participle phrase [$_{afP<i>}$*otrepetirovavšimi*$_{INST}$ *roli*$_{ACC}$] in (32a) is adjoined to a projection of the head noun *akterami*$_{INST}$ and its unlinked external theta role **i** is vertically bound inside nP$_{INST}$, which is itself the complement of the instrumental case assigning preposition *s* 'with.' The accusative case of the participle's direct object is not affected by the lexical case feature that is assigned to the participle, which conforms to the following descriptive generalization: the case feature assigned to nP percolates (spreads) nP-internally to the head noun and its modifiers (determiners, quantifiers, adjectives, and participles), but *not* to the arguments of these modifiers.[21]

Given the VP-in-afP$_{(i)}$ structure of verbal categories in (31), the nP-internal case distribution illustrated in (32) and (33) can be explained as follows: (i) all verbal categories have an encapsulated VP, which is a natural barrier to *percolation* of the matrix nP's case feature; (ii) case assignment to nP$_j$ in [$_{af'}$ [V-af]$_{af}$ [$_{VP}$ nP$_j$ V']] does not involve percolation from above. The VP node is a barrier to percolation of the case feature assigned to afP$_{(i)}$-in-nP because it is a verbal projection and thus has no *case receptor*, i.e., no unvalued case feature that can be valued by a contiguous valued case feature; this blocks the introduction of the matrix nP's case feature into the VP domain. Only [+N] nominal categories have case receptors. The assignment of accusative case to the direct object of transitive participles is thus maximally local, i.e., nP$_j$ in spec-VP is assigned accusative case by the functional head [V-af]$_{af}$ that is VP's sister: [$_{af'}$ [V-af]$_{af}$ [$_{VP}$ nP$_{j.ACC}$ V']] provided -**af**'s feature complex has +V.

140 Hybrid verbal adjuncts

The accusative case of the participle's direct object *roli* 'roles' in (32)–(33) cannot be explained in terms of a long-distance probe–goal relation: the matrix verb *napisal* in (34) assigns accusative only to the matrix direct object (*stat'ju*); we see in (35) that the accusative case of *roli* is entirely independent of accusative case assignment in its matrix clause.

(34)   Ja nedavno napisal stat'ju$_{ACC}$ o [xorošo otrepetirovavšix$_{LOC}$ roli$_{ACC}$ akterax$_{LOC}$].
      'I recently wrote an-article about [actors who rehearsed their roles very well].'

(35)   Nedavno byla napisana stat'ja$_{NOM}$ o [xorošo otrepetirovavšix$_{LOC}$ roli$_{ACC}$ akterax$_{LOC}$].
      'An article was recently written about [actors who rehearsed their roles well].'

(36) is the structure of the dative participle phrase in (32b); the participle-forming affix **-šč- (-af)** is realized as *-vš-*. The VP node blocks percolation of the lexical dative case into VP, thereby permitting structural accusative case to be assigned to the direct object in spec-VP.

(36)

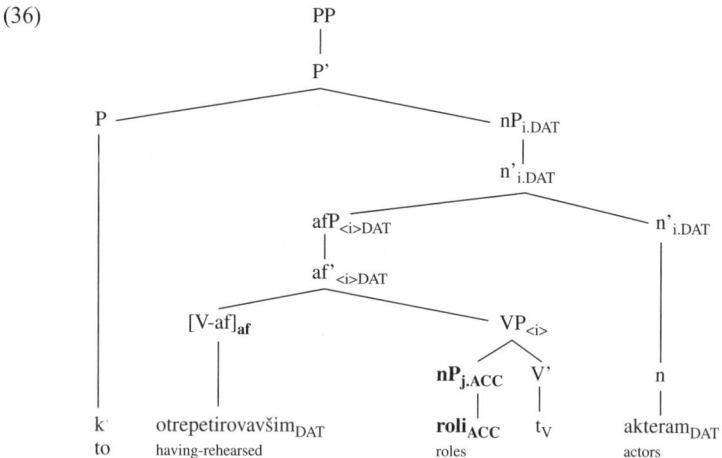

Summary: (37) is the schematic representation of structural accusative case assignment to direct objects: **-af** stands for the participle-forming suffix (-šč-), the infinitive-forming suffix (**-ti**), etc.; it makes no difference whether the maximal projection of **-af** is an s-clause [$_{afP}$ nP$_i$ af'$_{<i>}$], as in the case of object-controlled infinitive complements, or an s-predicate afP$_i$, as in the case of hybrid adverbials. The accusative case of nP$_j$ is assigned (checked) by any affixal head - **af** whose feature matrix includes [+V], which correctly excludes derived nominals, whose affixal head **-n** is [+N]/[–V] and thus assigns structural *genitive* case to the nP$_j$ in spec-VP, as in (38).[22]

(37)   Assignment (checking) of structural accusative case by -**af**$_{[+V]}$ to nP$_j$:²³

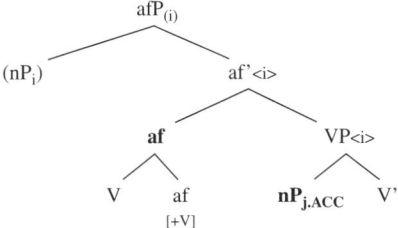

(38)   Assignment (checking) of structural genitive case by -**n**$_{[-V]}$ in derived nominals:

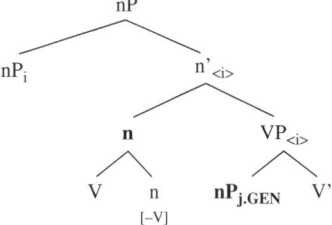

3.2.4   *Reflexive binding in participle phrases*

This section presents independent evidence supporting the s-predicate structure of -*šč*-participle phrases posited above: their putative unlinked external **i** is often the only potential binder of reflexive pronouns in sentences like (39) to (40) (coreferentiality is indicated by underlining or boldface).²⁴ *Mne* 'me' in (39a), which is the dative subject of the infinitive *podavat'* 'to-offer,' cannot be construed as the antecedent of the transitive participle's reflexive direct object *sebja*. *Generalu*, the infinitive's dative indirect object, is modified by the bracketed dative afP$_i$ participle phrase, making it the head of the smallest TBC in which afP$_i$ is vertically bound and, therefore, the unambiguous antecedent of *sebja* (see below for details); the interrogative enclitic particle *li* 'whether' is glossed as 'Q.'

(39) a. Podavat'   li   mne$_{DAT}$ ruku$_{ACC}$ [generalu$_{DAT}$, [$_{afPi}$ zapjatnavšemu$_{LF.DAT}$
        to-give   Q   me   hand   to-general   (who-has) sullied
        sebja$_{ACC}$ podlym postupkom$_{INST}$]]$_{nP}$?
        (him)self   by-vile deed
        'Should I offer my-hand to-the-general [having-sullied (him)self
        (*me/myself) by-a-vile deed]?' (Akunin)
     b. ... generalu$_{DAT}$, kotoryj$_{NOM}$ zapjatnal sebja$_{ACC}$ podlym postupkom$_{INST}$.
        'the-general, who sullied himself by a vile act'

142 *Hybrid verbal adjuncts*

(40) a. My govorim [$_{PP}$ o [$_{nP}$ gerojax, [$_{afP<i>}$ žertvujuščix soboj$_{<j>}$ radi rodiny]]].
'We speak [$_{PP}$ about [heroes [sacrificing themselves (*us/ourselves) for (their) country]]].'
b. Ves' gorod byl zatoplen [$_{nP}$ vodoj$_{INST}$, [$_{afP<i>}$ ostavšej$_{LF.INST}$ posle sebja$_{GEN}$ tolstyj sloj$_{ACC}$ grjazi$_{GEN}$]].
'(lit.) (The) entire city was inundated [with-water, [leaving after (it)self (a) thick layer of-mud]].'
c. **Oni** uveličivali rasstojanie$_{ACC}$ meždu **soboj**$_{INST}$ i [$_{nP}$ lavoj$_{INST.F}$, [$_{afP<i>}$nesšej$_{LF.INST.F}$ s soboj$_{INST}$ smert'$_{ACC}$]].
'**They** increased the-distance between **themselves** and the-lava, bringing death with-(it)self.'
d. **Ona** smotrela na [$_{nP}$ svjaščenika$_{ACC}$, [$_{afP<i>}$ pozvolivšego$_{LF.ACC}$ sebe$_{DAT}$ projavit' nepočtitel'nost'$_{ACC}$, [$_{gP<i>}$ xarakterizuja ee (***svoego**) otca$_{ACC}$]]].
'**She** looked at the priest, [having-allowed (him)self (*her(self)) to-show disrespect [when-characterizing **her** (***his**) father]].'[25]

It is clear from these sentences that reflexive pronouns in Russian are not canonically subject-oriented, as often assumed. A more empirically adequate generalization is this: reflexive pronouns are canonically bound by the most proximate asymmetrically c-commanding theta role.[26] This generalization can be formalized as follows:

(41) Reflexive binding as vertical binding:
The antecedent of a reflexive pronoun is the head of the *smallest* TBC in which the reflexive is the vertically bound tail, and the head and tail are coreferential.[27]

Given (41), let us now consider the reflexive binding in (40a)'s PP, which is represented in (42) (*žertvovat'* / *žertvujuščix* c-selects the quirky instrumental case of reflexive *soboj*).

(42)

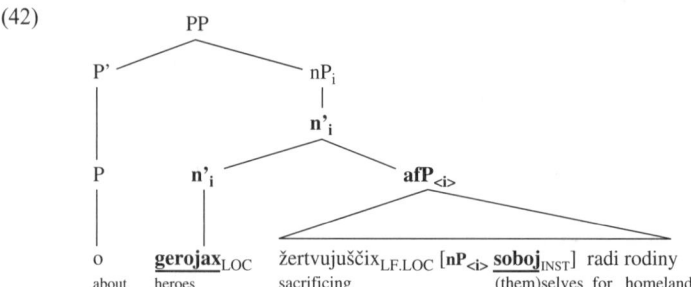

Since **-šč**-participles are s-predicates, (41) correctly predicts that a reflexive pronoun inside a **-šč**-participle phrase's encapsulated VP$_{<i>}$ is vertically bound by the participle phrase's (afP$_i$) unlinked external theta role **i** and thus canonically construed as coreferential with the head of the matrix nP, which is also the head of TBC in which the afP$_i$ is V-bound.[28] More specifically, *gerojax*$_{\text{LOC.PL}}$ 'heroes' is the head of the nP in (42)/(40a) and thus unambiguously construed as the antecedent of reflexive *soboj*: [$_{nPi}$ **soboj**$_{\text{INST}}$] is V-bound by the participle's encapsulated VP$_i$ (not shown here), which is V-bound by **afP$_i$**, which is in turn V-bound by **n'$_j$**, thereby making *gerojax* the head of the TBC in which *soboj*$_{<i>}$ is V-bound and, therefore, its antecedent. (41) correctly predicts that the nominative matrix subject *ja* 'I' in (40a) cannot antecede *soboj* in (40a)/(42). All the other sentences in (39) and (40) work in essentially the same way.

We cannot claim that *soboj* in (40a) is V-bound by the antecedent-bound PRO$_i$ subject of a participle s-clause headed by *žertvujuščix* because PRO$_i$ would be the head of the TBC in which the afP$_i$ participle-phrase was vertically bound, which would incorrectly predict that the participle would agree in case with PRO$_i$, which, however, is not in the locative case:

(43)

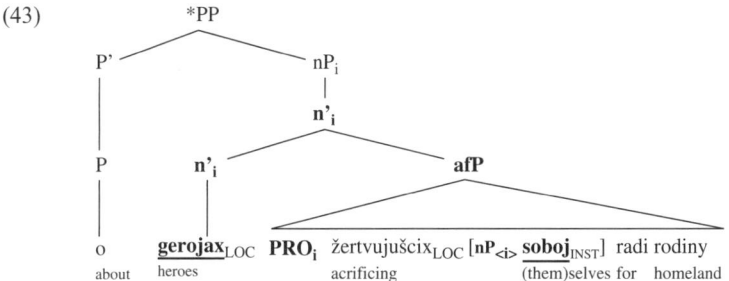

The ill-formedness of (43) is an important piece of evidence supporting my hypothesis that -**šč**-participle phrases are inherent s-predicates and, therefore, that (42) is the correct morphosyntactic representation of (40a).[29]

Note too that (41) also accounts for the fact that, although the nominative subject pronoun *ona* and direct object pronoun *ee* in (40d) are coreferential, *ee* cannot be replaced by reflexive *svoego (otca)* without changing the sentence's meaning because *ee* is the direct object of the gP$_i$, which is not vertically bound in a TBC in which *ona* is the head. If *ee* were replaced by *svoego*, the latter would, as predicted by (41), have *svjaščenika* as its antecedent, not *ona* (the masculine gender of the reflexive possessive adjective *svoego* is determined by *otca*, not by its antecentent).[30]

3.2.5 *-em-participles*

The -**em**-participle is of interest because, as we see in (44a–g), it combines properties of -**šč**- and -**en**-participles and is thus a 'hybrid hybrid' verbal category. See the examples in (45) to (47).

(44) (a) Like -šč-participles and unlike -en-participles, -em-participles compose with the LF only (see Timberlake 2004), which entails that they are exclusively s-predicates.[31] Thus only primary adjectives and -en-participles have SFs and compose with the copula.
 (b) Like -en-participles and unlike -šč-participles, -em-participles are formed from transitive verbs only.
 (c) Like -en-participles and unlike -šč-participles, the -em-participle's unlinked external theta role is always externalized **j**. Thus the derivation of -em-participles involves *dethematization* of **V**'s external **i** and the creation of a derived unaccusative diathesis.
 (d) -em-participles are canonically derived from prefixed imperfective verb stems, a restriction not shared by the other two participles.
 (e) -em-participles are the functional equivalent of -šč-participles affixed with the -sja suffix; see (45a–b) and (46a–b).
 (f) Like -en-participles, -em-participles do not compose with -sja (*V-em-LF-sja), which is what we expect: -en-, -em-, and -sja all derive unaccusative diatheses and thus cannot feed each other.
 (g) Unlike -en- and -šč + sja participles, -em-participles are *exclusively* passive, which means simply that dethematized **i** *obligatorily* relinks to {i^ [V-em-]}₄; there are accordingly no active or middle voice -em-participles. Recall that -en- and -šč + sja participles can be either passive or middle (cf. glosses of (46a–b)).

(45) a. [$_{nP}$ deti,   nakazyvaju-šč-ie-sja   roditeljami]
       children:NOM.PL   being-punished:LF.NOM.PL   by-parents:INST
       'children (who are) being-punished by (their) parents'
    b. [$_{nP}$ deti,   nakazyvaj-em-ye   roditeljami]
       children:NOM.PL   being-punished:LF.NOM.PL   by-parents:INST
       'children (who are) being-punished by (their) parents' (Livšic 1964: 164)

(46) a. Anna uslyšala [$_{nP}$ skrip$_{ACC}$ [otkryvaj-em-oj$_{LF.GEN.F}$ dveri$_{GEN.F}$]].
       'Anna heard the-creak [of-a-door being-opened].'
    b. Anna uslyšala [$_{nP}$ skrip [otkryvaju-šč-ej-sja dveri]].
       'Anna heard the-creak of a door opening/being-opened.'

(47) a. On uslyšal [zvuk$_{ACC}$ [ključa$_{GEN}$, [povoračivaj-em-ogo$_{LF.GEN}$ v zamke]]].
       'He heard [the-sound [of-a-key [being-turned in the-lock]]].'
    b. Nikita vspominal [vkus$_{ACC}$ [foreli$_{GEN.F}$ [podava-em-oj$_{LF.GEN.F}$ na zavtrak]]].
       N.   recalled   taste   of-trout   served   for breakfast
       'Nikita recalled the-taste of the-trout served for breakfast.'
    c. [$_{nP}$ Polovina$_{NOM}$ [$_{nP}$ [$_{afP<i>}$ vstrečaj-em-yx$_{GEN}$ mnoju$_{INST}$] ljudej$_{GEN}$]] kažutsja mne$_{DAT}$ znakomymi$_{INST}$.
       '[Half [of-the-people [met by-me]]] seem to-me (to be) familiar.'

Since we see in (44a–g) above that composition of -em-'s and **V**'s diatheses involves *both* dethematization, i.e., {{-^N}₁ {j^-}₂ ...} >> {{j^N}₁ {-^-}₂...},

3.2 Participles in Russian

and the obligatory deletion of **V**'s external **N**, i.e., $\{j\wedge N\}_1 > \{j\wedge-\}_1\}$, (48) is the simplest derivation capable explaining how **-em-**particples come to combine aspects of the derivations of both **-en-** and **-šč-**participles.

(48) The derivation of the **-em**-participle (*otkryvaj-em-oj* in (45a)):
    a. $\{\{i \wedge N\}_1 \{j \wedge N\}_2 \{- \wedge -\}_3 \{- \wedge \text{otkryvaj-}\}_4\}$ +
    b. $\{\{- \wedge \ \}_1 \{ \wedge -\}_2 \{ \wedge \ \}_3 \{ \wedge \text{-em-}\}_4\}$ >
    c. $\{\{- \wedge N\}_1 \{j \wedge -\}_2 \{- \wedge -\}_3 \{i \wedge \text{otkryvaj-em-}\}_4\}$ >>
    d. $\{\{j \wedge N\}_1 \{- \wedge -\}_2 \{- \wedge -\}_3 \{i \wedge \text{otkryvaj-em-}\}_4\}$ +
    ....
    e. $\{\{ \wedge -\}_1 \{ \wedge \ \}_2 \{ \wedge \ \}_3 \{ \wedge \text{-oj}_{\text{LF.GEN.F.SG}}\}_4\}$ >
    f. $\{\{j \wedge -\}_1 \{- \wedge -\}_2 \{- \wedge -\}_3 \{i \wedge \text{otkryvaj-em-oj}\}_4\}$ =>

(48a), the initial diathesis of the monotransitive **V**, composes with (48b), the proposed diathesis of the **-em**-suffix, creating the derived unaccusative, passive diathesis in (48c): dethematized **i** here *obligatorily* relinks to **otkryvaj-em-**; cf. optional (**i**) in the derivation of **-en-** and **-šč + sja-**participles, which accounts for their passive ~ middle ambiguity. Next, **j** in (48c) externalizes, creating the **-em-**participle stem in (48d), which obligatorily composes with the diathesis of the LF suffix in (48e), deriving the final, projectable diathesis in (48f). Note that, according to (48), it is the LF suffix, not the **-em-** suffix, that deletes **V**'s external N_1. Thus the derivation in (48) requires the stipulation that: (i) relinking dethematized **i** to $\{-\wedge V\text{-em-}\}_4$ is obligatory; (ii) **-em-** stems must compose with **af**$_{\text{LF}}$ but not **-af**$_{\text{SF}}$.

The alternative to (48) is to claim that **-em-** both passivizes **V** and deletes its N_1, as in (49). But (49) is ill-formed because **j** cannot externalize (there is no external N_1 relinking site) and it thus derives an impersonal $\{-\wedge-\}_1$ participle, which is ill-formed since it cannot be V-bound, and, therefore, cannot agree in case or be controlled. $\{j\wedge-\}_2$ in (49c) is also ill-formed.

(49)   a. $\{\{i \wedge N\}_1 \{j \wedge N\}_2 \{- \wedge -\}_3 \{- \wedge \text{otkryvaj-}\}_4\}$ +
    b. $\{\{- \wedge -\}_1 \{ \wedge -\}_2 \{ \wedge \ \}_3 \{ \wedge \text{-em-}\}_4\}$ >
    c. *$\{\{- \wedge -\}_1 \{j \wedge -\}_2 \{- \wedge -\}_3 \{i \wedge \text{otkryvaj-em-}\}_4\}$

According to (48), the LF suffix deletes **V**'s N_1, delinking externalized **j**, producing the LF **-em**-participle *otkryvaj-em-oj* in (48f), which projects to syntax as a well-formed passive s-predicate. Note that the LF here has the same N_1-deleting function as the LF suffix in the derivation of LF adjectives and LF **-en**-participles (see chapter 2). Thus all three are opposed to the derivation of **-šč-**participles, where it is the **-šč-** suffix that deletes **V**'s N_1 and affixation of the LF is determined by the $\{\theta\wedge-\}_1$ s-predicate stem; see (29) repeated as (50).

146 *Hybrid verbal adjuncts*

(50) The derivation of *otkryvaju-šč-aja-sja*:
 a. {{i ^ N}$_1$ {j ^ N}$_2$ {- ^ -}$_3$ {- ^ otkryvaju-}$_4$} +
 b. {{- ^ }$_1$ { ^ - }$_2$ { ^   }$_3$ { ^ -sja-}$_4$} >
 c. {{- ^ N}$_1$ {j ^ - }$_2$ {- ^ - }$_3$ {(i) ^ [[otkryvaju]-sja]}$_4$} >>
 d. {{j ^ N}$_1$ {- ^ - }$_2$ {- ^ - }$_3$ {(i) ^ [[otkryvaju]-sja]}$_4$} +
 ....
 e. {{ ^ - }$_1$ { ^ }$_2$ { ^ }$_3$ { ^ -šč-}$_4$} >
 f. {{j ^ - }$_1$ {- ^ -}$_2$ {- ^ - }$_3$ {(i) ^ [[otkryvaju-šč]-sja] }$_4$} +
 ....
 g. {{ ^ -}$_1$ { ^ }$_2$ { ^ }$_3$ { ^ -aja$_{LF}$-}$_4$} >
 h. {{j ^ - }$_1$ {- ^ -}$_2$ {- ^ - }$_3$ {(i) ^ otkryvaju-šč-aja-sja}$_4$}

We see in (51) that if **-šč-** is affixed to **V** before the **-sja** suffix, the derivation creates the diathesis in (51e), which projects an ill-formed (uncontrollable) syntactic structure.

(51) a. {{i ^ N}$_1$ {j ^ N}$_2$ {- ^ -}$_3$ {- ^ otkryvaju-}$_4$} +
 b. {{ ^ -}$_1$ { ^ }$_2$ { ^ }$_3$ { ^ -šč-}$_4$} >
 c. {{ i ^ -}$_1$ { j ^ N}$_2$ {- ^ -}$_3$ {- ^ otkryvaju-šč-}$_4$} +
 ....
 d. {{- ^ }$_1$ { ^ -}$_2$ { ^ }$_3$ { ^ -sja-}$_4$} >
 e. *{{- ^ -}$_1$ { j ^ - }$_2$ {- ^ -}$_3$ {(i) ^ otkryvaju-šč-sja}$_4$}

The only function of **-em-** in (48), other than making the composite **[V-em]** head adjectival, is to passivize **V**, which is parallel to the composition of **V** with **-en-** or **-sja**: all three are 'voice suffixes,' which alter **V**'s theta tier, and are the first to compose with **V**. The **-šč-** suffix in this respect stands alone: it is not a voice suffix since it leaves **V**'s theta tier intact, which explains why **-šč**-participle phrases and the finite clauses they correspond to have the same theta roles projected to the same positions (**i** is external in both). Thus the effect of affixing **-šč-** to **V** is: (i) **V**'s upper theta tier is unaffected; (ii) like **-en-** and **-em-**, it introduces the categorial features that make the **[V-šč-]** head adjectival; (iii) according to (50), it is the only participle-forming suffix that is responsible for the deletion of **V**'s external **N$_1$**.

There are two related weak points in the derivations proposed above:

(i) There is nothing in (48d) preventing the SF from entering the derivation instead of the LF at this point, which means that the exclusive use of the LF must be *stipulated* since SF **-em**-participles are no longer used, e.g.: **Deti nakazyva-em-y*$_{SF.NOM.PL}$ *roditeljami* 'The-children are-being-punished by-(their)-parents.'

(ii) The LF suffix is responsible for the deletion of **V**'s **N$_1$** except in the derivation of **-šč**-participles. The motivation for claiming that **-šč-** deletes **N$_1$** was to avoid having to stipulate that **-šč**-participles do not have SFs. But, since we must use this device (stipulation) in the derivation of **-em**-participles (cf. (48) and (50)), the question arises whether we might better capture the parallelism between these suffixes and the derivations they drive by eliminating one of these two instances of stipulation. Since the stipulation that the **-em**-participle stem cannot compose with the SF stem cannot be avoided, our only alternative is to consider the revised derivation of **-šč-**participles in (52) and (53), where **V**'s external N_1 is deleted by the LF suffix, which requires the stipulation that SFs cannot compose with **-šč-**participle stems.

(52) Revised derivation of [**V-šč-af**$_{LF}$]:
  a. {{i ^ N}$_1$ {j ^ N}$_2$ {- ^ -}$_3$ {- ^ V-}$_4$}   +
  b. {{ ^ }$_1$ { ^ }$_2$ { ^ }$_3$ { ^ šč-}$_4$}   >
  c. {{i ^ N}$_1$ {j ^ N}$_2$ {- ^ -}$_3$ {- ^ [V-šč-]}$_4$}   +
  d. {{ ^ -}$_1$ { ^ }$_2$ { ^ }$_3$ { ^ -af$_{LF}$}$_4$}   >
  e. {{i ^ -}$_1$ {j ^ -N}$_2$ {- ^ -}$_3$ {- ^ [V-šč-af$_{LF}$]}$_4$}   =>

(53) Revised derivation of [**V-šč-LF-sja**]
  a. {{i ^ N}$_1$ {j ^ N}$_2$ {- ^ -}$_3$ {- ^ V-}$_4$}   +
  b. {{- ^ }$_1$ { ^ - }$_2$ { ^ }$_3$ { ^ -sja}$_4$}   >
  c. {{- ^ N}$_1$ {j ^ - }$_2$ {- ^ -}$_3$ {(i) ^ [[V]-sja]}$_4$}   >>
  d. {{j ^ N}$_1$ {- ^ - }$_2$ {- ^ -}$_3$ {(i) ^ [V-sja]}$_4$}   +
  ....
  e. {{ ^ }$_1$ { ^ }$_2$ { ^ }$_3$ { ^ -šč-}$_4$}   >
  f. {{j ^ N}$_1$ {- ^ - }$_2$ {- ^ -}$_3$ {(i) ^ [[V-šč-]sja]}$_4$}   +
  ....
  g. {{ ^ -}$_1$ { ^ }$_2$ { ^ }$_3$ { ^ -LF}$_4$}   >
  h. {{j ^ -}$_1$ {- ^ - }$_2$ {- ^ -}$_3$ {(i) ^ [[V-šč-af$_{LF}$]-sja]}$_4$}

The derivations in (52)/(53) have the following advantages:

(i) **V**'s external N_1 is deleted by the LF suffix in the derivation of all s-predicate participles and adjectives.

(ii) The sole function of the **-šč-**suffix is to create a participle from **V**; both tiers of **V**'s initial diathesis remain intact, which is a highly desirable result since it captures the intuition alluded to above that **-šč-**participle phrases are more 'verbal', i.e., closer to the structure of finite clauses than **-en-** and **-em-** phrases.

The derivations in (52)/(53) have the following disadvantage: It must be stipulated that the SF suffix cannot compose with **-šč-**participle and **-em-**participle stems. However, given that **-šč-** and **-em-**participles did compose with the SF at an earlier stage of Russian, stipulation may be the appropriate mechanism to exclude them in the modern language.

We shall see in the following sections that the **-g-** suffix employed in the derivation of hybrid adverbials, which are gP$_i$ s-predicates, is responsible for the deletion of **V**'s external **N₁**: since the head of gP$_i$ is an uninflected adverbial and thus does not compose with adjectival suffixes, the LF is not available here to account for the deletion of **N₁**.

3.3   Hybrid adverbials in Russian

This section is devoted to the derivation, projected morphosyntactic structure, and control of the Russian hybrid adverbial phrase: [$_{gPi}$ [$_{g'<i>}$ [$_g$V-g] VP$_{<i>}$]], where **-g-** is the phrase's affixal head. I shall present empirical evidence that hybrid adverbial phrases are s-predicates (gP$_i$), not s-clauses: [$_{gP}$ PRO$_i$ [$_{g'<i>}$ [$_g$V-g] VP$_{<i>}$]]. This section is pivotal because it is both a particularly clear illustration of diathesis theory's explanatory power and because it sets the stage for the derivation of infinitive s-predicates and s-clauses in chapter 4 and the predicate instrumental of adjectives in chapter 5.

My argumentation that hybrid adverbial phrases are s-predicates (gP$_i$) is based primarily on the case-agreement of the pronominal s-predicate adjectives *sam* 'by oneself,' *odin* 'alone,' and *ves'* 'all' when adjoined to gP$_i$.[32] My analysis correctly predicts that SAM$_i$ in [$_{VPi}$ VP$_i$ [$_{gPi}$ gP$_i$ SAM$_{<i>}$]] (or [$_{VPi}$ VP$_i$ [$_{gPi}$ SAM$_{<i>}$ gP$_i$]]) agrees in case with the nP to which VP$_i$ assigns its **i** role because this nP is the head of the TBC in which [$_{gPi}$ gP$_i$ SAM$_{<i>}$] is V(ertically) bound. In other words, the case of SAM$_i$ in [$_{VPi}$ VP$_i$ [$_{gPi}$ gP$_i$ SAM$_{<i>}$]] is not fixed since it depends on the case and syntactic function of the nP head of its TBC in the matrix clause. In contrast, the s-clause analysis predicts, incorrectly, that SAM$_i$ V-bound in a hybrid adverbial *clause* should always have the *same case* since the head if its TBC would always be the PRO$_i$ subject of the putative hybrid adverbial clause.

The sentences in (54) illustrate the essential properties of gP$_i$ (the hybrid adverbial is in boldface, its maximal projection gP$_i$ is in square brackets, and gP$_i$'s controller – the head of its TBC – is underlined (**-g-** is realized as *-v* in (54a) and *-a-* in (54b), where **-sja** is realized as *-s'*).[33]

(54)   a. <u>Nikita$_i$</u>   zaartačilsja, [$_{gP<i>}$ **uslyša-v** cenu].
           N:NOM   balked   hearing   price:ACC
           'Nikita balked (upon) hearing the-price (when he heard the price).'
    b. <u>Nikita$_i$</u>   spal   [$_{gP<i>}$ ne   **razdevaj-a-s'**].
           N:NOM   was-sleeping   NEG   undressing
           'Nikita was-sleeping [without getting-undressed].'
    c. <u>Artem$_{i,NOM}$</u> udaril ženu$_{ACC}$, [$_{gP<i>}$ **vernuvšis'** domoj tol'ko k utru (p'janym$_{PI.M}$ / *p'janoj$_{PI.F}$)].
           'Artem struck (his) wife [when-he-(*she)-returned home toward morning (drunk$_{M.PI}$ / *drunk$_{F.PI}$)].'

Hybrid adverbials and **-šč**-participles (hybrid adjectivals) both project adjunct s-predicate structures, i.e., [$_{afPi}$ [$_{af'}$ [V-af]$_{af}$ VP]], where **-af** is the suffixal

3.3 Hybrid adverbials in Russian

head that contributes the adverbial or adjectival categorial features responsible for making afP$_i$ a hybrid category. More specifically, {{i^-}$_1$ {j^N}$_2$ {k^N}$_3$ {-^[V-af]}$_4$} => [$_{afPi}$ [$_{af'<i>}$[V-af]$_{af}$ [$_{VP<i>}$ nP$_j$ [$_{V'}$ t$_v$ nP$_k$]]]]. In what follows, -šč- participle phrases will be represented as afP$_i$ and hybrid adverbial phrases as gP$_i$. Since gP$_i$ and afP$_i$ both project an unlinked external {i^-}$_1$ that must be V-bound, it is the difference in the categorial features contributed by their respective affixal heads that determines the differences in their syntactic distribution. gP$_i$ has the following criterial properties:

(i) gP$_i$ is a prototypical hybrid category: it has an intact encapsulated VP$_{<i>}$ which is the complement of an affixal head which has nonverbal (adverbial) categorial features.

(ii) gP$_i$ is thus externally adverbial, and, like primary adverbs in Russian, its head is uninflected for number, gender, and case, which predictably creates *attachment ambiguities*.[34]

(iii) gP$_i$ fulfills many of the same functions as manner adverbs and finite adverbial clauses.

(iv) gP$_i$'s unlinked external theta role must be V-bound and gP$_i$ behaves in many respects like a verbal anaphor (see (41)); primary adverbs do not have an external theta role (see Williams 1994: 73).

(v) Evidence is presented that hybrid adverbial phrases do not have clausal structure.

(vi) We see in (54c) that gP$_i$ cannot be object-controlled, i.e., vertically bound in a TBC whose head is the matrix direct object nP$_j$.[35] In more general terms, gP$_i$ is syntactically well-formed only when it is V-bound by the matrix verb's external theta role. (54c) is thus not ambiguous: only the subject *Artem*$_{i.NOM}$ can control *vernuvšis'*.[36] More specifically, *gP$_i$ must adjoin to and be V-bound by the matrix VP$_i$* (VP$_i$ may itself be the complement of a finite (vP) or nonfinite affix head); thus only [$_{VPi}$ VP$_i$ gP$_{<i>}$] is well-formed.

(vii) Unlike infinitives and like **-šč-** participles, hybrid adverbial phrases can never have an overt subject nP.

(viii) The following two facts demonstrate that hybrid adverbial phrases cannot be contained in CP: (a) gP$_i$ cannot be introduced by a complementizer (C); (b) as we see in (55), the relative pronoun *kotoryj* 'which' cannot precede the head of gP$_i$ (*k*-words in Russian are the counterpart of *wh*-words in English); (56) and (57) are additional examples.[37]

(55)   a. *Vot kniga, **kotoruju**$_{ACC}$ **pročitav**, ja ubedilsja v nevinnosti osuždennogo.
'Here is the book, **which having-read**, I became convinced of the defendant's innocence.'
         b. Vot kniga, [$_{gP<i>}$**pročitav kotoruju**], ja ubedilsja v nevinnosti osuždennogo.

'Here is the book, **having-read which**, I became convinced of the defendant's innocence.'

(56) È. Sèpir predložil rjad$_{ACC}$ [$_{nP}$ priznakov$_{GEN}$, [$_{TP}$ [$_{gPi}$ **pol'zujus' kotorymi**$_{INST}$] možno oxarakterizovat' morfologiju jazyka s raznyx storon]]. '(lit.) E. Sapir proposed several parameters, **using which** it-is-possible to-characterize the-morphology of-a-language from various points-of-view.'

(57) Èto rešenie vypolnjalo rol' [$_{nP}$ prikaza, [$_{TP}$ [$_{gP<i>}$ **podčinjajas' kotoromu**], možno vystraivat' svoe suščestvovanie]]. '(lit) This decision fulfilled the-role of-an-order, **subordinating-oneself to-which** it is possible to arrange one's life.'

If a CP were present in (55a), *kotoruju* 'which' would move to its spec-position and be situated at the left-edge of the clause, which, as we see, is ungrammatical. Only the word order in (55b) is possible, which, together with the obligatory absence of complementizers, demonstrates that no CP is present: *kotoruju*, the direct object of *pročitav*, thus remains in situ in spec-VP of the VP$_i$ encapsulated in gP$_i$ because there is no spec-CP for it to move to.

The absence of CP in sentences like (55) is a direct consequence of my hypothesis that hybrid adverbials phrases are gP$_i$ s-predicates (but not from the hypothesis that they are s-clauses). Since gP$_i$ must be V-bound and since C is a functional category (functor), gP$_i$-in-CP is ill-formed because: (i) it cannot be vertically bound by C or its projection, which have no external theta role; (ii) the CP node is a V-binding barrier, i.e., not a possible link in gP$_i$'s TBC: unbound theta roles are syntactically ill-formed.[38] If hybrid adverbial phrases were s-clauses, their PRO$_i$ subject would always be the head of gP$_i$'s TBC and, therefore, the obligatory absence of a higher CP would be unmotivated.

Summary: Sentence pairs like (55a–b) provide direct evidence that hybrid adverbial phrases are not s-clauses. (55b) is well-formed because the s-predicate structure of gP$_i$ precludes its merging with CP, which in turn correctly predicts that the accusative direct object *kotoruju* of [$_{gP<i>}$ *pročitav kotoruju*] must remain in situ in spec-VP: without CP, there is no spec-position landing site for it to move to.

The derivation of gP$_i$ from the monotransitive stem **uslyša-** 'hear' in (54a) is represented in (58), whose final diathesis in (58c) projects the syntactic structure in (59):

(58) The derivation of Russian hybrid adverbials:
  a. $\{\{i \wedge N\}_1 \{j \wedge N\}_2 \{- \wedge -\}_3 \{- \wedge \text{uslyša-}\}_4\}$ +
  b. $\{\{\wedge -\}_1 \{\wedge\}_2 \{\wedge\}_3 \{\wedge -v\}_4\}$ >
  c. $\{\{i \wedge -\}_1 \{j \wedge N\}_2 \{- \wedge -\}_3 \{- \wedge [\text{uslyšav}]\}_4\}$ => (54a)

(59)   The syntactic projection of (58c) (= gP$_i$ in (54a)):

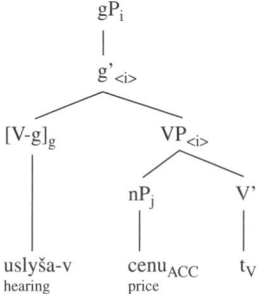

(58a), the initial diathesis of **uslyša-**, composes with (58b), the diathesis of the -**g**- affix (realized as -*v*), which deletes **V**'s initial **N$_1$** and supplies the adverbial features.

3.3.1   Earlier analyses of gP$_i$

The properties of hybrid adverbial phrases were accounted for in early generative theory by deriving them from underlying sentential structures like [$_{ADV}$ [$_S$ NP VP]], making use of the Equi-NP Deletion transformation, which deleted the subject NP of a constituent clause under identity to the matrix subject; S-node Deletion then pruned the nonbranching embedded S-node (see Babby 1979). But there are obvious problems with this type of structure-reducing derivation, e.g.:

(i) It violates the strong version of the lexicalist hypothesis: the -**g**- suffix was introduced as part of the *syntactic* derivation (see Babby 1974).

(ii) The Equi-NP Deletion rule eliminated the underlying adverbial clause's subject NP, which entails that hybrid adverbial phrases have neither an external theta role nor a subject NP (see Rappaport 1984); this renders them uncontrollable (unbindable).

(iii) The Equi-NP Deletion analysis incorrectly predicts that hybrid adverbial phrases should be object-controlled as well as subject-controlled. But we see in (60a) that [*vernuvšis' domoj tak pozdno*] 'upon-returning home so late' is obligatorily controlled by the matrix subject *ty* 'you' despite the fact that the matrix object *žene* 'wife' is closer, which looks like a Minimal Distance Principle (MDP) violation. An explicit analysis must be able to account for the fact that hybrid adverbials cannot be object-controlled: cf. (54c) and (60a).

152   *Hybrid verbal adjuncts*

(60) a. Čto$_{ACC}$ ty$_{NOM}$ skažeš' žene$_{DAT}$, [vernuvšis' domoj tak pozdno]?
what you say to-wife returning home so late
'What do you say to-(your)-wife when-(you)-return (*she-returns) home so late?'
b. Čto ty$_i$ skažeš' žene$_{DAT}$, [$_{gP_i}$ vernuvšis' domoj tak pozdno [$_{aP<i>}$ p'janyj$_{LF.NOM.M}$ / p'janym$_{PI.M}$]]?
'What do you say to-(your)-wife when-(you)-return home so late drunk?'
c. *Čto ty$_i$ skažeš' žene$_{DAT}$, [PRO$_i$ vernuvšis' domoj tak pozdno]?
d. *Čto ty$_i$ skažeš' žene$_{DAT}$, [PRO$_i$ vernuvšis' domoj tak pozdno [$_{afP<i>}$ p'janyj$_{LF.NOM.M}$]]?
'What do you say to-(your)-wife when-(you)-return home so late drunk?'

The GB analysis, which replaced the Equi-NP Deletion analysis, posits a gP clause with a PRO subject, which is antecedent bound by a proximate controller. But, as we have already seen, there is overwhelming independent evidence that hybrid adverbial phrases are s-predicates, not s-clauses. Second, the PRO$_i$-subject, clausal analysis in (60c–d) cannot account for the nominative case agreement of depictive LF adjectives adjoined to them (cf. (54c)).[39] Finally, given the structure in (60c/d), the MDP predicts that the object *žene* should be the controller (antecedent binder) of the PRO subject, not the matrix subject *ty*: we saw above that just the reverse is true.

3.3.2   The s-predicate analysis of hybrid adverbials
The basic problem with syntactic derivations of hybrid adverbial phrases is that *syntactic rules are not able to delete a subject nP without also deleting its theta role*. The derivation of gP$_i$ and of s-predicates in general requires an operation that deletes **V**'s external categorial head **N$_1$** but not the external **i** theta role linked to it in **V**'s initial diathesis. But this is precisely the kind of delinking operation that diathesis-based operations naturally perform (see (58)): given that the theta tier and the categorial tier of **V**'s diathesis are autonomous (see chapter 1), diathetic rules can operate on an argument's theta role without affecting the categorial head it is linked to (e.g., dethematization) or do just the opposite – delete a categorial head without affecting the theta role it is linked to (e.g., the derivation of s-predicates). Speaking in general terms, the existence of s-predicates presupposes the existence of the diathesis's two-tiered structure and of productive diathesis-level rules that can operate on individual slots (cells).

(61) represents the syntactic structure of (60a): gP$_i$ adjoins to and is vertically bound by the matrix VP$_i$, which assigns **i** to the subject nP *ty*. gP$_i$ is thus subject-controlled: *ty* is the head of the TBC in which gP$_i$ is vertically bound. (61) correctly predicts that gP$_i$ adjoined to matrix VP$_i$ is too high to be vertically bound by a VP$_i$-internal object. (63) is the structure of (60b), repeated as (62).

3.3 Hybrid adverbials in Russian 153

(61)

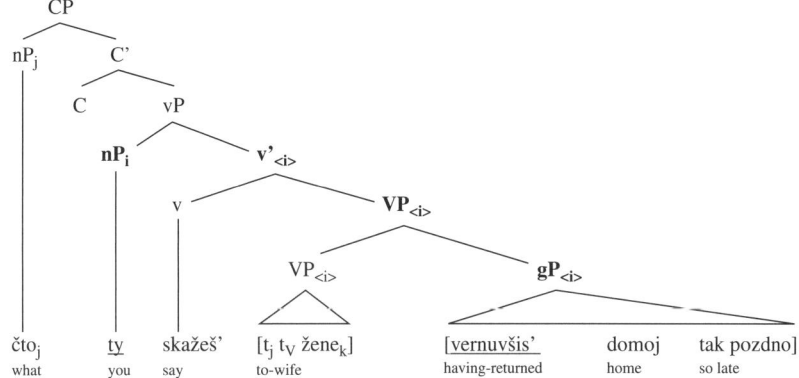

(62) Čto_j ty_i skažeš' žene_k [_{gP<i>} vernuvšis' domoj tak pozdno p'janyj_{LF.NOM.M}]]?
'What do you say to (your) wife when you return home so late drunk?'

(63)

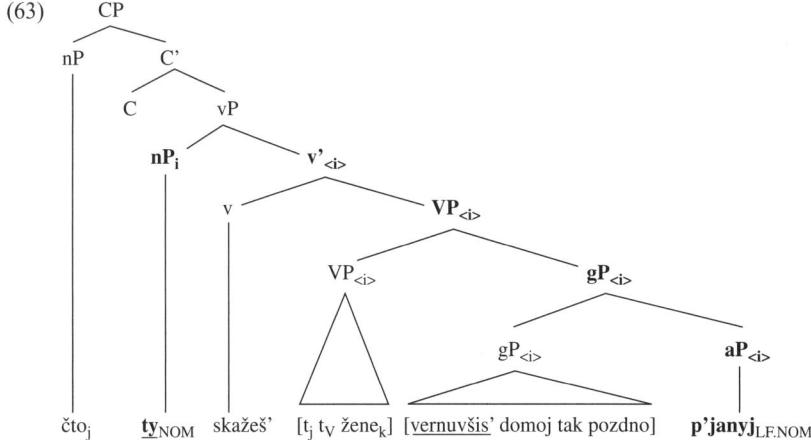

The TBC accounting for the control and nominative case agreement relation between the subject **ty** 'you' and the LF depictive adjective **p'janyj** in (63) is in boldface: nominative [_{aP<i>} *p'janyj*] 'drunk' is vertically bound by gP_i, which is vertically bound by the finite matrix VP_i, which assigns its external **i** theta role to **ty**, the subject of (63) and the head of the TBC in which *p'janyj* is V-bound: *p'janyj* therefore agrees with *ty* in case, gender, and number, and is *controlled* by it. The depictive adjective cannot agree with dative *žene* 'wife' (**Čto ty skažeš'* **žene**, *vernuvšis' domoj tak pozdno* [_{aP<i>} **p'janoj**_{LF.DAT.F}]? 'What do you say to your wife when she returns home so late drunk?') because

154 *Hybrid verbal adjuncts*

it is V-bound in gP_i, which obligatory adjoins to the matrix VP_i and is thus vertically bound in the TBC headed by the subject ty_i.

In the following examples, the underived s-predicate pronominal adjectives sam_i and *ves'* adjoin to gP_i: their nominative case, gender, and number agreement has the same explanation as that of *p'janyj* in (62)/(63). (65) is the structure of (64b). The case-agreement pattern in (62) and (64) is *not* predicted by the $[_{gP}\,[_{nP}\,PRO_i]\,[_g\,[V\text{-}g]_g\,[_{VP}\,nP_j\,[_{v'}\,t_v\,nP_k]]]]$ clausal analysis, according to which *sam*, *ves'*, and *p'janyj* should agree in case with the PRO_i subject.[40]

(64) a. **On** èto skazal, [**sam**_{<i>} ne znaja, počemu]$_{gP<i>}$.
 he:NOM.M that:ACC said himself:NOM.M not knowing why
 'He said that without knowing why himself.'
 b. **On** razdevalsja, [**ves'**_{<i>} vibriruja ot neterpenija]$_{gP<i>}$.
 he undressed, all:NOM.M vibrating from anticipation
 'He undressed, all trembling with anticipation.'
 c. **Sonja**$_{NOM.F}$ gromko rydala, [$_{gP<i>}$ kačajas' [$_{kP<i>}$ kak **p'janaja**$_{LF.NOM.F}$]].[41]
 'Sonia cried loudly, [staggering [as-though drunk]].'

(65)

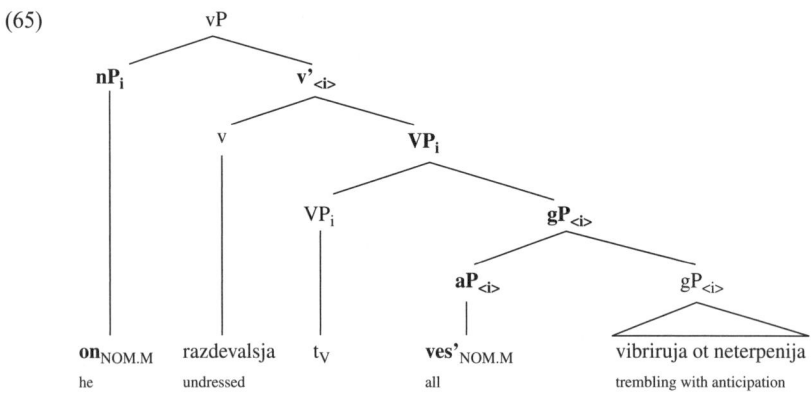

According to this analysis of gP_i, no *construction-specific* rules are required to account for its morphosyntactic properties: if the hybrid adverbial phrase is an s-predicate adverbial adjunct that cannot be adjoined lower than matrix VP_i, we have a ready-made explanation for the fact that it cannot be object-controlled.[42] Everything that is construction-specific about gP_i is encoded in the diathesis of its suffixal head **-g-** (its adverbial categorial features and the { ^-}$_1$-induced deletion of **V**'s external N_1); everything else in the derivation of gP_i and its syntactic control are entirely general and, it seems, universal.

The s-predicate analysis of gP_i correctly predicts the following systematic gap-in-paradigm: gP_i cannot be formed from impersonal verbs like *tošnit'* 'to feel nauseated': *stošniv / *tošnja are ill-formed because the initial external argument of the stem tošni- is {-^-}$_1$ and a hybrid adverbial formed from it cannot be controlled (V-bound); impersonal -šč-participles are ill-formed for the same reason. It is also predictable that gP$_i$ cannot compose with the copula, as in (66): since gP$_i$'s external argument is {i^-}$_1$, it cannot project a subject nP (see the deletion V's initial N$_1$ in (58)). Thus (66) violates the Projection Principle.

(66)   *On$_i$ byl   [$_{gP<i>}$ vozvraščajas' domoj$_{ADV}$].
          he:NOM.M   was:M   returning   home
          'He was returning home.'

gP$_i$ has two canonical positions in the matrix clause: postposed, i.e., adjoined to the matrix VP$_i$, as in (67a–b), and preposed, i.e., left-adjoined to TP, as in (67c); see (68) and Rappaport 1980, 1984:

(67)   a.   VP$_i$ b.   VP$_i$ c.   TP

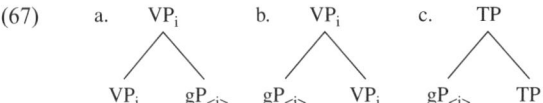

          VP$_i$ gP$_{<i>}$ gP$_{<i>}$ VP$_i$ gP$_{<i>}$ TP

(68)   a.   [$_{gP<i>}$Ostavšis' [$_{aP<i>}$ odna$_{NOM.F}$]], Anna$_{NOM.F}$ rasplakalas'.
          remaining   alone,   Anna   began-to-cry
          '[When-she-was alone], Anna began-to-cry.'
    b.   [$_{gP<i>}$ Sev sam$_{NOM.M}$ i priglasiv sest' Varju$_{ACC.F}$], on$_{NOM.M}$ zasmejalsja.
          '[Sitting-down himself and inviting Varya to-sit], he began-to-laugh.'
    d.   [$_{gP<i>}$ Pridja domoj p'janyj$_{LF.NOM.M}$ (*p'janaja$_F$)], Artem udaril ženu.
          'Coming home drunk, Artem hit (his) wife.' (see Neidle 1988: 130)

Since gP$_i$ cannot be V-bound when adjoined to TP, which has no external theta role to bind it, gP$_i$ in sentences like (68) must be V-bound in its lower VP$_i$-adjoined position in (67a–b) and only then moved to TP. Preposing bound phrases is not gP$_i$-specific. Compare the sentences in (68) and (69): the preposed PP in (69a) and the preposed nP$_{GEN}$ in (69b) contain a reflexive pronoun that is coreferential with and bound by the subject on 'he.' Here too these preposed phrases are merged and then moved from a lower position after the reflexives in them have been bound by the subject on, which precedes and c-commands them before they are preposed.

(69)   a.   [$_{TP}$ [$_{PP}$ K sčast'ju dlja [$_{nP<i>}$ **sebja**]], [$_{TP}$ **on**$_i$ otkazalsja ot ètoj bezumnoj zatei]].
          to luck   for   self   he rejected   that crazy scheme
          '(lit.) [Luckily for (him)self], he rejected that crazy scheme.'

156 *Hybrid verbal adjuncts*

    b. On utverždaet, čto [$_{TP}$ [$_{nPGEN}$ nikakogo davlenija na **sebja**$_{<i>}$] [$_{TP}$ **on**$_i$ ne
       he claims that no pressure on (him)self he NEG
       oščuščal]].
       felt
       'He maintains that [**he** did not feel [any pressure on **him(self)**]].'[43]

3.4   The syntactic distribution of gP$_i$

My analysis correctly predicts that gP$_i$ can be V-bound by any VP$_i$ it adjoins to, regardless of the category of the affixal head that VP$_i$ composes with, i.e., [$_{x'i}$ [V-x] [$_{VP<i>}$VP$_{<i>}$ gP$_{<i>}$]] should always be well-formed (x here is any affix that can compose with VP$_i$ and x's maximal projection can be either an s-clause [$_{xP}$ nP$_i$ x'$_{<i>}$] or an s-predicate [$_{xPi}$ x'$_{<i>}$]). The controller (antecedent) of gP$_i$ is always the head of the TBC in which [$_{VP<i>}$VP$_{<i>}$ gP$_{<i>}$] is vertically bound. This analysis thus predicts that: (i) gP$_i$ can modify finite verbs, participles, infinitives, other gP$_i$s, and derived nominals,[44] and, crucially, (ii) gP$_i$'s controller is therefore *not* always the subject of the finite matrix clause, which predicts that SAM$_i$ adjoined to gP$_i$ is not always nominative (see below).

When SAM$_i$ is adjoined to gP$_i$, creating [$_{VPi}$VP$_{<i>}$ [$_{gP<i>}$ gP$_{<i>}$ SAM$_{<i>}$]], it agrees in case, gender, and number with the head of the TBC in which VP$_i$ is vertically bound. If hybrid adverbials were s-clauses, SAM$_i$ would have to agree in case with their PRO subject and thus would *always be in the same case*; but if hybrid adverbials are gP$_i$ s-predicates, the case of SAM$_i$ is predicted to *vary*, depending on the case and grammatical function of the nP head of the TBC in which it is V-bound. These predictions are confirmed by the examples in the following sections, where we see that gP$_i$, [$_{aPi}$ SAM], kP$_i$, afP$_i$ (-**šč**-participle), infP$_i$ (infinitive s-predicate), and derived nominals merge to form complex structures, in much the same way that Lego pieces fit together, forming complex molecular structures.

3.4.1 gP$_i$ in participle phrases

The [$_{VPi}$VP$_{<i>}$ gP$_{<i>}$] configuration predicts that while gP$_i$'s controller cannot be the matrix verb's direct object, it need not necessarily be the matrix clause's dedicated subject nP$_i$. For example, in the case of gP$_i$ adjoined to the encapsulated VP$_i$ in -**šč**-participle phrases (= afP$_i$), which are themselves adjectival s-predicates (afP$_i$), gP$_i$'s controller is the head of the nP that afP$_i$ modifies, no matter what its function and case in the matrix clause may be (including direct object). These relations are schematically represented in (70) (α is a variable case feature); (71) is a concrete example and (72) is its syntactic structure.

3.4 The syntactic distribution of gP_i 157

(70)

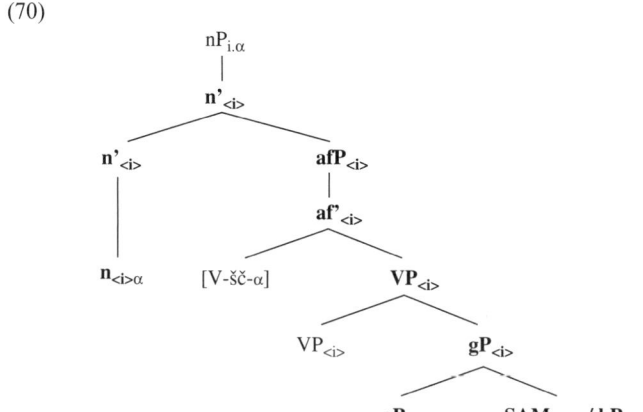

(71) My uvideli [šerifa, [$_{afP<i>}$ šestvujuščego k   nam [$_{gP<i>}$ razdvigaja tolpu]]].
      we saw   sheriff:ACC walking:ACC toward us   parting   crowd:ACC
      'We saw [the-sheriff [(who-was) walking toward us [parting the crowd
      (= as he parted the crowd)]]].'

(72)

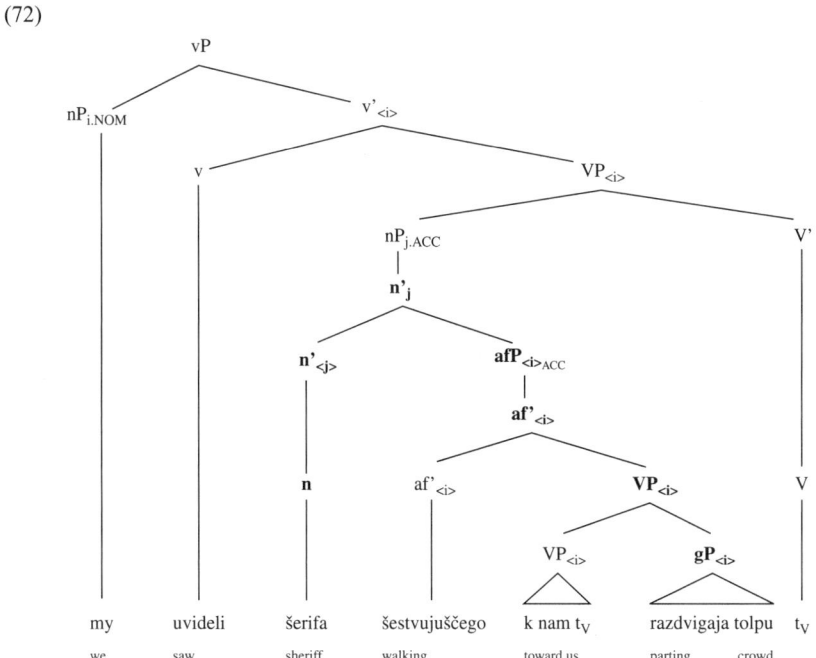

We see in (72) that [$_{gP<i>}$*razdvigaja tolpu*$_{ACC}$] is adjoined to and vertically bound by the VP$_i$ encapsulated in the -šč-participle phrase [$_{afPi}$ *šestvujuščego*$_{LF.ACC.M}$ *k nam*] '(who-is) walking toward us,' which itself adjoins to (modifies) the head of the matrix *direct object* nP$_{j.ACC}$ *šerifa* (see [$_{n'j}$ n'$_{<j>}$ afP$_{<i>}$]). Although the TBC head (controller) of gP$_i$ is the matrix direct object *šerifa* rather than the matrix subject *my* (see the boldface TBC), the sentence is perfectly well-formed because it conforms to the [$_{VPi}$ VP$_i$ gP$_{<i>}$] schema: gP$_i$ is *vertically bound by the external theta rol*e of a VP$_i$, which happens to be encapsulated in an afP$_i$ which happens to be adjoined to the direct object in this derivation. My analysis thus explains both why the matrix direct object *šerifa*, not the matrix subject *my*, is the controller of [*razdvigaja tolpu*]$_{gPi}$ in a sentence like (71), and why the sentence is well-formed.[45]

Sentences like (73) are ill-formed because gP$_i$ here is adjoined to matrix V'$_j$ rather than to VP$_i$ (see the depictive's FEM agreement) (cf. (54c)).

(73)   *Artem$_{NOM.M}$ udaril ženu$_{j.ACC.F}$, [$_{gP<i>}$ **vernuvšis'** domoj p'janoj$_{PI.F}$ /p'januju$_{LF.ACC.F}$].
        'Artem struck (his) wife [(when she) returned home drunk].'

If we delete [$_{afPi}$ *šestvujuščego k nam*] in (71), [$_{gPi}$ *razdvigaja tolpu*] is automatically reconstrued as having the matrix subject *my* as its understood subject, not the direct object *šerifa*: *My uvideli šerifa, razdvigaja tolpu* ~ *Razdvigaja tolpu, my uvideli šerifa* 'We saw the-sheriff [as-we-were-pushing-our-way-through the-crowd]': gP$_i$ here is V-bound by the VP$_i$ complement of finite vP and the matrix subject *my* is thus the head of the TBC in which gP$_i$ is the tail. In order for [$_{gPi}$ *razdvigaja tolpu*] to be object-controlled by *šerifa* in [*My$_i$ uvideli šerifa$_j$*, [$_{gP<i>}$ *razdvigaja tolpu*]], gP$_i$ would have to be adjoined to V'$_j$, i.e. *[$_{V'j}$ V'$_{<j>}$ gP$_{<i>}$], which, however, violates the [$_{VPi}$ VP$_{<i>}$ gP$_{<i>}$] schema posited above. Given the obligatoriness of [$_{VPi}$ VP$_{<i>}$ gP$_{<i>}$], the data in this section clearly demonstrates that the correct generalization is simply: *The antecedent (controller) of gP$_i$ is the head of the TBC in which it is vertically bound.*

Reflexive pronouns *in participial phrases* that modify the matrix direct object are construed as coreferential with and controlled by the matrix direct object rather than the matrix subject for essentially the same reason that hybrid adverbial s-predicates are (see (71)/(72) and the TBC-based definition of reflexive binding in (41)). For example, the reflexive pronoun *sebja*$_{ACC}$ in (74a) has the accusative direct object *šerifa* as its antecedent, not the nominative subject *my*: [$_{nPi}$ *sebja*] is V-bound by afP$_i$, which modifies *šerifa*; thus *šerifa* is both the head of the direct object nP$_j$ and the head of the TBC in which *sebja* is V-bound; cf. (74b), where *svoego* is a reflexive possessive pronoun (boldface and underlining here represent coreference, *svoego* in (74c) is the reflexive pronominal adjective).

(74) a. My uvideli [$_{nPj}$ šerifa$_{ACC}$, [$_{afP<i>}$ smotrjaščego$_{ACC}$ na sebja v zerkalo]].
'We saw the-sheriff [looking at himself (*us/ourselves) in the mirror].'
b. <u>Ona</u> smorela na **svjaščenika**$_{ACC}$, [$_{afP<i>}$ pozvolivšego$_{LF\cdot ACC}$ **sebe**$_{DAT}$ projavit' nepočtitel'nost'$_{ACC}$, [$_{gP<i>}$ xarakterizuja <u>ee</u> (*<u>svoego</u>) otca$_{ACC}$]].
'<u>She</u> looked at the-**priest** [(who) allowed **himself** to-express disrespect] [(while) characterizing <u>her</u> father]].'
c. <u>Ona</u> pozvolila <u>sebe</u>$_{DAT}$ [$_{infP}$ <u>PRO</u>$_i$ projavit' nepočtitel'nost'$_{ACC}$ [$_{gP<i>}$ xaraterizuja <u>svoego</u> otca$_{ACC}$]].
'<u>She</u> allowed <u>herself</u> to express disrespect [when-characterizing <u>her</u> father].'

3.4.2 gP$_i$ in gP$_i$

My analysis predicts that gP$_i$ can be adjoined to a higher gP$_i$, i.e., [$_{gPi}$ [g'$_{<i>}$ [V-g] [$_{VP<i>}$ VP$_{<i>}$ gP$_{<i>}$]]]: the external theta role of the lower gP$_i$ is vertically bound by the external theta role of the VP$_i$ encapsulated in the higher gP$_i$, which is vertically bound by the matrix VP$_i$, making the matrix subject the head of the TBC in which both gP$_i$s are V-bound: see (75).

(75) a. [$_{gP<i>}$ **Proglotiv**, [$_{gP<i>}$ ne **žuja**], kusok$_{ACC}$ buterbroda], on ustavilsja na
swallowing   NEG chewing piece of-sandwich he looked at
menja.
me
'[**Having-swallowed** a-piece of-the-sandwich [without **chewing** (it)]], he looked at me.'
b. Ja videl, kak on tanceval, [**derža**, [**prižav** k sebe], devušku].
I saw how he danced   holding pressed to self girl
'I saw him dancing, **holding** the-girl, **pressing** (her) to him(self).'
c. [$_{infP}$ Popast' v spal'nju] možno bylo by liš' [$_{gP<i>}$ **razbiv** okno, [$_{gP<i>}$ **nadelav** pri ètom šumu]].
'(It) was possible [to-get into the-bedroom] only [(by) breaking the-window, [making a-lot-of-noise doing it]].'
d. [Ne **toropjas' dopiv** kofe], ja naprivilsja k oknu.
'[Having-drunk the-coffee without rushing], I went to the window.'

3.5 gP$_i$ in infinitive projections

The syntactic structure of Russian infinitive *clauses* is schematically represented in (76) (see chapter 4 for details). Since gP$_i$ adjoins to the infinitive's encapsulated VP$_i$, its controller is the clause's dative subject, which is the head of the TBC in which gP$_i$ is V-bound. The subject of controlled Russian infinitive complement clauses is PRO$_{i.DAT}$ which is antecedent-bound by the closest argument of the matrix verb. See (77) to (80), where the infinitive is underlined and **-inf** represents the infinitive-forming affixal head, which is realized as *-t'*, *-ti*, or *-či*. In (80) we see overt dative *samomu* (SAM$_i$) agreeing in case, gender, and number with the infinitive clause's null dative subject.

(76)

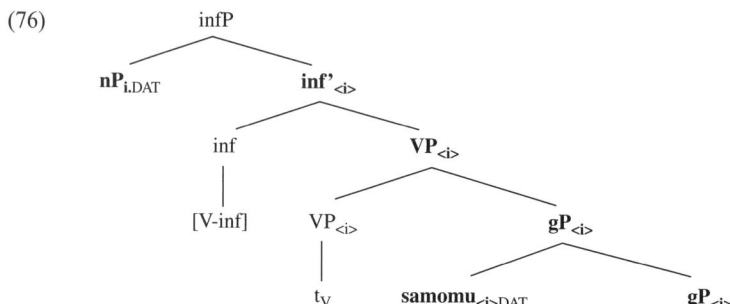

(77) Ob"jasnjajut ego uspexi [$_{nP}$ umeniem [$_{infP}$ **PRO**$_{i.DAT}$ pit' [$_{gP<i>}$ ne p'janeja]]].
explain:PL his success:ACC ability:INST to-drink NEG getting-drunk
'(PEOPLE) explain his success [(by-his)-ability [to-drink [without getting-drunk]]].'

(78) Menja$_j$ utomljalo [$_{infP}$ **PRO**$_{i.DAT}$ soprovoždat' ix povsjudu,
me:ACC exhausted:N to-accompany them:ACC everywhere
[$_{gP<i>}$ davaja ob"jasnenija]].
giving explanations:ACC
'(It) exhausted me [to-accompany them everywhere, [giving explanations]].'

(79) Kak **nam**$_i$ sdelat' èto, [$_{gP<i>}$ ne postaviv sebja$_{<i>}$ v glupoe položenie]?
how us:DAT to-do that:ACC NEG putting self:ACC in awkward position
'How (are) we to do that [without putting ourselves in an awkward position]?'

(80) [$_{CP}$Vmesto togo, čtoby [$_{infP}$ **PRO**$_{i.DAT}$ **samomu**$_{DAT}$ razryvat'sja na časti, [$_{gP<i>}$ dobyvaja den'gi na uplatu nalogov]]], ne lučše li razorvat' na časti sborščika nalogov?
'Instead of tearing yourself to pieces **yourself**, [trying-to-get money for the payment of (your) taxes], wouldn't it be better to tear the tax collector to pieces?'

(81) is the syntactic structure of (79), where the infP is not controlled: its *overt dative subject nam* 'us' controls [$_{gP<i>}$ *ne postaviv sebja$_{<i>}$ v glupoe položenie*]: the reflexive pronoun [$_{nPi}$ *sebja*$_{ACC}$] is vertically bound by gP$_i$, which is vertically bound by the **-inf**'s encapsulated VP$_i$ complement, which assigns its external theta role **i** to the dative subject *nam* in spec-infP. Note that the gP$_{<i>}$ and the reflexive pronoun [$_{nP<i>}$ *sebja*$_{ACC}$] are V-bound in the same TBC, whose head is *nam*, which accounts for the fact that *nam* is construed as simultaneously being the dedicated subject of infP, the controller of gP$_{<i>}$, and the antecedent of *sebja*$_{<i>}$.

(81)

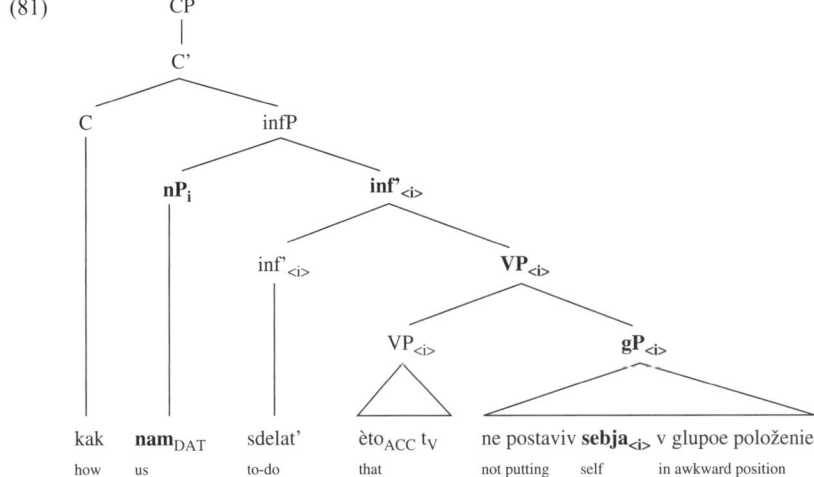

(82) is the schematic representation of the CP in (80): [$_{gP<i>}$ *dobyvaja den'gi na uplatu nalogov*] is V-bound by the external theta role **i** of the infinitive *razryvat'sja*, which is assigned to the clause's PRO$_{i.DAT}$ subject; *samomu*$_{DAT}$, which has a contrastive function here, is dative because it adjoins to inf'$_i$ and is thus vertically bound in the same TBC as gP$_i$, whose head is PRO$_{i.DAT}$.

(82)

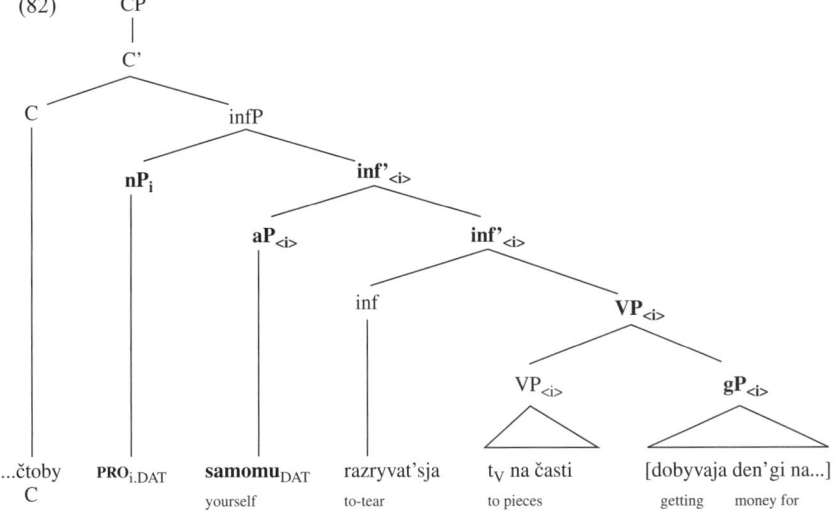

Bear in mind that although the preposed matrix direct object *menja*$_{ACC}$ 'me' in (78) *antecedent-binds* the infinitive clause's PRO$_{i.DAT}$ subject, it is nevertheless not

162 *Hybrid verbal adjuncts*

part of the TBC in which gP$_i$ is vertically bound: a TBC by definition cannot cross the infP node, which is a clause boundary. This can be demonstrated as follows: if a matrix nP were part of the TBC in which SAM$_i$ in an infinitive clause were bound, the nP would be the TBC's head, which makes the following incorrect prediction: SAM$_i$ would agree in case with the matrix nP rather than the infinitive's dative PRO subject. For example, if the direct object of an object-control verb were the head of the TBC in which the infinitive's subject were an intermediate link, grammatical sentences like (83a) would be predicted to be ungrammatical and ungrammatical sentences like (83b) would be predicted to be grammatical (boldface denotes links in the TBC in which SAM$_i$ is vertically bound).

(83)   a.   Anna   poprosila menja$_{ACC}$ [**PRO**$_{DAT}$ sdelat' uborku$_{ACC}$ **samomu**$_{DAT}$].
     Anna   asked   me   to-do   cleaning-up myself
     'Anna asked me to-do the-cleaning-up myself.'
   b.   *Anna poprosila **menja**$_{ACC}$ [PRO$_{i.DAT}$ sdelat' uborku$_{ACC}$ **samogo**$_{ACC}$].[46]
     Anna   asked   me   to-do   cleaning-up myself

3.5.1   SAM$_i$ *in infinitival complements*

In this section we see the single most compelling argument that hybrid adverbial phrases are s-predicates (gP$_i$), rather than s-clauses ([$_{gP}$ PRO$_i$ g'$_{<i>}$]). This argument makes crucial use of the fact that SAM$_i$ is an underived s-predicate adjective that always agrees in case, gender, and number with the nP head of the TBC in which it is V-bound (see (76), (80), (82), and (83)).[47] Our focus will be [$_{gPi}$ SAM$_{<i>}$ gP$_i$] or [$_{gPi}$ gP$_i$ SAM$_{<i>}$] adjoined to an infinitive phrase, which is schematically represented in (84): [V-inf]$_{inf}$ is realized morphosyntactically as either an infinitive s-clause, as in (84a) or an infinitive s-predicate, as in (84b), where α denotes nominative or dative case, α's value being determined by the case of the head of the TBC in which infP$_i$ is vertically bound (see chapter 4). TBCs are in boldface; the VP$_i$ encapsulated in gP$_i$ is not shown here.

(84a)   Infinitive s-clause:

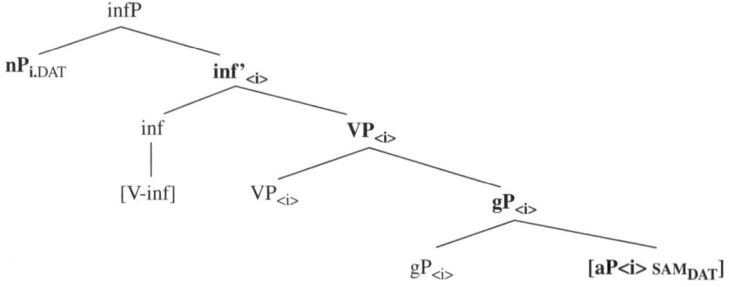

(84b)   Infinitive s-predicate:

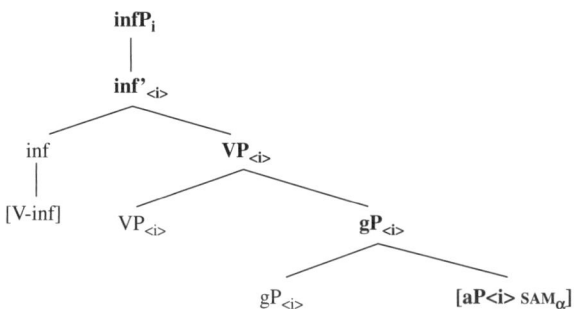

When SAM$_i$ is vertically bound in a TBC headed by the subject of its clause ('diagnostic SAM$_i$'), its case agreement is restricted to nominative and dative, which is precisely what we expect: SAM$_i$ adjoined to *subject-controlled* infinitive complements, which are canonically infP$_i$ s-predicates, are nominative when the matrix clause is finite, as in (85a) (cf. (84b)); in *object-controlled* infinitive complements and all other infinitive constructions, which are s-clauses, SAM$_i$ is dative, as in (85b–e) and (84a). The nominative ~ dative case of diagnostic SAM$_i$ in infinitive phrases follows from the fact that the subject of finite clauses is nominative and the subject of infinitive clauses is dative. Therefore, since there are no other types of clauses in Russian, and since diagnostic SAM$_i$ agrees with the subject of the clause it is vertically bound in, only diagnostic *sam*$_{NOM}$ and *samomu*$_{DAT}$ are possible.

(85) a. **On**$_{i.NOM}$ xočet [$_{inf'<i>}$ vse$_{ACC}$ sdelat' **sam**$_{NOM}$ (*samomu$_{DAT}$)].
      he   wants   everything to-do himself
      'He wants [to do everything (by) himself].'
   b. Oni$_{NOM}$ zastavili ego$_{ACC}$ [**PRO**$_{DAT}$ vse$_{ACC}$ sdelat' **samomu**$_{DAT}$].
      they   made   him   everything do himself
      'They made him [do everything (by) himself].'
   c. Dlja nas$_{GEN.PL}$ utomitel'no [**PRO**$_{i.DAT.PL}$ delat' èto$_{ACC}$ **samim**$_{DAT.PL}$].
      '(lit.) For us (it is) exhausting [to-do this (by) ourselves].'
   d. Nevozmožno [**PRO**$_{i.DAT}$ podnjat' ètot stol$_{ACC}$ **samomu**$_{DAT.SG}$].
      '(It is) impossible to-lift this table (by) oneself.'
   e. Ivan$_{NOM}$ znaet [$_{CP}$ kak [**PRO**$_{i.DAT}$ tuda dobrat'sja **odnomu**$_{DAT.SG}$]].
      'Ivan knows [how [to get there alone]].'

If all infinitive *clauses* have a dative subject, the dative case of *samomu*$_i$ in (85b), where there is no overt dative nP for it to agree with, is not in the least mysterious: the TBC in which *samomu*$_i$ is bound is headed by the clause's *null* (PRO$_i$) dative subject; the same is true for dative SAM$_i$ in (85c–e). The sentences in (86) demonstrate that infinitive clauses with *overt* dative subjects are entirely natural in Russian when the clause is not controlled. (86b) is particularly important since here we see dative *samomu* agreeing with the infinitive clause's *overt* dative subject *mne* 'me.'

(86) a. [Tebe$_{DAT}$ ujti na pensiju] značilo by [PRO$_{DAT}$ kapitulirovat' pered vragom].
'[(For) you to-go on pension] would mean [to-surrender to the-enemy].'
b. Počemu by   mne$_{DAT}$ ne prodat' ix$_{ACC}$ samomu$_{DAT}$?
    why   MOD me   NEG to-sell them (my)self
'Why shouldn't I sell them myself = Why shouldn't I be the one to sell them?'

Since *subject*-controlled infinitival complements are V-bound s-predicates (infP$_i$), we expect SAM$_i$ adjoined to infP$_i$ to agree in case with the subject of the matrix clause and, therefore, to be nominative when the clause is finite, which is precisely what we see in (85a). This prediction is confirmed in (87) to (88): if [$_{infPi}$ *vse delat' sam*$_{NOM}$], the infinitive s-predicate complement of *xočet* in (87), were made the complement of the object-control verb *zastavil* 'forced,' as in (88), we expect nominative *sam* to be replaced by dative *samomu* in [$_{infP}$PRO$_{i.DAT}$ *vse delat' samomu*$_{DAT}$] since object-controlled infinitive complements in standard Russian are s-clauses. Note that (87) is monoclausal and, therefore, the TBC headed by *on*$_{NOM}$ in which *sam*$_{NOM}$ is V-bound does not cross a clausal boundary; (88) is biclausal (coreference is indicated by underlining).

(87) [$_{vP}$ **On**$_{i.NOM}$ [$_{v'<i>}$ xočet [$_{infP<i>}$ vse$_{ACC}$ sdelat' [**sam**$_{NOM}$]aP$_{<i>}$]]].
     he   wants   all to-do self
'He wants to-do everything (by) himself.'

(88) [$_{vP}$Oni$_{i.NOM}$[$_{v'}$ zastavili ego$_{j.ACC}$[$_{infP}$**PRO**$_{i.DAT}$ [$_{inf'}$vse$_{ACC}$sdelat' **samomu**$_{<i>DAT}$]]]].
'They$_{NOM}$ made him$_{ACC}$ do everything$_{ACC}$ himself$_{DAT}$.'

More specifically, *sam*$_i$ in (87) is V-bound by infP$_i$, which is itself V-bound by the finite matrix verb's external theta role **i**, which is assigned to the matrix clause's subject *on*. Thus *on* is the head of the TBC in which *sam* is the tail, and they therefore agree in the nominative case. This structure accounts *explicitly* for the sentence's syntactic relations, i.e., for the fact that *on* is construed as: (i) the *antecedent* of *sam*, (ii) the *subject* of the finite verb *xočet*, and (iii) the *controller* of the infinitive complement. *On* is the head of the same TBC in all three relations. The case agreement of *sam* and *on* could not be accounted for if the subject-controlled infinitive complement in (87) were an infinitive clause.

Dative *samomu* in (88) agrees with the PRO$_{i.DAT}$ subject of the object-controlled infinitive clause complement. Thus, in both (87) and (88), *sam*$_{NOM}$ and *samomu*$_{DAT}$ agree with the subject of the minimal clause containing them, which is the head of their TBCs. PRO$_{i,DAT}$ in (88) is antecedent-bound by the proximate matrix accusative direct object *ego*, which determines its gender and number, but not its case, for precisely the same reason that the gender and number of a relative pronoun but not its case is determined by its matrix clause antecedent. As we saw above, the links in a TBC are forged by V-binding and predication, but not by antecedent binding, which explains why *samomu* in (88) does not agree in case with matrix *ego*$_{ACC}$: only maximally local, clause-internal relations create TBCs: the antecedent binding of PRO in (88) by *ego* is interclausal.

3.5.2 Agreement of SAM$_i$ adjoined to gP$_i$

We can now return to the crucial SAM$_i$-in-gP$_i$ structure in infinitive phrases schematically represented in (84a–b) above. The case agreement of SAM$_i$ described in the preceding section provides conclusive empirical evidence that hybrid adverbials are gP$_i$ s-predicates, not gP s-clauses. If they were s-clauses, i.e., [$_{gP}$ [$_{nPi}$ PRO$_x$] g'$_{<i>}$], where "x" denotes PRO's case, SAM$_i$ in [$_{gP}$ [$_{nPi}$ **PRO$_x$**] [$_{g'<i>}$ g'$_{<i>}$ [$_{aP<i>}$ **SAM$_x$**]]] would obligatorily agree in case with the PRO$_{i,x}$ subject of gP and its case realization would thus *not* depend on the case of the subject of gP's matrix clause. It makes no difference what the case of the hypothetical gP clause's PRO$_x$ subject might be; what is important is that the case of SAM$_i$ adjoined to a gP clause would obligatorily agree with its PRO$_x$ subject and therefore *not vary in case*.[48]

My hypothesis makes an entirely different, easily falsifiable prediction, namely, the case of SAM$_i$ adjoined to gP$_i$ should *vary*, i.e., depend on the case of the subject nP of the matrix clause gP$_i$ adjoins to. Thus SAM$_i$ in [$_{gPi}$ gP$_i$ [$_{aP<i>}$ SAM]] should be nominative when gP$_i$ adjoins to a finite clause or to the subject-controlled s-predicate infinitive complement of a finite verb: SAM$_i$ in both structures is V-bound in the TBC headed by the finite matrix clause's nominative subject (see (87) and (91)). The crucial prediction my hypothesis makes is this: SAM$_i$ in [$_{gPi}$ gP$_i$ [$_{aP<i>}$ SAM]] should be *dative* only when gP$_i$ adjoins to an *infinitive clause*, which has a dative subject. The following well-formed sentences demonstrate conclusively that only the gP$_i$ hypothesis correctly predicts the nominative ~ dative case distribution pattern of the SAM$_i$-in-gP$_i$-in-inf$_{(i)}$ construction described above.

(89) a. On ušel, sam (*samomu) ne znaja kuda.
 he:NOM left, himself:NOM (*DAT) not knowing where (to)
 'He left [without knowing himself where (he was going)].'
 b. Anna$_{NOM.F}$ položila trubku$_{ACC}$, [$_{gP<i>}$ [$_{aP<i>}$ vsja$_{NOM.F}$] droža].
 Anna put-down receiver, all trembling
 'Anna hung-up the-phone, trembling all-over.'

c. Ja uvidel vse, [gP<i> sam<i>NOM (*samomu_DAT) ostavajas' nezamečennym_PI]
'I saw everything, [remaining unseen myself].'

Let us begin by looking at (89c) and its structure in (90), which has the properties we expect to find only if hybrid adverbial phrases are s-predicates. S*am* in (90) is vertically bound by gP$_i$, which is itself vertically bound by finiteVP$_i$, which assigns its external theta role **i** to the nominative subject *ja*; *sam* thus agrees with the nominative subject *on*, which is the head of its TBC. The structure in (90) also accounts explicitly for (89c)'s control relations: *ja* is construed as the subject of the finite verb *uvidel*, the controller of the gP$_i$ *ostavajas' nezamečennym*, and the antecedent of *sam*.

(90)

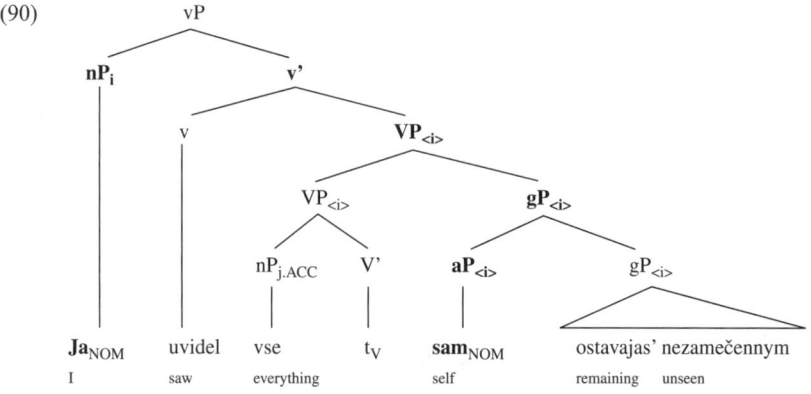

We see in (91) that SAM$_i$ adjoined to the subject-controlled infP$_i$ complement of a finite matrix clause is nominative, as predicted. (91) is monoclausal and the matrix subject *ja* is the head of the TBC in which *sam* is vertically bound.

(91) Ja$_{NOM.i}$ xotel [infP<i> uvidet' vse_ACC [gP<i> sam<i>NOM (*samomu_DAT) ostavajas' nezamečennym_PI]].
'I wanted [to-see everything, [remaining unseen myself]].'

We come now to the crucial object-control data. The s-predicate analysis of gP$_i$ and SAM$_i$ in (84a), repeated as (92), predicts that when [gPi gP$_i$ [aP<i> SAM]] is contained in an infinitive *clause*, SAM$_i$ should be *dative*, not nominative, because: (i) SAM$_i$ here is the tail of a TBC whose head is the infinitive clause's null or overt dative subject, (ii) as we saw above, SAM$_i$ obligatorily agrees in case with the head of its TBC. The well-formedness of the sentences in (93) to (95) demonstrates that this crucial prediction is correct.[49] The gP *clause* hypothesis incorrectly predicts that the case of SAM$_i$ in (91) and (93) should be the *same* since it would agree in case with the PRO_x subject of the gP s-clause in both.

(92)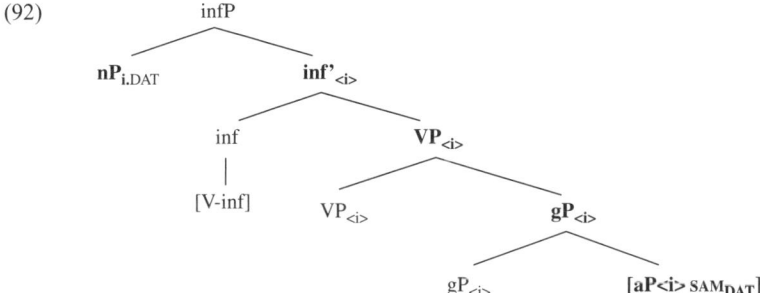

(93) a. Ščel' v doskax dala mne vozmožnost' vse videt', **samomu** ostavajas' nezamečennym.
'The-crack in the-boards gave me the-opportunity to-see everything, remaining unseen **myself**.'
b. Ščel'_NOM v doskax dala mne_DAT [_nP vozmožnost'_ACC [_infP **PRO**_i.DAT vse_ACC crack in boards gave me opportunity all videt', [_gP<i>[_aP<i> **samomu**_DAT] [_gP<i> ostavajas' nezamečennym_PI]]]]. to-see (my)self remaining unseen

(94) a. Mat'_NOM poprosila ego_ACC [_infP **PRO**_DAT žit' v dovol'stve, [_gP<i> **samomu**_DAT ne trevožas' o sud'be bednyx]].
'(His) mother bade him [live in contentment, [not worrying about the-plight of-the-poor [himself]]].'
b. Mat'_NOM.F poprosila ego_ACC.M žit' v dovol'stve, sama_NOM.F ne trevožas' o sud'be bednyx.[50]
'His mother bade him live in contentment, without worrying about the plight of the poor herself.'

(95) **Ona** kazdyj den' ždala pojavlenija otca, [_CP čtoby [_infP [_gP<i> **samoj**_DAT.F vytjanuvšis' na divane], [_infP **PRO**_DAT čitat' emu_DAT vslux **svoi** novye stixi_ACC]]].
'She each day awaited the-appearance of-her-father [so-that (she could) read him her new verses, [stretched-out on-the-sofa herself]].'[51]

When the infinitive *s-predicate* complement in (91) is made the infinitive complement of the noun *vozmožnost'* in (93), it must be realized as an infinitival *s-clause* because infinitive complements of nouns must be clauses (see §4.8.1).[52] Now, the fact that Russian infinitive clauses have dative subjects predicts the dative case agreement of *samomu*: see the internal syntactic structure of (93)'s matrix object nP in (96).[53] (97) represents the crucial TBC ("≈" denotes TBC's individual links).

168 *Hybrid verbal adjuncts*

(96)

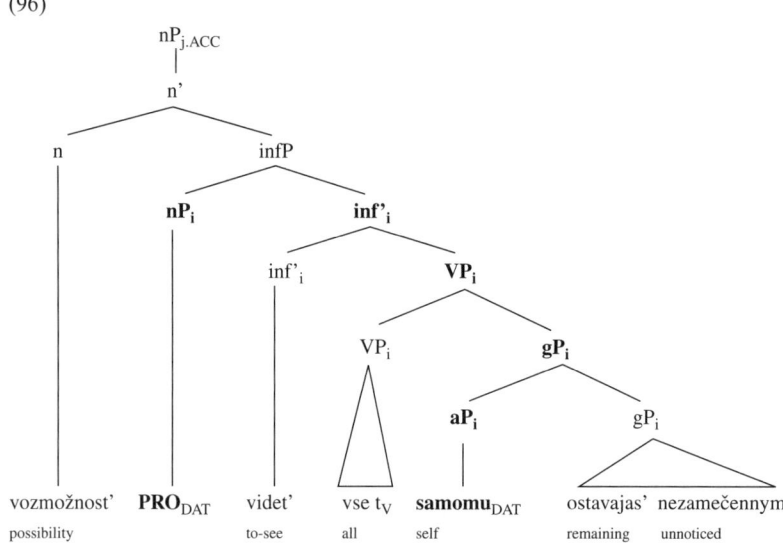

(97) TBC in (96): [$_{nPi}$ **PRO$_{DAT}$**] ≈ inf'$_{<i>}$ ≈ VP$_{<i>}$ ≈ gP$_{<i>}$ ≈ [$_{aP<i>}$ **samomu$_{DAT}$**]

Dative *samomu* in (96) is V-bound by [$_{gPi}$ *ostavajas' nezamečennym*], which is V-bound by [$_{VPi}$ *videt'*], which assigns its external theta role **i** to the infinitive clause's subject PRO$_{i.DAT}$.[54]

Summary: Demonstrating that hybrid adverbial phrases and subject-controlled infinitive phrases are s-predicates rather than clauses with PRO subjects is essential for diathesis theory because syntactic rules as presently conceived are not able to derive s-predicates, which involves deleting a subject nP but not the theta role assigned to it. Thus the existence of s-predicates entails the existence of the two-tiered representation of argument structure (diathesis) and the affix-driven rules that operate on them.

3.6 Hybrid adverbials in derived nominals

The [$_{nPi}$ [$_{n'}$ [V-n]$_n$ VP$_{<i>}$]] structure of derived nominals (DN) proposed in §1.11 correctly predicts that gP$_i$ can adjoin to the DN's encapsulated VP$_i$, just as it does in all other [$_{xP}$ [$_{x'}$ [V-x]$_x$ VP$_{<i>}$]] projections: gP$_i$ is vertically bound by VP$_i$ and its understood subject is therefore construed as VP$_i$'s external theta role, which is canonically *implicit* in DNs (see Grimshaw 1990, Babby 1997a). Thus in (98a), whoever is continuing the war is understood as relying on the allies.[55]

(98) a. [$_{nP}$ prodolženie vojny$_{j.GEN}$, [$_{gP<i>}$ opirajas' na pomošč'$_{ACC}$ sojuznikov$_{GEN}$]]
'[continuation of-the-war [relying on the-help of-the-allies]]'
 b. [$_{nP}$ perexod tverdogo veščestva$_{GEN}$ v gazoobraznoe$_{ACC}$, [$_{gP<i>}$ minuja židkoe$_{ACC}$]]
'the-change of-a-solid substance into a gaseous (one), [bypassing the liquid (one)]'

[$_{gP<i>}$ *opirajas' na pomošč' sojuznikov*] in (98a) is V-bound by the implicit agent **i** of *prodolženie*, not by overt *vojny*$_j$, which is in the DN's spec-VP$_i$ position and therefore too low to bind gP$_i$. (98a) is schematically represented in (99):

(99)

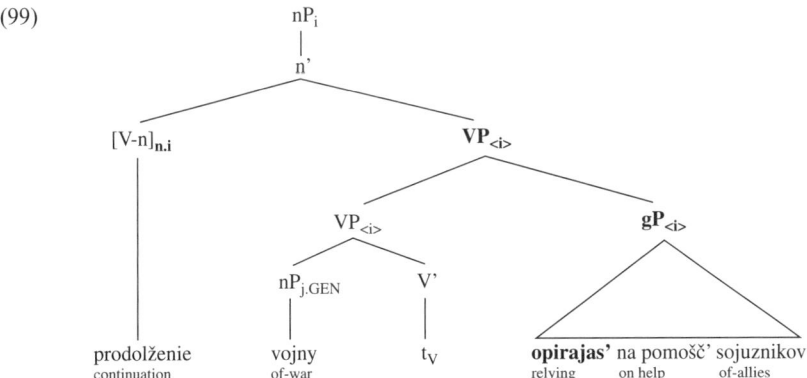

3.7 Hybrid adverbials in passive sentences

The analyses of gP$_i$ and of **-en**-participle passive sentences proposed above account for the following fact: gP$_i$ in passive sentences is *grammatical*, but is felt to be *infelicitous* (see Ickovič 1982: 135, 1968, 1974). gP$_i$ is *possible* in passive sentences because there is an encapsulated VP$_j$ to vertically bind it (see (23)/(24)). The reason passive sentences like (100b) are infelicitous is due primarily to the fact that, while it is the **j** (theme) theta role that is linked to the subject nP [$_{nPj.NOM}$ *samyj blagoprijatnyj moment dlja nanesenija udara*], it is the implicit agentive **i** that is understood as gP$_i$'s controller, i.e., the head of the TBC in which gP$_i$ is V-bound is implicit **i**, rather than the nP$_j$ subject.

(100) a. [$_{gP<i>}$ Polučiv dannye], my$_i$ vyberem [$_{nPj.ACC}$ samyj blagoprijatnyj moment dlja nanesenija udara].
'[(Upon) receiving the-data], we will-choose [the most propitious moment for striking the-blow].'
 b. [$_{gP<i>}$ Polučiv dannye], budet vybran [$_{nPj.NOM}$ samyj blagoprijatnyj moment dlja nanesenija udara].
'[(Upon) receiving the-data], [the most propitious moment for striking the blow] will-be chosen (by-us).'

In active sentences like (100a), the subject is the syntactic projection of **V**'s initial external $\{i{\wedge}N\}_1$ argument, which means that it is simultaneously the *external* argument, the *agent*, the *subject*, and the *head* of gP$_i$'s TBC (controller). However, in passive sentences, this prototypical *alignment* is disrupted, i.e., agent (**i**) and external argument/subject are *dissociated*: the subject nP of passive sentences is $\{j{\wedge}N\}_1$ => nP$_{j.\text{NOM}}$, while initial external **i** is made implicit, as in (100b), where [$_{gPi}$ *polučiv dannye*] 'receiving the data' is controlled by implicit **i**, not the subject [$_{nPj.\text{NOM}}$ *samyj blagoprijatnyj moment*...].

This means that in passive sentences, the speaker is faced with the choice of binding gP$_i$ by either the *implicit* agent **i**, as in (100b), *or* by the derived *external* **j** theta role (i.e., nP$_{j.\text{NOM}}$), which can also head a TBC in which gP$_i$ is V-bound, as in the infelicitous sentences in (101). Both options involve the misalignment of external ~ internal, and agent ~ theme, which is responsible for the infelicity of passive sentences containing gP$_i$.

(101) a. [$_{gP<i>}$ Podnjavšis' na 5 ètaz], my$_j$ byli vpuščeny v temnuju perednjuju.
'[Having-walked-up to the-5th floor], we were admitted into a dark foyer.'
b. [$_{nPj.\text{NOM}}$ Bol'šinstvo sudov] bylo potopleno, [$_{gP<i>}$ vypolnjaja rol' mišeni v voennyx učenijax].
'[The-majority of-the-ships] were sunk [fulfilling the-role of-target during military exercises].'

The ability of implicit **i** in passive sentences to head a TBC, on which this analysis is based, is independently motivated by (102), where it is the *implicit i* of the LF passive -*en*-participle *prinjatye* 'taken-on' that both licenses the *by*-phrase *pravitel'stvom GDR* 'by the government of the GDR' and *antecedes* the reflexive *na sebja* 'on itself,' i.e., implicit **i** is the head of the TBC in which *sebja* is V-bound. If *sebja* were bound by the participle's unlinked external **j** theta role, its antecedent would have to be *objazatel'stva* 'obligations,' which gives the wrong reading; the matrix subject [$_{nPi.\text{NOM}}$ *Novoe germanskoe pravitel'stvo*] 'the new German government' is not the intended antecedent of *sebja*. This leaves only implict **i** as the head of the reflexive's TBC, which gives the correct coreference relation: *sebja* is construed as coreferential with the by-phrase *pravitel'stvom GDR* 'by-the-government of-the-GDR'.[56]

(102) [$_{nPi.\text{NOM}}$ Novoe germanskoe pravitel'stvo]   staralos' sobljudat' [$_{nPj.\text{ACC}}$
new   German   government   tried   to-honor
objazatel'stva, [$_{afP<i>}$ prinjatye$_{\text{LF.J..ACC.PL}}$ na **sebja**$_{\text{ACC}}$ pravitel'stvom$_{\text{INST}}$ GDR]].
obligations   taken   on self   by-government of-GDR
'[The new German government] tried to honor [the-obligations [(which had been) assumed (lit. taken on **itself**) by-the-government of-the-GDR]].'

3.7 Hybrid adverbials in passive sentences 171

The only possible controller of the [$_{gP<i>}$ *sidja za stolom*] 'sitting at a-desk' in the imperfective passive sentence in (103) is the passive verb's implicitized external agent theta role {i^[raskryvajutsja]}$_4$: neither *naselernie* 'the public' nor *vse prestuplenija* 'all crimes' can be construed as sitting behind a desk.

(103) Naselenie$_{i.NOM}$ predpolagaet, čto vse prestuplenija$_{j.NOM}$ raskryvajutsja$_{PASS}$
       public   assumes   that all crimes   are-solved
       [$_{gP<i>}$ sidja za stolom].
              sitting at desk
       '(lit.) The-public assumes that all crimes are-solved [sitting at a-desk].'

4 *The derivation and control of infinitives*

4.0 Introduction

This chapter is devoted to the derivation of infinitives and to the control of their syntactic projections. Infinitive formation is a diathesis-based operation that composes the diathesis of a lexical verb stem **V**, which is common to all finite and nonfinite verbal categories, with the diathesis of the infinitive-forming suffix **-inf** (whose exponents are *-t'* ~ *-ti* ~ *-č'* in Russian). This entails that an infinitive's syntactic projection consists of VP embedded as the complement of **-inf**, which heads its own affixal projection, the infinitive phrase, i.e., [$_{infP}$...[$_{inf'}$ [$_{inf}$V-inf] [$_{VP}$ ...t$_V$...]]]. Although infinitive phrases have the same skeletal syntactic structure as the nonfinite verbal categories in chapter 3, it is not a hybrid category because **-inf** has the same set of verbal categorial features as **V**. Unlike participles and hybrid adverbials, infinitives are not inherently adjuncts. I will argue that infinitive complements are not all *infinitive clauses*, as assumed in earlier generative theory, which entails that the control of infinitives cannot be reduced to the antecedent binding of an infinitive clause's PRO$_i$ subject.[1]

Since Russian paradigmatic suffixes do not affect **V**'s internal arguments, our first step will be to determine how affixation of **-inf** affects **V**'s external {i^N}$_1$ argument. Given the derivation of adjectives and hybrid verbal adjuncts in chapters 2 and 3, we expect to find that an infinitive's final diathesis can project to syntax as: (i) the *infinitive s(mall)-clause* in (1a), where **V**'s external theta role **i** is assigned to its *dedicated* (c-selected) dative subject nP in spec-infP, which is canonically null (headed by PRO$_i$) when infP is controlled; (ii) the *infinitive s(econdary)-predicate* in (1b), where, in the absence of a subject nP, **V**'s delinked external theta role **i** passes up to the infP's root node, creating an infP$_i$ s-predicate; (iii) a *bare* infinitive phrase, which occurs only when the infinitive is the complement of an auxiliary verb. I shall present extensive empirical evidence that infinitive phrases have all three syntactic structures in Russian (bare infinitive phrases are discussed in §4.12).

4.0 Introduction   173

(1a)   Infinitive s-clause:

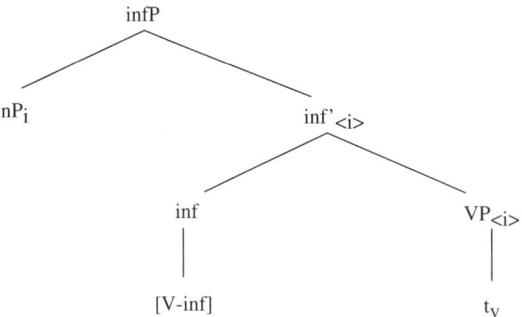

(1b)   Infinitive s-predicate:

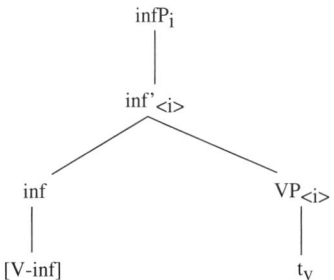

(1c)   Bare infinitive phrase:

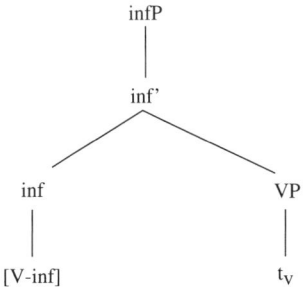

The unlinked external theta role of infP$_i$ in (1b) can be V(ertically)-bound by the **i** or **j** theta role of the controlling matrix verb: only matrix **i** and **j** are high enough in the matrix VP phrase to V-bind infinitive complements (matrix **j** is in spec-VP and matrix **i** in spec-vP).[2]

We see in (1a–c) that infinitive s-clauses, s-predicates, and bare phrases have the same phrasal architecture, i.e., they are *infinitive phrases*; they differ only with respect to the morphosyntactic realization of **V**'s initial $\{i\wedge N\}_1$ external argument; see the dative subject nP of the infinitive clause in (1a), the unlinked external theta **i** of the infinitive s-predicate in (1b), and the absence of both a subject nP and external theta role in (1c) (angle brackets denote a saturated theta role). The goal of this chapter is to present empirical evidence for the existence in Russian of infinitive s-predicates, s-clauses, and bare infinitive phrases (see Babby 1998a, Wurmbrand 2001).[3]

Although object-controlled infinitive complements are canonically s-clauses and subject-controlled complements are canonically infinitive s-predicates (see (87) and (88) in chapter 3), the relation between type of infinitive phrase and type of control is more complex. Given the two types of controllable infinitive phrase (s-predicate and s-clause) and the two types of control (subject and object), my analysis predicts the existence of the four possibilites represented in (2), according to which there could also be subject control of infinitive clauses and object control of infinitive s-predicates. We shall see robust evidence in this chapter that all four combinations do in fact exist in Russian and that all four involve V-binding, antecedent binding, or a combination of the two, which constitutes crucial evidence supporting the diathesis-based analysis of infinitives.[4]

	$infP_i$	infP
(2) subject control	+	+
object control	+	+

An important corollary of this analysis is that the s-predicate infinitive complement and its matrix clause form a *monoclausal* structure, whereas s-clause infinitive complements and their matrix clauses form *biclausal* structures.[5] This distinction plays a central role in explaining the nominative ~ dative case alternation of SAM_i in infinitive complements (see sam_{NOM} ~ $samomu_{DAT}$ in (3) and (4)) and the alternation of nominative and accusative direct objects of infinitives in Old Russian (see §4.10). Implicit in this theory of control is an argument against Hornstein's "control-as-movement" hypothesis: s-predicates do not have subject nPs and thus movement (raising) is not an option (see Hornstein 1999, Culicover and Jackendoff 2003).[6]

The hypothesis that an infinitive complement is either an s-clause, an s-predicate, or a bare phrase entails that an infinitive's missing subject can be either a dedicated subject nP_i headed by phonetically null PRO_i in the case of object-controlled infinitive clauses, an unlinked external theta role in the case of subject-controlled s-predicates ($[_{infPi}\ inf'_{<i>}]$), or nothing at all in the case of bare infinitive complement phrases (see (1c)). There is a great deal of empirical evidence in Russian for the existence of this three-way distinction. The presence of a null dative subject nP_i in spec-infP or its absence can be determined by

4.0 Introduction   175

observing the case agreement of SAM$_i$ in infinitive complements. As we saw in earlier chapters, SAM$_i$ can play this diagnostic role because it is an aP$_i$ adjunct and thus obligatorily agrees in case, gender, and number with the overt or null head of the nP heading the TBC in which it is V-bound (see Sigurdsson 1991 for Icelandic evidence). Consider the following examples.

(3) a. **On**   xočet èto   sdelat' **sam**   (*samomu).
        he:NOM.M wants that:ACC to-do   himself:NOM.M (*DAT.M)
        'He wants to do that himself.'
     b. **On**$_{i.\text{NOM.M}}$ xočet [$_{\text{infP}<i>}$ èto sdelat' [$_{\text{aP}<i>}$ **sam**$_{\text{NOM.M}}$]].
     c. *On$_{i.\text{NOM.M}}$ xočet [$_{\text{infP}}$ **PRO**$_{i.\text{DAT}}$ èto sdelat' [$_{\text{aP}<i>}$ **samomu**$_{\text{DAT.M}}$]].

(4) a. Ona poprosila ego   **samomu**   peredat' pis'mo   Anne.
        she asked   him:ACC himself:DAT to-give letter:ACC Anna:DAT
        'She asked him to-give the-letter to-Anna **himself**.'
     b. Ona$_{\text{NOM.F}}$ poprosila ego$_{\text{ACC.M}}$ [$_{\text{infP}}$ [**PRO**$_{i.\text{DAT.M}}$] [$_{\text{aP}<i>}$ **samomu**$_{\text{DAT.M}}$] peredat' pis'mo$_{\text{ACC}}$ Anne$_{\text{DAT.F}}$].
     c. Ty poprosila nas$_{\text{ACC.PL}}$ [$_{\text{infP}}$ **PRO**$_{i.\text{DAT.PL}}$ **samim**$_{\text{DAT.PL}}$ zanjat'sja tvoim delom].
        'You asked us [to-handle your case **ourselves**].'

(5) a. Vse èto zastavilo ego prinjat' [$_{\text{nP}}$ rešenie$_{\text{ACC}}$ [$_{\text{infP}}$ **PRO**$_{i.\text{DAT}}$ **samomu**$_{\text{DAT}}$ spustit'sja v pogreb]].
        'All this forced him to-make [$_{\text{nP}}$ the-decision [$_{\text{infP}}$ **PRO**$_{i.\text{DAT}}$ to-go-down to the-cellar **himself**]].'
     b. U nego$_{\text{GEN}}$ ne xvataet [$_{\text{nP}}$ mužestva$_{\text{GEN}}$ [$_{\text{infP}}$ **PRO**$_{i.\text{DAT}}$ prijti **samomu**$_{\text{DAT}}$]].
        'He does not have [the courage [to come himself]].'

(6) a. On podumyval [$_{\text{PP}}$ o [$_{\text{nP}}$ tom, [$_{\text{CP}}$ čtoby [**PRO**$_{i.\text{DAT}}$ **samomu**$_{\text{DAT}}$ zanjat'sja ètim biznesom]]]].
        'He was-thinking about getting-involved in-this-business **himself**.'
     b. Ja priletel včera, [$_{\text{CP}}$ čtoby [$_{\text{infP}}$ **PRO**$_{i.\text{DAT}}$ **samomu**$_{\text{DAT}}$ razobrat'sja]].
        'I flew-in yesterday [in-order [to-sort-things-out myself]].'

(7) Ja$_{\text{NOM}}$ rasskažu <u>vam</u>$_{\text{DAT}}$ vse$_{\text{ACC}}$, čto$_{\text{ACC}}$ mne$_{\text{DAT}}$ udalos' uznat' iz gazet, [$_{\text{CP}}$ čtoby [$_{\text{infP}}$ **vam**$_{\text{DAT}}$ **samomu**$_{\text{DAT}}$ podgotovit' <u>sebe</u>$_{\text{DAT}}$ temu$_{\text{ACC}}$ dlja razgovora$_{\text{GEN}}$]].
     'I will-tell <u>you</u> everything that I managed to-learn from the-newspapers [so-that [**you** (will be able) to-prepare (for) <u>yourself</u> a-theme for conversation **yourself**]].'

(8) Počemu by   **mne**   ne   prodat' ix   **samomu**.
     why   MOD me:DAT   NEG to-sell them:ACC myself:DAT
     'Why shouldn't I sell them myself.'

(9) **Vam**   **samoj**   ne   spravit'sja.
     you:DAT.F   yourself:DAT.F NEG to-cope
     'You won't-be-able to-cope (by) yourself.'

Sam is nominative in (3) because the subject-controlled infinitive phrase *èto sdelat' sam* 'to-do that himself' is an s-predicate and *sam* thus agrees in case with the nominative subject *on*, which is the head of its TBC. In biclausal object-controlled sentences like (4a), *samomu*, which is construed as coreferential with the overt *accusative* matrix direct object *ego* 'him,' is dative, despite the fact that there is no *overt* dative nP for it to agree with; this is because *samomu* agrees with the subject nP of the infinitive s-clause complement, which is obligatorily dative in Russian: [$_{infP}$ PRO$_{i.DAT}$ *samomu*$_{DAT}$ *peredat' pis'mo*$_{ACC}$ *Anne*$_{DAT}$]. PRO$_{i.DAT}$ in (4a) is antecedent-bound by the accusative matrix direct object *ego*. When an infinitive clause is not controlled, its dative subject can be overt, as in (8)–(9). (7) demonstrates that it is possible for a controlled infinitive clause to have an overt dative subject to avoid ambiguity. (Bold face indicates the head and tail of the TBC containing SAM$_i$; underlining in (7) indicates coreference.)

4.1   Independent infinitive clauses

(8) and (9) are so-called *independent infinitive clauses*, where the dative subject is canonically overt.[7] I will, however, not make extensive use of this construction in my analysis of the infinitive phrase's morphosyntactic properties and control since, as their glosses indicate, these sentences all have a deontic modal interpretation, which I assume is to be explained in terms of a higher modal projection mP, whose head m is normally null, as in (9), but can also be lexically realized as *nel'zja* 'it-is-impossible,' *nado* 'it-is-necessary,' enclitic *by* in (8), etc. The putative modal projection complicates the analysis of infinitive phrases and obscures the structural facts that are clear in infinitive projections that do not have a modal interpretation.[8]

The hypothesis that infinitives in sentences like (8) and (9) receive their modal meaning *compositionally* by virtue of being embedded in the modal mP projection correctly predicts that when an infinitive clause with an overt dative subject functions as an argument of a matrix lexical verb, it will not have a modal reading since the mP is not licensed here: see (10) to (12); the bracketed infinitive s-clause in (10a) is the subject of a finite matrix clause and does not have a modal meaning since it cannot be the complement of an mP in this position (the overt dative subjects are in boldface).

(10) a. [**Emu** polučat' takie podarki]$_{infP}$ bylo nepravil'no.
            him:DAT to-receive such gifts:ACC   was:N not-right:N
            '(It) was not-right [(for) him to-receive such gifts].'
       b. [$_{vP}$ [$_{infP}$ **emu**$_{DAT}$ [$_{inf'}$ polučat' takie podarki$_{ACC}$]] [$_{v'}$ bylo [$_{aP}$ nepravil'no]]].

(11) a. [CP Pered tem kak [infP im_DAT.PL vystupit']], plamennuju reč'_ACC skazal Nikita.
before   them   to-appear fiery   speech gave N.
'[Before they spoke], Nikita gave a fiery speech.'
b. Èto vse ravno [CP čto [infP Čexovu_DAT voskresnut' i v dom-muzej na Kudrinskoj javit'sja]].
'That is the-same-as [(for) Čexov to-come-back-to-life and show-up at the Čexov museum on Kudrinsky street].'

(12) a. Ja ne dumaju, čto èto xorošaja ideja – [infP vam_DAT sadit'sja za rul'].
'I don't think that it (is) a-good idea [(for) you to-get behind the-wheel].'
b. [infPVzroslomu čeloveku_DAT upast'] – užasno unizitel'no.
'[(For) a grown person to-fall] (is) terribly humiliating.'
c. Moskva ogromnyj gorod. [Čeloveku_DAT v nem zaterjat'sja] legče legkogo.
'Moscow is a huge city. [(For) a-person to-get-lost in it] (is) very easy.'
d. Ja sprašivaju ne pro to, čtoby [infP mne_DAT s"ezdit' tuda], a pro to, čtoby [infPnam_DAT vsem_DAT tam žit']. (E. Bonner)
'I'm asking not about [me going there] but about [us all living there].'

4.2 Control

There were essentially two approaches to control in earlier generative literature. According to the first, an infinitive complement is a *clause* whose subject PRO is *controlled* (antecedent-bound) by a proximate antecedent, which is an argument of the matrix verb. A sentence was said to exhibit *subject control* when the controller (antecedent) of the infinitive's PRO subject was the matrix clause's subject, and to exhibit *object control* when PRO's antecedent was the matrix object.[9]

There is no agreement in the literature about the formal properties of the infinitive clause's null pronominal subject. It has been argued that it is either the highly specialized ungoverned, caseless pronominal anaphor PRO, controlled small pro (see M. Petter 1998), or the copy/trace of movement (Hornstein 1999).[10] The fact that the null subject of infinitive clauses in Russian is dative argues against the classic GB PRO analysis (see Sigurdsson 1991), while the non-clausal, s-predicate analysis of subject control argues against Hornstein's copy/trace analysis. The fact that the subject of Russian infinitive clauses can be either null or an overt dative noun or pronoun argues for the controlled pro analysis. However, what is important for us here is not determining the precise nature of the infinitive clause's null subject but rather presenting empirical evidence that falsifies the hypothesis that *infinitive complements are obligatorily full nonfinite clauses*, which the PRO, pro, and copy/trace analyses all assume. However, I will, for expository purposes, continue to use PRO to designate the null subject of an infinitive clause, but with the understanding that it has case and thus does not have the properties originally attributed to its namesake in GB theory.[11] A Russian infinitive clause with a null subject will thus be represented in my framework by (13) (cf. (1)): $PRO_{i.DAT}$ is the clause's dedicated subject; it is the projection of the V's external argument $\{i{\wedge}N\}_1$ and its dative case is an external c-selectional property of the infinitive-forming suffix -**inf** (see (18)).

(13)

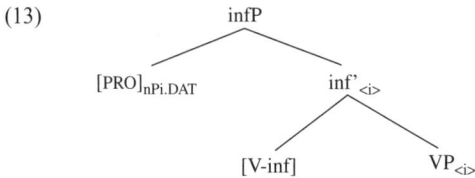

There is a great deal of evidence in Russian against the hypothesis that infinitives obligatorily have clausal structure. For one thing, impersonal (subjectless) transitive verbs like *tošnit'* 'to-experience nausea' are realized as infinitives when they compose with an auxiliary verb (see §4.12). Since subjectless verbs have no external nP and no external theta role (i.e., $\{-{\wedge}-\}_1$), they cannot be heading an infinitive clause with a PRO_i subject in sentences like (14a). (14b) is ill-formed because *zastavit'* 'to force' is an object-control verb and the infinitive of *tošnit'* cannot be object-controlled because it does not have a PRO_i subject to bind. We see in (14c) that finite forms of *tošnit'* head impersonal sentences (the direct object *menja*$_{ACC}$ has been preposed in syntax) (see Babby 2008 and Lavine and Freidin 2002 for details).

(14) a. Menja   perestalo   tošnit'   ot   zapaxa   tabaka.
         me:ACC   stopped:N   to-nauseate from smell:GEN of-tobacco:GEN
         'The-smell of-tobacco stopped making me feel-nauseated.'
      b. *Zapax   tabaka   zastavil   menja   tošnit'.
         smell:NOM tobacco:GEN made   me:ACC   to-feel-nauseated
         'The-smell of-tobacco nauseated me.'
      c. Menja   tošnilo   ot   zapaxa   tabaka.
         me:ACC   nauseated:N from smell:GEN of-tobacco
         'The-smell of-tobacco made me feel-nauseated.'

We shall see below that the strongest evidence against the clause-only approach to infinitive complementation comes from the case agreement of SAM_i.

According to the second approach alluded to above, an infinitive complement is precisely what it appears to be – a bare VP that has no null subject NP (see Culicover and Wilkins 1986, Larson *et al.* 1992: vii-xix, Babby

1974, Thomason 1976, Bach and Partee 1980, Klein and Sag 1985, Bresnan 1982).[12] The problem with this approach is that it cannot represent control in explicit terms.

The clausal and bare-VP analyses of infinitive complements share the following assumption: subject-controlled and object-controlled infinitive complements both have *the same syntactic structures*, i.e, they are *both* either infinitive clauses or bare (subjectless) infinitive phrases. We shall see below that the case agreement of SAM$_i$ in Russian infinitive phrases provides incontrovertible empirical evidence that this assumption is incorrect. The Russian data demonstrate that subject- and object-control infinitive complements have *different syntactic structures*: subject-controlled complements are canonically infinitive s-predicates whose unlinked external theta role **i** is syntactically V-bound; object-controlled complements are canonically infinitive s-clauses whose dative subject is antecedent-bound by the matrix object. Bare infinitive complements do exist, but only in composition with auxiliary verbs (see §4.12).[13]

4.3 Nonfinite verbal categories

This section is devoted to a concise comparison of hybrid adverbials (gP$_i$), -šč-participles (afP$_i$), and infinitives. While all three share many properties, which is due to their shared structure, i.e., [affix head + encapsulated VP], the syntactic distribution and function of infinitive phrases is radically different from that of the other two, which are exclusively hybrid s-predicate adjuncts (see chapter 3). The differences between them are a function of the properties of the suffixes that drive their derivations. Each suffix introduces different categorial features, which accounts for the differences in their function and distribution, and each suffix is responsible for differences in the realization of their common **V**'s external argument. Most important, **-šč**-participles and hybrid adverbials are always s-predicates. In contrast, **-inf** *optionally* deletes **V**'s external **N$_1$**, which accounts for the fact that the infinitive's final diathesis projects to syntax as either an s-predicate or an s-clause.

The derivation of hybrid verbal adjuncts is schematically represented in (15) (x here stands for both hybrid verbal adjunct forming suffixes); see chapter 3 for details.

(15) a. Diathesis of **V**: $\{\{i \wedge N\}_1 ... \{- \wedge V-\}_4\}$ +
      b. Diathesis of x-suffix: $\{\{ \wedge - \}_1 ... \{ \wedge -x \}_4\}$ >
      c. Composition of a + b: $\{\{i \wedge - \}_1 ... \{- \wedge [V-x] \}_4\}$ => (16)

(16)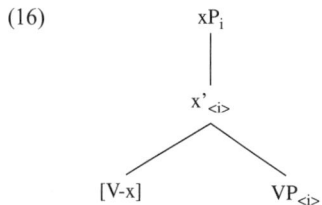

The x suffix carries the categorial features that determine whether xP_i is a participle or a hybrid adverbial. xP_i's external unlinked theta role must be V-bound: a sentence containing an unbound xP_i verbal anaphor is ill-formed.

Infinitives differ from hybrid s-predicate adjuncts in the following three ways. First, the infinitive-forming suffix **-inf** does not introduce non-verbal categorial features, and the infinitive in Russian is thus a homogeneous verbal category (see note 1). Second, the infinitive is the only verbal category in Russian that can function as the *argument* of a lexical head (e.g., the infinitive clause in (10a) is the subject of the finite clause).[14] (17), which is not impersonal, is more complex. Its word order is neutral, *smyla* (which is in the *genitive of negation*) is the direct object of matrix *imelo* 'had,' and the bracketed infinitive clause is the matrix subject: its extracted dative subject *emu* is preposed and the remnant of the subject infinitive clause is extraposed. *Imelo* is affixed with nonagreeing *-o* since infinitives do not have agreement features. Note that infinitive clause arguments do *not* have modal meaning (see §4.1).

(17)   Emu   ne   imelo   smysla [$_{infP}$ [t]$_{nPi}$ [$_{inf'<i>}$ igrat'   na skripke]].
       him:DAT.M NEG   had:N   sense:GEN   to-play   on violin
       '(It did) not make sense [(for) him to-play the-violin].'

The third difference is my main hypothesis: unlike the hybrid verbal adjuncts, which are always s-predicates, an infinitive phrase can have the structure of *either* an s-predicate, an s-clause, or a bare infinite phrase (cf. the LF and SF of adjectives in chapter 2).

(18) represents the derivation of infinitive s-clauses and s-predicates; the **-inf** suffix both c-selects external quirky dative case and makes external N_{DAT} optional, which is designated by the parenthesis-notation.

(18)   The derivation of infinitive phrases (**V**'s internal arguments are irrelevant):
       a. **V**'s diathesis: $\{\{i \wedge N\}_1 \ \ldots \ \{- \wedge V-\}_4\}$ +
       b. **-inf**'s diathesis: $\{\{ \wedge (N_{DAT})\}_1 \ \ldots \ \{ \wedge \text{-inf}\}_4\}$ >
       c. Composition of a + b: $\{\{i \wedge (N_{DAT})\}_1 \ \ldots \ \{- \wedge [\text{V-inf}]\}_4\}$ >>

d. N_{DAT} not selected: $\{\{i \wedge -\}_1 \quad ... \quad \{- \wedge [\text{V-inf}]\}_4\} \quad \Rightarrow$
e. Projection of d: $[_{infPi} [_{inf'} [\text{V-inf}]_{inf} \text{VP}_{<i>}]]$ (s-predicate)

....or...

f. N_{DAT} is selected: $\{\{i \wedge N_{DAT}\}_1 \quad ... \quad \{- \wedge [\text{V-inf}]\}_4\} \quad \Rightarrow$
g. Projection of f: $[_{infP} nP_{i.DAT} [\text{inf'} [\text{V-inf}]_{inf} \text{VP}_{<i>}]]$ (s-clause)

Summary: There are two kinds of *clauses* in Russian: finite clauses, which have nominative subjects $[_{vP} nP_{i.NOM} v'_{<i>}]$ (there are no *verbs* in Russian that select *external* quirky case), and infinitive clauses $[_{infP} nP_{i.DAT} \text{inf'}]$: the dative case here is an external c-selectional property of the **-inf** suffix (see (18b)). In the following sections I make explicit the complex relations between infinitive s-predicates, infinitive s-clauses, V_{aux} + bare infinitive phrase, subject control, object control, V-binding, and antecedent binding in greater detail.

4.4   Subject control and infinitive s-predicates

Consider the sentence in (3), repeated as (19): *sam* is nominative despite the fact that it adjoins to the infinitive projection; *èto* is the preposed direct object of *sdelat'* 'to-do.'

(19)   On   xočet   [èto   sdelat'   sam   (*samomu)].
       he:NOM.M wants   that:ACC to-do   himself:NOM.M (*DAT)
       'He wants [to do that by-himself].'

The structure of the bracketed infinitive complement in (19) can a priori be either an infinitive clause (as assumed in earlier theory), whose PRO subject is antecedent-bound by the matrix subject *on*, as in (20), or an infinitive s-predicate, whose unlinked external theta role **i** is V-bound by the external theta role **i** of the finite matrix verb *xočet*, as in (21). The obligatory nominative case agreement of *on* and *sam* in (19) demonstrates conclusively that the correct structure of (19) is (21): since *on* and *sam* agree in nominative case, *on* must be the head of the TBC in which *sam* is V-bound (antecedent binding does not involve case agreement); as noted above, TBCs do not cross clause boundaries, which means that the monoclausal structure in (21)/(22) is correct (the relevant TBC in (22) is in boldface):

(20)   a. *$On_{i.NOM.M}$ xočet $[_{infP} \textbf{PRO}_{i.DAT} \text{èto}_{ACC} \text{sdelat'} [_{aP<i>} \textbf{sam}_{NOM.M}]]$.
       'He wants to-do that himself.'
       b. *$On_{i.NOM.M}$ xočet $[_{infP} \textbf{PRO}_{i.DAT} \text{èto}_{ACC} \text{sdelat'} [_{aP<i>} \textbf{samomu}_{DAT.M}]]$.
       c. *$On_{i.NOM.M}$ xočet $[_{infP} \textbf{PRO}_{i.NOM} \text{èto}_{ACC} \text{sdelat'} [_{aP<i>} \textbf{sam}_{NOM.M}]]$.

(21) $On_{i.NOM.M}$ xočet $[_{infP<i>} \text{èto}_{ACC} \text{sdelat'} [_{aP<i>} \textbf{sam}_{NOM.M}]]$.
       'He wants to-do that himself.'

182 *The derivation and control of infinitives*

(22)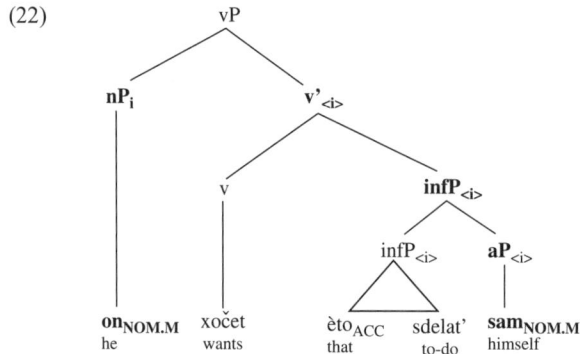

The unlinked theta role of [aP<i> *sam*] in (22) is V-bound by the unlinked external theta role of infP$_i$, which is in turn V-bound by the external theta role **i** of the finite verb *xočet*, which is assigned to the nominative subject *on*.

(20a) is ungrammatical because the head of *sam*'s TBC is the infinitive clause's dative PRO$_{i.DAT}$ subject, not the intended nominative *on*: *sam* here is not agreeing with the dative PRO head of its TBC but with *on*, which *antecedent-binds* dative PRO and therefore cannot be the head of *sam*'s TBC. The nominative case of *sam* cannot be explained in terms of case agreement with PRO$_{i.NOM}$ in (20c) because nominative case is not assigned to the subject of nonfinite clauses (see (24c)). Now consider (20b), repeated as (23)/(24b), which is ungrammatical despite the fact that *samomu* agrees with the dative PRO head of its TBC.

(23)   *On$_{NOM.M}$ xočet [$_{infP}$ **PRO**$_{i.DAT.M}$ èto$_{ACC}$ sdelat' [$_{aP<i>}$ **samomu**$_{DAT.M}$]].
        'He wants to-do that himself.'

(24a)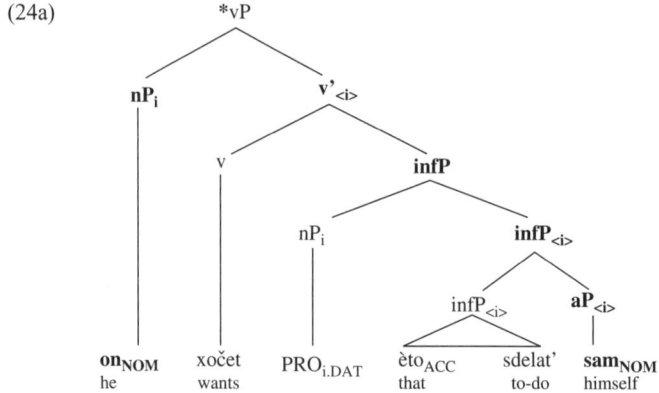

(24b)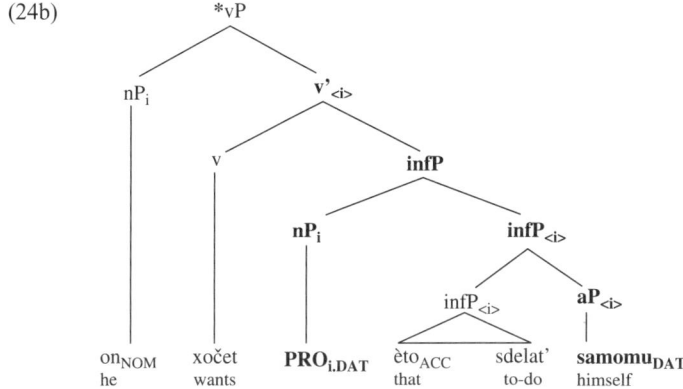

(24c)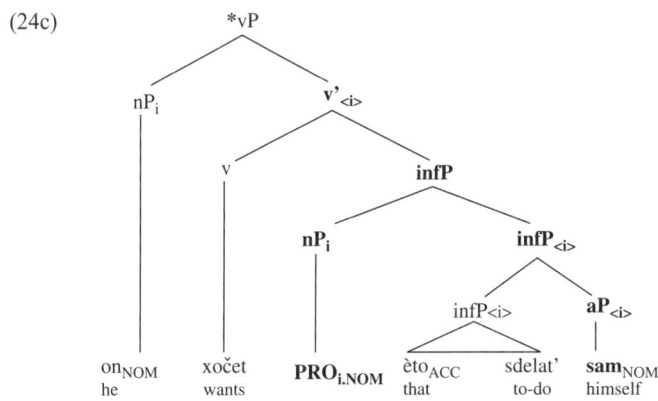

Summary: The nominative case of *sam* in (21)/(22) is direct empirical evidence against the clause-only analysis of infinitive control.[15] More specifically, (20a)/(24a) is ill-formed because *sam* agrees with the matrix subject *on*, which is not the head of its TBC. (20c)/(24c) is ill-formed becasue the subject of an infinitive clause cannot be asigned nominative case. We return to the ill-formedness of (20b)/(24b) in §4.4.1 directly below.

4.4.1 Subject-controlled infinitive clauses

Now consider sentnces like (25b/c) and (26), which involve subject control but whose infinitive complement is an *s-clause* rather than the expected s-predicate.[16] Compare (25a) and (25b/c): while both sentences involve subject control in the sense that the nominative matrix subject *my* 'we' is construed as the subject (controller) of the infinitive *vyžit'* 'to survive,' SAM$_i$ is nominative in (25a) but dative in (25b), which demonstrates that subject control does not

184 *The derivation and control of infinitives*

neatly correlate with an s-predicate complement and nominative *sam*: the dative case agreement of *samim*$_{DAT.PL}$ in (25b/c) and (26) demonstrates conclusively that the infinitive complements here are s-clauses.

(25) a. **My**$_i$ xotim [$_{infP<i>}$ vyžit' **sami**$_{<i>}$ (*samim)].
    we:NOM want   to-survive ourselves:NOM.PL (*DAT.PL)
    'We want to-survive ourselves.'
  b. My xotim najti sposob vyžit' **samim** (*sami).
    we:NOM want to-find way:ACC to-survive ourselves:DAT (*NOM)
    'We want to-find a-way to-survive ourselves.'
  c. My xotim [$_{infP<i>}$najti [$_{nP}$ sposob$_{ACC}$ [$_{infP}$ **PRO**$_{i.DAT}$ vyžit' **samim**$_{<i>DAT.PL}$]]].

(26) a. Ja ne vozražaju protiv togo, čtoby soobščit' **samomu**
    I NEG object against it:GEN C to-tell myself:DAT.M
    otkuda ona zvonila.
    from-where she:NOM called
    'I do not object to telling you myself where she was calling from.'
  b. Ja$_{NOM}$ ne vozražaju [$_{PP}$ protiv [$_{nP}$ togo, [$_{CP}$ čtoby [$_{infP}$ **PRO**$_{i.DAT}$ soobščit'
    I NEG object · against it that to-tell
    samomu$_{<i>DAT}$ otkuda ona zvonila]]]].
    myself from-where she called
  c. On$_{NOM.M}$ sliškom slab, [$_{CP}$ čtoby [$_{infP}$**PRO**$_{i.DAT}$ nesti ee
    he too weak to-carry her
    samomu$_{DAT.M}$]].
    himself
    'He (is) too weak (in-order) to-carry her by-himself.'
  d. Ona rasskazala ob étom, [$_{CP}$ čtoby, [$_{infP}$ [$_{gP<i>}$ napugav drugix], **PRO**$_{i.DAT}$
    [$_{aP<i>}$ **samoj**$_{DAT.F}$] izbavit'sja ot straxa]].
    'She spoke about this [in-order to-get-rid of (her own) fear [by-scaring others]].'

(25a) is straightforward: it has essentially the same derivation and syntactic structure as (21)/(22): the infinitive complement *vyžit'* projects an s-predicate, and *sami*$_{NOM.PL}$, which adjoins to it, predictably agrees with the nominative subject *my*$_{NOM.PL}$, which is the head of its TBC. The subject-controlled complement in (25b/c) is an infinitive s-clause whose dative PRO$_i$ subject is the head of the TBC in which *samim*$_{DAT.PL}$ is V-bound, which accounts for its dative case; PRO$_{i.DAT}$ is itself *antecedent bound* by the subject of the matrix clause. Subject control here is therefore a combination of V-binding inside the infinitive clause and the *antecedent binding* of PRO$_{i.DAT}$ by *my*$_{NOM.PL}$, which is not clause-bound. Thus, based on the data we have seen so far, control can be reduced to binding, i.e., to V-binding, which is clause-bound (since a TBC is clause-internal), to antecedent-binding, which is not clause-bound (see canonical object control below), and to the combination of V-binding and antecedent-binding, as in the case of (25b/c) and (26). The binding relations in (25b/c) and (26b) are represented in (27b) and (27c): the head and tail of the TBC in (27a–c) are in boldface and antecedent-binding is represented by underlining.

(27)   a. **My**$_{NOM}$ xotim [$_{infP<i>}$ vyžit' **sami**$_{NOM}$].
'We want to-survive ourelves.' (= (25a)
        b. <u>My</u>$_{NOM}$ xotim najti [$_{nP}$ sposob$_{ACC}$ [$_{infP}$ <u>PRO</u>$_{DAT}$ vyžit' **samim**$_{DAT}$]].
'We want to-find a-way to-survive ourselves.' (= (25b))
        c. <u>Ja</u>$_i$ ne vozražaju [$_{PP}$ protiv [$_{nP}$ togo, [$_{CP}$ čtoby [$_{infP}$ <u>PRO</u>$_{i.DAT}$ soobščit' **samomu**$_{<i>DAT}$ otkuda ona zvonila]]]].
'I do not object to telling you myself where she was calling from.'

The logical question now is why there must be an infinitive clause rather than an s-predicate in (27b–c). The answer is based on the fact that the infinitive complement *vyžit' samim*$_{DAT}$ (27b) is the complement of the noun *sposob* 'way,' not of *xotim najti* '(we) want to-find.' We will see below in §4.8.1 that the nP projection headed by *sposob* prevents the V-binding of its infinitive complement by the external theta role of matrix *najti*, which means that the infinitive s-clause [$_{infP}$ PRO$_{i.DAT}$ *vyžit'* **samim**$_{DAT}$] in (25b/c)/(27b) is the only possibility for assigning the infinitive's external **i** and is thus chosen by default: Russian infinitive *clauses* are self-sufficient with respect to both the satisfaction of **V**'s external theta role **i**, which is assigned to the infinitive clause's quirky dative subject and to the assignment of dative case to the infinitive's subject, which is selected by the infinitive suffix **-inf** (see (18b)).[17] Since V-binding occurs only in TBCs, an nP or CP cannot intervene between a potential V-binder and bindee. My version of the theory of control-as-binding thus correctly predicts that infinitive complements of nouns and of complementizers (C) must be s-clauses, in which SAM$_i$ agrees with the clause's PRO$_{DAT}$ subject and is therefore obligatorily dative. In (27c) there are three phrasal projections blocking the V-binding of the infinitive complement by the matrix subject *ja*.

The validity of my explanation for the obligatoriness of an s-clause infinitive complement in subject-control sentences like (27b–c) is supported by the fact that it can be generalized, i.e., it correctly predicts that *any* phrasal projection that intervenes between a potential V-binder and its infinitive s-predicate bindee blocks V-binding, requiring an infinitive *clause* in its stead and, therefore, dative SAM$_i$. In sentences like (26b)/(27c)), it is the complementizer projection CP headed by *čtoby* that blocks vertical binding.[18]

The ungrammaticality of ostensibly well-formed sentences like (23) (*On_{NOM} xočet [$_{infP}$ PRO$_{i.DAT}$ èto sdelat' [$_{aP}$<i> **samomu**$_{DAT}$]] 'He wants to-do that himself') suggests that the following 'principle' is at work in Russian:

186 *The derivation and control of infinitives*

An infinitive s-predicate complement is used wherever V-binding is possible; when it isn't, an infinitive s-clause complement is used instead.

Thus the sentence in (23) is ungrammatical because an infinitive clause has been used where an s-predicate can be V-bound. It remains to be seen whether this principle can be shown to be a special case of a more abstract, universal syntactic principle.

4.5   Object control

Below we see empirical evidence that object-controlled infinitive complements in standard Russian are s-clauses, whose PRO_{DAT} subject is antecedent-bound by the object in matrix spec-VP (antecedent binding is represented here by underlining); direct object in Russian can be assigned structural accusative or quirky dative case.

(28) $[_{vP} nP_{i.NOM} [_{v'} [V\text{-}v] [_{VP} \underline{nP_{j.ACC\ /\ DAT}} [_{V'} t_V [_{infP} \underline{PRO_{i.DAT}} \text{inf'}_{<i>}]]]]]$

The clearest evidence that object-controlled infinitive complements in standard Russian are s-clauses comes from the dative-case agreement SAM_i: see dative *samomu* in (4), repeated as (29), where the *accusative* matrix direct object *ego*, not the nominative matrix subject *Eva*, is construed as the controller of the bracketed infinitive clause; (30) is the syntactic structure of (29); additional examples are given in (31).

(29)   Eva   poprosila ego   [**samomu**   peredat' pis'mo Anne].
        Eva:NOM asked   him:ACC.M himself:DAT.M to-give letter:ACC Anna:DAT
        'Eva asked him to-give the-letter to-Anna himself.'

(30)
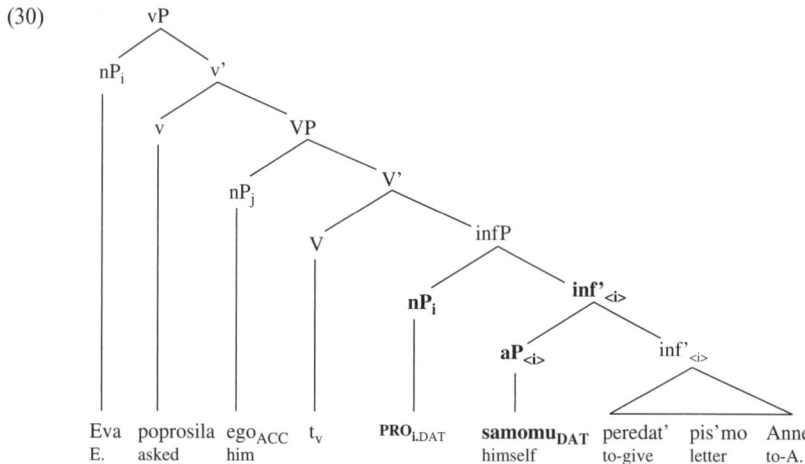

(31) a. Ona umoljala ego_ACC [_infP PRO_i.DAT ne ezdit' tuda **odnomu**_DAT].¹⁹
       she begged him   not to-go there alone
       'She begged him [not to-go there alone].'
    b. Nužno   zastavit' ego_ACC ob"jasnit' vse_ACC   **samomu**_DAT.
       necessary to-make   him   explain   everything   himself
       '(It is) necessary to-make him_ACC explain everything_ACC himself_DAT.'
    c. Ne vri: ty poprosila nas_ACC.PL **samim**_DAT.PL zanjat'sja tvoim delom.
       'Don't lie: you asked us to-handle your case ourselves.'
    d. Ja priglasil ee_ACC.F priexat' sjuda i **samoj**_DAT.F vse_ACC   osmotret'.
       I invited her   to-come here and herself   everything to-examine
       'I invited her to-come here and to-examine everything herself.'

[_aP<i> *samomu*_DAT] in biclausal (29)/(30) is adjoined to and V-bound by inf'_i, which assigns its external theta role **i** to the infinitive s-clause's PRO_DAT subject. This forms a TBC with PRO_DAT as the head and *samomu*_DAT as the tail. Since SAM_i obligatorily agrees in case, gender, and number with the head of its TBC, the dative case of *samomu* in (29) constitutes direct evidence that it is V-bound in a *clause* whose subject is dative. PRO_DAT itself is antecedent bound by the direct object *ego*_ACC.

The structure of (29) in (30) explains the fact that, although masculine dative *samomu* is construed as coreferential with matrix masculine accusative *ego*, there is no case-agreement relation between them: *ego*_ACC antecedent-binds PRO_DAT, and is thus not part of its TBC, which is clause-bound. If accusative *ego* were the head of *samomu*'s TBC rather than PRO_DAT, we could not account for the dative case of *samomu* in (30) in terms of agreement. Thus accusative *ego* and dative *samomu* are related to each other *indirectly* by means of their separate relations to PRO_i.DAT. We return to object control in §4.7, which is devoted to object control in colloquial Russian and to an explanation of the fact that infinitive *clauses* are used in standard Russian object-control constructions (see above) despite the fact that there is nothing here blocking infinitive s-predicates from being V-bound.

The fact that PRO in (29) is antecedent-bound by the matrix direct object *ego* rather than the matrix subject *Eva* is accounted for in the literature in terms of the Minimal Distance Principle, according to which PRO must be bound by the matrix clause's nearest c-commanding potential antecedent (see Bowers 1993, Bailyn 1995b: 30, Hornstein 1999: 76).²⁰

We now have a natural explanation for the initially baffling fact that the case of diagnostic (subject-oriented) SAM_i in standard Russian infinitive projections is restricted to nominative or dative case: it follows automatically from the fact that Russian has two kinds of clauses: finite clauses, which have nominative subjects, and infinitive clauses, which have dative subjects.

4.5.1 Infinitive clauses with overt dative subjects

This section is devoted to infinitive clauses with *overt* dative subjects (see the boldface in (32) to (39)), the existence of which supports my hypothesis that Russian controlled infinitive clause complements have *null* dative subjects. Sentences like (32) are crucial since here we see an infinitive's overt dative subject agreeing with *samim*$_{i.DAT.PL}$ (see (37) and (38)). (*skol'ko... ni* in (34) means 'however much'; *Vy*$_{NOM}$ 'you' and *vam*$_{DAT}$ in (35) are coreferential.)

(32) Prišlo vremja$_{NOM}$ [$_{infP}$ **nam**$_{DAT.PL}$ **samim**$_{DAT.PL}$ sebe$_{DAT.SG}$ pomoč'].[21]
came time us ourselves self to-help
'The-time has-come [(for) us$_{DAT}$ to-help ourselves$_{DAT}$ ourselves$_{DAT}$].'

(33) a. [**Tebe**$_{DAT}$ ujti na pensiju$_{ACC}$] značilo by [kapitulirovat' pered vragom].
'(For)[you to-go on pension] would mean [to-capitulate to the enemy].'
b. [$_{infP}$ [$_{nPi}$ **tebe**$_{DAT}$] [$_{inf'<i>}$ ujti [$_{PP}$ na pensiju]]]
'(for) you to-go on pension'

(34) [$_{infP}$ Skol'ko **verevke**$_{DAT}$ ni vit'sja$_{INF}$], a konec vse ravno pridet.
however-much rope to-twist, but end still comes
'However much a rope winds/twists, (its) end still comes.'

(35) Vy sami smožete rešit', [$_{CP}$ vospol'zovat'sja **vam**$_{DAT}$ našimi uslugami$_{INST}$ ili net].
'You$_{NOM}$ can decide yourself$_{NOM}$ [whether or not (for) you$_{DAT}$ to-use our services]=[whether or not to-use our services].'

(36) Začem bylo [**Ivanu** pytat'sja otravit' Ninu]?
why was.N Ivan:DAT to-try to-poison Nina:ACC
'Why did Ivan try to-poison Nina?'

(37) Počemu by [**mne** ne prodat' ix **samomu**]$_{infP}$?
why mod me:DAT NEG to-sell them:ACC myself:DAT
'Why shouldn't I sell them myself?'

(38) Ja rasskažu **vam**$_{DAT}$ vse$_{ACC}$, čto$_{ACC}$ mne udalos' uznat' iz gazet, [$_{CP}$ čtoby [$_{infP}$ **vam**$_{DAT}$ **samomu**$_{DAT}$ podgotovit' sebe$_{DAT}$ temu$_{ACC}$ dlja razgovora]]. (= (7))
'I will-tell you everything that I managed to-learn from the-newspapers [so-that [**you** (will be able) to-prepare (for) yourself a theme for conversation **yourself**]].'

(39) a. [**Emu** polučat' takie podarki] bylo nepravil'no.
him:DAT to-receive such gifts:ACC was:N not-right:N
'(It) was not-right [(for) him to-receive such gifts].' (see (10) and (11))
b. Ja ne dumaju, čto èto xorošaja ideja – [$_{infP}$ **vam**$_{DAT}$ sadit'sja za rul'].
'I don't think that it (is) a-good idea [(for) you to-get behind the-wheel].'

The dative pronoun *tebe* in (33) is the subject of the infinitive clause [$_{infP}$ *tebe*$_i$ *ujti na pensiju*] '(for) you to-go on pension,' which is itself the subject of the finite matrix clause. In (35), the dative subject of the infinitive clause *vam* 'you' is overt, despite the presence of coreferential *vy* in the matrix clause.

In (32), (37), and (38) we see dative SAM$_i$ agreeing with the *overt* dative subject of an infinitive clause. If the overt subject of an infinitive clause is dative, then so must the null subject of a controlled infinitive clause: the case assigned to nP does not depend on the overtness (phonetic realization) of its head. Thus the dative case of SAM$_i$ in object-control sentences like (29)/(30) is to be explained in precisely the same terms as the case of SAM$_i$ in finite clauses and in infinitive clauses with overt dative subjects: the overtness or covertness of the subject nP's head in infinitive clauses is irrelevant for case agreement. The dative case of SAM$_i$ in (32), (37), and (38) therefore provides conclusive evidence that object-control infinitive complements in standard Russian sentences like (29) are infinitive s-clauses with dative subjects, as in (30).

Let us now briefly consider the evidence from early nineteenth-century object-control sentences like (40), when it was still possible for SF adjectives and participles in object-controlled copula infinitive clauses to be *dative*, agreeing in case with the putative null dative subject (see (40)/(41)). The dative of SFs has been completely replaced in modern Russian by the predicate instrumental, as in (42) (see chapter 5).

(40)   Paša   prisudil   ego   byt'   posaženu na kol.
       Pasha:NOM condemned him:ACC.M to-be impaled:SF.DAT.M on stake
       'The-Pasha condemned him to-be impaled on a-stake.' (Puškin)

(41)   Paša$_{NOM}$ prisudil ego$_{ACC}$ [$_{infP}$ PRO$_{DAT}$ byt' **posaženu**$_{DAT}$ na kol]. (= (40))

(42)   Paša$_{NOM}$ prisudil ego$_{ACC}$ byt' posažennym$_{PI}$ (*posažennomu$_{LF.DAT}$) na kol.

We see in (40)/(41) that the SF dative **-en**-participle *posaž-en-u* agrees in gender, number, and case with the PRO$_{DAT}$ subject of the infinitive clause headed by *byt'* 'to-be'; PRO is antecedent-bound by the accusative matrix direct object *ego*. In (43), which is Old Russian, the dative predicate nominal *xristijaninu* 'Christian' agrees in case with the PRO$_{DAT}$ subject of the object-controlled clause (*že* is a discourse particle); the dative of predicate nominals has also been replaced in modern Russian by the predicate instrumental.

(43)   a. Ona$_{NOM}$ že učaše   syna$_{ACC}$ byti xristijaninu$_{DAT}$.
          she   prt taught son   to-be Christian
          'She was-teaching her-son to-be a-Christian.' (Lomtev 1954: 39)
       b. Ona$_{NOM}$ že učaše syna$_{ACC}$ [$_{infP}$ PRO$_{i.DAT}$ byti **xristijaninu**$_{DAT}$].

4.6 The case agreement and binding of kP_i

Here we see another kind of evidence that Russian infinitive clauses have dative subjects and controlled infinitive clause complements have null dative subjects. *Kak* 'as' is a functor and the *kak* phrase (i.e., $[_{kP_i} \textit{kak}+nP_{<i>}]$, where kP_i (= $kakP_i$)) plays the same diagnostic role as SAM_i.[22] Since kP_i is an adjunct s-predicate and its nP complement agrees in case with the head of the TBC in which kP_i is V-bound, my theory predicts that nP should be dative (i.e., $[_{kPi} \textit{kak}\ nP_{DAT}]$) when kP_i is contained in an object-controlled infinitive complement. (44) represents the internal structure of kP_i, where α denotes nP's variable-case feature.[23]

(44)

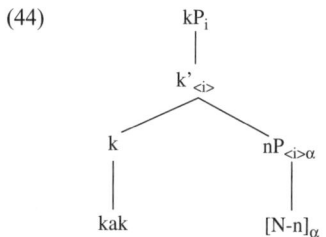

The case agreement between the nP complement of kP_i and the nP head of the TBC in which it is V-bound is illustrated in (45) to (48): $[\textit{kak geroja}_{ACC}]_{kP<i>}$ 'as a hero' in (45) is *object-controlled* and $[\textit{kak sel'di}_{NOM}...]_{kP<i>}$ 'like herrings' in (46) is *subject-controlled*; the subject in (47) is partitive genitive (boldface indicates the TBC's head and tail).

(45) **Ego**$_j$ vstretili [$_{kP<i>}$ kak **geroja**].
 him:ACC.M.SG met:PL as hero:ACC.M.SG
 '(UNSPECIFIED PERSON(S)) greeted him as a-hero.'

(46) **My** tesnilis' v vagone [$_{kP<i>}$ kak **sel'di** v bočke].
 we:NOM crowded in car as herrings:NOM in barrel
 'We (were) crowded (together) in the railway-car like herrings in a barrel.'

(47) **Narodu** nabilos' [$_{kP<i}$ kak **sel'dej** v bočke].
 people:GEN packed-in:N as herrings:GEN in a-barrel
 'People were-packed-in like herrings in a-barrel (= sardines in a can).'

(48) Začem **mne** naprjagat'sja kak **Ivanu**?
 why me:DAT exert-myself as Ivan:DAT
 'Why should I exert-myself like Ivan (the-way Ivan does)?'

The structure of the matrix VP in (45) is schematically represented in (49):

(49)

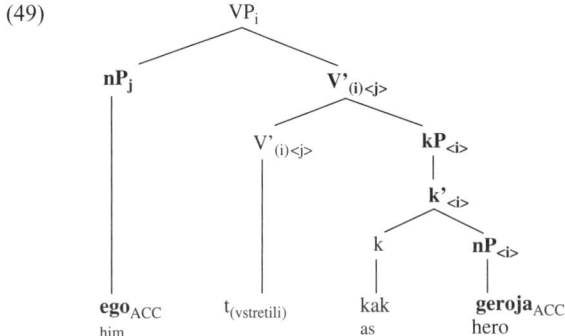

The s-predicate kP_i is V-bound by the internal **j** theta role of matrix $V'_{(i)j}$, which it adjoins to, and **j** is assigned to the matrix accusative direct object ego_j in spec-VP, making $ego_{j,ACC}$ the head of the TBC in which $[_{nP<i>ACC}\ geroja]$ is V-bound. The matrix V's external theta role **i** does not become available to V-bind kP_i until the internal theta role **j** has been assigned to $[_{VP}\ nP_j\ V']$, by which time kP_i has already been V-bound by **j**.[24] Since ego_{ACC} is the head of the TBC in which $[kak\ geroja_{ACC}]_{kPi}$ is V-bound, $geroja$ agrees with it in case.[25] (50) is the structure of the vP in (46), where kP_i is subject-controlled.

(50)

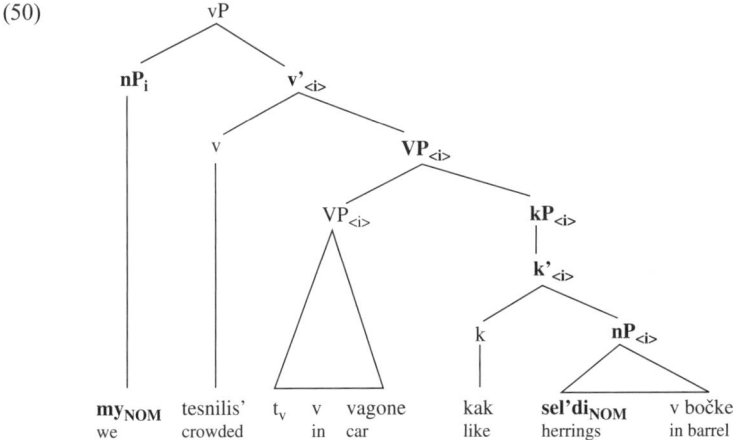

Sel'di 'herrings' in (46)/(50) is nominative because it agrees with the nominative subject *my*, which is the head of its TBC. Note that these examples of the subject and object control of kP_i do not involve infinitive complements, which demonstrates that my theory of control is not infinitive specific or PRO-specific: the control relation derives from the binding relation between the head and tail of their TBC (see the boldface TBC in (49) and (50)).

192 *The derivation and control of infinitives*

Subject controlled [*kak sel'dej*$_{GEN}$]$_{kP<i>}$ 'like herrings' in (47) is genitive because it agrees in case with the partitive genitive matrix subject *narodu*, which is the head of its TBC. The kP$_i$ in (48) is in an infinitive clause and dative [$_{kP<i>}$*kak Ivanu*$_{DAT}$] agrees in case with *mne*, which is the infP clause's overt dative subject and heads the TBC in which [$_{kP<i>}$ *kak Ivanu*$_{DAT}$] is V-bound.

Now we come to the crucial data: the internal [$_{infP}$ PRO$_{i.DAT}$ inf'$_{<i>}$] structure of infinitive clauses proposed above predicts that α in [*kak* nP$_α$]$_{kPi}$ should be dative when kP$_i$ is adjoined to an object-controlled infinitive complement since it should agree in dative case with the clause's PRO$_{DAT}$ subject. The following sentences demonstrate that this prediction is correct: if we embed (46)/(50) as the object-controlled infinitive complement of *zastavit'* 'to make/force' in (51), we find that [*kak* [$_{nP}$ *sel'di*$_{NOM}$]]$_{kPi}$ in (50) is realized as [*kak* [$_{nP}$ *sel'djam*$_{DAT}$]]$_{kPi}$ in (51), which agrees with the null PRO$_{DAT}$ subject of the infinitive clause (cf. SAM$_i$ in (29)/(30)). (52) is the structure of (51)'s finite VP:

(51) Nas   zastavili [tesnit'sja v vagone kak **sel'djam**   v bočke].
      us:ACC made:PL to-crowd in car   as herrings:DAT.PL in barrel
      'They made us squeeze (together) in the railway-car like herrings in a barrel.'

(52)

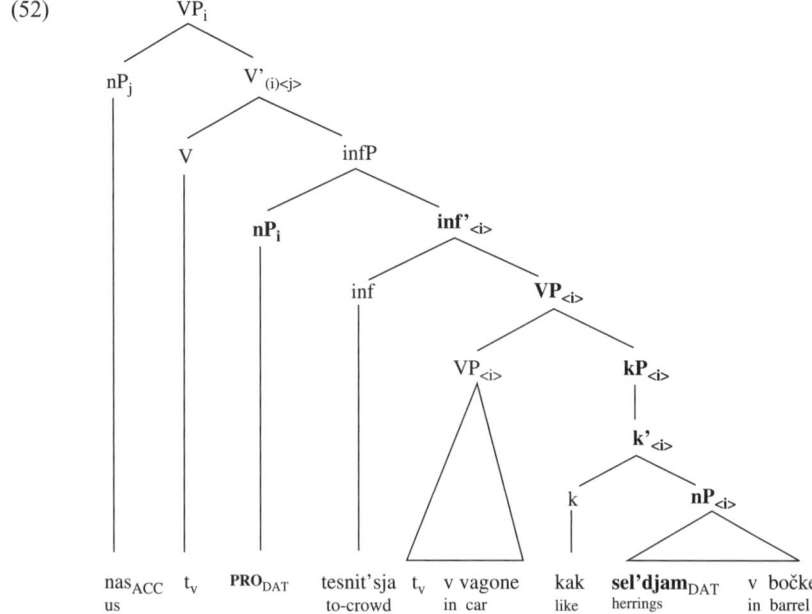

Nas, the matrix direct object of *zastavil*, antecedent-binds the infinitive clause's PRO$_{DAT}$ subject, which is the head of the TBC in which [*kak sel'djam*$_{DAT}$]$_{kP<i>}$ is V-bound.[26]

(53) is another example of the same phenomenon: [$_{nPNOM}$ *opasnost'*$_{NOM}$ [$_{infP}$ PRO$_{i.DAT}$ *isčeznut' kak vidu*$_{DAT}$] '(lit.) the-danger to-disappear as a-species' is the subject nP of finite *ugrožaet*, which assigns quirky dative case to its preposed object (*durakam* 'fools'). (54) is the structure of (53)'s subject nP.[27]

(53)   Durakam   ne   ugrožaet [opasnost'   isčeznut'   kak vidu].
       fools:DAT.PL NEG threaten danger:NOM to-disappear as species:DAT.SG
       '(lit.) [The-danger to-disappear as a-species] does not threaten fools.'

(54)   [$_{nP}$ opasnost'$_{NOM}$ [$_{infP}$ PRO$_{i.DAT}$ [$_{inf'}$ isčeznut' [$_{kP<i>}$ kak **vidu**$_{DAT.SG}$]]]]
       danger   to-disappear   as species

Dative *singular* [*kak vidu*]$_{kP<i>}$ does not agree in case with the preposed dative *plural* object *durakam*: [$_{nP.NOM}$ *opasnost'* [$_{infP}$ *isčeznut' kak vidu*$_{DAT}$]] is the subject of the sentence and, as we saw above in (25b), infinitive complements of nouns are obligatorily infinitive clauses (see §4.8.1). Thus the head of the TBC in which [$_{kPi}$ *kak vidu*$_{DAT}$] is V-bound must be the PRO$_{DAT}$ subject of the infinitive clause complement of the subject noun *opasnost'*, not the matrix verb's dative object *durakam*. This analysis is confirmed by (55), where *ugrožaet* has been replaced by *ispugaet* 'frighten,' which assigns *accusative* case to its object: *kak vidu*$_{DAT}$ remains dative because it still agrees with PRO$_{DAT}$ (*durakov* here is genitive rather than accusative because it is in the scope of negation).

(55)   Durakov   ne ispugaet [opasnost' [$_{infP}$ PRO$_{DAT}$ isčeznut'   kak **vidu**]].
       fools:GEN NEG frighten danger:NOM   to-disappear as species:DAT
       '(lit.) The-danger$_{NOM}$ [to-disappear as a-species$_{DAT}$] does not frighten fools$_{GEN}$.'

Glovinskaja (1996: 263) points out that there is a growing tendency in spoken Russian to replace the 'correct' [*kak* nP$_{DAT}$] in infinitive clauses like (56) with nominative [*kak* nP$_{NOM}$], as in (57); (58) is the structure of (56) ~ (57). Since there is no higher nominative singular nP in (57) for [$_{kPi}$ *kak xozjain*$_{NOM.SG}$] to agree with and since *xozjain* is construed as coreferential with PRO$_{DAT}$, it is safe to assume that the nominative case of *xozjain* in (57) is an instance of the *default nominative*, not of case agreement. The PRO$_{DAT}$ subject in (56)/(57) has arbitrary reference. (56) is 'correct' and (57) is colloquial Russian.

(56)   Nužny ljudi,   s   kotorymi možno   razgovarivat' kak **xozjainu**.
       needed people:NOM with whom   possible to-speak   as boss:DAT
       'People are needed with whom it is possible to speak as would a boss.'

194 The derivation and control of infinitives

(57) Nužny ljudi, s kotorymi možno razgovarivat' kak **xozjain**.
 needed people:NOM with whom possible to-speak as boss:NOM
 'People are needed with whom it is possible to speak as would a boss.'

(58) Nužny$_{SF.NOM.PL}$ ljudi$_{NOM.PL}$ [$_{CP}$ s kotorymi možno [$_{infP}$ PRO$_{i.DAT}$ razgovarivat'
 [$_{kP<i>}$ kak **xozjainu**$_{DAT.SG}$ / **xozjain**$_{NOM.SG}$]]].

4.6.1 The default nominative

Another example of the tendency noted in (57) to replace the expected dative case of agreeing s-predicate adjuncts in infinitive clauses with the nonagreeing or *default* nominative is discussed in Kozinskij 1983: 36, who cites the following examples.

(59) a. Ty uže dostatočno bol'šaja, [$_{CP}$ čtoby **samoj** xodit' v kino].
  you already enough big$_{LF.NOM.F}$ C by-self$_{DAT.F}$ to-go to movies
  'You$_{NOM}$ (are) already old enough [to-go to the-movies by-yourself$_{DAT.F.SG}$].'
 b. Ty uže dostatočno bol'šaja, [$_{CP}$ čtoby **sama**$_{NOM.F}$ xodit' v kino].
  'You$_{NOM.F.SG}$ are already old enough to-go to the-movies yourself$_{NOM.F.SG}$.'

(60) [$_{CP}$ čtoby [$_{infP}$ PRO$_{DAT}$ [$_{inf'}$ [$_{aP<i>}$ **samoj**$_{DAT}$ /**sama**$_{NOM}$] [$_{inf}$' xodit' v kino]]]]

(60) is the internal structure of the CP in (59a–b): infinitive projections introduced by a complementizer (*čtoby* 'in order to' here) are obligatorily infinitive clauses (see (6), (7), and §4.8.2). PRO$_{DAT}$ is antecedent-bound by the subject *ty*. Dative *samoj* in (59a) agrees with PRO$_{DAT}$, as expected; nominative *sama* in (59b) is the default nominative, agreeing with PRO$_{DAT}$ in gender and number but not case.

The object-controlled sentences in (61) demonstrate conclusively that the nominative of *sama* in sentences like (59b) does not agree in case with the matrix nominative subject (these examples and their acceptability judgments are from Kozinskij 1983, who indicates peripheral acceptability with "?"; all the sentences in (61) have the same meaning; (61d) is the structure of (61a–b).

(61) a. Ja$_{NOM}$ nauču vas$_{ACC.PL}$ [rešat' takie zadači$_{ACC}$ **samim**$_{DAT.PL}$].
  I will-teach you to-solve such problems yourselves
  'I will-teach you [to-solve such problems (by) yourselves].'
 b. ?Ja nauču vas$_{ACC.PL}$ [rešat' takie zadači **sami**$_{NOM.PL}$].
 c. ?Ja nauču vas$_{ACC.PL}$ [rešat' takie zadači **samix**$_{ACC.PL}$].
 d. Ja$_{NOM}$ nauču vas$_{ACC.PL}$ [PRO$_{i.DAT}$ rešat' takie zadači$_{ACC}$ **samim**$_{DAT.PL}$/
  sami$_{NOM.PL}$]

(61a) illustrates standard Russian object control: dative *samim* agrees in case with the infinitive clause's PRO$_{DAT}$ subject, which is the head of its TBC; PRO$_{DAT}$ is itself antecedent-bound by the accusative object *vas*. *Sami* in (61b) must be the default nominative since there is no higher nominative plural nP for it to agree with. The accusative case *samix* in (61c) is the topic of the next section.

4.7 Diachronic change in progress: object-controlled infinitive s-predicates

We saw in §4.4.1 that the diathesis-based analysis of infinitives and control predicts the potential existence of five infinitive control relations (see (2)): (i) subject control of s-predicates, (ii) object control of s-clauses, (iii) subject control of s-clauses (see (25b)), (iv) object control of s-predicates, and (v) auxiliary verb + bare infinitive complement (see §4.12). This section is devoted to (iv), object control of s-predicates.

If the complement of an object-control verb were an infinitive s-predicate infP$_i$ rather than an infinitive s-clause [$_{infP}$ nP$_{i.DAT}$ inf'$_{<i>}$], we would not expect the dative *samim*, which we find in standard object-control sentences like (61a); we would expect accusative *samix*, which would be agreeing with the accusative matrix direct object *vas*, the head of the TBC in which *samix* is V-bound. Examples like (61c) demonstrate that object-controlled s-predicates do exist and are in fact replacing the 'correct' infinitive s-clause complement in spoken Russian. This change is able to take place because there is no intervening maximal phrasal projection in sentences like (61c) to block the V-binding of infP$_i$ complements by the matrix nP$_{j.ACC}$ (*vas*). The structure of (61c) is thus monoclausal [$_{vP}$ *Ja*$_{NOM.SG}$ *nauču* **vas**$_{j.ACC.PL}$ [$_{inf<i>}$ *rešat' takie zadači* [$_{aP<i>}$ **samix**$_{ACC.PL}$]]], where **vas**$_{ACC}$ is the head of the TBC in which **samix**$_{ACC}$ is V-bound.

Recall the generalization at the end of §4.4.1: an infinitive s-predicate complement is used if V-binding is possible; if it is not possible, an infinitive s-clause complement is used instead. It is this tendency that is driving the replacement of object-controlled infinitive s-clauses by s-predicates wherever infP$_i$ can be V-bound. In the following example, accusative [$_{aPi}$ *odnogo*] 'alone' in (62a) is felt to be more colloquial than dative *odnomu* in (62b); (63) is the internal structure of the *čtoby*-clause's finite VP in (62a).

(62) a. Ja zakričal, [$_{CP}$ čtoby vy ne ostavili **menja**$_j$ zdes' [$_{infP<i>}$ pogibat' **odnogo**]].
 I shouted so-that you NEG leave me here to-die alone
 'I shouted so-that you$_{NOM}$ would-not leave **me**$_{ACC}$ here [to-die **alone**$_{ACC}$].'
 b. Ja zakričal, čtoby vy ne ostavili menjaj zdes' [$_{infP}$ PRO$_{i.DAT}$ pogibat' **odnomu**$_{DAT}$].
 'I shouted so-that you$_{NOM}$ would-not leave me$_{ACC}$ here to-die **alone**$_{DAT}$.'

196 *The derivation and control of infinitives*

(63)

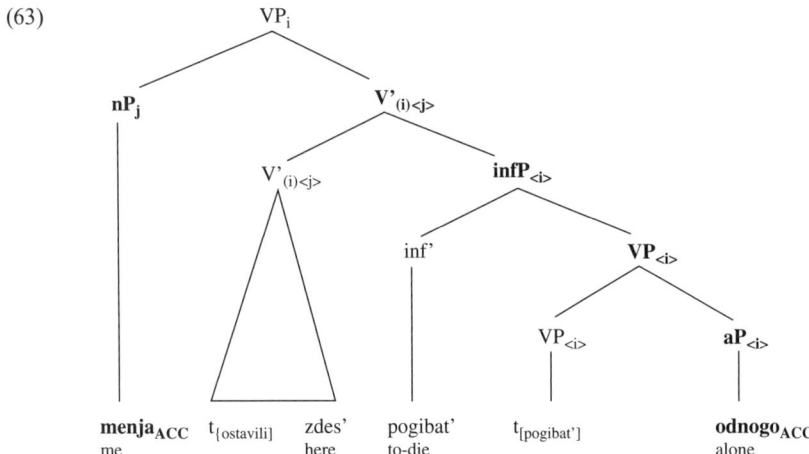

Accusative *odnogo* in (62a)/(63) adjoins to and is vertically bound by the infinitive's encapsulated **VP$_i$**, which is V-bound by **infP$_i$**, which is V-bound by finite V'$_{(i)j}$, which assigns its **j** theta role to the matrix direct object *menja*$_{j.ACC}$. *menja*$_{ACC}$ is thus the head of the TBC in which *odnogo*$_{ACC}$ is V-bound, and *odnogo* thus agrees in case with *menja*. This accusative-accusative case-agreement pattern leaves no doubt that the adjunct infinitive phrase *pogibat' odnogo* must be an infinitive s-predicate (see the boldface TBC in (63)).

The *menja*$_{ACC}$...*odnomu*$_{DAT}$ case-agreement pattern in biclausal (62b) tells a different story: *odnomu*$_{DAT}$ agrees in case with the PRO$_{DAT}$ subject of an infinitive clause, i.e., [$_{infP}$ PRO$_{i \cdot i.DAT}$ [$_{inf'<i>}$ *pogibat'* [$_{VP<i>}$ VP$_{<i>}$ [$_{aP<i>}$ **odnomu**]]]]; PRO$_{DAT}$ itself is antecedent-bound by accusative *menja*$_j$. The syntactic structure and case agreement of (62b) is essentially the same as (29)/(30) above. (64a)/(64b) is another example of an object-controlled infP$_i$.

(64) a. V sledujuščij raz mama$_{NOM}$ ne pustit menja$_{ACC.F}$ guljat' odnu$_{ACC.F}$.
      'Next time mom won't let me go-out alone.'
   b. ...mama$_{NOM}$ ne   pustit **menja**$_{ACC.F}$ [$_{inf'<i>}$ guljat' **odnu**$_{ACC.F}$]
      mom   NEG   let   me   go-out alone
   c. ...mama$_{NOM}$ ne   pustit menja$_{ACC.F}$ [$_{infP}$ PRO$_{I.DAT.F}$ guljat' **odnoj**$_{DAT.F}$]
      mama   NEG   let   me   go-out alone

4.7.1 *Depictive adjectives in infinitive complements*

Sentences like (65a) and (65b) provide additional evidence that infinitive complements in object-controlled sentences can be either s-predicates or s-clauses (*razrešila* and *predlagaja* select quirky dative case objects; the word order is neutral).

(65a) Ona$_i$ razrešila emu$_j$ leč' v postel' [$_{aP<i>}$ odetomu].
       she:NOM.F allowed him:DAT.M lie-down in bed   dressed:DAT.M
       'She allowed him to get in bed dressed.'

(65b) Ona otkryla dvercu, [$_{gPi}$ predlagaja svoemu šefu$_{DAT.M}$ sest' pervomu$_{DAT.M}$].
       'She opened the-car-door, [inviting her boss to-get-in first].'

It might seem at first glance that the LF dative depictive adjective *odetomu* in (65a) is agreeing with the PRO$_{DAT}$ subject of an object-controlled infinitive clause complement, i.e.: *Ona razrešila emu$_{DAT}$ [$_{infP}$ PRO$_{i.DAT}$ leč' v postel' odetomu$_{DAT}$]*. But, as we shall see in chapter 5, the dative case of *odetomu* in (65a) cannot be explained in these terms. Note that (66) has the same meaning; predicate instrumental *odetym* agrees with PRO$_{DAT}$ in gender and number, but not case.[28]

(66)   Ona razrešila emu leč' v postel' **odetym**.
       she:NOM.F allowed him:DAT.M to-get in bed dressed:PI.M
       'She allowed him to get in bed dressed.'

How can we explain the dative case of depictive *odetomu* in (65a), which is well-formed, if it does *not* agree with PRO$_{DAT}$? The existence of sentence pairs like (65a) and (66) is entirely predictable, given my hypothesis that an object-controlled infinitive complement can be either an s-clause or s-predicate: the finite matrix VP structures of (65a) and (66) are schematically represented in (67) and (68) respectively.

(67)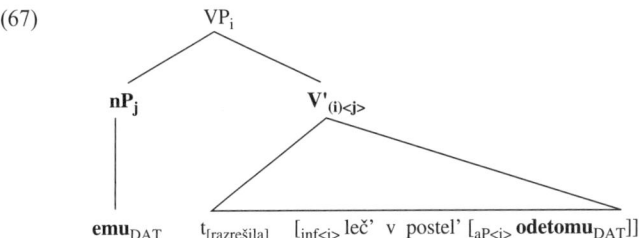

(68)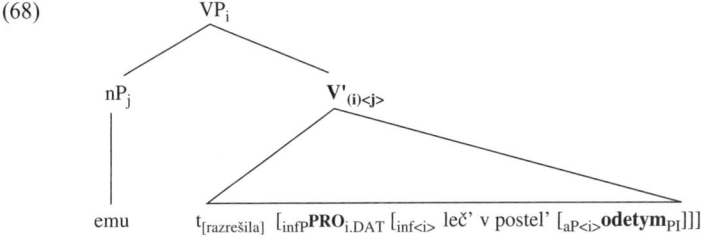

198 The derivation and control of infinitives

The infinitive complement of (66) in (68) is an infinitive clause and only the predicate instrumental depictive is possible: *[$_{VPi}$ *emu* t$_{[razrešila]}$ [$_{infP}$ **PRO**$_{i.DAT.M}$ [$_{inf<i>}$ *leč' v postel'* [$_{aP<i>}$**odetomu**$_{LF.DAT.M}$]]]] (see chapter 5). The infinitive complement of (65a) in (67) is an infinitive s-predicate, and dative *odetomu* therefore agrees in case with the dative matrix object *emu*, which is the head of its TBC.

It is a simple matter to confirm the infinitive s-predicate analysis of the infinitive complement in (67): if we replace the dative-assigning matrix verb *razrešila* with a verb whose direct object is accusative, my analysis correctly predicts that the depictive adjective will now be either predicate instrumental or *accusative*, but not dative:

(69)   Ona   poprosila **ego**   leč'   v postel' **odetogo/*odetomu**.
       she   asked   him:ACC to-get in bed   dressed:ACC/*DAT

(70)   Ona   poprosila ego   leč'   v postel' **odetym/*odetomu**.
       she   asked   him:ACC to-get in bed   dressed:INST/*DAT

The infinitive complement in (69) is an s-predicate whose unlinked external theta role **i** is V-bound by the accusative matrix object [$_{nPj.ACC}$ *ego*], which is the head of the TBC in which accusative *odetogo* is V-bound: *odetogo*$_{ACC}$ thus agrees with *ego*$_{ACC}$ in (69) for the same reason that *odetomu*$_{DAT}$ agrees with dative *emu*$_{DAT}$ (65a). Dative depictive adjectives are possible only when the infinitive complement in which they are V-bound is an infP$_i$ s-predicate and the matrix verb happens to assign quirky dative to its direct object. The structures of (69) and (70) are represented in (71) and (72) respectively.

(71)   Ona poprosila **ego**$_{j.ACC.M}$ [$_{inf<i>}$ leč'   v postel' **odetogo**$_{ACC.M}$].
       she asked   him   to-get in bed   dressed
       'She asked him to get in bed dressed.'

(72)   Ona poprosila ego$_{ACC}$ [$_{infP}$ **PRO**$_{DAT.M}$ [$_{inf<i>}$ leč' v postel' **odetym**$_{Pl.M}$]].
       'She asked him to get in bed dressed.'

(73)   *Ona poprosila ego$_{ACC}$ [$_{infP}$ **PRO**$_{DAT}$ [$_{inf<i>}$ leč' v postel' **odetomu**$_{DAT}$]].

I will argue in chapter 5, which is devoted to the relation of the predicate instrumental case of adjectives to the LF and SF, that the ungrammaticality of (73), which appears to be well-formed, has a diachronic explanation.

Summary: My theory correctly predicts that the case of SAM$_i$ adjoined to an infinitive s-clause is dative (or the default nominative, as in (61d)), whereas SAM$_i$ adjoined to an infinitive s-predicate can be nominative, dative, or accusative: The case of SAM$_i$ adjoined to infP$_i$ depends on whether the clause containing [$_{infPi}$ SAM$_{<i>}$ infP$_{<i>}$] is finite or an infinitive clause: in cases of subject control, SAM$_i$ is nominative in the former and dative in the latter. If [$_{infPi}$ SAM$_{<i>}$ infP$_{<i>}$] is object-controlled, SAM$_i$ agrees in case with the direct object of the finite matrix verb, which is accusative or dative (see (65a) and (74) below). These complex but entirely regular case and control patterns demonstrate that there is no direct, isomorphic relation between subject vs. object control and the case of SAM$_i$; but there is a direct relation between the case of SAM$_i$ (and kP$_i$) and the case of the head of its TBC.[29]

(74)   Ona posovetovala emu$_{j.DAT.M}$ [$_{infP<i>}$ poobeščat' [$_{infP<i>}$ ne ezdit' tuda [$_{aP<i>}$odnomu$_{DAT.M}$]]].
'She advised **him** [to-promise [not to-go there [**alone**]]].'

If all infinitives headed clauses, which have been demonstrated to have dative subjects in Russian, we would not expect the case agreement patterns of SAM$_i$ we have seen above: there would in fact be *no case variation* since SAM$_i$ would agree with PRO$_{DAT}$ and thus always be dative in infinitive phrases. It is unclear how Hornstein's 1999 raising-analysis of control can account for the Russian data since it assumes that all infinitive complements are clauses whose subjects raise to the matrix clause.

We have now seen that object control does not always involve the antecedent binding of an infinitive clause's PRO subject, and that subject control does not always involve the V-binding of an infinitive s-predicate's unlinked external **i** (see (25)). What is crucial is the fact that the four infinitive control possibilities predicted to exist by my theory in (2) are all attested (the fifth possibilty, the bare infinitive complement, is discussed below).

4.8   Locality restrictions on vertical binding

This section is devoted to demonstrating the explanatory power of my hypothesis that the syntactic distribution of infinitive s-predicates and s-clauses is directly dependent on whether or not the infinitive phrases are in a syntactic configuration that licenses V-binding.

4.8.1   Infinitive complements of nouns

We begin with (25), repeated here as (75a/b): *my* 'we' is construed as the subject of the infinitive *vyžit'* because it antecedent-binds the infinitive clause's PRO subject.

(75)   a.   My   xotim najti sposob vyžit'   samim.
             we:NOM must find way:ACC to-survive ourselves:DAT
             'We want to find a way to survive ourselves.'

b. My$_{NOM}$ xotim najti [$_{nP}$ sposob$_{ACC}$ [$_{infP}$ PRO$_{i.DAT}$ vyžit' [$_{aP<i>}$ samim$_{DAT.PL}$]]].
c. My$_{i.NOM}$ xotim [$_{infP<i>}$ vyžit' [$_{aP<i>}$sami$_{NOM.PL}$]].
'We want to survive ourselves.'

It was observed in §4.4.1 that the infinitive complement of a noun must be an s-clause because an s-predicate's unlinked external theta role **i** cannot be V-bound by the matrix verb in this position: nP, the maximal projection of the head noun *sposob* in (75a/b), blocks the V-binding of its infinitive complement by the matrix subject *my*$_i$. More specifically, *vyžit'* in (75a/b) cannot be an infinitive s-predicate V-bound by the external theta role of *xotim najti* because the maximal projection of the noun *sposob* intervenes between the potential vertical binder and bindee, breaking the TBC in which infP$_i$ would be V-bound. The links in a TBC must be maximally local, i.e., involve immediate domination; when this is impossible, the infinitive's external theta role must be assigned to an nP merged in spec-infP, which 'saves the derivation' by creating an infinitive clause whose dative subject is antecedent-bound (by the subject of the matrix sentence *my* in (75a/b)).

The sentences in (76) to (81) demonstrate that, when SAM$_i$ adjoins to the infinitive complement of nouns, it is *obligatorily dative*, which means that these infinitive complements must be s-clauses. We see in (81a–c) that the dative subject of infinitive s-clauses is *overt* when there is no higher antecedent-binder to control it.[30]

(76) (On očen' xotel, čtoby ego$_{ACC}$ ljubili$_{PL}$.) Pričem [$_{nP}$ potrebnosti$_{GEN}$ [$_{infP}$ PRO$_{DAT}$
 but need
 ljubit' kogo-to$_{ACC}$ **samomu**$_{DAT}$]] on ne ispytyval.
 to-love someone himself he NEG experienced
 '(He very much wanted people to love him). But he did not feel [the need [to love anyone **himself**]].' (A. Marinina)

(77) U nego$_{GEN}$ ne xvataet [$_{nP}$ mužestva$_{GEN}$ [PRO$_{DAT}$ prijti **samomu**$_{DAT}$]].
 at him NEG suffice courage to-come himself
 'He doesn't have the courage to come himself.'

(78) a. [$_{nP}$ želanie ženščiny$_{GEN}$ [$_{infP}$ PRO$_{DAT}$ **samoj**$_{DAT}$ uplatit' za sebja$_{ACC}$]] estestvenno$_N$.
 '[The-desire of-a-woman [to pay for herself$_{ACC}$ **herself**$_{DAT}$]] is-natural.'
 b. Ženščina$_{i.NOM}$ estestvenno želaet [$_{infP<i>}$uplatit' za sebja$_{ACC}$ [$_{aP<i>}$ **sama**$_{NOM}$]].
 'A-woman$_{NOM}$ naturally wants to-pay for herself$_{ACC}$ herself$_{NOM}$.'

(79) Anna$_{NOM}$ podala [$_{nP}$ ideju$_{ACC}$ [$_{infP}$ PRO$_{DAT}$ sobrat'sja tam **vsem**$_{DAT}$ vmeste]].
 'Anna suggested [the-idea [(for) **everyone** to-gather there together]].'

(80) Imeju [$_{nP}$ predpisanie$_{ACC}$ [$_{infP}$ dejstvovat' **odnomu**$_{DAT}$]].
 I-have order to-act alone
 '(I) have orders to-act alone.'

(81) a. Oni byli ošelomleny izvestiem o [$_{nP}$ vozmožnosti [$_{infP}$ uexat' **mne**$_{DAT}$ s det'mi]].
         possibility   to-leave me   with kids
'They were shocked by-news of [the-possibility [for me to leave with the-kids]].'
b. Možet, èto [$_{nP}$ edinstvennaja vozmožnost' [poznakomit'sja **ej**$_{DAT}$ s Nikitoj]].
'Perhaps this is [the only opportunity [(for) her$_{DAT}$ to-meet with Nikita]].'
c. Prišlo [$_{nP}$ [vremja [$_{infP}$ **nam**$_{DAT}$ **samim**$_{DAT}$ sebe$_{DAT}$ pomoč']].
   came   time   us   ourselves self   to-help
(lit.) 'The-time has-come (for) [us$_{DAT}$ to-help ourselves$_{DAT}$ ourselves$_{DAT}$].'

Is the generalization that a noun's infinitive complement must be an s-clause a construction-specific property of the NOUN + INFINITIVE COMPLEMENT collocation or is it the instantiation of a basic principle of grammar? I will argue for the latter hypothesis by presenting evidence that the distribution of infinitive s-clauses and s-predicates falls out naturally from a simple, construction-independent restriction on V-binding, namely, the infinitive s-clause is the only option in syntactic configurations where an infinitive s-predicate cannot be V-bound. The data demonstrate that V-binding must be maximally local in the sense that each contiguous link in the TBC must immediately dominate the lower link, which entails that the maximal projection xP in (82), no matter what its category, cannot intervene between the potential vertical bindee ZP$_i$ and its intended vertical binder YP$_i$ (xP=nP in (76)–(81)):

(82)   *YP$_i$ [$_{xP}$...x...ZP$_{<i>}$...]

Since we are interested here primarily in the V-binding of infP$_i$ by the external theta role of higher verbal projections, we will explore the predictive power of the version of (82) in (83), which predicts that the maximal projection of any category, not just nPs, intervening between V$^n_{i/j}$ (the vertical-binder) and infP$_i$ (the vertical-bindee) blocks V-binding and requires the replacement of an infP$_i$ s-predicate with an infinitive s-clause [$_{infP}$ PRO$_{i.DAT}$ inf'$_{<i>}$] and the antecedent-binding of PRO (V$^n_{i/j}$=VP$_i$ or V'$_j$). We shall see below that the schema in (83) accounts for many seemingly unrelated phenomena.

(83)   *V$^n_{i/j}$ [$_{xP}$...x...infP$_{<i>}$]

4.8.2 Infinitives with complementizers
(83) correctly predicts that when xP=CP (i.e., an infinitive phrase introduced by a complementizer), SAM$_i$ adjoined to the infinitive projection must be dative: since the CP phrase blocks the V-binding of infP$_i$, an infinitive introduced by a complementizer must be an s-clause whose PRO$_{i.DAT}$ subject is the head of the TBC in which SAM$_i$ is V-bound: [$_{CP}$ [$_{C'}$ *čtoby*$_C$ [$_{infP}$

PRO$_{i.DAT}$ ... [$_{aP<i>}$ samomu$_{DAT}$]]]]. InfP$_i$ in CP is ill-formed because its unlinked theta role **i** cannot be V-bound: *[$_{CP}$ [$_{C'}$ čtoby [$_{infPi}$ ... [$_{aP<i>}$ *samomu*]]]]. More generally: *[$_{CP}$ [$_{C'}$ C xP$_i$]] (see §3.3 for the discussion of *[$_{CP}$ [$_{C'}$ C gP$_i$]]). All the infinitives in the following examples are embedded in CP and all are s-clauses whose PRO$_{DAT}$ subject is the head of the TBC in which SAM$_i$ is V-bound. The dative subjects in (87) and (88) are overt because they are not antecedent-bound.

(84) Ja priletel včera, [$_{CP}$ čtoby$_C$ [$_{infP}$ PRO$_{DAT}$ **samomu**$_{DAT}$ razobrat'sja]].
      'I flew-in yesterday [in order [to-sort-things-out **myself**]].'

(85) Ona sliškom moloda, [$_{CP}$ čtoby$_C$ [$_{infP}$ PRO$_{DAT}$ nesti bremja stradanij **odnoj**$_{DAT}$]].
      'She is too young [to-bear the-burden of-suffering **alone**].'

(86) Odaryvat' drugix$_{ACC}$ gorazdo radostnee, [$_{CP}$ čem$_C$ polučat' **samomu**$_{DAT}$].
      '(It is) much more-joyous to-give to-others [than to-receive yourself$_{DAT}$].'

(87) [$_{CP}$Vmesto togo čtoby$_C$ [$_{infP}$ **ljudjam**$_{DAT}$ polagat'sja na pomošč' drugix]],...
      'instead of people relying on the help of others,...'

(88) Tak bylo [$_{PP}$ do [$_{nP}$ togo, [$_{CP}$ kak$_C$ [$_{infP}$ podnjat'sja **solncu**$_{DAT}$]]]].
                                              until   to-rise   the-sun
      'That's the way it was [until [the sun rose]].'

(89) Est' mnogo sposobov otpravit' pis'mo po počte, [$_{CP}$ krome kak$_C$ [$_{infP}$ PRO$_{DAT}$ **samomu**$_{DAT}$ brosit' ego v počtovyj jaščik]].
      'There-are many ways to-mail a-letter [other than [to-toss it into a mail box yourself]].'

(90) Prežde čem **samomu**$_{DAT}$ vyprygnut' iz samoleta, on velel vyprygnut' mne.
      'Before jumping (lit. to-jump) out of the plane himself, he ordered me to-jump.' (Comrie 1974: 130)

(91) Oni sobralis'[$_{CP}$ čtoby$_C$ [$_{infP}$ PRO$_{i.DAT}$ [$_{aP<i>}$**vsem**$_{DAT}$] vmeste rešit' ètu dilemmu$_{ACC}$]].
      'They gathered [(lit.) in-order-to-resolve this dilemma all together].'[31]

4.8.3 *Infinitive clauses as subjects*

The constraint in (83) predicts that an infinitive phrase functioning as a sentence's subject must be an s-clause because infP$_i$ cannot be V-bound in this position. The overt dative subjects of the bracketed infinitival subjects in (96) and (97), and the dative case of SAM$_i$ in (92) to (95) confirm this prediction. Since infinitives do not have agreement features, the matrix predicate adjectives and verbs have the default neuter singular nonagreeing form.[32]

(92) a. [Šastat' **odnomu** po   ulicam] bylo   nespodručno.
         to-walk alone:DAT around streets was.N awkward:N.SG
         'It was awkward [to-walk around the-streets **alone**].'
      b. [infP PRO_DAT šastat' **odnomu**_DAT po ulicam] bylo nespodručno.

(93) Dlja nas   utomitel'no [PRO_DAT delat' èto   **samim**].
      for us:GEN.PL tiring:N.SG   to-do this:ACC ourselves:DAT.PL
      'It is tiring for us [to do this **ourselves**].' (Comrie 1974: 129)

(94) Ostavalos'_N [infP PRO_DAT ždat' čuda_GEN ili že tvorit' ego_ACC **samomu**_DAT].
      'The-only-thing-left-to-do-was [to-wait-for a-miracle or to-create one **myself**].'

(95) U nego vošlo v obyčaj [PRO_DAT **samomu**_DAT otvečat' na nekotorye voprosy].
      'It became his habit [to-answer some questions **himself**].'

(96) Ty dumaeš', [**mne**_DAT tut s   toboj sidet'] – odno udovol'stvie?
      you think   me   here with you to-sit (is) a   pleasure
      'Do you think (that it is) a pleasure (for) [me_DAT to-sit here with you]?'

(97) Pora by [infP načat'sja **uroku**_DAT], a v klasse net   učitelja_GEN.
      time mod   to-begin lesson   but in class there-isn't teacher
      'It is time (for) [the **lesson** to-begin], but the-teacher isn't in class.'

4.8.4 *Conjoined subject-controlled infinitive complements*

This section deals with subject-controlled infinitive complements that are conjoined, e.g., *Olja xočet* [[*skinut' načal'nicu*] *i* [*zastupit' na ee mesto*]] 'Olja wants [[to-get-rid-of the-director] and [to-take her place]]'). The case of SAM_i in the second conjunct demonstrates the explanatory power of the constraint on V-binding in (82)/(83).

When two subject-controlled infinitive complements are conjoined by *i* 'and,' we expect them a priori to behave like the single, unconjoined infinitive complement in (98); i.e., if the conjunction of subject-controlled infinitive s-predicate is a symmetric structure like [infPi infP_<i> *i* infP_<i>], we expect SAM_i to agree in case with the nominative subject. However, this is not what happens: when SAM_i adjoins to the second conjunct of subject-controlled conjoined infinitive complement in standard Russian, *it is dative rather than the expected nominative*: compare (98) and (99); (100) to (103) are additional examples.[33]

(98) Ja sobirajus' **sam** (*samomu) vo vsem   razobrat'sja.
      I intend   myself:NOM(*DAT) in everything to-investigate
      'I intend to investigate everything myself.'

(99)   Ja sobirajus' otpravit'sja na mesto prestuplenija i   **samomu**
       I   intend   to-go   to scene of-crime   and myself:DAT
       vo vsem   razobrat'sja.
       in everything investigate
       'I intend to go to the scene of the crime and to investigate everything **myself**.'

(100) On   želaet ženit'sja na nej **sam** (*samomu).
       he:NOM wants to-marry on   her himself:NOM/*DAT
       'He wants to-marry her himself.'

(101) On želaet razvesti   Elenu s   Ivanom i   ženit'sja na nej
       he wants to-divorce Elena with Ivan   and marry   on her
       samomu (sam).
       himself:DAT (NOM).
       'He wants to-break-up Elena and Ivan and to-marry her **himself**.'

(102) Ja predpočitaju sprosit' i   **samomu**   že otvetit'.
       I   prefer   to-ask and myself:DAT prt to-answer
       'I prefer to-ask-questions and to answer (them) myself.'

(103) a. **Olja**$_{NOM.F}$ xočet zastupit' na mesto načal'nicy **sama**$_{NOM.F}$ (*samoj$_{DAT}$).
       'Olja wants to take the director's position herself$_{NOM\ (*DAT)}$.'
       b. Olja xočet skinut' načal'nicu i zatem zastupit' na ee mesto **samoj**.
       'Olja wants to-get-rid-of the-director$_{ACC}$ and then to-take her place
       herself$_{DAT}$.'

Given what we have already seen, the null hypothesis, assuming the validity of (83) (*$V^n_{i/j}$ [$_{xP}$...x...infP$_{<i>}$]), is that the second conjunct in these sentences is an infinitive s-clause, which occurs in the second conjunct instead of the expected s-predicate because V-binding is somehow blocked in conjoined infinitive complements. Our next step is to identify what is blocking it.

It has been proposed in Babyonyšev 1996, Munn 1993, and others that the coordinating conjunction, like all function words, heads its own functional projection, conjP, with the first conjunct in spec-conjP and the second in the lower, sister-to-head position. It follows naturally from (83) and the [$_{conjP}$ xP [$_{conj'}$ CONJ xP]] analysis of conjunction that if SAM$_i$ adjoins to the second conjunct of conjoined subject-controlled infinitives, it should be dative, not nominative, because, like CP, conjP intervenes between the potential vertical binder (the matrix verb's external theta role **i**) and bindee (infP$_i$), thereby blocking V-binding, in which case the second conjunct must by default be an infinitive clause, whose dative PRO$_i$ subject is the head of SAM$_{DAT}$'s TBC.[34] The dative case of SAM$_i$ in (99)–(103) thus provides independent evidence for the conjP treatment of conjunction as well as for the constraint on V-binding in (83).[35]

4.9 Hybrid adverbials in infinitive complements

In this section we return to the data in §3.5.2, which provide particularly strong independent evidence supporting my hypothesis that infinitives project to syntax as either the s-clause in (104) or the s-predicate in (105) (except when they compose with a form of V_{aux}). My theory of infinitive complementation and control makes the following prediction: when SAM$_i$ is adjoined to gP$_i$ (i.e., [$_{gPi}$ SAM$_{<i>}$ gP$_{<i>}$]), its case should depend on whether the matrix VP$_i$ that gP$_i$ adjoins to is finite or an infinitive and, in the latter case, whether the infinitive heads an s-predicate or an s-clause.[36] More specifically, SAM$_i$ adjoined to gP$_i$ should be: (i) nominative (*sam*) when [$_{gPi}$ SAM$_{<i>}$ gP$_{<i>}$] adjoins to a finite matrix clause or to the infinitive s-predicate complement of a finite subject-control verb, (ii) dative (*samomu*) elsewhere since V-binding is blocked elsewhere and, therefore, only infinitive s-clauses are possible: *samomu*$_{i.DAT}$ agrees with the PRO$_{i.DAT}$ subject (see (104)).[37] We shall see below that this complex prediction is correct and that the data are crystal clear.

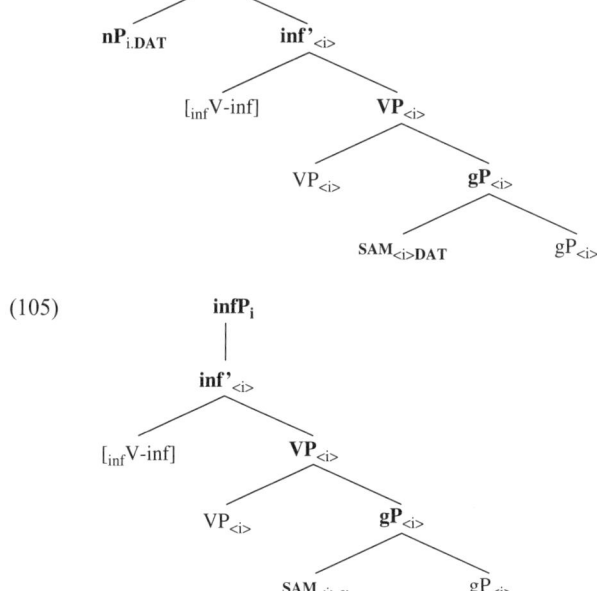

Let us begin with (106), the syntactic representation of (107) (small v is the finite suffix): *sam* is V-bound in the TBC headed by the subject *ja*$_{NOM}$ and is thus nominative.[38]

(106)

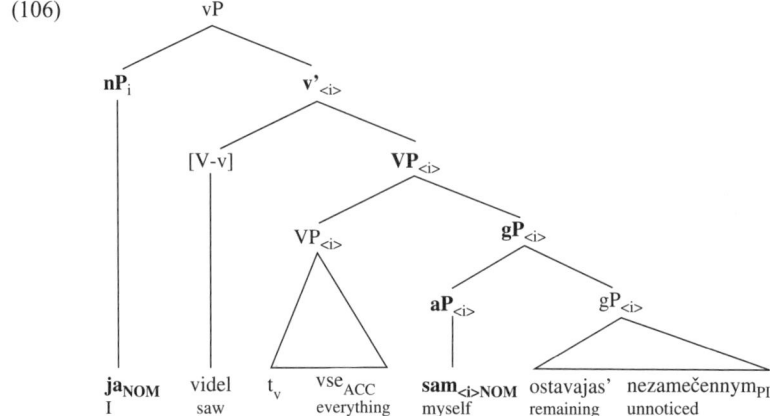

(107) Ja   vse   videl, [gP<i> **sam** (*samomu) ostavajas' nezamečennym].
       I:NOM all:ACC saw   self.NOM/*DAT   remaining unnoticed:PI
       'I saw everything, (while) remaining unseen myself.'

If (107) is embedded as the infinitive complement of a finite subject-control verb (*xotel* 'wanted' in (108)), *sam* is correctly predicted to remain nominative. This is because the infinitive complement of a subject-control verb is an infinitive s-predicate and, therefore, the sentence in (108) is monoclausal, with the subject *ja*$_{NOM}$ still the head of *sam*$_{NOM}$'s TBC: (109) is the syntactic structure of (108).

(108) Ja xotel vse videt', **sam** (*samomu) ostavajas' nezamečennym.
       'I$_{NOM}$ wanted to-see everything$_{ACC}$, (while) remaining unseen$_{PI}$ myself$_{NOM(*DAT)}$.'

(109)

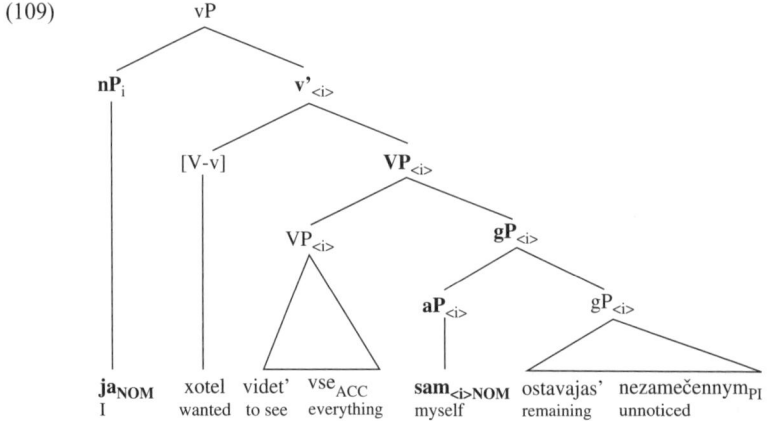

We come now to the crucial prediction: if my analysis is correct, it should be the case that, when [gPi SAM<i> gP<i>] adjoins to an infinitive *s-clause*, SAMi should be *dative* because it is the clause's dative PROi subject that now heads the TBC in which [gPi SAM<i> gP<i>] is the V-bound tail. This is precisely what we see in (110), in which the sentence in (106)/(107) has been embedded as the infinitive clause complement of the noun *vozmožnost'* 'opportunity,' whose nP projection is schematically represented in (111):[39] *samomu* is V-bound in the TBC headed by PRO$_{DAT}$ and thus agrees with it in dative case. PRO$_{DAT}$ is itself antecedent-bound by the matrix dative object *mne* 'me,' which is *not* part of the TBC in which *samomu* is bound; this is clearly demonstrated in (112) and (113).

(110) Sčel' v doskax dala mne vozmožnost' vse videt',
crack:NOM in boards gave me:DAT opportunity:ACC all:ACC to-see
[gP<i> **samomu** ostavajas' nezamečennym].
self:DAT remaining unnoticed:PI
'(lit.) A-crack in the-boards gave me the-opportunity to-see everything, remaining unseen **myself**.'

(111)

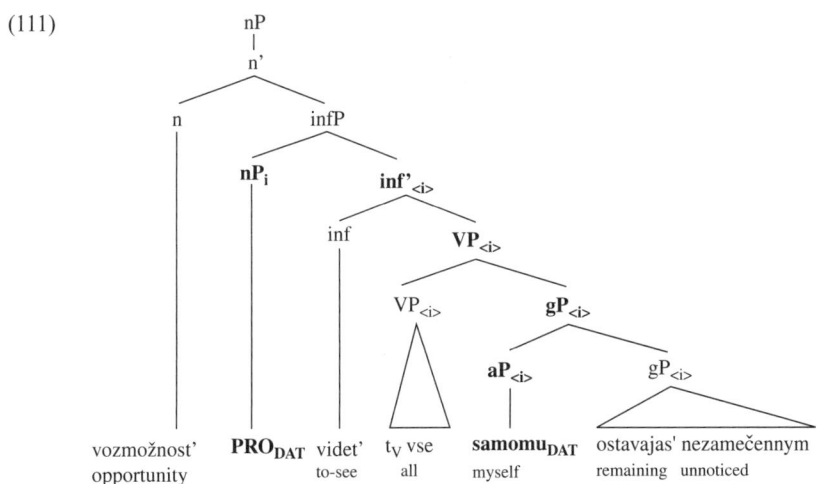

(112) Èto lišilo menja vozmožnosti vse videt', [**samomu** ostavajas' nezamečennym].
'That$_{NOM}$ deprived me$_{ACC}$ of-the-opportunity$_{GEN}$ to-see everything$_{ACC}$, [remaining unseen$_{PI}$ **myself**$_{DAT}$].'

(113) Mat' poprosila ego [$_{infP}$ PRO$_{i.DAT}$ žit' v dovol'stve, [$_{gP<i>}$ **samomu**$_{DAT}$ ne trevožas' o sud'be bednyx]].
'(His) mother$_{NOM}$ urged him$_{ACC}$ [to-live in-contentment, [not worrying about the plight of-the-poor **himself**$_{DAT}$]].'

4.10 Nominative direct objects in Old Russian infinitive clauses

This section presents Old Russian evidence supporting my analysis of infinitives. I will argue that the assignment of *nominative or accusative* case to the direct object of transitive infinitives in northern dialects of Old Russian (N-OR) depends directly on whether the infinitive heads an s-clause or an s-predicate. More specifically, if we assume that in Old Russian, just as in modern Russian, the infinitive complement of a subject-control verb is a V-bound s-predicate (infP$_i$) and that elsewhere, i.e., wherever V-binding is excluded, the infinitive projects an infinitive s-clause ([$_{infP}$ nP$_{i.DAT}$ inf'$_{<i>}$]), we can *explain* the distribution of the infinitive's nominative ~ accusative direct object in N-OR as well as the following closely related fact: the direct object of *finite* transitive verbs cannot be nominative. My analysis will be guided by the following question: Why is the assignment of the nominative case to direct objects in N-OR confined to infinitive s-clauses?

We begin with the following descriptive generalization: the accusative and nominative direct objects of infinitives in N-OR are in complementary distribution: nominative direct objects occur only in infinitive s-clauses; accusative direct objects occur elsewhere. Consider the data in (114)–(117) (the enclitic interrogative complementizer *li* 'whether' is glossed as "Q"; [$_{nPj:NOM}$ ta že čaša] is the direct object of the infinitive *pit'*).[40]

(114) i dast li vladyka   nam [$_{infP}$ ta   že čaša   pit'].
      and let Q bishop:NOM us:DAT that:NOM very cup:NOM to-drink
      'and will the-bishop permit us [to drink that cup]?'

(115) a. i   korolju$_{DAT.M}$ bylo$_N$ [$_{nP}$ ta   ruxljad'$_{NOM.F}$] dati.
        and king   was   that property   to-give
        'and (it) was (necessary for the) king$_{DAT}$ to-return that property$_{NOM}$.'
      b. i korolju$_{DAT.M}$ bylo$_N$ [$_{infP}$ t$_n$ [$_{inf'}$ [$_{nPNOM}$ ta ruxljad'] dati]].

(116) a. ino dostoit" mužu$_{DAT}$ [$_{nPNOM}$ žena svoja] nakazyvati
        'for it-is-fitting for-a-man$_{DAT}$ to-instruct [his wife$_{NOM}$]'
      b. ino dostoit" mužu$_{DAT}$ [$_{infP}$ PRO$_{DAT}$ [$_{nPNOM}$ žena svoja] nakazyvati]

(117) Bě že v to   vremja [$_{infP}$ PRO$_{DAT}$ viděti v" gradě [$_{nPNOM}$ pečal' gor'kaja]].
      was prt at-that-time   to-see in city   sorrow great
      '(One could) see [$_{nPNOM}$ great sorrow] in the city at that time.'

Since the assignment of *accusative* case to an infinitive's direct object is the same in Old Russian as it is in modern Russian (see §3.2.3), we will concentrate here on explaining the assignment nominative case to the direct objects in infinitive s-clauses, which arose in N-OR dialects under the influence of Finnish, which, like Icelandic and Lithuanian, has the following crucial property: the case of a verb's direct object depends on the case of the verb's subject, i.e., the direct object in these languages is accusative when the subject is nominative, but *the direct object is nominative when the subject is assigned oblique (quirky) case* (see Taraldsen 1986, Timberlake 1974, Lavine 2000, Franks and Lavine 2005).

There are essentially three structural case-assigning/checking domains in nominative-accusative languages: (i) the nP-internal domain, where the adnominal genitive is typically the only structural case (this domain plays no role here); (ii) the VP-internal domain, where the structural case is accusative; (iii) the VP-external domain, where the structural case is nominative. This allows for two types of nominative-accusative languages. English and modern Russian (Type I), in which all three case-assignment domains are autonomous and the case of the direct object does not therefore depend on the subject's case. In Type II languages like Finnish and Icelandic, and, I argue N-OR, VP is not an autonomous case domain: here the whole clause, $[_{xP}$ nP$_i$ $[_{x'<i>}$ $[_x$V-x$]$ $[_{VP}$ nP$_j$ V']]], is a single structural case domain, which necessarily involves a case-assignment hierarchy or *dependency* between nominative and accusative (see Yip, Maling, and Jackendoff 1987). Nominative is assigned to the syntactically *highest* available nP, which is normally the subject nP; accusative is assigned to the remaining (lower) nPs, if there are any: $[_{xP}$ nP$_{i.NOM}$ $[_{x'<i>}$ $[_x$V-x$]$ $[_{VP}$ nP$_{j.ACC}$ V']]]. However, when the subject nP is assigned quirky case, the highest available nP for structure case marking is now *the direct object*, and it is accordingly assigned nominative case: $[_{xP}$ nP$_{i.OBLIQ}$ $[_{x'<i>}$ $[_x$V-x$]$ $[_{VP}$ nP$_{j.NOM}$ V']]].

The oblique-subject/nominative-object Type II case-assignment pattern is illustrated in finite Icelandic sentences like (118), where the transitive verb *finnst* assigns quirky dative case to its subject (i.e., the external argument of *finnst* is $\{i{\char`\^}N_{DAT}\}_1$).

(118) Barninu   finnst   mjolk   góð.
       child:DAT finds   milk:NOM good:NOM
       'The-child finds the-milk good.'

210 *The derivation and control of infinitives*

When an Icelandic verb c-selects an external quirky (oblique) case, the highest nP available for structural case assignment is the direct object nP in spec-VP, and it is assigned nominative rather than accusative. Thus, since *finnst* 'finds' assigns quirky dative case to its subject, its direct object *mjolk* 'milk' is nominative. The dependent structural case assignment strategy at work in (118) can be stated informally as follows: assign nominative to the highest available nP. When the verb does not select an external quirky case, its subject is nominative, in which case its direct object is assigned accusative. In Finnish and Icelandic, *individual lexical verbs* c-select external quirky case, which accounts for the restriction in these languages of nominative objects to sentences headed by external quirky-case assigning verbs (see Yip, Maling, and Jackendoff 1987).

N-OR borrowed the Type II dependent case assignment strategy from its neighbors, but we actually see nominative direct objects in N-OR only in infinitive clauses because *lexical verbs in Russian do not assign quirky case externally* to $\{i^\wedge N\}_1$. The nominative direct object is confined to *infinitive clauses* in N-OR because, as we saw above, the infinitive-forming *suffix* **-inf** 'assigns' quirky dative case to [V-inf]'s subject nP, i.e., [V-inf] inherits the **-inf** suffix's c-selected external dative case when the diatheses of **V** and **-inf** compose: $\{\{i^\wedge N\}_1...\{-^\wedge V\}_4\}\} + \{\{ ^\wedge N_{DAT}\}_1...\{ ^\wedge\text{-inf}\}_4\} > \{\{i^\wedge N_{DAT}]_1...\{-^\wedge\{[V\text{-inf}]\}_4\}$ (see (18)).

In other words, it is only in infinitive clauses that direct objects are nominative in N-OR because they are the only kind of clause in Russian with an oblique subject. Since subject-controlled infinitive complements are s-predicates, not clauses, they do not have dative subject nPs: they merge with finite verbs, which have nominative subjects, to form *monoclausal* structures in which the subject-controlled infinitive complement's direct object nP is accusative.

To see how this works in vivo, let us look first at the syntactic structure of (115), which is schematically represented in (119) below: the infinitive clause has an overt dative subject (*korolju* 'king'); finite *bylo* 'was' is affixed with the nonagreeing neuter singular suffix. Since the infinitive s-clause [$_{infP}$ *korolju*$_{DAT}$ [$_{nPNOM}$ *ta ruxljad'*] *dati*] has a dative subject, its direct object *ta ruxljad'* 'that property' is the crucial 'first available nP' and it is assigned nominative case; *korolju* raises to spec-TP.[41] I assume that the nominative direct object *ta ruxljad'* left-adjoins to infP, which accounts for its neutral position to the left of the infinitive *dat'*. The infinitive phrase in (115)/(119) is an s-clause rather than an s-predicate, because there is no potential vertical binder for an infP$_i$.

(119)

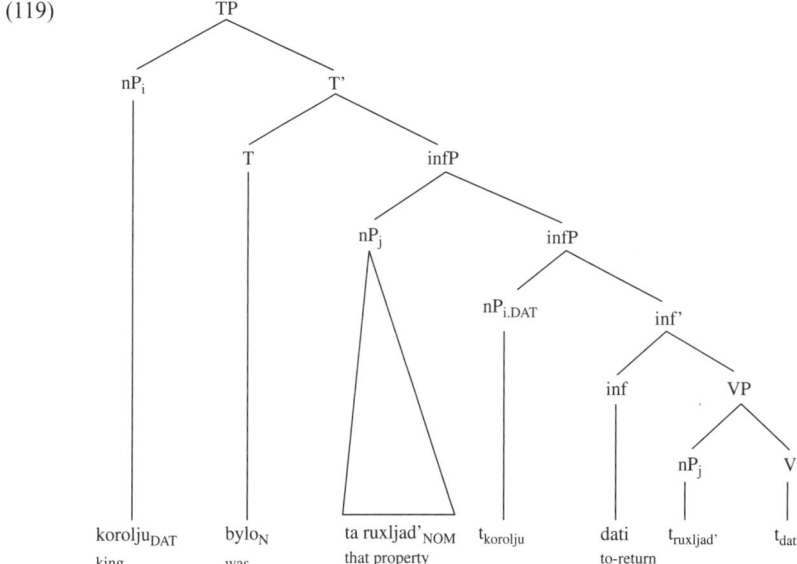

The sentence in (114), repeated here as (120)/(121), involves object control: the matrix direct object *nam* 'us' is the antecedent-binder of the infinitive clause's PRO$_{DAT}$ subject.

(120)   i   dast li vladyka   nam   ta   že čaša   pit'?
        and let   Q   bishop$_{NOM}$ us$_{DAT}$ that$_{NOM}$ very cup$_{NOM}$ to-drink
        'and will the bishop allow us to drink that very cup?'

(121)   i dast li vladyka$_{i.NOM}$ [$_{VP}$ nam$_{j.DAT}$ [$_{V'}$ t$_V$ [$_{infP}$ PRO$_{i.DAT}$ [ta že čaša]$_{j.NOM}$ pit']]]?

Since the object-control infinitive complement is an s-clause, which has a quirky dative PRO$_{i.DAT}$ subject, the infinitive's direct object *ta že čaša* is predictably nominative; the matrix quirky dative case direct object *nam*$_{DAT}$ is in the spec-position of the finite VP and it antecedent-binds PRO in the [$_{infP}$ PRO$_{i.DAT}$ *ta že čaša*$_{NOM}$ *pit'*] clause.

Note that the case marking in (120) provides another type of evidence that object-control structures are biclausal: a corollary of this analysis is that a *monoclausal* structure in N-OR cannot have both a nominative subject (*vladyka*) and a nominative direct object (*ta čaša*).

There is a great deal of empirical evidence supporting my hypothesis that nominative objects are found in N-OR only in infinitive clauses; some of this evidence is presented below.

We saw in §4.8.2 that infinitive phrases introduced by complementizers must have clausal structure because the CP projection blocks V-binding and,

212   *The derivation and control of infinitives*

therefore, infinitive s-predicates are excluded. This correctly predicts that *infinitives preceded by complementizers in N-OR should have nominative objects*: see (122), where *emu* is the overt dative subject of the infinitive clause headed by *vzjati* and *doč' tvoja* is the expected nominative direct object.

(122)   čtoby [_{infP} emu_{i.DAT} sobe_{DAT} [_{nPj} dočer_{NOM} tvoja_{NOM}] vzjati]
        C   him   to-self   daughter your   to-take
        'so-that-it-might-be-possible (for) [him to-take your daughter to-himself (in marriage)]'

My analysis of infinitives in modern Russian was based primarily on the nominative ~ dative case alternation of the SAM_i: SAM_i is dative in infinitive s-clauses because it agrees with the dative subject; SAM_i is nominative in subject-controlled infinitive s-predicates because it agrees with the nominative subject of the finite matrix verb. This analysis makes the following make-or-break prediction: if the occurrence of nominative direct objects in N-OR depends on the dative case of the subject in infinitive clauses, there should be N-OR infinitive s-clauses in which dative *samomu* and a nominative direct object cooccur. This prediction is borne out by (123), which is from Sprinčak 1960: 175: (124) is the structure of (123)'s second clause (*i* here is an emphatic particle not a conjunction); the dative subject is null in both clauses and *čaša* 'cup' in the second clause is ellipted.

(123)   [Kakova čaša]_{nP} drugu   nalit',   [takova]_{nP}   i   samomu pit'.
        kind-of_{NOM} cup_{NOM} friend_{DAT} to-pour such-a-one_{NOM} prt self_{DAT} to-drink
        'What you pour out for a friend (to-drink), you'll have to drink yourself.'

(124)

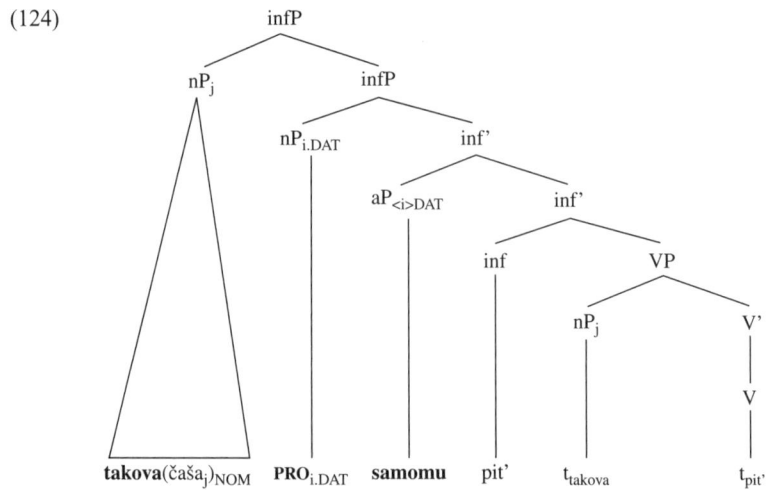

We see in (124) that dative *samomu* agrees with the infinitive clause's PRO_DAT subject and the direct object [*takova (čaša)*] is nominative because the subject is dative. My hypothesis also predicts that we will not find infinitive structures with dative *samomu* and accusative direct objects (***takovu_ACC i samomu_DAT pit'*), or nominative SAM_i and nominative direct objects (***takova_NOM i sam_NOM pit'*).

4.11   *obeščat'* 'to promise'

No theory of infinitives can be considered complete without an attempt to account for the anomalous behavior of *promise* (*obeščat'* in Russian). Larson (1991) notes that *promise* is "marked" because it is a subject-control verb whose optional object cannot control its infinitive complement, i.e., from the point of view of control, it's as though the object weren't there. For example, *I* is the controller of the infinitive in both *I promised to stay home* and *I promised him to stay home*; the latter sentence in standard English means *I promised him that I would stay home*, not *I promised him that he could stay home*. *Obeščat'* is anomalous in the same way:

(125)   a. Ja   obeščal   emu   ost'sja   doma.
            I:NOM   promised   him:DAT   to-stay   home_ADV
            'I promised him to stay home=I promised him that I would stay home.'
        b. Ja_NOM obeščal ost'sja doma_ADV.
            'I promised to-stay home.'

This verb is a problem for clause-only theories of infinitive control because, according to the Minimal Distance Principle, the infinitive complement's PRO subject should be antecedent-bound by the proximate matrix object (*him/emu* in (125)), which is the nearest c-commanding matrix argument. In other words, if a verb has an *optional* object argument, the MDP predicts that its infinitive complement should be *subject-controlled* when this object is not selected (the subject here is the closest potential controller), but that it should be *object-controlled* when the optional object is selected since now it is the closest controller. But we see in (125) that *obeščat'* 'promise' doesn't 'follow the rules.'

The verb *želat'* 'to-desire, wish,' however, has precisely the predicted control properties: the infinitive complement *byt' založnikom* 'to-be a-hostage' in (126a) is subject-controlled, whereas in (126b) it is object-controlled, i.e., here preposed dative *nikomu* 'anyone' is construed as the infinitive's controller (see Kozinskij 1983: 37, 1985: 113). The gender agreement of the **-en-** participle in (127) confirms that there is a control shift when the optional dative object *nikomu* is introduced.

(126)   a. Ja_NOM ne   želaju   byt'   založnikom_PI.
            'I (do) not   wish   to-be   a-hostage.'

b. Nikomu ne želaju byt' založnikom.
noone:DAT NEG I-wish to-be hostage:PI
'I do not wish anyone to-be a-hostage.'
c. Uxodja, doktor$_{NOM}$ poželal bol'nomu$_{DAT}$ vyzdorovet'.
leaving doctor wished patient to-get-well
'(lit.) When he was leaving, the doctor wished the-patient to-get-well.'
(Apresjan)

(127) a. On$_{NOM.M}$ poželal$_M$ byt' izbrannym$_{PI.M}$.
'He wished to-be elected.'
b. On$_{NOM.M}$ poželal ej$_{DAT.F}$ byt' izbrannoj$_{PI.F}$ (*izbrannym$_{PI.M}$).
'He wished$_M$ (for) her to-be elected$_F$.'

Thus *obeščat'* is classified as anomalous because it does *not* behave like *želat'*: its optional dative nP cannot control its infinitive complement.

Assuming that *obeščat'/promise* really is anomalous, our next step is see how diathesis theory can encode this verb's anomaly in its argument structure. Since *obeščat'* is a subject-control verb, we expect its infinitive complement to be an s-predicate, not an s-clause with a PRO$_{DAT}$ subject. So the problem shifts from violation of the MDP to V-binding: Why can't the dative object *emu* in (125) be the head of the TBC in which infP$_i$ is V-bound and, therefore, be infP$_i$'s controller? In other words, (129) cannot be the structure of well-formed (128a); here, as elsewhere, SAM$_i$'s case agreement points the way.

(128) a. **Ona** obeščala emu vse sdelat' **sama**.
she:NOM.F promised:F him:DAT everything:ACC to-do herself:NOM.F
'She promised him to-do everything herself.'
b. *Ona obeščala **emu**$_{j.DAT.M}$ [$_{infP<i>}$ vse sdelat' [$_{aP<i>}$ **samomu**$_{DAT.M}$]].
'She promised him to do everything himself.'
c. *Ona$_F$ obeščala emu$_M$ [$_{infP}$ PRO$_{DAT}$ vse sdelat' [$_{aP<i>}$ **samoj**$_{DAT.F}$]].
'She promised him to do everything herself.'
d. *Ona$_F$ obeščala emu$_M$ [$_{infP}$ PRO$_{DAT}$ vse sdelat' [$_{aP<i>}$ **samomu**$_{DAT.M}$]].
'She promised him to do everything himself.'

(129)

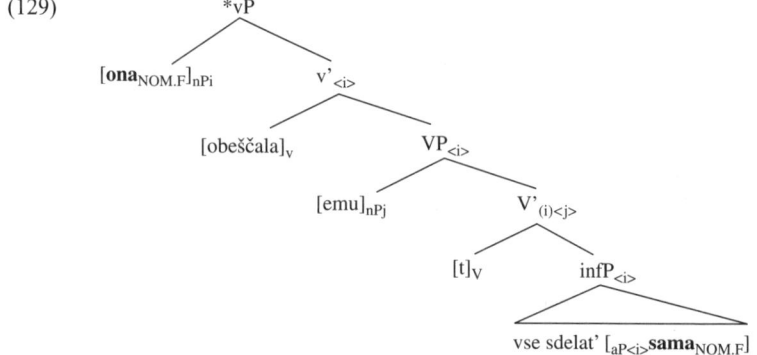

4.11 obeščat' *'to promise'* 215

The crucial question in terms of diathesis theory is this: Why doesn't the theta role **j** of dative *emu* in (129) V-bind infP$_i$, as it does in the derivation of colloquial object-control infinitive s-predicates (see §4.7)? If it did, we would get the ill-formed object control (128b) rather than well-formed (128a). So the problem for us reduces to this: How do we explain why it is the external theta role **i** of *obeščala* in (128a) that V-binds infP$_i$ rather than *emu*$_{j.DAT}$, which is in spec-VP and is thus the expected V-binder? In slightly different terms, why is nominative *ona* in (129) the head of SAM$_i$'s TBC rather than the more proximate dative *emu*$_j$? We see in (128c–d) that making the infinitive complement of *obeščat'* a clause does not solve the problem.

When the optional dative is not selected, control is unproblematic: *sama*$_{NOM}$ in (130) is vertically bound by the external theta role i of infP$_i$, which is V-bound by the external theta role i of the matrix verb *obeščala*, which is assigned to the subject *ona*$_{NOM}$; *sama* is nominative because it agrees with the nominative subject, which is the head of its TBC (see the boldface TBC in (131)).

(130)   Ona$_i$ obeščala [$_{inf'<i>}$ vse sdelat' [$_{aP<i>}$ sama]].
        'She$_{NOM.F}$ promised to-do everything$_{ACC}$ herself$_{NOM.F}$.'

(131)

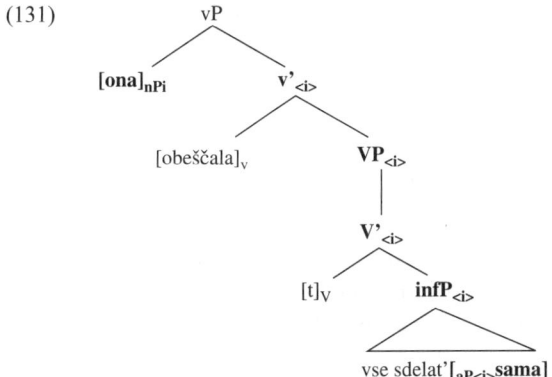

The problems begin in (128a) where the optional dative object *emu* is selected. According to what we have seen above, we expect the SAM$_i$ to be dative *samomu*, i.e., agree with the proximate matrix dative object *emu*. But this produces the ill-formed structure in (128b) (cf. ill-formed (128d)).

Up to this point my s-predicate + V-binding analysis has run into the same problems as the infinitive-clause + MDP analysis. I will argue below that the anomalous behavior of *obeščat'*/promise is a function of how the optional dative nP in sentences like (128a) (**Ona** *obeščala emu vse sdelat'* **sama** 'She promised him to do everything herself') is represented in argument structure.

216   *The derivation and control of infinitives*

Let us begin by comparing ill-formed (128b) (*Ona obeščala emu$_{j.DAT.M}$ [$_{infP<i>}$ vse sdelat' [$_{aP<i>}$ samomu$_{DAT.M}$]]) to the well-formed *object-control* sentence in (132a): (132b–c) represent (132a)'s structure in standard and colloquial Russian respectively; (133) is the structure of (132a) (cf. (129)).

(132) a. Ona   velela   emu   vse   sdelat' samomu.
         she:NOM ordered him:DAT everything:ACC to-do   himself:DAT
         'She ordered him to-do everything himself.'
      b. Ona velela [$_{VP}$ emu$_j$ [$_{V'}$ [t]$_V$ [$_{infP}$ PRO$_{i.DAT}$ [$_{inf'}$ vse sdelat' [$_{aP<i>}$ samomu$_{DAT.M}$]]]]]
      c. Ona velela [$_{VP}$ emu$_{j.DAT}$ [$_{V'}$ [t]$_V$ [$_{infP<i>}$ [$_{inf'}$ vse sdelat' [$_{aP<i>}$ samomu$_{DAT.M}$]]]]

(133)

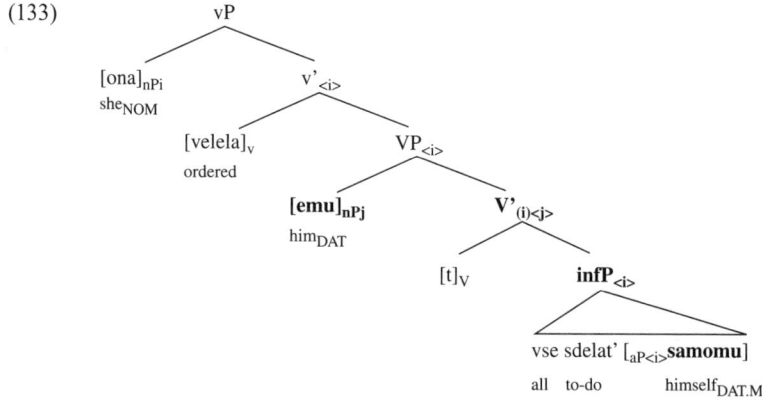

Returning to (128), we see that only (128a) (Ona$_{NOM.F}$ *obeščala emu$_{DAT.M}$ vse$_{ACC}$ sdelat' sama$_{NOM.F}$* 'She promised him to do everything herself') is well-formed, with the nominative case and gender agreement of *sama* showing that the infinitive complement must be an infP$_i$ and, therefore, that the nominative subject *ona* must be the head of *sama*'s TBC. This fact demonstrates that the dative nP *emu* in (128a)/*(129) and dative *emu* (132a)/(133) do not have the same grammatical status, i.e., *(128a) and (132a) must have different syntactic structures*. If the correct structure of (132a) is (133) and the structure of (128a) is *not* (129), what is the structure of (128a) and how does it explain the fact that dative *emu* behaves as though it were transparent or invisible with respect to the V-binding of infP$_i$ by the subject *ona*? We will consider the following two ways to capture the crucial fact that, while *emu*$_{DAT}$ controls (V-binds) infP$_i$ in (132a)/(133), it cannot V-bind infP$_i$ in (128a) (see the ill-formedness of (129)).

According to the first solution, which is deceptively simple, *obeščat'* is marked in the sense that its diathesis specifies that the infinitive is its 2-argument and the dative is its 3-argument, which means that *infP$_i$ is merged* *in the spec-VP position* of *obeščala/promised* and the optional dative argument is merged in the lowest, sister-to-V position, which is just the reverse of 'unmarked' object-control verbs like *velela* in (132a)/(133): see (134) below.

(134)

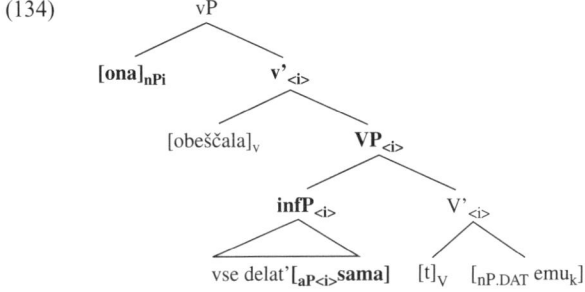

This would be the anomaly we are looking for: dative *emu* in (134), which is the first argument to merge with *obeščala*, is too low to V-bind infP$_i$ and, therefore, the dative argument's presence or absence is irrelevant for the V-binding of infP$_i$ and determining the case agreement of [$_{aP<i>}$ *sama*].

While this is just the effect we want, this analysis has a serious downside: to get the neutral [verb + dative + infinitive] word order, it must be stipulated that the dative object (*emu*) raises and adjoins to a higher position between the finite verb *obeščala* and the infinitive complement ([$_{infP<i>}$ *vse*$_{ACC}$ *sdelat' sama*$_{NOM}$]), which is along the lines suggested in Larson 1991 and Bowers 1993 (see Babby 2005). The main problem with this proposal is that the movement of *emu* in order to derive the neutral word order would have to be *obligatory*, and it is not clear how this type of movement can be justified in terms of feature checking or scrambling.

The second solution, which is, as far as I am aware, being proposed here for the first time, is this: the optional dative (*emu*) in **Ona** *obeščala emu vse sdelat' sama* 'She promised him to do everything herself' is not an *argument*, i.e., is not assigned a theta role by *obeščala*, and it is thus not a potential V-binder of the infP$_i$ complement. According to this proposal, dative *emu* 'him' in sentences like (128a) is an *adjunct* which, in traditional grammar, is called the *dative of interest or involvement*; we see in (135) that it is very productive in Russian and that *its neutral position is immediately after the matrix verb*, just as in (128a). Since the animate (human) datives in (135) are all adjuncts, they naturally correspond to possessive adjuncts or adverbial PPs in English.

(135)   a. On   soxranil   mne   žizn'.
           he:NOM   saved   me:DAT   life:ACC
           'He saved my life.'

b. Ona nastupila emu   na nogu (*na emu nogu).
   she stepped   him:DAT on foot:ACC
   'She stepped on his foot.'
c. Anna$_{NOM}$ pregradila Nikite$_{DAT}$ vyxod$_{ACC}$ iz gostinoj$_{GEN}$.
   A.   blocked   to-N.   exit   from living-room
   'Anna blocked Nikita from leaving (Nikita's leaving) the living room.'
d. On$_{NOM}$ položil ej$_{DAT}$ ruku$_{ACC}$ na taliju$_{ACC}$.
   he   put   to-her   hand   on waist
   'He put his hand on her waist.'
e. Èto$_{NOM}$ osložnjaet emu$_{DAT}$ žizn'$_{ACC}$.
   this   complicates to-him   life.
   'This complicates his life.'

If dative *emu* in (128a) has no *argument theta role*, the control problem vanishes: *emu* is transparent with respect to V-binding and the MDP, and its presence or absence does not affect the V-binding of infP$_i$ by the subject *ona*$_{i\text{-}NOM}$. Note that, according to this analysis, *emu* is merged by adjunction *in situ* in its basic position between the verb and its complements, i.e. [$_{VP_i}$ nP$_{DAT}$ VP$_i$]; no ad hoc obligatory movement rules are required to get the neutral word order.

But this explanation of the syntactic difference between (128a) and (132a) has two related problems: (i) it doesn't work for English, which does not have a productive dative of involvement (**She stepped him on the foot; *She spit him in the eye*); (ii) it doesn't account for the intuition that there is something marked or anomalous about this particular verb (*obeščat'*). My proposal is that what is 'special' about *obeščat'* is that it *subcategorizes* for an optional dative/human nP that is not linked to a theta role. The difference between an argument and a c-selected non-argument is easily captured by the 2×4 structure of the diathesis: the c-selected adjunct does not have a theta role linked to it in **V**'s diathesis, and it is therefore not a potential V-binder when projected to syntax.[42] The diathesis of *obeščat'* can thus be represented in (136), where {-^(**N**$_{dat}$)}$_2$ designates absence of the **j** argument theta role and, therefore, the dative nP's non-argument status. Since this dative adjunct is canonically human, it is interpreted as the dative of participation or involvement. The diathesis of an object-control verb with a quirky dative *argument* like *velet'* in (132a) is given in (137): the presence of the **j** theta role excludes the possibility of subject control. The crucial difference between (136) and (137) is the obligatory absence of **j** in the former and its obligatory presence in the latter.

(136)   The initial diathesis of *obeščat'* 'promise':
        {{i ^ N}$_1$ {- ^ (N$_{DAT}$)}$_2$ {infP$_i$}$_3$ {- ^ V}$_4$}

(137)   The initial diathesis of *velet'* 'order':
        {{i ^ N}$_1$ {j ^ N$_{DAT}$}$_2$ {infP}$_3$ {- ^ V}$_4$}}

4.11 obeščat' 'to promise' 219

Given (136), the syntactic representation of (128a) is (138).

(138) = (128a)

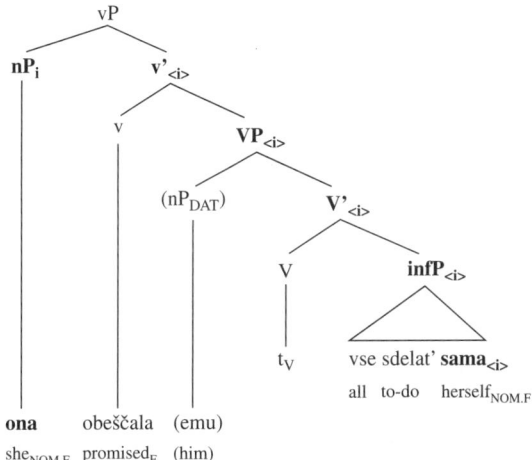

The TBC that accounts for the nominative case of *sama* in (138) is in boldface: [aP<i> **sama**] is V-bound by infP$_i$, which is vertically bound by VP$_i$, which assigns **i** to the subject *ona*$_{\text{NOM.F}}$; *sama* thus agrees with *ona*, which is the head of its TBC (cf. ill-formed (129)). Since dative *emu* in (138) has no argument theta role, it cannot V-bind the subject-controlled infinitive s-predicate complement of *obeščala*. Compare (138) to (140), the structure of the colloquial object-control sentence in (132), repeated as (139).

(139)   Ona velela emu vse sdelat' samomu (*sama).
         'She$_{\text{NOM.F}}$ ordered him$_{\text{DAT.M}}$ to-do everything$_{\text{ACC}}$ himself$_{\text{DAT.M}}$ (*herself).'

(140)

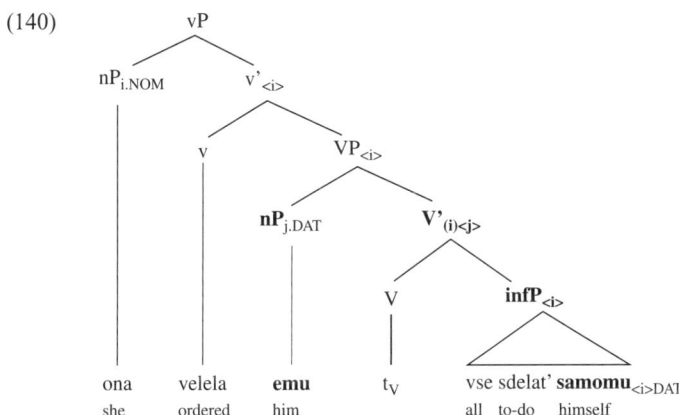

Emu in (138) has no argument theta role, while the argument *emu* in (139)/(140) is linked to the matrix verb's **j** and is merged in spec-VP, which is an argument position: [$_{nPj}$ *emu*] is thus the licit V-binder of infP$_i$. Since *emu*$_{DAT}$ in (140) is an argument and thus V-binds infP$_i$, it is the head of *samomu*$_{DAT}$'s TBC.

This analysis captures the intuition that *obeščat'* and *promise* are indeed marked: their anomalous property – selection of an optional human dative adjunct – is encoded in their diatheses; everything else, i.e, all the syntax, including control (binding) properties and neutral word order, is entirely regular since it is the direct projection of **V**'s final diathesis. The virtue of this analysis is that the anomaly associated with *promise* and *obeščat'* is lexical – a property of the verb's diathesis (cf. (136) and (137)), which is what we expect: the proper place for the stipulation of a particular lexical item's quirky, stem-specific properties is the diathesis, not the syntax, which is ideally the preserve of universal principles. What is significant for my theory of argument structure is that both the solutions outlined above involve *obeščat'/promise* having a 'marked' diathesis.[43]

4.12 The bare infinitive complement of auxiliary verbs

This section is devoted to the third, smallest type of infinitive projection, namely, the *bare* infinitive phrase, which has neither the unlinked external theta role of infinitive s-predicates nor the dedicated nP$_{i.DAT}$ subject of infinitive s-clauses. The bare infinitive is small in another sense: it has the most restricted syntactic distribution, occuring only as the complement of auxiliary verbs (V$_{aux}$), which entails that accounting for the derivation and morphosyntax of bare infinitives cannot be divorced from the unique properties of V$_{aux}$.[44] There is empirical evidence in Russian for the following three types of infinitive phrase:

(141) a. infinitive clause   [$_{infP}$ nP$_{i.DAT}$ inf'$_{<i>}$]
   b. infinitive s-predicate [$_{infPi}$ inf'$_{<i>}$]
   c. bare infinitive phrase [$_{infP}$ inf']

Bare infinitives have a third distinctive property, which will be the basis of my analysis: *impersonal (subjectless)* **V**s can be infinitives only in combination with V$_{aux}$, and, most significant, V$_{aux}$ in combination with the infinitive of an impersonal **V** is itself impersonal, i.e., the V$_{aux}$ obviously *inherits* the impersonal **V**'s {-^-}$_1$ external argument (see Williams 1994): *Morosilo*$_{N.SG}$ 'It was drizzling' ~ *Prodolžalo*$_{N.SG}$ *morosit'* 'It continued to drizzle.' This entails that: (i) infinitive complements formed from impersonal **V**s must be bare infinitives;

(ii) the diatheses of V_{aux} and lexical verb stems (**V**) *compose in argument structure* rather than merge in syntax, as do lexical subject- and object-control verbs and their s-predicate and s-clause infinitive complements: *inheritance* is a strictly diathesis-level operation; (iii) since V_{aux} and its bare infinitive complement compose, they have the 'tightest' syntactic bond: they form a *complex predicate* (cf. the properties of the French [causative V_{aux} + infinitive] construction in chapter 1).[45]

It was demonstrated in §2.16 that the short form (SF) of the adjective in the [V_{cop} + SF] construction is a *bare adjective phrase* (not an adjective s-clause with a raised subject), which means that bare phrases are auxiliary/copula specific, not infinitive specific. While the derivations involving V_{aux} and V_{cop} differ in several ways (see below), what is crucial is that the diatheses of both V_{aux} and V_{cop} *compose* with the diathesis of a **V** as part of a diathesis-level derivation, and that both *inherit* the external argument of the lexical **V** and **A** stems they compose with.

The routine assumption that auxiliary verbs are subject-control verbs is incorrect: subject-controlled infinitive complements are canonically s-predicates (infP$_i$) that are V-bound by the matrix subject's theta role; the infinitive complement of V_{aux} is a bare infinitive phrase, which has no external theta role and, therefore, cannot be *controlled* in the binding sense of the term developed in this and the preceding chapters (see §4.4.1 for discussion): cf. $On_{i.NOM}$ $može_{t AUX}$ [$_{infP}$ *prijti segodnja*] (cf. *[$_{infP<i>}$ *prijti segodnja*]) 'He can come today' and $On_{i.NOM}$ *xočet* [$_{infP<i>}$ *prijti segodnja*] (cf. *[$_{infP}$ *prijti segodnja*]) 'He wants to-come today.'[46]

My explanation of the unique properties of the [V_{aux} + bare infinitive] construction is based on the observation that the diathesis of V_{aux} is more like the diathesis of a diathesis-bearing (paradigmatic) suffix than the diatheses of lexical subject- and object-control verbs (cf. the parallels between the Turkish causative suffix and French causative auxiliary verb in §1.10): V_{aux} and paradigmatic suffixes both involve *inheritance*. More specifically, the diathesis of V_{aux} has *unspecified* slots (i.e., { ^ }) which are 'filled in' (valued) by the corresponding slots in the diathesis of the lexical verb stem (**V**) that V_{aux} composes with. Thus V_{aux}, whose external argument is always { ^ }$_1$, makes **V**'s external argument its own external argument. V_{aux} also *inherits* the remnant of **V**'s initial diathesis (i.e., positions 2–4, which Williams 1994 designates as **w**, treating them as the argument-structure analogue of a constituent): **w** becomes V_{aux}'s bare infinitive complement. It is thus 'bare' because V_{aux} in effect strips away **V**'s entire external argument whatever it is, leaving behind neither an external theta role nor an external **N** for its

222 *The derivation and control of infinitives*

infinitive complement (recall that diathetic operations do not leave traces or copies). Thus V_{aux} 'dismembers' **V**'s initial diathesis by inheriting its external argument as its own external argument and the rest of **V**'s diathesis as its bare infinitive complement. **V**'s bare infinitive complement is not uncontrolled because it always composes and forms a complex (compound) predicate expression with V_{aux}, which inherits **V**'s external argument; this produces the effect of subject control despite the fact that syntactic binding is not involved (see below).

(142) is a first approximation of the V_{aux} + bare infinitive derivation: Finite V_{aux}'s external argument $\{i\wedge N\}_1$ is *inherited* from **V**'s external diathesis in (142a); V_{aux}'s *inherited* internal diathesis $\{\{j \wedge N\}_2 \{k \wedge N\}_3 \{- \wedge V\}_4 \}$ in (142c) is **V**'s intact internal diathesis, i.e., (142a) minus $\{i \wedge N\}_1$ (cf. Williams' w).

(142)   a. **V**-'s diathesis: $\{\{i \wedge N\}_1 \; \{j \wedge N\}_2 \; \{k \wedge N\}_3 \{- \wedge V\}_4\}$ +
       b. V_{aux}'s diathesis: $\{\{ \wedge \}_1 \quad \{ \wedge \}_2 \quad \{ \wedge \}_3 \quad \{ \wedge V_{aux}\}_4\}$ >
       c. a + b: $\{\{i \wedge N\}_1 \; \{j \wedge N\}_2 \; \{k \wedge N\}_3 \{- \wedge V_{aux} \; V\}_4 \}$ =>
       d. $[_{auxP} nP_i \; [_{aux'} V_{AUX} \; [_{VP} nP_j \; [V] \; nP_k]]]$

But the derivation in (142) is obviously missing a crucial step. If the composition of **V** and V_{aux} is a diathetic operation in which V_{aux} 'splits' **V**'s initial diathesis, inheriting **V**'s $\{...\}_1$ as its own external argument and **V**'s remaining positions as its *bare* infinitive complement, how precisely do positions 2–4 (**w**) become an *infinitive* phrase? In other words, while it has been made explicit above how V_{aux} inherits **V**'s external argument and why its complement is thus bare, our next step is to account for the fact that the remnant of **V**'s initial diathesis becomes an infinitive.

We saw above that every **V** must compose with at least one paradigmatic affix and that the affix in V_{aux}'s derivation must be the infinitive-forming -t' suffix. But this is not a solution to the problem of how **V**'s remnant becomes the infinitive complement of V_{aux}: the infinitive suffix in Russian has the diathesis in (18), repeated here as (143).

(143)   The derivation of infinitive phrases (**V**'s internal arguments are irrelevant):
       a. **V**'s diathesis: $\{\{i \wedge N\}_1 \quad ... \{- \wedge V\}_4\}$ +
       b. -**inf**'s diathesis: $\{\{ \wedge (N_{DAT})\}_1 \; ... \{ \wedge \text{-inf} \}_4\}$ >
       c. Composition of a + b: $\{\{i \wedge (N_{DAT})\}_1 \; ... \{- \wedge [\text{V-inf}] \}_4\}$ >>

....

       d. N_{DAT} not selected: $\{\{i \wedge -\}_1 \quad ... \{- \wedge [\text{V-inf}] \}_4\}$ =>
       e. Projection of d: $[_{infPi} \quad [_{inf'} [\text{V-inf}]_{inf} \; VP_{<i>}]]$

....**or**....

       f. N_{DAT} is selected: $\{\{i \wedge N_{DAT}\}_1 \; ... \{- \wedge [\text{V-inf}] \}_4\}$ =>
       g. Projection of f: $[_{infP} nP_{iDAT} \quad [_{inf'} [\text{V-inf}]_{inf} \; VP_{<i>}]]$

4.12 The bare infinitive complement   223

We see in (143) that the composition of **V**'s diathesis with that of the infinitive suffix derives the diathesis of either an infinitive s-predicate (see (143d–e)) or an infinitive s-clause with a dative subject infinitive suffix (see (143f–g)). But the composition of the V_{aux}'s diathesis with either the diathesis of the infinitive s-predicate or s-clause, the final derived diathesis's syntactic projection, is ill-formed. More specifically: if the diathesis of V_{aux} (see (142b)) composes with (143d), the result is an auxiliary s-predicate, which is ill-formed (*finite* verbs cannot be s-predicates); if V_{aux}'s diathesis composes with the diathesis of (143f), the auxiliary's projected nP subject would be dative, which is also ill-formed. So we seem to be faced with a dilemma: the infinitive suffix must be selected in derivations involving V_{aux}, but selecting the infinitive suffix's diathesis in (143) invariably derives a nonviable diathesis (i.e., a diathesis that projects an ill-formed syntactic structure).

There is, however, an extremely simple way out of this dilemma that is perfectly natural in diathetic terms: a criterial property of auxiliary verbs is that they obligatorily *select the infinitive suffix* but not the infinitive suffix's diathesis in (143). In other words, the infinitive suffix of the bare infinitive complement is supplied by the V_{aux} itself, i.e., **-t'** but not its diathesis is encoded as a c-selectional property of auxiliary verbs (in much the same way that certain lexical verbs c-select quirky case). This accounts for all the morphosyntactic facts and, in addition, distinguishes auxiliary verbs from lexical and copula verbs (see §2.16).

When **V** in the derivation of [V_{aux} + bare infinitive] is affixed with the infinitive suffix **-t'**, it forms a complete word and [V-t'] is thus not available for any further diathesis-level operations. The only thing left to do is to provide the V_{aux} stem with a paradigmatic suffix, which is the finite suffix **-v-** in (144). Thus, in the derivation of bare infinitive complements, V_{aux} inherits **V**'s external argument intact and the remnant of **V**'s diathesis projects to syntax as V_{aux}'s *infinitivized bare VP*, i.e, a VP with no external theta role headed by [V-t']:

(144)   Final form of the derivation:
    a. V: $\{\{i \wedge N\}_1 \{j \wedge N\}_2 \{k \wedge N\}_3 \{- \wedge V\}_4\}$ +
    b. V_{aux}: $\{\{\wedge\}_1 \{\wedge\}_2 \{\wedge\}_3 \{\wedge V_{aux} [-t']\}_4\}$ >
    c. a + b: $\{\{i \wedge N\}_1 \{j \wedge N\}_2 \{k \wedge N\}_3 \{- \wedge V_{aux} [V-t']\}_4\}$ +
    d. -v-: $\{\{\wedge\}_1 \{\wedge\}_2 \{\wedge\}_3 \{\wedge -v-\}_4\}$ >
    e. c + d: $\{\{i \wedge N\}_1 \{j \wedge N\}_2 \{k \wedge N\}_3 \{- \wedge [V_{aux}\text{-v}] [V\text{-inf}]\}_4\}$ =>
    f. [$_{auxP}$ nP$_i$ [$_{aux'}$ V$_{aux}$ [$_{infP}$ nP$_j$ [$_{v'}$ t$_V$ nP$_k$]]]]   =(145)

224 *The derivation and control of infinitives*

(145)

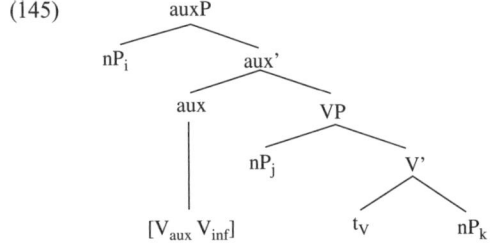

4.12.1 Infinitive complements of impersonal verbs

The derivation represented in (144)/(145) is clearly on the right track since it explains why impersonal **V**s are realized morphosyntactically as infinitives *only* when they compose with auxiliary verbs, and why the auxiliary verbs themselves become impersonal in the process.

V_{aux}'s { ^ }$_1$ external argument ensures that it inherits **V**'s external argument *no matter what it is*. V_{aux} thus inherits {-^-}$_1$ when it composes with an impersonal verb, projecting to syntax as an impersonal auxiliary verb, as in (147a) (*Ego*$_{ACC}$ *perestalo*$_N$ *tošnit'* 'He stopped feeling-nauseated'). The remnant of impersonal **V**'s diathesis is realized as V_{aux}'s bare infinitive complement, just as in derivations where V_{aux} inherits a 'personal' **V**'s {i^N}$_1$ argument. The composition of the diatheses of impersonal **V** and V_{aux} is schematically represented in (146): since the external {-^-}$_1$ argument inherited from impersonal **V** by V_{aux} does not project to syntax, the resulting impersonal V_{aux} stem must be affixed with the default **-o** suffix, which indicates non-agreement; **-l-** is the finite past tense suffixal realization of **-v-**.[47] Thus whether or not V_{aux} is impersonal or personal depends entirely on the external argument of the **V** it composes with.

(146)   The composition of V_{aux} and impersonal **V**:
   a. V: {{- ^ -}$_1$ {j ^ N}$_2$ {- ^ -}$_3$ {- ^ **tošni-**}$_4$}   +
   b. V_{aux}:   {{ ^ }$_1$ { ^ }$_2$ { ^ }$_3$ { ^ V_{aux} [**-t'**]}$_4$ }   >
   c. a + b: {{- ^ -}$_1$ {j ^ N}$_2$ {- ^ -}$_3$ {- ^ V_{aux} [tošnit']}$_4$ }   +
   d. **-v-**:   {{ ^ }$_1$ { ^ }$_2$ { ^ }$_3$ { ^ **-l-o**}$_4$ }   >
   e. c + d: {{- ^ -}$_1$ {j ^ N}$_2$ {- ^ -}$_3$ { ^ [V_{aux}-lo] [tošnit']}$_4$} =>

The infinitive of an impersonal verb (e.g. *tošnit'*) cannot merge with lexical subject- or object-control verbs because it is a bare infinitive and thus does not have an external **i** or nP$_i$ to bind (control) (see (149)); bare infinitives can cooccur with V_{aux} only.

Ego$_{j.ACC}$ 'him' in (147) is the preposed direct object of the bare infinitive of impersonal *tošnit'*; phasal verbs like *perestat'* 'stop' and *prodolžat'* 'continue' are formally auxiliary verbs in Russian.[48]

(147) a. Ego   perestalo tošnit'.
         him:ACC.M stopped:N to-nauseate
         'He stopped feeling-nauseated.'
      b. *On_{NOM.M} perestal_M tošnit'.
      c.

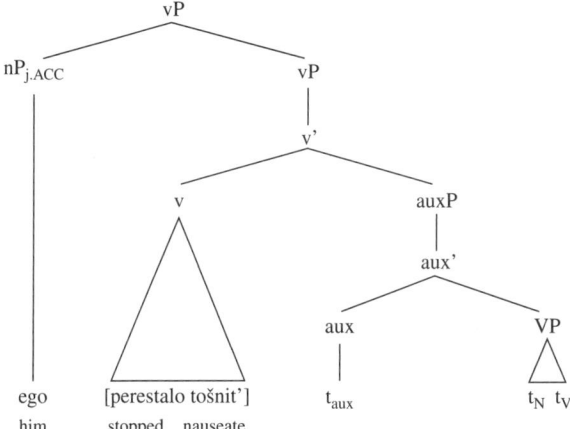

(148) The composition of *perestat'*_{aux} and impersonal *tošnit'*:
       a. V: {{- ^ -}₁ {j ^ N}₂ {- ^ -}₃ {- ^ **tošni-**}₄}   +
       b. V_{aux}: {{ ^ }₁   { ^ }₂   { ^ }₃   { ^ **perestan-** [-t']}₄} >
       c. a + b: {{- ^ -}₁ {j ^ N}₂ {- ^ -}₃ {- ^ **perestan-** [tošnit']}₄} +
       d. -v-:   {{ ^ }₁   { ^ }₂   { ^ }₃   { ^ **-l-o**}₄}   >
       e. c + d: {{- ^ -}₁ {j ^ N}₂ {- ^ -}₃ {- ^ [perestalo] [tošnit']}₄}} => (147c)

(149) *Zapax_{i.NOM} tabaka_{GEN} zastavljaet ego_{j.ACC} tošnit'.
        smell   tobacco   makes   him   feel-nauseated
       'The-smell of-tobacco makes him feel-nauseated.'

The bare infinitive complement of *perestalo* in (147) is not controlled because the {-^-}₁ initial diathesis of *tošnit'* has no external argument for *perestalo* to inherit. Inheritance of **V**'s external argument by V_{aux} produces the effect of subject control when it is {i^N}₁, i.e., if **V** has an {i^N}₁ external argument in its initial diathesis, V_{aux} inherits it when they compose and thus has a dedicated nominative subject. Thus *perestal and čitat'* in (150) share **V**'s external argument; see (150) and its derivation in (151).

(150) On   perestal   čitat'.
       he:NOM.M   stopped:M   to-read
       'He stopped reading.'

226 *The derivation and control of infinitives*

(151)   The derivation of (150):
   (a) čitaj-:   {{i ^ N}₁ {- ^ -}₂ {- ^ -}₃ {- ^ **čitaj-**}₄}   +
   (b) perestan-:   {{ ^ }₁   { ^ }₂   { ^ }₃   { ^ **perestan-** [**-t'**]}₄}   >
   (c) a + b: {{i ^N}₁ {- ^ -}₂ {- ^ -}₃ {- ^ **perestan-** [čitat']}₄} +
   (d) -v-:   {{ ^ }₁   { ^ }₂   { ^ }₃   { ^ **-l**}₄}   >
   (e) c + d   {{i ^N}₁ {- ^ -}₂ {- ^ -}₃ {- ^ perestal čitat'}₄}   => (150)

Summary: My hypothesis is that the morphosyntactic structure of [V$_{aux}$ + infinitive] sentences like (152) is different from the structure of [subject-control lexical verb + infinitive] sentences like (153).

(152)   a. On možet čitat'.
           'He can (*to) read.'
       b. On$_i$ možet [$_{infP}$ čitat'].

(153)   a. On xočet čitat'.
           'He wants to-read.'
       b. On$_i$ xočet [$_{infP<i>}$ čitat'].

While the infinitive complement *čitat'* in both sentences has no subject nP and *on* 'he' is construed as subject of the infinitive, the infinitive phrase in (153) is an s-predicate, i.e., it has an unlinked external theta role **i** that is vertically bound by the external theta role **i** of the lexical matrix verb *xočet* (see [$_{infP<i>}$ *čitat'*] in (153b)), i.e., the monoclausal structure in (154) has *two different external **i** theta roles* (one belonging to *xočet*, the other to *čitat'*) and a V-binding relation between them (*on$_i$* V-binds infP$_{<i>}$):

(154)

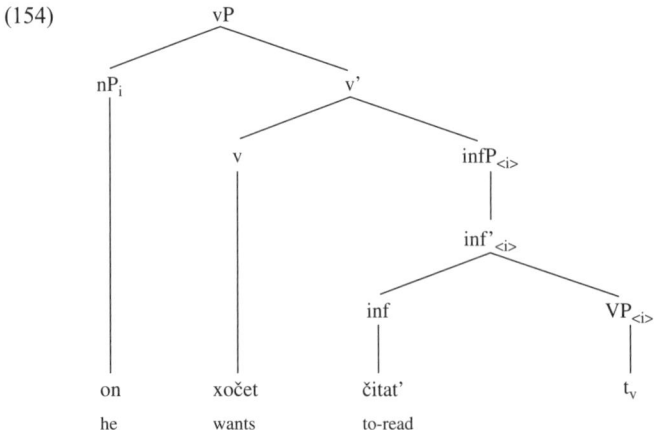

Compare (154) to (155), the syntactic structure of (152) (cf. (147c)).

(155)

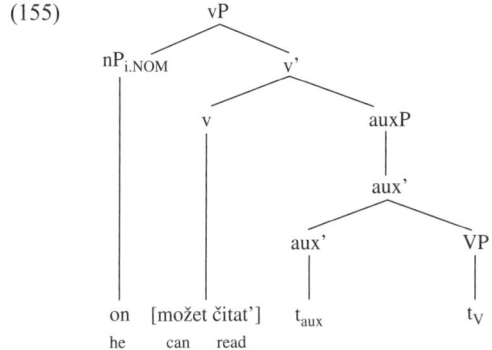

on [možet čitat'] t_{aux} t_V
he can read

The bare infinitive *čitat'* in (155) has neither an unlinked external theta role nor an external nP_i because *možet* inherited its external $\{i^\wedge N\}_1$ argument before the final diathesis projected to syntax. Thus the crucial difference between (152) and (153) is this: while (153)/(154) has two **i** theta roles, the higher V-binding the lower, we see in (155) that, since (152) has *only one external theta role* **i**, no *syntactic* binding is possible in such a sentence: the auxiliary verb *možet* and its bare infinitive complement *čitat'* quite literally *share* the external theta role **i**, which is the external theta role of *čitat'* in argument structure and the external theta role of finite *možet* (*čitat'*) in syntax. This relation has the *effect* of subject control.

Bare infinitive complements form the tightest bond with their obligatory matrix V_{aux} because this bond is established in argument structure when V_{lex} and V_{aux} compose. They project to syntax as components of a complex predicate, *sharing* V_{lex}'s external $\{i^\wedge N\}_1$ argument. Next comes the bond between infinitive s-predicate complements and their matrix controller: their unlinked external theta role is *vertically bound* by the head of their TBC, which is restricted to monoclausal syntactic structures. Infinitive s-clause complements form the loosest bond with their controller: the infinitive clause's PRO_i subject is *antecedent-bound* by an argument of the matrix verb, which involves a long-distance *interclausal* binding relation.

5 Deriving the predicate instrumental

5.0 Introduction

This chapter is devoted to the derivation of the predicate instrumental (PI) of adjectives and participles, and to the contribution diathesis-based theory makes to explaining the special status of *predicate case*.[1] The analysis presented below is based on the premise that the most insightful way to account for the unique morphosyntactic properties of the PI is in terms of its relation to the long form (LF) and short form (SF) of adjectives:[2]

(1) a. PI: Voda byla sliškom xolodnoj$_{PI.F}$, čtoby deti mogli kupat'sja.
water was too cold C the-children could swim
'The-water was too cold for the-children to-be-able to-swim.'
b. LF: Voda byla sliškom xolodnaja$_{LF.NOM.F}$, čtoby deti mogli kupat'sja.
c. SF: Voda byla sliškom xolodna$_{SF.NOM.F}$, čtoby deti mogli kupat'sja.

I shall argue that since the PI cannot be reduced to an instrumental-case instantiation of either the LF or SF, it is an independent affixal head with its own diathesis, which composes with **A**'s diathesis.[3] My main hypothesis is that the PI suffix neutralizes the morphological distinction between adjective s-predicate phrases and V$_{cop}$+ bare adjective phrases that the LF and SF suffixes lexicalize. In other words, evidence will be presented that the PI can head *either* an afP$_i$ s-predicate or, in tandem with V$_{cop}$, a bare afP. My argumentation once again makes crucial use of the case, gender, and number agreement of the s-predicate adjunct (aP$_i$) SAM$_i$, which *obligatorily* agrees with the head of the TBC in which it is V(ertically)-bound.[4]

5.1 The distribution of the PI, LF, and SF

(1) through (7) demonstrate the syntactic distribution of the PI, LF, and SF; (8) is a summary.

Depictive adjectives in finite and infinitive clauses:

(2) On   vernulsja domoj vzvolnovannyj / vzvolnovannym / *vzvolnovan.
     he:NOM.M returned:M home agitated:LF.NOM.M / PI.M /*SF.NOM.M
     'He returned home agitated.'

(3) Ona$_{NOM.F}$ poprosila ego$_{ACC.M}$ leč' v postel' odetym$_{PI.M}$ / *?odetomu$_{LF.DAT.M}$ /
     she   asked   him   to-get in bed dressed
     odetogo$_{LF.ACC.M}$ / *odet$_{SF.NOM.M}$.
     'She asked him to-get in bed dressed.'

Argument small clauses:

(4) Ja našel ego$_{ACC.M}$ p'janym$_{PI.M}$ / !p'janogo$_{LF.ACC.M}$ / *p'jan$_{SF.M}$.
     I   found him   drunk.

Predicate adjectives in infinitive (*byt'* 'to-be') clauses:

(5) a. Ja$_{NOM}$ prosil ego$_{ACC.M}$ byt' gotovym$_{PI.M}$ otpravit'sja v 5 časov.
        I   asked him   to-be ready   to-leave at 5 o'clock.'
     b. Ja prosil ego$_{ACC}$ [$_{infP}$ PRO$_{i.DAT.M}$ byt' gotovym$_{PI.M}$ otpravit'sja ...].
     c. *Ja prosil ego$_{ACC}$ [$_{infP}$ PRO$_{i.DAT}$ byt' gotovomu$_{LF.DAT.M}$ otpravit'sja ...].
     d. **Ja prosil ego$_{ACC.M}$ byt' gotovu$_{SF.DAT..M}$ otpravit'sja ....^{5}

(6) Èto polnyj mudizm – [$_{infP}$ sidet' posredi Germanii [$_{nP.DAT}$ trem vzroslym
     ljudjam] i byt' golodnymi$_{PI}$ (*golodnye$_{LF.NOM}$/ *?golodnym$_{LF.DAT}$)].^{6}
     'It (is) complete idiocy (for) [[three grown people] to sit in the middle of
     Germany and be hungry].' (A. Minčin)

Adjective complements of gP$_i$ headed by the copula:

(7) a. [$_{gP<i>}$ Buduči golodna],   devuška   pošla domoj.
        being hungry:SF.NOM.M girl:NOM.F went home
        'Because she was hungry, the-girl went home.'
     b. *Buduči golodnaja$_{LF.NOM.F}$, devuška pošla domoj.
     c. Buduči golodnoj$_{PI.F}$,   devuška pošla domoj.

(8) (1): PI ~ *LF ~ SF^7
     (2): PI ~ LF   ~ *SF
     (3): PI ~ (*)LF ~ *SF
     (4): PI ~ (*)LF ~ *SF
     (5): PI ~ *LF ~ (*)SF
     (6): PI ~ (*)LF ~ *SF
     (7): PI ~ *LF ~ SF

Assuming that the structure of PI phrases, like that of SF and LF phrases, is composed of an **A** (adjective stem) projection ([$_{AP}$...A...]) contained in an affix projection (afP or afP$_i$), my analysis will be guided by the following question: Does the PI, like the SF, have the structure of a *bare adjective phrase*: [$_{afP}$ [$_{af'}$

[A-af] AP]] (where "af" is af_{PI} or af_{SF}), or, like the LF, have the structure of an *s-predicate*: [$_{afPi}$ [$_{af'<i>}$ [A-af] AP$_{<i>}$]] ("af" here is af_{PI} or af_{LF})? Or does af_{PI} project both these structures?

The hypothesis that the PI can, like the LF, head an s-predicate or, like the SF, head a bare afP$_{PI}$ makes the following easily falsifiable prediction: if true, the PI should be restricted to constructions that license either the LF or the SF, i.e., there should be no constructions with the PI ~ *LF ~ *SF distribution. But the distribution in (8) does falsify this hypothesis. The data point to the following hypothesis, which I argue for below: although the PI shares certain distinctive morphosyntactic features with both the LF and SF, it is nevertheless distinct from them both and is thus a third type of **A**-stem suffix. The question posed in the preceding paragraph can accordingly be reformulated as follows: How does the structure and derivation of the PI differ from that of the LF and SF? Since the answer to this question is complex, I will first outline it here and then present the empirical evidence supporting it later in the chapter.

The PI, like the LF, can be realized as an s-predicate (see (9)), but with the following crucial difference: whereas LF adjectives obligatorily *agree in case* with the head of their TBC, PI s-predicates (PI$_i$) *never agree in case*.

(9)   [$_{afPi}$ [$_{af'<i>}$ [$_{af}$ A-af] AP$_{<i>}$]]

I account for this fact by arguing that the PI adjective suffix is an inactive, 'fossilized' case form and, therefore, cannot agree in case or be agreed with *in case*. Thus, most important for what follows, the PI does not behave like an adjective with a case feature. But the PI$_i$ does agree in gender and number with the head of its TBC.

The PI, like the SF (which has inherent nominative case), can be realized as (10), where the **A**'s external argument {i^N}$_1$ is inherited by the copula (V$_{cop}$) and realized as the sentence's nominative subject; afP in (10) is a bare adjective phrase: (10a) = (10b) and (10c).[8]

(10)   a. [$_{vP}$ nP$_{i.NOM}$ [$_{v'}$ V$_{cop}$ [$_{afP}$ [$_{af'}$ [$_{af}$ A-af] AP]]]]
        b. [$_{vP}$ nP$_{i.NOM}$ [$_{v'}$ V$_{cop}$ [$_{afPPI}$ [$_{af'}$ [$_{af}$ A-af$_{PI}$] AP]]]]
        c. [$_{vP}$ nP$_{i.NOM}$ [$_{v'}$ V$_{cop}$ [$_{afPSF}$ [$_{af'}$ [$_{af}$ A-af$_{SF}$] AP]]]]

I am thus claiming that the PI, LF, and SF have distinct case properties: the LF agrees in case with the nP head of the TBC in which it is vertically bound and thus occurs with the full range of case suffixes. The SF has an *inherent* nominative case feature only (see chapter 2). The PI, unlike the LF and SF, is a suffixal head that has no case feature associated with it and therefore cannot be involved in case-agreement relations.

There is a second important question, which I will pose here and answer later in the chapter: Why are *predicate adjectives* in standard Russian copula-infinitive *byt'* 'to be' clauses PI, never dative: [$_{infP}$ PRO$_{i.DAT}$ [$_{inf'}$ [$_{inf'}$ *byt'* afP$_{PI / *DAT}$] [$_{aP<i>}$ **samomu**$_{DAT}$]]]? We see in (11) to (14) that SAM$_i$ here is dative, which demonstrates conclusively that these copula infinitive phrases are s-clauses, which have PRO$_{i.DAT}$ subjects. Recall that infinitive complements of nouns and complementizers (*čtoby* in (13) and (14)) are always s-clauses (see §4.8.1 and §4.8.2).[9]

(11)   a. Ona   učityvala   ego sposobnost' byt'
          she   took-into-consideration his ability:ACC to-be
          sčastlivym samomu,   i   delat'   sčastlivymi drugix.
          happy:PI.M himself:DAT.M and to-make   happy:PI others:ACC
          'She took into consideration his ability to be happy himself and to make others happy.'
    b. *Ona učityvala ego sposobnost' byt' **sčastlivomu**$_{LF.DAT}$ samomu$_{DAT}$...
    c. *Ona učityvala ego sposobnost' byt' **sčastliv**$_{SF.NOM}$ samomu$_{DAT}$...
       (see note 5)
    d. *Ona učityvala ego sposobnost' byt' sčastlivym$_{PI}$ **samim**$_{PI}$...

(12)   Emu   ugrožaet [opasnost' [$_{infP}$ byt' **arestovannym samomu**]]$_{nP}$.[10]
        him:DAT threatens danger:NOM   to-be arrested:PI   himself:DAT
        '(lit) [The-danger to-be arrested himself] threatens him. = He is threatened by the danger of being arrested himself.'

(13)   Emu$_{DAT}$ prixoditsja skryvat'sja, [$_{CP}$ čtoby [$_{infP}$ PRO$_{DAT}$ **samomu**$_{DAT}$ ne   byt'
        him has   to-hide   C   himself   NEG to-be
    povešennym$_{PI}$ (*povešennomu$_{LF.DAT}$) za ubijstvo]].
    hanged   for murder
    'He has to hide [so-as not to-be hanged for murder himself].'

(14)   Mal'čik$_{NOM}$ ne xotel   znakomit'   šofera$_{ACC}$ s   parikmaxeršej, čtoby
        boy   NEG wanted to-introduce chauffer with hairdresser   C
    [$_{infP}$ PRO$_{DAT}$ ne stat'   **nenužnym**$_{PI}$ **samomu**$_{DAT}$].
                     NEG to-become unnecessary himself
    'The-boy didn't want to-introduce the-chauffeur to the-hairdresser [so-as not to-become unnecessary himself].' (M. Veller)

5.2 The Bailyn–Bowers hypothesis

In this section we consider an alternative hypothesis, namely, that the PI is a c-selected (quirky) case assigned to adjectives (and nouns) by Pr, which is the head of PrP (the "predicate phrase" in Bowers' theory), i.e., [$_{PrP}$ NP Pr AP$_{PI}$]:

NP is the subject of predication and AP is the predicate; they are in a predicational relation by virtue of the fact that NP is in spec-PrP and AP is the sister of Pr (see Bailyn 2001, Bowers 1993, 2001).

Although this hypothesis is initially appealing, it makes several incorrect predictions and is thus descriptively inadequate. For example, it assumes that the PI is a lexical case, which is at odds with the non-case behavior of the PI suffix described above. It is also unable to explicitly relate **A**'s PI realization with its LF and SF realizations, and assumes the validity of Bowers' dedicated PrP small-clause approach to predication.

Let us put these problems aside and examine the following prediction made by Bailyn's hypothesis. If all instances of predication are confined to the PrP, sentences like *Voda byla sliškom xolodna*$_{SF}$ 'The-water was too cold' in (1c) and *Vino bylo vkusno*$_{SF}$ 'The-wine was good' must have the structure schematically represented in (15), where *vino* raises from spec-PrP to spec-TP (cf. Bailyn 2001: 17). But there is an insoluble problem here: if all predication is restricted to PrP and its head Pr assigns PI case to AP, there is no way to derive the SF, which is the predicate adjective par excellence.

(15)

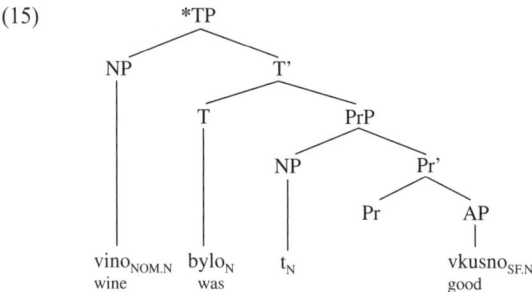

5.3 The PI in the light of the LF and SF

In the following sections I will (i) present empirical evidence that the PI heads either an s-predicate adjective phrase (PI_i or $afP_{PI.i}$) or a bare adjective phrase (afP_{PI}), (ii) make explicit the ways in which the PI is structurally different from both the LF and SF.

The PI suffix inherits **A**'s external argument as either an unlinked $\{i\wedge\text{-}\}_1$ external argument or its intact $\{i\wedge N\}_1$ external argument; the latter composes with a form of the copula, which inherits PI's inherited $\{i\wedge N\}_1$, creating a [V_{cop} + bare PI phrase]. This is parallel to the infinitive-forming suffix **-inf**, which heads either an infinitive s-predicate ($infP_i$) or an infinitive s-clause

5.3 The PI in the light of the LF and SF   233

([$_{infP}$ PRO$_{i.DAT}$ inf'$_{<i>}$]); see chapter 4. The structures I am proposing for the SF, LF, and PI are summarized in the schematic syntactic representations (16) to (19); (20) is the diathesis-based derivation of the PI from **A**.

(16)   V$_{cop}$ + SF bare afP structure: V$_{cop}$ inherits the SF's {i^N}$_1$ external argument:

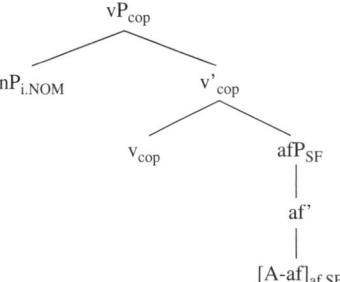

(17)   LF s-predicate structure (α ranges over all Russian case features):

afP$_{i.LF.α}$
|
af'$_{<i>}$
|
[A-af]$_{af<i>.LF.α}$

(18)   PI s-predicate:

afP$_{i.PI}$
|
af'$_{<i>}$
|
[A-af]$_{af<i>PI}$

(19)   V$_{cop}$ + PI bare afP:

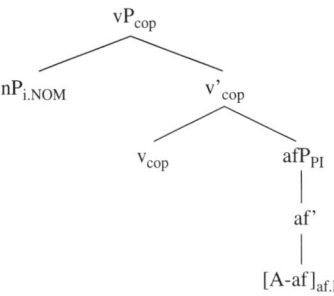

234   *Deriving the predicate instrumental*

(20)   Diathesis-based derivation of the PI:
(a) A's diathesis: $\{i \wedge N\}_1 \ldots \{- \wedge A\}_{\{4}$ +
(b) -af$_{PI}$'s diathesis: $\{ \wedge (-)\}_1 \ldots \{ \wedge -af_{PI}\}_4$ >
(c) a + b: $\{i \wedge (N)\}_1 \ldots \{- \wedge [A-af_{PI}]\}_4 =>$[11]

5.4   Evidence that PIs head bare adjective phrases: argument I

Below I present empirical evidence that -af$_{PI}$ can head a bare adjective phrase and make explicit how [copula + bare afP$_{PI}$] differs from [copula + bare afP$_{SF}$]. The most convincing piece of evidence that afP$_{PI}$ in the [*byt'* afP$_{PI}$] construction is a bare afP$_{PI}$ phrase, not an s-predicate (afP$_{PLi}$), is based on sentences like (11), repeated here as (21) (see (12) to (14) for additional examples).

(21)   Ona   učityvala   ego   sposobnost'   byt'
she:NOM took-into-consideration his   ability:ACC to-be
sčastlivym samomu,   i   delat'   sčastlivymi   drugix.
happy:PI.M himself:DAT.M and to-make happy:PI.PL others:ACC.PL
'She took into consideration his ability to be happy himself and to make others happy.'

The argument that *sčastlivym*$_{PI}$ in [$_{infP}$ *byt' sčastlivym*$_{PI}$ *samomu*$_{DAT}$] 'to-be happy himself' heads a bare afP$_{PI}$ has the five steps in (22). The syntactic structure of the matrix direct object phrase [$_{DP.ACC}$ *ego sposobnost'* [*byt' sčastlivym*$_{PI}$ *samomu*$_{DAT}$]] in (21) is represented in (23).

(22)   Argument that the PI *sčastlivym* in (21) heads the bare afP$_{PI}$ phrase in (23):
(i) The infinitive *byt'* 'to-be' is the complement of a noun (*sposobnost'*), which entails that [*byt' sčastlivym*$_{PI}$ *samomu*$_{DAT}$] must be an infinitive *clause* (see §4.8.1).
(ii) Infinitive clauses in Russian have dative subjects, which are null (PRO$_{DAT}$) when the clause is controlled: [$_{infP}$ PRO$_{i.DAT}$ [$_{inf'<i>}$ *byt' sčastlivym*$_{PI}$ *samomu*$_{<i>DAT}$]].
(iii) The claim that [*byt' sčaslivym samomu*] is an infinitive s-clause with a null dative subject is confirmed by the dative case of *samomu*, which agrees in case, number, and gender with PRO$_{DAT}$, which the head of its TBC.
(iv) The infinitive *byt'* is a copula, which is a functor and thus does not assign theta roles. As we saw in §2.16, its external argument is $\{ \wedge \}_1$, which entails that its subject in (21) is *inherited*, i.e., must be the external $\{i \wedge N\}_1$ argument of its PI complement *sčastlivym*:
[$_{infP}$ PRO$_{i.DAT}$ [$_{inf'}$ [$_{inf'}$ *byt'* [$_{afPPI}$ [$_{aP'}$ *sčaslivym*$_{PI}$]]][$_{aP<i>}$ **samomu**$_{DAT}$]]]
(v) It follows from (iv) that the diathesis of *sčastlivym*$_{PI}$ must have an $\{i \wedge N\}_1$ external argument, which is the source of the copula infinitive clause's dative subject. If *sčastlivym*'s external argument were $\{i \wedge -\}_1$ (s-predicate), the nP$_{i.DAT}$ subject of *byt'* in (21) would be unlicensed. Thus [$_{afPPI}$

sčastlivym] is 'bare' in syntax because its initial {i^N}$_1$ is inherited by *byt'* in argument structure.

(23) is the syntactic representation of the direct object DP in (21). In the diathesis phase of (21)'s derivation, which is naturally not present in the syntactic representation, A's initial {i^N}$_1$ was first inherited by the PI suffix's diathesis and then inherited by the diathesis of *byt'* 'to-be,' leaving the bare PI phrase we see in (23):

(23)

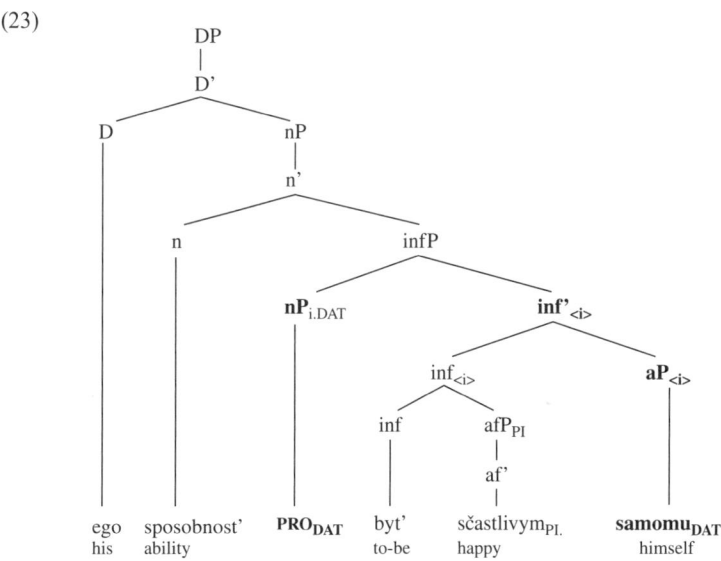

The copula *byt'* 'to-be' in (21) *inherits* the external argument of its PI adjective complement *sčastlivym* when their *diatheses compose*, the copula stem (**by-**) + *sčastlivym* then composes with the infinitive suffix and its diathesis, which accounts for the dative case of its PRO subject: the result is an infinitive clause: [$_{infP}$ PRO$_{i.DAT}$ [$_{inf'<i>}$ *byt' sčastlivym*]]. We do not see these operations reflected in syntactic representation (e.g., there is no trace in spec-afP$_{PI}$ in (23)) because these operations are diathetic not syntactic.

It is at this point that V$_{cop}$ and V$_{aux}$ part company: we saw in §4.12 that V$_{aux}$ selects the infinitive suffix **-t'** *but not its diathesis*, which accounts for the fact that the inherited subject of V$_{aux}$ is *not* dative. But V$_{cop}$ and its diathesis composes with **-t'** and its diathesis and the **-t'** suffix (= **-inf**) c-selects the infinitive clause's external dative case.

The diathesis-based derivation of [$_{infP}$ PRO$_{i.DAT}$ [$_{inf'<i>}$ *byt' sčastlivym*$_{PI}$]] in (21)/(23) is represented in (24).

(24) The derivation of [PRO$_{i.DAT}$ byt' sčastlivym$_{PI}$]; A = **sčastliv-** (see (20))

a. {i ^ N}$_1$ ... {- ^ **sčastliv-**}$_4$ + (A's diathesis)
b. { ^ }$_1$ ... { ^ **-ym$_{PI}$**}$_4$ > (-af$_{PI}$'s diathesis)
c. {i ^ N}$_1$ ... {- ^ [sčastlivym]}$_4$ + ({i^N}$_1$ was inherited by -af$_{PI}$)
....
d. { ^ }$_1$ ... { ^ **by-**}$_4$ > (copula diathesis)
e. {i ^ N}$_1$ ... {- ^ by- [sčastlivym]}$_4$ + ({i^N}$_1$ has been *inherited* by by-)
....
f. { ^ N$_{DAT}$}$_1$ ... { ^ **-t'**}$_4$ > (infinitive suffix diathesis)
g. {i ^ N$_{DAT}$}$_1$ ... {- ^ [byt'][sčastlivym]}$_4$ =>
h. [PRO$_{i.DAT}$ byt' sčastlivym$_{PI}$]]

5.4.1 The case of predicate adjectives in infinitive clauses

The PI is highly preferred in *byt'* + predicate-adjective structures, which creates the impression that the PI has become the 'default case' in *byt'* clauses (see Franks and Hornstein 1992). The explanation for this phenomenon is diachronic: as recently as the beginning of the nineteenth century, predicate adjectives in infinitive clauses could still be dative, agreeing in case with the PRO$_{DAT}$ subject. But these dative predicate adjectives were SFs, as in (25a), which are no longer possible in modern Russian. When the archaic oblique case forms of the SF were eliminated, creating the modern system where the SF is inherently nominative, the dative SF in *byt'* clauses was replaced with the PI, as in (25b) (see (25d) > (25e)). It was not replaced by the dative LF *sčastlivomu* because LFs in the modern language are exclusively s-predicate *adjuncts* and cannot function as predicate adjectives (see chapter 2).[12]

(25) a. Ona$_{NOM}$ učityvala ego sposobnost' byt' **sčastlivu**$_{SF.DAT}$ samomu$_{DAT}$.
     'She took-into-consideration his ability to-be happy himself.'
b. Ona$_{NOM}$ učityvala ego sposobnost' byt' **sčastlivym**$_{PI}$ samomu$_{DAT}$.
c. *Ona$_{NOM}$ učityvala ego sposobnost' byt' **sčastlivomu**$_{LF.DAT}$ samomu$_{DAT}$.
d. **[$_{infP}$ PRO$_{i.DAT}$ [$_{inf'}$ *byt'* [$_{afPSF}$ [$_{af'}$ **sčastlivu**$_{SF.DAT}$]]]]   (= (25a))
e. [$_{infP}$ PRO$_{i.DAT}$ [$_{inf'}$ *byt'* [$_{afPPI}$ [$_{af'}$ **sčastlivym**$_{PI}$]]]]   (= (25b))
f. *[$_{infP}$ PRO$_{i.DAT}$ [$_{inf'}$ *byt'* [$_{afPPI}$ [$_{af'}$ **sčastlivomu**$_{PLF.DAT}$]]]]   (= (25c))

Since SAM$_i$ was a separate class of underived pronominal aP$_i$ adjuncts in Old Russian and did not have SF endings, they were unaffected by these changes and continue to agree in case, number, and gender with the head of the TBC in which it is V-bound. The following are additional examples.

(26) a. Ona velela emu$_{DAT}$ byt' gotovym$_{PI}$ (*gotovyj$_{NOM.LF}$ / *gotovomu$_{LF.DAT}$) otpravit'sja.
     'She ordered him to-be ready to-depart.'

b. On byl gotov$_{SF}$ (*gotovyj$_{LF.NOM}$ / ?gotovym$_{PI}$) otpravit'sja.
   'He was ready to-depart.'
c. Ona$_{NOM}$ velela emu$_{DAT.M}$ [$_{infP}$ PRO$_{DAT.M}$ byt' gotovym$_{PI.M}$ otpravit'sja].
   she ordered him   to-be ready to-depart
   'She ordered him to be ready to-depart.'

(27) a. Ona delala vse vozmožnoe [dlja togo, čtoby [byt' arestovannoj]].
     'She$_{NOM.F}$ did everything possible [in-order [to-be arrested$_{PI.F}$]].'
   b. Ona$_{NOM.F}$ delala vse vozmožnoe$_{ACC}$ [$_{PP}$ dlja togo, [$_{CP}$ čtoby [$_{infP}$ PRO$_{DAT.F}$ byt' arestovannoj$_{PI.F}$]]].

(28) Policija vsegda preduprežḍaet naselenie$_{ACC}$ [$_{infP}$ PRO$_{DAT}$ byt' s terroristami **osmotritel'nymi**$_{PI.PL}$ i **samim**$_{DAT.PL}$ ix$_{ACC}$ ne trogat'].
   'The-police always warns the-public [to-be careful$_{PI.PL}$ with terrorists and not to-accost them$_{ACC}$ themselves$_{DAT.PL}$].' (Vojnovič)

5.4.2 The case of depictive adjectives in infinitive clauses

We now have an explanation for cooccurrence of dative *samomu* and PI *sčastlivym* in sentences like (21)/(23), but we do not yet have an explanation for the unacceptability in standard Russian of sentences like (3), repeated as (29), where the dative LF depictive adjunct *odetomu* 'dressed' agrees in case with the infinitive clause's PRO$_{DAT}$ subject. If the nominative depictive *odetyj*$_{LF.NOM.M}$ in (31) agrees in case with the nominative subject *on*, why can't the dative depictive *odetomu*$_{LF.DAT.M}$ agree with its dative subject in (29)? I put off answering this question until §5.10, when we will be able to fit all the pieces of the puzzle together.

(29) *?Ona poprosila ego$_{ACC}$ [$_{infP}$ PRO$_{i.DAT}$ leč' v postel' [$_{afP<i>}$ **odetomu**$_{LF.DAT}$]].
   'She asked him [to-get in bed dressed].'

(30) Ona poprosila ego$_{ACC}$ [$_{infP}$ PRO$_{i.DAT}$ leč' v postel' [$_{afP<i>}$ **odetym**$_{PI}$]].
   'She asked him to-get in bed dressed.'

(31) **On** leg v postel' **odetyj**$_{NOM.LF}$ / **odetym**$_{PI}$.
   he got in bed dressed
   'He got in bed dressed.'

5.5 *Buduči* + PI predicate adjectives: argument II

This argument that the PI *golodnoj*$_{PI.F}$ 'hungry' in (32c) heads a bare afP$_{PI}$ also makes use of the copula, only here it is realized as the hybrid adverbial (gP$_i$) *buduči* 'being,' whose adjective complement can be an SF or a PI, but not an LF.

(32) a. Buduči **golodna**, devuška otpravilas' domoj.
being hungry:NOM.F.SF girl:NOM.F went home
'Since she was hungry, the girl went home.'
b. *Buduči **golodnaja**$_{\text{NOM.F.LF}}$, devuška otpravilas' domoj.
c. Buduči **golodnoj**$_{\text{PI.F}}$, devuška otpravilas' domoj.

Given that *buduči*, like all gP$_i$s, is an s-predicate and that V$_{\text{cop}}$ inherits its adjective complement's external argument, we naturally expect the s-predicate LF in (32b) to be grammatical and the SF to be ungrammatical. But we see in (32) that the distribution is just the opposite and, most important, that *the PI patterns like the SF*, whose external argument is {i^N}$_1$. This SF ~ *LF ~ PI distribution is the basis of my second argument that the PI can head a bare afP$_{\text{PI}}$ phrase. We begin with the derivation of gP$_i$ in (33):

(33) The derivation of gP$_i$:
a. V's diathesis: {{i^N}$_1$ {j^N}$_2$ {k^N}$_3$ {- ^ V}$_4$} +
b. g-'s diathesis: {{ ^ -}$_1$ { ^ }$_2$ { ^ }$_3$ { ^ -g }$_4$} >
c. a + b: {{i ^ -}$_1$ {j^ N}$_2$ {k^N}$_3$ { - ^ [V-g]}$_g$}$_4$} => (34)

gP$_i$ in (34) is vertically bound by the matrix VP$_i$, which can be contained in a finite or nonfinite affixal projection. When this affix is finite (represented as small v in (34)), VP$_i$ assigns its external theta role to vP's nominative subject nP$_i$, which is the head of the TBC in which gP$_i$ and *sam* are V-bound.

(34)

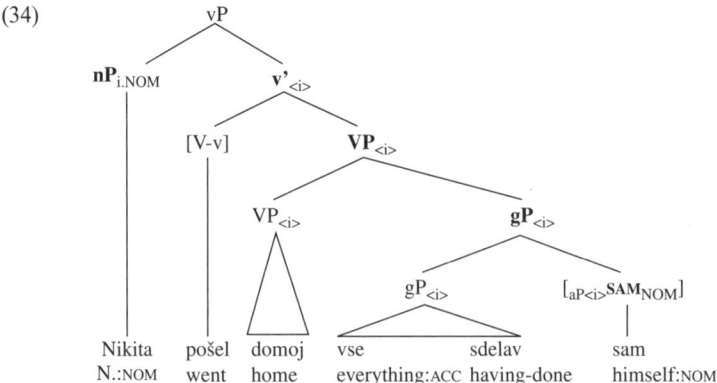

The grammaticality of the SF in (32a) and the PI in (32c) and the ungrammaticality of the LF in (32b) has the following explanation: the hybrid adverbial forming suffix **-g-** *selects* Vs (here **V$_{\text{cop}}$**) with a linked {i^N}$_1$

external argument, deleting **N**. Since $\mathbf{V_{cop}}$ inherits its external argument from the adjective it composes with, this adjective must have an intact $\{i\wedge N\}_1$, which is inherited first by $\mathbf{V_{cop}}$ and then by **-g-**: inheritance of **A**'s initial $\{i\wedge N\}_1$ creates a bare adjective phrase. This explains: (i) why [*buduči* + SF] and [*buduči* + PI] are well-formed and why the adjective phrases in both are bare phrases: the diatheses of both have inheritable external $\{i\wedge N\}_1$ arguments; (ii) why *buduči* + LF is ill-formed: the LF is an s-predicate and thus has no external $\{i\wedge N\}_1$ that can be inherited by the copula and selected by **-g-**.

This sequence of operations accounts for the *buduči* + PI ~ SF ~ *LF pattern in (32). More specifically: *golodnoj*$_{PI,F}$ in (32c) has an external $\{i\wedge N\}_1$ argument, which the copula inherits, thereby satisfying the **-g-** suffix's selection requirement; **-g-** deletes N_1, as it does in all gP$_i$ derivations (see (33c)). If the PI suffix's external argument were $\{i\wedge\text{-}\}_1$ (which projects s-predicates), the resulting sentence would be ill-formed for the same reason that [*buduči* + LF] is: it would violate **-g-**'s selectional restrictions.[13] Thus the well-formedness of sentences like (32c) provides a second empirical argument that the PI, like the SF, can head a bare adjective phrase.

Summary: (35) is the schematic diathesis-level derivation of (32a/c).

(35)   Derivation of (32a)/(32c):
    a. A's diathesis: $\{i\wedge\}_1$ ... $\{\text{-}\wedge A\}_4$ +
    b. **-af**$_{SF/PI}$'s diathesis: $\{\wedge\}_1$ ... $\{\wedge\text{-af}_{SF/PI}\}_4$[14]   >
    c. a + b: $\{i\wedge N\}_1$ ... $\{\text{-}\wedge [A\text{-af}_{SF/PI}]\}_4$[15] +
    ....
    d. V_{cop}'s diathesis: $\{\wedge\}_1$ ... $\{\wedge [\text{bud-}]\}_4$ >
    e. c + d: $\{i\wedge N\}_1$ ... $\{\text{-}\wedge [\text{bud-}][A\text{-af}_{SF/PI}]\}_4$ +
    ....
    f. **-g-**'s diathesis: $\{\wedge\text{-}\}_1$ ... $\{\wedge [_g\text{-uči}]\}_4$ >
    g. e + f: $\{i\wedge\text{-}\}_1$ ... $\{\text{-}\wedge [\text{buduči}][A\text{-af}_{SF/PI}]\}_4$ =>

5.5.1   Diathetic composition vs. syntactic merger

Since it was demonstrated in chapter 3 that gP$_i$-formation is a diathetic operation (the *composition* of the diatheses of the verb stem **V** and the paradigmatic suffix **-g-**) and, since we see in (35) that gP$_i$-formation must *follow* the composition of the copula and the PI suffix (hybrid adverbials can be formed only from *verb* stems), it must be true that the inheritance of the adjective's external argument by the copula is also diathesis-level *composition* rather than syntactic *merger* and *raising* (see §2.16 and §4.12). The cornerstone of the theory of the relation between argument-structure representation and morphosyntactic representation on which this book is based is that syntactic rules operate on the syntactic projections of **[V-af]**'s *final diathesis*, which entails that the output of syntactic operations cannot be the input to diathetic operations (which cannot 'read' syntactic trees). This means that the derivation of [*buduči* + PI/SF] provides another piece of evidence that the syntactic s-clause plus subject-raising analysis of the copula is incorrect. Derivations in the theory being proposed here are strictly *bipartite*: first the diathesis of **V** composes with the diatheses of affixes, auxiliary verbs, and copulas, creating a *final diathesis*, whose 2×4 structure projects to syntax as the clause's *initial syntactic structure* (i.e., its Extended Lexical Projection), which may then itself be involved in merger and move operations, which derive the clause's *final syntactic structure* (which, in a 'free word order' language like Russian, is the input to Information Structure).

Since the derivation of *buduči golodnoj* in (32c)/(35) involves consecutive *diathetic* operations, (36), the syntactic projection of the derivation's *final diathesis* in (35g), does not nor should it represent the intermediate steps in the sentence's *diathetic* derivation: projection-to-syntax is limited to the right-to-left projection (bottom-to-top merger) of the final diathesis's 2×4 structure to homologous positions in phrase structure (see chapter 1). For example, (36) does not reflect the inheritance of the PI's external $\{i^{\wedge}N\}_1$ argument by the copula nor the deletion of the copula's inherited external N_1 when it composes with the **-g-** affix (*-či*), thereby creating gP_i's s-predicate structure. We do not see these intermediate steps in the sentence's *syntactic* representation for the simple reason that they are diathetic not syntactic steps, which are accordingly explicit in (35), the representation of the diathetic phase of the derivation, and invisible in its syntactic phase; cf. the syntactic representations in well-formed (36) and ill-formed (37).

(36)

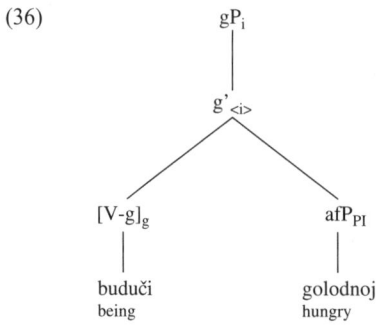

(37)

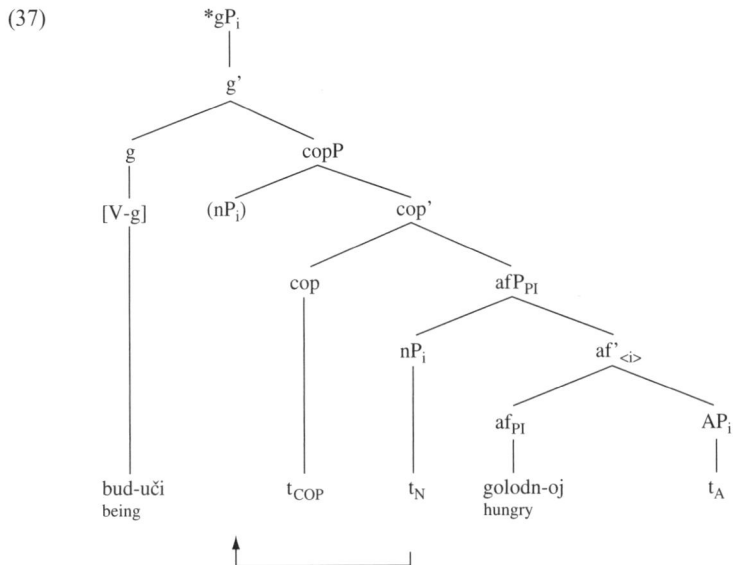

The more 'detailed' syntactic representation of (32c) in (37) is ill-formed because it is not the projection of the final diathesis in (35g); it represents as syntactic operations the intermediate derivational steps that were shown in (35a–g) to be diathetic operations.

Most important, it is not clear in (37) how the initial nP_i subject of the afP_{PI} clause in spec-afP_{PI} first *raises* to spec-vP_{cop} (see the arrow in (37)) and then is somehow deleted by the -g- suffix, leaving behind its now unlinked external **i** theta role, creating the gP_i s-predicate: these are not well-formed *syntactic* operations (cf. (35e–g)). One of the manifest advantages of the two-tiered representation of arguments in **V**'s diathesis is that it allows for precisely this type of argument-splitting operation, which can delete a categorial head in the lower tier without affecting its initially linked theta role in the upper theta tier (as in (35f–g)); or it can do just the opposite: a theta role may be acted upon without affecting the categorial head it is initially linked to in **V**'s diathesis (e.g., see the dethematization of **V**'s external theta role **i** in the diathetic derivation of passives). Speaking more generally, *only diathesis-based operations can effect delinking*. A corollary of this is that *s-predicates* (LF adjectives, -šč-participles, gP_i, $infP_i$, derived unaccusative in -*sja*, etc.), which have been shown above to play a crucial role in sentence structure, are created from **V**'s initial diathesis by *diathetic* operations, not *syntactic* rules. The latter are restricted to operating on words and phrases, whereas only the former is able to operate on stems, affixes, and their diatheses.

The copula and the auxiliary are different despite the fact that the diathesis of both has the crucial $\{\wedge\}_1$ external argument, which is responsible for *inheritance* of the lexical stem's external argument and thus for the creation of *bare complements*. We saw above that V_{cop} composes with nonverbal categories (adjectives and nouns), producing nonverbal bare phrases, whereas V_{aux} composes with verbal stems, producing verbal bare phrases. In addition to this complementarity, there is a systematic difference in their infinitive complements: the V_{cop}'s $\{\wedge\}_1$ external argument first inherits its nonverbal complement's external $\{i{\wedge}N\}_1$ argument; V_{cop}'s derived diathesis then composes *with the diathesis of any verbal suffix* (**-g-** as above, the **-inf** suffix, the finite suffix **-v-**, etc.). V_{aux} and its diathesis composes only with **V** and its diathesis, and V_{aux}'s diathesis itself *selects* its **V** complement's infinitive suffix **-t'** (**-inf**), *but not -t's diathesis* (cf. §4.12).

This analysis correctly predicts that V_{cop} and V_{aux} can both occur in the same derivation, as in (38), and, furthermore, that V_{cop} must compose before V_{aux} and that V_{cop} must therefore be the infinitive complement of V_{aux}.

(38) Starinnaja tarelka   dolžna$_{aux}$ byt'$_{cop}$ povešena na stene.
       antique   dish:NOM.F   should:F   to-be   hung:SF.F on wall
       '(An) antique dish should be hung on the wall.'

Since SF adjectives and participles cannot compose *directly* with V_{aux}, which selects only verbs, the SF (*povešena*) must first compose with the copula (*byt'*): *byt' povešena* 'to-be hung' is verbal and can compose with the auxiliary, giving *dolžna byt' povešena*. The copula's function here is to verbalize the SF adjective and, as predicted, it must be an infinitive (*byt'*) since, as we saw in §4.12, V_{aux}'s diathesis imposes the infinitive-forming **-t'** suffix on its complements. The diathesis-based derivation of sentences like (38), which can have an adjective in the SF or PI but not the LF, is schematically represented in (39).

(39)   The derivation of (38):
       a. A's diathesis: $\{i \wedge N\}_1 \ldots \{- \wedge$ **povešen-**$\}_4$ +
       b. **-af**$_{SF}$'s diathesis: $\{\wedge\}_1 \ldots \{\wedge$ **-a**$_{SF.F}\}_4$ >
       c. a + b: $\{i \wedge N\}_1 \ldots \{- \wedge$ [povešena$_{SF.F}$]$\}_4$ +
       ....
       d. V_{cop}'s diathesis: $\{\wedge\}_1 \ldots \{\wedge$ [by-]$\}_4$ >
       e. c + d: $\{i \wedge N\}_1 \ldots \{- \wedge$ [by-] [povešena]$\}_4$ +
       ....
       f. V_{aux}'s diathesis: $\{\wedge\}_1 \ldots \{\wedge$ **dolžn-** [**-t'**]$\}_4$ >
       g. e + f: $\{i \wedge N\}_1 \ldots \{- \wedge$ **dolžn-** [byt'] [povešena]$\}_4$ +
       ....
       h. **-af**$_{SF}$'s diathesis: $\{\wedge\}_1 \ldots \{\wedge$ **-a**$_{SF.F}\}_4$ >
       i. g + h: $\{i \wedge N\}_1 \ldots \{- \wedge$ dolžna [byt'] [povešena]$\}_4$ => (38)

5.6 Evidence that PIs head s-predicates: argument I

Evidence is presented in this section that there are sentences in which afP$_{PI}$'s external argument is {i^-}$_1$ and, therefore, the PI phrase is an s-predicate (PI$_i$), not a bare afP$_{PP}$. The most robust evidence comes from sentences like (40a), where the case agreement of SAM$_i$ reveals the sentence's 'hidden' syntactic structure: only accusative *odnogo* 'alone' is grammatical. The accusative case of the participle *ležaščego* 'lying' in (40c) instead of the PI *ležaščim* is felt to be somewhat archaic but not ungrammatical; (40d) is the finite sentence corresponding to the participle phrase in (40a). This is one of many constructions in which the PI is replacing the older agreeing LF: cf. (40a) and (40c); (40e–f) are additional examples.

(40) a. Ja uvidel **ego** ležaščim v bol'šoj komnate sovsem **odnogo**.
 I saw him:ACC.M lying:PI.M in big room all$_{adv}$ alone:ACC.M
 'I saw him lying in a big room all alone.' (M. Popovskij)
 b. *Ja uvidel ego$_{ACC}$ ležaščim$_{PI}$ v bol'šoj komnate sovsem odnomu$_{DAT}$.
 c. !Ja uvidel ego$_{ACC}$ ležaščego$_{LF.ACC}$ v bol'šoj komnate sovsem odnogo$_{ACC}$.
 d. [$_{vP}$ **On**$_{NOM.M}$ [$_{v'<i>}$ [$_{v'<i>}$ ležal$_M$ [$_{PP}$v bol'šoj komnate]] [$_{aP<i>}$sovsem **odin**$_{NOM.M}$]]]
 'He was-lying in a-big room all alone.'
 e. My$_{NOM}$ zametili ego$_{ACC.M.SG}$ vyxodjaščim$_{PI.M.SG}$ (!vyxodjaščego$_{LF.ACC}$) iz zdanija.
 'We saw him coming-out of the-building.'
 f. My videli **ego**.$_{ACC.M}$ perexodjaščim$_{PI.M}$ ulicu$_{ACC.F}$ **odnogo**$_{ACC.M}$.
 'We saw him crossing the-street alone.'

The accusative case agreement of *odnogo*$_{ACC.M}$ with the matrix direct object *ego*$_{ACC.M}$ in (40a) demonstrates conclusively that the PI projection [*ležaščim*$_{PI}$ ... *odnogo*$_{ACC}$] heads the PI s-predicate in (41), not the PI clause in (42).

(41) [$_{afPi}$ ležaščim$_{PI}$ v bol'šoj komnate sovsem [$_{aP<i>}$ odnogo$_{ACC.M}$]].

(42) *[$_{afP}$ [$_{nPi}$ PRO] ležaščim$_{PI}$ v bol'šoj komnate sovsem [$_{aP<i>}$ odnogo$_{ACC.M}$]].

While (42) is ill-formed for several reasons, the following piece of evidence is by itself sufficient to eliminate it as the structure of (40a): we saw conclusive evidence in chapter 3 that *šč*-participles are inherently s-predicates and, therefore, that there are no *šč*-participle *clauses*. This entails that *šč*-participles cannot have a subject nP in spec-afP$_{PP}$ as in (42), and that *the PI of šč-participles is always an s-predicate*.

The case agreement of *odnogo*$_{ACC}$ is another problem for the clausal structure in (42). Since SAM$_i$ obligatorily agrees in case with the head of its TBC, the accusative case of *odnogo* in (40a) must be agreeing with the accusative matrix

244 Deriving the predicate instrumental

object *ego*. If (40a) had the clausal structure of (42), *odnogo* would have to agree in case with the PRO subject of the putative PI clause, which, however, is not accusative because it is not in a configuration in which accusative case is assigned/checked.[16] Thus the s-predicate structure in (41) above and (43) below must be the correct structure of (40a): it accounts for the accusative case agreement between *odnogo* and *ego* in terms of the TBC headed by *ego*, which is in the spec-position of the matrix VP (see the boldface in (43)). PRO$_i$ in (42) would prevent *ego* from being the head of the TBC in which *odnogo* is V-bound since TBCs must be clause-internal.

In a bottom-to-top derivation, [$_{aPi}$ *(sovsem) odnogo*] first adjoins to the PI s-predicate phrase [$_{afPi}$ *ležaščim*$_{PI}$ *v bol'šoj komnate*], whose unlinked external **i** V-binds it, forming the first link in the boldface TBC in (43); next [$_{afPi}$ [$_{afP<i>}$ *ležaščim*$_{PI}$ *v bol'šoj komnate*] [$_{aP<i>}$ *sovsem odnogo*$_{ACC}$]] adjoins to matrix V'$_j$ and is V-bound by **j**, forming the second link; finally **j** of V'$_j$ is assigned to the accusative matrix direct object **ego**, which is the final link and therefore head of the TBC in which accusative **odnogo** is the tail, which accounts for their case agreement.

(43)

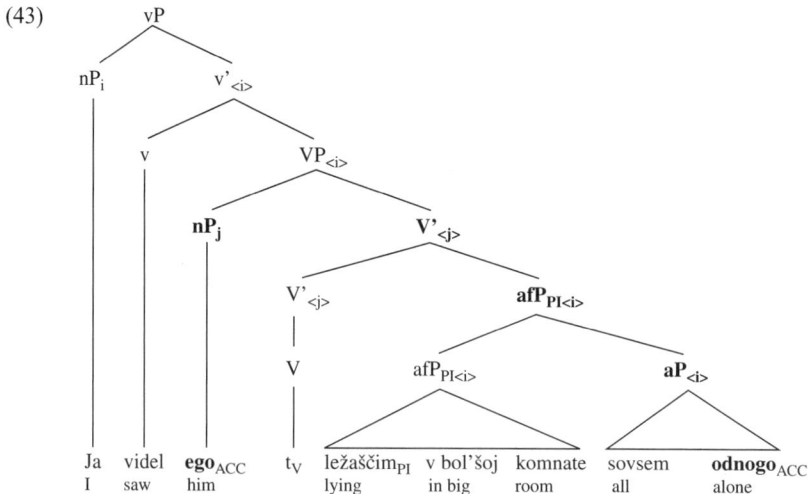

Note that the PI of *ležaščim* in (43) plays no role in determinimg the case agreement of *odnogo*: although *odnogo* is bound by the external theta role of [$_{afPi}$ *ležaščim*...], *ležaščim* itself is not the head of *odnogo*'s TBC nor is it a link in it.

We saw essentially the same agreement pattern in colloquial, object-control s-predicate *infinitive* complements like (44), whose partial syntactic structure is represented in (45); see §4.7.

(44) Ja_NOM zastavil ego_ACC.M ležat' v bol'šoj komnate sovsem odnogo_ACC.M.
　　　I　　　made　　　him　　　to-lie in large　　room　　all　　alone
　　　'I made him lie in a big room all alone.'

(45)

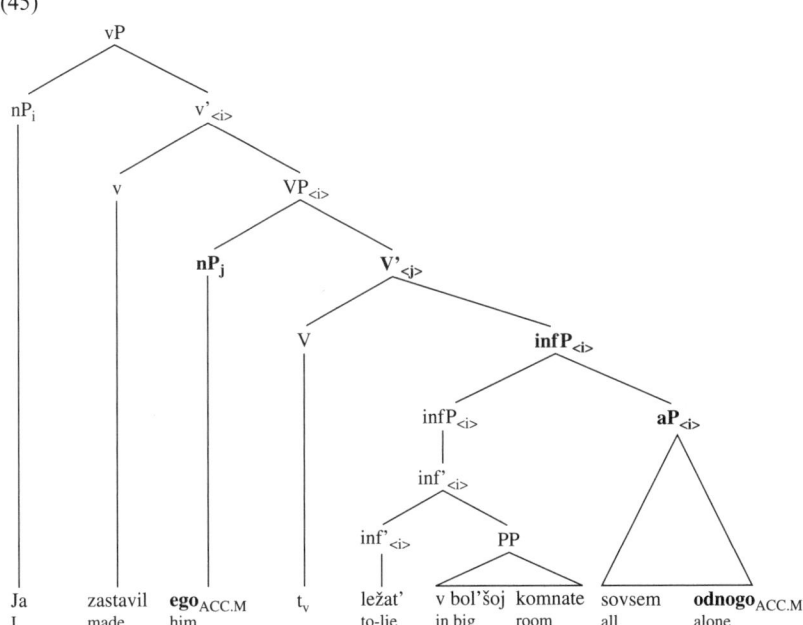

[sovsem odnogo]_aPi in (45) is V-bound by infP_i, which is V-bound by V'_j; **j** is assigned to the accusative direct object *ego*, which is the head of the TBC in which accusative *odnogo* is bound, accounting for its accusative case in now familiar terms.

5.7　*Byt'* + PI: argument II

The copula's infinitive *byt'* played an important role in §5.4 by demonstrating that [*byt' sčastlivym*_PI] 'to-be happy' in (23) is an infinitive s-clause with a bare afP_PI complement. The same properties of *byt'* are used below to demonstrate just the opposite, namely, that in subject-controlled structures like (46) to (50), [_infPi *byt'* PI] is an infinitive s-predicate, whose unlinked **i** is V-bound by the matrix subject, which is simultaneously the head of afP_i.PI's TBC. This analysis is bolstered by the nominative case of SAM_i in these sentences.

(46) Ona_NOM.F sovsem ne　　umeet　　　byt' gordoj_PI.F.
　　　she　　　entirely NEG know-how to-be proud
　　　'She just does-not know-how to-be proud.'

(47) Udača$_{NOM}$ prixodit tol'ko k tem, kto$_{NOM}$ umeet byt' terpelivym$_{PI}$.
success comes only to those who know-how to-be patient
'Success comes only to those who know-how to be patient.'

(48) Anna$_{NOM.F}$ staralas' byt' ob"ektivnoj$_{PI.F}$.
'Anna tried to-be objective.'

(49) a. On$_{NOM}$ xočet, [$_{CP}$ čtoby ego$_{ACC}$ priglasili$_{PL}$ na večer (**odnogo**$_{ACC}$)].
'(lit.) He wants [that (they) invite him to the-party (alone)].'
b. **On**$_{NOM.M}$ xočet [$_{infP<i>}$ byt' priglašennym$_{PI.M}$ na večer (**odin**$_{NOM.M}$)].
'He wants to-be invited to the-party (alone).'
c. On$_{NOM}$ xočet byt' priglašen$_{SF.NOM}$ na večer (odin$_{NOM}$).
'He wants to-be invited to the-party (alone).'
d. *On$_{NOM.M}$ xočet byt' priglasennyj$_{LF.NOM.M}$ na večer.

(50) Mne prosto neobxodimo byt' otvergnutoj vnačale, čtoby zatem
me:DAT.F simply essential:N to-be rejected:PI.F at-first so-as later
zavoevat' ljubov' otvergnuščego.
to-win love:ACC of-the-one-who-rejected:LF.GEN.M (me)
'(It is) simply essential (for) me to-be rejected at-first so-that I can later
win the-love of-the-man-who-rejected (me).' (I. Atamanenko)

It was demonstrated in chapter 4 on the basis of the nominative case agreement of SAM$_i$ that the infinitive complement of subject-control verbs like *umet'* 'to-know-how-to, to-be-able-to' and *starat'sja* 'to-try-to' is an *infinitive s-predicate* (infP$_i$), whose unlinked external theta role **i** is V-bound by the external theta role of the matrix verb: e.g., in (51), which is monoclausal, *on* and *sam* are the head and tail of the same TBC and thus agree in nominative case. If the infinitive complement of a subject-control verb were an infinitive clause [$_{infP}$ PRO$_{i.DAT}$ inf'$_{<i>}$], *sam* would have to agree with PRO$_{DAT}$, the head of its TBC, which, however, is ill-formed: see (52).

(51) **On**$_{NOM.i}$ umeet [$_{infP<i>}$ vse$_{ACC}$ delat' [$_{aP<i>}$ **sam**$_{NOM}$]].
'He knows-how [to-do everything [himself]].'

(52) *On$_{NOM.i}$ umeet [$_{infP}$ PRO$_{DAT.i}$ [$_{inf'<i>}$ vse$_{ACC}$ sdelat' **samomu**$_{DAT}$]].

Bearing these facts in mind, let us look more closely at [*byt' gordoj*] in (46), which, I argue, is an s-predicate. Since *umeet* is a subject-control verb, its infinitive complement [*byt' gordoj*] must be an infinitive s-predicate [$_{infPi}$ *byt' gordoj*], whose unlinked external theta role **i** is V-bound by the external theta role of *umeet*. Now, since the copula *byt'* inherits the external argument of its adjective complement, *gordoj*$_{PI.F}$'s external argument in (46) must be {i^-}$_1$. The syntactic representation of (46) is thus (53):

afP$_{PI}$ is a bare afP phrase because *byt'* inherits *gordoj*'s {i^-}$_1$ external argument.

(53)

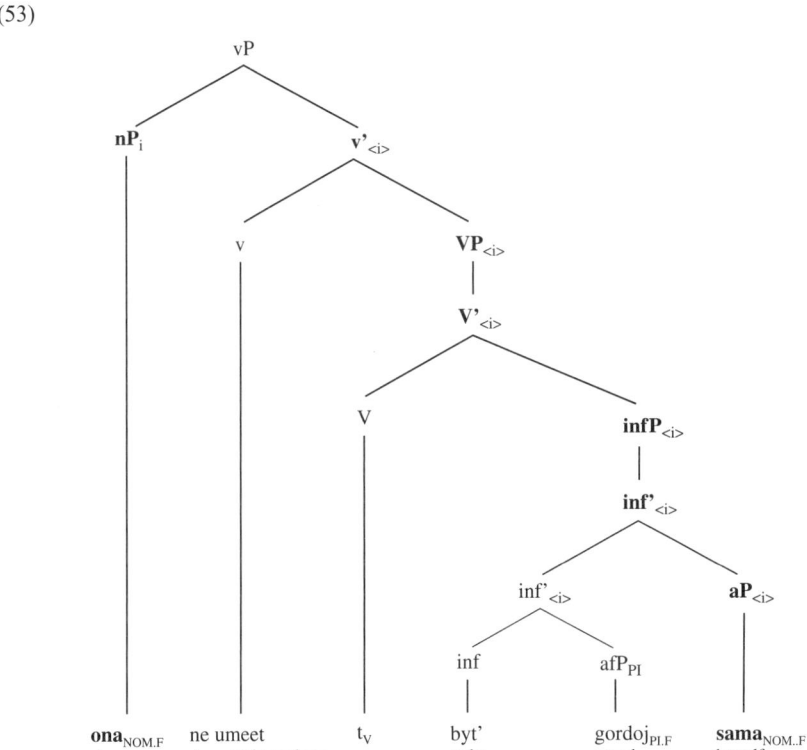

The structure in (53) is further supported by the well-formedness of (54) and the ill-formedness of (55): contrastive [$_{aPi}$ *sama*] in (53) and (54) is adjoined to [$_{infPi}$ *byt' gordoj*] and V-bound by it, which means that the head of the TBC in which *sama* is bound is the nominative subject *ona*, correctly predicting *sama*'s nominative case: cf. (55). If the infinitive complement in (54) were clausal and thus had a PRO$_{DAT}$ subject, dative *samoj* would agree with it, as in (55), which is ill-formed. (56) is the derivation whose final diathesis (56g) projects to (54).

(54) Ona$_{NOM.F}$ ne umeet byt' gordoj$_{Pl.F}$ sama$_{NOM.F}$.
 'She does-not know-how to-be proud herself.'

(55) *Ona$_{NOM.F}$ ne umeet byt' gordoj$_{Pl.F}$ samoj$_{DAT.F}$.[17]

248   *Deriving the predicate instrumental*

(56) The derivation of s-predicate [*byt' gordoj*] in (46):
  a. A's diathesis: $\{i \wedge N\}_1 \ldots \{- \wedge [\text{ gord-}]\}_4$ +
  b. -af$_{PI}$'s diathesis: $\{ \wedge \text{-}\}_1 \ldots \{ \wedge [_{af}\text{-oj}_{PI.F}]\}_4$ >
  c. a + b: $\{i \wedge \text{-}\}_1 \ldots \{- \wedge [\text{ gordoj}]\}_4$ +
  ....
  d. copula's diathesis: $\{ \wedge \}_1 \ldots \{ \wedge [\text{by-}]\}_4$ >
  e. c + d: $\{i \wedge \text{-}\}_1 \ldots \{- \wedge [\text{by- [gordoj]}]\}_4$ +
  ....
  f. **-inf** diathesis: $\{ \wedge \text{-}\}_1 \ldots \{ \wedge [\text{-t'}]\}_4$ >
  g. e + f: $\{i \wedge \text{-}\}_1 \ldots \{- \wedge [\text{byt'}] [\text{gordoj}]\}_4$ =>

Sentences like (49c), with the SF in place of the PI, are also well-formed ($On_{\text{NOM.M}}$ *xočet byt' priglašen*$_{\text{SF.M}}$ *na večer* 'He wants to-be invited to the-party'): its derivation is essentially the same as [*byt' gordoj*] in (56): the SF's external argument $\{i \wedge N\}_1$ is inherited by the copula stem *by-*, and **[[by-]** [*priglašen*]]'s inherited external N_1 in $\{i \wedge N\}_1$ is deleted by the $\{ \wedge \text{-}\}_1$ external argument of the s-predicate-forming infinitive suffix **-t'**, which composes with **by-** and projects to syntax as the s-predicate [$_{\text{infPi}}$ *byt' priglašen*$_{\text{SF.NOM}}$ *na večer*], which is V-bound by the matrix subject-control verb's external theta role.

On xočet byt' priglašennym$_{PI}$ *na večer* ~ *On xočet byt' priglašen*$_{SF}$ *na večer* 'He want to-be invited to-the-party' (see (49)), which do not differ in meaning, is another construction where the PI is challenging the SF (see (40a) and (40c), where the PI is replacing the LF). **On xočet byt' priglašennyj*$_{\text{LF.NOM}}$ *na večer* is ungrammatical because LFs are *adjuncts*, which cannot function as predicate adjectives.

5.7.1 An anomalous agreement pattern?

Consider the well-formed bracketed infinitive clause complements in (57) and (58). (59) is the structure of (57) and (58); recall that the infinitive complement of a noun is always a clause in Russian (§4.8.1).

(57) [$_{nP}$ ego sposobnost' [byt' sčaslivym$_{PI.M}$]]

(58) [$_{nP}$ ego   sposobnost' [byt' sčasliv$_{SF.NOM.M}$]].
         'his   ability   to-be happy'

(59) [$_{nP}$ ego   sposobnost' [$_{infP}$ PRO$_{i.DAT}$ [$_{inf'}$ byt' [$_{afP}$ sčasliv$_{SF.NOM.M}$/sčastlivym$_{PI.M}$]]]]
         'his   ability   to-be   happy'

Since the nominative case is an inherent property of the SF suffix in (58), [$_{afP}$ *sčastliv*$_{SF.M}$] is unaffected by the dative subject of the infinitive clause (PRO and *sčastliv*$_{SF.NOM.M}$ /*sčastlivym*$_{PI.M}$ agree in gender and number). The derivation of (58) is thus entirely regular. However, when we add SAM$_i$ to (58), it is (61) rather than the expected (60) that is well-formed. Compare (60) and (61) with (62) and

(63), where the expected agreement pattern emerges: dative *samomu* in (62) not nominative *sam* is well-formed.

(60) *[nP ego sposobnost' [infP PRO_{i.DAT} byt' sčastliv_{SF.NOM.M} **samomu**_{DAT.M}]]
     his ability   to-be happy   himself

(61) [nP ego sposobnost' [infP PRO_{i.DAT.M} byt' sčastliv_{SF.NOM.M} sam_{NOM.M}]]

(62) [nP ego sposobnost' [infP PRO_{i.DAT} byt' sčastlivym_{PI.M} **samomu**_{DAT.M}]]

(63) [nP ego sposobnost' [infP PRO_{i.DAT} byt' sčastlivym_{PI.M} *sam_{NOM.M}]]

(64) [nP ego sposobnost' [infP PRO_{i.DAT} byt' sčastlivym_{PI.M} *samim_{INST.M}]]

(61) is the only construction I am aware of in which SAM_i fails to 'follow the rules' and to agree with the head of its TBC (which is PRO_{DAT}; cf. (62)/(63)). While it is obviously the presence of the inherent nominative case of the SF that is responsible for the unanticipated agreement pattern in (61), we need to account for SAM_i's failure to agree in case with PRO_{DAT}. My best guess is that *sam* in (61) is simply the default use of the nominative case in an atypical s-clause whose null subject is quirky dative and whose predicate adjective is nominative (see notes 5 and 12; §4.6.1). We find a different argeement pattern in (62)/(63), which is patently related to the fact that the PI is a fossilized (inactive) case feature rather than the SF's inherent (active) case feature: SAM_i thus cannot agree with or be otherwise influenced by the proximate PI *sčastlivym* and therefore agrees with PRO_{DAT}.

5.8 Assigning the PI

Since it was assumed in earlier analyses that the PI of adjectives and participles is a case, the primary goal was to identify its case-assigner (e.g., see §5.2). If, however, the PI is not an active case feature, as proposed above, it is not assigned or checked, and there is no PI case assigner or probe. We shall see in the next section that the PI is licensed but not checked/assigned.

There is no paradigm of 'predicate case' with the PI realizing one of the possibilities.[18] My hypothesis is that the PI is an earlier instrumental case feature that split off from the inflectional case paradigm of adjectives and was reanalyzed as an independent adjective suffix that inflects for gender and number, but not case. This immediately accounts for the fact that the PI is never involved in case-agreement relations.

The PI and the SF have both become *specialized predicate adjectives*, and neither is assigned case. The morphological PI suffix has become a third type of adjective-forming suffix, which has its own diathesis and its own selectional and distributional properties; it is diachronically in competition with the LF and SF in all positions in which they cooccur and have not developed a semantic distinction. This three-way distinction is summarized in (65):

(65)   PI   LF   SF
    case   -   α   NOMINATIVE
    gender α   α   α
    number α   α   α

This type of reanalysis is relatively common in the history of highly inflected languages. For example, the Russian infinitive suffix **-t'** (from earlier **-ti**) is historically the dative case form of a derived nominal, which has been reanalyzed as a purely *verbal* category in modern Russian. The nominative SF of the Old Russian **-l-** participle in the [copula+ [**V-l**] participle] past tense construction was reanalyzed as the *verbal* past-tense suffix (thus $znal_{\text{M.SG.PAST}}$ 'knew' is no longer a nominative case *participle*, which explains why it can no longer compose with the copula; like the PI, it does agree in gender and number). The LF neuter singular *-oe* suffix has developed a specialized function and split off from the adjective paradigm: it has become a nominalizing suffix that converts adjectives and participles into substantivized adjectives, e.g, *On ne znal, kuda det' privez-enn-oe*$_{\text{LF.ACC.N.SG}}$ 'He didn't know where to-put *what-had-been-delivered*.' Russian thus has two homophonous *-oe* suffixes: one inflectional (*vkusn-oe*$_{\text{LF.NOM.N.SG}}$ *vino*$_{\text{N.SG.NOM}}$ 'good wine'), the other derivational. Essentially the same thing happened with the third person plural form of the verb, which, in addition to its primary inflectional function, can designate one or more unidentified/unidentifiable human agents; e.g.:

(66)   [$_{\text{PP}}$ Na drugom konce provoda] brosili$_{\text{3rd.PL}}$ trubku$_{\text{ACC}}$.
        at other end of-line threw-down receiver
        '(The-person) [at the other end] hung up (lit. threw-down the-receiver).'

(67)   Gromko postučali$_{\text{3rd.PL}}$ v dver.'
        '(Someone) knocked loudly at the-door.'

(68)   Ona$_{\text{NOM.F.SG}}$ ne ljubit, [$_{\text{CP}}$ kogda ee$_{\text{ACC}}$ celujut$_{\text{3rd.PL}}$].
        'She doesn't like (it) [when (anyone) kisses her].'

(69)   U odeždy byl tot neoprjatnyj vid, kotoryj ona priobretaet, esli ee **nosjat**$_{\text{3rd.PL}}$,
        [$_{\text{gP<i>}}$ ne snimaja (ee) mnogo časov podrjad].
        '(His) clothing had that messy look that it gets if **one wears** it [without taking (it) off for many hours at-a-stretch].'

Summary: As we saw above, the LF, SF, and PI occur in many of the same syntactic configurations. The semantic differences attributed to them often turn out to be stylistic, with the non-PI variant felt to be the more formal, colloquial, or archaic.[19] For example, object-controlled depictive adjuncts can be either a PI$_i$ or an accusative LF (see (70)/(71)): there is no semantic distinction here and the PI$_i$ is replacing the LF.

(70)   On   ostavil   knigu   raskrytoj / raskrytuju.
       he:NOM   left   book:ACC.F   open:PI.F / open:LF.ACC.F
       'He left the-book open.'

(71)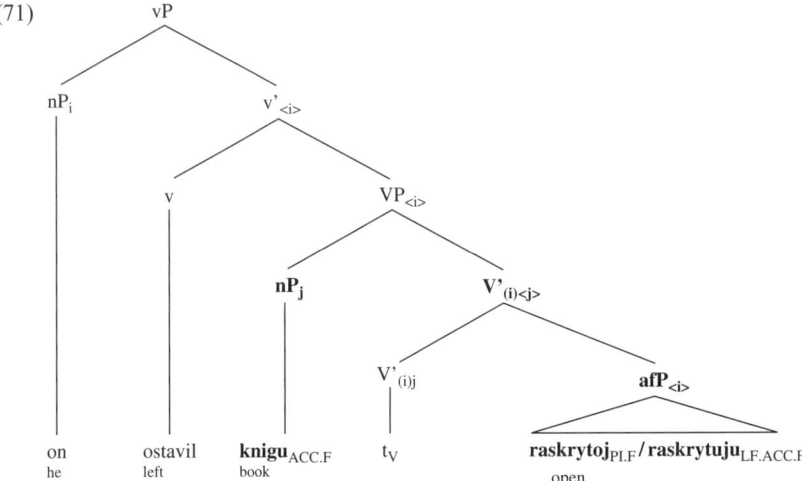

5.9   Licensing the PI

This section is devoted to the licensing and syntactic distribution of the PI. Since we have already seen the syntactic constructions in which the PI occurs, we now need to identify the structures in which it *cannot* occur and then, by comparing them, pinpoint the common denominator unifying the structures in which the PI is licensed. The most informative structures turn out to be those that license LFs but exclude PI s-predicates (PI$_i$), i.e. LF ~ *PI$_i$ ~ *SF. Consider the *kak* 'as' phrase in (72) to (76) (see the diagnostic use of kP$_i$ in §2.12 and §4.6).

(72)   a. **Ja** dolžen zaderžat' **vas**$_{ACC}$ na bortu kak **založnika**$_{ACC}$/*založnikom$_{INST}$.
       'I must detain you on board as a-hostage.'
       b. **Ja** byl zaderžan na bortu kak **založnik** (*založnika / *založnikom).
       'I$_{NOM}$ was detained on board as a-hostage$_{NOM}$ (*$_{ACC}$/*$_{INST}$).'

(73)   Ja   ne   vospol'zovalsja **Nikitoj**   kak **predlogom**.[20]
       I:NOM   NEG   used   Nikita:INST   as   excuse:INST
       'I didn't use Nikita as an excuse.'

(74) On obnaružil neskol'ko otpečatkov, **kotorye**$_{\text{ACC.PL}}$ on opredelil kak **prinadležaščie**$_{\text{LF.ACC.PL}}$ ej (*kak prinadležaščimi$_{\text{PI.PL}}$ ej).
'He found several fingerprints, **which** he identified as **belonging** to-her.'

(75) **Moja noga**$_{\text{NOM.F}}$ bolela$_\text{F}$ kak **slomannaja**$_{\text{LF.NOM.F}}$ / *slomannoj$_{\text{PI.F}}$
'My leg hurt as (though it were) broken.'

(76) Neskol'ko čelovek okazalis' v položenii, **kotoroe**$_{\text{ACC}}$ možno rassmatrivat' kak **komprometirujuščee**$_{\text{LF.ACC.PL}}$ /*komprometirujuščim$_{\text{PI.PL}}$.
'Several people were in a-position, which (it is) possible to-view as compromising.'

Given that an adjunct *kak* 'as' phrase is an s-predicate (kP$_i$) that inherits its unlinked external theta role **i** from its s-predicate complement, we expect the adjective/participle complement of *kak* to be either LF or PI$_i$. But we see in (72) to (76) that the predicate instrumental case of both nouns and adjectives is excluded in kP$_i$s. Since both the LF and PI$_i$ are s-predicates and are able to cooccur in other constructions (e.g., see (70)/(71)), the licenser of the PI we are looking for must be blocked by kP$_i$; to identify it, however, we need to look at other structures in which the PI$_i$ but not the LF is excluded.

Consider the PPs in (77) and (78) and the preposed nPs in (79) and (80): as in the case of the *kak*-phrase, only the LF can occur in these syntactic structures. In (79a–b), the preposed LF *golodnyj*$_{\text{NOM.M}}$ 'hungry' is V-bound by the external theta role of the subject, which it adjoins to: [$_{\text{nPi}}$ afP$_{<i>}$ nP$_{<i>}$] (afP$_i$ = LF~*PI$_i$).

(77) Ja ne ljublju smotret' [$_{\text{PP}}$ na sebja   goluju /*goloj].
I NEG like to-look at myself:$_{\text{ACC.F}}$ naked:$_{\text{ACC.F.LF}}$/*$_{\text{PI.F}}$)
'I don't like to look at myself (whem I'm) naked (in the mirror, etc.).'

(78) a. Naručniki snimut s nego mertvogo/*mertvym.
handcuffs:ACC remove:PL from him:GEN.M dead:GEN.M.LF(*PI.M)
'(Unspecified person) will-remove the-handcuffs from him (when he is) dead.'
b. Ego našli mertvym/!mertvogo.
him:ACC.M found:PL dead:PI.M / !LF.ACC.M
'(Unidentified person[s]) found him dead.'

(79) a. Golodnyj (*golodnym/*goloden), mal'čik otpravilsja domoj.
hungry:NOM.M.LF (*PI / *SF)), boy:NOM went home
'(Because he was) hungry, the boy went home.'
b. [$_{\text{nPi}}$ [$_{\text{afP<i>}}$ golodnyj], [$_{\text{nP<i>}}$ mal'čik]] otpravilsja domoj

(80) Imenno teper', [$_{\text{nP.DAT}}$ [$_{\text{afP<i>}}$ bol'nomu$_{\text{DAT}}$], [$_{\text{nP.DAT}}$ emu]] ponadobilas' Liza$_{\text{NOM}}$.
'Precisely now, [[(since he was) sick], he] needed Liza (lit. to-him was-needed Liza).'

5.10 Depictive adjectives 253

The exclusion of the PI_i and the obligatory use of the LF_i in the kP_i, the PP in (77) and (78), and the preposed nPs in (79) and (80) suggest the following descriptive generalization on which a principled explanation of the PI_i's syntactic distribution can be based: the PI is licensed by an *immediately* dominating *verbal* projection (either finite or nonfinite). This predicts that, in standard Russian, a nonverbal projection intervening between the licensing VP and afP_i blocks the occurrence of the PI_i, leaving the LF as the only option. In other words, afP_i embedded in a non-verbal phrase cannot be realized as the PI in standard Russian: *[VP [xP x [$afP_{PI.i}$]]], where x is a nonverbal category. Thus in (81), the LF *goluju* is V-bound in the nP complement of PP, which double-blocks the licensing of the PI_i:

(81)   Schematic representation of PP in (77):

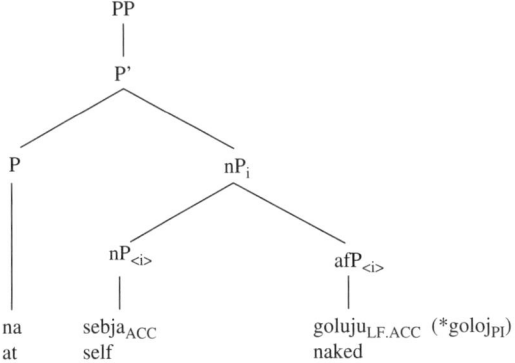

| na | sebja$_{ACC}$ | goluju$_{LF.ACC}$ (*goloj$_{PI}$) |
| at | self | naked |

The kP_i projection in (74) to (76) has the same effect as the PP and nP projections in (81), shielding its afP_i complement from the VP domain in which it is canonically licensed; only the LF is possible here because it is not sensitive to verbal vs. nonverbal environments (recall that only LFs, never PI_i, occur nP-internally).

My explanation of the PI's syntactic distribution seems correct because it is based on the fact that the PI must be *licensed*, but not in the way that cases are, which is precisely what we expect given my hypothesis that the PI of adjectives and participles is not an active case feature.

5.10 Depictive adjectives in infinitive clauses

There remains one more unsolved problem, namely, the morphosyntactic realization of *depictive* adjectives in infinitive clauses, which may appear at first to be dauntingly complex. However, we shall see below that the diathesis-based theory of morphosyntax elaborated in the preceding chapters is able to capture the data's underlying systematicity without resorting to ad hoc principles or additional null-headed functional categories. Our focus will be the initially baffling fact that the dative LF depictive adjective *odetomu* 'dressed' in (82a), which agrees in case, gender, and number with the dative subject of the infinitive clause, is rejected by speakers of standard Russian despite the fact that it does not violate any principles and its agreement pattern is identical to the well-formed depictive adjective *odetyj*$_{LF.NOM}$ in (82c), which is the corresponding finite clause.[21] Thus only the PI of depictive adjectives is acceptable in infinitive clauses, as in (82b); see §5.4.2.[22]

(82)   a. Ona poprosila ego$_{ACC}$ [$_{infP}$ PRO$_{i.DAT}$ leč' v postel' *?**odetomu**$_{LF.DAT.M}$].
           she asked him   to-get in bed dressed
       b. Ona poprosila ego$_{ACC}$ [$_{infP}$ PRO$_{i.DAT}$ leč' v postel' **odetym**$_{PI.M}$].
           'She asked him to-get in bed dressed.'
       c. On$_{i.NOM.M}$ leg v postel' **odetyj**$_{LF.NOM.M}$ / **odetym**$_{PI.M}$.
           'He got in bed dressed.'

It is crucial in what follows not to confuse *predicate* and *depictive* adjectives:

(83)   Predicate adjectives:
       Anna$_{NOM}$ poprosila menja$_{ACC}$ [$_{infP}$ PRO$_{DAT}$ byt' [$_{afP}$ gotovym$_{PI}$ / *gotovomu$_{LF.DAT}$ otpravit'sja]].
       'Anna asked me [to-be [ready to-leave]].'

(84)   Depictive adjectives:
       Anna poprosila menja [$_{infP}$ PRO$_{DAT}$ vernut'sja domoj gotovym$_{PI}$/*gotovomu$_{LF.DAT}$ k poezdke].
       'Anna asked me to-return home ready for the-trip.'

The LF predicate adjective *gotovomu* in (83) is ill-formed because it is an s-predicate adjunct (see chapter 2). But this does not explain the ill-formedness of LF dative *depictive* adjectives in infinitive clauses like (82a) and (84). Note that the LF *gotovomu* is ill-formed in both predicate and depictive functions in (83) and (84), but for different reasons: the predicate LF *gotovomu*$_{DAT}$ in (83) violates at least two grammatical rules whereas depictive *gotovomu*$_{DAT}$ in (84) does not violate any.

This section is devoted to explaining the unexpected ill-formedness in standard Russian of the dative depictive LF in infinitive clauses like (82a) and (84). We see in (85) that depictive adjectives in *finite* clauses are either nominative LFs or PI$_i$s.

(85)   a. On$_{NOM.M.SG}$ leg v postel' [$_{afPi}$ **odetyj**$_{LF.M.SG.NOM}$].
           'He got in bed dressed.'
       b. On$_{NOM.M.SG}$ leg v postel' [$_{afPi}$ **odetym**$_{PI.M.SG}$].
           'He got in bed dressed.'

c. *On_{NOM.M.SG} leg v postel' odet_{SF.M.SG.NOM}.
d.

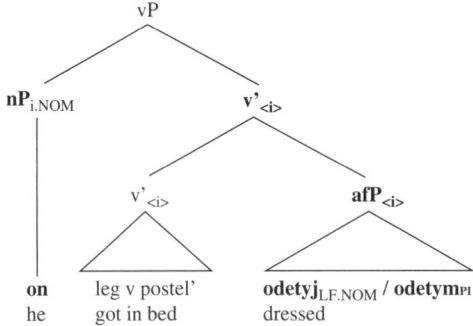

Depictive adjectives in infinitive clauses should a priori behave the same way they do in finite clauses like (85a–b), i.e., be realized as either a PI$_i$ or as an LF; see (86).

(86)

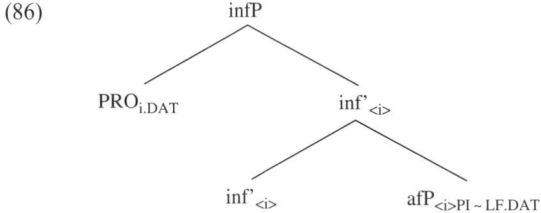

But, as we saw in (82a), dative depictive adjectives in infinitive clauses are, contrary to expectation, unacceptable in standard Russian.

Sentences like the following appear to contradict the generalization that dative depictive LFs are excluded in infinitive clauses: *odetomu*_{LF.DAT} in (87) and *odetym*_{PI} in (88) are both well-formed, the only difference being that (87) is more colloquial than (88) (*razrešit'* assigns quirky dative case to its direct object).

(87) Ona   razrešila   emu   leč'   v   postel' **odetomu**.
      she:NOM.F   allowed:F   him:DAT.M   to-get   in   bed   dressed:DAT.M

(88) Ona   razrešila   emu   leč'   v   postel' **odetym**.
      she:NOM.F   allowed:F   him:DAT.M to-get   in   bed   dressed:PI.M

However, we saw in chapter 4 that object-controlled infinitive complements in colloquial Russian can be s-predicates as well as s-clauses, which explains the well-formedness of the dative case of *odetomu* in (87): the infinitive complement here is an s-predicate and *odetomu* thus agrees with the dative matrix object *emu*, which, as we see in (89), is the head of its TBC: there is no PRO_DAT for *odetomu*_DAT to agree with.

(89)

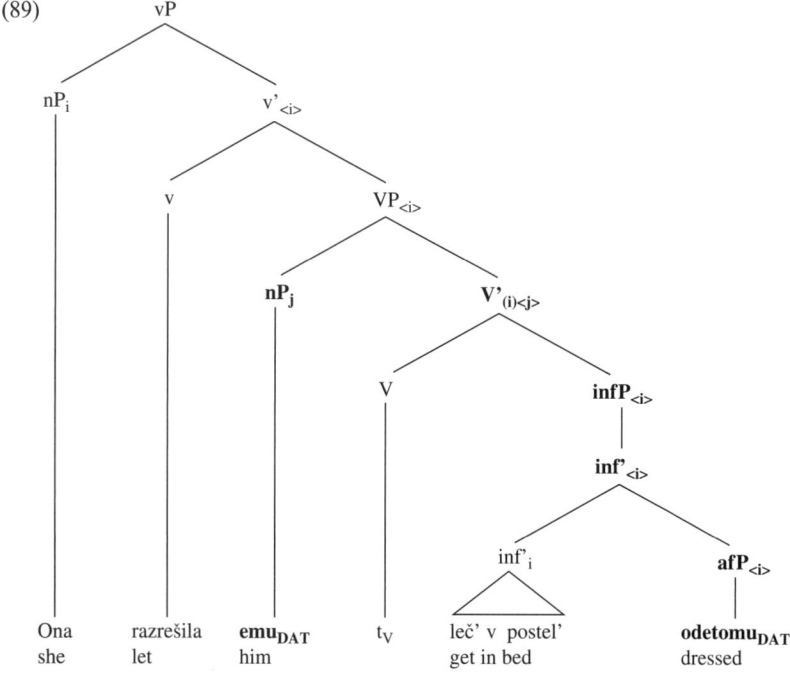

The syntactic representation of (87) in (89) correctly predicts the unacceptability of *odetomu*_LF.DAT in (82a) and its acceptability in (87): *odetomu*_LF.DAT in (89) agrees in case with the dative matrix object *emu*, which is the head of its TBC. But *odetomu*_LF.DAT in (82a)/(90) agrees with the PRO_DAT subject of an infinitive *clause* complement:

(90) Ona_NOM poprosila ego_ACC [_infP PRO_I.DAT leč' v postel' *?**odetomu**_LF.DAT.M].
      she   asked   him   to-get in bed   dressed

The infinitive s-predicate analysis of (87)/(89) is confirmed by (91):

(91) Ona   poprosila **ego**_jACC [_infP<i> leč' v postel' **odetogo**_ACC]
      she:NOM   asked   him   to-get in bed   dressed

The depictive adjective in (91) is accusative (*odetogo*) because the infinitive complement containing it is an infP_i *s-predicate* and the accusative matix object *ego* is the head of the TBC in which it is V-bound. Thus my empirical generalization holds: depictive adjectives in infinitive *clauses* cannot agree in case with the dative subject in standard Russian.

To see conclusive evidence that depictive adjectives cannot agree in case with the dative subject of infinitive *clauses*, all we have to do is observe the case of SAM$_i$ and a depictive adjective in an infinitive phrase which is in a syntactic environment excluding infinitive s-predicates: the prediction is that SAM$_i$ should agree in dative case with the PRO$_{DAT}$ subject of the infinitve clause but that the depictive adjective should be PI; both should have the same number and gender agreement, and the same TBC head. Bearing in mind that the infinitive complements of nouns and complementizers are always clauses (see §4.8), the sentences in (92) and (93) demonstrate that my prediction is correct: *samomu* agrees in case with PRO$_{DAT}$ subject but the depictive adjective is PI. (94) and (95) summarize the data.

(92) On podumyval o [$_{nP}$ vozmožnosti [$_{infP}$ PRO$_{DAT}$ samomu$_{DAT}$ leč' v postel' odetym$_{PI}$ /*?odetomu$_{LF.DAT}$]].
'(lit.) He was-thinking about [the-possibility [to-get in bed dressed himself]].'

(93) Šaljapin davno mečtal o tom, čtoby samomu$_{DAT}$
Chaliapin for-a-long-time has-been-dreaming about it C himself
sygrat' Mefistofelja$_{ACC}$ golym$_{PI}$ / *?golomu$_{LF.DAT}$.
to-play M. nude
'Chaliapin has-been-dreaming for-a-long-time about playing Mephistopheles nude himself.'

(94) a. Ona poprosila ego$_{j.ACC}$ [$_{infP<i>}$ leč' v postel' [$_{afP<i>}$ **odetogo$_{ACC}$**]].
b. *Ona poprosila ego$_{j.ACC}$ [$_{infP}$ PRO$_{i.DAT}$ leč' v postel' [$_{afP<i>}$ **odetomu$_{DAT}$**]].
c. Ona poprosila ego$_{j.ACC}$ [$_{infP}$ PRO$_{i.DAT}$ leč' v postel' [$_{afP<i>}$ **odetym$_{PI}$**]].
d. Ona poprosila ego$_{j.ACC}$ [$_{infP<i>}$ leč' v postel' [$_{afP<i>}$ **odetym$_{PI}$**]].
'She asked him to-get in bed dressed.'

(95) a. Ona razrešila emu$_{j.DAT}$ [$_{infP<i>}$ leč' v postel' [$_{afP<i>}$ **odetomu$_{DAT}$**]].
b. *Ona razrešila emu$_{j.DAT}$ [$_{infP}$ PRO$_{i.DAT}$ leč' v postel' [$_{afP<i>}$ **odetomu$_{DAT}$**]].
c. Ona razrešila emu$_{j.DAT}$ [$_{infP}$ PRO$_{i.DAT}$ leč' v postel' [$_{afP<i>}$ **odetym$_{PI}$**]].
d. Ona razrešila emu$_{j.DAT}$ [$_{infPi}$ leč' v postel' [$_{afP<i>}$ **odetym$_{PI}$**]].
'She allowed him to-get in bed dressed.'

Since the dative case of *samomu* in sentences (92) and (93) demonstrates that there must be a PRO$_{DAT}$ subject present, the ill-formedness of depictive *odetomu$_{DAT}$* in (94b) and (95b) cannot be accounted for by claiming that there is no dative subject for it to agree with. The final step in my analysis of the PI is therefore to explain the ungrammaticality of sentences with the structure of (94b), in which no grammatical rules or principles are violated.

We have to answer two complementary questions: (i) What prevents LF depictive adjectives in infinitive clauses from agreeing in case with the dative subject?' (11) Why does SAM$_i$, which is also an s-predicate adjunct, obligatorily agree in dative case with the subject of infinitive clauses?

The answer to both questions is diachronic, and we actually already have seen the answer to both above. The unacceptability of *odetomu* in (94b) is due to an ongoing diachronic change rather than to the violation of a synchronic morphological or syntactic principle. As we saw above, the PI$_i$ is incrementally, construction-by-construction, displacing the LF in all the syntactic environments in which they cooccur but have not developed a semantic distinction. The replacement of the LF by the PI$_i$ is proceeding at different rates in differrent constructions, which means that the agreement pattern (94b) is simply a special case of a broader phenomenon: the depictive PI$_i$ has all but replaced the depictive LF in infinitive clauses like (94a), but not in other constructions. For example, we saw above that the PI$_i$ is well on its way to replacing the LF in sentences like (96) and (97), but has not progressed as far as constructions like (94a).

(96) a. !Ja uvidel ego$_{ACC}$ ležaščego$_{ACC}$ v bol'šoj komnate sovsem odnogo$_{ACC}$.
      b. Ja uvidel ego$_{ACC}$ ležaščim$_{PI}$ v bol'šoj komnate sovsem odnogo$_{ACC}$.
      'I saw him lying in a large room all alone.'

(97) Ona našla ego$_{ACC.M}$ na polu p'janym$_{PI.M}$ / !p'janogo$_{LF.ACC}$.
      she found him   on floor drunk
      'She found him on the floor drunk.'

(98) My$_{NOM}$ zametili ego$_{ACC}$ vyxodjaščim$_{PI}$ / !vyxodjaščego$_{ACC}$ iz zdanija.
      we   saw   him   coming-out   from building
      'We saw him coming-out of the-building.'

(99) a. On$_{NOM.M}$ xočet byt' priglašennym$_{PI.M}$ na večer.
         'He   wants to-be invited   to the-party.'
      b. On$_{NOM.M}$ xočet byt' priglašen$_{SF.NOM.M}$ na večer. (see §5.7.1)
         'He   wants to-be invited   to the-party.'

We come now to the morphosyntax of SAM$_i$, which is the last piece of the puzzle. As noted above, the behavior of SAM$_i$ in infinitive clauses is the converse of the LF, despite the fact that both are vertically-bound s-predicate adjuncts:

(100) a. Ona poprosila ego [$_{infP}$ PRO$_{DAT}$ leč' v postel' **odetym**$_{PI}$ / *?**detomu**$_{DAT}$].
         'She asked him to-get in bed dressed.'
      b. Ona poprosila ego [$_{infP}$ PRO$_{DAT}$ leč' v postel' **samomu**$_{DAT}$ / *****samim**$_{PI}$].
         'She asked him to get in bed himself.'

The fact that SAM$_i$ in infinitive clauses must agree with the dative subject and is never PI$_i$ is also diachronic: unlike the SF and the LF, the pronominal adjectives *sam* 'himself,' *odin* 'alone,' and *ves'* 'all' were always declined according to the *pronominal declension* and they were therefore simply never affected by the morphosyntactic changes that created the modern three-way SF, LF, and PI system. Thus SAM$_i$'s most striking property from the diachronic point of view is that nothing has changed: SAM$_i$ has always agreed in case with the head of its TBC (see §4.10).

Notes

Introduction

1. What is said here of verbs holds for all *predicators* (verbs, adjectives, prepositions, specialized nonverbal predicate words), which are defined as lexical *stems* whose argument structure projects the sentence's *core syntactic structure*, i.e., the minimal syntactic projection in which all the predicator's theta roles are assigned (or bound). Core syntactic structure is also referred to as a predicator's Extended Lexical Projection.
2. Verbs are entered in the mental lexicon as lexical *verb stems* (**V**) with their own argument structures; this entails that each **V** must compose with at least one productive affix and its argument structure in order to form a *word*, the primitive category of syntactic structure. A derivation may involve the composition of **V**'s argument structure with the argument structures of several affixes (cf. agglutinating languages). Thus the derivation of every syntactic structure is based on (projected from) an argument-structure level derivation. An affix is defined as *productive* if it has its own argument structure. Thus the first 'cut' in the typology of affixes is + or − argument structure, not derivational vs. inflectional. In what follows, **V**'s *argument-structure representation* will be referred to as its *diathesis*.
3. The mapping between argument structure and morphosyntactic structure is monodirectional: while argument-structure operations have systematic syntactic effects, the converse is not true: *syntactic rules cannot affect argument structure*. Thus *projection*, in one of its meanings, may be thought of as monodirectional mapping from argument-structure representation to syntactic representation. I am of course not claiming that *all* syntactic operations are in reality projected argument-structure operations: e.g., *wh*-movement is a strictly syntactic rule. But all rules effecting a change of grammatical relations are by hypothesis argument-structure level operations.
4. These affixes will be referred to as *paradigmatic affixes* since they account for a given **V**'s syntactic paradigm. Another important source of language diversity is the parameterization of universal syntactic principles (e.g., the headedness parameter). See Baker 2001.
5. The stems themselves, which typically consist of roots, prefixes, and suffixes, are *not* assembled by productive rules. Stems are off-the-rack lexical entries whose meaning is typically not compositional, i.e., cannot be computed on the basis of the meanings of its components. For example, while the bracketed stem of the infinitive *izdavat'* 'to

publish' can be segmented into a root *-da-* 'give', a prefix *iz-* 'out from', and an imperfective aspect suffix *-va-*, i.e., *[iz-da-va]-t'*, it is, from the synchronic point of view, an idiomatic fossil whose meaning cannot be derived from *iz+da+va*; *[iz-da-va]-* is opaque with respect to the rules that operate at the levels of argument structure and syntax. Only the infinitive-forming suffix *-t'* is a productive paradigmatic suffix with its own argument-structure that composes with the lexical stem's argument structure (**V**'s diathesis); stem-to-infinitive derivations are treated in chapter 4.

6. The primary difference between *fusional* languages like Russian and *agglutinating* languages like Turkish thus boils down to the number of syntactic features an affix typically has: agglutinative suffixes canonically have one feature per suffix. Thus the dative plural suffix in Russian (*-am* in *korov-am* 'to-cows') corresponds to Turkish *inek*$_{stem}$-*ler*$_{plural}$-*e*$_{dative}$ 'to-cows'; *-ler-e* is not a dative plural suffix and *-am* cannot be segmented into *a-m*, corresponding to dative and plural features.

7. Strictly speaking, the sentence's *final syntactic representation* is the input into *information structure* (i.e., topic/comment, theme/rheme, focus/presupposition, etc.), which, in highly inflected languages like Russian, is realized by free word order (scrambling). Space does not permit me to treat this aspect of a sentence's derivation systematically, but this does not affect the book's focus, namely, the mapping between argument structure and morphosyntactic structure.

8. If an *event* in lexical-semantic representation has four *participants*, the **V** corresponding to this event will have three arguments and an adjunct (see below).

9. In what follows, the terms *argument structure* and *diathesis* are synonymous.

    Note that, according to the diathesis in (1), theta roles are not *assigned* to NPs in syntax: theta roles and their categorial heads are already *linked* in **V**'s initial diathesis. We shall see below that **V**'s internal and external c-selection *cannot* be predicted from its theta-selection: both tiers in (1) are autonomous.

10. I assume that the *order* of the theta roles in (1) is determined by a universal theta-role hierarchy (see the UTAH in Baker 1997); thus the *external* **i** role is an agent if one is selected, **j** is canonically the patient/theme, **k** is one of several oblique roles.

11. Italian *Piove* 'It is raining' has no arguments.

12. Grimshaw 1979 argues, as I do, that both theta-selection and categorial selection are necessary in argument-structure representation.

13. This entails that expletives like English *it* in *It is raining* do not project from **V**'s diathesis: they are syntactic place-fillers ('dummies').

14. The arguments' *cases* in (3) are predictable from **V**'s diathesis and, therefore, a separate case tier along the lines of Yip, Maling, and Jackendoff 1987 is unnecessary. Only *quirky case* needs to be represented in **V**'s diathesis (as a c-selectional feature).

15. "=>" represents the projection of **V**'s final diathesis to syntax; ">" represents an argument-structure level operation (composition), and "–>" represents a syntax-level operation.

16. An argument cannot be added to a diathesis that is *saturated*, i.e., when its three argument positions are occupied: there are no four-place predicators and no operations in natural language that can create 2×5, ten-slotted diatheses from 2×4, eight-slotted ones.

17. All the Russian examples, most of which are adapted from written sources, have been checked by native speakers.
18. See also Apresjan 1967, 1974, Padučeva 1974: ch. X, Diatezy i Zalogi 1975, Xrakovskij 1978, Xrakovskij 1981, Dolinina 1990, and Xrakovskij, Mal'čukov, and Dmitrenko 2004.

    The diathesis in the Russian School and my use of the term here are widely divergent. See Babby 1976.
19. I have of course noted in endnotes and references those aspects of diathesis-based theory that differ significantly from recent proposals in the generative literature.

1 The structure of argument structure

1. See Chomsky 1986: 81, 1989, Speas 1990: 1, Roberts 1987: 3, Cowper 1992: 17, Haegeman 1995, Bowers 2006; cf. the Projection Principle in earlier theory (Chomsky 1986: 82).
2. *Predicators* are verbs, nouns, adjectives, prepositions (On_{NOM} *byl* [$_{PP}$ *protiv vojny*$_{GEN}$] 'He was [against war]'), and hundreds of predicate words or phrases, which do not belong to any of the four major syntactic categories and cooccur with the copula (e.g. *nel'zja* + infinitive 'it is not possible to'). Chapter 1 deals primarily with verbs (verbal predicators). In what follows, **V** stands for lexical verb stem, to which are added productive affixes.
3. *Core syntactic structure* is vP, which is the smallest syntactic structure in which all **V**'s theta roles are satisfied.
4. A verb's *final derived argument structure* is the diathesis that results from the operation of all the argument-structure level rules applied to **V**'s *initial argument structure*, which is the form stored in the mental lexicon (see Jakobson 1957). I will use the term *diathesis* to refer to argument-structure representation; a diathesis-level *rule* canonically consists of the *composition* of **V**'s diathesis with the diathesis of a productive affix. *Merger* denotes the syntactic combination of fully formed words and phrases. Diathesis-level rules and syntactic-level rules are strictly segregated.
5. For example, *to be jealous* in English corresponds to the ditransitive verb *revnovat' kogo*$_{ACC}$ *k komu/ čemu*$_{DAT}$ in Russian (*k* is a c-selected preposition that itself selects dative case):

    On   revnuet   ženu   k svoemu drugu.
    he:NOM is-jealous wife:ACC to his   friend:DAT
    'He is-jealous of his friend (with respect to his wife).'

    While *to-be-jealous* is an event with three semantic participants, English and Russian differ with respect to the number of syntactic arguments (valence) the corresponding predicator can have: the verb *renovat'* has three arguments and thus cannot be translated directly into English, where *be-jealous* licenses only two arguments: the direct object (*ženu*) is rendered as the adjunct expression 'with respect to.' It is precisely this kind of unpredictable information that is encoded in the argument structure of particular **V**s in particular languages. Given that this type of mismatch between an event's semantic participants and the corresponding predicator's arguments abounds in the world's languages, it is not clear in what sense the lexical semantics of predicators predicts their syntactic structures.

6. I am using the term *map* in much the same way as Marantz 1984, i.e., as a function that *associates* each member of a set A (e.g. positions [arguments] in hierarchically arranged diathesis representation) with each member of a set B (e.g. positions [constituents] in hierarchical syntactic structure). 'Map' is neutral with respect to whether there is a derivational relation between A and B. I use the term *projection* (i) to describe how the information encoded in **V**'s diathesis determines and constrains the *merger* of its syntactic elements into consituent structure (thus the sentence is a *projection* of **V**'s diathesis); (ii) to describe the distribution (spreading, percolation) of **V**'s syntactic features to the nodes of the phrase it heads (see the Head Feature Convention and the notion of *feature percolation*).

7. The term *diathesis* is used widely in the Russian tradition (e.g. Mel'čuk and Xolodovič 1970, Padučeva 1974, Xrakovskij *et al.* 2004) as well as in generative grammar; see Levin and Rappaport-Hovav 1994: 47. The definition of *diathesis* that I propose below differs in essential ways from the way this term has been used by others.

8. As Rothstein (1985: 9, 2001) puts it:

> Knowing the number and type of theta roles that a head assigns is a matter of *lexical knowledge*. The thematic properties of lexical heads are idiosyncratic, and have to be learned as part of the process of learning "how to use a word."

My hypothesis is that the same is true of **V**'s c-selection, including external c-selection.

9. Since subject in English is obligatory, it was assumed in earlier generative theory that *external subcategorization* is unnecessary. Russian provides robust empirical evidence that having an overt or null subject is not a universal property of well-formed sentences (see discussion of the Extended Projection Principle in Babby 1989, 2002). Some **V**s in Russian cannot have a subject, some must have a subject, while for others, subject is optional (see the discussion of *korčit'* 'to convulse' below). Thus subject in Russian is a property of **V**s, not sentences, i.e., the occurrence of a subject in a Russian sentence depends on **V**'s external c-selection and external theta selection, which are autonomous.

We shall also see that diathetic operations that delete **V**'s *c-selected external N*, leaving its external **i** unlinked (stranded), play a central role in morphosyntax. External **N** deletion, which is responsible for the derivation of s(econdary)-predicates, is not a possible syntactic operation, i.e., an nP cannot be deleted in syntax, stranding its theta role. See chapters 2–5.

10. Russian has free word order and *menja* is not an accusative subject.

11. For discussion, see Bošković 1997: 4, Alsina 1996: 6, Stowell 1992: 10, Speas 1990: 11, Chomsky 1986, Grimshaw 1979, Pesetsky 1982.

12. We see below that a noun phrase has the following structure: $[_{nP} (nP_i) [_{n'} [_n \text{N-n}] \text{NP}]]$, which is parallel to vP: $[_{vP} (nP_i) [_{v'} [_v \text{V-v}] \text{VP}]]$. All lexical categories in Russian have the following core X-bar phrasal structure (X's Extended Lexical Projection): $[_{xP} (nP_i) [_{x'} [_x \text{X-x}] \text{XP}]]$, where X is the lexical stem and x is the first affix it composes with. See below for details.

13. "=>" represents the projection from diathesis to syntactic representation.
14. See Rosen 1984, Stowell 1992: 12, Moro 2000: 226, Speas 1990: 9, and Rappaport and Levin 1992: 140.
15. I am not arguing that syntax can be reduced entirely to argument structure: there are operations that can be performed only on diathesis representation (e.g., delinking: $\{i{\wedge}N\}_1 > \{i{\wedge}\text{-}\}_1$) and operations that can be performed only on syntactic representation (i.e. *wh*-movement; topicalization). Russian provides evidence that certain operations that are routinely assumed to be syntactic are in fact diathetic.
16. "^" = "|" = "is linked to." Note that fully formed words (the 'atoms' of syntax) are not in boldface. All the primitives of diathetic representation (stems, affixes, theta roles, etc.) are in boldface.
17. We see below that the 2×4 structure of **V**'s diathesis *constrains* the addition of new arguments: an additional argument can be added to **V**'s initial diathesis only if it has free or available {-^-} positions, which are not occupied by arguments. This will be illustrated below in causative derivations, where the diathesis of the causative *suffix* (or auxiliary verb in French) introduces a new external argument (the causer agent) and **V**'s initial external argument is displaced to the left-most available position in the diathesis. The causative derivation in Turkish, French, Italian, and other languages is our most cogent argument that **V** cannot have more than three arguments. If a *semantic situation* has four *participants*, one of them must be realized syntactically as an adjunct.
18. The nominative case of nP_i and the accusative case of nP_j are *structural* cases (see §3.2.3 for details). The case of nP_k, the only one of **V**'s three arguments not projected to a spec-position, is directly determined by the value of the **k** theta role, which is selected by **V**, e.g.: dative when **k** is an experiencer, instrumental when it is a material or substance, etc. (see Babby 1994a, Sadler and Spencer 2001: 213); I will use the term *theta case*. Quirky case and prepositions are c-selectional properties of **V**. Given this typology of case, there is no need for an autonomous *case tier* along the lines of Yip, Maling, and Jackendoff 1987. See Babby 1994a, Woolford 2006.
19. Much of this book can be read as an argument against proposals like Kratzer's that the external argument (subject of the sentence) is an argument of v rather than V (see Kratzer 1996).
20. The systematic neutral OVS word order derived from basic SVO order in sentences like the following make it seem probable that (8b) is correct: when an object moves to spec-TP, the verb moves to T; the subject remains in situ in spec-vP (provided that it is not a pronoun):

    (i) On ne ljubil, kogda [$_{PP}$ za nego] platili [$_{NP.NOM}$ ženščiny]
    'He didn't like (it) when women paid [for him] (lit. when for him paid women).'
    (ii) Knigu$_{ACC.F}$ pokrival$_M$ sloj$_{NOM.M}$ pyli$_{GEN}$.
    'A layer of dust covered the-book (lit. The-book$_{ACC}$ covered a-layer$_{NOM}$ of-dust$_{GEN}$).'

21. See Sadler and Spencer 2001: 212 for discussion of the ordering of theta roles in a hierarchy.
22. The argument structures in (9) do not exhaust the possibilities.

23. **V** in Russian impersonal sentences is affixed with the non-agreeing **-o** suffix, which is homophonous with the neuter singular agreement suffix; see *tošni-l-o* in (7), where *-l-* is the past tense suffix. For discussion of **-o** in impersonal sentences in Russian, Ukrainian, and Lithuanian, see Lavine 2000, Babby 2002 (= 1989), Babby 1996.
24. I will consider only **N** heads here for expository purposes.
25. [V-v] moves from the head of VP to the head of vP, which produces neutral SVO word order in Russian (see below for details).
26. ">>" denotes an automatic operation which is triggered by a specific diathesis configuration. I am claiming that relinking occurs in argument structure only and that a theta role can relink only if there is an {-^N} or {-^[V-af]}$_4$ 'landing site' for it to relink to in **V**'s diathesis. See below for independent evidence.
27. *Tošnilo* in (14a) is affixed with the nonagreement suffix **-o**, which is used whenever agreement is not possible, i.e., when there is no subject or the subject does not have agreement features and thus cannot be agreed with (see CP and infinitive-clause subjects). It is worth noting that expletives and default verbal agreement morphology appear to be in complementary distribution: a language typically (perhaps universally) has one or the other. This suggests that they fulfill the same function. If this observation is empirically correct, we do not expect there to be null or overt expletives in Russian.
28. The suffix *-sja /-s'* is responsible for creating *derived unaccusatives*:
    {{i^N}$_1$ {j^N}$_2$...{-^V}$_4$} > {{-^N}$_1$ {j^-}$_2$...{-^[V-sja]}$_4$} >> {{j^N}$_1$ {-^-}$_2$...{-^[V-sja]}$_4$}.
    A passivized V is a subtype of derived unaccusative: **i** relinks to {-^[V-sja]}$_4$, deriving {i^[V-sja]}$_4$.
29. Note that *externalization* is an argument-structure level operation.
30. Participle formation, which is a diathesis-based operation (see chapter 3), provides conclusive evidence that externalization of **j** in unaccusative derivations is a diathetic operation, not a syntactic one. The participle-forming suffix *-šč-* selects a verbal diathesis with an external theta role linked to an external N, i.e. {θ^N}$_1$. Since unaccusative verbs form *-šč*-participles, **j**-externalization, which gives {j^N}$_1$, must be diathetic since *the output of syntactic operations does not feed diathetic ones*. In other words, if externalization of **j** in unaccusative derivations were syntactic and participle-formation were diathetic, our grammar would predict (incorrectly) that unergative verbs but not unaccusative verbs form *-šč*-participles.
31. The verb *korčit' sja* 'to writhe' does have a {-^N}$_1$ external argument (see (55) and (58) in §1.8.1).
32. I am assuming that the PP headed by *ot* 'from' is an adjunct rather than a {k^N}$_3$ argument; this assumption has no effect on this discussion.
33. The only systematic record in syntax of a sentence's diathesis-level operations is the suffixes affixed to **V** and their order, which is especially clear in the case of agglutinative languages.
34. This entails that expletives merge in syntax, but are not projected from **V**'s diathesis.

35. Dative *emu* '(for) him,' which is the preposed subject of the postposed infinitive-clause matrix-subject in square brackets, occupies the same spec-TP position that the expletive *it* does in the corresponding English sentence. If there were a null expletive in Russian, we could not capture this correlation.
36. A comparison of weather verbs in Russian and other Slavic languages demonstrates dramatically that argument structure cannot be predicted from lexical semantics: it is unpredictable whether a 'same' weather verb will be impersonal in a particular Slavic language. For instance, the most common way to state that it is raining in Russian is *Idet dožd'* (lit. 'goes rain'), where *dožd'* 'rain' is the nominative subject, while in Czech the corresponding sentence is subjectless: *Prší*.
37. Although the s-predicate's unlinked external **i** is always derived in the case of verbs, there is a class of pronouns that have $\{i^\wedge\text{-}\}_1$ as their initial, underived external argument: the Russian pronominal adjectives *sam* 'by oneself,' *odin* 'alone,' and *ves'* 'all' are basic s-predicate adjectives, which accounts for the unique set of morphosyntactic properties that makes them an invaluable diagnostic tool (see chapters 3–5).
38. The affix, which is the head of the derived s-predicate (see Di Sciullo and Williams 1987), introduces the categorial features that determine afPi's category (here the features introduced are adverbial); see chapter 3 for details.
39. The hypothesis that a lexical rule is the composition of two diatheses raises the following question: Are all the non-lexical diatheses headed by an affix? In other words, are lexical rules as I have just defined them affix-driven or dia-thesis-driven?
40. Two theta roles cannot occupy the same slot in **V**'s final diathesis, which derives the Theta Criterion: an argument in syntax cannot be assigned two theta roles. The N_1 head in (26a) automatically deletes when $\{i^\wedge N\}_1$ is internalized because **[V-af$_c$]** takes precedence over **N** in the c-tier. In general, the contents of an affix slot takes precedence over the contents of a competing lexical slot.
41. An unergative verb's initial diathesis is $\{\{i^\wedge N\}_1 \ \{\text{-}^\wedge\text{-}\}_2 \ \{\text{-}^\wedge\text{-}\}_3 \ \{\text{-}^\wedge V\}_4\}$ (cf. (9c)).
42. See Jaeggli 1986, Babby 1993a, Brody and Manzini 1990, Roberts 1987, Stowell 1992: 12, Grimshaw 1990.
43. See §1.9 for an explanation of the crucial fact that the right-displaced (internalized) **i** in causative and passive derivations behaves differently: **i** in passive derivations *obligatorily* relinks to $\{\text{-}^\wedge[\textbf{V-af}]\}_4$, whereas in causative derivations, **i** canonically relinks to $\{\text{-}^\wedge[\textbf{V-af}]\}_4$ only when **V** is ditransitive and there are thus no other options.
44. An unergative verb's diathesis is: $\{\{i^\wedge N\}_1 \ \{\text{-}^\wedge\text{-}\}_2 \ \{\text{-}^\wedge\text{-}\}_3 \ \{\text{-}^\wedge V\}_4\}$. As the following examples show, passivized unergative sentences are impersonal because there is no $\{j^\wedge N\}_2$ argument in **V**'s diathesis to externalize when **i** is dethematized (unergative verbs in Russian do not passivize).

    (i) German: Sonntags wird nicht gearbeitet. (Roberts 1987: 512)
          'One does not work on Sundays.'
    (ii) Turkish: Bu   hava-da   çık-ıl-maz.
               this   weather-in emerge-passive-negative/aorist
          'One does not go-out (of the house) in such weather.'

45. Affixation of **-sja** to a transitive **V** creates a derived unaccusative diathesis, i.e.:
    $\{\{i\wedge N\}_1 \{j\wedge N\}_2 \ldots \{-\wedge V\}_4\} > \{\{-\wedge N\}_1 \{j\wedge-\}_2 \ldots \{i \wedge [V\text{-sja}]\}_4\} \gg \{\{j\wedge N\}_1 \{-\wedge-\}_2 \ldots \{i \wedge [V\text{-sja}]\}_4\}$.
46. There is no need here for a syntactic rule of nP (DP)-movement: the obligatory relinking of unlinked internal **j** to external $\{-\wedge N\}_1$ in derived unaccusative and passive derivations is the diathetic analogue of syntactic A-movement (see Bresnan 1978, 1982, Stowell 1992: 18, Baltin and Collins 2001: ch. 8). A basic theorem of diathesis theory is: Operations that change grammatical relations are diathetic, not syntactic.
47. The **-sja** (**-s'**) suffix, which is diachronically a reanalysed accusative enclitic reflexive pronoun, has not become a passive suffix since it has a number of nonpassive functions. Its most productive use is the derivation of derived unaccusatives, of which passive is a subtype (see below).
48. For example, the verbs in the following sentences are derived unaccusatives that are not passive:

    Jama   napolni-l-a-s' vodoj   (*rabočimi).
    pit:NOM.F fill-PAST-F-SJA water:INST.F workers:INST.PL
    'The-pit filled with-water (*by-workers).'
    Naša družba ukrepi-l-a-s'.
    'Our friendship got-stronger.'

49. *privezennoe* is the *long form* (LF) of the **-en-** participle, which modifies *oborudovanie* in (31). LFs are *s-predicates* as defined above (see chapter 2 for details). The **-en-** participle's externalized theta role **j** in (31) is not linked to an external **N**: $\{j\wedge-\}_1$ of [$_\text{afP<j>}$*privezennoe s soboj*] is vertically bound *oborudovanie* and is thus not a potential binder of *s soboj*.
50. See Williams 1994 for argumentation that it is the theta roles themselves rather than the syntactic categories they are linked to that are involved in binding relations. See Roberts 1987 and Brody and Manzini 1990 for discussion of implicit theta roles and their syntactic effects.
51. *soboj* 'with/by-themselves' is the instrumental-case reflexive pronoun, which inflects for case only. Note that, unlike the *adjunct* PP *s soboj* 'with them(selves)' in (30c), the bare instrumental reflexive *by*-phrase *soboj* 'by themselves' is ill-formed:

    *Vse oborudovanie$_\text{j.NOM}$ bylo privezeno soboj$_\text{INST}$.
    'All the-equipment was brought by-themselves.'

    Assuming that the adjunct *s soboj* is bound by implicit **i**, it is not clear why this **i** cannot also bind the *by*-phrase *soboj*; only the personal pronoun *imi* is possible (see (30b)). But, given that Russian can reflexivize adjuncts (see (30a)), *Vse oborudovanie*$_\text{j.NOM}$ *bylo privezeno* **soboj*$_\text{INST}$ / *imi*$_\text{INST}$ tells us that the *by*-phrase is not an ordinary adjunct; see Grimshaw's (1990) notion of *argument adjunct*. The facts seem to fall out if **i** in passive derivations were assigned directly to the *by*-phrase instead of being made implicit and licensing the *by*-phrase. But there are problems with this hypothesis that space prevents me from pursuing.

52. $\{i\wedge\text{-}\}_3$ projects an ill-formed syntactic expression because only unlinked *external* theta roles $\{i\wedge\text{-}\}_1$ can be V-bound.
53. "…" indicates that the positions in question are irrelevant for the definition of the diathesis type.
54. According to Baker 1988a–b, the verb stem **V** raises to and *incorporates* with (adjoins to) **v**, creating [V-v].
55. Cf. the theory of *bare phrase structure* (Chomsky 1995b).
56. The movement of the direct object in (47), which creates the sentence's neutral (discourse-free) word order, is not obligatory. A great deal depends on *information structure* (topic, focus, etc.).
57. Russian morphological case provides evidence that there are three distinct types of 'abstract' case assigned to argument nPs: *structural* case, *theta* (semantic) case, which is assigned to $\{k\wedge N\}_3$ only, and *quirky* (lexical) case, which is assigned any one of **V**'s three arguments as an unpredictable c-selectional property (see Babby 1994a). Only quirky case is marked in **V**'s diathesis as a diacritic feature on **N** in the lower tier; Russian **V**s assign quirky case only to internal arguments.

See the following argument realizations (morphosyntactic paradigm) of the initial ditransitive diathesis of *napolnit'* 'to fill', which theta-selects **k** = material/substance, which is realized as the instrumental case in Russian when it projects from $\{k\wedge N\}_3$ to $[_{V'}\ V\ nP_k]$.

    a. Rabočie$_{i.\text{NOM}}$ napolnili jamu$_{j.\text{ACC}}$ vodoj$_{k.\text{INST}}$.   ('active' sentence)
       'The-workers filled the-pit with-water.'
    b. Jama$_{j.\text{NOM}}$ byla napolnena vodoj$_{k.\text{INST}}$ (rabočimi$_{\text{INST}}$).   (passive)
       'The-pit was filled with-water (by-the-workers).'
    c. Jama$_{j.\text{NOM}}$ napolnilas' vodoj$_{k.\text{INST}}$ (*rabočimi$_{\text{INST}}$).   (derived unaccusative)
       'The-pit filled with-water.'
    d. Jamu$_{j\text{ACC}}$ napolnilo vodoj$_{k.\text{INST}}$ (*rabočimi$_{\text{INST}}$).   (impersonal)
    e. Voda$_{k.\text{NOM}}$ napolnila (soboj$_{\text{INST}}$) jamu$_{j\text{ACC}}$ (*rabočimi$_{\text{INST}}$). (pseudo-active [no standard name])
       'Water filled the-pit (with-itself).'

58. Sentences like the following are problematic since their analysis depends on whether there is anything like dative shift or double-object constructions in Russian (see Babby 2005 for preliminary discussion of the syntactic representation of these sentences in Russian and English):

    Ona napominaet mne sebja molodogo.
    she:NOM reminds me:DAT.M self:ACC.M young:LF.ACC.M
    'She reminds **me** (of) **myself** (when I was) young.'

59. The derivation in (53) needs at least one more affix before the **[V-sja]** stem becomes a well-formed word, which stops the argument-structure phase of the derivation. This additional suffix in Russian can be the finite suffix **v** or a nonfinite paradigmatic suffix (e.g., the infinitive suffix **-ti**).

60. *korčilos'* = **korči-l-o-s'**, where **korči-** is the verb stem **V**, **-l-** is the finite past tense suffix, **-o-** is the non-agreement suffix, and **-s'** is the realization of **-sja** after vowels.
61. In the case of transitive **V**s with an {i^N}$_1$ external argument, affixation of **-sja** must be accompanied by dethematization or deletion of **i**, which licenses externalization (relinking to **N$_1$**) of **j**. My generalization is thus: affixation of **-sja** to a transitive **V** always creates a derived unaccusative diathesis; passive, middle, and *korčit'* **V**s are all subclasses of derived unaccusative stems.
62. (60a) can be thought of as a single diathesis with an optional external **N** or as the result of conflating two diatheses with the same internal structures but with different external arguments ({-^-} and {-^N$_1$}) into one diathesis by the parenthesis notation. This distinction will make no difference in what follows: it is a well-known fact that many **V**s have more than one diathesis in the mental lexicon.
63. Recall that **-en-**participles are not inherently passive: they are passive only when dethematized **i** is relinked to {- ^ [V-en]}$_4$. When **i** is *deleted*, the **-en-**participle is a stative/resultative derived unaccusative. E.g.: *On prostuž-en* 'He has-a-cold' is normally construed as the stative form of *On prostudi-l-sja* 'He caught-cold' rather than the short passive of *prostudit'*; cf. *Frukty legko portjatsja* 'Fruit spoils easily' ~ *Frukty isporč-en-y*$_{SF.PL}$ 'The-fruit is spoiled.'
64. All causative auxiliary verbs and affixes have an external argument of their own, which *displaces* the lexical **V**'s initial external argument when the two diatheses compose (see Sadler and Spencer 2001:228, Baker 1988). This entails that true causative auxiliary verbs, like causative suffixes, *compose* with their infinitive complements in argument structure rather than *merge* with them in syntax (see §4.12). Russian and English have only an *analytic causative construction*, which does not differ formally from the biclausal object-control structures discussed in chapter 4.
65. {i^N}$_1$, which is always displaced in causative derivations, has different morpho-syntactic realizations depending on the lexical **V**'s initial internal valence (i.e. positions 2, 3, and 4). Since **af$_c$** is the head of **[V-af$_c$]**, its external argument displaces **V**'s external argument.
66. See transitive *spešit'* 'to dismount' in Russian, which selects both an external and internal agent theta role and whose syntactic projection predictably has a causative reading: *General*$_{NOM}$ *spešil vsadnikov*$_{ACC}$ 'The-general dismounted the-riders = the-general had/made the-riders dismount.' Since the corresponding derived unaccusative sentence has only one agent (**j**), it does not have causative meaning: *Vsadniki spešilis'* 'The-riders dismounted.'
67. For a different view of causativization, see the introduction to Seuren 1974.
68. Note that when **i** of {i^N}$_1$ links to {-^[V-af$_c$]}$_4$, giving {i^[V-af$_c$]}$_4$, the **N** that **i** is intially linked to deletes, which is what we expect. Recall the following corollary of diathesis theory: when the corresponding slots in the diatheses of **V** and an affix are both filled, the affix always wins out over **V**: the properties of the head's diathesis take precedence over those of its complement's diathesis under composition.
69. Note that Russian quirky case is typically assigned to **N$_3$**; e.g., *lišit'* 'deprive' assigns accusative case to nP$_j$ and quirky genitive to nP$_k$.

70. Compare the same sentence with a bivalent transitive verb whose direct object is assigned accusative case:

> Baba-m$_{NOM}$ çocuğ-a$_{DAT}$ kitab-1$_{ACC}$ oku-t$_{CAUS}$-tu$_{PAST}$.
> father-my boy   book   made read
> 'My-father made the-boy read the-book.'

71. The only way to escape the confines of the diathesis is to relink **V**'s initial external **i** to {-^[**V-af**]}$_4$. Implicit **i** licenses a variety of *adjuncts*: the canonical *by*-phrase, case doubling (adjunction to the dative indirect object), manner adverbs, and, as we shall see in §1.11, possessive adjectives and genitive nPs in derived nominals.
72. Position-skipping seems to be motivated by the need to avoid certain types of case-based ambiguity or homophony (see Guasti 1997: 149 for discussion).
73. We see the same phenomenon in Italian:

> Faccio riparare la macchina al / dal meccanico.
> I-make to-repare the car   to / by the mechanic
> 'I had the mechanic repare the car.'

74. See chapter 4 for discussion of the affix-like properties of the auxiliary verb's diathesis. The formal differences between auxiliary and copula verbs are discussed in chapter 5. Explicit derivations involving auxiliary verbs must be put off until §4.12, where the derivation and internal structure of the [V$_{aux}$ + bare infinitive] construction is presented.
75. Chapter 3 is devoted to hybrid verbal categories: [$_{xPi}$ [$_{x'}$ [$_x$ V-x] [$_{VP}$ nP$_j$ [$_{v'}$ t$_v$ nP$_k$]]]], where **x** is a suffix with nonverbal categorial features. In DNs, x = n = af$_n$.
76. Compare the following (only the DN is a hybrid category):

> Derived nominal: [$_{nP}$ [$_{n'}$ [$_n$ V-n] VP]]
> Finite clause: [$_{vP}$ [$_{v'}$ [$_v$ V-v] VP]]
> Simple noun phrase: [$_{nP}$ [$_{n'}$ [$_n$ N-n] NP]]

I am claiming that the derivations of DNs and causative sentences are *formally* parallel, not that DNs have causative meaning: the derivation of DNs does not introduce a second agent argument.

77. The morphosyntax of DNs in Russian has many facets that cannot be dealt with here. We will not consider the mapping between *possessive adjectives* and **V**'s arguments in DNs like the following (*svoego* is a possessive reflexive pronoun that has *Putin* as its antecedent) (see Babby 1997a–b for details and references):

(i) Pervoj stranoj, kotoruju Putin posetil [$_{PP}$ posle [$_{DN}$ **svoego**$_{j.GEN}$ **izbiranija**$_{GEN}$ **prezidentom**$_{k.INST}$]], stala Belorusija.
'(lit.) Belorussia was the first country that Putin visited [after **his election president**]. Cf.

(ii) Izbrali$_{PL}$ ego$_{j.ACC}$ prezidentom$_{INST}$.
'[Unspecified-agent(s)] elected him president.'

78. The parallelism between the grammatical relations in finite clauses and the corresponding derived nominals is obscured in Russian by the fact that **V**'s external

argument is always displaced and nPs have only one structural case (genitive) to realize nPs that would be either nominative subject or accusative direct object in the corresponding clause. E.g.:

Ona$_{NOM}$ živet v gorode$_{LOC}$, zakrytom$_{LF.LOC}$ [$_{PP}$ dlja [$_{nP}$ poseščenija$_{GEN.SG}$ inostrancev$_{GEN.PL}$]].
she lives in city closed for visiting foreigners
'She lives in a city which is closed to visits by foreigners.'
[$_{nP}$ poseščenie$_{NOM}$ goroda$_{GEN}$ inostrancami$_{INST.PL}$]
'the-visiting of-the-city by-foreigners'

79. There are three basic types of genitive case in Russian: (i) lexical (quirky) genitive (e.g. *svobody* in (89)); (ii) structural adnominal genitive (e.g. *prestupnika* in (89); (iii) adjunct (posesive) genitive: e.g., *Mendeleeva* in [*tablica èlementov*$_{GEN}$ *Mendeleeva*$_{GEN}$] 'Mendeleev's table of elements' (note the *fixed* order of the two genitives).

80. The fact that the adnominal genitive in DN phrases canonically realizes the external argument of intransitive **V**s and the direct internal argument of transitive **V**s (cf. absolute case), while the external argument of transitive **V**s is realized as the 'oblique' *by*-phrase (cf. ergative case) suggests that the DN's internal case marking follows an ergative-absolute pattern (see Williams 1987, Lebeaux 1986, Safir 1987, Nunes 1993; Babby 1997a: §4.1). However, this case pattern is epiphenomenal, and no special ergative /absolute case pattern need be posited for DNs.

81. The following is another example of quirky case inheritance: *avtorom* is the adjunct instrumental-case *by*-phrase and *metodom* is the quirky instrumental case selected by *ovladet'* and its DN *ovladenie*:

[nP ovladenie$_{GEN}$ avtorom$_{INST}$ [metodom$_{INST}$ socrealizma$_{GEN}$]]
the-mastering author [method of-socialist-realism]
'The-mastering by-the-author of-the-method of-socialist realism.'

82. n, the head of nP in (90), is the nominalizing suffix; it 'assigns' structural genitive case to the nP in spec-VP, which is the nP-internal analogue of accusative case assignment to nP$_j$ in spec-VP by **v** (the finite verbal suffix), as in (91b). See in §3.2.3 for discussion of structural case assignment/checking.

83. Recall that *dethematization* involves the right-displacement (or deletion) of **V**'s external **i** theta role only, leaving $\{-\wedge N\}_1$ behind. In contrast, *internalization* involves the right-displacement of **V**'s entire $\{i\wedge N\}_1$ external argument. Both are diathesis-based operations. **V**'s external theta role is *implicit* when it is dethematized and relinked to $\{-\wedge [V\text{-af}]\}_4$.

84. Dethematized **i** in *passive* derivations cannot link to **V**'s first available $\{-\wedge-\}$ position because there is no categorial head in its c-tier for it to link to. This explains why dethematization always involves the relinking of **i** to $\{-\wedge [V\text{-af}]\}_4$, which is always initially available because $\{-\wedge V\}_4$ is always initially unlinked.

85. The fact that we find position-skipping in both French causative sentences and Russian DN phrases lends additional support to my main hypothesis, namely, the correctness of the diathesis's 2×4 structure.

86. Note that DN phrases with one structural genitive and one quirky genitive are perfectly well-formed: see (89) above.
87. Another kind of attachment ambiguity is possible: the second genitive can be construed as a modifier of the first rather than as a second argument of the DN, i.e. [*zaderžanie èmisarov*$_{GEN}$ *mjatežnikov*$_{GEN}$] can be read as 'the-detaining of the rebels' emissaries' or 'the-detaining of the emissaries by the rebels' or 'the detaining of the rebels by the emissaries.'
88. **X** in (110) represents a quirky-case nP, a PP, or an infinitive argument, which all canonically occupy the 3-position in **V**'s initial diathesis (see *lišit'* 'deprive' + accusative + quirky genitive above).
89. The fact that the verb *upravljat'* 'to-govern' and its DN *upravlenie* both assign quirky instrumental case to their internal argument is an automatic consequence of my hypothesis that both share **V**'s initial diathesis. In (113), *podražat'* and *podražanie* assign quirky dative case. In (114), *pol'zovat'sja* and *pol'zovanie* assign quirky instrumental case.
90. The Same-Case Filter in Russian is thus sensitive to the *type* of abstract case. See Haegeman 1997a: 60, 62, whose constraint is on "adjacent occurrences of identical *forms*." See also Nunes 1993: 388 and Bylinskij and Rozental' 1961: 305 for discussion of Same-Case Filter effects.
91. Note that nPs like [*mužčina* [*srednx let*] [*prijatnoj naružnosti*]] '(lit.) a-man of-middle-age of-pleasant appearance' and *tablica elementov Mendeleeva* 'Mendeleev's table of-elements' are well-formed despite the fact that they have two structural genitive nPs because they are *not* DN phrases and thus have rigidly fixed word order. This avoids the kind of mapping opacity common in DN phrases, where the combination of **V**'s argument structure and morphological case license relatively free word order.
92. A given **V**'s *alternations* are the set of morphosyntactic structures projected from the set of diatheses derived from its initial diathesis.
93. The *o-* prefix in (123) is related to the preposition *o* 'around, about.' Many but not all verbal prefixes in Russian are related to prepositions.
94. See Babby 2005 for discussion of the Indonesian applicative construction and its relation to *spray/load* verbs and double object syntax. See Payne 2006: §8.1.2.
95. See Mel'čuk and Xolodovič 1970, Xolodovič 1974, and Xrakovskij *et al.* 2004, who explore the typology of argument realization in the world's languages.
96. For example, we see in chapter 4 that the infinitive-forming suffix **-t'** in Russian is responsible for assigning quirky dative case to the subject nP of infinitive clauses.
97. Strictly speaking, diathesis-level operations should be characterized as 'diathesis driven' rather than 'affix driven' since there are derivations that appear to involve *headless diatheses* (i.e. {...{-^-}$_4$} (e.g., the 'service causative' in Russian (Babby 1993b) and the applicative-like double-object construction in English (Babby 2005)). However, it will have to be left to future research to determine whether these operations involve headless diatheses or diatheses with null affixal heads.

2 The argument structure of adjectives

1. **A** composes with at least one paradigmatic affix to form a *word*, the smallest unit of syntax. <i> denotes an unlinked external theta role that has been vertically bound.

    Russian aP_i functions exclusively as an *adjunct* and its unlinked external **i** must be V(ertically) bound; Russian aPs obligatorily merge with a form of the copula.

2. The following are examples of copulative verbs other than *byt'* 'be':

    (a) Prosto čudo, čto ona ostalas' živa$_{SF}$.
    '(It is) simply a-miracle that she remained alive.'
    (b) Stolovaja okazalas' pusta$_{SF}$.
    'The-diningroom turned-out-to-be empty.'

3. In §2.16 we will encounter empirical evidence that the copula *byt'* 'be' is introduced presyntactically as an argument-structure level operation (composition) rather than in syntax (merger and subject raising). (1a) will be replaced by [$_{aP}$ [a' [A-a] AP]], where aP is a *bare* adjective phrase, which has neither an unlinked external theta role nor a dedicated nP_i subject: the V_{cop} 'inherits' **A**'s {i^N}$_1$, and argument-structure level operations do not leave traces (see V_{aux} + bare infinitive phrase in chapter 4). But we will assume the s-clause structure in (1a) plus subject nP_i raising analysis until §2.16 for expository purposes. Note that in both cases, **A**'s {i^N}$_1$ is projected as the sentence's nominative subject and *byt'* + aP is the predicate.

4. Note that the relation between aP and AP (and nP and NP) is identical to that of vP and VP. More generally, all the lexical stems X- of inflected words are complements of affix-headed projections xP ('small x' is the affixal head of [X-x]): [$_{xP}$ nP_i [$_{x'}$ X-x [$_{XP}$ nP_j [$_{x'}$ t_x nP_k]]]].

5. **A** in Russian is also realized as the *predicate instrumental* (PI), which is treated in chapter 5; I will include the PI data here for comparative purposes.

    There is a fourth possibility: **A** can compose with the *non-agreeing* **-o** suffix when: (i) **A** is used impersonally (there is no subject to agree with), as in [*V podvale*]$_{PP}$ *bylo temn-o i syr-o* 'It was dark and damp in the-basement'; (ii) **[A-o]** is used as a manner adverb, which does not agree; (iii) the subject does not have inherent agreement features as in the case of CP and infinitive-clause subjects.

6. All s-predicates in Russian are *derived* except for the small class of pronominal adjectives including sam_i 'by oneself,' $odin_i$ 'alone,' and ves'_i 'all'; they will play an important diagnostic role in the chapters to follow.

7. It is demonstrated in chapters 3 and 4 that *control* can be reduced to *binding*, i.e., to *vertical binding* (the relation between the head and tail of a TBC), to *antecedent binding*, which does not involve a TBC, and to combinations of the two.

8. The terminology here may be confusing: "s-predicate" refers to the adjective's *form* (it has an unlinked **i**), not to its *function*. LFs, which are always s-predicates, occur nP-internally as attributive adjectives that modify the head noun, and nP-externally as depictive adjuncts (secondary predicates).

    Bear in mind that since the word order in Russian is free, many of the examples to follow are not direct projections of the main predicator's final diathesis (its Extended Lexical Projection); discourse-oriented scrambling may have occured.

9. Since participles in Russian are morphosyntactically deverbal adjectives, I will make special reference to them only when they differ systematically from primarily (lexical) adjectives (see §2.15 below).
10. Diathesis-based operations in Russian do not normally affect the lexical stem's *internal diathesis*, i.e., positions 2 and 3. This is not true of other languages: see §1.12 for details.
11. LFs and SFs of the same stem have the same lexical meaning and the differences in meaning attributed to them in (8a–b) derive from the disparate syntactic structures they head. The LF and SF suffixes themselves have no inherent semantic content: they lexicalize the syntactic structures that are responsible for the difference in meaning in (8a–b).
12. 'Predicate LF' is a useful descriptive term that denotes an xP-internal LF, which modifies the head x; it is xP that combines with the copula.
13. Below and in the following chapters, 'subject' means 'dedicated subject' unless otherwise indicated.
14. This section is limited to a strictly morphosyntactic explanation of the complementarity of LFs and SFs. I will thus not discuss specific adjectives whose LF and SF have developed different lexical meanings, adjectives that have only one of the forms (e.g. rad_{SF} 'glad'), or the on going diachronic changes involving the replacement of the SF by the LF and PI in colloquial Russian (see chapter 5). Stylistic differences between SFs and predicate LFs are discussed in Švedova 1952.
15. Note that the TBC accounts for the relation between case, control, and binding.
16. SF depictive adjectives were still possible as recently as the first third of the nineteenth century (see Kubík 1982: 187, Švedova 1952: 119, Bulaxovskij 1954: 323–329):

> Ja vyšel iz   ego doma [očen' vesel].   (1814)
> I left from his home very happy:SF.NOM.M
> 'I left his home [very happy].'

Speakers of modern Russian no longer produce such forms.

17. We shall see evidence below that (25) needs to be revised, i.e., $nP_{i.NOM}$ does not *merge* in spec-aP and raise to spec-V_{cop} in syntax. Rather *bylo* inherits [A-a]'s external argument (*vino*) when the diatheses of **A** and $\mathbf{V_{cop}}$ *compose*, which means that aP in (25) should be a bare aP since diathesis-level operations do not involve traces. Thus (25) is correct except for the nP trace in spec-aP. Only finite verbs and infinitives project [$_{xP}$ nP$_i$ x'$_{<i>}$] clausal structures in Russian syntax. See note 3.
18. Sentences like *On okazatsja prav$_{SF}$* 'He turned-out-to-be right' are not counter examples: the SF *prav* here is the main predicate, not a depictive: *okazat'sja* is functioning as a copulative verb (see note 2).
19. Only Russian infinitive clauses have PRO subjects, which are dative (see chapter 4).
20. Thus *Identification* in diathesis theory is the nP-internal instantiation of vertical binding (see Grimshaw 1990:71 and Spies 1990 for discussion of *Identification*).
21. An argument nP$_i$'s external theta role **i** is bound by the corresponding theta role of the verb. See Williams 1985.
22. The structure in (35) will be revised in the same way as (25): see note 17 and (36).

23. xP in (36a) is an s-clause whose subject nP$_i$ has moved out of xP to spec-vP$_{cop}$. xP in (36b) is a bare phrasal projection, which is neither an s-clause nor an s-predicate; x's {i^N}$_1$ is inherited by V$_{cop}$ when their diatheses compose. These distinctions play no role in this section: only the existence of xP and x's category are relevant.
24. The LF cannot be the predicate of impersonal (subjectless) sentences for essentially the same reason: its unlinked external theta role would remain unlinked: *Bylo xolodnoe$_{LF.N.SG}$ '(It) was cold.' The correct impersonal form is Bylo xolodn-o '(It) was cold,' where -o here is the non-agreeing form that occurs when agreement fails to occur, not the homophonous neuter singular SF.
25. *Head-suppression* avoids the repetition of easily recoverable nouns, and is found in some form in all languages. The term 'suppression' is descriptive, referring to the absence of a noun that could appear but whose presence would make the discourse infelicitous, e.g.:

    (i) Vino bylo [$_{nP}$ vkusnoe vino].
    'The-wine was good wine.'
    (ii) Nikita kupil zelenuju knigu, a Anna (kupila) beluju (?knigu).
    'Nikita bought a green book and Anna bought a white one / ?book.'

26. The preposition *s* 'with' c-selects instrumental case.
27. The verb *predšestvovat'* selects an object with lexical dative case. The dative singular feminine suffix -*oj* of *vynutoj* (which is the **-en-** participle of *vynut'* 'to extract') makes it possible to unambiguously associate **n** with *stranic*$_{GEN.PL.F}$ 'pages' in the matrix clause.
28. *Botinki*$_{ACC.PL}$ is *topicalized* by extraction from the bracketed direct object nP, stranding the attributive LF *grjaznye*$_{ACC.PL}$ as the nP's only overt constituent. The head of an nP in Russian can be *extracted* from nP for the same reason that it can be *suppressed*: both extraction and suppression are licensed by the LF's agreement morphology. What I am calling suppression is undoubtedly a null pronoun (pro).
29. *U nego ne vse doma* is an idiomatic expression meaning 'He is not all there (lit. at him not everything (is) at-home).'
30. *Rasstroena* is the SF stative/resultative participle of *rasstroit'sja* 'to get upset'; (52) is not passive.
31. In this use, *vy* is semantically singular but formally plural.
32. (t$_n$) = (42) or (43), i.e. aP = small clause or bare adjective phrase.
33. *Takoj* does not have SFs:

    Vy vse takoj$_{LF.NOM.M.SG}$ že (*takie$_{PL}$ že / ** tak$_{SF}$ že)
    'You (polite) are still the same'.

    Since *takoj* is an inherent aP$_i$ (LF adjunct) and thus cannot license the subject *vy*, the structure of the predicate nominal nP must be [$_{nP}$ [n' [$_{aP<i>}$ *takoj* že] **n**]].
34. Assuming that only projections of the same category and case can be conjoined with the conjunction *i* 'and', sentences like the following provide another kind of evidence that the predicate genitive is the modifier of a predicate nominal nP's suppressed head:

Mašina$_{\text{NOM.F}}$ byla$_{\text{F}}$ [$_{\text{nP}_{\text{NOM}}}$ **n** [$_{\text{aP}<i>}$ bol'šaja$_{\text{LF.NOM.F}}$]] i [$_{\text{nP}_{\text{NOM}}}$ **n** [$_{\text{nP}_{\text{GEN}}}$ dorogoj marki$_{\text{GEN.F}}$]]

'The-car was [large] and [of expensive make].'

35. *Prenebregat'* selects quirky instrumental case.
36. **-šč-** participles have LFs only and are thus inherent s-predicates; see chapter 3 for details.
37. Cf.: Takuju gibel'$_{\text{ACC.F}}$ ne mogut$_{\text{PL}}$ rassmatrivat' kak slučajnuju$_{\text{LF.ACC.F}}$.
    '(Unidentified people) cannot view such destruction as accidental.'
38. Recall that "(t$_N$)" in (79a) and elsewhere is an abbreviatory device indicating a choice between the following two structures (we must wait until §2.16 to see the evidence that will enable us to make a principled choice):

    [vP$_{\text{cop}}$ Vino$_i$ [$_{\text{v'cop}}$ bylo [$_{\text{aP}}$ (t$_N$) [$_{\text{a'}<i>}$ vkusno$_{\text{SF}}$]]]] =
    [vP$_{\text{cop}}$ Vino$_i$ [$_{\text{v'cop}}$ bylo [$_{\text{aP}}$ t$_N$ [$_{\text{a'}<i>}$ vkusno$_{\text{SF}}$]]]] (s-clause with raised subject) or
    [vP$_{\text{cop}}$ Vino$_i$ [$_{\text{v'cop}}$ bylo [$_{\text{aP}}$ [$_{\text{a'}<i>}$ vkusno$_{\text{SF}}$]]]] (bare aP phrase with
                                                                                inherited subject)
            wine   was   good

39. For further discussion, see Švedova 1948 and 1952, Tolstoj 1966, Stepanov 1981: 152, Babby 1975a and 1999, and Siegel 1976.
40. See: a. Naša elka vysokaja$_{\text{LF}}$. 'Our fir-tree is (a) tall (one).'
    b. Naša elka samaja vysokaja$_{\text{LF}}$. 'Our fir-tree is (the) tallest (one).'
    c. Naša elka vysoka$_{\text{SF}}$ dlja gostinoj. 'Our fir-tree is (too) tall for the living-room.'

    A sentence like (a) can be glossed 'Our fir tree is tall with respect to the height-norm of this type of tree.' Thus the predicate LF's point of reference is the class that the subject belongs to; the SF's point of reference is canonically supplied by a complement or the discourse context; it is unmarked in the Jakobsonian sense.
41. The predicate nominal analysis of the predicate LF requires an *output constraint* or *filter* to ensure that an ill-formed sentence like (i) is not derived from the well-formed structure in (ii) underlying it.

    (i) * *Ona umnyj.* 'She$_F$ (is) smart$_{\text{LF.M}}$.'
    (ii) *Ona čelovek umnyj.* 'She$_F$ (is) a smart$_{\text{LF.M}}$ person$_M$.'

42. The semantic distinction described here is being lost in colloquial spoken Russian, where the LF and PI are replacing the SF (see chapter 5).
43. The right edge of phrases and sentences is the focus (rhematic) position in Russian.
44. The ill-formedness of the PI in sentences like (91) is explained in §5.9.
45. While Russian reflexive pronouns do not inflect for gender and number, these features are overtly realized on the aP$_i$s that agree with them.
46. **-en-** is realized as *-en-*, *-n-*, or *-t-*.

    Imperfective **V** forms the passive by composing with the diathesis of the **-sja** suffix, which has no categorial features and thus does not affect **V**'s category; **-en-** carries adjectival categorial features. Both **-en-** and **-sja** suffixes create derived unaccusative diatheses.

47. -šč-participles too can be reanalysed as adjectives:

> Glaza u nee byli takie raspolagajuščie.
> '(Her) eyes were so prepossesing (such prepossesing ones).'

Cf. *raspolagat'* 'to-make someone well disposed.'
48. See Chvany 1975 for a complete analysis of *byt'* 'to-be' in Russian.
49. Sentences like *Buduči golodnoj*$_{PLF,}$ *devuška otpravilas' domoj* are discussed in chapter 5.
50. The adjective stem **golodn-** and the SF suffix **-a** compose to form a complete word *golodna*, which is inert with respect to all subsequent diathetic operations. Inertness is indicated by not using boldface in diathetic derivations.
51. Compare the syntax-level nP-movement analysis in (104) and the diathesis-level inheritance analysis in (105): the copula syntactically *merges* with the SF *s-clause* in (104) and the clause's dedicated subject nP$_i$ moves (raises) to spec-vP$_{cop}$, leaving a trace; in (105) (and (117)), the diathesis of the copula *composes* with the diathesis of the SF presyntactically.
52. If **-g**'s diathesis is composed before *buduči*'s, a *nonviable diathesis* results, i.e., a diathesis that projects an ill-formed syntactic structure.

3 Hybrid verbal adjuncts

1. See the hybrid structure of Russian *derived nominals* in §1.11 and §3.6. Russian has no gerundive nominals.
2. See Baker 2003: 324–325. Jackendoff's 1977 *deverbalizing rules* are an early attempt to capture the bipartite, upstairs-downstairs XP-in-xP structure of hybrid categories.
3. This is what we expect to find given the fact that the final, right-most suffix is canonically the 'head of the word' (see DiSciullo and Williams 1987).
4. The following is an example (**-eli** 'since' is the hybrid adverbial forming suffix, **gid-** 'go' is the verb stem):

> [O Prinston-a gid-eli] biz onu gör-me-di-k.
> he:NOM Princeton:DAT go-since we:NOM him:ACC see-NEG-PAST-FIRST.PL
> 'Since he went to-Princeton, we haven't seen him.'

5. Recall that the unspecified (blank) positions { ^ } in the diatheses of affixes, auxiliaries, and the copula are filled in (valued) by corresponding positions in the lexical-stem diathesis they compose with; <i> denotes a satisfied (V-bound) external theta role.
6. See Lavine and Freidin 2002, Moro 1997: 55, Kratzer 1996, and Grimshaw 2005, who treat certain suffixes as heads of functional projections.
7. **-šč-** has the following allomorphs: *-šč- ~ -vš- ~ -š*; **-en-** has three allomorphs: *-en, -n,* and *-t*.
8. **-en-**participles can be middle or passive but never active voice. This follows from the fact that **V**'s external **i** is *dethematized* as part of **-en**-participle formation. In contrast, **-šč-**participle formation does not involve **i**'s dethematization.
9. I assume that *expletives* like *there* and *it*, which are 'dummy' subjects (i.e., neither assigned a theta role nor c-selected by V) are *not projected from* **V**'s *diathesis*: they

are merged as place-fillers *in the syntax* of configurational languages like English when **V** is impersonal or when **V**'s dedicated subject is postposed. Thus the question of whether Russian impersonal sentences have a null expletive subject is a purely syntactic matter. My opinion is that Russian does not have expletives because its non-agreement verbal morphology and free word order make expletives unnecessary; e.g., in Russian existential sentences the preposed locative PP occupies the position that *there* does in English. See Perlmutter and Moore 2002, Babby 2002 (= 1989).

10. (23) reflects my decision in §2.16 to treat copula-introduction as diathesis-level composition (rather than syntactic-level merger + raising), which entails that afP in (23) is a *bare phrase* (no unlinked theta role, subject nP_i, or subject trace) rather than an afP s-clause.

    Bear in mind that the criterial distinction between the SF and the LF is that, in the former, the lexical stem's initial external $\{i\wedge N\}_1$ or derived external $\{j\wedge N\}_1$ argument remains intact, whereas in the latter, the stem's initial $\{i\wedge N\}_1$ or derived $\{j\wedge N\}_1$ is realized as an s-predicate $\{i\wedge\text{-}\}_1$ or $\{j\wedge\text{-}\}_1$.

11. See Babby 1993a for discussion of the additional **-n-**suffix in LF **-en-**participles.

12. The derivation of the SF **-en-**participle *napoln-en-a* in (23) is essentially the same as the derivation of the SF adjective in (2.118/119): the V_{cop} stem's diathesis composes with the SF's diathesis, inheriting its $\{i\wedge N\}_1$ external argument, which is why afP in (23) is a bare **-en-**participle phrase.

13. Enclitics like interrogative *li* 'whether' are *sentence-level* enclitics and, predictably, do not interact with **-sja**: *Nravitsja li vam*$_{DAT}$ *èto*$_{NOM}$? 'Do you like it?' (cf. **Nravit li sja vam èto*). Russian words affixed with **-sja** have the following internal structure: $[[[V\text{-af}]\text{-af}]_W\text{-sja}]_W$. Thus **-sja** adjoins to $[[V\text{-af}]\text{-af}]_W$, where **-af** here denotes **V**'s non-enclitic suffixes. This is precisely how agglutinating and enclitic suffixes behave in Turkish.

14. The dotted lines demarcate the derivation's main phases and have a purely expository function; bear in mind that $\{\text{-}\wedge\text{-}\}$ in a final diathesis does not project to syntax.

15. **(i)** in (29c) indicates that dethematized **i** is either relinked to $\{\text{-}\wedge[[V]\text{-sja}]\}_4$ (in passive derivations) or deleted (in middle derivations). There is a strong tendency for voice affixes and their diatheses to compose early in the derivation.

16. Externalization is the argument-structure analogue of NP-movement (raising) in syntax. My hypothesis is that all operations that alter grammatical (syntactic) relations are diathesis-based operations. In contrast, *syntactic* movement rules leave traces and are *grammatical-relation preserving* (e.g., *wh*-movement).

17. Recall that **-sja** is a word-level enclitic suffix and thus occurs at the end of the word (i.e., $[W\text{-sja}]_W$) despite the fact that it is the first suffix to compose with **V**.

18. The infinitive s-clause is the only nonfinite phrasal projection in Russian with a subject nP, which is assigned lexical dative case (see chapter 4). A case is *structural* if its probe (assigner/checker) is a functional head. *Case assignment* is being used as a descriptive term: case is not 'assigned' in syntax, it is *checked*.

19. The **-en-** suffix does not assign accusative case because in Russian (and English) it creates derived unaccusative diatheses, which, according to my analysis, have no N_2 linked to the **j** theta role. This accounts for the absence of accusative case assignment

to the direct object of passivized (**V-en-**) verbs: there is no direct object to assign it to. In other words, **-en-** has a detransitivizing effect in standard Russian. This analysis eliminates the need to claim that the **-en-** suffix absorbs accusative case (see Babby 2004 for discussion of *case absorption*). However, in standard Ukrainian we find the [**-en-**participle + accusative direct object] impersonal transitive passive construction (see Lavine 2000), which means that **-en-** in Ukrainian does not obligatorily create derived unaccusative diatheses and that [**V-en-**] can assign accusative case when there is an intact $\{j^\wedge N\}_2$ to project in [**V-en**]'s final diathesis. If participles/adjectives are chacterized as +V/+N and nouns as −V/+N, then it is the feature +V that licenses accusative case.

[$_{PP}$ P nP$_{ACC}$] is not problematic if the accusative case assigned by specific prepositions is lexical or semantic case rather than structural.
20. (32) provides conclusive evidence against the Case Resistance Principle, according to which, words that assign case cannot themselves be assigned case (see Stowell 1981, Blake 1994, Culicover 1997: 51).

The preposition *k* 'to' assigns dative case.
21. *Case feature percolation* can be thought of as a chain reaction – a chain of case-feature valuations, i.e., the successive valuation of contiguous *unspecified case features*, which we refer to as *case receptors*. Adjectives, participles, determiners, and quantifiers in Russian are canonically case receptors; *nP-internal case agreement* in Russian is the result of case-feature percolation (see Babby 1987).
22. Bowers (2002) argues that accusative case is assigned to the direct object of transitive verbs by the specialized functional head Tr (transitive), which comes between vP and VP. However, if my analysis of accusative case assignment is correct, there is no need to make our grammar more complex by adding another null-headed functional projection if the ones we already have can do the job.
23. It is routinely assumed that structural case is assigned by *spec–head agreement*; e.g., see Hornstein, Nunes, and Grohmann 2006: §4.3. If [V-af], which is created by a diathetic operation, is projected as the head of VP and then moved to head the afP projection, as suggested above, then accusative case assignment can be explained in terms of spec–head agreement (before [V-af] moves out of VP's head position).
24. Reflexive pronouns in Russian are inflected for case only, which creates potential binding ambiguities not encountered in English.
25. *__svoego__ is a reflexive possessive pronoun whose antecedent is the matrix subject *ona*.

We shall see in the second part of this chapter that gP$_i$ (the hybrid adverbial phrase) obligatorily adjoins to VP$_i$. This fact provides additional evidence that there is an encapsulated VP in -šč-participle phrases: the gP$_i$ in (40d) is contained in the participle phrase (and V-bound by its external **i** theta role), which therefore must contain a VP$_i$ for gP$_i$ to adjoin to.
26. Williams 1994 argues that binding is a relation between theta roles, not between the nPs they are linked to, which correctly predicts the possibility that *unlinked external theta roles can bind reflexive pronouns* (as in (39)–(40) and in passive sentences like (31) in chapter 1; see §3.7 below).

27. (41) presupposes my analysis of *argument* noun phrases as nP$_i$ and *predicate nominal* noun phrases as nP (see (38) and §2.6.2).
    Subjects are felt to be the prototypical antecedent of reflexive pronouns for the simple reason that they are by far their most common antecedent by virtue of being the highest nP$_i$ in the sentence and thus asymmetrically c-commanding all the other object and adjunct nPs.
28. Given this analysis, bound reflexives are represented as [$_{nP<i>}$ *sebja*] and are thus 'controlled' in the sense that they are V-bound; their antecedent is the head of their TBC (cf. control of LF depictive adjuncts in §2.6.0, of gP$_i$ in §3.3, and subject-controlled infinitive s-predicates in chapter 4).
29. There are other problems with (43): LFs cannot be main predicates (see chapter 2). There is nothing preventing PRO$_i$ from having a non-local antecedent-binder, which, however, incorrectly predicts that the matrix subject is a potential binder. Only the maximally local s-predicate + V-binding analysis is descriptively adequate.
30. (41) also correctly predicts the absence of a reflexive pronoun in the following sentence (*my*$_{NOM}$ 'we' and *dlja nas* 'for us' are coreferential and *my* c-commands *dlja nas*):

    (i) My xranili v tajne [$_{nPj.ACC}$ [$_{aP<i>}$ unizitel'noe$_{LF.ACC.N}$ dlja nas$_{GEN}$] otkrytie$_{ACC.N}$].
        we kept in secret   humiliating   for us   revelation
        'We kept the revelation [(which was) humiliating for us] a secret.'
    (ii) *My xranili v tajne [$_{nPj.ACC}$ [$_{aP<i>}$ unizitel'noe$_{LF.ACC.N}$ dlja sebja$_{GEN}$] otkrytie$_{ACC.N}$].
        we kept in secret   humiliating   for ouselves revelation

    The sentence in (ii) is ungrammatical because the smallest TBC in which reflexive *sebja* is bound is headed by *otkrytie*, not its 'intended' antecedent *my*. Hence only a pronoun (*nas*) is possible here.
31. What appear to be SF **-em**-participles are *departicipial adjectives*, e.g.:

    Èlektron$_{M.SG}$ principal'no$_{ADV}$ nenabljuda-em$_{SF.M.SG}$.
    'The-electron (is) in-principle   unobserv- able.'

32. This small class of underived s-predicate adjectives will be referred to collectively as SAM$_i$. They are adjuncts and agree in case, gender, and number with the head of the TBC in which they are vertically bound.
33. The suffix **-g-** has the following exponents: *-a*, *-v*, *-všis'*, and *-či*, which are canonically predictable in terms of the V they compose with.
34. For example: *Vrač predpisal bol'nomu ležat'*, [$_{gP<i>}$ *ne vstavaja s posteli*] 'The-doctor ordered the-patient to-stay-in-bed [without getting up]': gP$_i$ can refer to either the matrix subject *vrač* 'doctor' or, in its most natural reading, to the PRO subject of the object-controlled infinitive *ležat'*, depending on whether gP$_i$ is low-adjoined to VP$_i$ in the infinitive clause or is high-adjoined to the VP$_i$ in the finite matrix clause. My analysis predicts that if a sentence contains three VP$_i$ nodes, it will be three ways ambiguous (when gP$_i$ is sentence-final). gP$_i$ is frequently left-dislocated to avoid this type of attachment ambiguity.
35. See Babby and Franks 1998 for discussion of hybrid adverbials in nonstandard Russian.

36. Bear in mind that while gP_i is always controlled by the external theta role **i** of the verbal category it adjoins to, this **i** may itself be $\{i^\wedge\text{-}\}_1$. See gP_i embedded in afP_i below.
37. See Franks 1995: 259–265, Greenberg 1996, and Babby and Franks 1998 for details.
38. See §4.8 for additional argumentation, based on infinitive s-predicates, that V-binding is a *maximally local relation* and, therefore, a maximal projection intervening between the bindee and potential binder blocks V-binding, creating an ill-formed (uncontrollable) structure.
39. Unless, of course, we were to claim that PRO, which would be the head of the TBC in which [$_{afP<i>}$ *p'janyj*] 'drunk' were V-bound and with which it would agree in case, is nominative. However, there is no evidence to support the hypothesis that subjects of nonfinite clauses can be nominative in Russian (see chapter 4).

    Note that *Čto ty skažeš' žene*, [$_{gP<i>}$ *vernuvšis' domoj tak pozdno* [$_{aP<i>}$ *p'janyj*$_{LF.NOM.M}$]]? is a grammatical sentence; I am claiming that it is the clausal structure in (60d) that is ungrammatical; cf. (60b).
40. PRO_i is never nominative in Russian (see chapter 4).
41. See §2.12 and §4.6 for discussion of kP_i and its diagnostic properties.
42. gP_i would have to adjoin to V'_j to be *object-controlled*, i.e, have the direct object as the head of its TBC.

    Must the fact that gP_i obligatorily adjoins to its matrix VP_i (giving [$_{VPi}$ $VP_{<i>}$ $gP_{<i>}$] or [$_{VPi}$ $gP_{<i>}$ $VP_{<i>}$]) be stipulated or can it be shown to follow from the general principles that determine the placement of adverbial expressions in the sentence? While an explicit answer to this question would take us too far afield, my impression is that gP_i's VP_i adjunction follows from the general rules governing the placement of all controllable adverbial adjuncts.
43. There is another piece of evidence that nP_{GEN} in (69b) must have moved from its initial lower position in spec-VP: its genitive case is the 'genitive of negation,' which is assigned (checked) by *ne* to nPs it precedes and c-commands (see Babby 1980).
44. According to the analysis proposed in §1.11.1, derived nominals have an encapsulated VP_i to which gP_i can adjoin: [$_{nPi}$ [$_{n'<i>}$ [V-n] [$_{VP<i>}$ $VP_{<i>}$ $gP_{<i>}$]]]. See §3.6.
45. Note that the gP_i in (71) can be preposed, just as it can in finite matrix clauses, left-adjoining to afP_i, i.e., [$_{afPi}$ $gP_{<i>}$ afP_i]:

    My uvideli šerifa, [$_{afP<i>}$ [$_{gP<i>}$ razdvigaja tolpu] [$_{afP<i>}$ šestvujuščego k nam]].
    we saw sheriff   parting   crowd   walking   toward us

    This word order avoids the potential attachment ambiguity inherent in gP_i's sentence-final position.
46. Vertical binding, which is a maximally local relation, always takes precedence over antecedent binding.

    We shall see in chapter 4 that *Anna poprosila menja*$_{ACC.M}$ *sdelat' uborku samogo*$_{ACC.M}$ is grammatical in colloquial Russian, where the object-controlled infinitive complement is a vertically bound $infP_i$ *s-predicate*, not an s-clause with a PRO subject.
47. See Comrie 1974, Schein 1982, Neidle 1988, Greenberg 1983, Franks and Hornstein 1992, and Franks 1995 for discussion. We will be concerned with SAM_i in TBCs

whose head is the matrix verb's external argument, which will be referred to as 'diagnostic SAM$_i$.'
48. Bear in mind that case assignment and agreement is clause-internal.
49. The dative case of the matrix object *mne* in (92a) is *not* responsible for dative *samomu* (underlining denotes coreference). In the following sentence, *lišit'* assigns quirky genitive case to nP$_k$; the infinitive complement of nouns is always an s-clause):

> Otsutstvie$_{NOM}$ ščeli$_{GEN}$ v doskax$_{LOC}$ lišilo menja$_{ACC}$ [$_{nP}$ vozmožnosti$_{GEN}$ [$_{infP}$ PRO$_{i.DAT}$ vse$_{ACC}$ uvidet', [$_{gP<i>}$ samomu$_{DAT}$ (*samogo$_{ACC}$) ostavajas' nezamečennym]]].
>
> 'The-absence of-a-hole in the-boards deprived me [of-the-opportunity [to-see everything [without being seen myself]]].'

50. In (94b) [$_{gP<i>}$ **sama**$_{NOM.F}$ *ne trevožas' o sud'be bednyx*] is high-adjoined to the finite VP$_i$ and the nominative subject *mat'* 'mother' is thus the head of the TBC in which gP$_i$ is V-bound. In (95a), however, [$_{gP<i>}$ **samomu**$_{DAT.M}$ *ne trevožas' o sud'be bednyx*] is low-adjoined to the infinitive VP$_i$ and the dative PRO subject is the head of the TBC in which gP$_i$ is V-bound.
51. In this sentence the gP$_i$ in the infinitive clause is preposed and adjoined to a position between the complementizer *čtoby* 'in order to' and the infinitive clause.
52. The following is an additional example of an infinitive clause complement of a noun:

> No bylo že [$_{nP}$ vremja [$_{infP}$ PRO naučit'sja žit'   **odnomu**, [$_{gP<i>}$ spravljajas'
> but was prt   time:NOM   to-learn to-live alone:DAT.M   coping
> so vsemi problemami]]].
> with all problems
>
> 'But (it) was indeed [time [to-learn to-live **alone**, [coping with all the-problems]]].'

53. PRO$_{DAT}$ in (93) is antecedent bound by the dative matrix object *mne* 'me,' which is not part of the TBC in which *samomu* is vertically bound.

For discussion of nonstandard uses of hybrid adverbial phrases, see Ickovič 1982, Babby and Franks 1998, and Lapteva 2003: 266–272.

54. The pronoun *vse* in (93) normally preposes and adjoins to inf' in the information-structure phase of the syntactic derivation. This is not shown in (97) for expository purposes.
55. The examples in (98) are from Ickovič 1982:145. DNs containing gP$_i$ are used primarily in written Russian.
56. See §2.6.2, where it is proposed that argument nPs have an external theta role and that the binding of reflexive [$_{nPi}$ *sebja*] can be reduced to V-binding by the head of its minimal TBC. It was pointed out above that gP$_i$ behaves like a verbal anaphor.

I assume without discussion that the *adjunct* by-phrase *pravitel'stvom GDR* 'by the government of the GDR' in (102) cannot directly bind *na sebja* 'on (it)self,' which is an *argument* of the **-en**-participle; cf. (100b), where implict **i** is the head of the gP$_i$'s TBC: there is no *by*-phrase here to bind gP$_i$.

4 The derivation and control of infinitives

1. I assume that cross-linguistic variation in the syntax of infinitives resides in the diatheses of the language-specific infinitive-forming affixes. For example, the infinitive suffix **-mek** in Turkish has nominal features, which accounts for the fact that it can be assigned case by the matrix verb; the infinitive in Turkish is thus a hybrid category:

   (O)   o-nu   sevmeğ-e   devam-ediyor.
   he:NOM her:ACC to-love:DAT continues
   'He continues to-love her.'

2. vP here designates the finite affix projection; 'small v' is the finite affixal head of vP.
   I assume that stems and affixes are not *syntactic* primitives, and, therefore, that **V** does not *raise* and adjoin to its affixal head **-inf**; rather, as in the preceding chapters, **V** and **-af (-inf)** compose as part of a diathetic operation, and **[V-inf]**, which is a syntactic primitive (fully formed word), starts the syntactic derivation as the head of infinitive's encapsulated VP and raises to head infP. We will see the motivation for this analysis in §4.12, where I discuss the 'bare VP' infinitive complement of auxiliary verbs.

3. We will be concerned initially only with infinitive s-predicates and s-clauses. The analysis of auxiliary verbs and their bare infinitive complements is presented in §4.12.

4. Given (1c), bare infinitive phrases cannot be bound; see §4.12 for discussion of their control.

5. This is an important distinction since the head and tail of a TBC must be clause mates.

6. Recall that a corollary of diathesis theory is that syntactic operations cannot alter a clause's grammatical relations or the cases that lexicalize them.

7. These sentences have a finite form of the copula, which is null in the present tense and is realized as the neuter singular *bylo* in the past:

   (a) V avtobus bylo ne vojti.
       in bus:ACC was:N NEG to-enter
       'It was not possible (for us, him, etc.) to get on the bus.'
   (b) Emu   ne   privykat'   bylo   k čudačestvam   svoix   kolleg.
       him:DAT NEG to-get-used was:N to peculiarities:DAT of-his(reflex) colleagues
       'He was not able to-get-used (it was not possible for him to-get-used) to the peculiarities of his colleagues.'

   The reflexive possessive pronoun *svoix* in (b) is coreferential with the infinitive's dative subject *emu*.

8. Sentences like the following seem to provide evidence that the overt dative subject in sentences like (8) and (9) is an argument of the modal head **m**. This would mean that the overt dative subject of **m** in (8) and (9) binds the PRO_{DAT} subject of its infinitive clause complement (note that *potušiš'* 'extinguish' in (a) is a *finite* form of the verb with a modal interpretation, not an infinitive):

   (a) Ploščad'   požara   byla   takoj,   čto **odnomu**   ne   potušiš'.
       area:NOM.F fire:GEN was:F such.PI.F that alone:DAT.M NEG extinguish.2nd.SG
       'The fire was so big that one could not put it out alone.' (Izvestija, July 23, 1981, p. 6)

The dative case of *odnomu* in (a) can be explained as agreement with the putative (null) dative subject in spec-mP. When *potušiš'* has simple future (non-modal) meaning, *odin* is predictably nominative since the mP is not present.

9. This approach requires a principle like the Minimal Distance Principle (MDP), which stipulates that PRO must be antecedent-bound by the closest matrix argument. In practice, this principle's function is to ensure that the matrix subject is not construed as PRO's antecedent when the matrix verb selects an object as well as the infinitive complement.
10. See Culicover and Jackendoff 2001 for argumentation against the raising analysis of control.
11. See Sigurdsson 1991 for Icelandic evidence that PRO is case-marked; Laurencot 1997 for a Russian-based discussion of Chomsky's proposal that PRO has "null case."
12. Both Generalized Phrase-structure Grammar and Lexical Functional Grammar posit a bare infinitive VP in control structures.
13. Don't confuse the bare VP hypothesis mentioned above with the bare complement of auxiliary verbs in §4.12.
14. A verbal category is an $[_{xP}...[V-x]\ VP]$.
15. Neidle 1988 attempts to save the clause-only analysis by claiming that the PRO subject of Russian infinitive clauses is nominative when subject-controlled and dative when object-controlled.
16. See [+subject control] and [+infinitive clause] in (2).
17. The overt subject nP of an infinitive clause in English is case-marked by *for*; see the glosses in (12a–c).
18. For additional examples, see (6), (7), and the following:

    $[_{PP}$Vmesto $[_{nP}$ togo $[_{CP}$ čtoby $[_{infP}$ **PRO**$_{DAT}$ pozvonit' **samomu**$_{DAT}$]]]], on načinaet u vsex sprašivat', vyzvali$_{PL}$ li miliciju.
    '[Instead of calling **himself**], he starts asking everyone whether anyone summoned the police.'

19. Cf. On$_{i,NOM}$ xotel $[_{infP<i>}$ ezdit' tuda odin$_{NOM}$ (*odnomu$_{DAT}$)] 'He wanted [to-go there alone].'
20. The MDP is superfluous in a theory with bottom-to-top syntactic merger (which is an automatic consequence of the right-to-left merger of **V** and its arguments encoded in the diathetic representation of argument structure [see chapter 1]): the matrix direct object merges with the infinitive phrase, both of which are arguments of matrix [V-v] *before* the subject merges in spec-vP. If binding takes place wherever its conditions are met ('cyclically'), the direct object nP$_j$ in ditransitive structures like (29)/(30) will bind the PRO subject of the infinitive clause before the subject *Eva* merges, at which point PRO is already bound by the matrix ego$_{ACC}$.
21. There are two independent sources of the dative case in (32): (i) the verb *pomoč'* 'to-help' assigns quirky dative case to its reflexive object *sebe* 'self'; (ii) the infinitive suffix assigns dative case to **V**'s external argument *nam*, and dative *samim* agrees with *nam*.

22. Since *kak* is a functor and does not assign theta roles or case, it inherits its unlinked external **i** from its nP$_i$ complement (see DiSciullo and Williams 1987: 37); see §2.6.2 and §2.12.
23. Bowers 1993 argues that *as* is the lexical realization of the head of the PrP (predicate phrase).
24. In *Ego vstretili kak geroi* '(UNIDENTIFIED PEOPLE)) met him$_{ACC.SG}$ like heroes-$_{NOM.PL}$,' kP$_i$ is adjoined to VP$_i$, not to V'$_{(i)j}$, i.e., [$_{VPi}$ VP$_i$ kP$_{<i>}$], and is thus V-bound by **i** (subject-controlled), not by **j** (object-controlled). Cf. gP$_i$, which obligatorily merges with VP$_i$, accounting for its obligatory control by matrix **i**.
25. Note that *ego* in (45) has been moved to spec-TP. *Vstretili* in (49) has already moved from VP to v, leaving a trace/copy.
26. Younger Russian speakers find sentences like (51) to be hypercorrect or infelicitous, preferring accusative *sel'dej* or even the default nominative *sel'di*; see §4.6.1 for discussion of this phenomenon. But see the following sentence from L. Vasil'eva (Kremlevskie Ženy 1992):

> ...na avtobuse, kotorogo$_{GEN}$ prixoditsja ždat' i [v nem tesnit'sja, kak **sel'-djam**$_{DAT}$ v bočke]
> '(lit.)...on a-bus, which (we) have to-wait-for and [to-crowd-together in it like **herrings** in a-barrel]'

27. The quirky-case dative object *durakam* has preposed to spec-TP and *ne ugrožaet* has raised to T; the postposed subject [*opasnost'*$_{NOM}$ *isčeznut' kak vidu*$_{DAT}$] is actually in situ in spec-vP. This word order is discourse neutral when an object is topicalized.

   In the following example, dative *kak rabyne* 'like a-slave$_{DAT}$' agrees in case with the dative PRO subject of the infinitive *rabotat'* not with matrix dative object *mne* 'me' because [$_{infP}$ PRO$_{DAT}$ *rabotat' kak rabyne*$_{DAT}$] is the matrix subject:

> Oni dumajut, čto mne$_{DAT}$ nravitsja [$_{infP}$ **PRO**$_{DAT}$ rabotat' kak **rabyne**$_{DAT}$].
> they think   that to-me   likes   to-work like a-slave
> 'They think that I like to work like a slave.'

We see in §4.8.3 that infinitive phrase subjects must be clauses.
28. *Pervyj* 'first' may behave as SAM$_i$ or an adjective (which means that *pervyj* is not a reliable diagnostic); cf. (a) and (b):

   a. Po zakonam gostepriimstva ona predostavila emu [$_{nP}$ pravo [$_{infP}$ **PRO**$_{DAT}$ **pervomu**$_{DAT}$ idti v duš]].
   'According to the rules of hospitality, she granted him [$_{nP}$ the right [$_{infP}$ to-shower **first**]].'
   b. Darvin$_{NOM}$ ponimal [$_{nP}$ važnost' [$_{infP}$ **PRO**$_{DAT}$ **pervym**$_{INST}$ realizovat' cennuju ideju$_{ACC}$]].
   'Darwin understood [the-importance [of-actualizing (lit. to-actualize) a valuable idea **first**]].'

   See Švedova and Lopatin 1989: 480.

29. The lack of an isomorphic mapping relation between case and control has been construed as evidence that control is not a basic component of the grammar (see Williams 2003).
30. The direct object [$_{nP}$ *potrebnosti*$_{GEN}$ *ljubit' kogo-to*$_{ACC}$ *samomu*$_{DAT}$] 'the-need to-love someone himself' in (76) has been preposed.
31. Reflexive binding in (a) and (b) provides additional evidence that *čtoby*+ infinitive phrases must be s-clauses: they have a PRO subject which binds the reflexive pronoun in C's complement (*ved'* is a discourse particle [prt]; subnumbers indicate coreference):

    (a) Ved' on   tjaželovat, čtoby ego   nesti   na **sebe**.
         prt he:NOM too-heavy C   him:ACC to-carry on self
         (lit.)'He is too-heavy (for one) to-carry him on self / He is too heavy to carry on your back.'
    (b) Ved' on$_1$ tjaželovat, [$_{CP}$ čtoby [$_{infP}$ **PRO**$_2$ ego$_1$ nesti na **sebe**$_2$]].

The PRO$_2$ subject of the infinitive clause is the only possible binder of the reflexive pronoun *sebe* (overt *on/ego* 'he/him' as binder gives the wrong reading); PRO$_2$ here is uncontrolled and has arbitrary reference.

32. Compare the following copula sentences: the dative of *samomu* could not be explained if the infinitive did not head an s-clause. Note too that the putative PRO subject in (b) is the head of the TBC in which the gP$_{<i>}$ is V-bound: there is no other option.

    a. [$_{nP}$ Čto-to novoe dlja Artema] – [$_{infP}$ **PRO samomu**$_{DAT}$ stat' žertvoj šantaža].
       '(It is) [$_{nP}$ something new for Artem] [$_{infP}$ to-become the-victim of-blackmail **himself**].'
    b. [$_{nP}$Lučšij sposob razgovorit' kogo-to$_{ACC}$] – [$_{infP}$ **PRO**$_{i.DAT}$ pomalkivat' **samomu**$_{DAT}$, [$_{gp<i>}$vynuždaja drugogo$_{ACC}$ govorit']].
       '[$_{nP}$ The best way to get someone to talk] (is) [$_{infP}$ to be silent **yourself** [(thereby) making the other (person) talk]].'

33. The following sentence demonstrates the same phenomenon with the *ni...ni* 'neither...nor' conjunction:

     Ja ne   xoču ni   terjat'   ee$_{ACC.F}$, ni byt'   poterjannym$_{PI.M}$ **samomu**$_{DAT.M}$.
     I   NEG want neither to-lose her   nor to-be lost   **myself**
     'I don't want to lose her nor (do I want) to-be lost **myself**.'

34. See Dubinskij *et al.* 2000 for discussion of conjunction as [XP *and* [$_{XP}$ PRO...]].
35. I leave it to future research to explain why Russian speakers find SAM$_i$ in conjoined infinitive complements natural only when it is adjoined to the second conjunct.
36. Recall that gP$_i$ always adjoins to its matrix VP$_i$, which is itself the complement of an affixal head. This explains the fact that gP$_i$ is always 'subject-controlled.'
37. In colloquial Russian, where the infinitive complement of an object-control verb can be an s-predicate, SAM$_i$-in-gP$_i$ is predicted to be accusative or dative, depending on the matrix direct object nP's case (see §4.7). Thus α in (105) can be nominative, dative, or accusative.

38. The pronominal matrix direct object *vse* 'everything' in (106) preposes and adjoins to matrix v', which produces the neutral word order. This is not shown in (107) for expository reasons.
39. Recall that the infinitive complement of a noun is always an s-clause (see §4.8.1).
40. See Timberlake 1974, which paved the way for the anlysis presented here. I am ignoring the modal meaning in sentences like (115) since it does not affect my conclusions.
41. The [nominative direct object + infinitive] word order in these sentences is the preferred order; see Franks and Lavine 2006 for an explanation of a similar phenomenon in Lithuanian. It is tempting to claim that the nominative direct object *ta ruxljat'* raises to spec-vP, where its nominative case feature can be checked by proximate T. But we see the same [nominative direct object + infinitive] word order in (122), which does not appear to be motivated by T's nominative checking ability (see Franks and Lavine 2006). I leave this problem to future research.
42. Another example of a subcategorized adjunct is *vosprinjat' ser'ezno (prinimat' vser'ez)* 'to-take seriously': *Ja ne vosprinjal ser'ezno istoriju*$_{ACC}$ 'I didn't take the-story seriously.' The distinction between subcategorized adjuncts and complex predicates is touched upon in §1.13.
43. Since (136) accounts for **V**'s syntactic behavior in more than one language, I assume that it must somehow be related to the lexical semantics of *obeščat'* and *promise*.
44. The term 'bare infinitive complement' is also used to refer to the *to*-less infinitive complements of auxiliary verbs in English: *I must (*to) go*. Since the distribution of the bare infinitive phrase is similar in both languages, I will assume below that the analysis proposed for Russian bare infinitives is valid for its English counterpart.
45. We know that V$_{aux}$ and lexical **V** *compose* presyntactically rather than merge in syntax because [V$_{aux}$ + bare infinitive] feeds passivization, which is an affix-driven diathesis-level operation: the output of syntactic operations cannot feed diathesis-level operations. In the following examples, *dolžen* 'must' is an auxiliary adjective and *nameren* 'intend' is an ordinary lexical adjective with an infinitive complement: *dolžen* inherits the passive diathesis's externalized {j^N}$_1$ whereas *nameren* cannot because it is not an auxiliary and has its own external argument.

    (i) a. On dolžen napisat' stat'ju   za nedelju.
          'He must write   the-article in a-week.'
       b. On nameren napisat' stat'ju   za nedelju.
          'He intends to-write the-article in a-week.'
   (ii) a. Stat'ja   dolžna byt' napisana im   za nedelju.
          'The-article must   be written   by-him in a-week.'
       b. *Stat'ja   namerena byt' napisana im   za nedelju.
          *'The-article intends to-be written   by-him in a-week.'

46. Cf. **On može*t/xočet* [$_{infP}$ PRO$_i$ *prijti segodnja*].
47. This derivation does not exclude the merger of a null expletive in syntax (see Perlmutter and Moore 2002). But it does assume that expletives are not projected from **V**'s diathesis. Expletives are lexical items that do not have diatheses and are

merged as syntactic place-holders in the syntax of configurational languages like English that realize the grammatical relations encoded in **V**'s diathesis in terms of syntactic positions. Note that {-^-} does not project to syntax from any position in a **V**'s final diathesis.

48. I am assuming that [*peresta-l-o tošnit'*] moves to v to check its tense (*-l-*) and agreement (*-o*) features.

5 Deriving the predicate instrumental

1. "PI" should be read as "the predicate instrumental of adjectives and participles"; whatever is said here of adjectives holds for participles unless otherwise indicated. See Bailyn 2001, Franks and Hornstein 1992, Nichols 1981, and Hinterhölzl 2001 for discussion of the PI's putative semantic contribution to the sentence, which I will only touch on. Implicit in this chapter is the assumption that the predicate instrumental of nouns needs to be treated separately.

2. According to native speakers, the PI and the LF in (1) are both natural, with no systematic difference in meaning; the SF is felt to be formal style. See chapter 2 for the analysis of the LF and SF.

    One of the most difficult problems encountered in analyzing the distribution of PI ~ LF ~ SF is that native speakers vary widely in their acceptability judgments. This is because the system is changing, with the PI spreading at the expense of the LF and SF (see below).

    Since it is difficult to tell whether copula + PI sentences like (1a) are, like the LF, a predicate nominal with a null head, i.e., copula + [$_{nP.PI}$ **n** PI], or, like the SF, copula + aP$_{PI}$ (where aP is a *bare* adjective phrase, not an adjective small clause; see §2.16), we will focus on the other constructions, where the relations are clearer.

3. It was shown in chapter 2 that LFs and SFs are both derived from the adjective stem's (**A**) diathesis. LFs project s-predicates (afP$_i$); SFs, which always compose with the copula, project bare adjective phrases ([$_{afP}$ af']), which have neither an external nP nor an unlinked external **i** since the copula *inherits* the SF's {**i^N**}$_1$ argument (see §2.16 and §4.12). In this chapter, PI = afP$_{PI}$, LF = afP$_{LF}$, and SF = afP$_{SF}$; **-af** heads the afP maximal projection in which the common AP projection is contained. **A** is the stem of the lexical adjective, which composes with **-af**, creating the composite head [A-af]$_{af}$ when their diatheses compose.

4. SAM$_i$ is never PI, which is an automatic consequence of the analysis of the PI proposed below.

5. Sentences like the following are discussed below:

    (a) Anna$_{NOM.F}$ prosila$_F$ ego$_{ACC.M}$ byt' **gotov**$_{SF.NOM.M}$ otpravit'sja.
    Anna   asked   him   to-be ready   to-depart.
    (b) Ona$_{NOM.F}$ učityvala$_F$ ego sposobnost'$_{ACC}$ byt' **sčastliv**$_{SF.NOM.M}$ **sam**$_{NOM.M}$. (*samomu$_{DAT}$).
    'She took-into-consideration his ability to-be happy himself.' (see (11c))
    (c) Anna prosila ego$_{ACC.M}$ byt' gotovogo$_{LF.ACC.M}$ otpravit'sja.

6. [$_{nP.DAT}$ *trem vzroslym ljudjam*] 'three grown people' is the dative subject of the conjoined infinitive clauses in (6).

7. We saw in chapter 2 that V_{cop} + LF is ungrammatical unless the LF is modifying the null head of a predicate nominal nP.
8. In sentences like (i), the predicate is a null-headed predicate nominal nP (see chapter 2), which is assigned the *predicate instrumental of nouns*. The overt adjective *vkusnym* thus agrees with the null head **n** of nP in instrumental case, which means that the predicate instrumental of nouns *is* an active case feature and that the adjective agreeing with it is an LF attributive adjective, which agrees in case, gender, and number with the head of its TBC. My hypothesis is that the PI of adjectives in (ii) is different from instrumental case LFs.

   (i) Vino$_{NOM.N}$ bylo [$_{nP.PI}$ [$_{n'}$ [$_{n'}$ **n**] [$_{afP<i.>LF}$ vkusnym$_{LF.INST.N}$]]].
   'The-wine was [good].'
   Note that (ii) is parallel to the SF.
   (ii) Vino$_{i.NOM.N}$ bylo [$_{afPPI}$ [af' vkusnym$_{PI.N}$]].

9. Boldface in these examples highlights the words under discussion; boldface in phrase-structure representation indicates TBC links.
10. The following sentence demonstrates that dative *samomu* in (12) does not agree in case with dative *emu*, which is the preposed matrix object of *ugrožaet*:

    (i) Ego$_{ACC}$ ustrašaet [$_{nPNOM}$ vozmožnost' [$_{infP}$ PRO$_{DAT}$ byt' arestovannym$_{PI}$ **samomu**$_{DAT}$]].
    '(lit.) [The-possibility [to be arrested himself]] scares him.'

    Here the matrix verb's preposed object nP is accusative rather than dative. See (53)/(54) in §4.6.
    I assume that *emu* in (12) preposes to spec-TP and is thus high enough to c-command and control (antecedent-bind) the PRO subject of the infinitive clause complement of the postverbal nominative subject noun *opastnost'*; (12) is the sentence's neutral word order:

    (ii) [$_{TP}$ Emu$_{DAT}$ [$_{T'}$ ugrožaet [$_{vP}$ [$_{nP.i}$ opasnost'$_{NOM}$ PRO$_{DAT}$ byt' arestovannym$_{PI}$ samomu$_{DAT}$] v']]].
    him threatens danger to-be arested himself

11. $\{ \wedge (\text{-})\}_1 = \{ \wedge \text{-}\}_1$ or $\{ \wedge \}_1$. Hence $\{ \wedge \text{-}\}_1 + \{ i \wedge N\}_1 > \{i \wedge \text{-}\}_1$; $\{ \wedge \}_1 + \{i \wedge N\}_1 > \{i \wedge N\}_1$.
12. The following sentence is grammatical but felt be to less felicitous than the same sentence with the PI :

    Ona$_{NOM}$ učityvala ego [$_{nP.ACC}$ sposobnost' [PRO$_{DAT}$ byt' sčastliv$_{SF.NOM.M}$ sam$_{NOM.M}$ (*samomu$_{DAT}$)]].
    'She took-into-consideration his ability to-be happy himself.'

    It is nominative *sam* that is problematic. We shall return to this type of sentence below.
13. It is this selectional restriction that accounts for the ill-formedness of hybrid adverbials formed from impersonal verbs, the external argument of which is $\{\text{-}\wedge\text{-}\}_1$.
14. See "(-)" in the derivation of the PI in (20).

15. [Λ af$_{SF/PI}$] in (35c) is a well-formed *word* and is thus *inert*, i.e., it cannot be affected by subsequent diathetic operations. This solves a potential problem later in the derivation: when the **-g-** suffix is introduced, only the copula stem **bud-** (V_{cop}) is available to compose with it.
16. There is no point in speculating about what the case of PRO in (42) might be since the only nonfinite verbal clause in Russian is the infinitive clause (whose dative subject is selected by the infinitive-forming suffix).
17. The corresponding masculine is:

    On$_{NOM.M}$ ne umeet byt' gordym$_{PI.M}$ sam$_{NOM.M}$ / *samomu$_{DAT.M}$.
    he NEG knows-how to-be proud himself

18. Cf. Babyonyshev 1996, who argues that genitive NPs are "caseless" in Russian, i.e, "genitive NPs do not check Case in the syntax at all" (see Harves 2002: 49–54).
19. See Hinterhölzl 2001, Bailyn 2001 for discussion of the putative semantic distinction in sentences like (2a–b).
20. *vospol'zovat'sja* selects quirky instrumental case.
21. Švedova and Lopatin 1989: 480 cite sentences like the following in which the depictive *-en*-participle can be either PI or dative (agreeing with overt dative subject *nam* 'us'); they note that the dative is both colloquial and archaic:

    Ne sidet' že nam$_{DAT.PL}$ zapertymi$_{PI.PL}$ / zapertym$_{DAT.PL}$.
    neg to-sit prt us locked-up
    '(lit.) We cannot just sit locked-up.'

22. We saw in chapter 2 that SFs cannot function as depictive adjectives.

Bibliography

Aissen, J. and D. Perlmutter. 1983. Clause reduction in Spanish. In D. Perlmutter (ed.), *Studies in Relational Grammar I*, 360–403. The University of Chicago Press.
Alsina, A. 1996. *The Role of Argument Structure in Grammar: Evidence from Romance*. Stanford, Ca.: CSLI Publications.
Ambrazas, Vytautas. 1997. *Lithuanian Grammar*. Vilnius: Baltos Lankos.
Anderson, S. 1982. Where's morphology. *Linguistic Inquiry* 13, 571–612.
Apresjan, Ju.D. 1967. *Eksperimental'noe Issledovanie Semantiki Russkogo Glagola*. Moscow: Nauka.
⎯⎯ 1974. *Leksičeskaja Semantika: Sinonimičeskie Sredstva Jazyka*. Moscow: Nauka.
Arad, Maya. 1995. On the projection of ditransitive verbs. *University College of London Working Papers in Linguistics* 7, 215–233.
Aranovich, Raúl and Jeffrey Runner. 2001. Diathesis alternations and rule interactions in the lexicon. In K. Megerdoomiam and L. Bar-el (eds.), *West Coast Conference on Formal Linguistics* 20, 15–28. Stanford: The Centre for the Study of Language and Information, Stanford University.
Babby, L.H. 1974. Towards a formal theory of 'part of speech'. In R. Brecht and C. Chvany (eds.), *Slavic Transformational Syntax*, 151–181. Ann Arbor: Michigan Slavic Materials.
⎯⎯ 1975a. *A Transformational Grammar of Russian Adjectives*. The Hague: Mouton.
⎯⎯ 1975b. A transformational analysis of transitive *-sja* verbs in Russian. *Lingua* 35, 297–332.
⎯⎯ 1976. Review of A.A. Xolodovič (ed.), *Tipologija Passivnyx Konstrukcij: Diatezy i Zalogi*. *Language* 52, 698–701.
⎯⎯ 1978. Participles in Russian: attribution, predication, and voice. *International Review of Slavic linguistics* 3, 5–25.
⎯⎯ 1979. The syntax of gerunds in Russian. In Linda Waugh and Frans Von Coetsem (eds.), *Contributions to Grammatical Studies*, 1–41. Leiden: E.J. Brill.
⎯⎯ 1980. *Existential Sentences and Negation in Russian*. Ann Arbor: Karoma.
⎯⎯ 1983. The relation between causative and voice: Russian vs. Turkish. *Wiener Slawistischer Almanach* 2, 61–88.
⎯⎯ 1986a. Departicipial adverbs in Russian. In A.L. Crone and C.V. Chvany (eds.), *New Studies in Russian Language and Literature*, 9–26. Columbus: Slavica Publishers.

1986b. The locus of case assignment and the direction of percolation: case theory and Russian. In R. Brecht and J. Levine (eds.), *Case in Slavic*, 170–219. Columbus: Slavica Publishers.

1987. Case, prequantifiers, and discontinuous agreement in Russian. *Natural Language and Linguistic Theory* 5, 91–138.

1989. Subjectlessness, external subcategorization, and the projection principle. *Zbornik Matice srpske za filologiju i lingvistiku* 32(2), Novi Sad, 7–40 (reprinted in *Journal of Slavic Linguistics* 2002).

1993a. A theta-theoretic analysis of *-en-* suffixation in Russian. *Journal of Slavic Linguistics* 1, 3–44.

1993b. Hybrid causative constructions: benefactive causative and adversity passive. In Comrie and Polinsky 1993, 343–367.

1994a. Case theory. In C. P. Otero (ed.), *Noam Chomsky: Critical Assessments*, Vol. I: *Linguistics (tome II)*, 630–652. London: Routledge.

1994b. Nestandartnye strategii vybora padeža, zadavaemogo sintaksičeskim kontekstom. *Voprosy Jazykoznanija* 2, 43–75.

1994c. A theta-theoretic analysis of adversity impersonal sentences in Russian. In S. Avrutin, S. Franks, and L. Progovac (eds.), *Formal Approaches to Slavic Linguistics: The MIT Meeting*, 25–67. Ann Arbor: Michigan Slavic Publications.

1996. Inflectional morphology and theta role suppression. In J. Toman (ed.), *Formal Approaches to Slavic Linguistics: The College Park Meeting*, 1–34. Ann Arbor: Michigan Slavic Publications.

1997a. Nominalization, passivization, and causativization. *Die Welt der Slaven* 42, 201–251.

1997b. Nominalization in Russian. In W. Browne (ed.), *Formal Approaches to Slavic Linguistics 4: The Cornell Meeting (1995)*, 54–83. Ann Arbor: Michigan Slavic Publications.

1998a. Subject control as direct predication: evidence from Russian. In Ž. Bošković, S. Franks, and S. Snyder (eds.), *Annual Workshop on Formal Appoaches to Slavic Linguistics (the Connecticut Meeting 1997)*, 17–37. Ann Arbor: Michigan Slavic Publications.

1998b. Adjectives in Russian: primary vs. secondary predication. In K. Dziverek, H. Coats and C. Vakareliyska (eds.), *Formal Approaches to Slavic Linguistics: The Seattle Meeting*, 1–16. Ann Arbor: Michigan Slavic Publications.

1999. Adjectives in Russian: primary vs. secondary predication. In K. Dziwerek, H. Coats, and C. Vakareliyska (eds.), *Annual Workshop on Formal Approaches to Slavic Linguistics: The Seattle Meeting (1998)*, 1–16. Ann Arbor: Michigan Slavic Publications.

2001. The genitive of negation: a unified analysis. In S. Franks *et al.* (eds.), *Formal Approaches to Slavic Linguistics 9 (The Bloomington Meeting)*, 39–55. Ann Arbor: Michigan Slavic Publications.

2002. Author's preface to reprint of Subjectlessness, external subcategorization, and the projection principle (= Babby 1989). *Journal of Slavic Linguistics* 10 (1–2), 341–388.

2005. Argument structure, case, double object syntax. In S. Franks *et al.* (eds.), *Formal Approaches to Slavic Linguistics: The South Carolina Meeting*, 27–41. Ann Arbor: Michigan Slavic Publications.

2006. Transitivity and antitransitivity. In Robert A. Rothstein, Ernest Scatton, and Charles E. Townsend (eds.), *Studia Caroliensia*, 13–26. Bloomington, Ind.: Slavica Publishers.

2008. Prolegomenon to any future typology of impersonal sentences in Russian. In D. Gerdts, J. Moore, and M. Polinsky (eds.), *Hypothesis A and Hypothesis B: Papers in Honor of David M. Perlmutter*. Cambridge, Mass.: MIT Press.

Babby, L.H. and S. Franks. 1998. The syntax of adverbial participles in Russian revisited. *Slavic and East European Journal* 42, 483–515.

Babyonyshev, M. 1996. Structural Connections in Syntax and Processing: Studies in Russian and Japanese. Doctoral Dissertation, MIT.

Bach, E. and B.H. Partee. 1980. Anaphora and semantic structure. In Jody Kreiman and Almerindo E. Ojeda (eds.), *Papers from the Parasession on Pronouns and Anaphora*, 1–28. Chicago Linguistics Society.

Bailyn, J. 1995a. A Configurational Approach to Russian "Free" Word Order. Doctoral Dissertation, Cornell University, Ithaca, N.Y.

1995b. Underlying phrase structure and "short" verb movement in Russian. *Journal of Slavic Linguistics* 3, 13–58.

2001. The syntax of Slavic predicate case. In G. Jager *et al.* (eds.), *ZAS Papers in Linguistics*, 22, 1–23.

2006. Against the scrambling anti-movement movement. In J. Lavine, S. Franks, M. Tasseva-Kutktchieva, and H. Filip (eds.), *Formal Approaches to Slavic Linguistics: The Princeton Meeting*, 35–49. Ann Arbor: Michigan Slavic Publications.

Baker, M. 1985. The mirror principle and morphosyntactic explanation. *Linguistic Inquiry* 16, 373–415.

1988a. Theta theory and the syntax of applicatives in Chichewa. *Natural Language and Linguistic Theory* 6, 353–389.

1988b. *Incorporation: A Theory of Grammatical Function Changing*. The University of Chicago Press.

1997. Thematic roles and syntactic structure. In Haegeman 1997a, 73–137.

2001. *The Atoms of Language: The Mind's Hidden Rules of Grammar*. New York: Basic Books.

2003. *Lexical Categories*. Cambridge University Press.

Baltin, M. and C. Collins. 2001. *The Handbook of Contemporary Syntactic Theory*. Oxford: Blackwell.

Birjulin, A.B. 1994. *Semantika i Sintaksis Russkogo Impersonala: Verba Meterologica i ix Diatezy (Specimina Philologiae Slavicae, Band 102)*. Munich: Verlag Otto Sagner.

Blake, Barry J. 1994. *Case*. Cambridge University Press.

1990. *Relational Grammar*. London: Routledge.

Bobaljik, J.D. 2001. The implications of rich agreement: why morphology doesn't drive syntax. In K. Megerdoomiam and L. Bar-el (eds.), *West Coast Conference on*

Formal Linguistics 20, 82–95. Stanford: The Centre for the Study of Language and Information, Stanford University.
Borer, Hagit. 2001. Morphology and syntax. In Spencer and Zwicky 2001, 151–190.
Bošković, Z. 1997. *The Syntax of Nonfinite Complementation*. Cambridge, Mass.: MIT Press.
Bowers, J. 1981. *The Theory of Grammatical Relations*. Ithaca, N.Y.: Cornell University Press.
    1993. The syntax of predication. *Linguistic Inquiry* 24, 591–656.
    2001. Predication. In M. Baltin and C. Collins (eds.), *The Handbook of Contemporary Syntactic Theory*, 299–333. Oxford: Blackwell.
    2002. Transitivity. *Linguistic Inquiry* 33, 183–224.
    2006. Arguments as relations. Cornell University manuscript.
    2007. Argument categories. Handout from the Workshop on Argument Structure and Syntactic Relations, University of the Basque Country Vitoria-Gasteiz, Spain, May 23, 2007.
Bowers, J. and U. Reichenbach. 1979. Montague grammar and transformational grammar: a review of *Formal Philosophy: Selected Papers of Richard Montague*. *Linguistic Analysis* 2, 195–245.
Brecht, R. and C. Chvany (eds.). 1974. *Slavic Transformational Syntax*. Michigan Slavic Materials 10. Ann Arbor: Michigan Slavic Publications.
Bresnan, J. 1978. A realistic transformational grammar. In M. Halle, J. Bresnan, and G. Miller (eds.), *Linguistic Theory and Psychological Relaity*, 1–59. Cambridge, Mass.: MIT Press.
    1982. The passive in lexical theory. In J. Bresnan (ed.), *The Mental Representation of Grammatical Relations*, 3–86. Cambridge, Mass.: MIT Press.
Brody, M. and M.R. Manzini. 1990. On implicit arguments. In R. Kempson (ed.), *Mental Representations*, 105–130. Cambridge University Press.
Bulaxovskij, L.A. 1954. *Russkij Literaturnyj Jazyk Pervoj Poloviny XIX Veka*. Moscow: Učpedgiz.
Butt, M. and T.H. King. 2000. *Argument Realization*. Stanford: CSLI Publications.
Bylinskij, K.I. and D.E. Rozental'. 1961. *Literaturnoe Redaktirovanie*. Moscow: "Isskustvo."
Channon, R. 1979. The status of 3–2 advancement in Russian. In P. Clyne, W. Hanks, and C. Hofbaur (eds.), *Papers from the Fifteenth Regional Meeting of the Chicago Linguistics Society*, 53–59. Chicago Linguistics Society.
Chomsky, N. 1970. Remarks on nominalization. In R. Jacobs and P. Rosenbaum (eds.), *Readings in English Transformational Grammar*, 184–221. Waltham, Mass.: Ginn and Co.
    1981. *Lectures on Government and Binding*. Dordrecht: Foris.
    1986. *Knowledge of Language: Its Nature, Origin, and Use*. New York: Praeger.
    1988. *Language and Problems of Knowledge: The Managua Lectures*. Cambridge, Mass.: MIT Press.
    1989. Some notes on economy of derivation and representation. In Itziar Laka and Anoop Mahajan (eds.), *Functional Heads and Clause Structure*, MIT Working Papers in Linguistics 10. Cambridge, Mass.: MIT Press.

1991. Some notes on economy of derivation and representation. In B. Freidin (ed.), *Principles and Parameters in Comparative Grammar*, 417–454. Cambridge, Mass.: MIT Press.

1995a. *The Minimalist Program*. Cambridge, Mass.: MIT Press.

1995b. Bare phrase structure. In G. Webelhuth (ed.), *Government and Binding and the Minimalist Program*, 383–439. Oxford: Blackwell.

Chvany, C. 1975. *On the Syntax of BE-sentences in Russian*. Cambridge, Mass.: Slavica.

Cinque, G. 1980. On the extraction from NP in Italian. *Journal of Italian Linguistics* 1, 47–99.

Clark, R. 1990. *Thematic Theory in Syntax and Interpretation*. London: Routledge.

Comrie, B. 1974. The second dative: a transformational approach. In R. Brecht and C. Chvany (eds.), *Slavic Transformational Syntax*, 123–150. Ann Arbor: Michigan University.

1980. Nominalization in Russian: lexical noun phrases or transformed sentences. In C. Chvany and R. Brecht (eds.), *Morphosyntax in Slavic*, 212–220. Columbus: Slavica Publishers.

1985. Causative verb formation and other verb-deriving morphology. In T. Shopen (ed.), *Language Typology and Syntactic Description III: Grammatical Categories and the Lexicon*, 309–48. Cambridge University Press.

1989. *Language Universals and Linguistic Typology: Syntax and Morphology*. The University of Chicago Press.

Comrie, B. and M. Polinsky (eds.). 1993. *Causatives and Transitivity*. Amsterdam: John Benjamins.

Cook, W.A. 1989. *Case Grammar Theory*. Washington, D.C.: Georgetown University Press.

Corbett, G., N. Fraser, and S. McGlashan (eds.). *Heads in Grammatical Theory*. Cambridge University Press.

Cowper, Elizabeth. 1992. *A Concise Introduction to Syntactic Theory*. The University of Chicago Press.

Culicover, Peter. 1997. *Principles and Parameters: An Introduction to Syntactic Theory*. Oxford University Press.

Culicover, P. and R. Jackendoff. 2003. Control is not movement. *Linguistic Inquiry* 34, 493–512.

Culicover, P. and W. Wilkins. 1986. Control, PRO, and the Projection Principle. *Language* 62, 120–153.

Diatezy i Zalogi. 1975. Tezisy konferencii "Strukturno-tipologičeskie metody v sintaksise raznosistemnyx jazykov" (21–23 oktjabrja 1975 goda). Akademija Nauk (Leningradskoe Otdelenie), Institut Jazykoznanija: Leningrad.

DiSciullo, A.M. and E. Williams. 1987. *On the Definition of Word*. Cambridge, Mass.: MIT Press.

Dolinina, I.B. 1990. Zalog i diateza: kriterii razgraničenija. In V.V. Klimov (ed.), *Soprjažennost' glagol'nyx kategorij*. 56–67. Leningrad: Leningradskoe Otdelenie Instituta Jazykoznanija AN SSSR.

Dubinsky, S. *et al.* 2000. Functional projections and predicates: experimental evidence from coordinate structure processing. *Syntax* 3, 182–214.

Epstein, S. D., E. M. Groat, R. Kawashima, and H. Kitahara. 1998. *A Derivational Approach to Syntactic Relations*. Oxford University Press.
Ferrell, P. 2005. *Grammatical Relations*. Oxford University Press.
Fillmore, C. J. 1968. The case for case. In E. Bach and R. Harms (eds.), *Universals in Linguistic Theory*, 1–89. New York: Holt, Rinehart & Winston.
Franks, S. 1985. Matrices and Indices: Some Problems in the Syntax of Case. Doctoral Dissertation, Cornell University.
  1995. *Parameters of Slavic Morphosyntax*. Oxford University Press.
Franks, S. and N. Hornstein. 1992. Secondary predication in Russian and proper government of PRO. In R. Larson, S. Iatridou, U. Lahiri, and J. Higginbotham (eds.), *Control and Grammar*, 1–50. Dordrecht: Kluwer.
Franks, S. and J. Lavine. 2006. Case and word order in Lithuanian. *Journal of Linguistics* 42, 239–288.
Freidin, R. 1975. The analysis of passives. *Language* 51, 384–405.
Giorgi, A. and G. Longobardi. 1991. *The Syntax of Noun Phrases*. Cambridge University Press.
Glovinskaja, M. Ja. 1996. Aktivnye processy v grammatike. In E. A. Zemskaja (ed.), *Russkij Jazyk Konca XX Stoletija (1985–1995)*, 237–302. Moscow: "Jazyki Russkoj Kul'tury."
Graudina, L. K., V. A. Ickovič, and L. P. Katlinskaja. 1976. *Grammatičeskaja Pravil'nost' Russkoj Reči*. Moscow: Nauka.
Greenberg, G. 1983. Another look at the second dative and dative subjects. *Linguistic Analysis* 11, 167–218.
  1996. Developments in linguistic theory: the analysis of gerunds and infinitives in Russian. *International Journal of Slavic Linguistics and Poetics* 39–40, 66–102.
Grimshaw, J. 1979. Complement selection and the lexicon. *Linguistic Inquiry* 10, 279–326.
  1990. *Argument Structure*. Cambridge, Mass.: MIT Press.
  2005. *Words and Structure*. Stanford, Calif.: CSLI Publications.
Guasti, M. T. 1997. Romance causatives. In Haegeman 1997b, 124–144.
Haegeman, L. 1995. *Introduction to Government and Binding Theory*. Oxford: Blackwell.
Haegeman, L. (ed.). 1997a. *Elements of Grammar: Handbook of Generative Syntax*. Dordrecht: Kluwer.
  1997b. *The New Comparative Syntax*. London: Longman.
Hale, Ken and Jay Keyser. 2002. *Prolegomenon to a Theory of Argument Structure*. Cambridge, Mass.: MIT Press.
Harves, S. 2002. *Unaccusative Syntax in Russian*. PhD Dissertation, Princeton University.
Hinterhölzl, L. 2001. Semantic constraints on case assignment in secondary adjectival predicates in Russian. In G. Jager *et al.* (eds.), *ZAS Papers in Linguistics* 22, 99–112.
Hoffman, M. C. 1991. The Syntax of Argument-structure-changing Morphology. Doctoral Dissertation, MIT.
Hornstein, N. 1999. Movement and control. *Linguistic Inquiry* 30, 69–96.
Hornstein, N., J. Nunes, and K. Grohmann. 2006. *Understanding Minimalism*. Cambridge University Press.

Ickovič, 1982. *Očerki Sintaksičeskoj Normy*. Moscow: Nauka.
Isačenko, A.V. 1963. Transformacionnyj analiz kratkix i polnyx prilagatel'nyx. In T.N. Mološnaja (ed.), *Issledovanija po Strukturnoj Tipologii*, 61–93. Moscow: Izd. Akademii Nauk USSR.
Jackendoff, R. 1975. Morphological and semantic regularities in the lexicon. *Language* 51, 639–671.
  1977. *X-bar Syntax: A Study of Phrase Structure*. Cambridge, Mass.: MIT Press.
  1987. The status of thematic relations in linguistic theory. *Linguistic Inquiry* 18: 369–411.
Jaeggli, O. 1986. Passive. *Linguistic Inquiry* 17, 587–622.
Jakobson, Roman. 1957 = 1984. Shifters, verbal categories, and the Russian verb. In L. Waugh and M. Halle (eds.), *Roman Jakobson: Russian and Slavic Grammar Studies*, 41–58. Berlin: Mouton.
Junghanns, U. and G. Zubatow. 1997. Syntax and information structure of Russian clauses. In W. Browne, E. Dornisch, N. Kondrashova, and D. Zec (eds.), *Formal Approaches to Slavic Linguistics: The Cornell Meeting*, 289–319. Ann Arbor: Michigan Slavic Publications.
Kamynina, A.A. 1980. O sintaksičeskoj svjazi deepričastij v sovremennom ruskom jazyke. In V.E. Krasnyx (ed.), *Problemy Učebnika Russkogo Jazyka kak Inostrannogo: Sintaksis*, 296–305. Moscow: "Russkij Jazyk."
Keenan, E. 1976. Towards a universal definition of "subject." In C.N. Li (ed.), *Subject and Topic*, 303–333. New York: Academic Press.
  1985. Passive in the world's languages. In T. Shopen (ed.), *Language Typology and Syntactic Description: Clause Structure*, 243–281. Cambridge University Press.
Keyser, S. and T. Roeper. 1984. On the middle and ergative constructions in English. *Linguistic Inquiry* 15, 381–416.
Klaiman, M.H. 2005. *Grammatical Voice*. Cambridge University Press.
Klein, E.H. and I.A. Sag. 1985. Type-driven translation. *Linguistics and Philosophy* 8, 163–201.
Kozinskij, I.Š. 1983. *O Kategorii "Podležaščee" v Russkom Jazyke*. Moscow: Institut Russkogo Jazyka AN SSSR.
  1985. Koreferentnye svjazi infinitivnyx oborotov v russkom jazyke. In V.S Xrakovskij (ed.), *Tipologija Konstrukcij s Predikatnymi Aktantami*, 112–116. Leningrad: Nauka.
Kratzer, A. 1996. Severing the external argument from its verb. In J. Rooryck and L. Zaring (eds.). *Phrase Structure and the Lexicon*, 109–136. Dordrecht: Kluwer.
Kubík, M. 1982. *Russkij Sintaksis v Sopostavlenii s Češskim*. Prague: Státní Pedagogické Nakladelství.
Kustova, G.I., K.I. Mišina, and V.A. Fedoseev. 2005. *Sintaksis Sovremennogo Russkogo Jazyka*. Moscow: Academa.
Lapteva, O.A. 2003. *Živaja Russkaja Reč's Teleèkrana*. Moscow: URSS.
Larson, R. 1988. On the double object construction. *Linguistic Inquiry* 19, 335–392.
  1991. *Promise* and the theory of control. *Linguistic Inquiry* 22, 103–139.

Larson, R., S. Iatridou, U. Lahiri, and J. Higginbotham (eds.). 1992. *Control and Grammar*. Dordrecht: Kluwer.

Lasnik, H. and J. Uriagereka. 2005. *A Course in Minimalist Syntax*. Oxford: Blackwell.

Laurencot, E. 1997. On secondary predication and null case. In M. Lindseth and S. Franks (eds.), *Annual Workshop on Formal Approaches to Slavic Linguistics (the Indiana meeting)*, 191–206. Ann Arbor: Michigan Slavic Publications.

Lavine, J. 1997. A lexicalist perspective of valency changing operations in Russian and Czech. *The Prague Bulletin of Mathematical Linguistics* 68, 5–34.

Lavine, J.A. 2000. Topics in the Syntax of Nonagreeing Predicates in Slavic. Doctoral Dissertation, Princeton University.

Lavine, J. and R. Freidin. 2002. The subject of defective T(ense) in Slavic. *Journal of Slavic Linguistics* 10 (1–2), 251–287.

Lebeaux, D. 1986. The interpretation of derived nominals. In A.M. Farley, P.T. Farley, and K.E. McCullogh (eds.), *Chicago Linguistics Society* 22, 231–247.

Lees, R.B. 1966. *The Grammar of English Nominalizations*. The Hague: Mouton.

Levin, B. and M. Rappaport-Hovav. 1994. A preliminary analysis of causative verbs in English. *Lingua* 92, 35–77.

1995. *Unaccusativity: At the Syntax-Semantics Interface*. Cambridge, Mass.: MIT Press.

2005. *Argument Realization*. Cambridge University Press.

Lieber, Rochelle. 1992. *Deconstructing Morphology*. The University of Chicago Press.

Livšic, V.A. 1964. *Praktičeskaja Stilistika Russkogo Jazyka*. Moscow: Vysshaja Shkola.

Lomtev, T.P. 1954. *Iz Istorii Sintaksia Russkogo Jazyka*. Moscow: Uchpedgiz.

Mairal, R. and J. Gil. 2006. *Linguistic Universals*. Cambridge University Press.

Marantz, A.P. 1984. *On the Nature of Grammatical Relations*, Cambridge, Mass.: MIT Press.

1995. The minimalist program. In G. Webelhuth (ed.), *Government and Binding Theory and the Minimalist Program*, 349–381. Oxford: Blackwell,.

Matushansky, Ora. 2006. Head movement in linguistic theory. *Linguistic Inquiry* 37: 69–109.

McCloskey, J. 1997. Subjecthood and subject position. In L. Haegeman (ed.), *Elements of Grammar: Handbook of Generative Syntax*, 197–235. Dordrecht: Kluwer.

Mel'čuk, I.A. 1980. Animacy in Russian cardinal numerals and adjectives as an inflectional category. *Language* 56, 797–811.

Mel'čuk, I.A. and A.A. Xolodovič. 1970. K teorii grammatičeskogo zaloga. *Narody Azii i Afriki* 4: 111–24.

Mixajlov, M.S. 1961. K voprosu ob aberracii zaloga v tureckom glagole. In S.G. Baxudarov, N.A. Baskakov, and A.A. Reformackij (eds.), *Voprosy Sostavlenija Opisatel'nyx Grammatik*, 211–232. Moscow: Izd. Akademii Nauk SSSR.

Moro, A. 1997. *The Raising of Predicates: Predicative Noun Phrases and the Theory of Clause Structure*. Cambridge University Press.

2000. *Dynamic Antisymmetry*. Cambridge, Mass.: MIT Press.

2008. *The Boundaries of Babel: The Brain and the Enigma of Impossible Languages*. Cambridge, Mass.: MIT Press.

Munn, Alan 1993. Topics in the Syntax and Semantics of Coordinate Structures. Doctoral Dissertation, University of Maryland.

Neidle, C. 1988. *The Role of Case in Russian Syntax*. Dordrecht: Kluwer.
Nichols, J. 1981. *Predicate Nominals: A Partial Surface Syntax of Russian*. University of California Publications in Linguistics, 97. University of California Press.
Nunes, M.L. 1993. Argument linking in English derived nominals. In R.D. Van Valin (ed.), *Advances in Role and Reference Grammar*, 375–432. Amsterdam: John Benjamins Publishing Co.
Odijk, J. 1997. C-selection and s-selection. *Linguistic Inquiry* 28, 365–371.
Padučeva, E.V. 1974. *O Semantike Sintaksisa: Materialy k Transformacionnoj Grammatike Russkogo Jazyka*. Moscow: Nauka.
Palmer, F.R. 1994. *Grammatical Roles and Relations*. Cambridge University Press.
Papangeli, Dimitra. 2004. *The Morphosyntax of Argument Realization: Greek Argument Structure and the Lexicon-Syntax Interface*. Utrecht: LOT Publishers.
Payne, T.E. 2006. *Describing Morphosyntax*. Cambridge University Press.
Perlmutter, D. (ed.) 1983. *Studies in Relational Grammar 1*. The University of Chicago Press.
Perlmutter, D. and J. Moore. 2002. Language-internal explanation: the distribution of Russian impersonals. *Language* 78: 619–650.
Perlmutter, D. and C. Rosen (eds.) 1984. *Studies in Relational Grammar 2*. The University of Chicago Press.
Pesetsky, D. 1982. Paths and Categories. Doctoral Dissertation, MIT.
Petter, M. 1998. *Getting PRO under Control*. The Hague: Holland Academic Graphics.
Pinker, S. 1984. *Language Learnability and Language Development*. Cambridge, Mass.: Harvard University Press.
  1989. *Learnability and Cognition: The Acquisition of Argument Structure*. Cambridge, Mass.: MIT Press.
Pylkkanen, L. 2002. Introducing Arguments. Doctoral Dissertation, MIT.
Rappaport, G. 1980. Deixis and detachment in the adverbial participles in Russian. In C.V. Chvany and R.D. Brecht (eds.), *Morphosyntax in Slavic*, 273–300. Columbus: Slavica Publishers.
  1984. *Grammatical Function and Syntactic Structure: The Adverbial Participle in Russian*. Columbus: Slavica Publishers.
Rappaport Hovav, M. and Beth Levin. 1992. -er nominals: implications for the theory of argument structure. In T. Stowell and E. Wehrli (eds.), *Syntax and the Lexicon*, 127–153. Syntax and Semantics, 26. New York: Academic Press.
Roberts, I.G. 1987. *The Representation of Implicit and Dethematized Subjects*. Dordrecht: Foris.
  1988. Predicate APs. *Linguistic Inquiry* 19, 703–710.
Rosen, C. 1984. The interface between semantic roles and initial grammatical relations. In D. Perlmutter and C. Rosen (eds.), *Studies in Relational Grammar*, Vol. II, 38–77. University of Chicago Press.
Rothstein, S. 1985. The Syntactic Form of Predication. Doctoral Dissertation, MIT. Distributed by the Indiana University Linguistics Club.
  2001. *Predicates and their Subjects*. Dordrecht: Kluwer.
Rozental', D.E. 1967. *Spravočnik po Pravopisaniju i Literaturnoj Pravke*. Moscow: "Kniga."

Rozwadowska, B. 1988. Thematic restrictions of derived nominals. In W. Wilkins (ed.), *Thematic Relations*, 147–165. Syntax and Semantics, 21. New York: Academic Press.

Ruwet, N. 1991. *Syntax and Human Experience*. Edited and translated by J. Goldsmith. The University of Chicago Press.

Sadler, L. and A. Spencer (eds.). 2001. Morphology and argument structure. In A. Spencer and A. Zwicky (eds.), *The Handbook of Morphology*, 206–236. Oxford: Blackwell.

Safir, K. 1987. The syntactic projection of lexical thematic structure. *Natural Language and Linguistic Theory* 5, 561–601.

Schein, B. 1982. Non-finite complements in Russian. *MIT Working Papers in Linguistics* 4, 217–244.

Seuren, P. (ed.) 1974. *Semantic Syntax*. Oxford University Press.

Siegel, M. 1976. Capturing the Russian adjective. In B. Partee (ed.), *Montague Grammar*, 293–309. New York: Academic Press.

Siewierska, A. 1988. The passive in Slavic. In M. Shibatani (ed.), *Passive and Voice*, 243–289. Amsterdam: John Benjamins.

Sigurdsson, H.A, 1991. Icelandic case-marked PRO and the licensing of lexical arguments. *Natural Language and Linguistic Theory* 9, 327–363.

Slioussar, N. 2005. Some properties of Russian scrambling. In A. Asbury, I. Brasileiro, and S. Mahanta (eds.), *Yearbook 2005: Utrecht Institute of Linguistics OTS*, 81–95. Utrecht: Utrecht Institute of Linguistics.

Sobin, N.J. 1985. Case assignment in Ukrainian morphological passive constructions. *Linguistic Inquiry* 16, 649–662.

Speas, M.J. 1990. *Phrase Structure in Natural Language*. Dordrecht: Kluwer.

Spencer, Andrew and Arnold Zwicky. 2001. *Handbook of Morphology*. Oxford: Blackwell.

Spenser, Andrew. 1991. *Morphological Theory*. Oxford: Blackwell.

Spinčak, Ja.A. 1960. *Očerk Russkogo Istoričeskogo Sintaksisa*. Kiev: Radjanska Shkola.

Stepanov, Ju.S. 1981. *Imena, Predikaty, Predloženija*. Moscow: Izd. "Nauka."

Stowell, T. 1981. The Origins of Phrase Structure. Doctoral Dissertation, MIT.

1992. The role of the lexicon in syntactic theory. In T. Stowell and E. Wehrli (eds.), *Syntax and the Lexicon*, 9–20. Syntax and Semantics, 26. New York: Academic Press.

Švedova, N.Ju. 1948. Vozniknovenie i rasprostranenie predikativnogo upotreblenija člennyx prilagatel'nyx v russkom literaturnom jazyke XV–XVII vv. *Doklady i Soobščenija Instituta Russkogo Jazyka* 1, 102–126. Izd. Akademii Nauk USSR.

1952. Polnye i kratkie formy imen prilagatel'nyx v sostave skazuemogo v sovremennon russkom literaturnom jazyke. *Učenye zapiski MGU* 150, 73–132.

Švedova, N.Ju and V.V. Lopatin. 1989. *Kratkaja Russkaja Grammatika*. Moscow: "Russkij Jazyk."

Taraldsen, T. 1986. On the distribution of nominative objects in Finnish. In P. Muysken and H. van Riemsdijk (eds.), *Features and Projections*, 139–161. Dordrecht: Foris.

Thomason, S.G. 1976. Some extensions of Montague Grammar. In Barbara H. Partee (ed.), *Montague Grammar*, 75–117. New York: Academic Press.

Timberlake, A. 1974. The nominative object in north Russian. In R.D. Brecht and C.V. Chvany (eds.), *Slavic Transformational Syntax*, 219–243. Michigan Slavic Materials, 10. Ann Arbor: The University of Michigan.

2004. *A Reference Grammar of Russian*. Cambridge University Press.

Tolstoj, E.V. 1966. Leksiko-grammatičeskie i stilističeskie osobennosti polnyx i kratkix prilagatel'nyx v funkcii imennogo sostavnogo skauemogo. In A.V. Abramovic et al. (eds.), *Voprosy Stilistiki*, 166–181. Moscow: Izd. MGU.

Ura, H. 2001. Case theory. In M. Baltin and C. Collins (eds.), *The Handbook of Contemporary Syntactic Theory*, 547–570. Oxford: Blackwell.

Wechsler, K. 1995. *The Semantic Basis of Argument Structure*. Stanford, Cal.: CSLI Publications.

Williams, E. 1981. Argument structure and morphology. *The Linguistic Review* 1, 81–114.

1985. PRO and the subject of NP. *Natural Language and Linguistic Theory* 3, 297–315.

1987. English as an ergative language: the theta structure of derived nouns. In B. Need, E. Schiller, and A. Bosch (eds.), *Chicago Linguistics Society* 23, 366–375.

1994. *Thematic Structure in Syntax*. Cambridge, Mass.: MIT Press.

2003. *Representation Theory*. Cambridge, Mass.: MIT Press.

Woolford, Ellen. 2006. Lexical case, inherent case, and argument structure. *Linguistic Inquiry* 37, 111–130.

Wurmbrand, S. 2001. *Infinitives*. Berlin: W. de Gruyter.

Xolodovič, A.A. 1974. *Tipologija passivnyx konstrukcij: diatezy i zalogi*. Leningrad: Nauka.

Xrakovskij, V.S. 1978. *Problemy Teorii Grammatičeskogo Zaloga*. Leningrad: Nauka.

1979. Diathesis. *Acta linguistica academiae scientiarum Hungaricae* 29, 289–307.

1981. *Zalogovye konstrukcii v raznostrukturnyx jazykax*. Leningrad: Nauka.

1990. Rol' zaloga i padeža pri markirovke izmenenija diatez. In V.V. Klimov (ed.), *Soprjažennost' glagol'nyx kategorij*, 112–124. Kalinin University.

Xrakovsky, V.S., A.L. Mal'čukov, and S.Ju. Dmitrenko (eds.). 2004. *40 Let Sankt-Peterburgskoj Tipologičeskoj Škole*. Moscow: Znak.

Yip, M., J. Maling, and R. Jackendoff. 1987. Case in tiers. *Language* 63, 217–250.

Zubizarreta, M.L. 1985. The relation between morphophonology and morphosyntax: the case of Romance causatives. *Linguisic Inquiry* 16, 247–289.

1987. *Levels of Representation in the Lexicon and in the Syntax*. Dordrecht: Foris Publications.

Index

active participle, *see* participles (-šč-)
adjectives (Russian), 74–122
    attributive (adjectives and participles), 91, 94, 108
    departicipial **-enn-** adjectives, *see* participles
    long form (LF) (*see also* s-predicate), 75, 78–80, 82, 83, 130, 236, 253
    meaning of SF and predicate LF, 103–107, 276
    predicate adjectives, 231, 232, 249, 254
    predicate long form, 89–93, 95, 106, 113
    short form (SF), 75, 82, 86, 120, 236
    small clause, 74, 81, 83
adjuncts, 67, 69–71, 217
    s-predicates, 148
    depictive adjectives and participles, 76, 80, 83, 84–88, 152, 196–199, 237, 251, 253–257
adjunction, 76, 218
    high adjunction, 139
    low adjunction, 140
advancement, *see* arguments
adverbials, *see* hybrid categories
affix, 13, 124
    affix-driven operations, 12 *see also* diathesis-level operations
    affixal head, 148, 228, 230
    paradigmatic affix, 15, 26, 73, 179, 222
    voice affix, *see* voice
agentless derived unaccusative (diathesis), *see* voice (middle derivation)
agreement (*see also* case agreement), 87, 93, 95–96, 100, 105, 153, 164, 165, 194, 224, 248–249
Alsina, A., 12, 263
alternations, 33, 40, 67, 71, 72, 174, 212
    typology, 68
ambiguity
    attachment, 149, 281
    unacceptable, 64, 176

anaphors (verbal), 149, 180, 282
    see also hybrid adverbials
antecedent binding, 37
antipassive construction, 69
antitransitive construction, 69
applicative construction, 69
arguments, 14, 15, 44, 69, 180, 217
    advancement (in diathesis), 36
    external, 14, 15, 18, 118, 134–137
    internal, 18
    merger, 15
    nominal, 92
    positions, 18
    projection, 15
    realization, 12
    sharing of external argument, 225, 227
    specified (in diathesis), 70
    splitting, 241
Argument Adjunct (*see also* causativization, passivization, *and* nominalization), 51, 66, 70
argument structure (*see also* diathesis), 11, 12, 14, 20, 78, 214
autonomous tiers (in diathesis), 42
atrofirovat'sja, 38, 43–44
auxiliary verbs (diathesis), 25, 52, 53, 172, 220–224, 242

Babby, L.H., 118
Babyonyshev, M., 204
Bach, E., 179
Bailyn, J., 232
Bailyn–Bowers hypothesis, 231
Baker, M., 14, 36, 49, 53, 59, 69, 268, 269
Baltin, M., 267
Bantu languages, 69

bare phrases (*see also under* infinitives *and* inheritance), 76, 91, 115, 118, 121, 221, 234–236
barrier, *see* binding
binary branching, 20, 34
binding (*see also* control and reflexive binding), 30, 37, 88, 150, 152, 165, 170, 174, 184
  binding domain, 30
  vertical binding (V-binding), 25, 42, 74, 142, 158, 185
bipartite structure of diathesis, *see* arguments
Birjulin, A., 25
Blake, B., 279
blocking mechanisms, 51, 253
Bobaljik, J., 32
Burzio's Generalization, 39
Bošković, Z., 20, 263
Bowers, J., 18, 217, 232, 262, 279
Bresnan, J., 179, 267
Brody, M., 266, 267
Bulaxovskij, L., 274
Bylinskij, K.I., 272
by-phrase, 28, 29, 49, 51, 54, 56

Canonical Structural Realization, 14
case, 11, 59, 189, 230
  absorption, 22
  accusative, 137–141
  adnominal genitive, 56, 62
  agreement, 80, 148, 230, 243
  assignment (checking) domains, 209, 249
  case doubling, *see* causativization
  caseless NP, 290
  default nominative, 193, 194–195, 236, 249
  Double Genitive Filter (*see also* Same-Case Filter), 67
  double instrumental, 66
  double structural genitive, 64, 65
  ergative-absolute, 69
  filter, *see* Same-Case Filter
  fossilized (inactive) case form, 230, 249
  inherent nominative, 76
  lexical case, *see* case; quirky
  percolation, 139
  possessive genitive, 56, 66–67
  predicate instrumental, *see* predicate case
  predicate genitive, *see* predicate case
  quirky case, 13, 37, 50, 57, 58, 81, 178, 181, 209, 231
  receptor (*see also* case percolation), 139
  spec-case, *see* case, structural case
  structural case, 34, 36, 49, 64, 137, 140
  theta role determined case (theta case) (*see also* prepositions), 15, 34, 37, 57, 64
Case Resistance Principle, 279
categorial features, 149
causativization, 28, 31, 32, 35, 45–54
  causative meaning, 47, 48
  causative-specific affixal diathesis, *see* construction-specific syntax
  faire (French causative auxiliary), 52, 53
  passive of causative, *see* passivization
  Romance causativization, 52–54
c-command, 37
Chvany, C., 277
Chomsky, N., 14, 22, 53, 55, 262, 263, 268
Cinque, G., 58
clausal structure, 274
clause union (syntax), 48, 53
clitics, 278
  climbing, 54
Collins, C., 267
complement, 36
complex predicates, 69, 221, 222, 287
composite head, 123, 128
composition of diatheses, 13, 26, 34, 48, 135, 221, 239–242
Comrie, B., 50, 51, 53, 58, 69
construction-specific syntax, 17, 23, 28, 33, 47, 50, 68, 124, 126, 154, 201
control (*see also* binding *and* infinitives), 26, 42, 75, 76, 84, 130, 148, 151, 166, 169, 174, 184, 191, 221, 222, 227
  GB control theory (*see also* PRO), 85
  infinitive control, 176
  object control, 52, 81, 87–88, 100, 149, 154, 166, 190
  subject control, 80, 88, 116, 126, 184, 190, 225
coordination (*see also* infinitives, conjoined subject-controlled infinitive complements), 204
copula verbs, 76, 115–122, 155, 278
  adjective and copula, 74, 76, 89, 235, 242, 283
core syntactic structure, 11, 15, 16, 17
Cowper, P., 262
crash (of a diathesis-level operation), 41
c-selection (category selection, subcategorization), 13, 222
Culicover, P., 174, 178, 279

default, *see* infinitives, subject control *and* case, default nominative
default suffix, *see* agreement
defective syntactic paradigm, 24
delinking, *see* diathesis-level operations
departicipial adjectives, *see* participles
depictive adjectives, *see* adjuncts
derivation (diathesis-level), 35, 235
derived nominals (DN), 89, 168–169
derived transitive verb (diathesis), 45
determiner phrase (DP), 55, 89
dethematization, 28, 30, 41, 58, 69, 131
detransitivization, 41, 69
deverbal adverbs, *see* hybrid adverbials
deverbalizing rules (Jackendoff), 277
diathesis, 11, 13–18, 45, 53, 72, 131, 148, 168, 174, 218, 221
  unlinked external N, 41
  unlinked internal theta role, 42
  unoccupied slots, 15, 46
  unspecified (blank) slots, 25, 53
diathesis-level operations (*see also* composition of diathesis), 11, 15, 55, 68, 71, 73, 111, 115, 118, 152, 223, 240, 241
diathesis structure (2×4 structure of the diathesis), 43–44
diathetic paradigm, 33, 124, 126
DiSciullo, A.M., 45, 53
ditransitive verbs, 16, 18, 19, 26, 28
Double Genitive Filter, 67
double-occupancy (of slot in diathesis), 28, 45
Dubinsky, S., 286
Dyirbal, 69

encapsulated VP, 126, 128, 131
enclitics, *see* clitics
English, 24, 125, 287
  causative, 52
-en- participle suffix, 30, 43
Equi-NP Deletion transformation, 151
ergative case, *see* case
expletive, 24, 277, 287
Extended Lexical Projection, 12, 13, 14, 19, 34, 124
Extended Projection Principle (EPP), 19, 39
external argument, *see* argument
External Subcategorization (c-selection), 14, 21, 23–24, 38, 39, 42, 75, 77, 119
externalization (of a verb's internal argument; diathesis-level), 14, 22, 29, 38, 110, 137

feature percolation, *see* head, Head Feature Convention
final derived argument structure (diathesis), 11, 12, 13, 19, 23, 118
Finnish, 209
fossilized case form, *see* case
Franks, S., 118, 209, 281
Freidin, R., 19
French, 18, 45, 51, 52, 95, 221

gerundive nominals, 123, 124
German, 95, 103
Giorgi, A., 55
grammatical relations, 11, 17, 19, 20, 23, 33, 55, 59, 73, 120, 164
Greenberg, G., 281
Grimshaw, J., 14, 36, 39, 51, 55, 58, 59, 70, 123, 168, 263, 266, 267
Guasti, M., 51, 54, 270

heterogeneous category (hybrid category), 124
Haegeman, L., 22, 262, 272
head
  head extraction, 275
  Head Feature Convention, 263
  head movement, 34
  head of a word, 26, 127, 137
  head suppression, 93–95, 98, 106, 275
  relativized head, 135
Hinterhölzl, L., 288
homogeneous category, 123
Hornstein, N., 86, 174, 199
hybrid categories, 124, 149
  derived nominals, 54
  hybrid adverbials, 115, 116, 123, 148–168
  hybrid category specific syntax, *see* construction-specific syntax
  hybrid hybrid category, 143
  hybrid verbal adjuncts, 25, 123–171

Icelandic, 175, 209
identification, 274
Ickovič, V., 169
impersonal verbs (impersonalization), 14, 16, 19, 24, 71, 130, 224–226
impersonal passive, 29
impersonal transitive verbs, 20, 21, 22, 36, 136, 137, 154, 178, 220, 278
implicit **i**, 28, 31, 59, 70, 132, 170–171
infinitives, 159–168, 172, 180, 199

bare infinitive phrase, 172, 220–224
complement of nouns, 199–201
conjoined subject-controlled infinitive
    complements, 203–204
control, 174, 177–179, 203–204, 213
  with nominative direct objects in Old
    Russian, 208–213
  object control: s-clause, 186–189;
    s-predicate, 195–196
  s-clauses (*see also* PRO), 172, 176–177,
    201, 202
  s-predicate, 172, 244
  subject control: s-clause, 183–185;
    s-predicate, 181–186
Information Structure, 240
inheritance (diathetic), 25, 76, 89, 117, 132,
    220, 232, 240, 246, 274
Isačenko, A., 103
intermediate passive rule, 50, 55, 58
internalization (of external argument in
    diathesis), 28, 32, 45, 46, 59
intrinsic ordering (diathesis composition), 137
Italian, 45, 54

Jackendoff, R., 264, 277
Jaeggli, O., 14, 266
Jakobson, R., 276
Japanese, 45–46

kP (*kak* phrase) (*see also* control), 190–194, 251
Klaiman, M., 69
Klein, E.H., 179
korčit', 37, 40, 41, 42
Kozinskij, I., 194, 213
Kratzer, A., 39, 264
Kubik, M., 274

language-specific diversity, 50, 73
Larson, R., 31, 178, 213, 217
Lavine, J., 19, 209, 265
law of diathesis conservation, 32
Lebeaux, D., 271
Lees, R., 55
Levin, B., 12, 14, 263, 264
lexical entry, 72
lexical rule, *see* diathesis-level operations
lexical semantics, 12, 24, 38
lexicon, 11
linking (of arguments in diathesis), 14, 16, 20
Lithuanian, 123, 124, 209

Livšic, V., 66
Lomtev, T., 189
long form, *see* adjectives
Longobardi, G., 55

Manzini, M.R., 266, 267
mapping opacity (between diathesis and
    syntax), 64, 66
Marantz, A., 32, 69, 263
Matushansky, O., 84
McCloskey, J., 80, 108
Mel'čuk, I.A., 272
merge (project), 17, 26, 33, 36, 118
middle, *see* voice
Minimal Distance Principle (MDP), 151,
    213, 284
Moro, A., 57, 82, 99, 264
Mirror Principle, 124, 134
modal meaning, 176, 180, 283
modification, 91, 93, 108, 139
monadic verbs (typology of), 37, 43
monotransitive verbs (diathesis), 31, 35
morphosyntactic structure (realization), 12, 23,
    45, 46, 57, 72, 174
Munn, A., 204

Neidle, C., 284
neutralization (morphological), PI suffix, 228
Nichols, J., 288
nominalization (derived nominals), 54–67
  monotransitive verbs, 62–66
  suffix, 250
nominative direct object, *see* infinitives
noun phrase (nP and NP), 88–89
  argument vs. predicate nominal, 89
NP movement, 11
null expletive, 24
Nunes, M., 271, 272

object control, *see* control *and* infinitives
operations (rules) (*see also* diathesis-level
    operations), 26

Padučeva, E., 263
Palmer, F., 69
paradigmatic affixes, 32, 73, 74, 127, 172
parameterization of syntactic principles, 72
participles, 75, 123, 127–137, 143
  comparison of **-en-** and **-šč-**, 131–134
  -en- participles, 110–113, 132

participles (cont.)
  -enn- departicipial adjectives, 114–115
  -šč (active) participles, 106, 126, 127, 130, 156–159, 243, 276, 277
  -em- participles, 143–148
  -l- participle (Old Russian), 250
passivization, 12, 28–32, 33, 39, 40, 41, 43, 48, 54, 58, 69, 110, 144, 169
Payne, T., 69, 272
percolation of case features, *see* case
Perlmutter, D., 24
Pesestsky, D., 263
Petter, M., 177
phase (in diathesis-level derivation), 41
PI (predicate instrumental), *see* predicate case
position (slot) skipping (in diathesis-level derivation), 51, 63, 64–65
predicate argument structure (*see also* argument structure *and* diathesis), 11
predicate case, 249
  predicate genitive, 98–100, 275
  predicate instrumental (adjectives), 228–259, 289
predicate long form of adjectives and participles (LF), *see* adjectives
predicate nominals (nP vs. nP$_i$), 89, 91, 103–107
predication, 108, 109
predicator, 11, 74
prefixes (with argument structure), 68
prepositions (PP), 68, 94
PRO (null subject of s-clause), 52, 85, 148, 161, 172, 177
Projection Principle, 80, 102, 155
promise (*obeščat'*), 213–220
pronoun (special use of Russian third person personal pronoun), 96–97
prosodic gap, 108

reference of noun phrase (R), 59
Rappaport, G., 151
Rappaport Hovav, M., 12, 14, 263, 264
reanalysis, 130, 249–250
reflexive binding, 30, 37, 141–143, 155, 158, 170, 280
relative clause (restrictive), 104
relativized head, *see* head
right-displacement (in diathesis), 68
Roberts, I., 262, 266, 267
Romance causativization, *see* causativization
Rosen, C., 264

Rothstein, S., 82, 263
Rozental', D.E., 64, 272
rule-schema, 136
Russian, 13–18
Ruwet, N., 25

s-clause, *see* small clause
s-predicate, *see* secondary predicate
Sadler, L., 12, 39, 264, 269
Safir, K., 271
Sag, I.A., 179
SAM$_i$ (pronominal s-predicate adjective), 148, 154, 156, 160, 176, 236, 243, 249, 258
Same-Case Filter, 272
secondary predicate (s-predicate, xP$_i$), 25, 33, 108, 119, 130, 152, 165
  adjective s-predicate, 74, 82, 91
  adverbial s-predicate, 118, 123
  finite s-predicate, 91
  infinitive s-predicate, *see* infinitives
  kP$_i$ s-predicate, 100
  -šč- s-predicate (*see also* participles), 141
Seuren, P., 269
short form, *see* adjectives
Siegel, M., 105
Sigurdsson, H., 175
-sja (unaccusative-forming suffix), 22, 29, 38–39, 40, 41, 43, 132, 134
slot skipping, *see* position skipping
small clause (s-clause), 74, 91, 111
Speas, M., 35, 36, 59, 262, 263, 264
specified argument, *see* arguments
Spinčak, Ja., 212
Stepanov, Ju., 104
Stowell, T., 12, 20, 32, 39, 263, 264, 266, 267, 279
subject, 24, 80–82, 91, 170
  dedicated subject, 14, 80, 85
  dative subject, 160, 178; overt, 163
  understood subject (*see also* control), 25, 80, 85, 116
  subject control, *see* control *and* infinitives
subjectless verbs, *see* impersonal verbs
suffix, *see* affix
syntactic operations (rules), 11, 23, 34, 118, 152, 241
syntactic relations, *see* grammatical relations
syntax, 15
subcategorized adjunct, *see* complex predicates
Švedova, N., 104

Taraldsen, T., 209
TBC, *see* theta binding chain
tense phrase (TP), spec of, 36
theta binding chain (TBC), 25, 85, 88, 118, 153, 164, 165, 181
Theta Criterion, 45, 137, 266
theta roles
   external, 131
   selection, 13, 18, 20
   theta-role conversion, 71
   theta-role sharing, 227
Thomason, S.G., 179
Timberlake, A., 132, 209, 287
tošnit', 41
trace, 89, 111, 274
Turkish, 18, 28, 45, 47–51, 67, 124, 278, 283
typology of alternations, *see* alternations

Ukrainian, 279
unaccusativity, 14, 20, 21, 22, 32, 38, 80, 131
understood subject, *see* subject
unergative, 20, 28, 29, 45, 47
universals, 12, 28, 44, 69, 71, 72, 154, 186, 220
UTAH, 14, 15

v (small v), 12
V_{aux}, *see* auxiliary verbs
V_{cop}, *see* copula verbs
V-binding, *see* binding, vertical
valence, 13, 15, 59
voice, 128, 132, 144, 146
   middle (voice) derivation, 38, 41, 110
Vy (*see also* agreement), 275

Williams, E., 18, 25, 26, 45, 53, 59, 135, 149, 221, 266, 271
Woolford, E., 57, 264
word, 117
word order, 19, 35, 52, 64, 150, 180, 217, 218
Wurmbrand, S., 174

x-bar structure, 89
Xolodovič, A.A., 263, 272
Xrakovskij, V., 263, 272

Yip, M., 209

Zubizarreta, M., 12, 14, 59, 66